The Contemporary Printed Literature
of the English Counter-Reformation
between 1558 and 1640

I

The Contemporary Printed Literature of the English Counter-Reformation between 1558 and 1640

An annotated catalogue by

A. F. ALLISON and D. M. ROGERS

Volume 1

(With the collaboration of W. Lottes)

Works in languages other than English

Scolar Press

First published 1989 by
Scolar Press
Gower Publishing Company Ltd.
Gower House
Croft Road
Aldershot
Hant GU I 1 3HR
England

Gower Publishing Company
Old Post Road
Brookfield
Vermont 05036
USA

Library of Congress Cataloging-in-Publication Data

Allison, A. F.
  The contemporary printed literature of the English counter-
reformation between 1558-1640: an annotated catalogue / by
A. F. Allison and D. M. Rogers.
        p.   cm.
    Bibliography: v. 1.
    Includes Index.
    Contents: v. 1. Works in languages other than English.
    ISBN 0-85967-640-4
  1. Counter-Reformation—England—Bibliography—Union lists.
  2. England—Church history—16th century—Bibliography—Union lists.
  3. England—Church history—17th century—Bibliography—Union lists.
  4. Bibliography—Early printed books—16th century—Union lists.
  5. Bibliography—Early printed books—17th century—Union lists.
  6. Catalogs. Union—England.   I. Rogers, D. M. (David Morrison)
II. Title.
Z7830.A46   1989
[BR375]
016.2742'06—dc19   88-39681
                          CIP

Typeset by Gloucester Typesetting Services
Printed and bound in Great Britain by
The Camelot Press Ltd, Southampton

Contents

Foreword

In 1956 the present editors published *A Catalogue of Catholic Books in English printed abroad or secretly in England, 1558–1640* (now commonly referred to as A&R). As that title indicates, our aim then was to survey the clandestine vernacular output of the English[1] Catholics during the chosen period. We left uncharted virtually the whole field of religious literature in Latin and other foreign languages published abroad by the English Catholics. We also left unexplored the extensive involvement of foreign Catholic governments and individual writers in English Catholic affairs. The object of the present two-volume catalogue is to list and describe, in Volume I, those books published during the same period, 1558–1640, that come within these last two, hitherto uncharted, categories, and by so doing to complete the survey of the period as a whole, and to present, in Volume II, an extended revision of the 1956 English catalogue, re-arranged according to the principles outlined in the present foreword. The re-arrangement of Volume II will entail a complete re-numbering of all the items contained in it. We have decided, however, since work on the preparation of Volume II is still proceeding, to refer in Volume I to books that will appear in Volume II by their old A&R numbers. When Volume II appears, it will be provided with a concordance at the front linking the old A&R numbers with the new numbers the same books will bear in Volume II.

The limits of the period over which this survey extends perhaps need some explanation. Although the Counter-Reformation as a whole European movement of reform and renewal began many decades before the death of Mary Tudor, it was by the accession of her half-sister Elizabeth in 1558 and the latter's deliberate choice of a Protestant path for the English Church that Catholic publishing became illegal in England and hence went underground or sought refuge abroad. If the historical break in religious continuity justifies our choice of 1558 as a commencing date, the reasons for stopping at 1640 are bibliographical rather than mainly historical. The decade which saw the outbreak of the civil war in England shows a sudden and rapid decline in the output of English Catholic publishing both at home and abroad which can be traced directly to the financial stresses which the troubles in England brought upon the Catholic minority. On the other hand, the very same period saw the release in England of a torrent of pamphlet literature of a size such that the editors of the Bibliographical Society's *Short-Title Catalogue* in 1926 were glad to terminate their work at a date which excluded the civil war and its vast contemporary literature. By 1926 the year 1640 had already become an accepted terminal year for bibliographers, and our concern is to chart the English Catholic share of the total output within the chosen period.

Categories of Material included in the Present Volume

All the books in this volume are in languages other than English.[2] They fall into ten main groups:

    1. Original works of a mainly religious character written by English Catholics in Latin or a modern foreign language. The writers of such works in English formed the subject-matter of our former catalogue, and those

of them who also appear here are signalled by the sign † after the name. Works of a purely secular nature are excluded: for example, mathematics, medicine, geography, astronomy, exploration, navigation, military science, trade and commence, archaeology and ancient history have no place here. Authors in this volume who published other works which are not included by us on grounds of subject-matter or date are signalled by the sign ‡ after the name to alert readers to the fact that our catalogue listings are not necessarily co-extensive with the writer's total output. Philosophy is included because of its close connection with theology. Some subjects are on the borderline; works on politics, law and modern history, for example, may be purely secular, but they may, on the other hand, have a religious dimension: the principle followed here is to include such works if they have a sufficiently close bearing on the politico-religious situation in England. The inclusion of works of a predominantly literary caste—poetry, drama, rhetoric—is determined by the subject-matter or, in certain cases, by the circumstances in which they were produced. Some well-known works by English Catholics will not be found here: More's *Utopia*, for example, and John Barclay's popular romance *Argenis* which is excluded because, although it contains an allegory on the French wars of religion, it can hardly be described as a religious work. Neither of these has any close bearing on the affairs of English Catholics. Complimentary verses and speeches to foreign dignitaries generally are included only if the person addressed played a prominent part in supporting the English Catholics in their struggle to preserve the faith: for example, John Colville's verses on the accession of Pope Paul V find a place here (no. 256) but an elegy by Adam Blackwood on the death of King Charles IX of France does not. All dramas performed at, and verses and other effusions produced for academic occasions at, English Catholic colleges abroad are included whatever the subject (e.g. nos. 958–61; 325; 1342.3). Music is excluded.

2. Translations into other languages of works that were originally published in English and that feature in our earlier catalogue (e.g. nos. 8–18; 1120–21). Two books are included here, no. 822 which is in Latin and English, and no. 1128.1 which is in Latin and Irish.

3. Translations into other languages of religious works by English Catholics of which the English original is either lost or exists only in manuscript. Many of the martyr relations belong to this class (e.g. nos. 313; 624).

4. Religious works by contemporary foreign authors of which English Catholics were the editors (e.g. nos. 549–77).

5. Mediaeval and post mediaeval spiritual texts edited for the use of English Catholics during this period (e.g. no. 1344).

6. Liturgical works in Latin printed specifically for use by English Catholics (nos. 336–336.9). These were listed in A&R and have been transferred.

7. Books in which the English author involved acted as translator (e.g. nos. 129; 252).

8. Works by foreign Catholics commenting on or replying to publications by English Catholics (e.g. nos. 69; 496–501).

9. Works by foreign Catholics concerning English Catholic affairs. These may relate to a particular person, institution or group (e.g. nos. 763–94; 323; 367), or to some more general theme (e.g. nos. 1429, *et seq.*). A work by a foreign Catholic is not included simply on the grounds that it is a reply to a theological work by an English Protestant. For example, works in the controversy arising out of the Oath of Allegiance of 1606 have their place here because that controversy directly affected the lives

of English Catholics, but contributions to the dispute about Antichrist (e.g. Lessius's *De Antichristo*, 1611, which is an answer to part of a work by King James) are excluded because that dispute has not the same relevance to our theme. For the same reason, where a work that is included here gave rise to a wider European controversy, later works in the controversy are included only if they have something further to contribute about the situation in England that originally occasioned it. Suarez's *Defensio fidei Catholicae*, for example, has its place here (nos. 1541–5) because it deals with the question of the loyalty of English Catholics posed by the oath of allegiance: the various French replies to Suarez, however, are excluded because the sole concern of these replies is the defence of Gallican liberties.

10. Twenty books in Latin (A&R nos. 63, 69, 70, 72, 140a, 192, 380, 552, 661–3, 666–9, 673–5, 677–8) and three books in French (A&R nos. 119–21) have been transferred from A&R to this volume.

Arrangement and Choice of Headings

The arrangement of Volume I differs in one important respect from that of *A Catalogue of Catholic Books in English*. There we followed the practice, common to most library catalogues and many bibliographies, of entering every book under the name of its author if known. When the author's name was not known, we took as the heading any pseudonym or initials masking his identity that appeared in the book itself, or, failing that, the first word of the title following the article. It followed that translations or editions of foreign works had to be entered under the foreign author and not under the English translator or editor. This, in a catalogue intended as a survey of the literary output of the English Catholics, had serious disadvantages. It meant that works by the same English Catholic writer could often become scattered throughout the catalogue and could only be linked by consulting the index of translators and editors at the end. Here we have abandoned that practice. Wherever possible, a book is entered under the name of the person, institution or group of people whose connection with it, as author, compiler, editor, translator or subject of study provides the justification for including it in the catalogue. Thus, all the works by or concerning a particular English Catholic person are now brought together under one heading. For example, all the foreign Catholic accounts of the trial and execution of Mary Queen of Scots are entered under her name and not under their various foreign authors.

Our headings fall into two parts, a personal section (Part I, pp. 1–188) and a subject section (Part II, pp. 189–211). In the personal section the headings are taken from the names of English Catholic persons, institutions or groups and are in a single alphabetical sequence. Where a book has an English Catholic author, editor, compiler or translator, and his name is known (whether revealed in the book or not) it is entered under him. If the name is not revealed in the book itself, the book is described in the note as 'Anon.'. Cross-references are given for initials and forms of name not used as main headings. Where there is no identifiable English Catholic author, editor, etc., but the subject of the book is an English Catholic, it is entered in an appendix entry under the English Catholic's name (e.g. nos. 194–204). Vernacular rather than Latinised forms of name are taken for the heading (e.g. Holywood rather than Sacrobosco) regardless of the form used in the book in question. A writer who uses a name in religion, an alias, a pseudonym or a set of initials is entered under his full name if this is known, otherwise under the name or initials used in the book. There are cross-references from initials and forms of name not adopted as the heading. Institutions are treated as persons and are entered in the personal section under the place where they were located, e.g. Douai, *English College*; Louvain, *Irish Franciscan College of St Anthony*. Groups are also entered in the personal section but under their own name preceded by the appropriate adjective of nationality, e.g. English Jesuits; Irish Regular Clergy. A list of all the institutions and groups used as headings is given at the beginning of the personal section (p. 1).

The subject section deals with all those books by English or foreign Catholic authors which concern English Catholic affairs but which cannot be allocated to any of the personal headings which form Part I. In this section each heading consists of a descriptive phrase indicating the main topic of the book or books entered under it. These subject headings are arranged in a chronological sequence, and an alphabetical list of them is prefixed to the section (p. 189).

Numeration

Main entries are numbered consecutively throughout the volume. An interpolated main entry bears a number with a decimal point.

Internal Arrangement within the Heading

The internal arrangement of an author heading normally follows this pattern:

1. Volumes (if any) comprising a group of the author's works. Such collectaneous volumes are listed in chronological order of publication.

2. Single original works in alphabetical order of title, the various editions, issues and significant variants being arranged in chronological order. When the same work was published in several different languages, the languages are normally arranged in the following order: (a) Original language of composition (other than English); (b) Latin; (c) Translations into other languages in alphabetical order of languages, irrespective of the opening words of the title of the particular translation, and irrespective of the chronological appearances of the various translations. Thus, for example, Persons's *Epistle of persecution* (A&R 629) was actually composed in Latin. It is entered here under Persons, Robert. *De persecutione anglicana*, where seven editions of the Latin are recorded (nos. 874, *et seq.*). Then a cross-reference to A&R 629 records the English text which is itself a translation, and is followed by entries for translations into French, German and Italian (nos. 879–84). Occasionally, for example under William Allen, when single works in English were the subject of multiple translations, the English titles have been used for sub-headings.

3. Works edited, translated, or with contributions by an English Catholic writer.

4. Academic disputations where the author acted as *Praeses*. (Where he was the *Respondens*, the publication concerned is generally treated as his original work; see no. 2 above). Where an Englishman was the *Praeses* and the *Respondens* a foreigner, the latter does not get a cross-reference, though he will be found in the General Index. Where both were English, the main entry is put under the *Respondens* and the *Praeses* gets a cross-reference.[3]

5. Finally, there may be an Appendix comprising contemporary Catholic biographical material about the author or comments and attacks on his writings. Under this part of the heading will sometimes be found cross-references to biographical and other material of which the author was also English and therefore the works are described under the latter's name. Non-author headings, for example anonymous relations concerning English martyrs which are entered under the martyr's name, consist entirely of Appendix entries.

Variations from the norm that may be called for because of problems peculiar to a particular heading are indicated within the heading itself.

Transcription of Title

Our object has been to give, in each entry, a transcription full enough to enable the book to be easily recognised and the nature of its contents understood. In general, we have given fuller transcriptions than those in the English catalogue of 1956, but, as before, long titles are regularly curtailed and we have not thought it necessary to indicate the fact in each case by '*etc.*'. Any omission from the body of the title, however, is indicated by the conventional ellipsis sign. *Capitalisation.* In transcribing, we have normally reduced capitals to lower-case characters except to begin the first word in each sentence, proper nouns and adjectives, and abbreviations. *Medial and initial 'i' and 'j', 'u' and 'v'.* These are transcribed according to the normal lower-case practice of the printer, as evidenced by the text of the book, *Accents.* In Latin titles they are omitted in the transcription. In other languages we have aimed at following the normal lower-case practice of the printer. A superscript letter 'e' indicating the umlaut in German is transcribed as if it followed the vowel modified.

Bibliographical Information

Following the transcription of the title of the book comes the format and a note of the number of parts (if more than one). In determining what constitutes more than one part to a book, we have applied the following rule: Independent, as distinct from continuative or subsidiary, signatures constitute a separate part, provided there is no continuous pagination linking them together. After that comes the imprint, namely the place of printing and the printer's name, both in the form as originally printed but omitting addresses, and the date in arabic numerals. If the book is undated, a date is supplied within square brackets. Next follows the citation of copies (*see* below: *Location of Copies*). All other information about the book is given in a note, which is indented and begins on a new line. We have aimed in these notes at providing much fuller bibliographical and historical information than was possible in our English catalogue. Collations are given among the notes only when other distinguishing factors are absent, e.g. when two editions of a book bear the same imprint and date, or no imprint and date at all. Square brackets are used to indicate information supplied by the editors. References to other bibliographies are given only when these afford fuller particulars. The phrase 'Not found' at the beginning of a note indicates that we have secured sufficient particulars of an edition to justify a numbered entry, but that no surviving copy has yet been located. The phrase 'Not seen' indicates that copies, the locations of which are known, have not been seen either by the editors or by librarians whom the editors have consulted; some books could not now be found in the libraries where they were recorded. For all the remainder of our entries at least one copy of the book has been examined, and generally the majority of copies cited has been seen and found to conform to the description given. In a small number of instances it has not been possible to determine the bibliographical status of a particular copy, usually because of the physical impossibility of comparing copies in widely scattered locations. When we could not ascertain to which of two editions or issues certain copies belong, these copies are quoted at the end of the location list: '*This or no. . . .*'

Location of Copies

Up to fifteen locations are given for each book when known. A list of symbols and the libraries they represent appears at the end of this Foreword. Whenever possible, we have used the same symbols as those appearing in our English catalogue and in STC (2nd edition). As in the English catalogue, in arranging the symbols we have cited first all or any of the three principal English libraries: the British Library, the Bodleian, and Cambridge University; all other symbols are in alphabetical order regardless of geographical location. Where more than fifteen copies of a book are known to us, a + sign follows the last symbol if the extra number does not exceed five; a double + sign if the extra number is more than five. In the case of the commoner books we have preferred, as a rule, to give English and European locations rather than American, since copies in America can usually be located in the United States Union Catallogue for which there is no equivalent on this side of the Atlantic. When a library possesses only a photocopy of a book of which few copies are known, the symbol for that library, inside square brackets and preceded by an asterisk, is placed at the end of the locations cited.

Indexes

We are confident that users of this volume will find the four indexes that we have provided very helpful. The Title Index (pp. 212–240) is comprehensive, embracing *all* the works described in this volume, together with such other contemporary publications as are cited in the annotations by their titles. It will afford a quick and easy means of finding any book wherever we have placed it. The Index of Publishers and Printers (pp. 241–272) assembles the materials in such a way as to illustrate both the concentration and the wide dispersal of the presses which made possible the publication and dissemination of this diverse range of books, and so gave expression to many aspects of the religious life of English Catholics in its various European ramifications. The Chronological Index (pp. 273–276) allows the output of any given year or years to be brought together, and hence to be related to its general European context. The General Index of Proper Names (pp. 277–289) covers all the persons and institutions (including foreign authors) mentioned in the whole volume, other than those whose names have been used as main headings.

A.F.A.   D.M.R.

[*Notes.*]

1. For the sake of brevity, the word 'England' is used here, as it was in our former catalogue, to denote all four countries of the British Isles: England, Ireland, Scotland and Wales, and the word 'English' to describe their respective inhabitants and vernaculars.
2. Books in other languages which also contain a small amount of English are treated as foreign.
3. Where no copy of the disputation has survived (e.g. nos. 253–5), because we lack the full title the main entry has been put under the *Praeses* instead of under the various *Respondentes* who are nevertheless all given cross-references.

Symbols and Libraries

A	University of Aberdeen.
A²	Blairs College, Aberdeen (deposited at E).
AAR	Aarau (Switzerland), Kantonsbibliothek.
AB	Augsburg, Staats-und Stadtbibliothek.
ABV	Abbeville, Bibliothèque Municipale.
AD	Père A. Dodin.
AIX	Aix-en-Provence, Bibliothèque Méjanes.
AMI	Amiens, Bibliothèque Municipale.
AMP	Ampleforth Abbey, York.
AMS	Amsterdam, Universiteitsbibliotheek.
AMS²	—, Theologische Hogeschool.
ANG	Angers, Bibliothèque Municipale.
ANG²	—, Université Catholique.
ANT	Antwerp, Stedelijke Bibliotheken.
ANT²	—, Museum Plantijn-Moretus.
ANT³	—, Ruusbroec Genootschap.
AR	Arras, Bibliothèque Municipale.
ASC	Ascoli, Capuchins.
AUG	Fort Augustus Abbey, Invernessshire.
AV	Avignon, Musée Calvet.
BA	Bamberg, Staatliche Bibliothek.
BAR	Barcelona, Biblioteca de Cataluña (Biblioteca Central.)
BAR²	—, Biblioteca Universitaria.
BAR³	—, Biblioteca del Seminario.
BER	Berlin, Deutsche Staatsbibliothek.
BEU	Beuron, Erzabteibibliothek.
BG	Bologna, Biblioteca Universitaria.
BG²	—, Biblioteca Communale del Archiginnasio.
BGS	Bourges, Bibliothèque Municipale.
BM²	Birmingham, Oratory.
BNE	Berne, Schweizerische Landesbibliothek.
BO	Boston, Public Library.
BON	Bonn, Universitätsbibliothek.
BOR	Bordeaux, Bibliothèque Municipale.
BOU	Boulogne, Bibliothèque Municipale.
BRG	Burgos, Biblioteca Publica Provincial.
BRN	Brno, Universitní Knihovna.
BRS	Brussels, Bibliothèque Royale.
BRS²	—, Société des Bollandistes.
BRS³	—, Musée d'Art et d'Histöire.
BRS⁴	—, Archives du Royaume.
BRU²	Bruges, Grootseminarie.
BRU³	—, Sint-Andriesabdij.
BRU⁴	—, Sint-Godelieveabdij.
BU	Budapest, Nationalbibliothek.

BUCK	Buckfast Abbey.
BUTE	Marquis of Bute.
C	Cambridge University.
C^2	—, Trinity College.
C^3	—, Emmanuel College.
C^4	—, Kings College.
C^5	—, St John's College.
C^7	—, Corpus Christi College.
C^8	—, Jesus College.
C^9	—, Gonville and Caius.
C^{10}	—, Magdalene College.
C^{11}	—, St Catherine's College.
C^{12}	—, Christ's College.
C^{13}	—, Clare College.
C^{15}	—, Pembroke College.
C^{16}	—, Queens' College.
C^{17}	—, Sidney Sussex College.
C^{18}	—, Selwyn College.
C^{19}	—, Peterhouse.
CAL	University of California.
CANT	Canterbury Cathedral.
CARL	Carlisle Cathedral.
CARP	Carpentras, Bibliothèque Municipale (Inguimbert.).
CASHEL	Cashel Cathedral, Co. Tipperary.
CAV	Cava dei Tirreni, Capuchins.
CB	John Carter Brown Library, Providence, R.I.
CHA	Chantilly, Les Fontaines, Jesuit Library.
CHAM	Chambéry, Capuchins.
CHI	Chicago, University.
CHICH[2]	Chichester Cathedral.
CHX	Chateauroux, Bibliothèque Municipale.
CLIF	Clifton, R.C. Diocese.
CML	Cartmell Priory, Lancs.
CMR	Colmar, Bibliothèque Municipale.
COI	Coimbra, Universidade.
COR	Cornell University.
CORD	Cordoba, Biblioteca Publica Provincial.
CU	Columbia University.
D	Dublin, Trinity College.
D^2	—, Archbishop Marsh's Library.
D^6	—, National Library of Ireland.
D^8	—, Royal Irish Academy. (=A&R D^9)
D^{10}	—, Gilbert Library, Pearse St.
D^{11}	—, Jesuits, Milltown Park. (=A&R D^8).
D^{12}	—, University College.
DAI	Douai Abbey, Woolhampton, Berks.
DE	Downside Abbey, Bath.
DET	Detmold, Lippische Landesbibliothek.
DI	Dillingen, Kreis-und Studienbibliothek.
DIJ	Dijon, Bibliothèque Municipale.
DMR	D. M. Rogers.
DNPK	Deene Park, Northants.
DOE	Donau-Eschingen, Fürstlich Fürstenbergische Hofbibliothek.
DOL	Dole, Bibliothèque Municipale.
DOU	Douai, Bibliothèque Municipale.
DRE	Dresden, Sächsische Landesbibliothek.

DUK	Duke University, Durham N.C.
DUR	Durham, University (including Cosin, Routh and Bamburgh Castle collections).
DUR^2	Durham, Cathedral.
DUS	Düsseldorff, Universitätsbibliothek.
E	National Library of Scotland.
E^2	Edinburgh University.
E^3	Signet Library, Edinburgh.
E^4	Edinburgh University, New College.
EH	T. Eyston, East Hendred
EI	Eichstätt, Staatliche Bibliothek.
ELY	Ely Cathedral (deposited at c).
EP	Epernay, Bibliothèque municipale.
ERL	Erlangen, Universitätsbibliothek.
ESC	Real Biblioteca del Escorial.
ETON	Eton College.
EV	Evora, Biblioteca Publica.
EX	Exeter Cathedral.
F	Folger Shakespeare Library, Washington.
FB	Frauenburg (Frombork), Bibliothek des Domkapitels.
FBH	Farnborough, Benedictine Abbey.
FER	Fernyhalgh Rectory, Lancs
FLO	Florence, Biblioteca Nazionale.
FLO^2	—, Biblioteca Riccardiana.
FLO^3	—, Biblioteca Marucelliana.
FOR	Fordham University.
FR	Freiburg i.B., Universitätsbibliothek.
FRA	Frankfurt, Jesuits.
FRI	Fribourg, Switzerland, Convent of La Maigrauge.
FU	Fulda, Landesbibliothek.
FU^2	—, Priesterseminar.
G^2	Glasgow University.
GAES	Gaesdonck, Klosterbibliothek.
GD	Gdansk, Biblioteka Gdanska.
GEI	Geistingen, Redemptoristenbibliothek.
GER	Gerona, Biblioteca Publica.
GETH	Gethsemani Abbey, Kentucky.
GN	Grenoble, Bibliothèque Municipale.
GNA	Genoa, Biblioteca Civica Berio.
GSN	Giessen, Universitätsbibliothek.
GT	Ghent, Universiteitsbibliotheek.
GTN	Göttingen, Universitätsbibliothek.
HA	Hague, Koninklijke Bibliotheek.
HAM	Hamburg, Stadtbibliothek.
HAN	Hannover, Niedersächsische Landesbibliothek.
HART	Pitts Theological Library, Emory University, Atlanta, Ga.
HD	Harvard University.
HD^2	—, Dunbarton Oaks Research Library.
HEI	Heidelberg, Universitätsbibliothek.
HER	Hereford Cathedral.
HEV	Heverlee, Theologische Bibliotheek, S.J.
HN	Huntington Library, San Marino, California.
HNC	Holy Name College, Washington D.C.
HP	Heythrop College, University of London.

HSA	Hispanic Society of America, New York.
ILL	University of Illinois.
IO	University of Iowa.
JE	Jena, Universitätsbibliothek.
JH	Johns Hopkins University, Baltimore.
JS	John Sparrow.
KA	Katowice, Biblioteka Slåska.
KAS	Kassel, Stadt-und Landesbibliothek.
KDN	Kaldenkirchen, Pfarrbibliothek.
KIE	Kiel, Universitätsbibliothek.
KL	Klagenfurt, Studienbibliothek.
KN	Köln, Universitäts-und Stadtbibliothek.
KN²	—, Erzbischöfliche Diözesan- und Dombibliothek.
KNY	Killiney, Eire, Franciscans.
KR	Krakow, Biblioteka Jagiellońska.
KR²	—, Biblioteka Czartaryskich.
L	London, British Library.
L²	—, Lambeth Palace.
L⁴	—, Sion College.
L⁸	—, Guildhall.
L⁹	—, Jesuits, Mount Street.
L⁹ᴬ	—, —, Archives.
L¹¹	—, Public Record Office.
L¹³	—, Westminster Abbey.
L²⁵	—, Middle Temple.
L²⁶	—, London Oratory.
L²⁷ᴬ	—, Westmins er Cathedral (Archives of the Archdiocese).
L³⁰ᴬ	—, London School of Economics.
L⁵⁰	—, King's College.
L⁵¹	—, School of Oriental and African S udies.
LAR	La Rochelle, Bibliothèque Municipale.
LC	Library of Congress, Washington.
LDS	Leeds University (Brotherton Library).
LEM	Le Mans, Bibliothèque Municipale.
LER	Lerida, Biblioteca publica.
LF	Lord Furness (Viscount Furness).
LGE	Liège, Bibliothèque Universitaire. (=A&R LIEGE).
LGE²	—, Bibliothèque Publique.
LGE³	—, Grand Séminaire.
LGE⁴	—, Jesuits.
LGO	Lugo, Biblioteca publica provincial.
LIL	Lille, Bibliothèque Municipale.
LIL²	—, Bibliothèque Universitaire.
LIL³	—, Faculté Catholique.
LINC	Lincoln Cathedral.
LIS	Lisbon, Biblioteca Nacional.
LIS²	—, Academia das sciencias.
LIV	Liverpool Cathedral.
LN	Leiden Universiteitsbibliotheek.
LOU	Louvain Universiteitsbibliotheek.
LOU²	—, St Anthony's Friary.
LOU³	—, Theological Faculty.
LW	Leeuwarden, Buma-Bibliotheek.
LX	Luxembourg, Bibliothèque Nationale.

LYN	Lyon, Bibliothèque Municipale.
LYN²	—, Bibliothèque Universitaire.
M	Manchester, John Rylands Library.
MAA	Maastricht, Bibliotheek Canisianum.
MAR	Maredsous, Belgium, Benedictine Abbey.
MD	Madrid, Biblioteca Nacional.
MD²	—, Academia de la Historia.
MD³	—, Biblioteca del Palacio Real.
MD⁴	—, Comillas, Jesuit University.
MFL	Münstereiffel, Klosterbibliothek.
MICH	Michigan University.
MIL	Milan, Biblioteca Ambrosiana.
MIL²	—, Biblioteca Brera (Braidense).
MIL³	—, Biblioteca Trivulciana.
MIN	Minnesota University.
MNS	Mons, Bibliothèque Publique Communale.
MONT	Montorges, Convent, Switzerland.
MOU	Moulins, Bibliothèque Municipale.
MP	Montpellier, Bibliothèque Municipale.
MR	Münster Universitätsbibliothek.
MR²	—, Priesterseminar.
MRB	Marburg, Universitätsbibliothek.
MSM	Mount St Mary's College, Derbyshire.
MST	Montserrat, Abadía di Santa Maria.
MTH	Maynooth, St Patrick's Seminary.
MU	München, Bayerische Staatsbibliothek.
MU²	—, Franziskanerbibliothek.
MU³	—, Deutsches Museum.
MZ	Mainz, Stadtbibliothek.
N	Newberry Library, Chicago.
NA	Navarra, Universidad de Pamplona, Navarra. Naworth Castle, Cumbria.
NB	Nürnberg, Universitätsbibliothek.
NBTS	New Brunswick Theological Seminary.
NCY	Nancy, Bibliothèque Municipale.
ND	University of Notre Dame, Indiana.
NEU	Neuburg a.d. Donau, Staatlichebibliothek.
NI	Nijmegen Universiteitsbibliotheek.
NI²	—, Berchmanianum.
NM	Namur, Bibliothèbue Universitaire.
NM²	—, Grand Séminaire.
NOR	Norwich Cathedral.
NP	Naples, Biblioteca Nazionale.
NP²	—, Biblioteca Universitaria.
NP³	—, Biblioteca Oratoriana.
NT	Niort, Bibliothèque Municipale.
NTS	Nantes, Bibliothèque Municipale.
NY	New York Public Library.
NY¹¹	—, General Theological Seminary.
O	Oxford, Bodleian Library.
O²	—, Queen's College.
O³	—, Christ Church.
O⁴	—, Brasenose College.
O⁵	—, Corpus Christi College.
O⁶	—, Worcester College.

O^7	—, Wadham College.
O^8	—, St John's College.
O^9	—, All Souls College.
O^{10}	—, Exeter College.
O^{11}	—, Merton College.
O^{12}	—, Magdalen College.
O^{13}	—, Lincoln College.
O^{14}	—, New College.
O^{16}	—, Trinity College.
O^{17}	—, Balliol College.
O^{18}	—, Jesus College.
O^{19}	—, Oriel College.
O^{24}	—, Pembroke College.
O^{25}	—, Pusey House.
O^{27}	—, University College.
O^{30}	—, Taylor Institution.
O^{31}	—, Keble College.
O^{35}	—, Blackfriars Priory.
O^{37}	—, Campion Hall.
O^{49}	—, Centre for Mediaeval and Renaissance Studies.
O^{41}	—, Greyfriars Priory.
OLD	Oldenburg, Landesbibliothek.
OP	Oporto, Bibliotheca Publica Municipal.
OR	Orléans, Bibliothèque Municipale.
OR^2	—, Bénédictines du Calvaire.
OS	Oscott, St Mary's Seminary.
P	Peterborough Cathedral (deposited at C).
PA	Paris, Bibliothèque Nationale, Imprimés.
PA^A	—, Bibliothèque Nationale, Manuscrits.
PA^2	—, Bibliothèque de l'Arsenal.
PA^3	—, Bibliothèque Mazarine.
PA^4	—, Bibliothèque Ste Geneviève.
PA^5	—, Bibliothèque de la Sorbonne.
PA^6	—, Collège des Irlandais.
PA^7	—, Bibliothèque de l'Histoire du Protestantisme.
PA^8	—, Bibliothèque de S. Sulpice.
PA^9	—, Capuchins.
PA^{10}	—, Dominicans.
PA^{11}	—, Benedictines.
PA^{12}	—, Archives Nationales.
PA^{13}	—, Bibliothèque de l'Institut.
PA^{14}	—, Bibliothèque de l'Histoire de la Ville.
PA^{15}	—, Franciscans.
PAL	Palma (de Mallorca), Biblioteca publica.
PAR	Parma, Biblioteca Palatina.
PAS	Passau, Stadtbücherei.
PBN	Paderborn, Erzbischöffliche Akademische Bibliothek.
PEN	Pennsylvania University.
PEN^3	—, Historical Society.
PER	Perpignan, Bibliothèque municipale.
PLU	Plume Library, Maldon, Essex.
PML	Pierpont Morgan Library, New York.
PN	Princeton University, N.J.
POI	Poitiers, Bibliothèque Municipale.
POI^2	—, Bénédictines du Calvaire.
PR	Prague, Statni Knihovna.
PR^2	—, Strahovská Knihovna.

PR^3	—, Knihovna Národního Muzea.
PRI	Prinknash Abbey, Gloucester.
R	Ripon Cathedral.
REG	Reggio Emilia, Collegio missionario dei Cappuccini.
RG	Regensburg, Staatlichebibliothek.
RG^2	—, Fürstlich Thurn- und Taxis'sche Hofbibliothek.
RMS	Rheims, Bibliothèque Municipale.
RNN	Roanne, Bibliothèque Municipale.
RNS	Rennes, Bibliothèque Municipale.
RO	Rome, English College.
RO^2	—, Biblioteca Nazionale (Vittorio Emmanuele).
RO^3	—, Biblioteca Alessandrina.
RO^4	—, Biblioteca Vallicelliana.
RO^5	—, Biblioteca Casanatense (=A&R ROME^2).
RO^6	—, Biblioteca Angelica.
RO^7	—, Capuchin International College.
RO^8	—, Franciscan College of S. Isidore.
RO^9	—, Archivum Roman, Societatis Iesu.
RO^{10}	—, Irish College.
RO^{11}	—, Dominican College of S. Clemente.
RO^{12}	—, Istituto Historico S.J.
RO^{13}	—, Biblioteca Corsiniana.
RO^{14}	—, S. Congreg of Propaganda.
ROT	Rottenburg, Priesterseminar.
ROT^2	—, Diözesanbibliothek.
ROU	Rouen, Bibliothèque Municipale.
RUT	Rutgers University.
SAI	Saintes, Bibliothèque Municipale.
SAL	Salamanca, Biblioteca de la Universidad (=A&R Salisbury Cathedral).
SALZ	Salzburg, Capuchins.
SBG	Strasbourg, Bibliothèque National and Universitaire.
SBG^2	Strasbourg, Grand Sèminaire.
SCG	San Cugat, Biblioteca Borja.
SEV	Seville, Biblioteca Colombina.
SEV^2	—, Universidad.
SEV^3	—, Archivo Municipal.
SEV^4	—, Biblioteca de las Indias.
SHT	s'Hertogenbosch, Capuchins.
SHT^2	—, Provinz Genootschap van Kunsten.
SIM	Simancas, Archivo General.
SJBD	Saint-Jean-de-Braye, Orléans.
SJU	St John's University, Collegeville.
SMA	S. Malo, Bibliothèque Municipale.
SMI	S. Mihiel, Bibliothèque Municipale.
SO	Soest, Stadtbibliothek.
SOI	Soissons, Bibliothèque Municipale.
SOL	Solesmes, Bibliothèque de l'Abbaye Benedictine.
SOR	Soria, Biblioteca Publica Provincial.
SOU	Southwell Cathedral.
SP	Speyer, Priesterseminar.
SPS	S. Pieter, Schwarzwald, Priesterseminar.
ST	Stonyhurst College.
STAN	Stanford University, California.
STG	Stuttgart, Württembergische Landesbibliothek.
STI	Santiago de Compostela, Biblioteca Universitaria.

STL	St Louis University, Missouri.
STM	Stockholm, Kungl. Biblioteket.
STO	Saint Omer, Bibliothèque Municipale.
STR	S. Trond, Franciscans.
STU	S. Andrews University
SWAF	Swaffham Parish Library, Norfolk.
TAG	Taggia, Capuchins.
TAL	Tallaght, Co. Dublin, Irish Dominicans.
TAR	Tarragona, Biblioteca Publica Provincial.
TB	Tübingen, Universitätsbibliothek.
TDO	Toledo, Biblioteca Provincial.
TEX	Texas, University.
TI	Tilburg, Theologische Facultheit.
TNI	Tournai, Grand Séminaire.
TNI²	—, Bibliothèque de la Ville.
TOU	Toulouse, Bibliothèque Municipale.
TRI	Trier, Stadtbibliothek.
TRO	Troyes, Bibliothèque Municipale.
TUR	Turin, Biblioteca Nazionale Universitaria.
U	Union Theological Seminary, New York.
UD	Udenhout, Capuchins.
UEB	Überlingen, Leopold-Sophien-Bibliothek.
ULM	Ulm, Stadtbibliothek.
UP	Uppsala, Universitetsbibliotek.
USH	Ushaw College, Durham.
UT	Utrecht, Bibliotheek Rijksuniversiteit.
UT²	—, University, Franciscan Library.
V	Virginia, University.
VAL	Valladolid, English College.
VAL²	—, Scots College.
VAL³	—, Abadía di Silos
VCE	Venice, Biblotheca Nazionale Marciana.
VCE²	—, Bibliotheca Correr.
VER	Versailles, Bibliothèque Municipale.
VES	Vesoul, Biblothèque Municipale.
VI	Vienna, Österreichische Nazionalbibliothek.
VI²	—, Universitätsbitliothek.
VI³	—, Priesterseminar.
VIL	Villanova College.
VNS	Valenciennes, Bibliothèque municipale.
VT	Vatican, Biblioteca Apostolica Vaticana.
VT²	—, Archives.
VV	Villa Viçosa, King Manuel II's Library.
W	Ware, St Edmund's College.
WA	Warsaw, Biblioteka Narodowa.
WB	Walberberg, Albertus Magnus Akademie (O.P.).
WIE	Wiesbaden, Nassauische Landesbibliothek.
WLC	Washington and Lee College, Lexington V.A.
WN	Winchester Cathedral.
WO	Wolfenbüttel, Herzog-August-Bibliothek.
WOR	Worcester Cathedral.
WR	Wroclaw, Biblioteka Uniwersytecka.
WR²	—, Biblioteka Zakładu Narodowego im. Ossolinskich.
WVS	W. Vincent Smith (now at USH).

WZ	Würzburg, Universitätsbibliothek.
X	Xanten, Stifts- und Pfarrbibliothek.
Y	Yale University.
YK	York Minster.
ZA	Zaragoza, Biblioteca Publica de la Ciudad.

See also Addenda & Corrigenda

Signs and Abbreviations

[*]	*See* Foreword, p. xii.
†	*See* Foreword, p. viii.
‡	*See* Foreword, p. viii.
[ ]	Information given within square brackets is not contained in the book itself. A serial number in the left-hand margin enclosed in square brackets indicates a deletion.
—	without
Ⓐ	*See* Addenda & Corrigenda, p. 290
a.a.	all after
a.b.	all before
abr.	abbreviated/abbreviation
Anon.	anonymous
anr.	another
Brs.	broadside
c.	*circa*
col.	column
coll.	collection
coloph.	colophon
cp.	compare
Ded.	dedication/dedicated/dedicatory epistle
ed.	editor/edited by/edition
e.g.	*exempli gratia*
esp.	especially
et seq.	*et sequitùr*
f./ff.	folio/folios
facs.	facsimile
Fol.	folio (format)
imp.	imperfect
l./ll.	line/lines
mutil.	mutilated
n.	note
n.a.	not after
n.b.	not before
n.d.	no date
no./nos.	number/numbers
n.p.	no printer or place of publication
n.p.d.	no printer, place of publication or date
p./pp.	page/pages
pr.	printer/printed
pref.	preface
pseud.	pseudonym
pt./pts.	part/parts
sgd.	signed
s.sh.	single sheet
soc.	society
t./tom.	tomus/tome
tp.	titlepage
transl.	translator/translated/translation
v./vol.	volume

Short References

The following shorter references are used. Other works referred to in the Catalogue are cited in full where they occur.

AAW — Archives of the Archdiocese of Westminster, 16A Abingdon Road, London W8 6AF.

A&R — A. F. Allison and D. M. Rogers, A Catalogue of Catholic Books in English printed abroad or secretly in England, 1558–1640. *Bognor Regis*, 1956. (*Biographical Studies*, vol. 3, nos. 3, 4.)

AGULLÓ — Mercedes Agulló y Cobo, Relaciones de sucesos. *Madrid*, 1966, *etc.* (*Cuadernos bibliográficos*.)

ALBAREDA — A. M. Albareda, Bibliografía dels monjos de Montserrat (segle XVI). *Montserrat*, 1933.

ALEGAMBE — P. Alegambe, Bibliotheca scriptorum Societatis Iesu. *Antwerpiae*, 1643.

ANGLIA — Anglia. Zeitschrift für Englische Philologie. *Halle*, 1877, *etc.*

ANST — Godfrey Anstruther, The Seminary Priests. A dictionary of the secular clergy of England and Wales, 1558–1850. 4 vols. *Ware, etc.* [1968–77.]

APC — Acts of the Privy Council. *Public Record Office, London*, 1890. *etc.*

APSI — Archivum Provinciale Societatis Iesu (i.e. the archives of the English Province, 114 Mount Street, London W1).

ARCHIVIUM HIBERNICUM — Archivium Hibernicum. Irish historical records. (Catholic Record Society of Ireland.) *Dublin*, 1912, *etc.*

ARSI — Archivum Romanum Societatis Iesu (i.e. the Jesuit General Archives at Rome).

ASCARELLI — Fernanda Ascarelli, Le cinquecentine romane. *Roma*, 1972.

BAUDRIER — Julien Baudrier, Bibliographie Lyonnaise. 12 ser. *Lyon*, 1895–1921.

BCNI — Bibliotheca catholica neerlandica impressa 1500–1727. *Hagae Comitis*, 1954.

BELLENGER — Dominic Aidan Bellenger, English and Welsh Priests 1558–1800. A working list. *Bath*, 1984.

BENZING — J. Benzing, Die Buchdrucker des 16. und 17. Jahrhunderts im deutschen Sprachgebiet. 2 Auflage. *Wiesbaden*, 1982.

BL — British Library.

BLISS — S. D. Bliss, Collection relative à Marie Stuart. *Paris*, 1931.

BNB — Biographie nationale ... de Belgique. 15 tom. *Bruxelles*, 1866–1983.

BRADSHAW

Henry Bradshaw, A Catalogue of the Bradshaw Collection of Irish Books in the University Library, Cambridge. *Cambridge,* 1916.

CAL SPD

Calendar of State Papers Domestic. *Public Record Office, London,* 1856, *etc.*

CATÁLOGO COLECTIVO

Catálogo colectivo de obras impresas en los siglos XVI al XVIII existentes en las bibliotecas españolas. Seccion I. Siglo XVI. *Madrid,* 1972, *etc.*

CHADWICK

Hubert Chadwick, St Omers to Stonyhurst. A history of two centuries. *London,* 1962.

CHANEY

Edward Chaney, The Grand Tour and the Great Rebellion. Richard Lassels and 'The Voyage of Italy' in the seventeenth century. *Geneve,* 1985. (*Bilbioteca del Viaggio in Italia.* 19.).

CHAUSSY

Yves Chaussy, Les Bénédictins anglais refugiés en France au XVIIe siècle (1611–1669). *Paris,* 1967.

CLANCY

T. H. Clancy, English Catholic Books 1641–1700: a bibliography. *Chicago,* 1974.

CLEARY

Gregory Cleary, Father Luke Wadding and St. Isidore's College, Rome: biographical and historical notes. *Rome,* 1925.

COLLECTANEA HIBERNICA

Collectanea Hibernica. Sources for Irish History. *Dublin,* 1958, *etc.*

CORCORAN

T. Corcoran, Studies in the History of Classical Teaching, Irish and Continental, 1500–1700. *Dublin and Belfast,* 1911.

CORDES

Jean de Cordes, Bibliothecae Cordesianae catalogus. [By Gabriel Naudé.] *Parisiis,* 1643.

CRS

Publications of the Catholic Record Society. *London,* 1905, *etc.*

CSPD

See above: CAL SPD.

DD

Doway College Diaries. (vols. 1, 2, ed. T. F. Knox. *London,* 1878; vols. 3, 4, 5, *Publications of the Catholic Record Society,* vols. 10, 11. *London,* 1911.)

DESGRAVES

Louis Desgraves, Les livres imprimés à Bordeaux au XVIIe siècle, *Genève,* 1971. (*Histoire et civilisation du livre.* 4.)

DESMAZIÈRES

Emile Desmazières, Bibliographie Tournaisienne. *Tournai,* 1882.

DILWORTH

Mark Dilworth, The Scots in Franconia, *Edinburgh and London,* 1974.

DNB

Dictionary of National Biography. *London,* 1882, *etc.*

DODD

Charles Dodd, *pseud.*, The Church History of England from 1500 to ... 1688. 3 vols. *Brussels,* 1737–42.

DR

Downside Review. *London,* 1880, *etc.*

DUTHILLOEUL

H. R. Duthilloeul, Bibliographie Douaisienne. 2nd. ed. *Douai,* 1842.

ERL

English Recusant Literature, 1558–1640. ed. D. M. Rogers. (Modern facsimile reprints of works listed in A&R.) 1967, *etc.*

ESCUDERO

F. Escudero y Perosso, Tipografía Hispalense. *Madrid,* 1874.

ESTREICHER

K. J. T. Estreicher, Bibliografija Polska. *Cracow,* 1870, *etc.*

FOLEY

Henry Foley, Records of the English Province of the Society of Jesus. 7 vols. *London,* 1877–82.

FOPPENS	J. F. Foppens, Bibliotheca Belgica. *Bruxelles*, 1739.
FORBES-LEITH	W. Forbes-Leith, (1) Memoirs of Scottish Catholics during the XVIIth and XVIIIth centuries. *London*, 1909. (2) Narratives of Scottish Catholics under Mary Stuart and James VI. *Edinburgh*, 1885.
GALLARDO	B. J. Gallardo, Ensayo de una biblioteca española de libros raros y curiosos. 4 tom. *Madrid*, 1863–89.
GARDINER	S. R. Gardiner, Prince Charles and the Spanish Marriage, 1617–1623. 2 vols. *London*, 1869.
GIBSON	R. W. Gibson, St. Thomas More: a preliminary bibliography . . . to the year 1750. *Yale*, 1961. For an updating, *see* under Smith.
GILLOW	Joseph Gillow, A Literary and Biographical History, or Bibliographical Dictionary of the English Catholics. 5 vols. *London* [1885–1902].
HAY	M. V. Hay, The Blairs Papers (1603–1660). *London and Edinburgh*, 1929.
HMC	Historical Manuscripts Commission. Reports. *London*, 1870, *etc.*
HOUDOY	J. Houdoy, Les imprimeurs lillois. *Paris*, 1879.
IER	Irish Ecclesiastical Record. *Dublin*, [1864, *etc.*]
INDEX AURELIENSIS	Index Aureliensis. Catalogus librorum sedecimo saeculo impressorum. *Aureliae Aquensis*, 1965, *etc.*
IRISH THEOLOGICAL QUARTERLY	Irish Theological Quarterly. *Dublin*, 1906, *etc.*
KING MANUEL	Catalogue of a Collection of Early Portuguese Books in the Library of H.M. King Manuel of Portugal. 3 vols. *London*, 1928, *etc.*
KNUTTEL	W. P. C. Knuttel, Catalogus van de pamfletten-verzameling berustende in de Koninklijke Bibliotheek. 6 dl. *s'Gravenhage*, 1889–1910.
LABARRE	Albert Labarre, (1) Répertoire bibliographique des livres imprimés en France au seizième siècle. no. 53. Douai. 1972. (*Bibliotheca bibliographica Aureliana*. 44). (2) Repertoire bibliographique des livres imprimes en France au XVIIe siecle. Tome 4. Douai. 1982. (*Bibliotheca bibliographica Aureliana*. 86.)
LA NOUE	Franciscus de La Noue, Chronicon generale ordinis Minimorum. *Lutetiae Parisiorum*, 1635.
LAW	T. G. Law, Historical Sketch of the Conflicts between Jesuits and Seculars in the Reign of Queen Elizabeth. *London*, 1889.
LE LONG	Jacques Le Long, Bibliothèque historique de la France. *Paris*, 1719. nouvelle édition. *Paris*, 1768–78.
LETTERS AND NOTICES	Letters and Notices. [A privately printed periodical of the English Province of the Society of Jesus.]
LIBRARY	The Library. A quarterly review of bibliography. New ser. *London*, 1900, *etc.* 4th ser. vol. 1. 1920, onwards, amalgamated with the Transactions of the Bibliographical Society.
MACNEILL	Charles MacNeill, Publications of Irish Interest published by Irish Authors on the Continent of Europe prior to the eight-

teenth century. *Dublin*, 1930. (*Bibliographical Society of Ireland*, vol. 4.)

MADAN — Falconer Madan, Oxford Books. 3 vols. *Oxford*, 1895–1931.

MANSI — G. D. Mansi, Sacrorum conciliorum nova et amplissima collectio. 55 vols. *Florentiae*, etc., 1759–1962.

MANZI — Pietro Manzi, La tipografía napoletana nel '500. *Firenze*, 1974. (*Biblioteca di bibliografía italiana.* 73.)

MAYER — Anton Mayer, Wiens Buchdrucker Geschichte, 1482–1882. 2 Bde. *Wien*, 1883–87.

MEYER — A. O. Meyer, England and the Catholic Church under Queen Elizabeth. tr. J. R. McKee. *London*, 1916.

MIL — Peter Milward, (1) Religious Controversies of the Elizabethan Age. A survey of the printed sources. *London*, 1977. (2) Religious Controversies of the Jacobean Age. A survey of the printed sources. *London*, 1978.

OPTAT — Optat de Veghel, Benoît de Canfield (1562–1610). Sa vie, sa doctrine et son influence. *Romae*, 1949.

ORCIBAL — Jean Orcibal, Benoît de Canfield. La règle de perfection. The rule of perfection. Edition critique. Paris, 1982. (*Bibliothèque de l'Ecole des Hautes Etudes. Section des sciences religieuses.* 83.)

O'REILLY — Myles W. P. O'Reilly, Lives of the Irish Martyrs and Confessors. *New York*, 1878.

PALAU — A. Palau y Dulcet, Manual del librero hispanico-americano . . . segunda edicion. *Barcelona*, 1948, *etc.*

PBSA — Papers of the Bibliographical Society of America. *New York*, 1906, *etc.*

PÉRENNÈS — F. Pérennès, Dictionnaire de bibliographie catholique. 5 tom. 1858–60. (*J. P. Migne, Troisième et dernière Encyclopédie théologique.* tom. 39–43).

PETTI — A. G. Petti, A Bibliography of the Writings of Richard Verstegan. (*Recusant History*, April 1963, pp. 82–103.)

PITS — John Pits, Ioannis Pitsei . . . Relationum historicarum de rebus Anglicis tomus primus. (De illustribus Angliae scriptoribus.) *Parisiis*, 1619. No more published.

POLLEN — J. H. Pollen, The English Catholics in the Reign of Queen Elizabeth . . . 1558–1580. *London*, 1920.

PRO — Public Record Office, London.

RENOUARD — P. Renouard, Imprimeurs & libraires parisiens du XVIe siècle. 3 vols. *Paris*, 1964–79.
—, Fascicule Brumen. *Paris*, 1984.

REUSENS — E. Reusens, Documents relatifs à l'histoire de l'Université de Louvain (1425–1797). tom. 1–5. *Louvain*, 1881–1903.

RH — Recusant History. A journal of research in post-Reformation Catholic history. *Bognor Regis*, etc., 1951, *etc.*

RIVIÈRE — E. M. Rivière, Corrections et additions à la Bibliothèque de la Compagnie de Jésus. 2 tom. *Toulouse*, 1911–30.

ROBERTI — G. M. Roberti, Disegno storico dell'ordine dei Minimi. 3 vols. *Roma*, 1902–22.

ROMBAUTS — Edward Rombauts, Richard Verstegen. Een polemist der

Contra-Reformatie. *Brussel*, 1933. (*Koninklijke Vlaamsche Academie voor Taal-en Letterkunde*. Reeks 6, nr. 54.)

SALVÁ   Vicente Salvá y Perez, Catálogo de la biblioteca de Salvá. 2 tom. *Valencia*, 1872.

SANCHEZ   J. M. Sanchez, Bibliografía Aragonesa del siglo XVI. 2 tom. *Madrid*, 1913–14.

SBARALEA   J. H. Sbaralea, Suppelementum et castigatio ad Scriptores trium ordinum S. Francisci. 3 tom. *Romae*, 1908–36.

SCOTT   John Scott, A Bibliography of Works relating to Mary Queen of Scots. *Edinburgh*, 1895. (*Publications of the Edinburgh Bibliographical Society*. 2.)

SHAABER   M. A. Shaaber, Check-list of Works of British Authors printed abroad, in languages other than English, to 1641. *Bibliographical Society of America, New York*, 1975.

SIMON DIAZ   José Simon Diaz, Bibliografía de la literatura hispanica, *Madrid*, 1960, *etc.*

SIMPSON   Richard Simpson, Edmund Campion. A biography. *London*, 1867. New ed. *London*, 1896.

1632 CATALOGUE   [A MS list preserved in the archives of the English College, Rome (Scritture XXX 2), of 39 English Jesuit writers and their works. It is undated but can be assigned on internal evidence to 1632.]

SMITH   Constance Smith, An Updating of R. W. Gibson's St. Thomas More: a preliminary bibliography. *St. Louis University*, 1981. (*Sixteenth Century Bibliography*. no. 20.)

SOMMERV   Carlos Sommervogel, Bibliothèque de la Compagnie de Jésus. 11 tom. *Bruxelles, etc.*, 1890–1932. For corrections and additions, *see* under Rivière.

SOUTHWELL   Nathaniel Southwell, Bibliotheca scriptorum Societatis Jesu. *Romae*, 1676.

STALLA   Gerhard Stalla, Bibliographie der Ingolstädter Drucker des 16 Jahrhunderts. 1971, etc.
(*Bibliotheca bibliographica Aureliana*. nos. 34, 41, 46, 56, 61, 67, 71, *etc.*)

STC   A Short-Title Catalogue of Books printed in England, Scot-Land, & Ireland and of English Books printed abroad 1475–1640. First compiled by A. W. Pollard & G. R. Redgrave. Second edition, revised and enlarged, begun by W. A. Jackson & F. S. Ferguson, completed by Katharine F. Pantzer. Volume 2 I–Z. *Bibliographical Society, London*, 1976. (Volume 1 A–H. *London*, 1986.)

STRYPE   John Strype, Annals of the Reformation. New ed. 4 vols. *Oxford*, 1824.

STUDIES   Studies: an Irish quarterly review of letters, philosophy and science. *Dublin*, 1912, *etc.*

THEUX   Le chevalier de Theux de Montjardin, Bibliographie Liégoise. 2nd ed. *Bruges*, 1885.

THOMASON   British Museum, Catalogue of the Pamphlets, Books, Newspapers, and Manuscripts . . . collected by George Thomason, 1640–61. Ed. G. K. Fortescue. 2 vols. *London*, 1908.

TOBOLKA   Z. V. Tobolka, Knihopis československých tisků. 8 vols. *v Praze*, 1925–63.

URIARTE	P. J. E. de Uriarte, Catálogo razonado de obras anónimas y seudónimas de autores de la Compañía de Jesús pertenecientes á la antigua asistencia española. 5 tom. *Madrid*, 1904–16.
VINDEL	Francisco Vindel Angulo, Manual, gráfico-descriptivo del bibliófilo Hispano-Americano. *Madrid*, 1930–34.
WADDING	Luke Wadding, Scriptores ordinis minorum. *Romae*, 1906. (Original ed. 1650.) For the Supplementum *see* under Sbaralea.
WADDING PAPERS	Brendan Jennings, Ed. Wadding Papers 1614–38. *Irish Manuscripts Commission, Dublin*, 1953.
WALSH	M. On. Walsh, Irish Books printed abroad, 1470–1700. *Dublin*, 1963. (*The Irish Book*, vol. 2, no. 1.)
WELDON	Benet Weldon, Collections. [A MS collection (with some printed material) on the history of the English Benedictine Congregation from 1607 to 1707. Compiled by Benet Weldon, O.S.B., 1647–1713. Preserved at Douai Abbey, Woolhampton.]

Catalogue
Part I (Personal)

In addition to personal names, the following institutions and groups figure as headings in this section:

Douai, *English College.*
Douai, *Irish College.*
Douai, *Scots College.*
England, *Catholic Church.*
English Benedictines.
English Bridgettines.
English Carthusians.
English Catholics.
English Catholic Seminaries.
English Dominicans.
English Jesuits.
English Secular Clergy.
Ireland, *Catholic Church.*
Irish Regular Clergy.
Liège, *English Jesuit College.*
Liège, *English Jesuit Novitiate.*
Lisbon, *English Bridgettine Convent.*
Lisbon, *English College.*
Lisbon, *Irish College.*
Louvain, *English Jesuit College.*
Louvain, *Irish Franciscan College of St Anthony.*
Madrid, *English College.*
Paris, *Arras College.*
Paris, *Irish College.*
Rheims, *English College.*
Rome, *English College.*
Rome, *Irish College.*
Rome, *Irish Franciscan College of St Isidore.*
Saint Malo, *English Benedictine Priory.*
Saint Omer, *English Jesuit College.*
Salamanca, *Irish College.*
Scotland, *Catholic Church.*
Scottish Catholics.
Seville, *English College.*
Seville, *Irish College.*
Valladolid, *English College.*

A., A. Carta, escrita a vno de los colegiales ingleses que residen en Madrid. *See* no. 1247.

1 **A., A.** Copia de vna carta de vna señora inglesa catolica . . . escrita a su marido exortandole, que aunque pierda su hazienda y hijos, no dexe de confessar el ser catolico. Fol. (a bifolium) [Coloph.] *Madrid, por Diego Flamenco,* 1623. L(2).; MD.MD²(Jes. 153/33).

Letter sgd.: A.A. Though the text provides some family details the author has not been identified. The English original was published [in 1611] as part of A&R 265. The Spanish version had previously appeared as part of nos. 280.1 and 1065 of this catalogue.

2 —[Anr. ed.] Fol. (a bifolium). *En Madrid, por Diego Flamenco, y en Sevilla por Francisco de Lyra,* 1623. CU.HD.MD²(3-Jes.75/97; 93/32; 117/94).SEV.

Sgd.: A.A. A reprint of no. 1.

3 —[*Italian transl.*] Copia d'vna lettera d'vna signora inglese catholica . . . scritta a suo marito. Essortandolo, che anco con la perdita de suoi beni, e figli non lasci di confessare d'essere catholico. Tradotta dalla lingua spagnola. 4°. *Milano, nella Reg. Duc. Corte, per Gio. Battista Malatesta,* 1623. DMR.MIL².NY.

Sgd.: A.A.

A., G. G. R., *Peregrin Roman. See* no. 931.

A., R. [Letter to William Allen concerning the surrender of Deventer]. *See* nos. 14–17.

A., T.W. *See* nos. 1419–24.

4 **Abercromby, Robert.** 'Εξέτασις epistolae, nomine Regis Magnae Britanniae, ad omnes Christianos monarchas, principes, & ordines, scriptae; quae praefationis monitoriae loco, ipsius Apologiae pro iuramento fidelitatis, praefixa est . . . a Bartholo Pacenio I.C. 4°. *Montibus, impressore Adamo Gallo,* 1609. L.; O⁴.WO.

Answers James I's 'Praefatio monitoria' in STC 14405. Bartholus Pacenius, *pseud.* [R. Abercromby?] *See* CSPD 1611–18, nos. 16, 39, under Passenius. APC 1613–14. Lib. 1927, pp. 141–6. Imprint false; *pr.* [Mainz, Joannes Albinus].

4.1 —[Anr. ed.] 8°. *Montibus, impressore Adamo Gallo,* 1610. BRS².LOU³. UT.WO.

Bartholus Pacenius, *pseud.* Imprint false; *pr.* [Mainz, Joannes Albinus.]

5 **Alabaster, William.‡** Apparatus in reuelationem Iesu Christi. Noua & admirabilis ratio inuestigandi prophetiarum mysteria ex scriptura seipsam interpretante. 4°. *Antuerpiae, ex officina Arnoldi Conincx,* 1607. L.O.C.; ANT².D.GTN.KN(2).L².LGE³.PA.PR.TRO.VI.VT.YK. + +

Declared heretical by the Roman Inquisition in Jan. 1610. *See* Story & Gardner, *The Sonnets of William Alabaster,* 1959, p. xix, n. 4. For works published after he left the Catholic Church, *see* STC 246–51.

Alanus, Gulielmus. *See* Allen, W.

Albus, Joannes Jacobus. *See* Whyte, J. J.

Alford, Michael, *alias. See* Griffiths, M.

Allen, William, *Cardinal.†*

WORKS WRITTEN IN LATIN

6 —Gulielmi Alani angli . . . libri tres. Id est, De sacramentis in genere, lib. I. De sacramento eucharistiae. lib. I. De sacrificio eucharistiae. lib. I. 4°. *Antuerpiae, apud Iohannem Foulerum anglum,* 1576. [Coloph.] *Duaci, excudebat Ludouicus de Winde, cura et impensis Iohannis Fouleri.* L.O.C.; AMS.D.DAI.DI.DMR.HP.MD.MU.OS.PA.RO².USH.VT. + +

7   —[Anr. issue with title:] Opus aureum. De sacramentis in genere, de eucharistiae sacramento, de sacrificio eucharistiae. *Duaci, ex officina Baltazaris Belleri*, 1603. C².FR.FU.MNS.O²⁷.PA.RO².RO⁵.TB.TRO.VI.
The sheets of no. 6 except for the first quire (*⁴) which is reprinted. The original colophon on the verso of the final leaf is covered by a paste-over errata slip.

TRANSLATIONS OF HIS ENGLISH WORKS

Apologie and True Declaration (A&R 6)

—[*Latin*] Duo edicta Elizabethae Reginae Angliae contra sacerdotes . . . vna cum Apologia Gulielmi Alani, 1583 [*etc.*] = pt. 2 of nos. 524–7.

Briefe Historie of the Glorious Martyrdom (A&R 7)

—[*Latin*] [A conflated text corresponding to that of no. 8 following. *Tr.* John Gibbons.] 1583, [*etc.*] *In* nos. 524–7.

8   —[*Italian*] Historia del glorioso martirio di sedici sacerdoti martirizati in Inghilterra . . . Tradotta . . . da vno del collegio Inglese di Roma. S'e aggiunto il martirio di due altri sacerdoti, & vno secolare inglesi. 8°. *Macerata, appresso Sebastiano Martellini*, 1583. L.O.; C².CHA.D⁸. DE.HAN.L².NP.OS.RO.RO²(2).RO⁶.SOL(-*plates*)VT(2) +
Anon. Comprises, in fact, nineteen martyr relations (of which the first fifteen had appeared in the English original although the title had called for only twelve, and the last four are added). The translator has not been identified. With 6 pl. reprinted from no. 876.

9   —[Anr. ed.] 8°. *Milano, per Paolo Gottardo Pontio*, 1584. [Coloph.] *Milano, per Pietro Tini*. L.O.; BRS².DMR.FLO.L⁹.MD³.NP.ST.VT.W(2).
Anon. Without plates.

10   —[Anr. ed.] 8°. 2 pts. *Napoli, appresso Horatio Saluiani, & Cesare Cesari*, 1584. O. (*pt. 2*); RO² (*both pts. but wanting K of pt. 2*). W (*pt. 2*).
Anon. Pt. 1 contains Allen's preface, pt. 2 the martyr relations. Each part has its own t.p. and they may have been issued separately. Without plates.

11   —[Anr. ed. enlarged.] Historia del glorioso martirio di diciotto sacerdoti, et vn secolare, fatti morire in Inghilterra . . . S'è aggiunto al presente il martirio di cinque altre sacerdoti inglesi. 8°. *Macerata, appresso Sebastiano Martellini*, 1585. L(-*plates*).O.; AIX(2:-1-plates).C².CHA. D⁸.DE.MD.NCY.O¹⁴.PA.(2).RO.RO².RO⁶.RO⁸.W. +
Anon. Five new martyr relations are added to the former nineteen. With the same plates as no. 8.

12   —[*Supplement by an unidentified author*]. De iustitia Britannica, siue Anglica, quae contra Christi martyres continenter exercetur. 8°. *Ingolstadii, ex officina typographica Dauidis Sartorii*, 1584. L(2).O.C.; D⁸.DE.DI(2).E.FU.L³.L²⁶.O⁸.OS.PA.SOL.UP.VI.YK.
Anwers Lord Burghley's *Iustitia Britannica*, 1584 (STC 4904). The text contains substantial extracts from Sander's *De visibili monarchia* (nos. 1013–16). Sometimes erroneously stated to be a translation of A&R 13. The anonymous author indicates that he intends the work as a supplement to Allen's *Brief Historie*. Scott 125.

Copie of a Letter . . . concerning the Yeelding vp of . . . Dauentrie (A&R8)

13   —[*Latin*] Epistola de ciuitate Deuentriensis reddita suo legitimo regi per illustrem virum Gul. Stanleium. 12°. *Cracouiae*, 1588.
Not found. Description from Simpson, p. 513, no. 43. Dodd (vol. 2, p. 53) records what is probably the same edition but calls it 8°. Not found in Estreicher.

14 —[*French*] Iustification pour le catholique, noble cheualier anglois, le sieur Guillaume Stanlay . . . sur la rendition de la ville de Deuenter & autres lieux à l'obeyssance de sa Majesté Catholique. 8° (in fours). *Paris, chez. Didier Millot,* 1588. O.; AIX.HA.PA(2).
   As in the English original, the letter, signed R.A. [Roger Ashton], to which Allen's work is a reply, is printed before Allen's text. Neither letter bears any date in this edition.

15 —[Anr. ed.] Copie d'vne missiue, escripte par vn gentil-homme anglois, estant au camp de sa Majesté Catholique és Pays-Bas. Au reuerend Monsr. Guillaume Allain . . . sur le faict de la reduction de la ville de Deuenter . . . Ensemble la response & resolution d'iceluy. 8°. *n.p.d.* [1588]. O¹¹. [*DMR.]
   The gentleman's letter, signed R.A., is here dated 20 March 1587. Allen's reply is dated from Rome, 20 July 1587.

16 —[*Italian*] Copia d'vna lettera scritta all'illustrissimo . . . cardinal d'Inghilterra, prima ch'egli fosse promosso al cardinalato, con la risposta del medesimo. 4°. *Roma, per Iacomo Ruffinelli,* 1588. L.; FLO.PA.RO²(2).RO³.RO⁶.RO⁹.(Anglia 30.I.561).VT(4:-2 *imp.*).
   The gentleman's letter, signed R.A., is dated 20 March 1587. Allen's reply is dated 20 April 1587. Translator's *ded.* sgd.: F. Andrea Vuisse Irlandese [Andrew Wise] and dated from Rome 22 Dec. 1587.

17 —[Anr. ed.] 8°. *Firenze, appresso Giorgio Marescotti,* 1588. L.; RO³.
   The gentleman's letter is here signed A.R. instead of R.A. Otherwise this is a straight reprint of no. 16.

   True Report of the Late Apprehension . . . of John Nicols (A&R 12).

   —[*Extracts, Latin.*] 1583 [etc.] *Tr.* [John Gibbons.] *In* nos. 524–7.

   True Sincere and Modest Defence (A&R 13).

18 —[*Latin*] Ad persecutores anglos pro catholicis domi forisque persecutionem sufferentibus; contra falsum . . . libellum, inscriptum; Iustitia britannica, vera, sincera, & modesta Responsio. 8°. *n.p.d.* [1584] L.O.C.; D.D².DE.E.L⁴.L²⁶.MD.PA.PA⁶.RO³.TRO.VT.WO. +
   Anon. *Tr.* [William Rainolds] *Pr.* [Rouen, Fr. Persons's press]. *See* Pits, pp. 790–1; CRS 9, pp. 220, 226, 230, 255. Scott 126.
   —[Anr. ed.] 1588. *In* no. 525.
   —[For *De iustitia Britannica,* 1584, sometimes erroneously stated to be a translation of A&R 13, *see* no. 12.]

APPENDIX

   —Fitzherbert, N. De Alani Cardinalis vita libellus, 1608. *See* no. 476.

19 **Allot, William.** Thesaurus bibliorum, omnem vtriusque vitae antidotum secundum vtriusque instrumenti veritatem & historiam succincte complectens. 8°. *Antuerpiae, in aedibus Petri Belleri,* 1576. [Coloph.] *Typis Aegidii Radei.* BRS.DI.HA.MU.RO².RO⁵.UT².VT.
   A selective subject-index to the Bible arranged alphabetically.

20 —[Date vaiiant.] 1577. L.; AMS.FR.HA.LYN.MD.MU.SAL.STG.STI.WR.X.YK.

21 —[Anr. ed.] 8°. *Lugduni, apud Alexandrum Marsilium,* 1580. 8°. AMI. ANG.AV.BAR².FR.FRA.MD.MIL.MU.PA.RO².RO³.STG.STI(2).TB.VT.ZA.

22 —[Anr. ed.] 8°. *Antuerpiae, in aedibus Petri Belleri,* 1581. [Coloph.] *Typis Andreae Bax.* L.O.; BG².BRS.CHA.DI.FR.GT.HP.L².LYN.O⁷.PA.RO². TB. + +

23 —[Anr. ed.] 8°. *Lugduni, sumptibus Ludouici Ganaraei,* 1583. BAR²(2). BRN.CMR.LGE.MD.MU.PA.RO².RO⁶.SAL.TNI.TOU.TRO.VI.WO. +
   A close reprint of no. 21.

24   —[Anr. ed.] 8°. *Lugduni, in offi. Q. Phil. Tinghi, apud Simphorianum Beraud, et Stephanum Michaelem,* 1585. [Coloph.] *Vimiaci, excudebat Ioannes Symonetus,* 1584. O.C.; A.B.AV.BAR².BRN.CHA.CMR.D.DMR.FLO. MU.NCY.PA⁵.PR.STG. +

     —[Supposititious ed. *Antwerp, Bellerus,* 1586. BCNI 3880. The copy cited, formerly at Alverna now at UT², is in fact a copy of no. 15 with the date in the imprint altered from 1576 to 1586 by pen.]

25   —[Anr. ed.] 8°. *Coloniae Agrippinae, apud Petrum Henningum,* 1612. BA.CMR.FLO².MR².NI.PA⁵.PR².ROT².SPS.STG.

     Alsuortus, Danielis. *See* Holdsworth, D.

26   **Anderson, Patrick.**† Copia de las cartas que se embiaron de Escocia a nuestro padre Claudio Aquauiua. Fol. *n.p.d.* [1612]. MD²(Jes. 47/32). RO⁹(3:-Anglia 42, ff. 266–75; Anglia 42, ff. 249–58; Fondo Jesuitico 446, ff. 689–98). [*L.]

     A translation of a letter to the Jesuit General by Anderson giving an account of his missionary work in Scotland from 24 Dec. 1609 to the time of writing. Dated 4 Jan. 1612. *Pr.* [Spain?] A Latin letter from Anderson to the General, giving a similar account, but dated 30 July 1611, is preserved in holograph at Stonyhurst (A.II 3. No. 2). An English translation from the Stonyhurst MS was printed in *Letters & Notices,* vol. 11, 1876, pp. 98–126.

27   **Anderton, James,** *of Lostock.* [Translation of *The Protestants Apologie.* A&R 132–3.] Apologia Protestantum pro Romana ecclesia ... Per Ioannem Brerleium sacerdotem anglum ... composita, & per Guilielmum Raynerum Latine versa. 4°. *Lutetiae Parisiorum, e typographia Ioannis Ducarroy,* 1615. O.; A.AUG.BOR.C⁵.CHA.D.FU².HP. L⁴.MD.MU.OS.PA.PA³.WO. +

     Ioannes Brerleius, *pseud.* Printed at the expense of Arras College, Paris, the house of writers of the English secular clergy, of which the translator, William Rayner, was a member. For the identity of the author and for the background, *see* RH, May 1982, pp. 17–41.

28   —[Anr. issue.] Ioannis Brerlei sacerdotis angli pro Romana ecclesia aduersus nouam Protestantum doctrinam libri tres. *Lutetiae Parisiorum, ex officina Niuelliana, sumptibus Sebastiani Cramoisy,* 1617. O.; D.HAN.MTH.O¹²(imp.).PLU.RO².RO⁶.STG.VI.VT.

     The sheets of no. 27 except for the titleleaf (a1) which has been cancelled and replaced by a bifolium (a²) comprising the new title-leaf and a leaf containing 'Elenchus tractatuum'.

29   —[Anr. issue with title:] Apologia siue propugnatio Catholicae Romanae religionis ex testimoniis authorum Protestantum clarioris famae & eruditionis. *Lutetiae Parisiorum, apud Michaelem Sonnium,* 1617. AMI.F.MD.

     The sheets of no. 28 except for a² which has been reprinted.

     Anderton, Lawrence.† [For *Apologia Protestantium,* sometimes erroneously ascribed to L. Anderton, *see* nos. 27–9] .

     Angelus, *a S. Francisco, name in religion. See* Mason, R.

     Anne, *Countess of Argyll. See* Campbell, A.

30   **Ansley, Henry.** Disputatio theologica, de virgine incomparabili, et sacrosancta Dei genitrice Maria. 4°. *Ingolstadii, excudebat Dauid Sartorius,* 1589. L.; MU.PR.PR².SBG.TRI.VI.

     A thesis for the licentiate in theology at Ingolstadt. For Ansley *see Anglia,* 1973, pp. 357–62.

30.1 **Appleton, Thomas,** *alias* Neville. Vsrini heroes immortalitatis in templo dedicati atq. ad modos dicti in Collegio Anglicano inter philosophicas theses auspiciis Alexandri Vrsini Cardinalis publice defensas a Thoma Neuello eiusdem collegii alumno. 4° (a gathering of twelve). *Romae, typis Iacobi Mascardi,* 1620. MIL².NP.RO².(3).RO³.RO⁸.

     Poems on the occasion of Cardinal Alessandro Orsini's presiding over the philosophical disputations at the English College. Sommerv. (tom. 6, col. 738) records this work under the name of Silvester Petrasancta (Pietrasancta) a Jesuit who perhaps actually wrote the Latin verses for this occasion while he was teaching at Rome.

—[*A disputation in which he acted as Praeses.*] Sankey, W. Conclusiones theologicae de Incarnatione, 1637. *See* no. 1024.

Aquipontanus, Joannes, *pseud. See* Gibbons, J. (nos. 524–7).

Archangel, *name in religion. See* Forbes, J.

Argyll, Anne, *Countess of. See* Campbell, A.

31 **Arrowsmith, Edmund,** *Saint.* [*Appendix.*] Recit veritable de la cruauté et tyranie faicte en Angleterre, à l'endroit du pere Edmond Arosmith de la Compagnie de Iesus. 8° (in fours). *Paris, chez la vefue Abraham Saugrain*, 1629. PA.PA⁴.ST.

> Arrowsmith was executed on 28 August 1628. The author of this account has not been identified, but it is probably derived from an anonymous English *Relation* of which an edition, dated 1630, is recorded, though no copy is now known. A second, enlarged edition of the English *Relation* was printed at London in 1737.

31.1 **Arundell, Charles.** Discours de la vie abominable, ruses, trahisons, meutres, impostures . . . & autres tres iniques conuersations, desquelles a vsé & vse iournellement le my Lorde de Lecestre . . . Traduict d'Anglois en François & mis en forme de dialogue. 8°. *n.p.*, 1585. L.O; AIX.BOR.BRS.CARP.DMR.LINC.MD.O⁹.PA(2).PA⁴.TOU.WO.

> Anon. A translation of the English work usually known by the title of its second edition, printed in 1641: *Leicesters common-wealth.* The first edition, printed in 1584, entitled *The copie of a letter, wryten by a master of arte of Cambridge*, is entered in A&R (no. 261) under COPY. The principal author has been identified as [Charles Arundell]. *See* L. Hicks S.J. in *Studies*, Spring, 1957, pp. 91–105. The anonymous translator, reported at the time to be Thomas Throckmorton, says in his preface that he has added at the end some further details about Leicester based on his own knowledge acquired when he was living in England. *Pr.* [Paris?] For a Latin work including an account of Leicester based on the English and French versions of *Leicestors common-wealth, see* nos. 115–16.

Ashton, Roger, *Ven.* [Letter written to William Allen concerning the surrender of Deventer, 1587.] *See* nos. 13–17.

B., A. *See* no. 1416.

B., R.V. *See* nos. 1366–7.

B., T.W. *See* nos. 1419–24.

32 **Babthorpe, Ralph,** *alias* Smith. Quinquennale peplum ad modos Palladi oblatum Rodolphus Smitheus Colleg. Anglicani alumnus dedicat . . . Antonio Burghesio S. D. N. Pauli V fratris filio Sulmonis Principi cuius auspiciis de vniuersa philosophia publice disseruit in Collegio Anglicano. 4°. *Romae, apud Bartholomaeum Zannettum*, 1614. O.; DMR.RO²(2).VT.

> Complimentary verses addressed to the Cardinal under whose auspices Babthorpe defended his thesis. This work is also recorded by Sommerv. (tom. 6, col. 632) under the name of the Jesuit professor at Rome, Hieronymus Petruccius, who perhaps actually wrote the Latin verses for this occasion.

33 **Bacon, Thomas,** *alias* Southwell. Regula viua seu analysis fidei in Dei per Ecclesiam nos docentis auctoritatem. 4°. *Antuerpiae, apud Ioannem Meursium*, 1638. L.O.C.; D.DE.DUR.HP.L²⁶.LGE³.MTH.OS.ST.TRI.VT.W. + +

34 —Vindiciae pro Nicolao Smithaeo contra censuram nomine Facultatis Parisiensis editam in eiusdem librum, cui nomen, Modesta & breuis

discussio, &c. ... Auctore R.D. Antonio Goffar, S. Theologiae Doctore, & Protonotario Apostolico. 12°. *Leodii, typis Leonardi Streel*, 1631. C(2).; RO[8]. *This or no.* 34.1 : AMI.LGE.PA[3].PA[4].

A defence of Matthew Wilson's *Modesta ac breuis discussio*, 1631 (no. 1400) against the *Censura* of the Sorbonne, 1631 (no. 684). For the Belgian secular theologian, Antoine Goffar, whose name appears as author on the titlepage, and who signs the dedicatory epistle, *see* J. H. Zedler, *Grosses vollständiges Universal Lexicon*, 1732, *etc.*, Bd. 11, col. 93; also *Biographie Nationale ... de Belgique*, tom. 7, 1880–83, col. 84. The *Vindiciae* was probably a work of collaboration between Goffar and the English Jesuits at their college of Liège. Alegambe (p. 432) attributes it to Thomas Bacon, alias Southwell, S.J., who was a professor at the College. This first issue was probably published soon after 13 June 1631 when the Bishop's acting Vicar-General gave his approbation. Collation: ✚[12] 2✚[8] A–O[12] +2 unsigned leaves, the first with Errata, the second blank. *See* RH October 1987, pp. 373–5.

34.1 —[Anr. issue.] *Leodii, typis Leonardi Streel*, 1631. PA(D11975). *See also no. 34 above.*

The sheets of no. 34 with two additional quires at the end (9¶[12]2¶[6]) containing further approbations for *Modesta ac breuis discussio*. Documentary evidence shows that this issue appeared near the end of 1631. *See* RH October 1987, p. 389.

35 **Badduley, Robert,** *alias* Ignatius Stafford. Historia de la celestial vocacion, missiones apostolicas, y gloriosa muerte, del padre, Marcelo Franco Mastrili. 4°. [Coloph.] *Lisboa, por Antonio Aluarez*, 1639. L.; HP.HSA.MD(2).MTH.NI.RO[2](2).VI.VT.

Written by Badduley in Spanish. Mastrili's martyrdom took place at Nagasaki on 17 October 1637. Titlepage engraved, and with an additional engraved plate depicting the martyrdom.

36 —[*French transl.*] Histoire de la miraculeuse guerison, celeste vocation, missions apostoliques, et glorieuse mort du pere Marcel François Mastrilli ... mise en françois par ... Laurent Chifflet. 8°. *Douay, chez la vefue Baltazar Bellere*, 1640. L.; ANT[3].CHA.DOU.GT.HEV.LOU[3].

Another edition, printed at Lyon, 1640, reported by Sommervogel, tom. 2, col. 1133, has not been found. An Italian translation published at Viterbo in 1642 falls outside the scope of this catalogue.

37 —[*A disputation in which he acted as Praeses.*] Saa y Meneses, B. Magnae Matri Virgini Immaculatae, Caelorum Reginae; assertiones caelestes, sub praesidio P. M. Ignatii Stafford. Fol. (a bifolium). *Vlissipone, typis Matthiae Rodrigues*, 1632. MD[2](Jes.86/69).

The subject is astronomical and philosophical.

37.1 **Bagshaw, Christopher.**† Relatio compendiosa turbarum quas Iesuitae Angli, vna cum D. Georgio Blackwello Archipresbytero, sacerdotibus seminariorum populoq; Catholico cōciuere. 4°. *Rothomagi, per Iacobum Molaeum, n.d.* [1601.] L.O.C.; C[3].F.KNY.L[2](2).L[30].O[4].P.USH. W.YK.

Anon. Imprint false; *pr.* [London, Thomas Creede.] Law 5. Lib. 1947, p. 180. A&R 63. STC 3106. ERL 71. Mil. vol. 1, pp. 116, *etc.*

38 **Bagshaw, Robert,** *in religion* Sigebert Bagshaw. [*Begin :*] In nomine Sanctissimae Trinitatis Patris et Filii et Spiritus Sancti. Amen. Fr. Sigebertus Bagshaw presbyter & monachus Congregationis anglicanae ordinis nigrorum Sancti Benedicti eiusdemque Congregatinois Praeses ... 4° (a quadrifolium). *n.p.d.* [1632.] DAI(Weldon III, pp. 749–55. [*DMR].

An excommunication by Bagshaw, as President General of the restored English Benedictine Congregation, on Ildephonsus (Hanson) of St. Gregory for refusing to submit to his authority.

Dated from Douai, 28 May 1632. *Pr.* [Douai, Balthasar Beller?]
The DAI copy bears Bagshaw's signature in MS attested by two
notaries apostolic of whom one was the Douai printer, Balthasar
Beller.

39 —[*Documents published by him as President General.*] Ildefonsus, de San
Victores, *President General of the Spanish Benedictine Congregation.*
[*Begin :*] Nos Magister Fr. Ildefonsus de San Victores totius Sanctae
Congregationis Nigrorum monachorum S. Benedicti . . . Generalis . . .
4° (a quadrifolium). *n.p.d.* [1633.] DAI(2-Weldon III, pp. 757–64; 1,
unpaged). [*DMR].

A mandatum requiring English Benedictines professed in the
Spanish Congregation to submit to the authority of the restored
English Congregation. Dated 6 May 1633. *Pr.* [Douai, Balthasar
Beller?] One DAI copy is attested in MS by two notaries apostolic of
whom one was Balthasar Beller (*See* note to no. 38.)

40 —Pacheco, Placido, *President General of the Spanish Benedictine Con-
gregation* [and others]. [*Begin :*] IHS. MRA. BNDS. Frater Sigebertus
Bagshaw presbyter & monachus Ordinis S. Benedicti Congregationis
Preses . . . 4°. *n.p.d.* [1631]. DAI(Weldon III, pp. 725–48).PA(Lk 6868).
VAL(XII, ff. 123 *et seq.*) [*DMR].

Documents by Pacheco and others relating to the restored English
Benedictine Congregation. The whole dated from Douai, 12 March
1631. *Pr.* [Douai, Balthasar Beller.] The DAI copy is signed in MS
by Bagshaw and attested by two notaries apostolic of whom one was
Balthasar Beller. (*See* note to no. 38.)

41 —Urban VIII, *Pope.* [*Begin :*] Fr. Sigebertus Bagshaw presbyter &
monachus S. Benedicti Ordinis nigrorum Congregationis Angliae,
eiusdemque pro tempore Praeses . . . 4° (a bifolium). *n.p.d.* [1631].
DAI(Weldon IV, pp. 191–4).PA(Hp451). [*DMR.]

An edition, for use by the English Benedictines, of the Brief
Britannia of 9 May 1631, with an exhortation by Bagshaw to submit
to it. Dated from Douai, 26 September 1631. For a translation into
English, by an anonymous Benedictine, of the text of the Brief
alone, *see* A&R 833. *Pr.* [Douai, Balthasar Beller].

Bagshaw, Sigebert, *name in religion. See* Bagshaw, R.

42 **Baird, Andrew.** L'entretien de l'ame deuote sur les excellences,
grandeurs, et perfections de Dieu. *Lugduni, apud Ludouicum Muguet,*
1625.

Not found. Description from F. La Noue, *Chronicon generale
Ordinis Minimorum*, 1635, pp. 575–6. G. M. Roberti, *Disegno storico
dell'ordine de'Minimi*, 1902, vol. 2, pp. 619–20, gives the imprint in
French, which is probably correct.

Baker, Augustine, *name in religion. See* Baker, D.

Baker, David, *in religion* Augustine Baker. [*A work of which he was part
author.*] Reyner, C. Apostolatus Benedictinorum in Anglia, 1626.
See no. 934.

42.1 **Balfour, Robert.**‡ Commentarius R. Balforei in Organum logicū
Aristotelis ad Illustrissimum Cardinalem de Sourdis. 4°. *Burdigalae,
apud S. Millangium*, 1616. [Coloph.] *Acheué d'imprimer le 23 Septembre
1615.* L(*date in imprint altered by pen to 1618.* O(*date in pen 1618*);
ANG.BOR.O²⁴.PA.

t.p. engraved. The '1618' edition listed by Shaaber (B101) is a
'ghost' based on a misreading of the imprint of the L. copy (520.d.2).

42.2 —Commentariorum in lib. Arist. de philosophia tomus secundus, quo
post Organum logicum, quaecumque in libris Ethicorum occurrent
dificilia, dilicide explicatur. 4°. *Burdigalae, apud I. Millangium et Cl.
Mongiroud*, 1620. BOR.O²⁴.PA.

43 —[*Works edited and translated by him.*] Gelasius, *Cyzicenus.* Γελασιου

Κυζικηνου Σύνταγμα . . . Gelasii Cyziceni Commentarius actorum Nicaeni Concilii, cum Corollario Theodori Presbyteri, de Incarnatione Domini. Nunc primum Grece prodeunt . . . Interprete Rob. Balforeo Scoto, cum eiusdem notis. 8° (in fours). *Lutetiae, apud Federicum Morellum,* 1599. L.P(3); A.BG.C².C³.D.DE.DUR.E.O².O³.PA(2). PA.WO. + +

The Greek originals and Balfour's Latin translation in parallel columns, followed at the end by Balfour's Latin commentary. In some copies, the verso of the titleleaf carries a large woodcut device of the publisher, F. Morel; in others it is blank.

44 —[Anr. ed. of the Greek text of Gelasius with Balfour's Latin translation.] *In :* Gelasii Cyziceni Commentarius actorum Nicaeni Concilii, Roberto Balforeo . . . interprete [and other Greek texts with Latin translations by various hands]. Fol. 2 pts. *In Bibliopolio Commeliniano,* 1604. L.; D.DET.E.E².O².PA.PA⁴.WO.

Omitting Balfour's Latin commentary and his preface and dedication to no. 43. This collection does not include the work by Theodorus on the Incarnation. Some copies lack the general titlepage and have only the titlepages to the individual parts. *Pr.* [Heidelberg.]

44.1 —Theodorus, *Presbyter.* Theodori . . . Commentarius de Incarnatione D.N. Iesu Christi. Nunc primum Graece & Lat. prodit, interprete Rob. Balforeo Scoto. Cum eiusdem notis. 8° (in fours). *Lutetiae, apud Federicum Morellum,* 1599. C¹⁸.PA.PA⁴.

The Greek original and Balfour's Latin translation in parallel columns, followed at the end by Balfour's Latin commentary. Also published as part of no. 43.

45 **Barclay, John.**‡ De rebus Britanniae nouis. I. Barclei ad suos gentiles epistolae. 8°. *Francopoli, ex officina Matriniana, n.d.* [between 1606 and 1616]. DUR.NCY.PA.PA⁴.PBN.RMS.

A collection of letters by Barclay to various unnamed correspondents, mainly on religious persecution in England and the need for toleration. None of the letters is dated but all probably belong to the period 1606 to 1616 when he was living in England under King James I's protection. The imprint is fictitious.

46 —Ioannis Barclaii Paraenesis ad sectarios. Libri II. 8°. *Romae, ex typographia Bartholomaei Zannetti,* 1617. A².AV.BOR.DUR(2).E.FU².L²⁵. MD.MTH.PA.PA².RO²(2).RO⁵.STI.TRO + +

Repudiating his earlier Gallican views expressed in no. 52. Dedicated to Pope Paul V.

47 —[Anr. ed.] 8°. *Coloniae, apud Ioannem Kinckium,* 1617. O(2).; AMI. AMP.C⁵.CHA.DI(3).DMR.FLO.HA.KN(2).L².L⁴.LOU.MU.O².PA.USH + +

48 —[Anr. ed.] Editio tertia. 12°. *Coloniae, apud Ioannem Kinckium,* 1625. L.O.; A².AUG.C⁵.D.DE.GT.GTN.KN.KNY.LOU.MU.O⁶.PA.VT.WO +

49 —[Anr. ed.] Editio quarta. 12°. *Coloniae, apud Ioannem Kinckium,* 1638. AUG.D.D²E.².L⁴.LOU.MD.PLU.PR.STI.ULM.USH.VAL².VI.X. +

50 —[*French transl.*] La parenese aux sectaires . . . c'est à dire, aduertissement aux religionaires, auquel sont contenuz . . . les poincts principaux des controuerses du iourd'huy. Traduict du latin en françois par Iean Walteri de Castro, chanoine de Visé sur Meuse. 4°. *Liege, chez Leonard Streel,* 1634. GT.LGE³.

51 —[*Polish trans.*]. Iana Barklaiusza Paraenesis, to iest, napominania y przestrogi nowowiernych, kśiag dwoie. Przez Lukasza Gornickiego, kánoniká Wilenskiego, wármienskiego, proboszcza xieskiego, sekret: I.K.M. 4°. *w Krakowie, w drukárni Franciszka Cezárego,* 1628. BER. FB. [*L.]

52 —Ioannis Barclaii pietas. Siue publicae pro regibus, ac principibus, et priuatae pro Guilielmo Barclaio parente vindiciae. Aduersus Roberti S.R.E. Cardinalis Bellarmini tractatum, De potestate Summi Ponti-

ficis in rebus temporalibus. 4°. *Parisiis, ex typis P. Mettayer*, 1612.
L.O.C.; AUG.E.FLO.FU.L^2.MD.MTH.NCY.O^3.PA.RO^5.VT.YK + +

A defence of no. 53.1 against no. 1505. For the controversy, *see* Mil vol. 2, pp. 101 *et seq.* Reprinted in Melchior Goldast's anti-Catholic compilation, *Monarchia S. Romani Imperii*, 1611–14.

53 —[*Appendix.*] Eudaemon Ioannes, A. R.P. Andreae Eudaemon-Ioannis . . . epistola monitoria, ad Ioannem Barclaium, Guillelmi filium de libro ab eo pro patre suo contra . . . Robertum Bellarminum S.R.E. Card. scripto. 8°. *Coloniae Agrippinae, apud Ioannem Kinckium*, 1613. L.O(2); ANT^2.C^2.D^2.DUR.FLO.LYN.MU.PA(3).STG.TB.TRO.VT.WO.YK + +

Answering no. 52.

53.1 **Barclay, William.** De potestate Papae: an & quatenus in reges & principes seculares ius & imperium habeat. 8°. *n.p.* 1609. L.O.C(3).; A.F.HP.L^2.M.MU.O^3(2).PA.VAL.YK. + +

Published posthumously. The unsigned preface is by [John Barclay the Author's son]. *Pr.* [London, Eliot's Court press.] The Jesuit annual letter for 1610 from the English mission says the work was edited under the direction of the Archbishop of Canterbury, Richard Bancroft (Foley, vol. 7, Addenda, p. 1006). A&R 69. STC 1408 ERL 136. English transl. STC. 1409. Answered by nos. 1505, 1534. *See* Mil, vol. 2, p. 101.

53.2 —[Anr. issue.] *Mussiponti, apud Franciscum du Bois, & Iacobum Garnich*, 1609. DE.ERL.HAM.LIL^3.LIV.MD(2).MU(2).PA.VT. (*some of these possibly no. 53.3*)

The sheets of no. 53.1 with only the imprint added. Although du Bois and Garnich were genuine printers at Pont-à-Mousson in Lorraine, there appears to be no evidence that they had any connection with this London printed book. A&R 70 (not differentiated from no. 53.3 below). STC 1408.3.

53.3 —[Anr. issue.] *Mussiponti, apud Franciscum du Bois, & Iacobum Garnich*, 1609. L.

The sheets of no. 53.2 except for the first quire (originally π^8, now π A^8) which has been reprinted, though without textual alteration.

54 —[Anr. ed.] 8°. *Mussiponti, apud Iacobum Garnich*, 1610. C.; AMP.AUG. BRS.CARP.CHA.DUR^2.LN.LOU.NCY.O^6.OR.PA.VT.W. + +

A reprint of nos. 53.1–53.3. Imprint false; probably *pr.* [in France, rather than Lorraine].

55 —[Anr. ed. with anr. ed. of no. 58.] Guilielmi Barclaii de potestate Papae . . . Eiusdem de regno et regali potestate . . . Editio nunc primum in Germania adornata emendatior. 8°. *Hanouiae, impensis ac typis Willerianis, & consort.*, 1612. O.C.; A.D^2.DE.E.FU.GTN.HA.HAN. PA^5.RMS.SBG.STG.W. + +

A non-Catholic reprint of the two books.

56 —[Anr. issue.] Editio nunc secundo in Germania adornata emendatior. *Hanouiae*, 1617. L.O.; A^2(2).E.FRA.HAN.L^{26}.LGE.^{3}.LYN.MD.MU.PA.STG.VT. WO(2). + +

A reissue of the sheets of no. 55 except for the first gathering which is reset. The new first gathering *pr.* Hanau [Petrus Antonius].

57 —[*French transl.* of no. 53.1 alone.] Traicté de la puissance du Pape. Scauoir, s'il a quelque droict, empire, ou domination sur les rois & princes seculiers. Traduit du Latin. 8°. *Pont à Musson, par Helie Huldric*, 1611. L.O.; A.AIX.AV.DMR.LOU.LOU^3.LYN.NCY.NTS.PA.PA^7.STO. TOU.WO. +

Imprint false and probably fictitious; *pr.* [in France?]

58 —Guilielmi Barclaii . . . De regno et regali potestate aduersus Buchananum, Brutum, Boucherium, & reliquos monarchomachos, libri sex. 4°. *Parisiis, apud Guillielmum Chaudiere*, 1600. L.O.C(3).; A.AUG.C^3.C^5. CARP.CHA.D(3).DUR(2).GT.HP.L^2.PA.USH.VT. + +

Later editions are included in nos. 55–6.

—[*Appendix.*] Bellarmine, R., *Saint, Cardinal.* Tractatus de potestate Summi Pontificis in rebus temporalibus. Aduersus Gulielmum Barclaium, 1610. *See* nos. 1505–8.

Barlow, Rudesind, *name in religion. See* Barlow, W.

59 **Barlow, William,** *in religion* Rudesind Barlow. Epistola R. Adm. P. Praesidis Generalis et Regiminis totius Congregationis Angliae Ord. S. Benedicti ad RR. Prouinciales et ad Definitores eiusdem Congregationis in apostolica missione laborantes. 8°. *n.p.d.* [1627, *n.b.* 5 Nov.] AMP(-*approbation leaf*)DMR.L⁴(-*approbation leaf*).

Rejecting the claims of Richard Smith, Bishop of Chalcedon, to jurisdiction over the English Benedictines. For the background *see* RH 1971, pp. 1–20. Commonly known from the opening word of the text as Barlow's 'Mandatum'. This is the first issue, intended for private circulation within the Congregation; it has an approbation dated from Douai, 5 November 1627. The author's name is given (sig.₊2ʳ) in the form: F. Rudesindus. *Pr.* [Douai, Balthasar Beller.] Collation: π² (π2 =approbation leaf)₊2A–P⁸Q⁴ (A1 blank).

60 —[Anr. state, with imprint and date:] *Duaci, typis Baltazaris Belleri,* 1627. VT.

Identical with no. 59 except that the titlepage is partly reset to allow for the inclusion of the imprint and date.

61 —[Anr. issue, with additions.] *n.p.d.* [1628, *n.b.* 28 Jan.] PA⁴(−*approbation leaf*).

The sheets of no. 59 (including the title-leaf) unaltered but with the addition at the end of a section (signed: A–C⁴) containing fresh material and ending with a 'Testimonium notarium' dated 28 January 1628.

62 —[Anr. issue, with further additions and with altered title:] Epistola R.A.P. Praesidis Generalis, et Regiminis totius Congregationis Anglicanae: Ordinis S.E. Ad RR.PP. Prouinciales, & ad Definitores eiusdem Congregationis in apostolica missione laborantes. *Duaci, ex officina Baltazaris Belleri, n.d.* [1628, *n.b.* 14 May.] DE.ST.

Intended for general circulation outside the Order. In thi issue, the original bifolium (π²) is replaced by a new bifolium consisting of a fresh unsigned title-leaf (with title and imprint as above) and a leaf signed R2. The verso of the titleleaf bears a new approbation, dated 14 May 1628. The leaf signed R2 contains on the recto the original approbation of 5 Nov. 1627 and on the verso a Privilegium dated 18 Feb. 1628. This bifolium is followed by a reissue of the remaining sheets (₊2A–P⁸Q⁴) of no. 59 which in turn are followed by freshly printed material (signed R–Y⁴Z²) comprising 'Epistola Secunda' (which reprints the material added in no. 61) and 'Epistola Tertia' (which is a further addition). The text ends (Z2ʳ): Duaci ex Conuentu S. Gregorii die 10 mensis April. 1628. Finis.

63 —[Anr. issue.] *Duaci, ex officina Baltazaris Belleri, n.d.* [1628, *n.b.* 10 June.] L.; AMP.DAI.DE(2).PA.W(*imp.*)

A reissue of the sheets of no. 62 except for the last (Z²) which has been reprinted to allow the addition of Barlow's printed signature at the end of the text and a printed notarial testimony dated 10 June (in some copies, 11 June) 1628. The latter is signed in MS by the two Douai printers B. Beller and P. Auroi acting as Notaries apostolic. In some copies errors in the setting of the last page have been corrected in the course of printing. In some copies sig. X4 is a cancel but the text does not appear to vary.

Barnes, John.

ORIGINAL WORKS

Apologie pour l'Autheur des Chroniques.

64 —Apologie pour l'autheur des Chroniques, sur ce qui est mentionné en l'an 703. par laquelle sont demonstrées trois verités qu'il a insinuées en cet endroict, & autres de ses Chroniques . . . Contre vn moderne qui a publié le contraire. [1624.] *In:* Yepes, A. de. Chroniques generales de l'ordre de S. Benoist. [French transl. by Olivier Mathieu.] *Paris, Denys Langlois,* 1619, 24. ANG.PA.

Anon. An attack on no. 757. The evidence for Barnes's authorship is given in no. 40. Not published separately but added as an appendix to Mathieu's translation of Yepes where it occupies pp. 1209–33 of vol. 2, published in 1624.

Dissertatio contra Aequivocationes

65 —Dissertatio contra aequiuocationes. 8°. *Parisiis, apud Rollinum Baragne & Iacobum Villery,* 1625. L.; DAI.DE.DUR(2).LOU³.U. *This or 66 or 67 :* AMI.D.LEM.LYN.TOU.VT.VT²(*a fragment*).

Attacking, in particular, two Jesuit works: *De Antichristo* by L. Lessius, and A&R 641. *Pr.* [Denis Langlois.] Set up in type in 1624 but held up at the request of the Paris Nuncio who sent a copy of the text to Rome. Though it was condemned by the Holy Office on 24 Dec. 1624 the French authorities subsequently gave permission for publication to proceed. *See* Chaussy, pp. 108–14. VT²(Nunz. di Francia, 418, ff. 183, *et seq.,* microfilm at PA¹²) has the text sent to Rome by the Nuncio: it is mainly in MS but includes pp. 129–43 and 257–72 of the sheets printed by Langlois. The setting of the imprint differs from that in no. 66: here the titlepage ends:—Cum licentia Superiorum./[Ornament.]/PARISIIS,/Apud Rollinum Baragne & Iacobum Villery,/veneunt in Palatio./M.DC.XXV./[Rule.] *Cum approbatione & Priuilegio Regis.*

66 —[Anr. state, with imprint reset.] O.C(2); AIX.C².DE.PA(D25014).

The titlepage ends:— . . . *abscondita eius.*/[Ornament.]/PARISIIS, /Apud Rollinum Baragne & Iacobum Villery,/vaeneunt in Palatio. /M.DC.XXV./[Rule]/*Cum approbatione Doctorum,/& Priuilegio Regis.*

67 —[Anr. issue.] *Parisiis, apud Rollinum Baragne & Iacobum Villery,* 1625. *With imprint set as in no. 65:* D².DAI.PA(D25015).RMS. *With imprint set as in no. 66:* C³.E³.HP.PA(D13481).PA³.

The bifolium A1.8 has been cancelled and replaced. In the cancellans the second paragraph of the Preface has been rewritten. The cancellans may be recognised by its having no row of type-ornament across the top of sig. A1ʳ (p. 1). In some copies the cancellans is found in combination with the imprint of no. 65, in others with that of no. 66.

68 —[*French transl.*] Traicté et dispute contre les equiuoques. Traduit du latin. 8°. *Paris, chez Rolin Baragnes . . . et Iacques Villery,* 1625. C.; AMP.AV.D².DE.HD.LEM.LYN.O³.O¹¹.PA(2),PA².SBG².TOU.VI.

With the revised version of the second paragraph of the Preface. (*See* no. 67.)

69 —[*Appendix.*] [Raynaud, T.] Splendor veritatis moralis collatus cum tenebris mendacii et nubilo aequiuocationis ac mentalis reseruationis . . . Per Fr. S. Emonerium Ord. Min. Conuent. 8°. *Lugduni, apud Antonium Berlerium,* 1627. O.; PA.

Answering Barnes's treatise on equivocation. S. Emonerius, *pseud.* A reprint of what appears to be this work was appended to a Lyon edition, dated 1630, of Lessius's *Dissertatio de montibus pietatis.* (*See* Southwell, p. 553.)

Examen Trophaeorum

70 —Examen Trophaeorum Congregationis praetensae anglicanae Ordinis
S. Benedicti. 12°. *Remis, ex officina Eubuli Cordati typographi iurati,*
1622. LYN².PA(*imp.*).VT.
  Preface sgd.: Johannes S. Andreae [fictitious name in religion
  assumed by Barnes]. Imprint fictitious; *pr.* [Paris?]. An attack on
  no. 757 which had begun to appear in 1619. Apparently written at
  the instigation of [F. Walgrave]. Answered in no. 934. For the controversy, *see* Chaussy, pp. 103, *et seq.*

Supplicatio exhibita . . . Urbano VIII

71 —Supplicatio exhibita SS.D.N. Vrbano 8. a Primario Definitore
Missionis anglicanae Congregationis hispanicae, & Vicario generali
eiusdem missionis & Congregationis in Anglia pro declaratione
cuiusdam breuis SS.D.N. Pauli V. dati anno 1619. die 23. Augusti.
s.sh. 4°. *n.p.d.* [1623.] PA.VT²(Nunz. di Francia, 412, f. 254, microfilm
at PA).
  Written in collaboration with Robert Hadock. Both authors sign the
  text. *Pr.* [Paris?] For the background, *see* Chaussy, p. 112.

Syllabus Actorum . . . 1620

72 —Syllabus actorum ex definitorio Benedictinorum Anglorum. 4°.
Augustae, apud Baptistam Fabrum, 1620.
  Not found. Description taken from Cordes Catalogue, p. 66. It
  appears to be a collection of documents put together earlier than
  no. 73. The imprint, clearly false, is shared with three books published by Thomas Preston in London with the connivance of the
  English government in 1620–21 (nos. 925.3, 926.1, 927.1) and
  compare the false imprint of no. 885.

Syllabus Actorum . . . 1623

73 —Syllabus actorum a Definitorio et superioribus Congregationis
hispanicae Ordinis Sancti Benedicti in casu excommunicationis &
publicae denuntiationis religiosorum anglorum in suburbio San-
Germanico degentium per apostasiam indebite resilientium a superiorum debita subiectione & obedientia. Editus per R. P. Maurum
S. Crucaeum presbyterum Benedictinum, & notarium Definitorii
Congregationis hispanicae. 4°. *Parisiis,* 1623. PA(4⁰LK⁷6867).PAᴬ(MSS.
Franc. 15769, ff. 252, *et seq. Imp.*).
  A collection of documents covering the years 1612–23, put together
  by [Barnes]. Maurus de S. Cruce [Maurus Hames] to whom the
  compilation is attributed on the titlepage probably played only a
  minor part in the work. *See* Chaussy, pp. 106–7.

PROGRAMMES ANNOUNCING THESES TO BE DEFENDED
BY BARNES AT THE UNIVERSITY OF DOUAI

74 —De Antichristi aduentu. Q. theologica. Vtrum ante finem saeculi
venturus sit Antichristus? . . . pro priore ad baccalaureatum . . . die
23. Aprilis 1619. *s.sh.*fol. *Duaci, typis viduae. L. Kellami,* 1619.
BRU³(EA 25/423).
  This and the following four items (nos. 75–8) not seen. Description
  taken from Labarre, vol. 2, pp. 171–2, nos. 849–53, who cites the
  copies shown here.

75 —De verbo Dei incarnato. Q. theologica. Vtrum homine non peccante
filius Dei incarnatus fuisset? . . . pro posteriore ad baccalaureatum . . .

die 5. Iunii 1619. *s.sh.*fol. *Duaci, typis viduae L. Kellami*, 1619. BRU³ (EA 25/245).
See note to no. 74.

76 —De oratione. Q. theologica. Vtrum oratio sit necessaria ad salutem?...
pro secunda ad licentiam ... die 2. Septembris 1619. *s.sh.*fol. *Duaci, typis viduae L. Kellami*, 1619. BRU³(EA 25/231).
See note to no. 74.

77 —De vsuris & mutuo. Q. theologica. An vsus sit prohibita iure diuino?
... pro tertia ad licentiam ... die 9. Septemb. 1619. *s.sh.*fol. *Duaci, typis viduae L. Kellami*, 1619. BRU³(EA 25/208).
See note to no. 74.

78 —De S. Ioanne Baptista. Q. theologica. An S. Ioannes habuerit priuilegium vitandi omnia peccata venalia? ... pro quarta et vltima ad licentiam ... die 16. Septemb. 1619. *s.sh.*fol. *Duaci, typis viduae L. Kellami*, 1619. BRU³(EA 25/285).
See note to no. 74.

WORKS EDITED BY BARNES

79 —Jimenez de Cisneros, Garcia, *Abbot of Montserrat*. Exercitatorium spirituale, et directorium horarum canonicarum. 8°. *Duaci, typis viduae Laurentii Kellami*, 1615. AMI.AMP(*imp.*).HP.PA.RO⁶.TNI.TRO.
The Latin text of the directions for the spiritual life and of the directions for the observance of the canonical hours first published by Cisneros in Latin, and also in Spanish, in 1500. *See* Albareda, pp. 43, *et seq.*

79.1 —[Scupoli, L.] Pugna spiritualis. Tractatus vere aureus: de perfectione vitae christianae. Olim hispanice a R. P. Ioanne Castaniza ... editus ... tandem reditus Latine a R. D. Iod. Lorichio ... Editio secunda ad exemplar Hispanicum autoris castigata, & aucta. 16°. *Duaci, ex officina Laurentii Kellami*, 1612. AMP.LIL².
An edition of the Latin translation by Lorichius of the work by [Scupoli] here attributed by [Barnes] to Castaniza. The authority for Barnes is Pits, p. 868. This edition has a dedicatory letter by the English printer Lawrence Kellam.

79.2 —[Anr. ed.] Editio nouissima ad exemplar Hispanicum. 12°. *Duaci, ex typographia Baltazaris Belleri*, 1625. O.; PA.
Without Kellam's dedicatory letter.

79.3 —[Anr. ed.] 32°? *Herbipoli, typis J. Volmari*, 1626. PA.STAN.
This edition also contains a work by Antoine Sucquet. Further editions with the false attribution to Castaniza lie outside the period of this catalogue.

80 **Barnes, Stephen.** Quaestio theologica. Vtrum idolatria sit species superstitionis: ac mortale peccatum, idemque grauissimum? ... 19. Septembr. 1609. *s.sh.*fol. *Duaci, typ. viduae Iac. Boscardi, n.d.* [1609]. DOU(Rec. A. 1609/27).
For Stephen Barnes *see* Anst., vol. 1, p. 24.

Barnestapolius, Obertus, *pseud. See* Turner, R. (nos. 1271–4.)

Barnewell, John. Vniuersa theologia iuxta mentem Doctoris subtilis, 1620. *See* no. 752.

81 —[*A disputation at St. Anthony's College, Louvain in which he acted as Praeses.*] Ferrall, F. Sententia diui Augustini ... de gratia, lib. arb. praedestinatione, et reprobatione, ac simul proponitur disputatio de iustificatione ac merito bonorum operum. 4°. *Louanii, typis Henrici Hastenii*, 1627.
Not found. Description taken from Reusens (tom. 5, p. 427) who saw a copy in the old library of Louvain University which was destroyed in 1914. Reprinted in 1641 with a different respondent, Patrick Brenan (copies at L.KNY.).

82   **Baron, Bartholomew.** [*Begin :*] Reuerendo admodum Patri P. F. Lucae Waddingo . . . auunculo suo plurimum colendo. Fr. Bartholomaeus Barronius D.D.C.Q. Conclusiones philosophicae. Ad mentem Doctoris subtilis . . . Praeside Fr. Patritio Flemingo . . . Defendet Fr. Bartholomeus Barronius. In Collegio S. Antonii de Padua Fratrum Minorum Hibernorum. Fol. (2 sheets) *Louanii, apud viduam Henrici Hastenii*, 1630. RO⁸.

      A programme announcing his forthcoming defence of his thesis.

83   **Baron, Bonaventure.**‡ [*Begin :*] Eminentissimo, et Reuerendissimo Principi Francisco Card. Barberino . . . Fr. Bonauentura Baronius Collegii S. Isidori F.F. Min. Hibernorum alumnus. S.P.F. Conclusiones theologicae iuxta mentem Doctoris Subtilis. De peccatis . . . [*End :*] defendentur Romae in Collegio S. Isidori . . . a F. Bonauentura, qui supra. Praesidente R. P. F. Ioanne Ponce Hiberno S. Theologiae Lectore. Anno 1635. *s.sh.*fol. *Ramae* [sic], *ex typographia Ludouici Grignani*, 1635. RO⁸.

      A programme announcing his forthcoming defence of his thesis. The printer has left spaces for the date and time to be filled in by pen.

84   —[*Begin :*] Eminentissimo, et Reuerendissimo Principi Alphonso de la Cueua S.R.E. Cardinalis amplissimo Fr. Bonauentura Baronius Collegii Sancti Isidori alumnus felicitatem exoptat. Conclusiones theologicae . . . [*End :*] Disputabuntur publice in Collegio S. Isidori . . . Praesidente Reu. Fr. Francisco a S. Maria [F. Tully] . . . 1633. Mense Nouembris. *s.sh.*fol. *Romae, ex typographia Ludouici Grignani*, 1634. RO².

      A similar programme to no. 83. Text and part of the setting are the same as in nos. 128, 271, 414.

      Barret, Richard. [Catalogue of martyrs]. *See* nos. 312, 1004–9.

84.1   **Barret, William.** Ius regis, siue de absoluto & independenti secularium principum dominio & obsequio eis debito . . . Libri tres. In quibus. Summo Pontifici ius non esse principes deponere . . . probat Guil. Barret, Anglus. 8°. *Basileiae, apud Hieronomum Pistum*, 1612. L(2,1 *imp*.).O.C.; ANT.C³.D.E.F.MTH.PA³.PN.W.WOR.YK.

      Entered in Stationers' Register to W. Burre, 5 September 1612. Imprint false; *pr.* [London, Nicholas Okes.] For Barret, *see* DNB. A&R 72. STC 1501. ERL 224. Mil. vol. 2, pp. 115–16. Some copies (e.g. 1 at L) have a cancel errata leaf.

85   —[Anr. issue with imprint.] *Francofurti, prostant apud Societatem Bibliopolarum Londinensium*, 1617. L.; DRE.KAS.KIE.MU.WO.

      The sheets of no. 84.1 reissued with a cancel title.

      Barreus, Didacus. *See* Barry, J.

      Barronius, Bartholomaeus. *See* Baron, B.

86   **Barry, James.** [*Begin :*] Admodmu Reuerendo . . . Basilio Nouello de Stronchio . . . Prouinciae Diui Francisci . . . Cōmissario Visitatori . . . eius humilis filius Frater Didacus Barreus Hybernus eiusdem Ordinis, ac Reformationis lector generalis F.P. . . . Theologicae conclusiones ex quatuor libris Sent. Scoti selectae . . . [*End :*] Disputabuntur publice Syracusis in comitiis prouincialibus Fratrum Minorum regularis, ac strictioribus obseruantiae . . . Obiectis satisfaciet Frater Didacus qui supra. M.DCXXIX. *s.sh.*fol. *Messanae, typis Petri Breae*, [1629]. RO⁸.

      A programme announcing his forthcoming defence of his thesis. The printer has left spaces for the date and time to filled in by pen. For Barry *see* Cleary, p. 124.

87   —[*Begin :*] Illustrissimo Principi Hieronymo Columnae S.R.E. Card. Ampliss. Fr. Didacus Barry S. . . . Conclusiones theologicae . . . [*End :*] Defendet Fr. Didacus Barry, in Collegio S. Isidori Fratrum

Minorum Strict. Obseru. S. Francisci, nationis Hibernicae. Anno 1628. *s.sh.*fol. *Romae, apud Ludouicum Grignanum*, 1628. RO⁸.
A programme similar to no. 86.

Bathe, William. Aparejos para administrar el sacramento de la penitencia, [1614]. *See* no. 272.

—Breuis ac methodica institutio continens praecipua Christianae fidei mysteria, 1617. *See* no. 1358.

88 —Ianua linguarum, siue modus maxime accommodatus, quo patefit aditus ad omnes linguas intelligendas. Industria patrum hibernorum Societatis Iesu, qui in collegio eiusdem nationis Salmanticae degunt, in lucem edita: & nunc ad linguam latinam perdiscendam accommodata. In qua totius linguae vocabula, quae frequentiora, & fundamentalia sunt continentur: cum indice vocabulorum, & translatione hispanica eiusdem tractatus. 4°. *Salmanticae, apud Franciscum de Cea Tesa*, 1611. L.; AB.D⁵.D¹⁰.DMR.O².O³⁰.PA.PEN.STG.

> Anon. Compiled at the Irish College, Salamanca, for the use of students preparing for the priesthood. *See* S. P. O'Mathúna, William Bathe. *Amsterdam*, 1986. (*Amsterdam Studies in the Theory and History of Linguistic Science*. ser. 3. vol. 37.) Later adaptations of this linguistic work published in other parts of Europe fall outside the scope of this catalogue. Some copies (e.g. L.PEN.) were originally bound without the Latin–Spanish vocabulary called for in the title.

—Sacra Tempe, 1622. *See* no. 273.

89 **Batt, Anthony.**†‡ Thresor caché au champ du Seigneur nouellement trouué. Diuisé en deux parties. La premiere comprenant les prieres deuotes, & actions de graces. La seconde de pieuses meditaciõs, & exhortations, tirées de la Ste Escriture. 12°. *Paris, aux despens de l'Autheur, de l'imprimerie de Iean Laquehay*, 1640. PA.

> Probably not a translation but written in French by the Author. A Latin version was published in 1641. For an English translation, also published in 1641, *see* Clancy no. 81. For the background to the work *see* Chaussy, p. 202.

90 **Beaton, James,** *Archbishop of Glasgow.* [*Appendix.*] Cayet, J. P. L'oraison funebre de hault et puissant Monseigneur . . . l'Archeuesque de Glasco, Melort Iames de Bethune, ambassadeur pres la Maiesté tres-Chrestienne, pour . . . le Roy Iacques, premier d'Escosse, d'Angleterre & d'Irlande. 8° (in fours). *Au faux-bourgs S. Germain lez Paris, par Fleury Bourriquant*, 1603. L(-*sig. E4 containing complimentary poems*).O.; E⁴.PA(2).PA³.Y. Scott 195.

Beech, Anselm. *See* no. 340.

Benedetto, *Inglese. See* Fitch, W.

Benedictus, *Anglus, de Canfeld. See* Fitch, W.

Benested, Tomas. *See* Benstead, T.

Benet, *of Canfield, name in religion. See* Fitch, W.

Benoist, *Anglois, de Canfeld. See* Fitch, W.

91 **Benstead, Thomas,** *alias* Hunt, *Bl.* [*Appendix.*] Relacion del martirio de los dos sacerdotes, el padre Tomas Benested, que fue del Colegio Ingles de Seuilla; y de N. Sprat del Seminario de Duay en Flandes, que padecieron en Linconia de Inglaterra primero de Iulio del año del Señor 1600. Con la desastrada muerte del iuez, que los sentencio. Fol (a bifolium). [Coloph.] *Seuilla, en casa de Clemente Hidalgo*, 1600. MD²(3-Jes.102/39; 117/60; 129/26). [*L.]

> This narrative, based on eye-witness accounts, appears to be taken from the same source as that published in English in A&R 917. A French version mentioned by Raisse (this catalogue no. 323), p. 62, does not appear to be extant. The 'N. Sprat' of the title is an error: the martyr was Thomas Sprat or Sprott.

Bethune, James. *See* Beaton, J.

Bishop, William, *Bishop of Chalcedon.*† [*A work edited by him.*] Pits
J. Ioannis Pitsei . . . Relationum historicarum de rebus Anglicis tomus
primus, 1619 [*etc.*]. *See* nos. 907, 909.
Blackwell, George. [*Appendix.*] [For a papal letter to him:] *see* no. 395.
Blackwood, Adam.††
  *A collected edition of Blackwood's Opera Omnia was published at Paris
  in 1644.*

92 —Aduersus Georgii Buchanani dialogum, De iure regni apud Scotos,
  pro regibus apologia. 4°. *Pictauis, apud Franciscum Pagaeum,* 1581.
  L.O(3).; AIX.C³.D(2).DE.E(2).FLO.HAN.L².O³.PA(2).PA⁴.RO².VT.WO. + +
  Answers STC 3973. Dedicated to Mary, Queen of Scots, and her son.
  Scott 117.

93 —[Anr. ed.] Hac secunda editione per auctorem recognita, multis
  partibus aucta & emendata. 8°. *Parisiis, apud Arnoldum Sittart,* 1588.
  L(2).O.C(2).; A.D.DUR.E(2).GTN.L⁴.O¹².PA.PA⁴.RO³.USH.VT. + +
  This edition reprints the dedication to Mary, Queen of Scots, and
  her son. In some copies (e.g. L(2)) there is also a dedication, not
  present in no. 92, to Ioannes Saracenus, Archbishop of Arras: this
  is printed on a bifolium, signed a.2.3, inserted among the preliminaries. In some other copies (e.g. DUR.PA⁴) this insertion is
  replaced by a bifolium, also signed a2.3, carrying a dedication to
  Philippus Huraltus.

94 —De coniunctione religionis et imperii libri duo, quibus coniurationum
  traducuntur insidiae fuco religionis adumbratae. Ad illustrissimam
  . . . Mariam Scotiae Reginam, & Galliae dotariam. 8°. *Parisiis, apud
  Michaelem de Roigny,* 1575. L(*imp.*).O(3).C(4).; E(2).GTN.HD.HP.L².
  L¹³.O⁵.OS.PA(3).PA⁴(2 -*1 imp.*).USH.VT. +

95 —[Anr. ed. enlarged, with title:] De vinculo religionis et imperii libri
  tres, quorum duo priores ante annos prope quadraginta publicati,
  tertius nunc primum editur. 12°. *Augustoriti Pictonum, ex praelo
  Antonii Mesnerii, n.d.* [*c.* 1613]. O(2).C.; A.E².L².LAR.NP.PA³.PA⁴.TOU.
  VT.WO.
  The evidence for the date of printing is the statement on the titlepage that the first edition of bks. 1, 2 had appeared nearly forty
  years earlier.

96 —De Principis Augustissimi Francisci Ducis Guisiani obitu, ad
  Iohannem Florettum senatorem regium, Adami Blacuodaei elegia.
  4° (a quadrifolium). *Parisiis, ex typographia Thomae Richardi,* 1563.
  NCY.PA.
  François de Lorraine, second Duke of Guise, was uncle of Black-
  woods' patroness, Mary, Queen of Scots. The verses bear witness to
  Blackwood's devotion to the cause of the Guise family.

 —De vinculo religionis et imperii. *See* no. 95.

97 —In nouae religionis asseclas carmen inuectiuum ad virum illustrissimum Ioannem Florettum, consiliarium regium, Adamo Blacdouaeo
  [*sic*] Scoto authore, eiusdem varia aliquot ad varios poemata. 4°.
  Parisiis, ex typographia Thomae Richardi, 1563. E³.G².HA.WO.
  Many of the poems in this collection are addressed to Scottish
  Catholic exiles in France. Also containing Blackwood's 'Epigrammata sacra' addressed to Mary, Queen of Scots.

98 —In psalmum Dauidis quinquagesimum, cuius initium est, Miserere
  mei Deus . . . meditatio. 12° (in eights). *Augustoriti Pictonum, ex
  officina Iuliani Thorelli typographi Vniuersitatis,* 1608. E.POI.

98.1 —Martyre de la Royne d'Escosse, douariere de France. Contenant le
  vray discours des traisons a elle faictes a la suscitation d'Elizabet
  Angloise, par lequel les mensonges, calomnies & faulses accusations
  dressees contre ceste tresuertueuse . . . princesse sont esclaircies &
  son innocence auerée. 8°. *A Edimbourg, chez Iean Nafeild,* 1587.

L.O.C.; A.A^2.C^3.DE.E.E^2.F.G.HD.HN.NY.PML. +
Anon. Imprint false; *pr.* [Paris.] A&R 119. STC 3107. Scott 144.

98.2 —[Anr. ed.] Auec son oraison funebre prononcée en l'Eglise nostre dame de Paris. 12°. *A Edimbourg, chez Iean Nafeild,* 1588. L.O.; AIX.BO.DMR.E.E^2.F.HD.HN.LDS.PA.PA^2.PML.
Anon. Imprint false: *pr.* [Paris.] The funeral oration is by [R. de Beaulne, Archbishop of Bourges]. With poems in Latin and French from the anonymous collection at no. 798. A&R 120. STC 3108. ERL 391. Scott 175.

99 —[Anr. ed.] Martyre de la Royne d'Escosse ... Sont adioustées deux oraisons funebres, l'vne Latine, & L'autre Françoise: & vn liure de poemes Latin & François. 8°. *En Anuers, chez Gaspar Fleysben,* 1588. L.O.; A^2.AB.ANT^2(2,1 *imp.*)BRS.E.GT.L^2(-*t.p.*).PA.PA^2.RMS.RO^2.TOU.VER. +
Anon. Imprint false. The funeral oration in French by [R. de Beaulne, Archbishop of Bourges] had appeared in no. 98.2; that in Latin, of which the author is not known, is added. The poems in Latin and French, some of which had also appeared in no. 98.2, are from the anonymous collection at no. 798. Scott 174.

99.1 —[Anr. ed.] Martyre de la Royne d'Escosse ... Auec deux oraisons funebres ... Et plusieurs poemes. 12°. *A Edimbourg, chez Iean Nafeild,* 1589. L.C.; E(formerly E^3).F.LIV.O^3.PA^2(2).
Anon. Imprint false; *pr.* [Paris.] In fact containing only one funeral oration, as in no. 98.2. A&R 121. STC 3109. Scott 176.

100 —[Anr. ed., with 'La mort de la Royne d'Escosse', and with title:] Histoire et martyre de la Royne d'Escosse ... Auec vn petit liure de sa mort, concernant la procedure & malice des Anglois. 16°. 2 pts. *Paris, chez. Guillaume Bichon,* 1589. L(2).O(*pt.1 only, wanting tp. and prelims., bound into a copy of no. 808*).; DMR(pt.1).E.ETON(*wants folding plates*).MIN.PA(Bliss 165).PA^2(2:–*H10922, pt.1 only, bound with a copy of no. 807; H10923, pt.1 only, wanting t.p. and prelims., bound into a copy of no. 808*).PA^4.
Anon. Without the funeral orations and the poems. Collation: (pt.1.) a^{4}A-Kk^{8}Ll^4. (pt.2.) A^{4}A-O^8(O7,8 blank). Pt.2, entitled 'La mort de la Royne d'Escosse', though possibly by Blackwood, is not included in the 1644 edition of his works. It has its own titlepage, without imprint but bearing the date 1589, and four folding wood-cut plates. For independent editions of pt.2, *see* nos. 806–8. Pt.1, without its titlepage and preliminaries is sometimes found inserted in copies of no. 808. Scott 180. Renouard III.524.

101 —Sanctarum precationum prooemia, seu mauis, eiaculationes animae ad orandum se praeparantis. Quibus addita sunt eiusdem argumenti varii generis odae, cum aliis quibusdam poematiis. 8° (in fours). *Augustoriti Pictonum, ex officina Ioannis Blanceti,* 1598. O.; E.GT.PA.POI.
Dedicated to James Beaton, Archbishop of Glasgow.

102 —[Anr. ed.] 8°. *Augustoriti Pictonum, ex officina Iuliani Thorelli, typographi Vniuersitatis,* 1608. E.KN^2.PA^3.POI.
Scott 202.

103 —Varii generis poemata. 8°. 2 pts. *Pictauis, ex officina libraria Iuliani Thorelli,* 1609. E.LAR.
Some of the poems are addressed to Scottish and English Catholic exiles in France. Pt.2 includes a long prose passage on religion addressed to King James I of England, signed by Blackwood and dated from Paris, 12 June 1606. Scott. 203.

Blaclous, Thomas, *alias. See* White, T.
Blacuodaeus, Adamus. *See* Blackwood, A.
[*104–5 cancelled*]
Boece, Hector. Scotorum historiae a prima gentis origine ... libri XIX. Accessit & huic editioni ... continuatio, per Ioannem Ferrerium,

1574. *See* no. 734.

Boethius, Hector. *See* Boece, H.

106   **Bourchier, Thomas.** Historia ecclesiastica de martyrio fratrum ordinis
diui Francisci . . . qui partim in Anglia sub Henrico octauo rege:
partim in Belgio sub Principe Auriaco, partim & in Hybernia tempore
Elizabethae . . . passi sunt. 8°. *Parisiis, venundantur apud Ioannem
Poupy*, 1582. L.O.C.; CHA.D.DMR.DUR.GT.GTN.KNY.L²⁶.MD.MU(2).PA.PA³.
RO.VT. + +

The account of the Belgian martyrs is by Florentinus van Oyen
Leydanus.

107   —[Anr. ed.] 12°. *Ingolstadii, ex officina Wolfgangi Ederi*, 1583. L(2).O(2).
C(4).; AB.ANT.CHA.D.DIL(3).KNY.L².L²⁶(2).MU(2).OS.STG.TB. + +

108   —[Anr. ed.] 8°. *Parisiis, apud Guillielmum Bichonium*, 1586. L.; AB.AIX.
AR.AUG.C².C⁴.L⁸.PA.PA⁴.STR.

A reissue of no. 106 with the bifolium a1.8 reset. Renouard III.474.

109   —[*German abridgment.*] Catalogus vnd ordentliche Verzeichnuss der
newgekroenten anderthalbhundert streitbarn Barfuesser Martyrer
. . . an jetzo aber kuertzlichen vnnd summarischer Weiss aus dem
Latein ins Teutsch getrewliches Fleiss vertiert: durch F. Valentinum
Friccium. 4°. *Ingolstadt, durch Wolffgang Eder*, 1584. L.C.; AB.BER.EI.
MU.SBG.STG.ULM.UT².VI.WO.

110   —[Anr. ed.] An jetzo zum andern mal im Truck aussgangen. 4°. *Ingolstatt, durch Wolffgang Eder*, 1585. C(2).; AB.BER.MU.PR.UT².WO(3).

A close reprint of no. 109.

111   —[*Italian abridgment.*] Martirio, e morte d'alcuni frati di San Francesco
de'minori osseruanti, che . . . furono martirizati in Inghilterra, in
Fiandra, & in Hibernia . . . Tradotto di Latino in volgare, & in compendio dal padre Fra Danielle Perugino. 4°. *Bologna, per Bartolomeo
Cochi*, 1607. L²⁶.SOL.

Anon.

112   —Oratio doctissima et efficacissima ad Franciscum Gonzagam Minis-
trum Generalem pro pace, et disciplina regulari magni conuentus
Parisiensis instituenda. 8°. *Parisiis*, 1582.

Not found. Cited by Wadding, p. 215. Wadding also has an entry
(p. 216) for what appears to be the same work under the heading
Thomas Lanctonus which he thinks may be a pseudonym for
Bourchier. A note in the Supplement to Wadding (p. 221) gives the
Latin form Lanius, a late Latin word for Butcher (=Boucher).

113   —[*A work edited by Bourchier.*] Socolovius, S. Concio de Eucharistiae
sacramento, 1584. *In:* Hieremias II, *Patriarch of Constantinople.*
Censura Orientalis Ecclesiae. De praecipuis nostri seculi haereticorum
dogmatibus . . . a Stanislao autem Socolouio . . . in Latinum conuersa
. . . Accessit eiusdem Auctoris Concio de Eucharistiae sacramento,
coram Poloniae Rege habita. 8°. *Parisiis, apud Arnoldum Sittart*, 1584.
O.; PA.

Bourchier's name does not appear in the book but according to
Wadding the 'Concio de Eucharistiae sacramento' was edited by
him. A 1582 Dillingen edition of Socolovius's translation of the
work by Hieremias does not contain the 'Concio'.

114   **Bray, Edmund.** [*Begin:*] Excellentissimo, ac Illustrissimo D. D.
Georgio Comiti de Tenczyn Osolinski . . . sacrae regiae Poloniae et
Sueciae Maiestatis intimo camerario, et ad S. D. N. Vrbanum VIII.
extraordinario Oratori. Fr. Edmundus Braius Hibernus Collegii
Sancti Isidori alumnus O.F.P. . . . Conclusiones theologicae . . .
[*End:*] Disputabuntur publice in Collegio S. Isidori . . . Praesidente
Reu. P.Fr. Ioanne a S. Francisco [J. Punch] . . . 1633. *s.sh.*fol. *Romae,
ex typographia Ludouici Grignani*, 1634. RO⁸.

A programme announcing his forthcoming defence of his thesis.

114.1 **Braye, Roger.** Poemata. *Courtrai*, 1627.
Not found. There was a copy in the Campbell Library at Beaumont College, now dispersed. Its present whereabouts are not known.

114.2 **Brehun, Maurice.** Parayso del crhistiano [*sic*] donde se trate los Exercicios espirituales practicados de los varones mas perfectos de nuestros tiempos. [Format unknown]. *En Paris, en casa de Denys L'Anglois*, 1616.
Not found, but described by H. Watrigant in his reprint of no. 273 (see note to that entry), who quotes from a copy that he saw himself. Brehun reveals in the book that he was a native of Kilkenny and had taken a degree in theology under the Jesuits at Salamanca.

Brerleius, Ioannes, *pseud. See* Anderton, J.

Bridgewater, John. [For 'Concertatio Ecclesiae Catholicae', sometimes erroneously attributed to an author of this name:] *See* Gibbons, J.

115 **Briegerus, Julius,** *pseud.*? Flores Caluinistici decerpti ex vita Roberti Dudlei comitis Lecestriae in Anglia; Hollandiae ac Zelandiae pro Elizabetha Angliae Regina gubernatoris. Ioannis Caluini, Thomae Cranmeri, Ioannis Knoxii; aliorumque protectorum & apostolorum sectae Zwinglianae & Caluinianae in Anglia, Scotia, Gallia, Belgio & Germania. Per Iulium Briegerum . . . collecti ex variis scriptoribus. 8°. *Neapoli, apud Ioannem Baptistam Zangarum*, 1585. L(2).O.; DUR(2). HA.L⁴.MD.PA.PA².STA.VI. [*DMR.] *This or no. 116*: BOR.DUS.PA⁴(3).SO. TB.TRI.
The name Julius Briegerus appears to be a pseudonym, perhaps masking an English Catholic, though this is not certain. No foreign writer of this name has been found. The work is a reply to Lawrence Humfrey's attack on Campion and Durie in tom. 3 of *Doctrinae Iesuiticae praecipua capita*, 1585. It contains an account of Robert Dudley, Earl of Leicester based on A&R 261 and this catalogue no. 31.1. Imprint fictitious; *pr.* [Cologne, Maternus Cholinus.] This edition may be distinguished from no. 116 by ll. 5–6 of the title (. . . COMITIS LE-/CESTRIAE . . .) and the date in the imprint which is not italicised (Anno M.D.LXXXV.).

116 —[Anr. ed.] 8°. *Neapoli, apud Ioannem Baptistam Zangarum*, 1585. L.; D. *See also note to no. 115.*
Iulius Briegerus, *pseud.*? Imprint fictitious; *pr.* [at the same press as no. 115.]. This is an inferior reprint of no. 115 from which it may be distinguished by ll. 5–6 of the title (. . . COMITIS LECE-/STRIAE . . .) and the italicised date in the imprint (*Anno M.D. LXXXV*).

117 **Bristow, Richard.**† Richardi Bristoi . . . Motiua, omnibus Catholicae doctrinae orthodoxis cultoribus pernecessaria; vt quae singulae omnium aetatum ac praesentibus maxime temporis haereses funditus extirpet. 4°. 2 vols. *Atrebati, ex officina typographica Roberti Maudhuy*, 1608. C.; BOR.D(*vol. 2 dated 1607*).FU.L².L⁴.LYN.MD.MU.OS.PA.PA³.RO³. USH.VI.WO(*vol. 2 dated 1607*). +
Not a translation of A&R 146 but a recasting of the same material with additions. *See* Mil., vol. I, pp. 39–41. The two volumes comprise twenty-five numbered 'Motiva'. *Ed.* Thomas Worthington, President of Douai College.

118 —[*Motiva*, Vol. 3, entitled:] Veritates aureae S. R. Ecclesiae auctoritatibus veterum omnium patrum, historicorum, ac conciliorum, ita stabilitae et confirmatae. 4°. *Duaci, ex officina typographica Baltazaris Belleri*, 1616. AAR.MU(2).PA(2).PA³.W.
Described on p. 1 as 'Motiovrum tomus tertius'. It comprises 'Motiva' nos. 26–51. With a life of the author by Richard Huddleston. Probably *ed.* [Matthew Kellison, Worthington's successor as President of Douai College].

119   —[Anr. issue of vol. 3, with title:] Motiuorum antihaereticorum tomus tertius. Omnibus doctrinae Catholicae orthodoxis cultoribus pernecessarius, auctoritatibus veterum S. R. Ecclesiae patrum atque historicorum ita confirmatus, vt pefectissimum opus vnusquisque sibi
Ⓐ   polliceri audeat. *Duaci, ex officina typographica Baltazaris Belleri,*
119.1 1616. PA.
120   **Brown, Richard.** S. Thomae Cantuariensis, et Henrici II. illustris. Anglorum Regis monomachia, de libertate ecclesiastica cum subiuncto eiusdem argumenti dialogo. Vtrumque publicabat Richardus Brunaeus. 8°. *Coloniae Agrippinae, apud Cornelium ab Egmundt,* 1626. L(2).O(2).C(2).; BM².CARP.D².DMR.DUR.FRA.L²⁵.O².O⁶.PA.RO³.U.VT. +
A university thesis. The approbation, given at Cologne, calls it 'Monomachia haec a Richardo Brunaeo laudabiliter suscepta, feliciterque depugnata'. The author, who has not been identified, describes himself (p. 100) as a Catholic born and brought up in London.
121   **Bruce, William.**‡ Ad principes populumq. christianum, de bello aduersus Turcos gerendo . . . consilium . . . Ferdinando . . . Archiduci Austriae . . . dicatum. 4°. *Cracouiae, in officina Lazari,* 1595. BU.GD. HEI.KR.KR².MU.STM.WR².
For the author, *see* Kot, S., *William Bruce,* Krakow, 1937.
122   —[Anr. ed.] 8°. *Lipsiae.* [Coloph.] *Imprimebat Michael Lantzenberger, impensis Henningi Grosii,* 1595. L.O(2).; D.E².F.HD.MU.O⁵.PA.RO⁶.STG. WO(2).
123   —Epistola . . . ad illustrem D. Iohannem Gostomium a Lezenica . . . Qua breuiter refutatur responsusm oppositum ad summa consilii de bello aduersus Turcos gerendo capita. 4°. *Gorlicii,* 1596. KR.KR².WR.
The printer is identified in *Index Aureliensis* as [Hans Rambau].
Ⓐ   **Bruin, Paul.** Conclusiones theologicae, 1639. *See* no. 253.
(Bru-   **Brunaeus, Richardus.** *See* Brown, R.
nus)   **Brussaeus, Gulielmus.** *See* Bruce, W.
124   **Bullock, George.** Oeconomia methodica concordantiarum Scripturae sacrae. Fol. *Antuerpiae, ex officina Christophori Plantini,* 1572. [Coloph., dated 30 April 1572:] *Excudebat Christophorus Plantinus.* L(L.17.h.13).O.; ANT³.C².C⁵.DIL.L¹³.LOU³.MD.MU.O².PA.PA².RO³.WO. + +
Though the approbation is dated from Louvain, 28 October 1567, no earlier edition than this of Antwerp, 1572, is known.
125   —[Anr. ed.] Nunc recens ab innumeris erroribus . . . cura, ac industria R.P.M. Liuii . . . repurgata. 4°. 2 vols. *Venetiis, apud haeredes Simonis Galignani de Karera,* 1585. [Coloph. to vol. 2:] *Georgius Angelerius & Alexander Gryphius excudebant.* L.O.; BG.DMR.LOU³.MD(*vol. 2*).MST.VI (*vol. 2*). *This or no. 126:* LER.MD³.STI.TB.ZA.
126   —[Anr. state, with imprint:] *Venetiis, apud haeredes Melchioris Sessae,* 1585. C¹³.LIL.PA.RO⁶. *See also note to no. 125.*
Forms part of a shared edition with no. 125 with which it is identical except for the imprint on the titlepage.
127   —[An abridgment.] *In:* Eulard, P. Bibliorum sacrorum concordantiae morales et historicae. 4°. *Antuerpiae, ex officina Plantiniana [etc.],* 1625. O; BRS.HA.LGE³.PA.WO.
C., A.H.L.N.H.E.V.E.A. *See* no. 638.
127.1 **Caddell, Peter, and Harris, Paul.** Illustriss. Archiepisc. & R. Episcopis per vniversam Hiberniam: praecipue vero Episcopis comprovincialibus Provinciae Dubliniensis honorandis suis Dom. Dauidi Osoriensi, Ioan. Fernensi, Rosso Kildar. & Math. Vicario Apostolico Ledinensi. Fol. *Impressum Lugd. ad insignia Apost. Petri & Pauli sumptibus Vplai Euridici, n.d.* [1632.] L²⁷ᴬ(A26 no. 65).
Complaints against Thomas Fleming, Archbishop of Dublin. Text dated, Dublin 3 May 1632. An English version is at A&R 189. Imprint false; *pr.* [Dublin, Soc. of Stationers?].

128   **Cahan, Eugene.** [*Begin :*] Eminentissimo, ac Reuerendissimo Principi
       Augustino Oregio . . . Cardinali Amplissimo . . . F. Eugenius Cahanus
       Collegii S. Isidori alumnus. P. felicitatem exoptat. Conclusiones
       theologicae . . . [*End :*] Disputabuntur publice in Collegio S. Isidori
       . . . Praesidente Reu. P. Fr. Francisco a S. Maria [F. Tully] . . . 1634.
       Mense Martii. *s.sh.*fol. *Romae, ex typographia Ludouici Grignani,*
       1634. RO².
           A programme announcing the forthcoming defence of his thesis.
       Text and part of the setting are the same as in nos. 84, 271, 414.
       Cahill, Patrick. Censura propositionum ad sacram facultatem theo-
       logiae Parisiensem allatarum, per D. Patricium Cahill, 1631. *See* nos.
       683–5.
       Camerarius, David. *See* Chalmers, D.
       Camerarius, William. *See* Chalmers, W.
129   **Campbell, Anne,** *Countess of Argyll.* [*A work edited and perhaps
       translated by her.*] Augustine, *Saint.* El alma del incomparable San
       Augustin sacada del cuerpo de sus Confessiones. 4°. *Amberes, por
       Geraldo Wolschaten,* 1622. C(*imp.*); ANT².GT.L⁹(*imp.*).
           A translation of extracts from the *Confessiones* compiled for the
       Archduchess Isabella, Governor of the Netherlands.
       Campianus, Edmundus. *See* Campion, E.

       Campion, Edmund, *Saint.*†

                               OPUSCULA

       —Edmundi Campiani . . . orationes, epistolae, tractatus de imitatione
       rhetorica, 1602. *In* no. 1263.
       —[Anr. ed.] 1615. *In* no. 1265.
130   —[Anr. ed. enlarged.] Edmundi Campiani . . . Opuscula omnia nunc
       primum e M.S. edita. 24°. *Parisiis, ex officina Niuelliana, sumptibus
       Seb. Cramoisy,* 1618. C(2:-1-*t.p.*).; E.FU.LI.MD.MU.O¹⁴.O¹⁵.PA(2).RO².
       RO⁴.ST.VAL².VT.WO. +
           This edition adds *Rationes decem* and Robert Turner's Latin
       translation of the anonymous account of Campion's capture, trial
       and death. (*See* nos. 196, *et seq.*).
131   —[Anr. ed.] *Pisa,* 1618.
           Not found. Listed in Simpson, p. 503.
132   —[Anr. ed.] 32°. *Lugduni, sumptibus I. Petri Charlot,* 1619. CHA.DMR.
       MAA.RO³.
           Contents as in no. 130. This appears to be a reissue of an edition not
       so far found. The titleleaf is a cancel.
133   —[Anr. ed.] 24°. *Mussiponti, apud Sebastianum Cramoisy,* 1622. O.;
       A.ANT.BRS².C.CHA.DE.DUR(2).HAN.L²⁶(2).O⁶.P⁴.RO².SP.U.W. +
           A close reprint of no. 130.
134   —[Anr. ed.] 16°. *Mediolani, apud Io. Baptistam Bidellium,* 1625. L.;
       D⁵.L²⁶.NP.RO⁴.
       —[Anr. ed.] 1625. *In* no. 1269.
       —[Anr. ed.] 1631. *In* no. 170.

                       DE IMITATIONE RHETORICA

       —*In Opuscule* and in no. 168.

                               LITANIAE

135   —Litaniae Deiparae Virginis Mariae ex Patribus et Script. collectae a
       RR.PP. Edmundo Campiano, in Anglia pro fide Catholica mortuo, et
       Laurentio Maggio, Societatis Iesu sacerdotibus, et ab iisdem per
       singulos hebdomadae dies distributae. 16°. *Parisiis, apud Sebastianum
       Cramoisy,* 1633.

No copy found. A reprint of this edition, edited by P. de Roche-monteix, was published by E. Cagniard at Rouen in 1887 (copy at PA). The unsigned dedicatory epistle to the Reader, reprinted by Cagniard from the original edition of 1633, says that Campion's autograph MS of the work was then still preserved at the Jesuit College at Pont-à-Mousson.

NARRATIO DE DIVORTIO

—Narratio de diuortio Henrici VIII, 1622. *In* no. 639.
—[Anr. ed.] 1631. *In* no. 170.

RATIONES DECEM

For an English translation printed in 1632 see A&R *193. The following list covers editions and translations published abroad either separately or as part of small collections of which Campion's work forms a substantial section.*

Latin

135.1 —Rationes decem: quibus fretus, certamen aduersariis obtulit in causa fidei, Edmundus Campianus ... allegatae ad clarissimos viros, nostrates academicos. 8° in fours. *n.p.d.* [1581.] BUTE.DUR(Bamborough).O^{37}.ST.W(formerly WN^4).
   Pr. [secretly at Stonor Park, Oxfordshire, 'Greenstreet House' press.] A&R 192. STC 4536.5. ERL 1. Mil. vol. 1, pp. 57, *etc.*

136 —[Anr. ed.] 12°. *Romae, apud Franciscum Zanettum,* 1582. BG.D^{11}.F.FLO.MD.NP.PA.PAR.PM.RO^2(2).TRI.

137 —[Anr. ed.] 8°. *Mediolani, apud Pacificum Pontium,* 1582. FLO^3.MIL^2.

138 —[Anr. ed.] 8°. *Mussiponti, excudebat Martinus Mercator,* 1582. KN^2.PA^4.TB.TRO.

139 —[Anr. ed.] Edmundi Campiani ... Rationes decem ... & ad eas Guilielmi Whitakeri ... responsio. 8°. *Antuerpiae, excudebat Aegidius Radaeus,* 1582. L(2).O.C.; BER.C.^{5}C^9.D^2.E^2.LN.MU(2).P.STG.UT.WR.YK. ++

   A Protestant edition comprising Campion's work and William Whitaker's *Responsio* (the latter first published in London in 1581: STC 25358). Antwerp was under Calvinist domination from 1577 to 1585.
—[Anr. ed.] 1582. *In* no. 334.
—[Anr. ed.] 1583. *In* no. 524.

140 —[Anr. ed.] Edmundi Campiani ... Rationes decem redditae academicis Angliae. 12°. *Ingolstadii, excudebat Dauid Sartorius,* 1583. L(2).O.C.; AB.DIL.FR.FU^2.KN^2.MU(3).RO^4.RO^{12}.ROT^2.STG.W.
   Collation: A–D^{12}E^6(E6 blank).

141 —[Anr. ed. enlarged.] Addita est breuis narratio vitae & martyrii eiusdem Campiani. 12°. *Ingolstadii, excudebat Dauid Sartorius,* 1583. W.
   Collation: A–I^{12}. For the 'Breuis narratio' *see* note under [*Appendix.*] Vita et martyrium ... 1583.

142 —[Date variant of no. 141.] 1584. L.; BER.D^{11}.DI.FLO^2.KR.L^9.L^{26}.MD.MFL.MU(2).O^5.RO^5.VI.YK. +

143 —[Anr. ed.] Rationes decem quibus fretus, certamen aduersarii obtulit in causa fidei, Edmundus Cāpianus. 12°. *Romae, ex typographia Bartholomaei Bonfadini & Titi Diani,* 1584. BER.CARP.L^{13}.PM.RO.RO^2(3).RO^3.RO^5.UP.VAL.VI.

144 —[Anr. ed.] Raitones [*sic*] decem ... 8°. *n.p.d.* [1585?] KR(2).UP(2). [*L.O.].
   Pr. [Wilno, M. K. Radziwill.] The printer is identified in *Index Aureliensis,* VI.375.

145 —[Anr. ed.] 1585. *In tom. 2 of :* Doctrinae Iesuiticae praecipua capita.
8°. *Rupellae, apud Theophilum Regium,* 1585. L.C.; BA.RO⁵.
A Protestant edition in which Campion's work is accompanied by
Whitaker's answer. *See* no. 139.
—[Anr. ed.] 1585. *In* no. 335.

146 —[Anr. ed.] Edmundi Campiani . . . Rationes decem redditae academicis Angliae. Addita praefatione Petri Muchitsch. 12°. *Graecii,
excudebat Georgius Vuidmanstadius,* 1588. C².MU.
—[Anr. ed.] 1588 (1589). *In* nos. 525–6.

147 —[Anr. ed.] Rationes decem quibus fretus certamen aduersariis obtulit
in causa fidei Edmundus Campianus. 12°. *Herbipoli, apud Henricum
Aquensem,* 1589. L.C.; BER.EI.HAN.NI².P.PR².RO(*imp.*)SO.WA.X.

148 —[Anr. ed.] Edmundi Campiani . . . Rationes decem redditae academicis Angliae. 12°. *Pragae, typis Michaelis Peterle,* 1592. BRN.BU.KR.
PR.PR³.WR(2). [*L.]

149 —[Anr. ed.] 12°. *Viennae Austriae, excudebat Franciscus Kolb,* 1594.
BER(2).WR. [*L.]

150 —[Anr. ed.] 1594. *In* Tertullianus, Q. Tres grauissimi, perpetuae
Catholicae fidei constantiae, testes. 16°. *Coloniae Agrippinae, in
officina Birckmannica sumptibus Arnoldi Mylii,* 1594. L.; DMR.E.F.
FLO².FRA.FU².HAN.MU.NP.PA⁴.TB.VT.
—[Anr. ed.] 1594. *In* no. 527.
—[A 'ghost'. 'Augustae Taurinorum, 1594.']
There is no Turin edition of this year. The imprint of the two
copies cited in the PA printed catalogue which is the source of
Shaaber C.70 should read *Augustae Trevirorum* and refers to no. 527
of this catalogue.

151 —[Anr. ed.] 1600. *In* Vincent, of Lerins, Saint. S. Vincentii Lerinensis
. . . aduersus prophanas haeresewn nouationes . . . Item R. P.
Edmundi Campiani . . . Rationes decem. 12°. *Coloniae, in officina
Birckmannica sumptibus Arnoldi Mylii,* 1600. L.C.; AMP.ANT.C³.CHA.
DE.E².FR.HP.MU.OS.PA.USH.VT.W. +

152 —[Anr. ed.] Rationes decem . . . allegatae ad clarissimos viros, nostrates
academicos. 32°. *Parisiis, apud Iacobum Rezé,* 1600. O.; D².SOL.

153 —[Date variant.] 1601. HP(*missing*).LW.ST.USH.

154 —[Anr. ed.] Rabsaces Romanus id est: Edmundi Campiani Jesuitae
Rationes decem . . . & ad eas Guilielmi Whitakeri . . . responsio. 8°.
Lichae Solimorum, excudebat Wolgangus Kezelius, 1601. O.; BER.BG.
DMR.HD.LC.PA.PA⁶.PR.
A Protestant edition in which Campion's work is accompanied by
Whitaker's answer. *See* nos. 139, 145.

155 —[Anr. ed.] 1602. *In* Calvin, Justus [*otherwise* Justus Baronius]. Iusti
Baronii . . . praescriptionum aduersus haereticos perpetuarum . . .
tractatus VI. 8°. *Moguntiae, ex officina typographica Ioannis Albini,*
1602. CHA.LX.PA(2).PR.RO⁵.VT.

156 —[Anr. ed.] Edmundi Campiani Jesuitae Rationes decem . . . et ad eas
Guil. Withakeri . . . responsio. 4°. *Lichae, typis Guolgangi Kezelii,*
1604. O.; BER.BUCK.CHA.PR.RO¹².VT.WASH².WO.
A Protestant edition in which Campion's work is accompanied by
Whitaker's answer. *See* nos. 139, 145, 154.

157 —[Anr. ed.] Rationes decem: quibus fretus certamen aduersariis obtulit
in causa fidei Edmundus Campianus. 12°. *Mussiponti, apud Melchiorem
Bernardum,* 1605. PA.UP.

158 —[Anr. ed.] Edmundi Campiani . . . Rationes decem redditae academicis Angliae. 24°. *Cracouiae, ex officina Andreae Petrocouii,* 1605.
L.O.; BRS².GTN.KR.MU.PR.PR².UP.VI.

159 —[Anr. ed.] 1605. *In* Calvin, Justus [*otherwise* Justus Baronius]. Iusti
Baronii . . . praescriptionum aduersus haereticos perpetuarum . . .

tractatus VI. 8°. *Moguntiae, apud Ioannem Albinum*, 1605. O.; U.
    A reissue of no. 155.

160   —[Anr. ed.] 1606. *In* Tertullianus, Q. [*etc.*] Trium nobilium auctorum
    . . . opuscula tria. 12°. 2 pts. *Rorschachii, excudebat Bartholomeus
    Schnell*, 1606. L.; DI(6).FR.FU.HEI.MU.O³⁷.SBG.STG.TB.U.

161   —[Anr. ed.] Rationes decem . . . 8°. *Biturigibus, apud Germanum
    Lauuerjatium*, 1607. [Coloph.] *Excudebat Mauricius Leuez.* PA.

162   —[Anr. ed.] 1608. *In* Tertullianus, Q. [*etc.*] Tres grauissimi testes . . .
    8°. *Rorschachii, Snell & Crasebomius*, 1608.
        Anr. ed. of no. 160. Not found. Description from Simpson, p. 502,
        no. 4B(3).

163   —[Anr. ed.] 1613. *In* Vincent, *of Lerins, Saint.* S. Vincentii Lerinensis
    . . . aduersus prophanas haereseωn nouationes. . . Item R. P. Edmundi
    Campiani . . . Rationes decem. 12°. *Coloniae, in officina Birckmannica,
    sumptibus Arnoldi Mylii*, 1613. L.O.; A.C⁹.DMR.FR.FU².GTN.HA(2).HP.
    LGE³.O¹².OS.PA.ST.TRI. +
        A reprint of no. 151.

164   —[Anr. ed.] 1613. *In* Peter, *Canisius, Saint.* Institutio christiana siue
    paruus catechismus . . . vna cum fasciculo precum & meditationum
    . . . Accesserunt his perelegantes Rationes decem fortissimi martyris
    Edmundi Campiani. 12°. *In officina Lamberti Ratsfeldii*, 1613. X.
        Pr. [Münster.] Campion's work has its own titlepage, with imprint:
        Monasterii Westphaliae, in officina Lamberti Ratsfeldii, 1613.

165   —[Anr. ed.] Edmundi Campiani . . . Rationes decem quibus fretus
    certamen aduersariis obtulit in causa fideii. 8°. *Rhemis, ex officina
    Nicolai Constant*, 1615. PA.

166   —[Anr. ed.] 12°. *Cadomi, ex typographia Adami Cauelier*, 1616. O⁸.RO⁶.
167   —[Anr. ed.] Edmundi Campiani . . . Rationes decem . . . et ad eas Guil.
    Withakeri . . . Responsio. 4°. *Per Wilhelmum Wesselium. Prostat
    Francofurti apud Iohannem Carolum Vnckelium*, 1617. ERL.PA³.PR.SO.U.
        A Protestant edition in which Campion's work is accompanied by
        Whitaker's answer. *See* nos. 139, 145, 154, 156. *Pr.* [Kassel].

    —[Anr. ed.] 1618. *In* no. 130.
    —[Anr. ed.] 1619. *In* no. 132.

168   —[Anr. ed. With *De imitatione rhetorica.*] Edmundi Campiani . . .
    Rationes certaminis oblati academicis Anglis cum elegantissimo
    tractatu de imitatione rhetorica. 12°. *Flexiae, apud Ludouicum Hebert*,
    1620. BOR.HP.MSM.PA³.SAI.
        Other editions of Campion's *De imitatione rhetorica* are included in
        the *Opuscula* (nos. 130 *et seq.*)

    —[Anr. ed.] 1622. *In* no. 133.

169   —[Anr. ed.] 1622. *In* Tertullianus, Q. [*etc.*] Sandapila silicernio
    quinti ac sexti euangelii efferendo . . . Tertullianus libro de prae-
    scriptionibus . . . Edmundus Campianus . . . libro rationum acade-
    micis Oxoniensibus oblatarum. 16°. *Lugduni, sumptibus Claudii
    Landry*, 1622. A.BOR.DAI.FR.KN.LYN².PA⁸.PA⁸.PR.SAL.X.

    —[Anr. ed.] 1625. *In* no. 134.
    —[Anr. ed.] 1625. *In* no. 1269.

170   —[Anr. ed., with *Opuscula.*] Edmundi Campiani . . . Decem rationes
    propositae in causa fidei, et opuscula eius selecta . . . auctiore editione.
    12°. *Antuerpiae, ex officina Plantiniana Balthasaris Moreti*, 1631.
    L.O.C.; AMS.ANT².D¹⁰.DE.E.FU².HP(3).PA.RO⁶.ST.USH.VT. + +
        Editor's *ded.* sgd.: Silvester Pietrasancta. This edition of the
        Opuscula adds Campion's work on the divorce of Henry VIII
        (reprinted from no. 639) but omits Robert Turner's Latin transla-
        tion of the anonymous account of Campion's capture, trial and
        death (*See* nos. 196, *et seq.*)
    —[A 'ghost'. 'Ingolstadii, David Sartorius, 1631'.]

There is no Ingolstadt edition of this year. The imprint of the copy cited in the YK printed catalogue which is the source of Shaaber C.91 reads *Antuerpiae, ex officina Plantiniana* . . . and refers to no. 170 of this catalogue.

171 —[Anr. ed.] 1632. *In* Vincent, *of Lerins, Saint.* Vincentii Lirinensis . . . Aduersus prophanas haereseon nouationes. 12°. *Duaci, typis Ioannis de Fampoux*, 1632. D.

Czech

172 —Spis krátký Edmunda Kāpiana Societatis Iesu . . . Podaný. Z Latinske řeči na Czesko přeložený . . . S. dowolenijm wrchnosti. 12°. *w starém Městě Pražském v G.N. Léta*, 1601. [Coloph.] *Datum w Kolegi S.M.C. Societatis Iesu v Swatého Klimenta w Starém Městě Pražském Den Zelencho Cžtwrtku ginak Wečeře Páne Letha, MDCI.* PR. (*Tobolka, vol. 2, no. 1420, also cites two other copies, one in the Zemský Archiv, the other in the Knihovna Nàrodniho Museo.*)

The dedication to the Archduke Ferdinand (whose arms are printed on the verso of the titlepage) is dated from the Collegium Clementinum of the Jesuits in Prague, 19 April 1601, and signed by the translator: O.M. [Ondřej Modestin]. *Pr.* [Giřika Nygrina.]

173 —[Anr. ed. with title:] Wssech Pikartských, Luteryanských, y ginác zrotilých Prewytkantů, Hostides, To gest: Deset podstatných přjčin, kterychž gistotau, welebný Knez, a zmužilosrdnaty Mučedlnijk Edmund Kampian. 12°. *wytisstěno w Holomúcy*, 1602. PR. (*Tobolka, vol. 2, no. 1419 also cites a copy in Lobkowiczova Knihovna.*) *Pr.* [Jiř Handle].

Dutch (*See also* Flemish)

174 —Thien redenen van Edmundus Campianus . . . met de weder legginghe vanden seer geleerden . . . Guilielmus Whitakerus . . . uyt de Latijnsche inde Nederduytsche tale ghetrouwelijck ouer-gheset door Jacobum Triglandium. 8°. *Amstelredam, door Marten Iansz Brandt*, 1624. AMS.UT².

A translation of the Protestant editions incorporating Whitaker's answer at nos. 139, 145, 154, 156, 167.

Flemish (*See also* Dutch)

175 —De thien redenen, van Edmondus Campianus . . . door de welcke hy seer claer ende sterckelijcken bewijst, het een, heylich, Catholijck ghelooue der H. Roomscher Kercken. Nu wt den Latijn in Nederlandts duyts ouerghesedt. 8°. *t'Hantwerpen, gheprint by Hieronymus Verdussen*, 1591. L.; ANT.GT.HEI.LN.

176 —[Anr. ed.] 8°. *t'Hantwerpen, gheprint by Hieronymus Verdussen*, 1592. BRS.C².

177 —[Anr. ed.] Thien redenen, van Emondus Campianus . . . Seer claer bewijsende het een heylich, Catholijck ghelooue de H. Roomscher Kercken. 8°. *Louen, by Jan Maes*, 1609. AMS.ANT³.UT². [*L.]

A reprint of the same Flemish translation of *Rationes decem*, but omitting the anonymous editorial preface of nos. 175–6 and a translation of Campion's address to the doctors of Oxford and Cambridge which was appended to those editions.

178 —[Anr. ed. of no. 177.] 8°. *Tot Louen, by Jan Maes*, 1622. L.; BRS².TIL.

French

179 —Bref discours du P. Edmond Campian . . . contenant dix points & fondemens principaux de l'Eglise Catholique, Apostolique, Romane, contre les heresies de Luther, Caluin, Beze, & autres de la religion

pretendue reformée. Traduit du Latin en François par R.P. Baulduin Deglen Abbé de Hennin Lietard. 12°. *Douay, chez Iean Bogard,* 1582. CHA.

180 —[*A different transl.*] Les dix raisons, pour lesquelles M. Edmond Campian . . . s'est faict fort d'entreprēdre la dispute pour la religion Catholique cōtre les aduersaires d'icelle . . . mises de Latin en François par M. Pierre Madur. 16°. *Lyon, par Iean Pillehotte,* 1584. L.; PA.

181 —[*A different transl.*] 1601. *In* Panigarola, F. L'art de prescher . . . par R. P. F. François Panigarole . . . Dix raisons contre les heretiques par R. P. Emond Campián . . . traduict, par Gabriel Chappuis. 12°. *Paris, chez Regnauld Chaudiere,* 1601. BRS.LX.
A 1604 edition of Panigarola's work published at Paris by Chaudière does not include Campion's work.

182 —[*A different transl.*] Les dix raisons sur lesquelles se fondoit Aymond Campian . . . presentant le combat en la cause de la foy aux aduersaires . . . traduittes du Latin de l'autheur: et dediées à la Royne Regente. Par le Sieur de la Brosse. 8°. *Paris, veufue Matthieu Guillemot & Samuel Thiboust,* 1612. AMI.BER.PA(2).PA³.PA⁵.PA⁷.POI.

German

—1583. *Tr.* Johann Christoff Hueber. *In* no. 882.

183 —[*A different transl.*] Zehen wolgegruendte Vrsachen, warumb man bey dem alten Catholischen Glauben bestendig bleiben, vnd kcinem andern mit rhuwigem gewissen beypflichten soll. Erstlich durch den H. Edmundum Campianum kuertzlich in Latein, jetzo aber durch Vitum Gamundanum etwas aussfuerlicher beschrieben. 8°. *Meyntz, durch Casparum Behem,* 1589. BER.FU².MU.UP.VI.WR. [*O.]
Translator's foreword sgd.: Vitus Miletus Canno, zu S. Seuer in Erfurt. Including a translation from St. Vincent of Lerins, *Aduersus prophanas haereseon novitates.*

184 —[Anr.ed] 8°. 1594. [Coloph.] *Neyss, durch Andream Reinheckel.* BER.KA. [*L].
Title and contents as in no. 183.

185 —[*A different transl.*] Der Lutherischen Caluinischen vnd anderer sectischen Predicanten. Schraeckengast. Das ist. Dess Ritterlichē Engellēdischen Martyrers Edmundi Campiani . . . Zehen . . . Motiff vnd Vrsachen . . . Jetzund auff ein Newes mit fleiss verteutscht vnd widerumb in Truck zugeben. 8°. *Ingolstatt, durch Elisabeth Ederin,* 1598. BER.DI.MU.TB.VT. [*O.].
Tr. [Conrad Vetter.]

186 —[Anr. ed.] Jetzund auff ein newes mit fleiss verteutscht, durch Conradum Vetter. 4°. *Ingolstatt, in der Ederischen Truckerey, durch Andream Angermayer,* 1599. L.O.; DI.FR.HD.MU.RG.ROT².VI.VI³.WO.Y.Z.

187 —[Anr. ed.] Jetzund auff ein Newes mit Fleiss verteutscht, vnd widerumb in Truck zugeben. 12°. *Wien, bey Frantz Kolben,* 1599. KL.
Not seen. Description from Mayer (no. 157) who cites the copy at KL. The copy said by Shaaber (C. 74) to be at Milwaukee does not exist. It would appear from the title that this edition was reprinted from no. 185 which does not reveal the translator's name.

188 —[Anr. ed.] 1600. *In* Rassfeldt, L. Zeugnuss bestendiger Wahrheit Catholischer Religion, durch . . . Tertullianum . . . Vincentium Lirinensem . . . Edmundum Campianum. 12°. *Coellen, bey Johan Gymnicus im Einhorn,* 1600. BER.BRN.DI.MU.VI.WO.
A German translation of the Collection at nos. 150, 160, 162.

189 —[Anr. ed.] 1602. *In* Vincent, *of Lerins, Saint.* Das Gueldene Warnungbuechlein, dess heyligen . . . Vincentii Lirinensis . . . Item Edmundi Campiani . . . zehen vnterschiedtliche vrsachen. 12°.

28

Ingolstadt, in der Ederischen Druckerey, durch Andream Angermayer, 1602. L.O.; BER.DI.KN.MU.NEU.PR².ROT².

190 —[Anr. ed.] Aller Sectischen Predicanten Schraeckengast . . . Jetzund auff ein Newes mit fleiss verteutscht, vnd widerumb in Truck zugeben. 12°. [Coloph.] *Bruenn, bey Bartholomeo Alberto F.*, 1610. PR.PR².
A reprint of no. 185.

Hungarian

191 —Campianus Edmondnac Iesus neve alat vitezkedet theologusnak, es nem régen Angliaban az Közönsèghes keresztien hitét martyromsaggal koronazotnac, Tiz Magiarul irot okai . . . Balassa Bálinttol iratot. 8°. *Viennae Austriae, typis Margarethae Formicae*, 1607. BU.PR².
According to the dedicatory epistle the translation was begun by Balassa and completed by Dobokay Sandor.

Polish

192 —Dzieśieć wywodow. Dla ktorych Edmundus Kampianus z Londynu Societatis Iesu wszystkie heretiki co naucześnsze w Angliey, ná dysputatia około wiáry wyzwał, pisane od niego do Akademiey Oksonienskiey y Kantabriyskiey. 8°. *w Vilnie, w drukarni Mikołaia Chrystofá Radźiwila*, 1584. KR².
Translator's *ded.* sgd.: Petrus Skarga.

193 —[*A different transl. with additional material.*] Dźieśiec mocnych dowodów, jz adwersarze kośćioła powszechnego, w porządney o wierze dysputácyey, vpáś́c musza Edmunda Kampiana Societatis Iesu. Z láćinskiego ná Polski ięzyk z pilnośćia przetłumáczone y potrzebnie wydáne, z krotką spráwa iego meczenniczego dokonánia, y odpisu Witákierowego. A przytym, na antidotum Kálwińskíe odpowiedź, y z nowokrzczeńcámi rosprawá, z strony przyczyn nawrocenia Gaspra Wilkowskiego, rokv, M.D.LXXXIIII. 4°. *n.p.d.* [1584–85.] KR².WA.WR².
Translator's *ded.* sgd. at Wilno on 13 December 1584. Pr. [Wilno, M. K. Radziwill.]

APPENDIX

I. *Works about Campion published under the author's name or pseudonym*

194 Bombino, P. Vita et martyrium Edmundi Campiani martyris Angli. 8°. *Antuerpiae, apud heredes Martini Nutii, & Ioannem Meursium*, 1618. L(2).O.; AIX.ANT.BRS.CHA.DE.E.HP.L²⁶.LGE.LOU.MU.OS.PA.RO².ST.VT. + +

195 [Anr. ed. revised and enlarged.] Editio posterior ab Auctore multis aucta partibus, & emendata. 8°. *Mantuae, apud fratres Osannas ducales impressores*, 1620. [Coloph.] *Ex officina Aurelii, & Ludouici Osannae fratrum.* L(2): 1 *imp.*).O.C(2).; BRU.D.DI.DUR.HP.L²⁶.MU.PA. PA³.RO².UP.VI. + +
With a *ded.* by the author to Ferdinando Gonzaga, Duke of Mantua, whose arms appear on the titlepage. A Paris ed. of 1626 recorded by Sommerv. (tom. 2, col. 1683) and a Naples ed. of 1627 noted by Simpson (p. 500, no. 33) have not been found.

—Briegerus, J., *pseud.*? Flores Caluinistici decerpti, 1685. A reply to Lawrence Humfrey's attack on Campion and Durie in tom. 3 of *Doctrinae Iesuiticae praecipua capita*, 1585. See nos. 115–16.

—Durie, J. Confutatio responsionis Gulielmi Whitakeri . . . ad Rationes decem, 1582. *See* nos. 334–5.

II. *Works about Campion published anonymously and of
which the author has not been identified*

—Lettere venute d'Inghilterra, 1582. *See* no. 363.1.

196   —L'histoire de la mort que le R. P. Edmund Campion, et autres ont
souffert en Angleterre pour la foy Catholique & Romaine le premier
iour de Decēbre mil cinq cens quatre vingts vn. Traduict d'Anglois en
François. 8° (in fours). *Lyon, par Iean Pillehotte*, M[   ]i [1582].
CHA(C. 59, *mutil.*).
> The other priests executed with Campion were Ralph Sherwin and
> Alexander Briant. As far as is known, the English original from
> which this French translation was made is not extant either in print
> or in MS. The work is that of an eye-witness to Campion's disputes
> in the Tower before his trial. It is not the same as Alfield's *True
> report* (A&R 4). In the only known copy of this edition the date in the
> imprint is partly torn away.

197   —[Anr. ed. enlarged.] 8° (in fours). *Paris, chez Guillaume Chaudiere*,
1582. L.; BUTE.CHA(also at C. 59).DE.PA(2).RMS.
> This edition has, at the end of the original text, some further details
> about the three priests, together with a short account of the execu-
> tion of Everard Hanse (31 July 1581).

198   —[Anr. ed., with title:] Discours des cruautés et tirannyes qua faict la
Royne d'Angleterre, à l'endroict des Catholecques [*sic*], Anglois,
Espagnolz, François, & prestres Catholicques, qui soutenoient la foy
& le tourmant qui l'ont [*sic*] soufert . . . Plus y est adiousté la mort
d'Edouard Hance prestre Anglois & le martyre qui la [*sic*] soufert.
8° (in fours). *Paris, iouxte la coppie imprimée à Londres par Pierre le
Sage imprimeur, n.d.* [1582]. CARP.PA.
> Including the additions made in no. 197. No London edition, either
> in English or in French, is known. In spite of the Paris imprint, the
> typographical errors suggest that the compositor was ignorant of
> French.

199   —[*Italian transl.*] Martirio del Reuer. P. Emondo Campione . . . patito in
Inghilterra per la fede Catholica . . . Tradotto dall'Inglese in lingua
Francese, & poi dal Francese in Italiano. 4°. *Turino, appresso gl'heredi
del Beuilacqua*, 1582. L.; AB.FLO.TUR.
> This translation omits the additions made in nos. 197–8.

200   —[Anr. ed.?] Historia della morte di P. Emondo Campiano ed alteri due
che hanno patito in Inghilterra per la fede. *Milano, Giacomo Piccaria*,
1582. MIL[2](*missing 1976*).
> Not seen. Description from card catalogue at MIL[2] and Simpson,
> p. 497.

201   —[Anr. ed.?] Auuiso della sua morte, tradotto dell'Inglese. 12°. *Milano,
[e] Bologna, Pellegrino Bonardo*, 1581 [1582]. CARP(*missing 1979*).
> Not seen. Description from card catalogue at CARP. The date 1581
> would appear to be a cataloguing error.

202   —[Anr. ed., with title as in no. 199.] 4°. *Venetia, appresso Domenico, &
Gio. Battista Guerra, fratelli*, 1582. CHA.RO[3].VI.VT.
> A reprint of no. 199 without the dedicatory epistle.

203   —[*Latin transl. by Wilhelm Est.*] Martyrium R. P. Edmundi Campiani
. . . qui cum duobus aliis presbyteris, Radulpho Sherwino & Alexandro
Briano in Anglia . . . mortis supplicio affectus est . . . Per G. Estium e
Gallico Latine redditum. 8°. *Louanii, ex officina Iohannis Masii*, 1582.
L.; BRS[2].LINC.PR.W.
> This translation omits the additions made in no. 197. Following the
> account of Campion and his companions there is a shorter work:
> *Martyrium Petri Elcii Madridiensis, ex epistola P. F. Francisci de
> Castro*, and three Latin poems, one of them 'Ad martyres Anglicanos'.

—[*Latin transl. by James Laing.*] Historia de morte ... Edmundi Campionis ... et aliorum qui in Anglia ... passi sunt mortem ... traducta ex sermone Gallico in Latinum, 1585. Including the additions made in no. 197 but not those made in no. 203. *In* no. 711.

—[*Latin transl. by Robert Turner.*] Narratio de morte, quam in Anglia pro fide Romanè Catholica Edmundus Campianus ... aliiq; duo constanter oppetierunt, ex Italica sermone facta Latine a R.T., 1599 [*etc.*]. Omitting the additions made in nos. 197, 203. *In* nos. 130–4, 1262, 1264.

—[*A work based in part on the foregoing account.*] Vita et martyrium Edmundi Campiani, 1853 [*etc.*]. Based partly on the foregoing account and partly on Allen's life of Campion in A&R 7 and this catalogue nos. 8–11. Not the same as the work of similar title by Bombino (nos. 194–5). This text is appended to some editions of *Rationes decem.* *In* nos. 524–7.

204 —[*German transl. of 'Vita et martyrium'.*] Leben vnd Leyden, dess edlen Martyrers ... Edmundi Campiani ... Erstlich Englisch, nachmal Lateinisch beschriben ... Jetzo ... in vnser Hochteutsch auffs trewlichst gebracht. 12°. *Dilingen, durch Iohannem Mayer*, 1588. L.; AB.

Campion, John, *alias. See* Poyntz, J.
Campion, Richard, *alias. See* Wigmore, R.
Canfield, *Benet of. See* Fitch, W.
Cantwell, Michael. Censura propositionum ... obsignatarum ... per Michaelem Cantuelem, 1631. *See* nos. 683–5.

204.1 **Carier, Benjamin.†** [*Appendix*] Pelletier, Thomas. Discours sur la mort du sieur Carier, cy devant ministre du ... Roy de la Grande-Bretagne, et décédé en la foy catholique, à Paris le 20 juin. 8°. *Paris, François Huby*, 1614. PA.
Not seen. Carier, who had been a chaplain to King James I, made public his conversion to Catholicism in a letter dated from Liège 12 December 1613 (A&R 207). He was invited to Paris and there died in June 1614.

Caron, Raymund. [Roma triumphans septicollis, 1635.]
Has no place in this catalogue because the titlepage date is a misprint. The dedication is correctly dated: 1653.

205 **Carue, Thomas.‡** Itinerarium R.D. Thomae Carue Tripperariensis, sacellani maioris in ... legione strenuissimi Domini Colonelli D. Walteri Deueroux ... Opera studio et impensis Authoris. 12°. *Moguntiae, imprimebat Nicolaus Heyll*, 1639. L(2).O.C.; D⁶.D¹¹.DI.E.HA. HAN.L²⁵.MU(2).ST.TRI.UP.VI. + +
Pt. 1 of the Author's account of his experiences as chaplain to various regiments on the Catholic side in the Thirty-Years' War. Pt. 2 (*Moguntiae*, 1641) and pt. 3 (*Spirae*, 1646) may be found accompanying this or other editions of pt. 1.

206 —[*Anr. ed. of pt. 1, enlarged.*] Editio tertia auctior & correctior. 12°. *Moguntiae, imprimebat Nicolaus Heyll, sumptibus Joann. Baltasari Kuntzen*, 1640. L(2).O.; D.D⁶.D¹¹.DI.ERL.FR.GER.HA.MTH.PA.ST.VI.VT. WO. +
The second edition has not been found.

207 —[*German transl. of pt. 1, with further additions.*] Reyssbuechlein dess erwuerdigen Herrn Thomae Carue ... auss dem Latein: ins Teutsch vbersetzt durch P. R. Jetzo aber biss auffs Jahr 1640 continuirt vnd fortgesetzt ... studio Wolffgangi Sigismundi a Vorburg. 12°. *Maeyntz, bey Nicolao Heyll, in verlegung Joan: Balthasar Kuntzen*, 1640. L.; D.D⁶.ERL.MU.WO.
With nine additional chapters not found in any of the three Latin parts. A German translation of pt. 2 was printed at Mainz in 1642.

Cavellus, Hugo. *See* MacCaghwell, H.

208   **Chalmers, David.** Dauidis Camerarii ... de Scotorum fortitudine,
        doctrina, & pietate, ac de ortu & progressu haeresis in regnis Scotiae
        & Angliae libri quatuor. Nunc primum in lucem editi. 4°. *Parisiis,*
        sumptibus Petri Baillet, 1631. O.C.; D.E. *This or no. 209 :* BG.CARP.D⁶.
        LINC.LOU³.PA⁴.RO⁶.VAL².
            Seen through the press, probably during the Author's absence from
            France, by Jean Morin of the Paris Oratory; the Privilege grants
            Morin permission to have the work printed. For Chalmers *see* ref.
            under his brother William, no. 213, and Hay, pp. 110, *et seq.* This
            issue has a dedicatory epistle to Cardinal Francesco Barberini,
            Protector of Scotland.

209   —[Anr. issue.] *Parisiis, sumptibus Petri Baillet,* 1631. L(2).O(2).C(2);
        A.DUR.E(2).E².(3).L².L²⁶.PA.PA².PA³.RMS.STA. *See also note to no.* 208.
            The dedicatory epistle of no. 208 has been replaced by one to King
            Charles I of England, and an 'Index rerum' and an 'Index alpha-
            beticus omnium sanctorum' have been added; otherwise this is a
            reissue of the sheets of no. 208. Scott 227.

210   —De statu hominis veteris simul ac nouae ecclesiae, et infidelium con-
        uersione. Libri tres. 4°. 3 pts. *Catalauni, apud Iacobum Theuenym,*
        1627. C(2).; A².D.E(2).KNY.L².LIL.NP³. *This or no. 211 :* RO.²RO³.RO⁶.
        Pts. 2 and 3 have separate titlepages. Pt. 2 is entitled: 'De virtutibus
        requisitis in concionatore euangelico'; pt. 3: 'De quibusdam con-
        trouersiis Christianae religionis inter Catholicos et haereticos nostri
        temporis'. In this issue the preliminaries to pt. 1 occupy an unsigned
        bifolium.

211   —[Anr. issue.] *Catalauni, apud Iacobum Theuenym,* 1627. RO.
            The original bifolium containing the preliminaries to pt. 1 has been
            replaced by an unsigned quadrifolium containing the same pre-
            liminaries reprinted together with an epistle to the reader warning
            that, in the printed text, liberties were taken with the Author's MS.
            Apart from the first quire of pt. 1 this is a reissue of the sheets of
            no. 210.

212   —[Anr. issue of no. 210, with a cancel title to pt. 1.] *Rothomagi, apud*
        Carolum Osmont, 1628. PA².
            Except for the cancel title to pt. 1 this is a reissue of the sheets of
            no. 210 including the titleleaves of pts. 2 and 3 which bear the
            original Chalons imprint. It does not include the epistle to the
            reader of no. 211.

213   **Chalmers, William.** Antiquitatis de nouitate victoria. Siue iusta
        defensio praemotionis physicae, contra impetitiones pseudo-Eugenii
        Philadelphi Romani. 4°. *Fastemburgi, apud Petrum Baretium, & Ioh.*
        Astemium, 1634. D².G².UT.
            A defence of the Thomistic doctrine of *Praemotio physica* against
            the *Scientia media* of the Molinists. For Chalmers, a Scotsman who
            became a priest of the Paris Oratory, *see* F. Ferrier, *William*
            Chalmers ... *Etude bio-bibliographique,* Paris, 1968 (*Le mouvement*
            des idées au XVIIe siècle. 7.). Eugenius Philadelphus Romanus was
            the pseudonym of François Annat S.J. who had attacked Chalmers's
            opinions in *Exercitatio scholastica tripartita* ... *Cum appendice ad*
            Gulielmum Camerarium, Scotum, 1632 (copies at O.PA.). The imprint
            is fictitious; *pr.* [Paris?].

214   —Dissertatio theologica. An confessarius absoluere possit Catholicum
        pie viuentem ita sensibus destitutum, vt nullum dare possit contri-
        tionis vel poenitentiae signum? 16°. *Parisiis, apud Carolum Rouillard,*
        1637. PA³.

215   —[Anr. ed.] 16°. *Brixiae Catacorum, ex officina Caroli Pensae,* 1638.
        D.PA.PA².

Imprint false ?; *pr.* [in France ?].

216 —Gulielmi Camerarii ... Disputationes theologicae de discrimine peccati venialis & mortalis. De perfecta obseruatione diuinae legis ... Oppositae Disputationibus Roberti Baronis ... de iisdem materiis. 8°. *Parisiis, apud Dionysium Houssaye,* 1639. A.A².LYN.

An answer to Robert Baron's *Disputatio* ... *de vero discrimine peccati mortalis et venialis,* 1633 (STC 1495).

217 —Gulielmi Camerarii ... Selectae disputationes philosphicae in tres partes distributae. Pars prima (– tertia). Fol. 2 pts. *Parisiis, typis Caroli Chappellain,* 1630. O.C.; E².G².NP².O².O⁸.O¹².O¹⁹.PA⁵.RO⁵.RO⁶. SAL.STU.

Pt. 1 contains 'Pars prima', pt. 2 'Pars secunda' and 'Pars tertia'. Each of the three 'Partes' has its own titlepage.

218 —Gulielmi Camerarii ... Tractatus, in quo, omnium animarum indiuisibilitas luculenter probatur. 8° (in fours). *Parisiis, apud Carolum Roulliard,* 1638. PA.PA³(2).

The author says in his preface to the reader that he wrote the work ten years ago but has not published it until now.

219 —[*Works edited by him.*] [Various authors.] Sanctorum patrum Augustini, Fulgentii et Anselmi monimenta ... nunc primum ex vetustissimis manuscriptis eruta, ad [*sic*] adnotationibus illustrata, studio et opera R. Patris Guilielmi Camerarii, Scoti. 12°. *Parisiis, apud Fiacrium Dehors,* 1634. PA.

220 —[Imprint variant.] *Parisiis, apud Sebastianum Huré,* 1634. PA³.

Forming part of a shared edition with no. 219.

221 —Muhammad Ibn Muhammad, *al Farabi.* Alpharabii, vetustissimi Aristotelis interpretis, opera omnia, quae, Latina lingua conscripta, reperiri potuerunt ... eruta. Studio et opera Guilielmi Camerarii, Scoti. 8°. *Parisiis, apud Dionysium Moreau,* 1638. L.O.C.; D.PA.PA³.

222 **Chamberlin, Christopher.**‡ Christoph. Chamberlini Naenia in obitu perillustris, ac nobilissimi herois, D. Ioannis Flemingi, Baronis Slaniensis fillii. 4°. *Bruxellae, ex typographejo Mommartiano,* 1636. D.D⁷.

Dedicated by the Author to William Fleming, Baron Slane, whose son John died while a student at the Irish College, Douai. Chamberlin was encouraged to write this tribute to John Fleming by Nicholas Aylmer, President of the Irish colleges at Douai and Tournai.

223 —Christophori Chamberlini Epigrammatum liber I. 8°. *Duaci, typis viduae Petri Telu,* 1623. L.; ANT².NI(*v.imp.*).

—Elegiae funebres in exequiis Serenissimi ... Principis Alberti, Archiducis Austriae, 1622. *See* no. 225.

—Expositio tabulae emblematicae, 1622. *Part of* no. 324.

224 —Laetitia Belgarum in aduentu Serenissimi Principis Ferdinandi Austriaci ... elegiis & elogiis adumbrata. 4°. *Louanii, apud Ioan. Oliuerium, & Corn. Coenestenium,* 1634. ANT².BRS.HA.

An address by Chamberlin in Latin prose, followed by several unsigned Latin poems. At the end is a quadrifolium containing a poem 'Virtutum et Musarum Triumphus' which is signed by Chamberlin. Ferdinand of Austria took up office as Viceroy of the Netherlands in the autumn of 1634.

225 —Laudatio funebris Serenissimi et pientissimi Principis Alberti, Archiducis Austriae ... Auctore Christoph. Chamberlino Iberno. Collegii Ibernorum Duaceni nomine. 4°. 2 pts. *Duaci, typis Petri Telu,* 1622. [Imprint to pt. 2:] *typis viduae Petri Telu,* 1622. L(pt. 1).; ANT². DOU(1622/16–17).

Pt. 1 comprises the 'Laudatio' which is in prose; pt. 2 consists of Latin verses, 'Elegiae funebres', which are also by Chamberlin.

The approbations cover both parts. The Archduke Albert died on 15 July 1621.

226 —Optatae electioni Illmi. ac Rmi. Domini F. Hugonis Cauelli ... ad Archiepiscopatum Ardmachanum totiusq; Iberniae Primatum ... assumpti hoc aeternae gratulationis & gratitudinis monumentum L.M.P. studiosi Iberni Romae. Stylo Christoph. Chamberlini. 8°. *Romae, ex typographia Cam. Apost.*, 1626. RO⁸.

Chamberlin's address, in Latin prose, is followed by Latin verses by members of the Irish College at Rome. The Franciscan, Hugh MacCaghwell (Hugo Cavellus), was nominated Archbishop of Armagh and Primate of Ireland on 17 March 1626.

227 —Virtutis et nobilitatis plausus honori Reuerendissimi Domini F. Bonauenturae Magnesii ex Seraph. Or. ad episcopatum Dunensem promoti. 8°. *Romae, typis Francisci Corbelletti*, 1630. L.

An address by Chamberlin in Latin prose, followed by Latin verses by various members of the Irish College at Rome. Bonaventure Magennis (Magnesius) was nominated to the see of Down on 22 April 1630.

—Virtutum et musarum triumphus, 1634. *Part of no. 224.*

228 —Xenium ianuarium ad Ampliss. Virum D. Franciscum Kinschotium Summum Belgicae Thesaurarium. Gratitudinis ergo Christophorus Chamberlinus. D.D.D. 4° (a single quadrifolium). *Romae, apud Grignanum,* 1628. RO⁸.

An address in Latin prose followed by two 'Elogia' which are also by Chamberlin. François de Kinschot, Trésorier Général at Brussels, appears to have been a patron of the newly founded Irish College at Rome.

229 —Xenium ianuarium, siue dissertatio historico-poetica de Januarii et strenarum origine, annisq; antiquorum. 4°. *Bruxellae, e typographia Ioannis Mommartii,* 1631. BRS².PA.

'Xenium ianuarium', in Latin prose, is followed by a Latin poem entitled 'Christo nato strena ianuaria'. The whole dedicated by Chamberlin to his patron, Fabio de Lagonissa, Papal Nuncio at Brussels.

Chambers, David, *Lord Ormond.* Discours de la legitime succession des femmes. *See no. 230.*

230 —Histoire abbregée de tous les roys de France, Angleterre et Escosse, mise en ordre par forme d'harmonie. 8°. 3 pts. *Paris, chez Iean Feurier,* 1579. L.P(pts. 2, 3, with pt. 1 of no. 231).; A.AIX(pt. 2).BOR(pt. 3).C². (pts. 1, 3).D.E(2).E².F.HD.LAR.LINC(pt. 2).N.TOU.UT.VT.Y. + +

Pt. 2 is entitled: 'Discours de la legitime succession des femmes aux possessions de leurs parens: & du gouuernement des princesses aux empires & royaumes'; pt. 3: 'La recerche des singularitez plus remarquables, concernant l'estat d'Escosse'. Pts. 2 and 3 have each their own titlepage and are sometimes found separately. The Privilege mentions all three parts and grants permission to Jean Feurier, Michel Gadoulleau and Robert Coulombel to print and sell the book. The dedication reveals that pts. 1 and 3 were written and ready for printing several years before publication. Scott 107–9.

231 —[Imprint variant.] *Paris, chez Robert Coulombel,* 1579. O(pt. 1, with pts. 2, 3 of no. 230).; A.A².E.PA.PA².PA³.

Part of a shared edition with no. 230. On the tp. to pt. 1 only the imprint has been reset; on those to pts. 2, 3 the imprint and lower part of the title, including the printer's device (here the Aldine dolphin and anchor) are altered.

232 —[Imprint variant.] *Paris, chez Michel Gadoulleau,* 1579. C.; C²(pt. 2). NCY.PA.PA⁴.RMS.

Part of a shared edition with no. 230.

—Recerche des singularitez plus remarquables, concernant l'estat d'Escosse. *See* no. 230.

Chambers, David, *of Fintry. See* Chalmers, D.

Chambers, William. *See* Chalmers, W.

Chambre, David. *See* Chambers, D., *Lord Ormond.*

233 **Champney, Anthony.†** Anthonii Champnaei ... De vocatione ministrorum tractatus. Quo vniuersos cuiusuis praetensae reformationis ministros omni penitus legitima vocatione destitui ... clare ostenditur. 8°. *Lutetiae Parisiorum, ex officina Niuelliana. Sumptibus Sebastiani Cramoisy,* 1618. L.O.C.; AMP.C⁵.D.DE.DUR.GTN.HP.L².MD. MTH.PA.VT(2).WO.YK. + +

The Author's own translation of a work that he wrote in English and published in 1616 (A&R 233). Some copies have an index (occupying sig. Ddd-Eee⁸); others appear to have been issued without it.

234 —Enchiridion controuersiarum. Quo fides catholica & romana, in omnibus praecipuis horum temporum controuersiis ex Sacra Scriptura probatur. 12°. *Parisiis, apud Petrum Burey,* 1614. PA(D. 29646).

This pamphlet of only fourteen leaves appears to be a prospectus for a proposed Latin translation by Champney of a work that he wrote and published in English in 1614 (A&R 231). It is doubtful whether the full Latin translation ever appeared.

Channaeus, Mauritius. *See* Chauncy, M.

Chauncy, Maurice. Historia martyrum Angliae, 1573. A reprint of the 1550 edition of *Historia aliquot nostri saeculi martyrum*, including the first part, on More and Fisher, as well as the second which concerns the Carthusians put to death under Henry VIII. *In* no. 1455.

235 —[Anr. ed.] Historia aliquot nostri saeculi martyrum ... nunc denuo typis excusa. 8°. *Burgis, apud Philippum Iuntam,* 1583. O.; DMR.VAL. *This or no. 236:* EV.MD.SEV².W(-t.p.).

Without engravings.

236 —[Anr. issue.] *Burgis, apud Philippum Iuntam,* 1583. L(2).; NY.SOL.

The sheets of no. 235 with an additional gathering (*⁸) inserted in the preliminaries. This contains a letter from the Archbishop of Evora to the Pope saying that he is subsidising the printing. The catchwords show that it has been inserted as an afterthought. Some copies also have at the end an unsigned leaf containing a Tassa and Errata.

237 —[Anr. ed., abridged, with title:] Vitae ac martyrii Cartusianorum aliquot, qui Londini, pro vnitate Ecclesiae aduersus haereticos strenue depugnantes varie trucidati sunt, pia narratio. 8°. *Mediolani, apud Petrum Martyrem Locarnum,* 1606. L.; CHA.DMR.L⁸.L⁹.L²⁶.PA.RO².RO³. RO⁵.ST.VT(2).

This and subsequent editions omit pt. 1 on More and Fisher. *Ed.* Franciscus Turrianus. Without engravings.

238 —[Anr. ed. enlarged, with title:] Innocentia et constantia victrix; siue commentariolus; de vitae ratione et martyrio 18. Cartusianorum; qui in Angliae regno ... trucidati sunt ... Nunc recensita ... in Cartusia, horti Angelorum, Wirceburgi. 8°. 2 pts. *n.p.,* 1608. L.O.C.; CHA(-t.p.). D⁸.DMR.DUR.GT.GTN.KN(2).LOU.MU(2).OS.PA(2).RO.VI. + +

Pr. [Cologne, Bernard Gualterus.] The titlepage is engraved and there are two additional engraved plates. Pt. 2 comprises A. Havensius's *Historica relatio duodecim martyrum Cartusianorum, qui Ruraemundae ... agonem suum compleuerunt,* which is mentioned in the dedication to the whole collection. Sig. A1 is a cancel.

239 —[Anr. issue of no. 238, with title:] Commentariolus de vitae ratione et martyrio octodecim Cartusianorum qui in Anglia sub Rege Hērico VIII ... trudidati sunt ... Vna cum noua historica relatione duo-

decim martyrum Cartusianorum Ruraemundensium . . . auctore
V. P. Arnoldo Hauensio. 8°. 2 pts. *Gandaui, apud Gualterum Manilium,*
1608. L(2).O.; ANT.ANT³.DMR.GT.HA.KN².L²⁶(2).MZ.ST.U.UT².
The preliminaries are reprinted. In no. 238 they collate as follows:
∗⁸††⁴ (††4 = A1 cancellans, signed A). In this reissue the original
∗⁸, comprising title and dedication, is discarded and a new quire
∗⁴, printed by Manilius at Ghent, comprising the reprinted title and
a new dedication, inserted in its place. This issue is dedicated to the
Prior of Sheen Anglorum at Malines. Of the original ††⁴ only the
'Index capitum' (††2ᵛ–††3ᵛ) was needed for the reissue, so ††1
(dedicatory verses) is discarded and ††2ʳ (end of dedicatory verses)
covered over with a new, folding, engraved plate, and ††4 (=A1
cancellans) is also discarded, A1 being here in its uncancelled state.
A comparison of A1 with ††4 in no. 238 shows no differences of
setting. After this the book is a reissue of the original sheets. In
some copies the two parts are bound in reverse order. In pt. 2 the
title is cancelled and replaced by a bifolium consisting of a new title
printed by Manilius and an engraved plate.

240   —[*A work edited by Chauncy.*] Sutor, P. De vita Cartusiana libri duo . . .
nunc vero denuo . . . Mauritii Chancaei . . . opera in lucem restituti,
ac a pluribus mendis repurgati. 8°. *Louanii, apud Ioannem Foulerum
Anglum,* 1572. [Coloph.] *Ioanni Foulero excudebat Reinerus Velpius.*
O.; ANT.DMR.O⁵.
An edition of Sutor printed at Cologne in 1609 does not contain
Chauncy's editorial emendations.

241   —[*Appendix. A poem based on Chauncy's 'Historia martyrum'.*] Tamariz,
C. Historia de los sanctos martires de Cartuxa, que padescieron en
Londres: dirigida a los religiosissimos padres prior y monges del
monasterio de Cartuxa de Seuilla. 8°. *Seuilla, en casa de Alonso de la
Barrera,* 1584. *A costa de Antonio Biuas mercader de libros.* L.; DMR
EV.HSA.PA.SEV⁴.
A poem of eight-line stanzas in six cantos.

Cheisholmus, Gulielmus. *See* Chisholm, W.

241.1 **Cheyne, James.**‡ Iac. Cheyneii . . . analysis in XIIII libros Arist. de
prima seu diuina philosophia. Eiusdem in eosdem libros scholia . . .
Eiusdem scholae duae, vna de perfecto philosopho, altera de praedictionibus astrologorum. 8°. 2 pts. *Duaci, ex officina Ioannis Bogardi,*
1577[1577–78]. O.; A.BOR.DOU.ETON.O²⁴(2).PA(3).TRO.
Some copies (BOR.ETON.O.²⁴(1).PA(1).TRO.), have imprint date
variant 1578 to pt. 1.

241.2 —[*Anr. ed.*] Analysis, siue resolutio et quaestionum difficiliorum in
XIIII libros Aristotelis de diuina philosophia dilucida explicatio.
Authore D. Iacobo Cheyneio I.V.L. Eiusdem scholae duae, vna de
perfecto philosopho, altera de praedictionibus astrologorum. 8°.
Duaci, sumptibus Baltazaris Belleri, 1599. CB.PA.
Reprinted in the *Opera* of J. R. Lavater at Hanau in 1607 and 1616.

242   **Chisholm, William,** *Bishop of Vaison, the younger.* Examen con-
fessionis fidei Caluinianae quam Scotis omnibus ministri Caluiniani
subscribendam et iurandam proponunt. 8°. *Auenione, apud Iacobum
Bramereau,* 1601. L.C.; A.CMR.D.E.E².(3).FLO.G².KN.L¹³.LYN.O⁷.RO⁶.
TRO.VI.
On the Scottish Calvinistic confession of faith of 1581. Including
the text of the confession in English and Latin. Dedicated by the
author to King James VI of Scotland. Titlepage engraved.

243   —[*French transl., enlarged by the translator.*] Examen d'vne confession de
foy, publiée nagueres en France, sous le nom du Roy d'Angleterre . . .
fait premierement en Latin . . . et puis en François, & plus au long,
par F. N. Coeffeteau. 8°. *Paris, chez Iean Gesselin,* 1603. BOR.E.PA⁶.

The original dedication to King James is here replaced by one to the Duc de Guise, signed by the translator, and the English and Latin texts of the confession are replaced by a French translation made from the 1603 English edition published by order of King James just after his accession to the throne of England.

244 —[Date variant.] 1604. L.; DMR.O⁹.PA⁷.VT.

245 **Christopherson, John,** *Bishop of Chichester.* [*Works translated by him.*] Eusebius [and others]. Historiae ecclesiasticae pars prima (-tertia). 8°. 3 pts. *Louanii, excudebat Seruatius Sassenus, sumptibus haeredum Arnoldi Birckmanni* [Cologne], 1569. L.O.C(pt. 1).; A.ANT³.BRS.D(pt. 2). DE(pt. 3).FU².HAN.KN.LOU.MD.MTH.MU.PA.PA³.USH. + +

Comprising Christopherson's Latin translation of Eusebius's Church History together with Latin translations of other Greek ecclesiastical historians. Edited posthumously by Edward Godsalve. Christopherson's translation of the Church History was incorporated in the collected works of Eusebius printed at Paris and elsewhere from 1581 onwards.

246 —[Anr. ed., with title:] Historiae ecclesiasticae scriptores Graeci. Fol. *Coloniae Agrippinae, apud haeredes Arnoldi Birckmanni,* 1570. L.C.; DI.F.FU².KN.LGE.MD.NCY.O³.O⁴.O¹³.PA.VER.VT. +

247 —[Anr. ed.] Fol. *Parisiis, apud Claudium Fremy,* 1571. [Coloph.] *Ex chalcographia Nicolai Brusle ... impensis ... Claudii Fremy, & Nicolai Chesneau ... 1571 die 19 Aprilis.* ANT².LOU.STI. *This or no. 247.1* : LIL³.MD.NCY.TOU.VT.

247.1 —[Imprint variant.] *Parisiis, apud Nicolaum Chesneau,* 1571. PA(2). The colophon is unchanged.

248 —[Anr. ed.] Fol. *Coloniae Agrippinae, apud haeredes Arnoldi Birckmanni,* 1581. D.DI.DNPK.FU.L².L²⁶.MD.MU.O⁵.O⁷.O⁹.TNI.VT.WLC.

249 —[Anr. ed.] Fol. *Basileae, per Sebastianum Henricpetri,* 1611. DE.KN.O¹⁸. A non-Catholic edition.

250 —[Anr. ed.] Opera & studio ... Seuerini Binii. Fol. *Coloniae Agrippinae, apud Arnoldum Quentelium,* 1612. C.; DI.FU².L².Y. *This or no. 251* : NCY.TB.

251 [Anr. ed., with title:] Ὁι τῆς Ἐκκλησιαστικῆς ἱστοριας Συγγραφεις Ἑλληνικοι. Historiae ecclesiasticae scriptores Graeci. Fol. *Coloniae Allobrogum, excudebat Petrus de la Rouiere,* 1612. A.C³.CHA.D.DMR. FLO².FRA.KNY.KNY.L⁴.LOU³.MD.O³.MD.PA.PH.VT.WO. + + *See also no. 250.*

A non-Catholic edition printed at Geneva, it nevertheless reprints the original dedicatory epistle and note to the reader by Edward Godsalve from no. 245.

—Philo, *Judaeus.* [Christopherson's translation of four of the writings of Philo, first published in 1553, falls outside the scope of this catalogue. Though incorporated in the edition of Philo's works published at Lyon in 1561, it was not reprinted separately between 1558 and 1640.]

Clanchy, Bernardin. Conclusiones theologicae, 1639. *See no. 253.*

Claudius, *de S. Benedicto, name in religion of* William White. Constitutiones missionis Benedictinorum, 1633. *See no. 338.*

252 **Clement, Caesar.** [*A work translated by him.*] Numan, P. Historia de los milagros que en nuestra Señora de Monteagudo cerca de Sichen, en el Ducado de Brabante, nuestro Señor ha sido seruido de obrar ... Traduzida aora de frances en romance, y dirigida a la Sereniss. ... Señora, Doña Ysabel Clara Eugenia, Infante de España, nuestra señora. 8°. *En Brusselas, en casa de Rogero Velpio,* 1606. BRS.BRS³.L²⁵. MD.PA².

A translation into Spanish of *Histoire des miracles aduenuz ... au lieu dit Montaigu.* For an English version of the same work *see*

A&R 578. Translator's *ded.* sgd.: Cesar Clemente. For Clement *see* Anst., vol. 1, p. 79.

Cleremond, D. B. de, *pseud. See* no. 280.1.

Clery, Daniel. Theses ex vniuersa theologia, 1639. *See* no. 254.

252.1 **Coffin, Thomas.** De S. Stephano Protomartyre laudatio habita in Vaticano in Pontificio Sacello, die eiusdem martyris natali, a Thoma Cofino, Anglicani Collegii Alumno. Ad Gregorium XIII. Pont. Max. 4°. *Apud Iacobum Ruffinellum,* 1591.

  Not found. Description from Sommerv. (tom. 7, col. 106). Because Coffin was sent from Rome for the English mission in May 1591 (Anst. vol. 1, p. 82), this sermon must have been delivered on St Stephen's Day (26 December) 1590; it was only three weeks previously, on 5 December, that Gregory XIV had been elected Pope. *Pr.* [Rome.]

Cofinus, Thomas. *See* Coffin, T.

Coghlan, Terence. Censura propositionum . . . obsignatarum . . . per . . . Terentium Coghlanum, 1631. *See* nos. 683–5.

253 **Colgan, John.** [*Disputations at St. Anthony's College, Louvain in which he acted as Praeses.*] Bruin, P., Ward, F., Conway, A., Clanchy, B. Conclusiones theologicae de sacramentis in genere et tribus primis in specie ad mentem Doctoris Subtilis. 4°. *Louanii, typis Cornelii Coenestenii,* 1639.

  Not found. Description from Reusens (tom. 5, p. 427) who saw a copy in the old library of Louvain University destroyed in 1914.

254 —Clery, D., Sirenus, T. Theses ex vniuersa theologia ad mentem Doctoris Subtilis disputandae. 4°. *Louanii, typis Everardi de Witte,* 1639.

  Not found. *See* note to no. 253.

255 —Dormer, J., Mellaghlin, C., Conway, L., Donnelly, A. Conclusiones theologicae de Deo vno ad mentem Doctoris Subtilis. 4°. *Louanii, typis Cornelii Coenestenii,* 1640.

  Not found. *See* note to no. 253.

Colley, Aegidius. [The writer of this name who published *De quatuor hominis nouissimis* at Liège in 1630, sometimes taken to have been an Irishman, was, in fact, a Belgian. *See* J. F. Foppens, *Bibliotheca Belgica,* 1739, tom. 1, p. 28. No copy of Colley's book has been found.]

256 **Colville, John.**†‡ In felicissima inauguratione beatissimae Papae Pauli Quinti gratulatio Ioannis Coluilli Scoti. 8° (a quadrifolium). *Parisiis, apud Dionysium Binet,* 1605. HD.PA.VT.

  Latin verses. Paul V was elected on 16 May 1605.

257 —In obitu beatiss. Papae Clementis Octaui lacrymae Ioannis Coluilli Scoti. Eiusdem in felicissima assumptione beatiss. Papae Leonis Vndecimi gaudia. 8°. *Parisiis, ex typographia Steph. Preuosteau,* 1605. L.; PA.PA[4].RO[5].VT.

  Latin verses. Clement VIII died on 5 March and Leo XI was elected on 1 April 1605.

258 —Paraenesis Ioannis Coluilli Scoti (post quadraginta annorum errores in gremium sanctae Catholicae Romanae Ecclesiae quasi postliminio reuersi) ad suos tribules & populares. 8°. *Parisiis, e typographia Steph. Preuosteau,* 1601. L(2).O.; A.BOR.E.E[2].FLO.L[3].MTH.PA.PA[3].RO[4].TRO.VER. VT(3).YK. +

  Justifying his reconciliation to the Catholic Church. The approbation is signed by three priests, two of them English and one Scottish, living in Paris: William Bishop, John Bosvile and James Laing. For a Scottish version of this work, altered and enlarged by the author and published at Paris in the following year, *see* A&R 249.

Comerford, Patrick, *in religion* Patricius ab Angelis, *Bishop of Waterford.* [A letter from Ireland, dated 31 October 1618.] *In* no. 1074.

—[*Appendix.*] Rome, *Irish College.* Coronatae virtuti reuerendiss. D. Patritii Quemerfordi ... Episcopi Waterfordiensis, & Lismorensis, inaugurati plausus Seminarii Hibernorum de Vrbe, 1629. *See* no. 948.

Conn, George. Assertionum Catholicarum libri tres. *See* no. 261.

—De duplici statu religionis apud Scotos. *See* no. 262.

259   —De institutione Principis, tractatus breuis, in quatuor partes diuisus. 8°. *Regii, apud Flaminium Bartolum,* 1621. N.

Including chapters on the relations between Catholic princes and the Holy See.

260   —[Anr. ed.] 8°. *Regii, apud Flaminium Bartolum,* 1628. VT.

A reprint of no. 259 including the original dedicatory epistle and approbation.

261   —Georgii Conaei assertionum Catholicarum libri tres. In quibus ex solo scripto Dei verbo praecipua haeresum aetatis nostrae dogmata refelluntur. 4° (in eights). *Romae, apud haeredem Bartholomaei Zannetti,* 1629. L.O.C.; A².C⁵.D.DMR.E.PA³.PR³.RO².RO³.RO⁴.U.VAL².VT(2).

Dedicated by the author to Pope Urban VIII whose arms are engraved on the titlepage.

262   —Georgii Conaei de duplici statu religionis apud Scotos libri duo. 4°. *Romae, typis Vaticanis,* 1628. L(2).O(2).C(2).; A(2).AIX.C⁵.DE.E.E²(3). FLO.GTN.L².L²⁶.MTH.PA(2).PA³.RO²(4).VT(3). + +

Dedicated to Cardinal Francesco Barberini whose arms are printed on the titlepage. Scott 223.

263   —Praemetiae siue calumniae Hirlandorum indicatae, et Epos. Deipara Virgo Bononiensis ad xenodochium vitae. 8°. *Bononiae, typis Nicolai Tebaldini,* 1621. L(2).O.; GTN.PA.PA³.

Defending Thomas Dempster's *Nomenclatura,* 1620 (no. 297) against attacks by the Irish clergy.

264   —Vita Mariae Stuartae Scotiae Reginae. 12°. *Romae, apud Ioannem Paulum Gellium,* 1624. [Coloph.] *Ex typographia Andreae Phaei.* L(3).O.; A.AIX.D.DMR.E.E².GTN.HA.PA(3).PA³.RO²(2).ST.VT. + +

With an engraved portrait of Mary, unsigned. Scott 214.

265   —[Anr. ed.] 8°. *Wirceburgi, apud Stephanum Fleischmann,* 1624. L.; DI.FR.HEI.KN².L²⁶.MU.N.NTS.PA.PA⁶.STG.ULM.VT.WO.

With a different engraved portrait, signed by I. Leipoldt, 1587. Scott 213.

266   —[*Italian transl.*] Vita di Maria Stuarda Regina di Scozia ... dalla latina tradotta nell'italiana lingua da Tadeo di Negro. 12°. *Genoua, per Giuseppe Pauoni,* 1630. CARP.GTN.

267   **Conry, Florence,** *Archbishop of Tuam.*‡ Tractatus de statu paruulorum sine baptismo decedentium ex hac vita: iuxta sensum B. Augustini. 4°. *Louanii, ex officina Henrici Hastenii,* 1624. L.O.; BRS². CH.D.D⁶.D¹⁰.F.KNY(2).LEM.LYN(*with imprint date altered in MS to 1635*). MD.MTH(2).PA.RO³.VT.

Reprinted at Louvain in 1641, and again reprinted, together with the *Augustinus* of Cornelius Janssen, in 1643.

Constable, Henry.† [Examen pacifique de la doctrine des Huguenots, 1589.]

Has no place in this catalogue. It was written before Constable became a Catholic and was printed in England under false French imprints. *See* RH 1960, pp. 224–35; & 1962, pp. 228–37. STC 5638.7 & 5638.9.

Conuaeus, Richardus. *See* Conway, R.

Conway, Anthony. Conclusinoes theologicae, 1639. *See* no. 253.

Conway, Lewis. Conclusiones theologicae, 1640. *See* no. 255.

268   **Conway, Richard.** Quaedam sanctorum quorundam, & grauiorum virorum de sanctitate, & literis Ibernorum testimonia. 4°. (A single quire of eight leaves signed A), *n.p.d.* [*b.* 1621.] VT(Stamp. Barb. U VII 54/4).

On early Celtic saints and other illustrious persons. There is a prefatory note signed: Richardus Conuaeus Ibernus Societatis Iesu Sacerdos. Included in the work is a catalogue headed: 'Cathalogus quorundam sanctorum, virorumque illustrium Ibernorum, alias Scotorum, seu Irlandorum . . .' This differs from FitzSimon's catalogue (no. 480). *Pr.* [in Spain?].

—[Anr. ed.] 1621. *In* no. 864 (together with an edition of FitzSimon's catalogue).

269   **Cope, Alan.** Syntaxis historiae euangelicae, in qua res Domini nostri Iesu Christi, quo ordine gestae fuerant . . . narrantur. 4°. *Louanii, apud Johannem Foulerum Anglum,* 1572. O.C.; BRS.C².C⁹.D.DMR.FLO. L¹³.LOU.LYN.MD.O¹².PA.RO³.RP⁵.UP.WO. +

270   —[Anr. issue, with title:] Historiae euangelicae vnitas. Seu singularia vitae Domini nostri Iesu Christi, eo ordine quo gesta fuerunt recensita. *Duaci, ex officina Baltazaris Belleri,* 1603. O.; AMI.BRS.CMR.DOU. LYN.O³.O⁷.PA.PA³.PA⁴.VI.VT.WO.

The sheets of no. 269 except for the first quire which has been entirely reset.

—[*A work edited by him.*] Harpsfield, N. Dialogi sex contra summi pontificatus . . . oppugnatores, 1566 [*etc.*] *See* nos. 636–8.

271   **Cornin, Joseph.** [*Begin:*] Eminentissimo, ac Reuerendissimo Principi Tiberio Muti S.R.E. Card. amplissimo F. Iosephus Corninus Collegii S. Isidori . . . alumnus S.P.F. Conclusiones theologicae . . . [*End:*] Disputabuntur publice in Collegio S. Isidori . . . Praesidente Reu. P. Fr. Francisco a S. Maria [F. Tully] . . . 1634. Mense Martii. *s.sh.*fol. *Romae, ex typographia Ludouici Grignani,* 1634. RO².

A programme announcing the forthcoming defence of his thesis. Text and part of the setting are the same as in nos. 84, 128, 414.

Courtney, Edward, *alias. See* Leedes, E.

Cr., G., *Scotus.*† [Latin verses signed by him]. *See* no. 1305.1.

Creswell, Joseph.†

Original Works

272   —Aparejos para administrar el sacramento de la penitencia con mas facilidad y fruto: y receuir los admirables efectos, que suele obrar la santa Eucharistia en los que llegan a ella bien dispuestos. Recogidos por el licenciado Don Pedro Manrique. 4°. *En Milan, en Real y Ducal Palacio, por Marco Tulio Malatesta,* CIƆ IƆC IV [misprint for 1614]. CHA.MIL².NEU.NP.PA.PA⁶(*imp.*).RO².

Pedro Manrique, *pseud.* Written in Spanish by [Creswell] using retreat notes left by [William Bathe]. *See* RH, Oct. 1979, pp. 81–2. A Latin version indicated by Sommerv. (tom. 1, col. 1012) as having been printed by Malatesta at Milan in 1604 appears to be a 'ghost'.

273   —[*Latin transl.,* with title:] Sacra Tempe seu de sacro exercitiorum secessu, exempla collecta a D. Petro Manrique Hispano primum hispanice tum italice edita nuper latine versa & pro xenio sodalibus academicis maioribus oblata. 12°. *Ingolstadii, typis Gregorii Haenlin,* 1622. CHA.MU.

Petrus Manrique, *pseud. See* note to no. 272. *Tr.* Wolfgang Schoensleder. The Italian translation mentioned in the title has not been found. A modern edition of *Sacra Tempe* was published by H. Watrigant, in 1910 (*Collection de la Bibliothèque des Exercises de Saint Ignace,* no. 26).

273.1   —[Breve modo de rezar el rosario de Nuestra Señora, 1613.]
Not found. This anonymous pamphlet, referred to by Uriarte (no. 6218), may possibly be the little work on the rosary which Creswell wrote in Spanish and published at Barcelona in 1613. An English

translation, with a prefatory note by Creswell, saying how he came to write and publish the original, is included in a collection of spiritual writings published at the English College press, S. Omer, in 1620 (A&R 334, STC 11313, ERL 37). *See* RH Oct. 1979, pp. 81–2. Uriarte describes the original as 'pliego en folio'.

274 —Carta escrita al embaxador de Inglaterra, residēte en la corte de la Magestad Catolica, en que se deshazen las calumnias, inuentadas para dar color a la iniqua y artificiosa persecucion, que padecen, los que en aquel reyno professan nuestra santa fé, y la obediencia deuida a la Yglesia Romana. Traduzida en lengua Castellana. 4°. *n.p.d.* [1606] MD (pressmark: 3–6463).

Signed by Creswell at the end. *Pr.* [Madrid?]. For the background, *see* A. J. Loomie, *Guy Fawkes in Spain* (*Bulletin of the Institute of Historical Research*, Special Supplement no. 9, Nov. 1971, pp. 47–51). A MS of the English original is at BL MS Cotton Vespasian C XII, ff. 342–71; an edition of it by A. J. Loomie is currently in preparation.

275 —Exemplar literarum, missarum, e Germania, ad D. Guilielmum Cecilium, consiliarium regium. 8°. *Impressum, n.p.*, 1592. L(3).O.C(2).; DMR.FLO.HA.L².L²⁶.MD.MU².OS.PA(2).RO.RO⁶.VAL.VT. +

Ded. sgd.: Ioannes Pernius [*pseud.*]. A defence of the English Catholic colleges abroad, answering the Royal Proclamation of 18 October 1591 (STC 8207–09). The authorities for Creswell's authorship are Pits (p. 813), the 1632 Catalogue, and Alegambe. *Pr.* [Rome, Vincenzo Accolti.]

276 —Historia de la vida y martyrio que padecio en Inglaterra, este año de 1595. P. Henrique Valpolo . . . el primer martyr de los seminarios de España. Con el martyrio de otros quatro sacerdotes. 8°. *Madrid, en casa de Pedro Madrigal*, 1596. DMR.ESC.L²⁶.MD.MD².(*imp.*).RO³.RO⁴.USH (-*t.p.*).

The author's name is given in the 'Tassa' on A2ʳ. Written by Creswell in Spanish. The account of Walpole is reprinted in no. 284.

277 —[Anr. ed.] 8°. *Çaragoça, por Lorenço de Robles, a costa de Angelo Tauano*, 1596. PA(*Res. Nx. 2373, formerly the Salvá copy*). Sanchez also cites a copy in the Bibl. Municipal, Mahón.

278 —[*French transl.*] Histoire de la vie et ferme constance du pere Henry Valpole anglois prestre, de la Compagnie de Iesus, premier des seminaires d'Espagne martirizé pour la confession de la foy Catholique . . . Faite françoise de l'espagnol. 8° (in fours). *Arras, de l'imprimerie de Robert Maud'huy*, 1597. BRS².ETON.HP.PA².W.

279 —Informacion a la ciudad de Seuilla, por parte del Colegio Ingles de la misma ciudad. Fol. [Coloph.] *Seuilla, en casa de Clemente Hidalgo*, 1604. L.; MD²(Jes. 112/38).SEV³. (Siglo XVII, seccion IVa, t. 20, no. 31).

Signed by Creswell at the end. Asking the municipality not to discontinue the allowance granted to the College since its foundation in 1592. Text dated 26 April 1604. For the debate in the Seville chapter on the matter *see* no. 1072.

Single Translations by Creswell

280 —Salvianus, *Bishop of Marseille*. Quis diues saluus. Como vn hombre rico se puede saluar. Escrito a la Iglesia Catolica . . . cerca del año de Christo 480. 8°. [Coloph.] *Emprimado en Flandes, en el Colegio de los Yngleses de Sant Omer . . . Por Ricardo Britanno impressor*, 1620. MD(3–10704).

A translation of *Ad ecclesiam adversus avaritiam*. *Tr.* [J. Creswell.] The authorities for Creswell are the 1632 Catalogue and Alegambe.

His English translation of the same work is at A&R 748. The preface to the English Catholics of the English translation is here replaced by a dedicatory epistle to the Infanta Maria whose proposed marriage to Prince Charles was being negotiated at this time. *See* RH, Oct. 1979, pp. 123–4. This and no. 392 are the only extant books printed at the College press, S. Omer, during the period covered by the present catalogue, that bear the College imprint. 'Ricardus Britannus' is probably the Welshman, Richard Floyd, who was employed at the press; *see Library*, Dec. 1926, p. 315, and Downshire MSS (Berkshire County Record Office, Reading), vol. 37, nos. 115, 116.

280.1 —[Unidentified Author.] Vando y leyes del Rey Iacobo de Inglaterra contra la fe catolica. Con su respuesta, y aduertencias al letor para la auerigacion e inteligencia deste caso, prouechosas para el mismo Rey, y para todos ... traduzidas de Latin en varias leguas [*sic*] por el D. B. de Cleremond [*sic*]. 4°. *n.p.d.* [1611.] L(2).O.; HSA.MD.O⁹.PA.RO³. RO¹².VAL.VI.

A translation into Spanish [by Joseph Creswell?] of A&R 265 which is itself a translation into English by [John Wilson] of a Latin work (apparently not now extant and probably never published) answering STC 8447. The author of the Latin original is designated in the English as B. D. de Clerimond, almost certainly a pseudonym masking an English Catholic. The identification of de Clerimond as Creswell, accepted by A&R, is now known to be mistaken. In spite of the wording of the titlepage, the Spanish translation was made from the printed English text and not direct from the original Latin. The translator has added to the confusion by concealing his own identity under a variant form of the pseudonym used in the English for the author of the original. *Pr.* [Madrid, Luis Sanchez]. *See* RH, Oct. 1985, pp. 348–57.

Collections of Documents translated into Spanish
by Creswell and others and edited by him

281 —De vna de Londres de los ocho de nouiembre de 1611, recibida a 25 de enero de 1612. Fol. (a bifolium). *n.p.d.* [1612.] SIM(*E 626/278. With the MS of Creswell's covering letter to the Spanish Council of State*).
Extracts from a letter from England describing the persecution of Catholics, together with two other documents. The name of the letter-writer is not given. Creswell's name does not appear in the printed text but his letter to the Council of State implies that he had put the collection together. *Pr.* [Madrid?].

282 —[Anr. ed. with title:] Carta embiada de Londres de vn religioso Catholico, a otro de España, de los ocho de nouiembre de 1611. Recebida a 25. de enero de 1612. en que da noticia de lo que passa a cerca de la persecucion de los Catholicos en dicho reyno. Fol. (a quadrifolium). *Barcelona, en casa Sebastiā de Cormellas*, 1612. LIS (Reg. 254¹). [*L.]

[283 *cancelled*]
—[Las leyes nueuamente hechas en el Parlamēto de Inglaterra, [1606].] This collection, formerly thought to have been put together by Creswell with the help of Andrew Wise, is now known to have been the work of James Wadsworth, the Elder. *See* no. 1342.2.
—Relacion de cinco martyres en Ynglaterra este año de 1616. Traducida de Latin, 1616. *See* no. 320.

Works compiled in part by Creswell

—Floyd, J. Deus et Rex, 1618. *See* no. 487.

284 —Yepes, D. de, *Bishop of Tarazona*. Historia particular de la persecucion de Inglaterra, y de los martirios que en ella ha auido, desde el año del Señor, 1570. 4°. *Madrid, por Luis Sanchez*, 1599. L(2).O(3). C.; BAR².DE.E.FLO³.HP.L²⁶.MD.OS.PA.ST.VAL.VI.W(*imp.*). + +
Creswell's name is not revealed in the book. For the history and contents of this work see the introduction by D. M. Rogers to the Gregg reprint of 1971.

Crichton, George.‡ [Latin verses probably by him.] *See* no. 1305.1.
285 **Curcy, John.** [*Begin:*] Eminentissimo Principi Bernardino Cardinali Spadae ... Ioannes Curcaeus Seminarii Ludouisiani alumnus F.P.S. Conclusiones theologicae ... [*End:*] Disputabuntur publice in Collegio S. Isidori ... Praesidente Reu. R. P. Francisco a S. Maria [F. Tully] ... Mense Maio ... 1633. *s.sh.*fol. *Romae, apud Ludouicum Grignanum*, 1633. RO².
A programme announcing the forthcoming defence of his thesis.
Curle, Hippolitus. Serenissimae Augustissimaeque Mariae Stuartae, 1618. *See* no. 325.
Cusack, Christopher. Exhibitio consolatoria, 1622. *See* no. 324.
Daniel, *a Jesu, pseud. See* Floyd, J. (nos. 481–3).
Darcy, Peter. Disputatio theologica de praedestinatione et gratia, [1621]. *See* no. 1342.
286 **Davenport, Christopher,** *in religion* Franciscus a Sancta Clara. Apologia episcoporum, seu sacri magistratus propugnatio. 8°. *Coloniae Agrippinae, apud Bernardum Brunum*, 1640. O.C.; C⁵.D.DMR.DUR.E. HER.O².O⁴.O⁵.O⁶.PA.PA⁴.PLU.VT. +
Imprint false; *pr.* [at Paris].
287 —Deus, natura, gratia. Siue tractatus, de praedestinatione, de meritis & peccatorum remissione, seu de iustificatione, & denique de sanctorum inuocatione. Vbi ad trutinam fidei Catholicae examinatur Confessio Anglicana. 4°. *Lugduni, sumptibus Antonii Chard*, 1634. L.O.C(2).; C⁵. D.D².DMR.DUR.E.E².HP.L⁴.PLU.MD.PA.ST. + +
For the background to this work see J. B. Dockery, *Christopher Davenport*, [1960], ch. 4.
288 —[Anr. ed.] Secunda editio. 8°. *Lugduni, sumptibus Anthonii Chard*, 1634. O.; A.AUG.DAI.KN.L².O⁵.PA.
289 —[Date variant.] 1635. C.; C⁵.D.DE.ETON.O¹².O¹⁸.O¹⁹.O³¹.
290 —Epistolium continens confutationem duarum propositionum astrologicarum cum principiis aduersus iudiciariam astrologiam ... Notata sunt commercia haereticorum cum Magis quamplurimis. 8°. *Duaci, ex typographia Balthazaris Belleri*, 1626. DOU.
291 **Dempster, Thomas.‡** Apparatus ad historiam scoticam lib. II. Accesserunt martyrologium scoticum sanctorum DCLXXIX. scriptorum scotorum MDCIII. nomenclatura. 4°. *Bononiae, typis Nicolai Tebaldini*, 1622. L(2).O(2).C.; A²(2).AIX.CHA.D(3).DMR.E.E².GTN.MD.O⁶.PA. PA³.RO⁵.USH.VT(3).WO. + +
292 —Asserti Scotiae ciues sui. S. Bonifacius. rationibus. IX. Ioannes Duns rationibus. XII ... excerptum e libris de scriptoribus scotis eiusdem. 4°. *Bononiae, typis Nicolai Tebaldini*, 1621. L(2).; A².CARP.E.O¹².PA. PA³.VT(2).
293 —De iuramento lib. III. Locus ex antiq. Rom. retractatus. 8°. *Bononiae, apud Nicolaum Tebaldinum*, 1623. [Coloph.] *Sumptibus Auctoris.* L.O.; D.E.GTN.HD.L⁴.O¹².PA.YK.
A historical treatise on oath-taking.
294 —Historia ecclesiastica gentis Scotorum lib. XIX. 4°. *Bononiae, typis Nicolai Thebaldini*, 1627. L(2).O.C.; A.A².D(2).E.GTN.PA.PA³.RO³.RO⁵. USH.VI.VT(2). + +
Titlepage engraved. This ed., published two years after the author's

death, is the earliest known, but some version of the text, whether printed or MS, was evidently in circulation as early as 1620. *See* note to no. 297.

295 —Menologium Scotorum. In quo nullus nisi Scotus gente aut conuersatione, quod ex omnium gentium monimentis, pio studio . . . colligit publicat & inscribit . . . Thomas Dempsterus. 4°. *Bononiae, typis Nicolai Tebaldini*, 1622. L(2).O(2).C.; A(2).A².DMR.DUR.E.E².O².O⁵.O⁶. PA.RO³.RO⁵.WO. +

Dedicated to Cardinal Maffeo Barberini (later Pope Urban VIII) as Cardinal Protector of Scotland, whose arms are printed on the titlepage.

296 —Scotia illustrior, seu mendicabula repressa, modesta parecbasi Thomae Dempsteri . . . Qua libelli famosi impudentia detegitur; mendacia ridicula confutantur; Scotiae sancti sui vindicantur. 4°. *Lugduni, apud Petrum Ronsier, n.d.* [1620]. L(2).C.; D.E.F.GT.M.PA.PA³. PA⁴.VT.

Claiming that various early Celtic saints were Scottish. It answers no. 953 and was in turn answered by nos. 396.1, 955. The dedication is dated 4 Oct. 1620.

297 —Scotorum scriptorum nomenclatura . . . Ex Historiar. lib. XIX excerpta. 4°. *Bononiae, typis Sebastiani Bonomii*, 1620. L.; BG(*with date variant* 1619?).F.O².O⁶.VT.

An index of mainly ecclesiastical writers extracted, apparently, from an earlier version, either printed or MS, of no. 294.

298 —[Anr. ed., enlarged, with title:] Scotorum scriptorum nomenclatura. Quartum aucta . . . ex suis Historiarum lib. XIX excerpsit Thomas Dempsterus. 4°. *Bononiae, typis Nicolai Tebaldini*, 1622. L.O(2).; A(2).A².DMR.E.E².O².O⁶.

299 —Votum diuae Virgini Sanlucianae. Peregrinorum nomine. Detectis & supplicio iusto affectis iconoschatomachis. 8°. *Bononiae, typis Nicolai Tebaldini*, 1623. *Impensis Peregrini Golsarini.* L.; BG.GTN.

A poem.

300 —[*A work edited by him.*] Accolti, B. Benedicti Accolti de bello a Christianis contra barbaros gesto, pro Christi sepulchro, & Iudea recuperandis. Libri IIII. Thomas Dempsterus . . . cum aliis scriptoribus collatos, & mendis expurgauit, & notis non vulgaribus, illustrauit. 4°. *Florentiae, apud Zenobium Pignonum*, 1623. L.; D.E.FLO.PA.RO².

Dermicius, *Thadaei filius, pseud. See* Hicky, A. (no. 669).

Didymus Veridicus, *Henfildanus, pseud. See* Stapleton T. (no. 1141).

301 **Digby, John,** *alias* Salisbury. Panacrides apes musicis concentibus aduocandae. Ad philosophicas theses Ioannis Salisburii Coll. Angl. Conv. 4°. *Romae, apud Franciscum Corbellettum*, 1627. L(2).; MIL² (XX.5.11. no. 11.) PA.VT.

Complimentary verses, preceded by a prose dedication, to Cardinal Francesco Barberini on the occasion of his presiding over philosophical disputations at the English College, Rome. For Digby *see* CRS, vol. 37, p. 204, and Anst, vol. 2, p. 85. Titlepage engraved.

[302 *cancelled*]

303 **Dillon, Thomas.** Leccion sacra en la fiesta celebre que hizo el colegio de la Compania de Iesu de la ciudad de Cadiz in hazimiento de gracias a Dios nuestro Señor por el cumplimiento del primer siglo de su sagrada religion. 4°. *Seuilla, [Francisco] de Lyra*, 1640.

Not found. Description from Sommerv. (tom. 3, col. 83). Dillon, of Irish origin, was brought up in Spain and joined the Andalucian Province of the Society of Jesus.

Dodritius, Joannes, *pseud. See* Persons, R. (no. 871).

304 **Dolabella, Horatius,** *pseud.* Prurit-anus, vel nec omne, nec ex omni.

Siue apologia pro Puritanis, & nouatoribus vniuersis. In qua et mores, & opiniones nouorum hominum nostri temporis, auctoritate Scripturae affirmantur & infirmantur ad reformatos huius saeculi fratres, Germanos, Gallos, & Britannos. Per Horatium Dolabellam Neapolitanam. 4°. *Lutetiae Britannorum, apud Isaacum Iacobi*, 1609. O(*a fragment consisting of sig. F² only*. Douce fragments, e.42/37).; L².

A satire ridiculing the Protestant Reformation in England by posing questions and answering them with scriptural quotations taken out of context in the manner attributed to the Puritans. The author has not been identified but was suspected at the time to be an English Catholic. Collation: A–E⁴F². Imprint fictitious; *pr.* sig. A–E⁴ [S. Omer, François Bellet]; sig. F² [secretly in England]. *Prurit-anus* ends on E4ᵛ; F² contains a satirical passage in English headed 'A Puritans Grace' which is not mentioned in the table of contents. *See* RH, Jan. 1966, pp. 202–3, and *Library*, 1919, pp. 188–9.

305 —[Anr. issue, with sig. F² cancelled, and with a cancel title adding the words:] Addita est etiam, per appendicem, similis apologia pro libro Ser. Iacobi Regis Magnae Britanniae nuperrime edito & inscripto Praefatio monitoria ad omnes monarchas, & principes Christianos &c. *Lutetiae Britannorum, apud Isaacum Iacobi*, 1609. O(I.d.137); HP. L². (*cancelland F² not removed*). NY (*cancelland F² and cancelland title not removed*).

A reissue of the sheets of no. 304 with a cancel title on which the words cited above are added, and with a new bifolium F² cancelling the old one which had contained 'A Puritans Grace'. The new F² contains an extension of *Prurit-anus*, in Latin, applying the same method to pour ridicule on James I's 'Praefatio Monitoria' prefixed to STC 14405. The cancels *pr.* [S. Omer, F. Bellet].

306 —[Anr. ed.] Editio altera correctior. 8°. *Intercatiae Orniacorum, apud Ioannem Simonis*, 1610. C.; LC.

A reprint of no. 305. Imprint fictitious; *pr.* [S. Omer, Charles Boscard].

Donnelly, Anthony. Conclusiones theologicae, 1640. *See* no. 255.

Donovan, Patrick. [*A work edited by him.*] Thirry, W. Discursus panegyrici de nominibus . . . S. Patricii, 1617. *See* no. 1250.

Dormer, John. Conclusiones theologicae, 1640. *See* no. 255.

Douai, *English College.*

AN APPEAL BY THE COLLEGE FOR ALMS

307 —A la inuicta y catholica España: y en particular a los varones nobles y generosos della, en quien por tantos siglos ha conseruado su piedad y religion pura e incorrupta. El Seminario Ingles de Duay . . . dessea todo bien y prosperidad. 4° (a single quadrifolium). [Coloph.] *Madrid, por Francisco Abarca de Angulo*, 1621. HSA.L²⁷ᴬ.(16/1 n.2).

An appeal by thè College for alms. Addressed to the nobility and gentry of Spain.

DOCUMENTS ISSUING FROM THE COLLEGE

Documents of 1579

308 —Auisi notabili intorno al progresso della religione catholica Estratta parte dalle lettere annali del Seminario Inglese di sua Santita in Fiandra per l'anno 1578. parte da lettere fidelissime riceuute da i Catholici d'Inghilterra. 4° (a quadrifolium + 2 leaves). *Bologna, per Alessandro Benacci*, 1579. L.C.; PA.

An Italian translation of documents sent to Rome by the English College (now temporarily removed to Rheims). They describe the sufferings of Catholics in England in 1578. No printed Latin or English original has been found.

309 —[Anr. ed.] Auuisi notabilissimi intorno al progresso della religione catholica . . . 4° (a single quadrifolium). *Oruieto*, 1588. L.; RO[3].

A poor reprint, with some omissions, of no. 308. *Pr.* [Antonio Colaldi?] The date printed at the end of the text, 8 January 1588, refers to the completion of printing and not to the contents of the documents.

309.1 —[Anr. ed.?] Avvisi notabilissimi intorno al progresso della religione cattolica . . . 12°. pp. 8. *In Milano e in Ferrara, per il Baldini*, 1590. BG[2](A.V.K. IX.11/5. *Missing 1980*).

Not seen. Description from BG[2] card catalogue. The Milan edition has not been found.

310 —[Anr. ed.] Auisi notabili intorno al progresso della religione catolica . . . 8° (a quadrifolium made up from a half-sheet). *Bologna, per Fausto Bonardo, n.d.* [1598?] RO[3].

Although the title follows that of no. 308 the text is that of no. 309 except that the date at the end is omitted. In the only copy found the date 1598 has been added in early MS under the imprint on the titlepage.

311 —[*Latin transl.*] Acta quaedam insignia anglica ad catholicam religonem pertinentia. Ex Seminario Rhemensi allata, in Latinum conuersa Io. Antonio Guarnerio . . . interprete. 4° (a quadrifolium). *Bergomi, typis Comini Venturae vrbis impressoris*, 1580. O.; MIL[2].MIL[3].PA.RO. RO[9](Anglia 30. I. ff. 160–74).VT.

A translation made from no. 308. Dedicated by the translator to Francesco Bonhomio, Bishop of Vercelli, formerly Apostolic Delegate in Switzerland, who had commissioned the work so that the sufferings of the English Catholics might become known to non-Italian-speaking Swiss.

Documents of 1590

312 —Relatione del presente stato d'Inghilterra. Cauata da vna lettera de li 25. di Maggio scritta di Londra, et da vn'altra, scritta da vna persona di qualità, venuta di frescho d'Inghilterra, data in Anuersa alli 27. di Giugno, & altre. 4°. *Roma, appresso Francesco Zannetti*, 1590. L.; FLO. FLO[3].RO[4].RO[5].RO[6].RO[9].(Anglia 31. I. n. 7).VT.

An Italian translation of documents sent to Rome by the English College at Douai together with a list in Latin of 91 martyrs who suffered in England between 1577 and 1590 compiled by Richard Barret, President of the College. No printed English or Latin original of the documents in Italian has been found. An extended version of Barret's list is at no. 1004.

Documents of 1616

313 —Vita et martyrium D. Max-fildaei Collegii Anglorum Duaceni sacerdotis, Londini ob sacerdotium capitis damnati 11. Iulii anno D. 1616. Ex litteris Anglice datis aucta & Latine reddita. 12. *Duaci, typis viduę Laurentii Kellami*, 1616. OS.

Probably prepared for publication under the direction of the President of the College, Matthew Kellison. The identity of the writer of the letter is not known.

314 —[Anr. ed., *with accounts of other alumni of the College martyred in the same year :*] Exemplar literarum a quodam sacerdote Collegii Anglorum Duaceni quondam alumno ex Anglia ad idem Collegium transmissarum. De martyriis quatuor eiusdem Collegii alumnorum ob sacerdotium hoc anno 1616. in Anglia morte damnatorum. 8°. *Duaci, typis Petri Auroi*, 1616. D[11].DAI.MD(MSS 18420).

315 —[Anr. ed. of no. 314.] 8°. *Duaci, typis Petri Auroii,* 1617. L.; A.DE.DOU.
316 —[Anr. ed. of no. 314.] 8°. *Dilingae, apud viduam Ioannis Mayer,* 1617. L.C.; AAR.BRS².FR.MU(4).PR.VI.
   Shaaber, who records only this edition and the French translation of 1616 (no. 317), enters both in error under Joseph Creswell (C. 409, 410).

317 —[*French transl.*] Coppie d'vne lettre enuoyée d'Angleterre au semi-maire [*sic*] des Anglois à Douay. Par vn prestre qui auoit esté autrefois de leur compagnie . . . Traduicte du latin en françois, par le Sieur D. D. 8° (in fours). *Douay, chez Pierre Auroy,* 1616. L(2).; DMR.DOU. OS.PA.PA².
   A translation of no. 314 with additional material at the end. The translator has not been identified. For Shaaber's misattribution of the work *see* note to no. 316.

318 —[Anr. ed., *abridged.*] Histoire veritable du martyre de trois prestres du College de Douay. Lesquels ont esté condamnez & mis à mort en Angleterre. 8° (in fours). *Paris, iouxte la coppie imprimée à Douay, chez Pierre Auroy,* 1617. L.; PA.
   Omitting the account of Maxfield and much other material. In spite of the Paris imprint this is probably a pirated edition printed in the Spanish Netherlands. It is a very careless piece of printing.

319 —[Anr. ed., *abridged, with title :*] Histoire veritable du martyre de quatre prestres du College de Douay, cruellement & inhumainement mis à mort en Angleterre. 24°? *Paris, chez Pierre de la Fosse,* 1618. L.
   In spite of the reworded title, this is a verbatim reprint of no. 318. It is probably another pirated edition printed in the Spanish Netherlands. As far as is known, there was no printer named Pierre de la Fosse at Paris at this period.

320 —[*Spanish transl.*] Relacion de cinco martyres en Ynglaterra este año de 1616. Traducida de latin. 4°. *n.p.* 1616. RO⁹.(Anglia 32/1 no. 9). [*L⁹].
   The text is basically that of no. 314 but this Spanish translation was published a few months before the Latin original appeared in print. *Tr.* [Joseph Creswell.] *Pr.* [S. Omer, Eng. Coll. press.] *See* RH Oct. 1979, pp. 119–20, 141 (note 141).

APPENDIX

Papal Letters of Recommendation

321 —Gregory XIII, *Pope*, Litterae S.D.N.D. Gregorii Papae XIII. hor-tatoriae ad subueniendum pauperibus Collegii Anglicani Rhemis, & caeteris Anglis pro fide Catholica dispersis. *s.sh.*fol. *Romae, apud haeredes Antonii Bladii, impressores camerales,* 1582. L.
   This is the Bull *Omnipotens Deus* of 21 Jan. 1582 (Cherubini, *Bullarium,* 1617, t. 2, p. 454, no. 72). Reprinted in no. 878.

322 —Sixtus V, *Pope.* Copia della bolla del Santissimo S.N. Sisto Papa V. oue si essortano i fedeli a souuenire alle necessità del Collegio Inglese gia instituto in Duaco della Germania inferiore, et che al presente si troua in Rhemis di Francia. Alla quale va congionata vna breue dichiaratione dello instituto, frutto et presente necessità di detto Collegio. *Roma, per gl'heredi d'Antonio Blado,* 1586. VT(Rossiana 4312, int. 21. *Missing 1980*). *Ascarelli cites another copy at* RO¹³.
   Not seen. Description from VT card catalogue. This is the Italian translation of the Bull *Afflictae et crudeliter,* 3 Sept. 1586. (Cheru-bini, *Bullarium,* 1617, t. 2, p. 541, no. 39).

Martyrology of the College

323 —Raisse, A. Catalogus Christi sacerdotum, qui ex nobili Anglicano Duacenae ciuitatis Collegio proseminati, praeclarum fidei Catholicae

testimonium in Britannia praebuerunt. Collectore Arnoldo Raissio
Duaceno. 8°. *Duaci, typis Martini Bogardi*, 1630. L.; DAI.DMR.DOU(2).
HA.PA.USH.VI².X.

A chronological list of 132 martyrs and confessors from the College
between 1577 and 1628, with some others, compiled from various
sources including documents at that time in the College archives.

323.1 —Hierogazophylacium Belgicum, siue thesaurus sacrarum reliquiarum
Belgii. 8°. *Duaci, apud Gerardum Pinchon*, 1628. L.; AMS.ANT³.D.DMR.
HD.PA.PN.

Under the heading of the English College, Douai, the author prints
a numbered list of 135 English martyrs between 1577 and 1618.
This was used in preparing the revised catalogue of 1630 (no. 323).
The book also contains lists of the relics possessed by the English,
Irish and Scots establishments throughout the Netherlands.

Plays performed at the College

—Drury, W. Aluredus, 1620. *See* nos. 329–30.

Theses defended at the College

—Savage, F. Conclusiones logicae, 1624. *See* no. 1025.

324   **Douai,** *Irish College.* Exhibitio consolatoria tabulae emblematicae
Serenissimae Principi Isabellae de gemino interitu, et fratris Regis, et
Archiducis mariti: cui subnectitur catalogus eorum, qui e Collegio
Ibernorum Duaceno ad messem dominicam prodierunt, praeside
Reuerendo Domino Christoforo Cusaco. Per alumnos Collegii. 4°.
Duaci, ex typographia Baltazaris Belleri, 1622. L(-plate).; ANT.D¹².
DOU.

On the death in 1622 of Philip III of Spain and the Archduke
Albert of the Netherlands. Consisting of Latin verses (one of them
by Christopher Chamberlin) explaining an emblematic engraved
plate which precedes the text, followed by an address to the Archduchess Isabella by the Irish College and a list of alumni of the
College who have gone on the mission to Ireland. Modern reprint
in *Archivium Hibernicum*, 14, 1949, pp. 66–83.

—Laudatio funebris . . . Alberti, Archiducis Austriae, 1622. *See* no. 225.
—*[Appendix. Discourses delivered at the College.]* Thirry, W. De prouida
status electione oratio theologica, 1624. *See* no. 1249.
—Thirry, W. Discursus panegyrici de nominibus . . . S. Patricii, 1617.
See no. 1250.

325   **Douai,** *Scots College.* Serenissimae Augustissimaeque Mariae Stuartae,
Reginae Scotiae . . . Catholicae fidei inuictae martyri, suas ex vniuersa
philosophia assertiones dedicanti perquam nobili et generoso juueni
D. Hippolyto Curle, Scoto beneuolentiae, & gratitudinis ergo accine-
bant Seminarii Scotorum Duacensis alumni. 4°. *Duaci, apud Balta-
zarem Bellerum*, 1618. BRS.DOU.

Poems, Latin and Greek, composed for the occasion of Curle's
defence of his thesis which he dedicated to the memory of Mary
Queen of Scots. Curle, who was both student and benefactor of
the College, later became its Rector. *See* Foley, vol. 5, p. 189.

326   —*[Appendix. A Papal Letter of Recommendation.]* Clement VIII, *Pope.*
Litterae hortatoriae Smi. D. N. Clementis VIII. Pro Seminario
Scotorum Duaci. *s.sh.*fol. *Romae, apud Impressores Camerales, n.d.*
[1593]. RO⁹.(Fondo Gesuitico, 446², f. 615).

Dated at the end, from Rome 16 February 1593.

—*[An appeal on behalf of the College.]* Thomson, G. De antiquitate
Christianae religionis apud Scotos, 1594. *See* nos. 1251–2.

327 —[*An account of celebrations by the College.*] 1622. *In :* Narratio eorum quae Duaci pro celebranda sanctorum Ignatii et Francisci canonizatione gesta sunt. 8°. *Duaci, typis viduae Petri Telu,* 1622. DOU.LIL.
St. Ignatius of Loyola and St. Francis Xavier were canonised on 22 May 1622. This account by an unidentified author of the celebrations at Douai marking the event includes (pp. 3–6) the part played in them by the Scots College which was under Jesuit direction. With ten unnumbered engraved plates.

Doulaeus, Georgius, *pseud.* See Warford, W.

Dovenius, Cornelius. See O'Devany, C.

328 **Dowley, James.** [*Begin :*] Clero, Senatui, Populoq; Lymericenae vrbis vtramque felicitatem exoptat. Vester Iacobus Dulaeus. Quaestio theologica. Quis est Pastor bonus qui dat animam suam pro ouibus suis? [*End :*] ... [ ]dis Apostolicae Protonotarius, Constantissimae Germanorum Nationis [ ]mia Paris. apud Plessaeos Philosophiae Professor. [ ], Anno M.DC.XL. *s.sh.*fol. *n.p.d.* [1640]. RO⁸. (*v.imp.*).
A programme announcing the forthcoming defence of his thesis. *Pr.* [Paris?].

Dractan, Carlos. See Tancred, C.

329 **Drury, William.** Aluredus siue Alfredus tragico-comoedia ter exhibita, in seminario Anglorum Duaceno ab eiusdem collegii iuuentute, anno Domini MDCXIX. 16° (in eights). *Duaci, ex officina Ioannis Bogardi,* 1620. L.; BRS.CAL.COR.HD.Y.X.
Including also another play, entitled 'Mors' and a poem 'De venerabili Eucharistia ab apibus inuenta'. All are in Latin verse. For Drury *see* RH., April 1966, pp. 293–7.

330 —[Anr. ed., with an additional play, and with title:] Dramatica poemata ... Editio secunda ab ipso authore recognita, & ... auctior reddita. 12°. *Duaci, typis Petri Bogardi,* 1628. L.O.C.; BRS.CHI.DOU.DUR.F.HN. LIL.MAA.MU.OS.PEN.PN.Y.
The added play, also in Latin verse, is entitled 'Reparatus siue depositum'. A third edition of the collection, printed at Antwerp in 1641, falls outside the scope of this catalogue.

331 **Dudley, John,** *Duke of Northumberland.*‡ Ioannis Dudlaei, Northumbriae nuper in Anglia Ducis, iam tum securi persecutiendi, ad populum Londinensem concio. 4°. *Romae, apud Paulum Manutium Aldi F.,* 1570. L.; L⁵⁰.VT(5).
A free translation of Northumberland's speech on the scaffold in 1553, professing himself a Catholic. For the English original *see* STC 7283. A contemporary MS note on the titlepage of the L. copy reads: 'Interprete Richardo Scelleio Anglobritanno' [probably Sir Richard Shelley who was living in Italy when this translation was published]. A MS of the translation is in the British Library (MS Royal 12 A xxvi). For the background see W. K. Jordan & M. R. Gleason, *The Saying of John late Duke of Northumberland upon the Scaffold, 1553,* Cambridge, Mass., 1975.

332 —[*Italian version of the same speech.*] Questa e la confessione, che Giouanni Duca di Northomberlando fece, essendo egli sopra il palco per essere giustitiato. 4°. *n.p.d.* [*c.* 1570?] L(1203.i.10); F.RO².RO⁵.
Pr. [Rome, heirs of Antonio Blado?] The date [1570] is assigned to this publication by D. Bernoni, *Catalogo delle edizioni romane di Antonio Blado ed eredi,* [1891]. It may, however, have been printed much earlier [*c.* 1553–54] by Antonio Blado himself, for the text is much closer to the English original of [1553] than to the Latin version of 1570 (no. 331). *See* Jordan & Gleason, p. 65.

333 —[*French version.*] De l'execution faicte à Londres du duc de Nortomberlan ... auec la cöfession qu'il fit sur l'escharfaut auät sa mort. 4°.

Paris, Iacques Gregoire, n.d. [*c.* 1589]. L(C.57.a.23, *misdated* [*1554*] *in catalogue*); PA(Nc.156, *misdated* [*1571*] *in catalogue*).PA³(37233/22, *misdated* [*1606*] *in catalogue*).

> The printer's name in the imprint is followed by the statement 'demeurant pres de la porte S. Victor, à l'image S. Iean', an address at which he is known to have been active only in 1589. This edition may be a reprint of an earlier one, no longer extant, for the text keeps close to the English original of [1553] and reveals stylistic similarities with the Italian version (no. 332). *See* Jordan & Gleason, p. 69.

Dulaeus, Jacobus. *See* Dowley, J.

334   **Durie, John.** Confutatio responsionis Gulielmi Whitakeri ... ad Rationes decem, quibus fretus Edmondus Campianus ... certamen Anglicanę Ecclesię ministris obtulit in causa fidei. 8°. *Parisiis, apud Thomam Brumennium,* 1582. O.C.; A.C³.C⁹.D.DI.E.HP(2).LOU³.O³.O⁵.PA³. USH.VT.YK. + +

> Incorporating the text of Campion's work. Answers STC 25358. Whitaker replied in STC 25362. Renouard (Brumen) 269.

335   —[Anr. ed., enlarged.] 8°. *Ingolstadii, ex typographia Dauidis Sartorii,* 1585. L.O.C.; A².AUG(2).C¹⁵.DI.E.MD.O⁴.PA.ST.VI.X. + +

> Including a reply to STC 25362 in which Whitaker had answered no. 334.

—[*Appendix.*] Briegerus, J., *pseud*? Flores Caluinistici decerpti, 1585.

> A reply to Lawrence Humfrey's attack on Campion and Durie in tom. 3 of *Doctrinae Iesuiticae praecipua capita,* 1585. *See* nos. 115, 116.

Eclesal, T., *pseud. See* no. 899.

335.1 **Elder, Adam.** Ad Reuerendum in Christo Patrem Robertum Reid strenae, siue conciones capitulares. 4°. *Parisiis ex typographia M. Dauidis,* 1558. A.E(2,1 *imp*.).STU.

> Adam Elder was a monk of Kinloss and this work is addressed to Robert Reid who was formerly Abbot of Kinloss and became Bishop of Orkney in 1541.

Elisaeus, *a Sancto Michaele, name in religion. See* Pendryck, W.

England, *Catholic Church.*

Missals for use in England

336   —Missae aliquot pro sacerdotibus itinerantibus in Anglia. Ex Missali Romano reformato. 4°. *n.p.* 1615. L.O.C.; AMP.DE.HP.N.OS.RO.ST.STL. TEX.USH.W(3).

> *Pr.* [S. Omer, Eng. Coll. press.] The reformed Roman missal of 1570 had been further revised by Pope Clement VIII in 1604. A&R 542. STC 16225.

336.1 —[Anr. issue, with a cancel title and the addtiion of pt. 2 *Ordo baptizandi* also printed at the College press.] Missale paruum pro sacerdotibus in Anglia itinerantibus. Ordo etiam baptizandi, aliaq; sacramenta ministrandi, & officia quaedam ecclesiastica rite peragendi. Ex Pontificali, & Rituali Romano, iussu Pauli PP. Quinti editis, extractus. 4°. 2 pts. *n.p.* 1623. L.O.; ILL.

> A&R 543 & 720. STC 16226. Pt. 2 is the earliest non-Sarum Ritual.

336.2 —[Anr. ed. enlarged.] Missale paruum pro sacerdotibus in Anglia, Scotia, & Ibernia itinerantibus. 4°. 3 pts. *n.p.* 1626. L.O(2).C.; AMP.D. DE.DUR.E.F.HP.M.ST(2).TEX.USH(2).W. + +

> *Pr.* [S. Omer, Charles Boscard.] Pt. 2 contains *Ordo baptizandi* and pt. 3, without a separate title, adds six supplementary masses. A&R 544. STC 16227. ERL 235.

Primers in Latin and English

—*See* vol. 2 under English Catholics. *Liturgical and semi-liturgical Books.*

Rituals for use in England

336.3 —Sacra institutio baptizandi: matrimonium celebrandi: infirmos vngendi: mortuos sepeliendi . . . iuxta vsum insignis ecclesiae Sarisburiensis. 4°. *Duaci, excudebat Laurentius Kellam*, 1604. L.O(5).C.; C³.DE.DOU.HD(*imp.*).PRI.TEX.Y.

  Copies should have ā²; ā1 has an index on the recto and approbation dated 5 July 1604 on the verso; ā2 is blank. A&R 717. STC 16157.5. *Ed.* E. Maihew.

336.4 —[Anr. issue, with 8 additional leaves of 'Annotationes' by the same editor.] L.O.C.; DE.HN.HP.LIV.M.NY¹¹.PML.ST.TEX.USH.W. A&R 718. STC 16158. ERL 345.

336.5 —[Anr. ed. with title:] Manuale sacerdotum hoc est. ritus administrandi sacramenta baptismi, matrimonii, et extremae vnctionis . . . iuxta vsum insignis ecclesiae Sarisburiensis. 8°. *Duaci, excudebat Laurentius Kellam*, 1610. [1610/11]. L.O(2).C.; C³.C¹⁷.CASHEL.DAI.DE.EX.HD.NLW. NY¹¹.ST.TEX.USH.W.

  Imprimatur dated 9 Feb. 1611. A&R 719. STC 16159.
—Ordo baptizandi, 1623. A&R 720. = pt. 2 of no. 336.1.
—Ordo baptizandi, 1626. = pt. 2 of no. 336.2.

336.6 —Ordo baptizandi aliaque sacramenta administrandi, & officia quaedam ecclesiastica rite peragendi: ex rituale Romano iussu Pauli Quinti edito, extractus. Pro Anglia, Hibernia, & Scotia. 12°. *n.p.* 1632. OS. A&R 721. STC 16161.5. *Pr.* [S. Omer, Eng. Coll. press.]

336.7 —[Anr. ed.] 24°. *Parisiis*, 1636. L(destroyed).O.; DMR.FER.USH.W.
  Pr. [widow of Jerome Blageart.] A&R 722. STC 16162. ERL 338.

336.8 —[Anr. ed.] 12°. *n.p.* 1639. O.; DAI(-*t.p.*).L⁹.ST.TEX.W.
  Pr. [S. Omer, Eng. Coll. press.] A&R 723. STC 16162.3.

336.9 —[Anr. ed.] 32°. *Per Ioannem Cousturier*, 1639. DE.
  Pr. [Rouen.] A&R 724. STC 16162.7.

Appendix

336.10 —Clement VIII, *Pope.* Litaniae et preces recitandae pro fide Catholica Romana in regnis Angliae, & Scotiae restituenda, & propaganda, & antiquae eorundem regnorum cum eadem Romana Catholica Ecclesia vnitatis restitutione. 4° (a single quadrifolium). *Romae, ex typographia Camerae Apostolicae*, 1603. VT (Capponi IV 907/12).

  Prayers for general use to be said for the restoration of the Catholic faith in England and Scotland. With a woodcut of the arms of Clement VIII on the titlepage.

English Benedictines.

Constitutional Documents

337 —Breue Santissimi D. N. Pauli Papae V. Pro continuatione & restauratione Congregationis Anglicanae, cum extensione priuilegiorum, & gratiarum, quaecunque Congregationi Hispanicae de obseruantia, & veteri Congregationi Anglicanae, aut Ordini S. Benedicti in Anglia concessa sunt. 4° (a bifolium). *n.p.d.* [1633.] DAI(Weldon III, pp. 623–6. *With MS signatures of three Notaries Apostolic, including Balthasar Beller, the Douai publisher and printer).*

  The Brief *Ex incumbenti* of 23 August 1619 by which Pope Paul V restored the English Congregation. This printing of the Brief was ordered by the President General in 1633 because of opposition to

his authority by some of the English monks who had originally
joined the Spanish Congregation. Following the text is a printed
note reading: 'Praesens copia desumpta est ex originali authentico
... quod testamur nos infrascripti Notarii Apostolici Duaci com-
morantes ad hoc specialiter vocati, die 14. Ianuarii 1633'. *Pr.*
[Douai, Balthasar Beller.]

338 —Constitutiones missionis Benedictinorum Congregationis Anglicanae.
16°. *Duaci, typis L. Kellami,* 1633. VT(Barb.D.I.23).
With a prefatory letter signed by the President General Claudius
de S. Benedicto [name in religion of William White].

339 —[Anr. issue, with title:] Constitutiones missionis Benedictinorum
Congregationum Anglicanae et Hispanicae. *Duaci, typis L. Kellami,*
1633. DE(11266).
The title and the beginning of the prefatory letter are partly reset.

Other Documents issued by Presidents General

—*See* nos. 38–41; 59–63.

A Work issued on Instructions from the General Chapter

—Apostolatus Benedictinorum in Anglia, 1626. *See* no. 934.

Appendix

Maihew, E. Congregationis Anglicanae Ordinis Sanctissimi Patriarchae Benedicti. Trophoea, 1619 [*etc.*]. *See* nos. 757, 759.

340 —Spinola, I. D. [*Begin:*] Ioannes Dominicus Spinola Protonotarius
Apostolicus ... Pro parte, & ad instantiam Venerabilis Congregationis
Sancti Benedicti Regni Hispanorum, nec non RR.DD. monachorum
missionis Anglicanae eiusdem Congregationis ... fuit inita quaedam
concordia ... *s.sh.*fol. *n.p.d.* [1614.] DAI(Weldon VI, f. 639). [*DMR.]
A statement by the Procurator of the Spanish Benedictines at Rome
to the effect that the prior consent of the Spanish Congregation (to
which many English monks belonged) was required before an independent English Congregation could be formed. It aimed to
nullify the efforts of Anselm Beech to see such a congregation
established. Dated from Rome, 3 October 1614. *See* Justin McCann,
Ampleforth and its Origins, 1952, p. 103. *Pr.* [Rome].

English Bridgettines. [*Appendix.*] Relacion que embiaron, 1594. *See*
no. 741.
—Sander, E. Traslado de vna carta, [*c.* 1590.] *See* no. 965.
English Carthusians. [*Appendix.*] Chauncy, M. Historia martyrum
Angliae, 1573 [*etc.*]. *See* nos. 235–9, 241.

English Catholics.

PLEAS FOR TOLERATION

Plea of 1603 to James I

341 —Requeste et supplication des Catholiques Anglois. Au Roy d'Angle-
terre leur souuerain Prince, pour la tolerance de la religion Catholique,
en son royaume. 8° (a quadrifolium). *Paris, chez Estienne Colin,* 1603,
Iouxte la copie imprimée à Londres, en langage Anglois. PA(Nf.628).
The only printed text of the English original know to have survived
is contained in the Protestant answers to it: STC 18292 and 20141.
For the background to this and other petitions to King James by
English Catholics, *see* Mil., vol. 2, pp. 72–6.

342 —[Anr. ed.] 8°. *Paris,* 1604. L(C.110.*c.*19/1); PA(Nf.308B).

343   —[Anr. ed.] 4°. *Paris, pour Syluestre Moreau,* 1604. L(G.1747/3); PA
      (Nf.308A); PA³(37233/7).
      A close reprint of no. 342 by the same printer.
344   —[Anr. ed.] 8° (a quadrifolium). *Paris, pour Abraham de Meaux,* 1605.
      CARP.PA³(2: 6506/1; 36118/1).
345   —[Anr. ed.] 8° (a quadrifolium). *Paris, iouxte la copie d'Abraham de
      Meaux,* 1605. PA³(37260/21).
      A close reprint of no. 344 by the same printer.
346   —[Anr. ed.] 8° (in fours). *Paris, par Claude Percheron iouxte la copie im-
      primée à Rouan par Estienne Mallasis, n.d.* [1613]. L(C.110.c.19/2).;
      PA(Nf.308).
      The approbation is dated 16 March 1613. The Rouen edition cited
      in the imprint has not been found.
347   —[Anr. ed.] 8°. *Iouxte la coppie imprimée à Londres, par Clement
      Cheualier. Paris,* 1625. PA(Nf.808C).PA³.
      It seems probable that the petition originally presented to James I
      in 1603 was reprinted in London on the accession of Charles I in
      1625, but no copy of any edition of the English is known. The
      'Clement Chevalier' cited in the above imprint is evidently Clement
      Knight who is known to have been active as a publisher in London
      from 1594 to 1629. In spite of the claim in the imprint, the French
      is not a new translation but a reprint of that at nos. 341–6.
348   —[Anr. ed.] 8°. *Lyon, par Claude Armand, dit Alphonse,* 1625. WO.
349   —[Anr. ed., with minor changes and with title:] Remonstrance et de-
      claration des Catholiques anglois, faite au Roy d'Angleterre, à son
      corronnement du royaume d'Escosse. Pour obtenir de sa Maiesté la
      liberté de la religion Catholique dans l'estendue de ses royaumes.
      Traduit en françois, par le Reuerend Pere Patrice Chenart. 8° (in
      fours). *Paris, par P. Meetayer* [sic], 1633. PA(Nf.330).PA⁷.
      Except for the introduction of one or two perfunctory references to
      Scotland the text is the same as that of the petition originally pre-
      sented to James I in 1603. It seems probable that there was an
      edition in English to mark the occasion of Charles I's coronation as
      King of Scotland, 18 June 1633, but no copy has been found. Apart
      from the new Scottish references, the translation is the same as that
      of nos. 341–8.

Plea of 1604 to James I

350   —Seconde requeste presentée au Roy d'Angleterre, par les Catholiques
      Anglois. Auec la responce de sa Maiesté faicte ausdits Catholiques,
      le 4. iour de Ianuier 1604. Translatée d'Anglois en François. 12°?
      Imprimé à Paris, sur la coppie de Londres, 1604. CARP(M.208/6).
      The English original has not been found.

Plea of 1621 to James I

351   —Declaration presentée au Roy d'Angleterre; par les Catholiques
      Anglois, sur les presentes affaires de son royaume. Ensemble tout ce
      qui a esté ordonné par sa Maiesté, sur icelle declaration. 8° (in fours).
      Sur la coppie imprimée à Poictiers. Paris, chez Matthieu le Blanc, 1621.
      L.; CARP.PA.PA⁴.
      A plea drawn up under eighteen heads together with a statement
      that King James has consented to them. In 1621, following an
      appeal by Louis XIII of France, James agreed to a measure of *de
      facto* toleration of Catholics. *See* no. 368. No printed English
      original is known. The Poitiers edition of the French, referred to
      in the imprint, has not been found. The slovenly presswork of the
      present edition suggests that the Paris imprint may be false.

352 —[Anr. ed.] 8° (in fours). *Troyes, par Pierre Cheuillot*, 1621. N.

353 —[Anr. ed., with title:] Declaration presentée au Roy d'Angleterre, par les Catholiques Anglois, sur les presentes affaires de son royaume. Auec la liberté rendue aux religieux prestres, & autres Catholiques Anglois. Par le commandement du Roy d'Angleterre. En faueur de sa Maiesté tres Chrestienne. Ensemble tout ce qui a esté ordonné par sa Maiesté sur icelle declaration. 8° (a quadrifolium). *Paris, chez Pierre de la Fosse*, 1621. O.

The imprint appears to be false; no Paris printer of this name is recorded at this period.

Plea of 1623 to Prince Charles

354 —Memorial, en el qual suplican los Catolicos de Inglaterra, al Serenissimo Principe de Gales . . . despues de concluydos los casamiētos, que su Alteça se sirua de darles vna vniuersidad en cada reyno de los suyos . . . y otro que dieron los Escoceses a V.M. Fol. (a bifolium). *Valladolid, por Geronimo Morillo, n.d.* [1623]. L.

Two petitions drawn up at the time of the marriage negotiations with Spain. The first, by English Catholics to Prince Charles, asks for Catholic universities in England, Ireland and Scotland. No English original of this has been found. The second, by [Hugh Semple] to the King of Spain, asks for a seminary for Scottish Catholics in Madrid.

355 —[Anr. ed.] Fol. (a bifolium). [Coloph.] *Impresso por Matias Clauijo*, 1623. MD².(3: Jes.75/86; 108/70; 117/69).
Pr. [Seville].

356 —[Anr. ed.] Fol. (a bifolium). *n.p.d.* [1623.] HSA.
Pr. [Spain?]

357 —[*Italian transl.*] Due suppliche date in Spagna L'vna dalli regni d'Inghilterra, di Scotia, & d'Irlanda, al Precipe di Gales, per mettere l'vniuersità, & studi in ciascuno d'essi a beneficio de Catholici. L'altra al Re Catholico, per far hauer a gli Scozzesi vn seminario nelli regni di Spagna. Tradotte dalla lingua spagnuola nell italiana. 4° (a single quadrifolium). *Milano, nella Reg. Duc. Corte, per Gio. Battista Malatesta*, 1623. L.; DMR.DUR.

DECLARATIONS CONCERNING THE AUTHORITY OF RICHARD SMITH, BISHOP OF CHALCEDON

358 —Declaratio Catholicorum laicorum Angliae circa auctoritatem quam Reuᵐᵘˢ Dominus Episcopus Chalcedonensis in eosdem vendicat et quae ad hanc spectant acta. 4°. *Antuerpiae, ex officina Plantiniana Balthasaris Moreti*, 1631. L.O.C.; BRS.PA.PA³.ST.VAL.VI.VT.WO.

A translation of A&R 248. For the background *see* RH Oct. 1982, pp. 111–45, especially p. 134. Answered by the Bishop in no. 1095.

359 —[Anr. ed.] 4°. [Coloph.] *Leodii, excudebat Leonardus Streel*, 1631. LINC.

360 —[Anr. ed.] Fol. [Coloph. sig. Ff1ᵛ:] *Ipris, typis Ioannis Belleti*, 1631. [2nd coloph. sig. Ff2:] *Bruxellae, apud viduam Huberti Anthoni*, 1631. RO⁹.(Anglia 33 I. no. 9). [*L⁹.]

The second colophon is probably repeated from a Brussels edition not found.

361 —[*French transl.*] Declaration des Catholiques laiques du royaume d'Angleterre, touchant l'authorité que Monsieur l'Euesque de Chalcedoine s'attribue sur eux. 4°. *n.p.d.* [1631.] BRS(2).PA(Nf324). PA³.VT.

pr. [Tournai?] The approbation is dated from Tournai, 29 April 1631.

362 —[*A disavowal of the foregoing declaration.*] General desadueu des Catholiques lais d'Angleterre, contre vne Declaration qui a esté faussemēt publiée à leur nom. 4° (a bifolium). *n.p.d.* [1631]. L²⁷ᴬ.(A24/99). The names of the individual English Catholics disavowing the declaration are not given. *See* the reference in the note to no. 358. *Pr.* [Paris, at the press of Jérome Blageart.]

PURPORTED WARNING BY THE CATHOLICS OF ENGLAND
TO THE CATHOLICS OF FRANCE

—[Auertissement des Catholiques Anglois aux François Catholiques du danger où ils sont, 1586, *etc.*]
This anonymous work, first printed in France in 1586 and later reprinted, has no place in this catalogue. Though it purports to be written by English Catholics, this is merely a fiction: it is a League tract by [Louis d'Orleans] opposing the claims of Henry of Navarre to the French throne.

APPENDIX (*Arranged chronologically*)

1575

363 —Gregory XIII, *Pope.* [*Begin :*] Indulgentia. Sancti. Iubilei. Pro Catholicis Anglis tam in Anglia, quam extra eam existentibus. Gregorius Papa XIII. vniuersis Christi fidelibus praesentes literas inspecturis salutem . . . *s.sh.*fol. *Romae, apud heredes Antonii Bladii Impressores Camerales,* 1575. RO⁵.(Per.Est.18/2³.n.730).
The indulgence is dated at the end, from Rome 30 March 1575.

1582

363.1 —Lettere venute d'Inghilterra tradotte in Italiano, doue si hanno alcuni auisi della crudel persecutione di quel Regno verso i Catholici, et della morte d'alcuni che per la Fede sono stati martirizati. 4°. *In Brescia, Appresso Vincenzo Sabbio,* 1582. VT(Racc.I.IV.1242 Int. 10).
Includes translations of a letter of Anthony Tyrrell written from prison in London, 18 July 1581, a letter from Dr Allen at Rheims (another version of Knox, *Letters and Memorials of . . . Allen* (1882) no. XLV, p. 101) and other letters from France and England, ending with an account of the martyrdom of Edmund Campion and his two companions [1 Dec. 1581].

1583

364 —Cartas muy verdaderas de Ynglaterra, en las cuales se refiere y cuenta lo mucho que han padecido y padecen los Christianos por la confession de nuestra sancta fe Catholica. 4°. *n.p.* 1583.
Not found. Description from Uriarte 2416. *Pr.* [Spain?].

1585

—Crudelitas Caluinianae exempla duo . . . Quorum primum, continent barbarum ac saeuum Caluinianorum edictum recenter editum contra Catholicos, 1585. *See* nos. 1457–59.

1599

—Nueuos auisos de Inglaterra . . . de sucessos, y persecuciones de los Catholicos, [1599]. *See* no. 1063.

1606

365 —Breuiculus duorum nuper in publicis comitiis Anglicanis actorum,

anno Christi M.DC.VI. Iacobi Angliae Regis tertio. 8°. *Londini*,
[1606.] L.

Extracts from the statutes enacted against Catholics following the
Gunpowder Plot of 1605, with a Catholic commentary. The author
has not been identified. Imprint false; *pr.* [Douai, Pierre Auroi.] In
the only known copy the date has been cropped away. A 1606 edition
with a Rouen imprint, mentioned by Bellarmine in no. 1491 (p. 145)
has not been found. A&R 140a (p. 186). STC 9504. ERL 60.

366   —[Anr. ed.] 8°. *Herbipoli*, 1609. BRS².

The title as in no. 365 except that the word 'nuper' is omitted.
Imprint false?

—Las leyes nueuamente hechas en el Parlaméto de Inglaterra este año
de M.DC.VI contra los Catolicos Ingleses, [1606]. *See* no. 1342.2.

1607

367   —Cristanovitch, S.‡ Examen Catholicum edicti Anglicani, quod contra
Catholicos est latum, auctoritate Parlamenti Angliae. Anno Domini
M.D.C.VI. Auctore Stanislao Cristanovic. 8°. *Parisiis, apud Franciscum
Huby*, 1607. L.O.C.; D⁸.DMR.F.HER.L²⁶.LINC.PA.PA³.PA⁴.(*2 : 1 imp.*).WO.

On the penal legislation enacted against Catholics following the
Gunpowder Plot. The author refers to himself being in England
'anno praeterito' (f. 5v.). The book was publicly burned at Paris at
the request of the English Ambassador.

1612

—De vna de Londres . . ., [1612]. On the persecution of Catholics in
England. *See* nos. 281–2.

1621

368   —La liberté rendue aux religieux, prestres, & autres Catholiques Ang-
lois. Par le commandement du Roy d'Angleterre. En faueur de sa
Maiesté tres-Chrestienne. 8°. *Paris, chez Pierre Ramier*, 1621. L.;
DUKE.PA(2: Nf.316; Lb.1553).

An address to King Louis XIII thanking him for having intervened
with James I on behalf of the English Catholics. *See* also no. 351.
From internal evidence the author appears to have been a French-
man.

369   —[Anr. ed.] 8°. *Rouen, chez Iacques Besogne, iouxte la copie imprimée à
Paris*, 1621. PA(Nf.316A).

1622

370   —Recit veritable de ce qui s'est passé en Angleterre sur l'eslargissement
des Catholiques, qui y estoient detenus prisonniers pour auoir professé
la religion Catholique . . . Auec la lettre du Grand Chancelier addres-
sée aux iuges dudit pays, par commandement du Roy. 8°. *Paris, chez
Antoine Vitray*, 1622. PA(Nf.317A).

By letters patent of 11 August 1622 James I instructed his judges to
release from gaol all Catholics imprisoned solely for religion. His
instructions were conveyed to the judges by the Lord Keeper (the
'Grand Chancelier'), John Williams, Bishop of Lincoln, the text of
whose letter to the judges is here printed in French. No contemporary printed edition of the English original is known but the text
survives in MS (*see* CSPD 1619–23, p. 436). Collation: A–B⁴ (B4
blank).

371   —[Anr. ed.] 8°. *Paris, chez Antoine Vitray*, 1622. L.
Collation: A⁸ (A8 blank).

372 —[Anr. ed.] 8°. *Lyon, pour François Yurad,* 1622. PA(Nf.317).
—[Anr. ed.] 1623. *In :* nos. 1606–07.

373 —[*A supposititious speech by King James concerning the English Catholics.*]
Razonamiento que hizo el Rey de Inglaterra al Parlamento, en su villa
de Londres, a quinze de Febrero deste año . . . Acerca de lo tocante a
los Catolicos de su reyno, vso de los oficios diuinos, y predicacion del
Euangelio publicamente: y casamiento del Principe su hizo con la
Señor Infanta de España . . . Impresso por mandado del mismo
Rey en Londres, por Hercules Vvolfangho . . . y traducido en Español
por el licenciado Iuan Dimas de Aresticona. Fol. *Madrid, por Diego
Español,* 1622.
Not found. Description from Palau 248825. There appears to be no
record of any such speech by James or of any English edition of the
text.

374 —[Anr. ed.] Fol. (a bifolium). *Madrid por Diego Español, y por su
original en Cadiz por Monoel Gracian,* 1622. MD(R-varios.201, *etc.*).
MD²(Jes.117/4).

375 —[Anr. ed.] Fol. (a bifolium). *Barcelona, en casa de Esteuan Liberos, en
presente año* [1622]. MD²(Jes.72/27, *formerly* 72/23).

376 —[Anr. ed.] Fol. (a bifolium). *Barcelona, en casa de Esteuan Liberos, en
este dicho año de* 1622. MD(MSS 18400/15).

377 —[*French version.*] Harangue prononcée par le Roy de la grande Bretagne
à l'ouuerture du Parlement tenu en la ville de Londres le XV. de
Feburier dernier. Touchant la liberte donnée aux Catholiques Anglois. L'Alliance du Prince de Galles son fils, auec la fille de sa Maiesté
Catholique. Et la declaration contre les Estats d'Hollande pour la
nauigation & traffic des Indes Orientales. 8°. *Iouxte la copie imprimée à
Londres, chez Hercules François au Cimetiere sainct Paul,* 1622. F.NCY
(280446/6).
The London imprint is fictitious.

378 —[*A different French version.*] Harangue celebre prononcée par le Roy
d'Angleterre, à Lassemblée generalle du Parlement conuocqué en la
grand Salle du Palais Royal de Vvestmunster à Londres ville capitale
du Royaume dAngleterre. Pour le restablissement de la religion
Catholique Apostolique & Romaine. Traduite d'Anglois en François.
12°. *Bruxelles, chez Henry Bosck,* 1623. NCY(280446/1).

379 —[*Italian version.*] Ragionamento fatto al Rè della Gran Bertagna, al
Parlamento nella città di Londra, a 15. di Febraro dell'anno 1622.
Stampato in Londra per Hercole Francese, nel Cimiterio de San
Paolo, e tradotto d'Inglese in Spagnuolo per il Dottor Giouanni
Dimas, e stampato in Barcelona in casa di Stefano Liberos. Tradotto
di Spagnuolo in Italiano, e ristampato in Mantoua l'anno sodetto.
[1622.] 4° (a bifolium). L¹¹(SP.14/127, no. 52A.) [*L.] *Pr.* [Mantau].
There is no imprint or date except in the form shown above.

380 —Anr. ed.] 4° (a quadrifolium). *Stampato in Mantoua, & poi in Bolog.
per Nicolò Tebaldini,* 1622. L.; DUR.
Dedicated by the printer to Thomas Dempster 'in Bologna Lettore
Eminentiss'.

381 —[*A different Italian version.*] Il famoso ragionamento fatto dal Re
d'Inghilterra, all'Assemblea generale del Parlamento, congregato nella
gran sala del Palazzo Regio di Vestmonster in Londra . . . sopra lo
ristabilimento della religione Catolica, Apostolica, Romana. Tradotto
dall'Inglese in Francese, & stampato in Brusseles . . . & hora tradotto
in Italiano. 4°. *Milano, per Pandolfo Malatesta,* 1623. A di 27 Giugno.
L(2).; F.

1623

382 —Relacion de vn caso en que murieron muchos Catolicos oyendo la palabra de Dios. Sucedio en la ciudad de Londres, a cinco de nouiembre de 1623. Fol. (a bifolium). *Valladolid, por Geronimo Morillo, n.d.* [1623]. HD.MD²(Jes.72/44, *imp.*) [*L.].

A Catholic account of the accident at Blackfriars (known as the 'Fatal Vespers', 26 Oct./5 Nov. 1623) caused by the collapse of the floor of the room in which Robert Drury S.J. was preaching to a large crowd, and resulting in the death of many of those present. Presumably translated from an English original but this has not been found. For another Catholic account *see* A&R 333.

383 —[Anr. ed.] Fol. (a bifolium). *n.p.d.* [1623.] MD²(Jes.178/10). *Pr.* [Spain].

—[For works dealing with the question of toleration for Catholics in England in connection with the proposed Anglo-Spanish marriage treaty of 1623: *see* nos. 1562.1 – 1607].

1625

—[For the articles of the Anglo-French marriage treaty of 1625 which included toleration for Catholics in England: *see* nos. 1608–15.]

1626

384 —Relacion cierta de las nouedades del Reyno de Ingalaterra, y su Corte, embiada por vn Catolico de la ciudad de Londres a Paris Corte del Rey de Francia. Fol. (a bifolium). *Madrid, en casa de Bernardino de Guzmã,* 1626. ESC.F.MD.MD²(Jes.204/20, *missing 1976*).

A newsletter of which the first part describes the renewed persecution of Catholics in England in spite of the articles of toleration contained in the Anglo-French marriage treaty of the previous year. The author has not been identified. Neither the English original nor any French version has been found.

385 —[Anr. ed.] Fol. (a bifolium). *Lisboa, impressa por Geraldo de la Viña,* 1626. MD.

386 —[Anr. ed., with title:] Verissima relacion en que se da quenta en el estado en que estan los Catolicos de Inglaterra por parte de los hereges, y con el zelo que la Reyna los fauorece. Fol. (a bifolium). [Coloph.] *Seuilla, por Iuan de Cabrera,* 1626. L(593.h.17/57).

387 —[Anr. ed.?] Noticias de Ynglaterra y sobre el estado de los Catolicos. Presa que hicieron las naos de Unquerque prendiendo al Duque de Buquingan. Fol. (2 leaves). *Seuilla, por Iuan de Cabrera,* 1626.

Not seen. Description from Escudero 1371 citing 'Coleccion de varios de la Biblioteca de Sevilla'.

1628

388 —Remonstrance au Roy d'Angleterre. Sur la miserable condition des Catholiques ses subiects, en comparaison du fauorable traictement que les Huguenots reçoiuent en France. 8° (in fours). *Paris, chez Iacques Brisson,* 1628. L.O.; CARP.D⁷.DMR.E².F.PA.PA³.(*imp.*).RO⁶.

The author has not been identified. Pp. 9–19 set out the various penal enactments in force against English Catholics.

389 —[Anr. ed., or anr. issue.] 8° (in fours). *n.p.,* 1628. LGE.

390 **English Catholic Seminaries.** Las causas que han mouido al Rey Catolico don Felipe II. nuestro señor, para admitir y fauorecer a los seminarios de clerigos Ingleses en los reynos de España, y en sus estados de Flandes. Fol. (a bifolium). [Coloph.] *Impresso por mandado del señor Presidente de Castilla, por Luis Sanchez: en Madrid 14 de Deziembre, de 1597.* L(Add.MSS. 28470, ff. 113–14).

An appeal for alms for the English seminaries in Spain and the Spanish Netherlands, issued under the authority of King Philip II. It was evidently intended to send copies to various prominent persons, for space has been left in the printed text for the name of the addressee to be inserted in MS.

[391 *cancelled.*]

English Dominicans. [Faculties granted by Pope Urban VIII to the English Superior, Thomas Middleton, 15 August 1627. The printed text cited by Anstruther (*A Hundred Homeless Years*, 1958, p. 131) has no place in this catalogue. It is not contemporary but forms part of a *summarium* of documents prepared over a century later for a special congregation set up by Pope Benedict XIV. (VT². S.S. Inghilterra 22, p. 72).]

392   **English Jesuits.** [*Appendix.*] Ignatius, *of Loyola, Saint.* Exercitia spiritualia B.P. Ignatii Loyolae. 12°. *Audomaropoli, in Collegio Anglicano Societatis Iesu,* 1610. L.; HA.HE.HP(2).LOU.MAA.NM².ST.
       Printed at the College press for the use of the Jesuits of the English mission. This and no. 280 are the only two extant books printed at the press during this period that openly bear the College imprint.

393   —[Anr. ed.] 32°. *n.p.,* 1619. DAI(2).ST.
       Pr. [S. Omer, Eng. Coll. press.]

394   —Vitelleschi, M. Epistola Reuerendi P.N. Generalis Mutii Vitelleschi ad patres et fratres Societatis Iesu. 8°, *n.p.d.* [1639 or 1640.] L.; ST.
       The General's letter, dated from Rome, 15 November 1639, is addressed to all members of the Society. This edition was printed for the use of those belonging to the English Province. *Pr.* [S. Omer, Eng. Coll. press.]

       —[*A work sometimes misattributed to the English Jesuits.*] [Corona Regia, 1616.]
       This satire on King James I, put out spuriously under the name of Isaac Casaubon, with a false London imprint, has no place in this catalogue. Though rumoured at the time to have been the work of the English Jesuits at Louvain, its author it now known to have have been C. Breda, a Belgian student of Louvain University, and there is no evidence to connect it with the Jesuits. *See* I. G. Philip, 'Dragon's Teeth', Honald Library Society, Claremont, Ca., 1970. For editions of the work, *see* STC 4744–4744.7.

       —[*Works defending the English Jesuits against the charge of complicity in the Gunpowder Plot.*] Eudaemon Ioannes, A.   R. P. Andreae Eudaemon-Ioannis . . . ad Actionem proditoriam Edouardi Coqui, Apologia, 1610. *See* no. 521.

       —Eudaemon Ioannes, A.   R. P. Andreae Eudaemon-Ioannis . . . Responsio ad caput IV primae Exercitationis Isaaci Casauboni, 1615. *See* no. 522.

394.1 —Eudaemon Ioannes, A.   R. P. Andreae Eudaemon-Ioannis . . . Responsio ad Epistolam Isaaci Casauboni. 8°. *Coloniae Agrippinae, apud Ioannem Kinckium,* 1612. L.; BRS².C².D.D².DI.DMR.E.L²(2).PA.RO⁶.(2).TRO.WO.
       Answers STC 4742 and deals specifically with charges against the English Jesuits. Answered by STC 20344. *See* Mil., vol. 2, p. 125. Reprinted as part of the author's *Epislola ad amicum gallum . . . item Responsio ad Epistolam Isaaci Casauboni,* published by Kinckius at Cologne in 1613. (*See* Sommerv. tom. 3, col. 484, no. 8).

395   **English Secular Clergy.** [*Appendix.*] Clement VIII, *Pope.* [*Begin:*] Dilecto filio Magistro Georgio Blackuello, nostro & Sedis Apostolicae notario, regni Angliae Archipresbitero . . . *s.sh.*fol. *n.p.d.* [1602.] O.; L²⁷ᴬ(A.7/64).
       The Brief *Venerunt nuper* of 5 October 1602 limiting the powers of

the Archpriest, George Blackwell. This printed version does not bear the papal arms. It was probably printed from a MS of the original Brief at the instigation of the Appellant party among the secular clergy. *Pr.* [Paris, Widow of Guillaume de la Noue].

396   —[*A plea on behalf of the secular clergy*.] Rationes reditae, pro impressione librorum in causa sacerdotum Anglorum quos quidam eiusdem nationis Iesuitae schismatis aliorumque scelerum iniquissime insimularunt, cum quibus solis (eorum importunitate coacti) & nullo modo cū toto ordine aut ipsa Societate in arenam descenderunt. 8°. *n.p.d.* [1631.] KNY.PA.PA³.USH.VT.

A plea for the right of the secular clergy to answer attacks by the Jesuits on the Bishop of Chalcedon. Probably published after the issue of the Brief *Britannia* (dated 9 May 1631) by which Pope Urban VIII sought to silence the controversy over the Bishop's authority. *Pr.* [Paris.] For other works in the controversy, *see* under Smith, R., *Bishop of Chalcedon*.

Estevão, Thomas. *See* Stephens, T.

Estuarda, Maria. *See* Mary, *Queen of Scots. See* also O'Donnell, Mary Stuart.

396.1   **F., G.,** *Veridicus Hibernus.* Hiberniae siue antiquioris Scotiae vindiciae aduersus immodestam Parecbasim Thomae Dempsteri ... nuper editam ... His accessit nomenclatura Scotorum & Scotiae, &c. Authore G. F. Veridico Hiberno. 8°. *Antuerpiae, apud Hermannum Copman,* 1621. L(2).O(2).C.; D.D⁶.E.F.GT.PA.PA³.PA⁴.ST.VT.

Answering no. 296 of Thomas Dempster. Imprint false; *pr.* [Paris, Jérome Blageart.] Sometimes attributed to [David Rothe] but this is unlikely: there appears to be no early evidence to support the attribution, and Rothe published his own answer to Dempster's work in no. 955 printed in the same year by the same Paris printer. Including (pp. 83–121) a reprint of the 1619 Liège edition of Henry FitzSimon's *Catalogus praecipuorum sanctorum Hiberniae*, reproducing both the license and the colophon of that edition (*see* no. 480). Sir James Ware (*De Scriptoribus Hiberniae*, 1639, p. 26) attributes this work to a certain 'J. Roche'.

Fallon, James. Censura propositionum ... obsignatarum ... per ... Iacobum Fallonum, 1631. *See* nos. 683–85.

Faunt, Lawrence Arthur. Apologia Assertionum ... contra falsas Antonii Sadeelis criminationes. *Part of* no. 403.

—Apologia libri sui de inuocatione ... sanctorum. *See* no. 409.

397   —Assertiones rhetoricae et philosophicae. 4°. *Posnaniae, ex typographia Ioannis Wolrab,* 1582. UP.WR².

398   —Assertiones theologicae de Christi in terris ecclesia. 4°. *Posnaniae, per Ioannem Wolrab,* 1580.

Not found. Description from Sommerv., tom. 3, col. 554. Perhaps =399.

399   —[Anr. ed.] 4°. *Posnaniae, per Ioannem Wolrab,* 1582. UP.WR².

Answered by A. Sadelius in *Posnaniensium assertionum ... analysis et refutatio,* 1583, to which Faunt replied in no. 403.

—Assertiones theologicae. De ordinatione ac vocatione ministrorum Luther. *See* no. 411.

400   —Assertiones theologicae. De trino et vno Deo aduersus nouos Samosatenicos. Ex praelectionibus Collegii Posnaniensis praeteriti semestris excerptae. 4°. *Posnaniae, in officina Ioannis Wolrhabi,* 1581. DI.

401   —Coenae Lutheranorum et Caluinianorum oppugnatio, ac Catholicę Eucharistię defensio, comprehensa thesibus in Collegio Posnaniensi Societatis Iesu in publica disputatione propositis. Anno. M.D.LXXXVI. Octobris [space] die. A Laurentio Arturo Faunteo. 4°. *Posnaniae, in officina typographica Ioannis Wolrabi, n.d.* [1586.] O.;

AUG.C[5].C[19].FLO.HP.MD.O[7].PR.ST.UP.WR[2].
> In some copies the word 'Aprilis' printed on a slip is pasted over the word 'Octobris'.

402 —Coenae Lutheranorum, et Caluinianorum oppugnationis ... pars altera: de augustissimo Missae sacrificio. Comprehensa thesibus ... Anno M.D.LXXXVI. Octobris [space] die. A Laurentio Arturo Faunteo. 4°. *Posnaniae, in officina Ioannis Wolrhabi*, 1586. O.; C[19].DI. HP.MD.MU.NP.RO[5].ST.TRI.UP.VI.WA.WR[2].
—Confutatio thesium Zachariae Schilteri. *Part of* no. 408.

403 —De Christi in terris ecclesia ... libri tres. In quibus Caluinianos, Lutheranos, et caeteros, qui se euangelicos nominant, alienos a Christi ecclesia esse ... demonstratur, & simul Apologia Assertionum eiusdem inscriptionis contra falsas Antonii Sadeelis criminationes continetur. 4°. *Posnaniae, per Ioannem Wolrab*, 1584. [Coloph.] *In officina typographica Ioannis Wolrabi.* L(2 : 1 *imp.*).; BRN.C[19].DI.MTH. PR.PR[2].UP.WA.WR[2].
> The *Apologia Assertionum* is a defence of nos. 398–9 against Sadelius's *Posnaniensium assertionum ... analysis et refutatio*, 1583.

404 —De controuersiis inter ordinem ecclesiasticum & saecularem in Polonia ... tractatio. In qua refellitur libellus quidam famosus & mordax, contra querimoniam & postulata cleri, in postremi Regni Comitiis Regi, Regniq. ordinibus publice oblata conscriptus. 4°. *n.p.*, 1587. L.; KR.UP.WA.WR[2].
> The text ends: 'Laus Deo. A.H.L.E.L.A.F.' [Auctor huius libri est Laurentius Arturus Faunteus.] In his preface the author says that the work to which he is replying (the 'libellus ... famosus & mordax' of the title) was published anonymously. *Pr.* [Poland]

405 —[Anr. ed.] Nunc demum recognita et aucta. 4°. *n.p.*, 1592. KR.KR[2]. WA.WR[2]. Anon. There are no initials at the end of the text. *Pr.* [Poland].

406 —[Anr. ed.] Nunc demum recognita & aucta. 4°. *Cracouiae, in officina Andreae Petricouii*, 1632. L.; KR.LC.WA.WR[2].
> Anon. There are no initials. This edition forms one of a collection of Catholic tracts, *Opuscula tam ecclesiastici quam equestris ordinis*, put together by Melchior Stephanides and published at Cracow in 1632. It is bibliographically independent and so may also have been issued separately.

407 —Doctrina Catholica de sanctorum inuocatione & veneratione. Per theses explicata, et contra Lutheranos, Caluinianos, caeterosque sanctorum honoris et implorationis oppugnatores defensa. A Laurentio Arturo Faunteo ... in publica disputatione proposita, anno M.D.LXXXIIII. Octobris [space] die. 4°. *Posnaniae, excudebat Ioannes Wolrab, n.d.* [1584.] DI.FR.KR[2].PR.RO[2].UP.VT.WA.WR[2].[*O.]
> Answered by D. Tossanus in *Disputatio de doctrina catholica orthodoxa de sanctorum spiritum legitima et illegitima veneratione*, 1587, to which Faunt replied in no. 409.

408 —L. Arturi Fauntii ... Refutatio descriptionis Coenae Dominicae a Daniele Tossano ... contra librum oppugnationis Coenae Caluinianae et Lutheranae eiusdem Fauntii, editae. Adiecta est eiusdem Auctoris breuissima confutatio thesium Zachariae Schilteri. 4°. *Posnaniae, typis Ioannis Wolrabii*, 1590. KR.KR[2].UP.WA.WR[2].
> Answers Tossanus's *Coenae Dominicae* ... 1589, which had attacked no. 402. Answered by Tossanus in *Contra Laurentium Arturum Iesuitam Posnaniensem Disputationes II*, 1590.
—Refutatio descriptionis Coenae Dominicae a Daniele Tossano ... editae. *See* no. 408.

409 —R. P. Laurentii Arturi Fauntii ... Apologia libri sui de inuocatione, ac veneratione sanctorum, contra falsas Danielis Tossani ... criminationes. Adiunctus est Apologiae liber ipse, cuius defensio suscipitur,

in Germania nunquam editus. 8°. *Coloniae Agrippinae, in officina Birckmannica sumptibus Arnoldi Mylii*, 1589. L.O.; C⁹. FR.FU².HP.KN. KR².MD.MU(3).O⁷.PA.RO³.UP.VI. + +

A defence of no. 407 which is here reprinted. Tossanus answered the *Apologia* in *Contra Laurentium Arturum Iesuitam Posnaniensem Disputationes*, II, 1590.

410 —[Anr. ed.] 4°. *Posnaniae*, 1590.
Not found. Described by Gillow, vol. 2, p. 227 as having pp. x. 130. Not in Sommerv. *Pr.* [J. Wolrab?]

411 —[*Disputations in which he acted as Praeses.*] Sierakowski, S. Assertiones theologicae. De ordinatione ac vocatione ministrorum Luther. et Caluin. eorundemque sacramentis ... Praeside Laurentio Arturo Faunteo. 4°. *Posnaniae, in officina typographica Ioannis Wolrabi*, 1590. KR.WA.WR².

412 —Disputatio theologica de D. Petri, et Romani Pontificis successoris eius in Ecclesia Christi principatu. In Collegio Posnaniensi Societatis Iesu, anno M.D.LXXXIII. Die Octob: 4 publicae proposita. Praeside Laurentio Arturo Faunteo. 4°. *Posnaniae, ex typographia Ioannis Vuolrabi*, 1583. C.; KR.KR².PR.PR².UP.WR².

413 **Fay, Francis.** Martyrium Rmi. D. F. Cornelii Douenii, Dunensis et Connerensis Episcopi, ex Seraphica D. Francisci Reg. Obseruant. familia assumpti, et R. D. Patritii Luchrani, presbyteri Dublinii in Hybernia, sub Arthuro Chichestriensi Prorege anno M.D.CXII. 1 Februarii Dublini faeliciter consummatum. 4°. *Coloniae Agrippinae, excudebat Arnoldus Kempensis*, 1614. L.; HA.PA³.RO³.STG.VT.

Anon. For the identification of the author and for the sources used by him, *see RH*, Oct. 1985, pp. 358–61. *See also Collectanea Hibernica*, vol. 26, 1984, pp. 13–19.

Fen, John.† Concertatio ecclesiae catholicae, 1583 [*etc.*] *See* nos. 524–7.
—[*translations by him.*] *See* no. 415.
Ferrall, Francis. Sententia diui Augustini ... de gratia, 1627. *See* no. 81.

414 **Ferrall, James.** [*Begin.*] Reuerendissimo Patri Fr. Ioanni Baptistae a Campanea totius ordinis Minorum Ministro Generali ... Iacobus Ferallus Collegii S. Isidori alumnus. Humili dicat obsequio. Conclusiones theologicae ... [*End.*] Disputabuntur publice in Collegio S. Isidori ... Praesidente Reu. P. Fr. Francisco a S. Maria [F. Tully] ... 1633. Mense Februarii. *s.sh.fol. Romae, ex typographia Ludouici Grignani*, 1634. RO².

A programme announcing the forthcoming defence of his thesis. Text and part of the setting are the same as in nos. 84, 128, 271.

Fidelis Annosus, *Verementanus, pseud. See* Floyd, J. (nos. 492–4).
Fierbertus, Nicolaus. *See* Fitzherbert, N.
Filchius, Gulielmus. *See* Fitch, W.
Fischerus, Joannes. *See* Fisher, J.

Fisher, John, *Saint, Cardinal, Bishop of Rochester.*††

COLLECTIONS

415 —R. P. D. Ioannis Fischerii ... opera, quae hactenus inueniri potuerunt omnia. Fol. *Wirceburgi, apud Georgium Fleischmannum*, 1597. L.O.C.; BAR.².D.DI.DUR(2).HP.L².LGE.MD³.PA.PA⁴.VT.WO. + +

This collection includes Latin translations, some by John Fen, of works written by Fisher in English.

SINGLE WORKS

Assertionis Lutheranae Confutatio

416 —Assertionis Lutheranae confutatio. 8°. *Coloniae, apud Maternum Cholinum*, 1558. C.KN.OS.PA.VI. *This or no. 417 :* PR.
First published in 1523.

417 —[Titlepage variant.] *Coloniae, apud haeredes Arnoldi Birckmanni*, 1558. O.; C⁵.CHA.CHI.DI.RO². *See also note to no. 416.*
With Birckmann's device above the imprint. Forms part of a shared ed. with no. 416.

418 —[Date variant of no. 416.] *Coloniae, apud Maternum Cholinum*, 1559. D.L².NP.X. *This or no. 419 :* TB.

419 —[Date variant of no. 417.] *Coloniae, apud haeredes Arnoldi Birckmanni*, 1559. C.; C⁵.D.E.GAES.MD.

420 —[Anr. ed.] 8°, *Coloniae, apud Maternum Cholinum*, 1564. L.; BEU.C⁵. C⁹.DI.F.GAES.ILL.MD.P.PA.TB.TRO.

421 —[Titlepage variant.] *Coloniae, apud haeredes Arnoldi Birckmanni*, 1564. O.; ANT².C¹⁶.DE..F.FU².GT.HER.L¹³.MD.O²⁷.R.W.X.
With Birckmann's device above the imprint. Forms part of a shared ed. with no. 420.

Assertionum Regis Angliae . . . Defensio

—Assertionum Regis Angliae . . . defensio, 1562. *In :* no. 665.

422 —[*German transl. of chapter 11.*] Vom Vrteil des gemaeynen Volcks. Dass nicht die Gemeynde, oder die Laeien, sondern die Vaetter vn̄ vorsteher Christlicher Kyrchē, von der Glauben laehre vn̄ Religions sachē zu vrteilen . . . macht haben . . . verdeutschet durch Georg. Wiceliū den jungern. 8°. *Zu Coeln durch die Erben Johan Quentels vnd Gerwinum Calenium*, 1561. BER.HAN.[*L.]

Biblisch Betbüchlein

—*See* no. 431.

Breve Trattato . . . del Modo di pregare Iddio

—*See* nos. 439–40.

Christliche und andechtige Gebet und Psalmen

—*See* no. 432.

De orando Deum

—*See* Tractatus de orando Deum.

Devot(e) Psalmen

—*See* nos. 428–9.

Guldin Fewerzeug

—*See* no. 433.

Psalmen oder schoene Gebet

—*See* no. 430.

Psalmi seu Precationes

423 —Psalmi seu precationes . . . Item: Psalmi aliquot selecti ex Dauide. 24°. *Coloniae, apud haeredes Arnoldi Birckmanni*, 1561. C.; MIN.PA.
First published *c.* 1525.

424   —[Anr. ed.] 24°. *Coloniae, apud haeredes Arnoldi Birckmanni*, 1568. L².
       For an edition printed in London in this year *see* STC 2995a.

425   —[Anr. ed.] 24°. *Coloniae, excudebat Petrus Ho[rst]*, 156[ ]. JS.(*t.p. mutil.*).
       In the only known copy the last three letters of the printer's name
       and the last digit of the date are torn away. For Horst *see* Benzing,
       p. 242, no. 44.

426   —[Anr. ed.] Psalmi, seu precationes . . . Accessit Imploratio diuini
       auxilii contra tentationem ex psalmis Dauidis, per Th. Morum. 16°.
       Lugduni, apud Sebastianum Gryphium, 1572. L(*2 : 1 imp.*); C².C³.(2).
       C⁸.DMR.ELY.L.¹⁵.NM².P.VAL.
       More's 'Imploratio' is here added to the contents for the first time.
       Imprint false; *pr.* [London, Thomas Vautrollier.] STC 2995a.2.

427   —[Anr. ed. of no. 426.] 16°. *Lugduni, apud Sebastianum Gryphium*, 1598.
       C⁵.HART.[*DMR.]
       Imprint false; *pr.* [London, Thomas Creede for Gabriel Cawood.]
       STC 2995a.3.

428   —[*Flemish transl.*] Deuot psalmen oft ghebeden . . . Met een deuote
       wtlegginge op dat Vader onse. Met noch een schoone vermaninghe
       Ioannis Chrysostomi om God te bidden. Ouergeset wt den Latine in
       Duytsch door H. Antonium van Hemert, Regulier by Eyndouen. 12°.
       T'Antwerpen, by Christoffel Plantin, 1583. SHT².[*DMR.]

429   —[*A different Flemish transl.*] Deuote Psalmen . . . met andere schoone
       ghebeden vergadert door Franc. Sweertium Antwerp. 16°. *t'Ant-
       werpen, by Guilliam Verdussen*, 1622. ANT².
       The titlepage is engraved.

430   —[*German transl.*] Psalmen, oder schoene Gebet, in Latein aussgangen
       . . . Jetzund durch einen Catholischen guethertzigen Priester . . .
       verdeutscht. 12°. 1559. [Coloph.] *Dilingen, durch Sebaldum Mayer.*
       MU(*imp.*)[*O.]

431   —[*A different German transl.*] Biblisch betbüchlein Joannis Roffensis.
       Darinnen die fuernemsten Trost vnd Heuptsprueh, inn Psalmsweise
       zusammen getragen sind, verdeutscht durch Valen. Winsheim
       Pfarherrn zu Dennstat. *Leipzig, n.d.* [1564.] [Coloph.] *Bey M. Ernesto
       Voegelin.* DRE.HD.VT.
       A non-Catholic version. The preface is dated from Denstedt, St.
       John the Baptist's day, 1564.

432   —[*A different German transl.*] Christliche vnd andechtige Gebet vnd
       Psalmen . . . aus dem Latein ins deutsche versetzet, vnd mit etlichen
       andechtigen gebetlein vermehret. *Gedruckt zu Dantzigk, bey Iacobo
       Rhodo*, 1597. [Coloph.] *In Verlegung Balthasaris Andreae.*
       Not seen. Description from Estreicher, Bd. 16, pp. 229–30, who
       cites a copy at WA.

433   —[*A different German transl.*] Guldin Fewerzeug: Christlicher Lieb
       vnnd Andacht . . . auff ein newes widerumb mit Fleiss corrigiert,
       gemehrt und gebessert in Truck geben. 12°. *Ingolstadt, bey Wilhelm
       Eder*, 1623. DI.[*O.]
       A Catholic translation. The foreword is headed: 'Vorred Christian
       Fu[ ]n Pfarrherrn S. Quintin zu Mayntz, ersten Dolmetschern
       dess guldin Fewerzeugs'. No copy of any earlier edition of this
       translation has been found.

Sacri Sacerdotii Defensio

434   —Sacri sacerdotii defensio contra Lutherum . . . Addita est epistola
       Diui Cypriani ad Cornelium fratrem. 16°. *Parisiis, apud Michaelem
       Iulianum*, 1562. L.O.; E.L²⁵.LOU³.MU.N.PA.PA².PA⁴.R.SAL.VT.
       First published in 1525.

Tractatus de Orando Deum

435 —Tractatus de orando Deum, et de fructibus precum, modoq; orandi, nunquam antehac Latine editus. 16°. *Duaci, ex officina Ioannis Bogardi,* 1567 [1576]. AMS.C³.LIL².

The date in the imprint is misprinted; the correct date is given in the approbation. With a dedicatory apistle signed by Richard Hall and dated from Marchiennes College at Douai, 16 December 1575. For editions in English *see* STC 10888–90 and A&R 305.

436 —[Anr. ed.] Ioannis Roffensis . . . Tractatus de orando Deum, & de fructibus precum, modoq. orandi. 16°. *Romae, apud Franciscum Zannettum,* 1578. FLO.RO³.RO⁴.VT.

A reprint of no. 435 including Hall's dedication.

437 —(Anr. ed.) 24°. *Placentie, — Bazachius,* 1593. MIL² (*missing 1976*).

Not seen. Description from MIL² card catalogue.

438 —[Anr. ed.] Reumi. D. D. Ioan. Fisheri . . . De orando Deum, & de fructibus precum, modoque orandi. 12°. *Iuxta exemplar Romae impressum. Pariisis, apud Nicolaum & Ioannem de la Coste,* 1631. C⁵.KN². PA.VAL.

439 —[*Italian transl.*] Breue trattato . . . Del modo di pregare Iddio, e de'frutti che si cauano dall'oratione. 12°. *Ex officina Horatii Saluiani. In Napoli, Appresso Gio. Giacomo Carlino, & Antonio Pace,* 1592. RO⁴(S. Borr. I. III. 28.)

Not seen. Description from Manzi (no. 173) who records the above copy.

440 —[Anr. ed.? or a different transl.?] Breue trattato . . . del modo di pregare Iddio, e de'frutti che si cauano dall'oratione. Tradotto dalla lingua latina nella italiana, da Antonio Massa. 16°. *Venetia, appresso Bartholomeo Carampello,* 1593. VI.

Vom Urteil des Gemaeynen Volcks

—*See* no. 422.

MISTAKEN ATTRIBUTION

—Expositio breuis dictorum selectorum ex libris Veteris Testamenti, 1598.

This Protestant work, published under the pseudonym 'Piscator' is sometimes mistakenly attributed to Fisher. It has no place in this catalogue.

APPENDIX

—[For an account of the martyrdom of Fisher.] *See* nos. 235–6, 1455.

Fitch, William, *in religion* Benet of Canfield.†

LE CHEVALIER CHRESTIEN

441 —Le cheualier chrestien contentant vn dialogue entre vn chrestien & vn payen, diuisé en deux parties. 8°. *Rouen, chez Iean Osmont,* 1609. L.; PA(2). *This or no. 442* : N(*imp.*).NM²(*imp.*).PA⁹(*imp.*).

Written by the author in French. The Privilege states that the Paris publisher Charles Chastellain who owned the rights to the book made over half of them to Jean Osmont at Rouen. It was printed at Rouen, as the typography reveals, and the printing was completed on 28 July 1609 (*see* sig. a8ᵛ).

442 —[Imprint variant.] *Paris, chez Charles Chastellain,* 1609. O.C.; DUS. L²⁶.TRO.VER. *See also no. 441.*

Forms part of a shared edition with no. 441 with which it is identical except for the imprint.

REGLE DE PERFECTION

Fitch wrote pts. 1 and 2 in English and then translated them into French. For editions of the English *see* A&R 306–8. He wrote pt. 3 in French. For a modern edition of the whole work, *see* Jean Orcibal, *Benoît de Canfield, La règle de perfection. The rule of perfection*, Paris, 1982.

French

443   —Reigle de perfection, contenant vn bref & lucide abregé de toute la vie spirituelle ... diuisée en trois parties. 8°. *Paris, chez Charles Chastellain*, 1609. ANT³.PA.
In spite of the wording of the title this edition contains only pts. 1 & 2 of the *Règle*. These are followed by two minor works by the author: 'Lettre contenant la response à vn doute touchant l'obiect de la volonté de Dieu' and 'Coppie d'vn aduis donné touchant l'oraison.' With two engravings. Optat 6.

444   —[Anr. ed.] 32°. *Arras, de l'imprimerie de Guillaume de la Riuiere*, 1609. ANT³.AR(*imp.*).
A reprint of no. 443. Without the engravings. Optat 7.

445   —[Anr. ed., with the addition of pt. 3.] Troisiesme edition. 24°. *Paris, chez Charles Chastellain*, 1609. TRO. *Copy reported but not seen:* FRI.
Pt. 3, which appears to have been added to this edition without authorisation, contains some passages omitted in the revised version at no. 446 and lacks others that were added in no. 446. *See* Orcibal, pp. 19–20. Optat 8.

446   —[Anr. ed.] Cinquiesme edition reueue & corrigée par l'Autheur, des fautes eschappées aux autres impressions. 8°. *Paris, chez Charles Chastellain*, 1610. PA.
Containing all three parts. Published by the Author at the bidding of his superiors. Pt. 3 has been revised and corrected: it now includes 'Traité de la Passion' (forming ch. 16–20) which was not included in no. 445. *See* Orcibal, pp. 19–20. With the two engravings. Optat 9. No edition claiming to be the fourth has yet been found.

447.   —[Anr. ed., with additions.] Augmentée en ceste sixiesme edition de sa miraculeuse conuersion, & vn sommaire discours de son heureuse vie & mort, plus vne sienne methode & addresse de l'oraison, auec vne lettre qu'autrefois il a escrit au Pere Ange de Ioyeuse. 12°. *Paris, chez Charles Chastellain*, 1614. AD.LOU³.PA⁹. (*t.p.* only). SMI.USH. *Copy reported but not seen:* FRI.
Containing all three parts of the *Règle*. This posthumous edition contains some alterations to pt. 3. The account of the Author's conversion is by Fitch himself: it has a short biographical introduction by 'le Sieur de Nantilly' who has not, apparently, been identified. *See also* no. 466.1. Optat 10.

448   —[Anr. ed.] Septiesme edition. 12°. *Paris, chez la veufue Charles Chastellain*, 1622. ANT³.NM².PA⁹.RO⁴.RO⁷. *Copy reported but not seen:* FRI.
A reprint of no. 447. The titlepage of pt. 3 of the *Règle* (sig. M3ʳ) bears the date 1621 in the imprint. Optat 11.

449   —[Anr. ed.] Spetiesme [*sic*] edition. 12°. *Paris, chez la vefue Charles Chastellain*, 1627. CHAM.TI.
Not, in fact, the seventh edition (for which *see* no. 448), but a reprint of it. The titlepage of pt. 3 bears the date 1626 in the imprint. Optat 12.

450   —[Date variant?] 1628. Copy reported by Optat (13) at PA⁹. Not found there in 1976.

451   —[Anr. ed.] 12°. *Douay, chez Gerard Pinchon*, 1632. CHA.DOU.

A reprint of no. 446. It does not include the additions of nos. 447–9. Optat 14.

452 —[Anr. ed.] Spetiesme [*sic*] edition. 12°. *Paris, chez Charles Chastellain*, 1633. L^{26}.PA.PA^3.

A reprint of no. 449. The titlepage of pt. 3 bears the date 1626 in the imprint. Optat 15.

453 —[Anr. ed.] *Paris, chez Charles Chastellain*, 1636. *Copies reported but not seen:* MONT.OR^2.

Description from Optat 16. A reprint of no. 452?

Latin

454 —Regula perfectionis, continens breue & lucidum compendium totius vitae spiritualis . . . in tres partes diuisae . . . Gallice primum & Anglice composita, postmodum . . . typis . . . Latine mandata. 8°. *Parisiis, apud Carolum Chastellain*, 1610. AMP(*imp.*).ASC.L^{26}.PA.PA^8 (*v.imp.*).PBN.RO^6.SBG^2.SPS.X.

Containing all three parts. A translation made from the French edition of 1610 (no. 446). Optat 26.

455 —[Anr. ed.] R. P. F. Benedicti Angli de Canfeld . . . Regula perfectionis. 18°. *Coloniae, apud Ioannem Crithium*, 1610. L.C.; ANT^3.CHA.DUR.KN. L^4.LOU^3.MU.O^7.O^{41}.PA^9.RO^6.SAL.TB.WO. +

A reprint of no. 454. Optat 27.

456 —[Anr. ed.] Regula perfectionis. 12°. *Romae, apud haeredem Bartholomaei Zannetti*. 1625. CAV.DE.L^{26}.RO^4.RO^7.TAG.

A reprint of no. 454. Optat 28.

456.1 —[Anr. ed.] *Romae, apud haeredem Bartholomaei Zannetti*, 1628.

Not found. Description from Optat 29 citing Bernardus a Bononia, *Bibliotheca Scriptorum*, p. 40.

457 —[Anr. ed.] 8°. *Duaci, ex officina Gerardi Pinchon*, 1630. AMP.BRS.ELY. L^{35}.

A reprint of no. 454. Optat 30.

Flemish

458 —Den reghel der volmaecktheyt. Inhoudende een cort begrijp van het gheheel gheestelijck leuen, besloten in dit punt alleen van den wille Godts. Ghedeelt in drij deelen. 12°. *t'Hantwerpen, by Guilliam Lesteens*, 1622. AMS^2.ANT^3(2).MAA.NI.SHT.STR(*imp.*).

Pts. 1 & 2 only. Translated from the Latin version of 1610 (no. 454). Optat 43.

459 —[Anr. issue?] *Men vintse te coope tot Dendermonde, by Joos van Langhenhove, n.d.* [1622.]

Not found. A copy formerly at SHT (pressmark: 098 248 ben C) is described in *Franciscaansch Leven*, Helmond, 1934, pp. 459–60. This collection is now at TI but the book is missing. The catalogue slip for it gives some details that suggest that it is another issue of no. 458 rather than a new edition. It presumably predates the enlarged Antwerp edition of 1623 (no. 460). Not in Optat.

460 —[Anr. ed., with the addition of pt. 3.] Den tweeden druck, van nieuws ouersien ende verbetert. 12°. *tot Antwerpen, by Guillam Lesteens*, 1623. [Coloph.] *wt de druckerye van Hieronymus Verdussen.* L.; ANT. ANT^3(2).CHA.FRA.LOU.NI.TI(2).STR.

A reprint of no. 458 with the addition of pt. 3 which is also translated from the Latin version of 1610 (no. 454). Some copies have the table to pts. 1 & 2 in a different typesetting from others. Optat 44.

461 —[Anr. ed.] Den derden druck, van nieus ouersien ende verbetert. 12°.

tot Antwerpen, by Guilliam Lesteens, 1631. ANT.ANT².ANT³(2).NI.
SHT.STR(2).TI(2).UT².
Containing all three parts. A reprint of no. 460. Optat 45.

German

462   —Regel der Vollkommenheit, &c. Erster Theyl: welcher die Vollkommenheit dess wuercklichen Lebens, auff ein einigen Puncten dess
Goettlichen willens gestellt, in sich begreift. 12°. *Ingolstatt, bey Wilhelm Eder*, 1625. MU.[*O.]
      A translation of pt. 1 only, made from the Latin version of 1610
(no. 454). Without the minor works. Not in Optat.

463   —[Anr. ed.] 12°. *n.p.*, 1627. MU.[*O.]
      Pt. 1 only. A close reprint of no. 462. *Pr.* [Ingolstadt, Wilhelm
Eder?] Not in Optat.

464   —[Anr. ed.] Regel der Volkommenheit, oder Kurtz begriff dess wuercklichen Geistlichen Lebens, auff ein einigen Puncten dess Goettlichen
willens gestellet. 12°. *Coelln, durch Ioannem Kinckium*, 1633. GAES
(*destroyed*).MU.[*O.]
      Pt. 1 only. A reprint of nos. 462–3. Optat 47.

Italian

465   —Regola di perfettione, laquale contiene vn breue, & chiaro compendio
di tutta la vita spirituale ridotta ad vn solo punto della diuina volontà,
& diuisa in tre parti. 12°. *Venetia, presso Marco Guarisco*, 1616. L.;
FLO.RO³.RO⁷.SALZ.
      This translation follows the Latin of 1610 (no. 454) but omits pt. 3
except for the chapters on the Passion (here numbered 1–5 but in
the Latin 16–20). It also omits the minor works published with the
Latin. Optat 39.

Spanish

466   —Regla de perfecion reducida al punto vnico de la volundad de Dios
... Traducida en Español y dedicada a la Serenissᵃ Sᵃ Infanta Sor
Margarita de la Cruz. Por el D. Bartolome Leonardo de Argẽsola.
12°. *Çaragoça, por Iuan de Lanaja*, 1629. PR².[*L.]
      A translation of all three parts made from the Latin version of 1610
(no. 454) but omitting the minor works. Margarita de la Cruz,
daughter of the Empress Maria of Austria and niece of Philip II of
Spain, was a Carmelite nun of the royal convent at Madrid; the
translator had been chaplain to her mother. *See Enciclopedia Universal*, tom. 30, pp. 6–11. The book was suppressed by order of the
Spanish Inquisition (*Novissimus librorum prohibitorum ... index*,
Madrid, 1640, p. 115). No copy found by Optat.

VERITABLE ET MIRACULEUSE CONVERSION

466.1   —Veritable et miraculeuse conuersion du R. P. Benoist de Canfeld ...
Plus vn Eloge ou sommaire discours de son heureuse vie & mort, auec
vne sienne methode & addresse de l'Oraison, & vne lettre qu'autrefois
il a escrit au deffunct P. Ange de Ioyeuse. Par le sieur de Nantilly.
12°. *n.p.d.* [*after* 1614.] L(4902.aa.26).
      See note to no. 447. Nantilly is the editor. Collation: a–h¹²i⁶ (i6
blank), pp. 204. The absence of imprint and date, together with
the use of a lower-case register in the collation, indicates that it was
not issued separately but forms part of an edition of the *Règle*. The
edition has not been identified.

APPENDIX

467 —Brousse, J. La vie du reuerend pere, P. Ange de Ioyeuse, predicateur Capucin, autrefois duc, pair, et mareschal de France ... Ensemble les vies des RR. PP. P. Benoist Anglois, & P. Archange Escossois, du mesme ordre. 8°. *Paris, chez Adrian Taupinart*, 1621. O.; AV(-*t.p.*). CHA(*imp., wanting the lives of P. Benoist and P. Archange*).HNC(-*t.p. The second t.p., introducing the lives of P. Benoist and P. Archange is that of no. 468*). NCY.O⁶.PA.

Only the lives of P. Benoist [W. Fitch] and P. Archange [J. Forbes] concern this catalogue. Collation: π^8 A–Vv⁸Xx²A–T^8. With a quadrifolium signed 2Dd⁴ [*sic*] containing a table to the life of P. Ange de Joyeuse and titlepage and preliminaries to the lives of P. Benoist and P. Archange inserted between sig. Dd6 and Dd7. The titlepage to these last two lives reads: 'La vie, conuersion, et conuersation miraculeuse du reuerend Pere P. Benoist Anglois ... Ensemble celle du R.P. Archange, Escossois ... composée en Latin par le R.P. Faustinus de Diest ... Traduite en nostre langue, & augmentée ... Le tout par M. Iacques Brousse'. This titlepage bears the same imprint and date as the main titlepage. For the Latin original of the life of P. Archange *see* nos. 502–4. An English translation of all three lives, made from the French, is at A&R 170.

468 —[Anr. issue of the lives of P. Benoist and P. Archange, with a cancel title.] *Paris, chez Louis Boulenger*, 1621. AIX.CHA.PA². *See also no 467.* The sheets of no. 467 from sig. 2Dd2 onwards, except that the original title for these two lives (2Dd2) has been replaced. Except for the imprint, the wording of the cancel title is the same as that of the title it replaces.

469 **Fitzgerald, James.** [*A disputation in which he acted as Praeses.*] Nierowny, D. and Glebhoffmann, S. D.O.M.A. Conclusiones theologicae, de sacramentis in genere, baptismo & confirmatione in specie ad mentem Doctoris Subtilis ... Praeside Fr. Iacobo Geraldino studii theologici Conuentus S. Hieronymi Viennae lectore ordinario. *s.sh.*fol. *Viennae*, [   ], 1640, RO⁸(*imprint partly torn away*).

470 **Fitzgerald, James FitzMaurice.** Edictum Illustrissimi Domini Iacobi Geraldini, de iustitia eius belli, quod in Hybernia pro fide gerit. *s.sh.*fol. *n.p.d.* [1579?]. L².(Carew MSS, 607, f. 41).[*L.*DMR.] Probably printed in [Spain or Portugal] shortly before FitzGerald's expedition to Ireland set sail in June 1579. The expedition is represented as a Catholic crusade. *See* M. V. Ronan, *The Reformation in Ireland*, 1930, p. 560. *pr.* [Lisbon?]

471 —[*Appendix.*] Gregory XIII, *Pope*. Copia Breuis Sanctissimi Domini nostri Gregorii Papae XIII super facultate concessa Iacobo Geraldino ... gerendi bellum aduersus Elisabetham praetensam Angliae Reginam, in fidei Catholicae fauorem. *s.sh.*fol. *n.p.d.* [1579?] L.(Lansdowne MSS, 96, no. 53.)[*L.*DMR.] *Pr.* [Lisbon, Antonio Ribeiro]. Probably printed shortly before the expedition set sail (*see* note to no. 470).

472 **Fitzgerald, William.** Le psaultier de Iesus. Contenant de tres deuotes prieres et pretitions reueues, corrigées, et amplifiées, auec embellissement des figures. 12°. *Paris, chez Rolin Thierry*, 1600. LIL².VER. In addition to the psalter, the collection includes 'Letanies de Iesus', 'Exercise du Matin', 'Exercise du Soir', and a paraphrase in French verse of the 'Libera me, Domine'. *Ded.* to the Princess Louise de Lorraine sgd.: 'Vostre tres-humble & affectionné Orateur, G. FitzGerald Prestre'. In Nov. 1593 the widow of John Fowler was licensed to print at Douai 'Plusieurs dévotes pétitions

communément appellées *le psaultier de Iesus* nouvellement traduit [*sic*] de l'anglois en françois'. Titlepage engraved, and with 15 other engravings. For editions of the *Jesus Psalter* in English *see* A&R 413–19.

473   —[Anr. ed., abridged, with title:] Certaines deuotes et pieuses petitions communiment appelés [*sic*] le psaultier de Iesus. 12°. *Douay, chez Pierre Borremans*, 1605. [Coloph.] *De l'imprimerie de la vefue Ia. Boscard, aux depēs de Pierre Borremans.* LIL².

       Omitting the author's dedication and the paraphrase of the 'Libera me, Domine'. With engravings (including the titlepage) crudely copied from no. 472. Pérennès (II. 70) cites what may be an imprint variant (*Douai, Iac-Boscard*, 1605) but gives no location. Approbations given at Paris, 1596 and 1598 are here reprinted.

474   —[Anr. ed., with title as in no. 472.] 12° *Liege, chez Christian Ouuerx*, 1623. LGE.

       The titlepage is not engraved.

475   **Fitzherbert, Nicholas.**‡ Nicolai Fierberti, Oxoniensis in Anglia Academiae descriptio. 8°. *Romae, apud Guglielmum Facciottum*, 1602. L(3).O(3).C.; BM².C².D.D².DE.E.HP.L².PA.PA⁴(2).RO⁵.ST.VT. +

       Containing some material on ecclesiastical history.

476   —Nicolai Fizerberti de antiquitate & continuatione Catholicae religionis in Anglia, & de Alani cardinalis vita libellus. 8°. *Romae, apud Guillelmum Facciottum*, 1608. L(4).O(3).C.; D.DE.E.GTN.HP.PA.PA⁴(2).RO.RO². ST.USH.VT. + +

477   **Fitzherbert, Thomas.**† An sit vtilitas in scelere vel de infelicitate principis Macchiauelliani, contra Macchiauellum & politicos eius sectatores. 8°. *Romae, apud Gulielmum Facciottum*, 1610. L.O(2).; BG.D. DUR.FLO.GTN.MD.OS.PA.RO²(2).RO⁶.USH.VT.W. +

       A veiled attack on the anti-Catholic policies of the English government.

478   **Fitzsimon, Henry.**†‡ Britannomachia ministrorum, in plerisque et fidei fundamentis, et fidei articulis dissidentium. 4°. *Duaci, ex officina Baltazaris Belleri*, 1614. D¹⁰. (*sig. A2.3 crossed through in MS for cancellation but not replaced.*)

       Collation: A–Aaa⁴Ccc² (Ccc2 errata); Bbb is omitted from the register. The bifolium A2.3 contains a prefatory letter from Fitz-Simon to the Jesuit General, Claudio Acquaviva, beginning: 'Dedisti ad me literas, Magnae Pater . . .' In some copies of this and no. 479 the IHS device on the titlepage is engraved, with the caption 'Laudabile Nomen Domini'; in some others it is a woodcut, of different design, without a caption; in yet others it is a woodcut, of different design again, without a caption. Apart from the device, the titlepages show no differences of setting. Pp. 303, *et seq.* contain an 'Appendix de ordinatione ministrorum' attacking STC 17597. *Britannomachia* is answered in STC 13540, 17598, 20914a. *See* Mil., vol. 2, pp. 172, *et seq.*

479   —[Anr. issue.] *Duaci, ex officina Baltazaris Belleri*, 1614. L(3).O.C(2).; BAR³.C².D(2).HA.HD.HP.L².L⁴.MTH(2).PA.ST.YK. *This or no. 478 :* BRS. C³.D⁶.KN.RO.RO².TB.VT. + +

       The sheets of no. 478 but with the bifolium A2.3 cancelled and replaced by a quadrifolium signed A⁴ containing an expanded version of the same letter to Acquaviva now beginning: 'Dedisti ad me, Optime Pater . . .'. The first gathering now collates: A⁴(—A2.3 +²A⁴). In some copies the cancelland A2.3 has not been removed, and in some sig. A4 containing the beginning of the epistle 'Christiano Lectori' is also a cancel.

480   —Catalogus praecipuorum sanctorum Hiberniae recognitus & auctus. Per R. P. Henr. Fitz-Simon. 8°. [Coloph.] *Leodii, typis Ioannis Ouv-*

verx, 1619. LGE². (*cited by Theux col. 69, but now missing*).
Not found. Description from the reprint in no. 396.1. This catalogue was adapted and enlarged by FitzSimon from an unpublished
list by [Richard Fleming]; *see* Rothe's statement in no. 955, p. 21.
Editions earlier than 1619 cited by McNeill (p. 28) and others have
not been found.

—[Anr. ed.] 1621. A reprint of no. 480 with the original Liège colophon
and date 1619 unaltered. *In* no. 396.1.

—[Anr. ed., abridged, with title:] Catalogus aliquorum sanctorum
Iberniae, 1621. *In* no. 864.
An Antwerp edition of 1627 cited by Sommervogel (tom. 3, col.
766) has not been found.

Fleming, Patrick. [*A disputation in which he acted as Praeses.*] Baron, B.
. . . Conclusiones philosophicae, 1630. *See* no. 82.

Fleming, Richard. [An unpublished catalogue of Irish saints.] *See*
no. 480.

Florus, Carolus. *See* Waldegrave, C., *alias* Flower.

Flower, Charles, *alias. See* Waldegrave, C.

Floyd, John.†

Single Works

481 —Apologia Sanctae Sedis Apostolicae quoad modum procedendi circa
regimen Catholicorum Angliae tempore persecutionis cum defensione religiosi status. Authore Daniele a Iesu . . . Ex Anglico in
Latinum fideliter conuersa. Cui accessit Epistola ad . . . Galliae
episcopos, qui de eodem libro censuram tulerunt. 8°. *Coloniae, sumptibus Symonis Fabritii,* 1631. L(2).O.C.; D.PA.PA³.PA⁴(2).RO².WO.
Daniel a Iesu, *pseud.* Imprint fictitious; *pr.* [Rouen, Nicolas
Courant.] A translation of A&R 322, with the addition of the 'Epistola' which answers no. 1405 of this catalogue. The 'Epistola' is
signed: G. W. Euulgator [George Wright], for whom *see* also nos.
1400–4. For the controversy of which this work (together with
nos. 484–5, 488–9) forms part, *see* RH, Oct. 1987, pp. 329, *et seq.*

482 —[Anr. issue.] *Rothomagi, typis Nicolai Courant,* 1631. A.G².L⁴.L²⁶.
The sheets of no. 481 except for the title and conjugate leaf which
are reprinted, and with the addition of an unsigned leaf at the end
bearing a new approbation.

483 —[Anr. ed., corrected and enlarged.] Editio altera emendatior. Cui
praefixa est Admonitio ad lectorem admodū R. Domini Hermanni
Loemelii. 8°. *Audomaropoli, typis Georgii Seutin,* 1631. O.; AMI.D.D².
HP.L².L⁴.L²⁶.N.
Daniel a Iesu, *pseud.* With the 'Epistola', signed as before. The
'Admonitio ad Lectorem', here printed for the first time, is by
[Floyd] using the pseudonym Hermannus Loemelius which he also
uses in nos. 485, 486, 488–91.

484 —Censura symboli apostolorum ad instar nuperrimae Censurae quarundam propositionum, ex duobus libris, anglicano idiomate conscriptis, excerptarum, Parisiis latae. 4° (a bifolium). *n.p.d.* [1631.]
HP.PA³. *This or no. 484.1 :* MD².VAL.
Anon. A mock censure of articles of the Apostles' Creed, parodying
the method used by the Sorbonne in its censure (no. 684) of works
by Floyd and Wilson. Floyd adumbrates it in a passage in no. 488
and defends it, along with his other works in the controversy, in
no. 485. This edition can be distinguished from no. 484.1 by the
last line of sig. Al^r which here ends '. . . Trinitati communes'. The
text was included in a work by [Caspar Schoppe] attacking the
Jesuits, *Societatis Iesu nouum fidei symbolum,* 1636.

484.1   —[Anr. ed.] 4° (a bifolium). *n.p.d.* [1631.] L(E.236/32).C.; O¹². [*DMR.]
This edition can be distinguished from no. 484 by the last line of
sig. Al^r which here ends: '. . . est impia blasphe—'. The L. copy is
bound with the Thomason Tracts for 1642 but bears no date in
MS by Thomason, and the typography is earlier than that of the
other tracts in the volume. [Printed abroad?] On 14 June 1631,
Richard Smith, Bishop of Chalcedon, reported from London to the
Cardinals of Propaganda that the Jesuits had arranged to have the
work publicly sold by the heretics in England, but his letter does
not say where it was printed. *See* RH, Oct. 1987, pp. 374–5, 399,
n. 139.

485   —Defensio decreti Sacrae Congregationis . . . ad Indicem . . . pro sup-
pressione librorum quorumcumq. vtriusq. partis in controuersia Rmi.
Episcopi Chalcedonensis; dati Romae XIX. Martii Anno 1633. Qua
contumax eiusdem sacri decreti Disquisitio refutatur. Per Hermannum
Loemelium. 8°. *Coloniae,* 1634. O¹⁸(-N4).PA(-N4).USH.
Hermannus Loemelius, *pseud.* Alegambe (p. 242) cites this as a
work by Floyd. Imprint false; *pr.* [S. Omer?] The approbation on
sig. N4^r is dated from S. Omer, 24 Jan. 1634. For the decree of the
Index, *see* no. 1103. For the 'Disquisitio' criticising it, *see* no. 1102.
The final quire (o⁴) contains an 'Epilogus' in which [Floyd] names
and describes some works of his own which the decree of the Index
has prevented him from publishing.

486   —[Anr. issue, with additions.] *Coloniae,* 1634. O.; C².PA⁴.
The sheets of no. 485 unaltered, but with the addition at the end
of a quire (P⁸) containing the text of the decree of the Index and of
the 'Disquisitio'.

487   —Deus et Rex siue dialogus, in quo agitur de fidelitate . . . Iacobo Regi
in regnis suis praestanda. 12. *Coloniae, sumptibus Authoris,* 1619. O.C.;
A.AIX.D(2).HP.KN².L²⁵(2).PA⁶.SBG.ST(3).VAL(2).VER.VT.
Anon. By [Floyd, probably in collaboration with Joseph Creswell].
A translation [by Henry More] of A&R 325, though the English was
not published till 1620. *See* RH, Nov. 1979, p. 95. Answering STC
14415. Imprint false; *pr.* [in the Spanish Netherlands.]

488   —Ecclesiae Anglicanae querimonia apologetica de censura aliquot epis-
coporum Galliae, in duos libros Anglicanos. &c. Authore Hermanno
Loemelio. 4°. *Audomaropoli, typis Georgii Seutin,* 1631. O.; DUR.HP.
L²⁶.O⁵.O¹².VAL.
Hermannus Loemelius, *pseud.* Answers no. 1405. *Pr.* by Seutin [at
the English College press]. Reprinted in no. 491.

489   —Hermanni Loemelii . . . Spongia, qua diluuntur calumniae nomine
facultatis Parisiensis impositae libro qui inscribitur, Apologia sanctae
sedis apostolicae. 4°. *Audomaropoli, apud Georgium Seutin,* 1631.MD.
Hermannus Loemelius, *pseud.* Answers part of no. 684. Floyd's
authorship is attested by Alegambe (p. 242) and also by a MS note
in a copy of no. 490 at USH once in the library of the English College,
S. Omer. Collation: *⁴**²A–R⁴S² (S2 errata).

490   —[Anr. issue, with an addition.] *Audomaropoli, apud Georgium Seutin,*
1631. L.O.C.; AMP.L²⁶.LGE³.PA².USH(2).VAL. *This or no. 489* : PA⁴.UT.VT.
A reissue of the sheets of no. 489 except for the errata leaf (S2)
which has been cancelled and replaced with four new quires
(T-X⁴Y²) containing 'Parathesis circa duo breuia apostolica ad
Rmum Episcopum Chalcedonensem' and with a new errata list
(unsigned) covering both works. The 'Parathesis' includes an
answer to no. 1088. In some copies the cancelland S2 has not been
removed.

491   —[Anr. ed., with anr. ed. of no. 488.] Hermanni Loemelii . . . Spongia
. . . Nec non, Ecclesiae Anglicanae querimonia. 8°. 2 pts. *Audomaro-*

poli, apud viduam Caroli Boscardi, 1631. O.; AMI.FLO.HP.LINC.O¹².PA. PA⁴.RO².

A reprint of nos. 490, 488, with some of the misprints corrected. *Ecclesiae Anglicanae querimonia* has its own titlepage, signatures and pagination.

492 —Hypocrisis Marci Antonii de Dominis detecta, seu censura in eius libros de republica ecclesiastica, praeambula pleniori responsioni. Auctore Fideli Annoso Verementano theologo. 8°. *Antuerpiae, ex officina Plantiniana, apud Balthasarem Moretum, & viduam Ioannis Moreti, & Io. Meursium,* 1620. L.O(2).; ANT².C⁵.CARP.DUR(2).E².GT. HP. KN.L⁴.L⁹.MD.PA(2).RO²(2).VT + +

Fidelis Annosus Verementanus, *pseud.* The authorities for [Floyd] are the 1632 Catalogue and Alegambe (p. 242). Answers STC 6994. The fuller answer promised in the title is no. 493. *See* RH, Nov. 1979, pp. 126–30.

493 —Monarchiae ecclesiasticae, ex scriptis M. Antonii de Dominis . . . demonstratio . . . seu Respublica ecclesiastica M. Antonii de Dominis, per ipsum a fundamentis euersa. Auctore, Fideli Annoso Verementano theologo. 8°. *Coloniae Agrippinae, sumptibus Bernardi Gualteri,* 1622. O.; A.D.GT.GTN.KN(2).L².L¹³.LOU³.MD.NCY.PA.RO².SBG.VT. + +

Fidelis Annosus Verementanus, *pseud.* This is the fuller answer to STC 6994 promised in no. 492. *See* RH, Nov. 1797, pp. 126–30.

—Parathesis circa duo breuia apostolica ad Rmum Episcopum Chalcedonensem, 1631. *Part of* no. 490.

—Spongia, qua diluuntur calumniae nomine facultatis Parisiensis impositae, 1631. *See* nos. 489–91.

494 —Synopsis apostasiae Marci Antonii de Dominis . . . ex ipsiusmet libro delineata, auctore Fideli Annoso Verimentano theologo. 8°. *Antuerpiae, apud heredes Martini Nutii & Ioannem Meursium,* 1617. L.O.C.; BG².C².CARP.DUR(2).E².GT.KN(2).O².PA.PA⁴.RO².VI.VT. +

Fidelis Annosus Verimentanus, *pseud.* The authorities for [Floyd] are the 1632 Catalogue and Alegambe (p. 242). Answers STC 6996. An English version published in the same year is at A&R 331. *See* RH, Nov. 1979, pp. 126–7.

495 —Syntagma de imaginibus manu non factis deque aliis a Sancto Luca pictis, 1625. *In:* Codinus, G. De officiis et officialibus magnae ecclesiae et aulae Constantinopolitanae. *Parisiis, apud Sebastianum Cramoisy,* 1625. L.O.; D.HD².LC.PA.VI.

This edition of Codinus was edited by Jakob Gretser S.J. and published after the editor's death. The 'Syntagma', which forms part of the apparatus criticus, is attributed in the book to Gretser, but Alegambe (p. 242) enters it under Floyd ('Syntagma de imaginibus manu non factis, deq. aliis a S. Luca pictis').

Appendix

496 —[Duvergier de Hauranne, J.] [A1ʳ, head-title:] Assertio Epistolae Illustrissimorum ac Reuerendissimorum Galliae Antistitum, qua libros Nicolai Smithaei & Danielis a Iesu damnarunt, aduersus libellum cui titulus Querimonia ecclesiae Anglicanae, &c. 4°. *n.p.d.* [1632.] O.; D.G².O⁴.PA⁶.

Petrus Aurelius, *pseud.* All copies seen are without titlepage and preliminaries. The *Assertio* is an attack on no. 488. It is followed by an attack on no. 489 headed 'In octo causas quibus Iesuita quasi praeuiis exceptionibus Censurarum Parisiensium autoritatem eludere conatur'. *Pr.* [Paris].

497 —[Duvergier de Hauranne, J.] Confutatio collectionis locorum, quos Iesuitae compilarunt, tanquam sibi contumeliosos & iniuriosos, ex

defensione epistolae, illustrissimorum & reuerendissimorum Galliae Episcoporum, & Censurae Sacrae Theologiae Facultatis Parisiensis, a Petro Aurelio edita. 8°. *n.p.*, 1633. O.; ANT.D.^{2}.HAN.PA.TRO.WO.

> Petrus Aurelius, *pseud.* Answering a 'scheda, cui titulus erat, Calumniae, mendacia, & conuitia Petri Aurelii'. *See* 'Argumentum operum Petri Aurelii' prefaced to the 1646 edition of his works. The 'scheda' [by Floyd?] may have circulated only in MS; no printed edition has been found. *Pr.* [Paris.]

—[Duvergier de Hauranne, J.] In octo causas quibus Iesuita quasi praeuiis exceptionibus Censurarum Parisiensium autoritatem eludere conatur, [1632]. *Part of* no. 496.

498   —[Duvergier de Hauranne, J.] Vindiciae Censurae Facultatis Theologiae Parisiensis seu, Responsio dispunctoria ad libellum cui titulus Hermanni Loemelii . . . Spongia . . . Auctore Petro Aurelio theologo. 4°. *Parisiis, apud Carolum Morellum,* 1632. L.O.; D.G^2.MTH.O^4.O^{12}.O^{16}. PA(2).PA^2.PA^4.RO^2.VT.

> Petrus Aurelius, *pseud.* Defending no. 684 against Floyd's attack on it in no. 489.

498.1   —[A partial re-issue.] *Parisiis, apud Carolum Morel,* 1634. HAN.O^4.

> A partial re-issue of the 1632 sheets (no. 498) with certain quires reset, no doubt to make up shortages for a complete re-issue with a fresh titlepage. About a quarter of the whole has been reset but without textual changes.

—France, *Bishops.* Epistola Archiepiscoporum et Episcoporum Parisiis nunc agentium, 1631. Including a censure of no. 481. *See* nos. 1405–6.

—France, *Jesuits.* Declaration et desadueu des Peres Iesuites, [1633]. Disavowing positions maintained in several of the works of [Matthew Wilson] and [J. Floyd]. *See* no. 1408.

499   —Hallier, F. Defensio ecclesiasticae hierarchiae, seu, vindiciae censurae Facultatis Theologiae Parisiensis, aduersus Hermanni Loemelii Spongiam. 4°. *Parisiis, apud Carolum Morellum,* 1632. L.O.; AIX.AV. CMR.D.D^2.DMR.L^2.LGE^3.LYN.MD.O^2.PA.PA^6.RO^6.VT(2). +

> Defending no. 684 against no. 489.

500   —Le Maistre, N. Instauratio antiqui episcoporum principatus, et religiosae erga eosdem monachorum & clericorum omnium obseruantiae. Cui praemissa est confutatio rationum quas Sorbonicae censurae obiecit Spongia. 4°. *Parisiis, apud Guillelmum Pelé,* 1633. L.O.; O^2.O^{12}.PA.

> Defending no. 684 against no. 489.

501   —Normandy, *Parlement.* Arrest du Parlement de Rouen donné en la Chambre des Vaccations le septiesme iour d'Octobre 1632. Par lequel est ordonné que le liure intitulé Hermani Loemelii Spongia, sera lacéré & bruslé dans la cour du palais. Publié en l'Audience & executé le huictiesme dudit mois. 8°. *Paris, de l'imprimerie de Pierre Durand,* 1632. L(5423, h.1/10).; L^{27A}.(16/1 no. 8, *formerly* A26/148).

> The arrêt states that 150 copies of *Spongia* (no. 489), together with some books in English, had been illegally brought to Rouen by André Boscard, publisher at S. Omer, and delivered to Stephen Duffy, head of a community of Irish priests at Rouen. *See* M. E. Gosselin, *Glanes historiques normandes,* Rouen, 1869, pp. 169–72.

—Paris, *Sorbonne.* Censura propositionum quarumdam, 1631. Including a censure of 15 Feb. 1631 of propositions taken from the English original of no. 481. *See* no. 684.

—[Author unknown.] Deprauationes deprehensae, 1631. Including criticism of no. 481. *See* no. 1410.

Forbes, Archangel, *name in religion. See* Forbes, J.

502   **Forbes, John.** *in religion* Archangel Forbes. [*Appendix.*] Faustinus,

Diestensis. Alter Alexius natione Scotus, nobili familia oriundus, nuper in Belgium felici S. Spiritus afflatu delatus, & in familiam Seraphici Patris S. Francisci Capuccinorum adscriptus, sub nomine F. Archangeli. 12°. *Coloniae Agrippinae, excudebat Ioannes Christophori,* 1620. L(3).O; E.FR.FRA.LYN.KN(2).PA.RG.RO[10].(*mutil.*).UT[2].VT.X(*imp.*).

A French translation of this work, published in 1621, forms part of no. 467. An English translation, made from the French, is in A&R 170.

503 —[Anr. ed., with title:] Conuersio et conuersatio P. F. Archangeli regio sanguine clari nuper in Belgium felici S. Spiritus afflatu delati, & in familiam Seraphici S. Francisci Capucinorum adscripti, atque in eadem beata morte consummati. 12°. *Leodii, apud Arnoldum a Corsvvaremia,* 1623. KN.LGE.

504 —[*Italian transl.*] Narratiua della vita d'vn figlio, et d'vna madre Scozzesi di patria, & nobilissimi per nascita; il figlio fù vn'altro Alessio Romano, il quale guidato dallo Spirito Santo ... andò in Fiandra ... & poi fù ascritto nella fameglia del Serafico Padre S. Francesco de'Capuccini sotto il nome di Fr. Arcangiolo. 4°. *Modona. appresso Giulian Cassiani,* 1634. L.; G[2].

505 **Forcer, Francis.** [*Appendix.*] Armenta, J. de. Relacion sumaria, de la insigne conuersio de treynta y seys cossarios, Ingleses de nacion, y de profession hereges, y de la iusticia que se hizo de algunos dellos en puerto de Santa Maria. 4°. *Cadiz, por Hernando Rey,* 1616. MD[2] (9–556bis/8).

The conversion of the captured English pirates was largely the work of Francis Forcer S.J.

—Madrid, *English College.* La fiesta que su Alteza de la serenissima Señora Infanta Maria de Austria mandó hazer, [1623]. The ceremonies were organised by the Superior, Francis Forcer. S.J. *See* nos. 753–4.

506 **Ford, Edward.** [*Begin.*] Illustrissimo, ac Reuerendissimo Domino Fr. Martino de Leone, et Cardenas, Episcopo Triuentino ... Odoardus Fordus Ibernus Seminarii Ludouisiani alumnus. S.P.S. Conclusiones ex uniuersa philosophia ... [*End.*] Disputabuntur publice Romae in Collegio S. Isidori Fratrum Min. Hibernorum Strict. Obseru. ab Odoardo Fordo ... Praesidente P. Fr. Ioanne Ponce [Punch]. *s.sh.*fol. *Romae, apud Ludouicum Grignanum,* 1630. RO[8].

A programme announcing the forthcoming defence of his thesis.

Forest, John. *Bl.* [*Appendix.* For an account of his martyrdom:] *See* no. 1010.

507 **Fortescue, Adrian,** *alias* Talbot. Regalis domus Sabaudiae nexus Gordio validior nullius manu ac ne ferro quidem soluendus imperium sua magis firmitate quam dissolutione portendens Serenissimo Principi Mauritio Cardinali a Sabaudia theses inter philosophicas ab Hadriano Talbotto Anglicani Collegi conuictore publice disputatas dithyrambico carmine ad modos dictus. 8° (a single quire). *Romae, apud Alexandrum Zanettum,* 1624. MIL[2]. (&&5 99/21).RO[2](3).VT.

For Fortescue, *see* Foley, vol. 7, p. 277. Titlepage engraved. Sommerv. (tom. 2, col. 193) records this work under Franciscus Brivius, a noted Jesuit professor at the Roman College, who perhaps actually wrote the Latin verses for this occasion.

507.1 **Fortescue, George.** Chori inter publicas disputationes auditi: sive Emblematis explicatio, quo gentilitia Illustriss. Principis Odoardi Farnesii S.R.E. Card. Ampliss. insignia exornavit Georgius de Fortiscuto Angl. Coll. Alum. Dum propositas de universa Philosophia theses, sub felicissimis illius auspiciis defendebat in Collegio Anglicano. 4°. *Romae, apud Bartholomaeum Zannettum,* 1612.

Not found. Description from Sommerv. (tom. 7, col. 107). For

Fortescue *see* DNB. The subject matter of his book of Latin essays, *Feriae academicae*, published at Douai in 1630, does not bring it within the scope of the present catalogue.

Fortiscutus, Georgius de *See* Fortescue, G.

508 **Foster, Seth.** [*Begin.*] Ilustrissimo Philippo Boncampagno Cardinali S. Sixti vtriusque collegii Anglicani Protector optimo, Sethus Fosterus collegii Anglorum alumnus, felicitatem ... Assertiones de vera hominis iustificatione contra haereticos huius temporis. *s.sh.*fol. *n.p.d.* [1583.] L(Landsdowne MSS 96/56).[*L.*DMR.]
A programme announcing the forthcoming defence of his thesis at the English College then at Rheims. Foster was at the College from 1582 to 1584. *Pr.* [Rheims, Jean Foigny.]

—[*Appendix.*] Lisbon, *English Bridgettine Convent.* Relacion que embiaron las religiosas del monasterio de Sion, 1594. With a 'Preambulo' by Robert Persons based on material supplied by Foster. *See* no. 741.

509 **Fowler, John.** [*Works edited or translated by him.*] Frarinus, P. Oratio Petri Frarini ... Quod male, reformandae religionis nomine, arma sumpserunt sectarii nostri temporis. Habita in scholis artium, Louanii, 10, Calendas Ianuarii. Anno 1565. 8°. *Louanii, apud Ioannem Foulerum*, 1566. L.O.C(2).; ANT².BRS.C².
After publishing the Latin original Fowler made an English translation which he published in the same year (A&R 344).

510 —Génébrard, G. Chronographia in duos libros distincta. Prior est de rebus veteris populi, auctore Gilb. Genebrardo ... Posterior recentes historias, praesertimque ecclesiasticas complectitur, authore Ar. Pontaco Burdegalensi: nunc primum ... in minorem formam redacta. 12°. *Louanii, apud Ioannem Foulerum Anglum*, 1570. BRS.ETON.KN. PA.VI.X.
Edited and abridged by Fowler. Editions of the unabridged text, of which several were published at Paris and Cologne, are not by him.

511 —[Anr. ed. enlarged.] 12°. *Louanii, apud Ioahnnem Foulerum Anglum*, 1572. L.C.; A²(*imp.*).BRS.DMR.KN.LX.PA.ST.VI.WO.X.
Brought up to 1571 by Fowler.

512 —Marulic, M. M.Maruli Spalatensis Dictorum factorumque memorabilium libri sex ... infinitis mendis diligenter repurgati ... per Ioan. Foulerū Bristolien. 8°. *Antuerpiae, apud eundem Iohan. Foulerum*, 1577. [Coloph.] *Typis Gerardi Smits.* L.; AIX.AMS.ANT².BRS.CHA.O⁷.OR. PA.PA⁴.RMS.TRI.UT².VI.VT. +
A redaction by Fowler of Marulic's *Bene vivendi instituta.*

513 —[Anr. ed.] 8°. *Antuerpiae, ex officina Aegidii Steelsii*, 1584. ANT³.CMR. GT.PA.V.
In this posthumous edition Fowler's name is suppressed; in the dedicatory epistle (reprinted from no. 512) it is replaced by that of the new publisher, Aegidius Steelsius.

514 —[Anr. ed.] 8°. *Parisiis, apud Hieronymum de Marnef, & viduam Gulielmi Cauellat*, 1585. [Coloph.] *Excudebat Petrus Hury.* AIX.DMR. PA.VT.
This edition bears Fowler's name.

515 —[Date variant.] 1586. L.; BG.C².F.FLO.ILL.MD.PA.PA⁴.VT.
516 —[Anr. ed.] 8°. *Antuerpiae, excudebat Martinus Nutius*, 1593. [Coloph.] *Typis Danielis Veruliet.* C.;ANT².AV.BG.BRS.N.PA.RUT.
In this edition Fowler's name is suppressed.

517 —[Anr. ed.] 8°. *Coloniae Agrippinae, sumptibus Bernardi Gualtheri*, 1609. [Coloph.] *Excudebat Stephanus Hemmerden, sumptibus Bernardi Gualtheri.* CMR.
In this edition Fowler's name is suppressed.

517.1 —Thomas, *a Kempis.* De Christi imitatione libellus vere aureus, ex fontibus sacrae Scripturae totus excerptus, ab Authore D. Thoma

Kempensis olim conscriptus ... Accessit opusculum Ioannis Gersonis de cordis meditatione, cum speculo euangelici sermonis B. Anselmi. 12°. *Louanii, apud Ioannem Foulerum Anglum*, 1570. L.; DMR.
A note headed 'Typographus Lectori' on the verso of the titlepage shows that Fowler was editor as well as publisher of the work.

517.2 —[Anr. ed.] 12°. *Louanii, Iohanni Foulero excudebat Ioh. Masius*, 1575. ANT³.DMR.

518 —Thomas, Aquinas, *Saint*. Ex vniuersa Summa sacrae theologiae ... S. Thomae Aquinatis, desumptae conclusiones. 8°. *Louanii, apud Ioannem Foulerum Anglum*, 1570. L.; ANT³.ILL.MD.VT(-*t.p.*).
Ded. to Thomas Goldwell, Bishop of St. Asaph, sgd.: Ioannes Foulerus Bristoliensis. This text of the 'Conclusiones' (which are not by St. Thomas himself) is taken from the 1576 Antwerp edition of the *Summa theologica*.

519 —[Anr. ed.] 8°. *Venetiis, apud Franciscum, Gasparem Bindonum, & fratres*, 1572. O.; ANT².DMR.RO¹¹.VT.
A reprint of no. 518 including Fowler's signed dedication.

520 —[Anr. ed., with title:] Conclusiones ex vniuersa summa sacrae theologiae. 8°. *Antuerpiae, in aedibus Petri Belleri*, 1589. C(*imp.*); LYN(2). O⁴.O⁷.PA.
This posthumous edition reprints the dedication of nos. 518–19 but suppresses Fowler's name at the end of it.

520.1 —[*A work published by him for the English market?*] Pius V, *Saint, Pope*. Bulla S.D.N.D. Pii diuina prouidentia Papae V. Lecta in die Coenae Domini. Anno M.D.LXVIII. Cuius transsumptum omnes ordinarii, curati, ac confessores debent penes se habere, & diligenter legere, vt in eadem Bulla habetur. 12° (in fours). *Louanii, apud Ioannem Foulerum*, 1569. BRS.VT.[*L.]
A reprint of the Roman edition of 1568 (Ascarelli, p. 220). The papal anathemas pronounced annually on Maundy Thursday were aimed not only against heretics, apostates and schismatics but also against all laymen who infringed clerical rights and privileges without papal sanction. Pius V's efforts to persuade Catholic princes to publicise them in their dominions met with little success and local reprints of the Roman editions are rare. It seems probable that Fowler published this principally for the English Catholic market, to coincide with the rising of the Northern Earls in 1569. There are no editorial preliminaries.

—Stapleton, T. [A work translated by Fowler.] 1565. *See* no. 1158.

Franciscus, *a Sancta Clara, name in religion. See* Davenport, C.

Franciscus, *de S. Maria, name in religion. See* Tully, F.

François, R.P. *Hybernois. See* Nugent, F.

G., D. *See* no. 953.

G., R. *See* no. 1347.

Gabriel, *de Ste Marie, name in religion. See* Gifford, W.

521 **Garnet, Henry.**† [*Appendix.*] Eudaemon Ioannes, A. R.P. Andreae Eudaemon-Ioannis ... ad actionem proditoriam Edouardi Coqui, Apologia pro R.P. Henrico Garneto Anglo. 8°. *Coloniae Agrippinae, apud Ioannem Kinckium*, 1610. L(3).O(4).C(2).; ANT².BRS.C²(3).D.DE. DUR.GTN.HP.L².MD.MTH.PA(4).ST.USH. + +
Answers STC 11620 which was largely the work of Sir Edward Coke. Answered by STC 45 and also in STC 4745 and 20344. Eudaemon Ioannes replied to the first two in no. 522. *See* Mil., vol. 2, pp. 86–9. With a plate depicting 'Garnet's Straw'. Some copies also have a portrait of Garnet inserted. Includes a list of martyrs from 1573 to 1608 divided into priests and layfolk.

522 —Eudaemon Ioannes, A. R.P. Andreae Eudaemon-Ioannis ... Responsio ad caput IV primae Exercitationis Isaaci Casauboni, et ad Anti-

77

logiam Roberti Abbati aduersus Apologiam P. Garneti. 8°. *Coloniae Agrippinae, apud Ioannem Kinckium*, 1615. L.; L².LGE³.MD.MU.PA.RO³. RO⁶.TRO.UP.VI.VT.

Defending no. 521 against the attacks on it in STC 4745 and 45 and answering allegations of Jesuit complicity in the Gunpowder Plot.

523   **Gascoigne, Henry.** Theses ex vniuersa theologia disputandae. In Coll. Anglicano Societatis Iesu Louanii, Anno Domini CIƆ IƆC XXIII. Praeside Rdo Patre Georgio Morleo Soc. Iesu ... Defendet P. Henricus Gascoigne eiusdem Societatis. Die 7 Augusti. 4°. [Coloph.] *Louanii, ex officina Bernardini Masii*, 1623.

Not found. Description based on Sommerv., tom. 5, cols. 1326–7.

Geraldinus, Jacobus. *See* FitzGerald, J. *See* also FitzGerald, J. F.

524   **Gibbons, John.** Concertatio ecclesiae Catholicae in Anglia. 8°. 2 pts. *Augustae Treuirorum, apud Edmundum Hatotum*, 1583. L.O(2).; AIX. DE.FB.HP.L²(pt. 2).L²⁶.LGE³.PA.ST.USH.VAL.VI.VT(2).WO(pt. 2) +

Anon. A collection edited by [J. Gibbons and J. Fen]. Pt. 1 includes the text of nos. 135.1, 874 and *Vita et martyrium* (Campion, *Appendix*), and Latin versions of no. 8 and A&R 12; pt. 2 includes a Latin version of A&R 6. The editorship was for long erroneously ascribed to John Bridgewater; for the correct identification see the introduction by D. M. Rogers to the 1970 facsimile reprint by Gregg International. Pt. 2 of the collection, entitled 'Duo edicta Elizabethae Reginae Angliae contra sacerdotes' is sometimes found on its own but was not issued separately.

525   —[Anr. ed., enlarged.] Nunc denuo centum et eo amplius martyrum, sexcentorumque insignium virorum rebus gestis ... aucta, & in tres partes diuisa. 4°. *Augustae Treuirorum, excudebat Henricus Bock*, 1588. L.; DUR²(-*tertia pars*).HP(-*tertia pars*).KNY.L²⁶.MD.MTH(-*tertia pars*). O⁵.RO.ST.VAL(-*t.p.*).VT.

Anon. This edition includes, among other additions, in the 'Tertia pars' a reprint of no. 18. Although the 'Tertia pars' has its own titlepage, the signatures and pagination are continuous throughout all three 'Partes'.

526   —[Date variant.] 1589. L.C.; C⁵.DE(-*tertia pars*).GTN.LGE³.O³.PA.PA⁶.USH. VI.W(-*tertia pars*).WO.

527   —[Anr. issue.] *Augustae Treuirorum, excudebat Henricus Bock*, 1594. O.; ANT.L⁹.MD(*tertia pars only*).MD³.O⁸.PA.

The sheets of no. 525 except for the outer four leaves of the first quire of 'Pars prima' and the whole of the first quire of 'Pars tertia', all of which have been reset.

528   —Confutatio virulentae disputationis theologicae, in qua Georgius Sohn ... conatus est docere Pontificem Romanum esse Antichristum ... Authore Ioanne Aquipontano. 4°. *Augustae Treuirorum, excudebat Henricus Bock*, 1589. L.O.C.(*imp.*); VI.

Ioannes Aquipontanus, *pseud.* For the identification of the author *see* the reference given in the note to no. 524. Answering Sohn's *Disputatio theologica quod Papa Romanus sit Antichristus.*

529   —[*Disputations in which he acted as Praeses.*] Arresdorffius, N. Disputatio theologica de sanctis, complectens omnes fere nostri temporis controuersias ... Praeside R.P. Ioanne Gibbono Anglo. 4°. *Augustae Treuirorum, ex officina Emundi Hatoti*, 1584. L.O.; DI(2).FR.FU.L²⁶.MU. MZ.PA.

530   —Schanaeus, P. De sacrosanctae Eucharistiae communione sub vna specie. Disputatio theologica ... Praeside R.P. Ioanne Gibbono Anglo. 4°. *Augustae Treuirorum, in officina Emundi Hatoti*, 1583. DI. DMR.FR.

Gibbons, Richard.

WORKS EDITED BY HIM

Aelred, Saint, Abbot of Rievaulx

531 —Opera diui Aelredi Rhieuallensis ... omnia ope et studio R.P. Richardi Gibbonii ... ex vetustis M.S. nunc primum in lucem producta ... additi anonymi rhythmi de laude virginitatis. 4°. *Duaci, apud viduam Laurentii Kellam,* 1616. O.; DOU.O⁶.PA.TRI. *This or no. 532 :* PA⁴.

532 —[Anr. state, with titlepage reset to read:] Diui Aelredi Rieuallensis ... opera quae inueniri potuerunt omnia ope et studio R.P. Richardi Gibboni ... in lucem producta ... [then as before]. PA².RO. *See also note to no. 531.*

533 —[Anr. issue, with title as in no. 531.] *Duaci, ex typographia Gerardi Pinchon,* 1631. L.O.C.; CMR.D.KN.MU.NI.PA.PA³.RO².RO⁶.USH.VT.WO. + The sheets of no. 531 except for the title and preliminaries which have been reset.

Amadeus, Saint, Bishop of Lausanne

534 —Diui Amadei ... De Maria Virginea matre homiliae octo. Recognitae per R.P. Richardum Gibbonum. 12°. *Audomaropoli, ex typographeio Caroli Boscard,* 1613, BRU.CHA.LGE.RO². With an addition by Gibbons, 'Scriptores de B. Virgine'. There is a colophon with the same imprint as that on the titlepage.

535 —[Imprint variant.] *Audomaropoli, apud Antonium Crabbe bibliopolam iuratum,* 1613. CHA. The second word of the title is also reset to read 'Amedei'. The colophon is unchanged.

536 —[Imprint variant.] *Antuerpiae, apud haeredes Martini Nutii,* 1613. PA³.PR.RO².VT. Forms part of a shared edition with nos. 534–5. The colophon is unchanged. The second word of the title reads 'Amedei'. The text was republished by the house of Nutius at Antwerp in 1625 as part of *De laudibus B. Mariae Virginis* by Richardus a S. Laurentio.

Androzzi, Fulvio

537 —R.P. Fuluii Androtii ... opuscula spiritualia ... in Latinum conuersa. 12°. *Duaci, typis Petri Auroy,* 1615. L.; ANT³.DOU.MAA.NI.PA.RO².ST (*2 : 1 -t.p.*). An edition of Jean Busée's Latin translation of both parts of Androzzi's *Opere spirituali*. Gibbons's name appears in the heading of the dedicatory epistle.

Diez, Felipe

538 —R.P.F. Philippi Diez ... Summa praedicantium, ex omnibus locis communibus locupletissima tomus primus (secundus). Nunc recens castigata & aucta ... opera ac studio R.P. Richardi Gibboni. 4°. 2 vols. *Antuerpiae, ex officina haeredum Martini Nutii,* 1613. C.; BRS.D. L²⁶.LYN.MD.NI.PBN.PR.UT². Vol. 2 is dated 1600, a date copied from an earlier ed. by the same printer, not edited by Gibbons.

539 —[Anr. issue, with a cancel title.] *Audomaropoli, ex officina Caroli Boscardi,* 1613. PA.

Giovanni, da S. Geminiano

540 —Sermones funebres R.F. Ioannis de Sancto Geminiano, Ordinis Praedicatorum ... Opera & studio R.P. Richardi Gibboni. 8°.

Antuerpiae, sumptibus viduae & haeredum Petri Belleri, 1611. [Coloph.] *Excudebat Andreas Bacx.* PA.PA³.VI.WB.X.

541 —[Imprint variant.] *Duaci, apud Petrum Borremans*, 1611. DOU.PA⁴.
Forms part of a shared edition with no. 540. The colophon is unchanged.

542 —[Anr. ed.] 8°. *Antuerpiae, sumptibus Petri & Ioannis Belleri*, 1616. [Coloph.] *Excudebat Andreas Bacx.* C.; ANT³.LOU³.
A reprint of no. 540. Sommerv. (tom. 3, col. 1407) cites another edition or issue with this imprint, dated 1618, but this has not been found.

543 —[Anr. ed.] 8°. *Antuerpiae, apud Ioannem Bellerum*, 1630. ANT.KNY.NI. OR.PA.VER.

Goswin, Saint

544 —[*Appendix.*] Beati Gosuini vita celeberrimi Aquicinctensis monasterii abbatis septimi, a duobus diuersis eiusdem coenobii monachis separatim exarata, e veteribus MS. Nunc primum edita. Cura R.P. Richardi Gibboni. 8°. *Duaci, ex officina Marci Wyon*, 1620. L.C.; AIX. AMI.CHA.DOU.GN.HA.HAN.HP.LIL.PA.PA⁴.RO³.RO⁶.USH. +

Harpsfield, Nicholas

—Historia Anglicana ecclesiastica . . . Nunc primum in lucem producta studio & opera R.P. Richardi Gibboni, 1622. *See* no. 639.

Nider, Johann

545 —R.P.F. Ioannis Nider . . . Praeceptorium: siue orthodoxa et accurata Decalogi explicatio . . . In lucem et nitorem restitutum per R.P. Rich. Gibbonum. 8°. *Duaci, typis Ioannis Bogardi*, 1611. C.; DOU.LGE³.MU. O³.TRO.

546 —[Date variant.] 1612. O.; C².HA.LOU³.PA.RO².TRO.

Ribera, Francisco de

547 —R.P. Francisci Riberae . . . In librum duodecim prophetarum commentarii . . . Hac omnium postrema editione ab infinitis mendis typographicis expurgati . . . opera R.P. Richardi Gibboni. Fol. *Duaci, ex officina typographica Baltazaris Belleri*, 1611. BGS.BRS².DIJ.EP.HA. LN.LOU³.MD.MNS.O⁴.TNI.
Other editions of Ribera's work, published at Paris and Cologne, are not edited by Gibbons.

548 —[Date variant.] 1612. L.; DOU.L²⁶.MD⁴.MU.NM².OR.PA.

Toledo, Francisco de

549 —Francisci Toleti . . . de instructione sacerdotum, et peccatis mortalibus libri VIII . . . Omnia opera & studio R.P. Richardi Gibboni. 8°. *Duaci, ex officina Baltazaris Belleri*, 1608. BRS.CHX.HA.MU.NM².PR³.WB.
Earlier editions of Toledo's work were not edited by Gibbons.

550 —[Date variant.] 1609. CHA(2).DOU.MU.NM².

551 —[Anr. ed.] Francisci Toleti . . . de instructione sacerdotum et peccatis mortalibus lib. VIII. Quibus accessit suo loco interiectus Martini Fornarii . . . de ordine tractatus . . . Opera R.P. Richardi Gibboni. 8°. 2 pts. *Duaci, ex typographia Baltazaris Belleri*, 1613. DOU.MNS.PA.X.
Pt. 2, which has its own titlepage, contains the *Annotationes* to Toledo's work, by Andrea Vitorelli.

552 —[Anr. ed.] Francisci Toleti . . . de instructione sacerdotum et peccatis mortalibus lib. VIII. Quibus suis locis interiectae accesserunt annotationes et additiones Andreae Victorelli, necnon P. Martini

Fornarii . . . de Ordine tractatus. 8°. *Duaci, ex typographia Baltazaris Belleri,* 1615. GTN.

In this edition, Toledo's work, Vitorelli's *Annotationes* and Fornari's tract *de Ordine* all form part of a single volume. pp. 1317.

553 —[Date variant.] 1616. LOU[3].

554 —[Anr. ed.? or anr. issue?] 8°. *Rothomagi, sumptibus Stephani Vereul,* 1617. X.

The title follows that of no. 552. pp. 1317.

555 —[Anr. ed.] 8°. *Duaci, ex typographia Baltazaris Belleri,* 1617. ANT[3]. FRA.UT.

The title follows that of no. 552. pp. 1214.

556 —[Anr. ed.? or anr. issue?] 8°. *Duaci, ex typographia Baltazaris Belleri,* 1619. DOU.MNS.PA.SBG[2].WB.

The title follows that of no. 552. pp. 1214.

557 —[Anr. ed.] 8°. *Antuerpiae, apud Petrum & Ioannem Belleros,* 1619. ANT[3].AUG.X.

The title follows that of no. 552. pp. 1168.

558 —[Anr. ed., with title:] Francisci Toleti . . . Summa casuum conscientiae absolutissima. Siue de instructione sacerdotum et peccatis mortalibus lib. VIII . . . Opera Richardi Gibboni. Quibus suis locis interiectae accesserunt annotationes & additiones Andreae Victorelli necnon R.P. Martini Fornari . . . de Ordine tractatus. 8°. *Duaci, ex typographia Baltazaris Belleri,* 1622. L.; CHA.LGE[4].MAA.MNS.

pp. 1182.

559 —[Date variant.] 1623. DMR.KN[2].LIL.LIL[3].MP.VES.

560 —[Anr. ed.] 8°. *Antuerpiae, apud Petrum & Ioannem Belleros,* 1623. O.; ANT[3].FU.KN[2].MAA.MTH.PBN.PR.

Title as in no. 558. pp. 1187.

561 —[Anr. ed.] Francisci Toleti . . . de instructione sacerdotum . . . 8°. *Rothomagi, apud Ioannem Osmont,* 1625. CHA.PA.PA[6].

Title as in no. 552. pp. 1317.

561.1 —[Anr. ed.] 8°. *Rothomagi, apud Ioannem Osmont,* 1628. DMR.

Title as in no. 552. pp. 1317.

562 —[Imprint variant.] *Rothomagi, apud Adrianum Ouyn,* 1628. PA.

Part of a shared edition with no. 561.1.

563 —[Imprint variant.] *Rothomagi, apud Dauidem du Petit Val,* 1628. PLU.

Part of a shared edition with no. 561.1. Sommerv. (tom. 3, col. 1405) cites a 1628 Rouen edition with the imprint of R. Lallemand, which may be another imprint variant of the same shared edition, but no copy of it has been found.

564 —[Anr. ed.] Francisci Toleti . . . Summa casuum conscientiae . . . 8°. *Antuerpiae, apud Petrum & Ioannem Belleros,* 1628. FU.KDN.KN[2].NI. SBG.WO.

Title as in no. 558.

565 —[Anr. ed.] 4°. *Coloniae Agrippinae, apud Ioannem Gymnicum,* 1629.
Ⓐ C[2].PR[2].

565.1 Title as in no. 558.

566 —[Anr. ed.] Francisci Toleti . . . de instructione sacerdotum . . . 8°. *Rothomagi, apud Adrianum Ouyn,* 1630. O.

Title as in no. 552.

567 —[Imprint variant.] *Rothomagi, apud Ioannem Le Cousturier,* 1630. DIJ.

Forms part of a shared edition with nos. 566, 568.

568 —[Imprint variant.] *Rothomagi, apud Carolum Osmont,* 1630. L[26].

Forms part of a shared edition with nos. 566–7. Sommerv. (tom. 3, col. 1405) cites a 1630 Rouen edition with the imprint of L. Dumesnil, which may be another imprint variant of the same shared edition, but no copy of it has been found.

569 —[Anr. ed.] Francisci Toleti . . . Summa casuum conscientiae . . . 8°.

Duaci, apud Gerardum Patté, 1633. O.; BRU.BRS².DMR.DOU.
Title as in no. 558.

570   —[Anr. ed.] Francisci Toleti ... de instructione sacerdotum ... 8°.
Rothomagi, apud Ioannem Berthelin, 1636. CHA.
Title as in no. 552.

571   —[Imprint variant.] *Rothomagi, apud Ioannem Baptistam Behourt*, 1636.
O.
Forms part of a shared edition with no. 570.

572   —[*French transl.*] L'instruction des prestres, qui contient sommairement
tous les cas de conscience ... mise en François par M. A. Goffar ...
Auec les sommaires du R.P. Richard Gibbon. 4°. *Lyon, chez Antoine
Chard*, 1628. PA.PA¹⁰.

573   —[Imprint variant.] *Lyon, chez Antoine Pillehotte*, 1628. ANG.CHA(2).PA.
Part of a shared edition with no. 572. With Pillehotte's device
substituted for Chard's on the titlepage.

574   —[Anr. ed.] 4°. *Lyon, chez Antoine Pillehotte*, 1632. AV.
575   —[Anr. ed.] 4°. *Rouen, chez Iean Berthelin*, 1634. OR.PA.
576   —[Anr. ed.] 4° (in eights). *Lyon, de l'imprimerie de Simon Rigaud*,
1637. AV.

577   —[Anr. ed.] 4°. *Lyon, chez Antoine Chard*, 1638.
No copy found. Description from Sommerv. (tom. 3, col. 1406).

Torsellino, Orazio

578   —Horatii Tursellini ... Historiarum ab origine mundi vsque ad annum
1598. epitomae libri X. Accessit ex Auctario Henrici Spondani, ad
Annales C. Baronii liber XI ab anno 1598. vsque ad annum 1622.
12°. *Duaci, ex typographia Baltazaris Belleri*, 1623. ANT.ANT².DMR.
DOU.ETON.GT.PA.TRI.
Editor's *ded.* sgd.: Richardus Gibbonus. Collation: †¹²A–T¹²
(T12 blank).a,e,i,o¹² Sponde's continuation begins on sig. al. It has
its own pagination and a separate index.

579   —[Anr. issue? of Torsellino's work alone.] Horatii Torsellini ...
Historiarum ab origine mundi vsque ad annum 1598. epitomae libri
decem. 12°. *Duaci, ex typographia Baltazaris Belleri*, 1624. BRS.²
DOU.LX.
Collation: †¹²A–T¹² (T12 blank). This appears to be a reissue, with
a different titlepage, of the sheets of the first section of no. 578. The
second section of no. 578, containing Sponde's continuation, is not
present and is not called for on the titlepage.

580   —[Anr. ed. of no. 579.] 12°. *Duaci, ex typographia Baltazaris Belleri*,
1626. AAR.BRS².DOU.VI.
581   —[Date variant.] 1627. DOU.
582   —[Anr. ed. of no. 578.] 12°. *Parisiis, iuxta exemplar Duaci*, 1628. O.; CHA.
583   —[Anr. ed. of no. 579.] 12°. *Duaci, ex typographia Baltazaris Belleri*,
1630. ANT³.DOU(2).GT.LIL².LIL³.MU.O⁷.

584   —[Anr. ed. of no. 579.] 12°. *Parisiis, apud Maturinum Henault*, 1631. PA.
585   —[Anr. ed. of no. 578, with additions to 1630.] Horatii Tursellini ...
Historiarum ab origine mundi, vsque ad annum 1630 epitome libri X.
12°. *Parisiis, apud Mathurinum Henault*, 1631. A.PA⁶.
The additions from 1622–1630 are contained in a separately paged
section at the end headed 'Res memorandae, quae ab anno 1622
vsque ad annum 1630 contigerunt' described as compiled by I. L.

586   —[Anr. ed. of no. 585, but with title:] Horatii Tursellini ... Historiarum ab origine mundi vsque ad annum 1598. Epitomae libri
decem. 12°. *Parisiis, sumptibus Michaelis Soly*, 1631. PA.
In spite of the title, this edition contains the full text of no. 585.
The type appears to be at least in part reset.

587   —[Imprint variant.] *Parisiis, apud Ioannem Branchu,* 1631. PA.
       Forms part of a shared edition with no. 586.
588   —[Anr. ed., with title as in no. 585.] 12°. *Parisiis, sumptibus Guillelmi
       Pelé,* 1637. LYN².PA².WIE.
589   —[Anr. ed., with title as in no. 585.] 12°. *Parisiis, sumptibus Guillelmi
       Pelé,* 1640. O⁷.

Vigerio, Marco, Cardinal

590   —Historia admiranda de Iesu Christi stigmatibus sacrae sindoni
       impressis, ab Alphonso Paleoto . . . explicata . . . Auctore R.P.F.
       Daniele Mallon. (Historiae admirandae tomus alter. Complectens M.
       Vigerii . . . de praecipuis incarnati Verbi mysteriis decachordum
       Christianum. Eiusdem lucubratio de instrumentis dominicae pas-
       sionis. Omnia ad vetera exemplaria castigata: sacrae Scripturae
       auctoritatibus, & indicibus adiectis, per R.P. Richardum Gibbonum.)
       4°. 2 vols. *Duaci, ex typographia Baltazaris Belleri, n.d.* [1607]. [vol. 2.]
       Duaci, ex officina Baltazaris Belleri, 1607. C(2).; CHA.DOU.GT.KN.L⁴.
       LAR.LN.LOU³.O⁴.PA(2).ST.TRO.UT.VI. + +
       Gibbons edited vol. 2 (Vigerio); he appears to have had no hand in
       editing vol. 1 (Paleotti).
591   —[Date variant.] Vol. 2 bears the date 1608 in the imprint. BRS².
592   —[Anr. ed.] 4°. 2 vols. *Duaci, ex typographia Baltazaris Belleri,* 1616.
       [vol. 2.] *Duaci, ex officina Baltazaris Belleri,* 1616. O.; ANT³.BOR.D.
       DOU.HA.L²⁶.LOU.LOU³.PA.RO².WO.
       Vol. 1 has both an engraved titlepage which bears the imprint and a
       printed one which is without it. Vol. 2 has a printed titlepage only.
593   —[Anr. issue.] *Antuerpiae, apud Ioannem Keerbergium,* 1616. [Vol. 2.]
       Duaci, ex officina Baltazaris Belleri, 1616. L.O.; PA².
       A reissue of the sheets of no. 592 except that, in vol. 1, the original
       engraved titlepage bearing Beller's imprint at Douai has been
       cancelled and replaced by a printed titlepage with Keerberg's
       Antwerp imprint. Apart from the imprint, the wording of the title
       is similar. The titlepage of vol. 2 is unchanged.

594   **Gifford, Edward,** *alias* White. Dithyrambus in draconem gentilitiū
       Ilustriss. Principis Francisci Boncompagni S.R.E. Card. Ampliss. in
       Collegio Anglicano philosophicas inter theses Odoardi Viti eiusdem
       Collegii alumni emodulatus. 4°. (a single quire signed: A¹²). *Romae,
       apud haeredē Bartholomae Zannetti, n.d.* [1621]. RO⁸.
       A Latin poem in honour of the dragon family emblem of the
       Cardinal. Gifford left the College in May 1620 to enter the Jesuit
       novitiate in Rome (*see* Foley, vol. 7, p. 301) but Boncompagni was
       only created Cardinal on 19 April 1621.
595   **Gifford, William,** *Archbishop of Rheims, in religion* Gabriel de Ste
       Marie. Conciones aduentuales super Missus est. In quibus honor
       Deiparae propugnatur contra impios & blasphemos haereticos . . . &
       praerogatiuae Diuae Virginis ample explicantur. 8°. *Remis, apud
       Nicolaum Constant . . . Nicolaum Hecart, & Franciscum Bernard,
       dicti Illustriss. Archiepiscopi typograph.,* 1625. LYN.NM².RO³.TRO.
       Gifford's own Latin translation of sermons given by him in French
       at Paris. *See* Chaussy, p. 188.
596   —[*Begin:*] Illustrissimo Principi et Cardinali amplissimo Lodouico a
       Lotharingia Archiepiscopo et Duci Rhemensi . . . Gulielmus Giffordus
       Collegii Anglorum Rhemensis alumnus felicitatem . . . Theses theo-
       logicae de cultu externo contra haereticos. [*End:*] Defendentur publice
       [space] Mense [space] Die [space]. *S.sh.*fol. *n.p.d.* [1583.] L(Lans-
       downe MSS 96/54). [*L.*DMR].

A programme announcing the forthcoming defence of his thesis. Gifford was at this period a student at the English College, then at Rheims. *See* DD 1 & 2, p. 195. *Pr.* [Rheims, Jean Foigny.]

597 —Oraison funebre, prononcée en l'Eglise S. Pierre aux Nonnains de Reims, le 26 Iuillet, à la ceremonie de l'enterrement du coeur de feu Monseigneur . . . Louys Cardinal de Guise, Archeuesque, Duc de Reims. 8°. *Reims, chez Simon de Foigny,* 1621. L.; NCY.PA.PA[11].RMS.

Gifford had been coadjutor to Louis de Guise since 1618 and was to succeed him as Archbishop.

598 —Oratio funebris in exequiis venerabilis viri domini Maxaemiliani Manare praepositi ecclesiae D. Petri oppidi Insulensis. 4°. *Duaci, ex officina Ioannis Bogardi,* 1598. DOU.

For Maximilien Manare and other friends of Gifford's in the Low Countries, *see* Chaussy, p. 15.

599 —Traitté singulier, pour l'esclarcissement et resolution de quelques controuerses de ce temps: specialement touchant la predestination, & l'autorité de la Ste Escriture. Pour response à la lettre du Sieur de Tesserant. 8°. *S. Malo, par Pierre Marcigay,* 1613. NM[2].PA[2].PA[4](*imp.*) PA[6].SMA.

The controversy with de Tesserant arose out of sermons given by Gifford as Theologal of Saint Malo. *See* Chaussy, pp. 185–6.

600 —[*Works edited by Gifford,*] [Benedictine Rule.] Regle des religieuses de l'ordre de S. Benoist, reformées par R.P. Mre. Estiẽne Poncher Euesque de Paris. Traduite du Latin en François par R.P. D. L. Bernard . . . Prieur du College de Cluny à Paris 1608. Et depuis reueue & examinée par R.P.F. Gabriel de Ste Marie. 32°. 2 pts. *Paris chez Michel Soly,* 1621. BRU[4].CHA.GETH.SJBD.SOL.

With an additional titlepage, engraved.

—Rainolds, W. Caluino-Turcismus, 1597 [*etc.*]. *See* nos. 929–30.

—Rainolds, W. De iusta reipub. Christianae . . . authoritate, 1590 [*etc.*]. *See* nos. 931–2.

601 —[*Appendix.*] Marlot, G. Discours funebre sur la mort de feu Monseigneur . . . Gabriel de Saincte Marie, Archeuesque Duc de Reims . . . Auquel est monstré comme par deux mouuemens, apparemment contraires, on se peut disposer à la mort. Dedié à Monseigneur l'Illustrissime Prince Henry de Lorraine . . . Par Dom Guillaume Marlot . . . Prieur de ladite Abbaye de S. Nicaise. 4°. *Reims, chez François Bernard,* 1629. RMS.

602 —Maupas, H. de. Discours funebre, prononcé en l'Eglise de Saint Pierre aux Nonnes de Reims le xi iour de May 1629. A l'enterrement du coeur de feu Monseigneur Gabriel Gifford Archeuesque Duc de Reims . . . Par Messire Henry de Maupas Abbé de Sainct Denys dudit Reims. 8°. *Reims, chez Simon de Foigny,* 1629. PA.RMS.

603 —Morel, J. Hymni sacri. Item pleraque alia poematia, quae ad pietatem Christianam pertinent. Ad R. Antistitem D.D. Guillelmum Gifortium Archiepiscopum Ducem Remensem . . . Authore Ioanne Morello, Scholę Remensis in Academia Parisiensi moderatore. 4°. *Parisiis, apud P. Ludouicum Feburier . . . et Ioannem Bessin,* 1623. PA(3).PA[3].RMS.

Sacred poems, dedicated to Gifford.

604 —[Various authors.] Musarum Remensium applausus, pro magnifico Illustrissimi Dñi D. Gabrielis a S. Maria Archiepiscopi Ducis Remensis . . . in vrbem ecclesiamq. suam aduentu 11. & 12. Februarii diebus celebrato. 8° (in fours). *Remis, typis Simonis de Foigny,* 1623. RMS.

Poems, Latin, French and Greek, in honour of Gifford on the occasion of his taking possession of the see of Rheims. With an engraving of his arms on the verso of the titleleaf.

Giovanus, Joannes. *See* Young, J.

Godsalve, Edward. [*A work edited by him.*] Christopherson, J. Historiae ecclesiasticae pars prima, 1569. *See* no. 245.

Good, William. Ecclesiae Anglicanae trophaea, [1584, *etc.*]. *See* nos. 944–6.

605   **Gordon, James,** *of Huntley.*† Iacobi Gordoni . . . Controuersiarum epitomes, in qua de quaestionibus theologicis hac nostra aetate controuersis breuiter disputatur: idque ex sacris praesertim literis, tomus primus. 4°. *Augustoriti Pictonum, ex praelo Antonii Mesnerii,* 1612. O; A².CHA(2).D.E.E².L².L¹³.MD.PN.PR.RO¹¹.TRI.TRO.VI.VT.
Containing the first two controversies: 1. 'De verbo Dei'; 2. 'De Ecclesia'. There is an abridged English translation at A&R 360–4. Some copies have on the titlepage an engraved device of a wheat-sheaf with motto 'Acervus de parvis grandis', others are without it.

606   —[Anr. issue, with a cancel title.] *Augustoriti Pictonum Venundantur Parisiis. Apud Iacobum Barrois,* 1618. N(*with the cancel title pasted over the 1612 cancelland*).

607   —Iacobi Gordoni . . . Controuersiarum epitomes tomus secundus. In quo de augustissimo Eucharistiae sacramento contra Caluinianos breuiter disputatur. 4°. *Lutetiae Parisiorum, ex officina Niuelliana, sumptibus Sebastiani Cramoisy,* 1618. BAR³.PA.TRI.TRO.
Comprising the third controversy, 'De sacramento Eucharistiae'. No English translation of this appears to have been published.

608   —[Imprint variant.] *Lutetiae Parisiorum, sumptibus Nicolai Buon,* 1618. CHA.
Part of a shared edition with no. 607.

609   —[Anr. ed. of tom. 1, 2, with the addition of tom. 3 comprising controversies 4–9.] Controuersiarum Christianae fidei aduersus huius temporis haereticos epitome: Auctore R.P. Iacobo Gordono. 8°. 2 pts. *Coloniae Agrippinae, apud Ioannem Kinchium,* 1620. L.; D².E(2). HAN.HP.MD⁴.MTH.N.PA.PA⁶.PA⁸.ST(2). *This or no. 610 or no. 611 :* FU.O¹³.RO².
Pt. 1 contains tom. 1–2 comprising controversies 1–3; pt. 2 contains tom. 3 comprising controversies 4–9. Collation: (Pt. 1) ⁎⁸ A–S⁸T⁴V–Ii⁸Kk⁴. (Pt. 2) ⁎⁴A–Y⁸. Pt. 1 has a dedicatory epistle by the Author to Pope Paul V whose arms appear on the titlepage. At the end of Pt. 2 some copies have two additional quires: Z⁸, containing an index, and ²⁎², containing a letter from the publisher to the Pope saying that Gordon is dead, while in others these are lacking.

610   —[Anr. ed. of pt. 1 of no. 609, with anr. issue of pt. 2.] R.P. Iacobi Gordoni Huntlaei . . . Controuersiarum epitomes tomus primus (– tertius). 8°. 2 pts. *Coloniae Agrippinae, apud Ioannem Kinchium,* 1620. C(*pt. 1*).; CHA.DNPK.HP.LGE³.LX(*pt. 1*).MD.WO. *See also note to no. 609.*
In this edition pt. 1 is without the dedicatory epistle to the Pope whose arms on the titlepage are replaced by the printer's device. Pt. 1 collates: ⁎⁶A–Ff⁸. In some copies a bifolium signed R6.7 containing half-title and approbations for 'tomus secundus' is inserted between the original R5 and R6, making the whole gathering appear to be R¹⁰. Pt. 2 is a reissue of the sheets of pt. 2 of no. 609 and some copies have the index and letter at the end, while others are without them.

611   —[Anr. issue of both parts.] *Coloniae Agrippinae, apud Ioannem Kinchium,* 1620. L⁹.O². *See also note to no. 609.*
Identical with no. 610 except that the titleleaf (⁎1) of pt. 1 has been cancelled and replaced with a bifolium (⁎1.2) comprising a reprint of the first two leaves (⁎1,2) of no. 609. The title (⁎1ʳ), therefore, now follows that of no. 609 and has the arms of Paul V on it, and its

conjugate leaf ($*2^{r-v}$) contains the Author's dedicatory epistle to the Pope which does not appear in no. 610.

612 —[*Disputations in which he acted as Praeses.*] Marchesinus, P. De puro Dei verbo. Assertiones theologicae, quas authoritate & consensu inclytae facultatis theolog: Vniuersitatis Vien, defensurus est . . . Paulus Marchesinus . . . Praeside Iacobo Gordono. 4°. *Viennae Austriae, ex officina Caspari Stainhoferi,* 1572. PR.VI(*with an additional bifolium containing a dedication by Marchesinus*).

613 —Muchitsch, P. De vera et gratuita iustificatione hominis peccatoris coram Deo, per Iesum Christum. Assertiones theologicae, quas authoritate & consensu inclytae facultatis theologicae Vniuersitatis Viennensis, defensurus est . . . Petrus Muchitsch . . . Praeside Iacobo Gordono. 4°. *Viennae Austriae, in aedibus Collegii Caesarei Societatis Iesu,* 1572. PR.

The College no longer did its own printing after 1565. Probably *pr.* [Caspar Stainhofer].

614 **Gordon, James,** *of Lesmore.* Chronologia annorum seriem, regnorum mutationes, & rerum memorabiliū sedē, annumque ab orbe condito ad ñra vsque tempora cōplectens. Tomus prior. 8°. *Burdigalae, apud Sim. Milangium,* 1611. A.BAR³.BOR.CMR.DUR.FLO.GN.GTN.KN².LGE.PA. PA⁴.PA⁵.PR.TRO.VT. +

Titlepage engraved. With 3 folding tables.

615 —[A continuation.] Operis chronologici tomus posterior. Rerum per vniuersum orbem gestarum sedem, breuemque a Christo ad annum vsque M.DC.XIII. Fol. *Augustoriti Pictonum, ex officina Antonii Mesnerii,* 1613. A.BRS.CARP.FLO.KN².LOU³.LYN.MTH.PA(2).PA⁵.RO³.VT.

Titlepage engraved. In some copies a printed slip bearing the words 'Opus Chronologicum' is pasted over either the first two words ('Operis chronologici') or the first four words ('Operis chronologici tomus posterior') of the engraved title. In one copy seen (A) the words 'tomus posterior' are erased from the engraved title, leaving a space. With a folding engraved map.

616 —[Anr. ed. of both parts together.] Opus chronologicum, annorum seriem, regnorum mutationes, et rerum toto orbe gestarum memorabilium sedem annumque . . . complectens. Fol. 2 vols. *Coloniae Agrippinae, apud Ioannem Crithium,* 1614. L(2).; A.AIX.C⁸.CHA.CMR. D.D².DUR.FLO.FU.GT.KN.HP.O³.O⁵.OS.RO².VT.WO. + +

617 —[Anr. ed. of both parts, with a continuation to 1617.] Fol. 2 vols. *Augustoriti Pictonum, ex officina Antonii Mesneri,* 1617. L.O.C.; A(2). ANT.BAR².BRS.CMR.E.L⁴.MTH.O⁴.PA.PA⁴.SBG.VT. + +

What appears to be a third volume, printed at Poitiers in 1618, cited by Sommerv. (tom. 3, col. 1613) has not been found.

618 —De Catholica veritate diatriba. Pro epithalamio. Ad Serenissimum Valliorum Principem. 12°. *Burdigalae, apud Petrum de la Courm* [sic], 1623. L.O.C.; A.A².DE.DUR.E.E².HP.NM².O⁵.ST.VAL.VT. +

Dedicated to Prince Charles at the time of the proposed Anglo-Spanish marriage treaty.

619 —Iacobi Gordoni . . . Theologia moralis vniuersa octo libris comprehensa. Fol. *Lutetiae Parisiorum, sumptibus Sebastiani & Gabrielis Cramoisy,* 1634. L.O.C.; ANG.BG².BRS.L²⁶.LYN.O⁴.O⁸.PA.PA³.PR.RO². SBG². +

620 —Opuscula tria. Chronologicum, historicum, geographicum, curis tertiis nouissime lustrata & aucta ab ipso Auctore. 12°. *Coloniae Agrippinae, ex officina Bernardi Gualteri,* 1636. L.; ANT².DUR.E.E².GT. GTN.LOU³.MAR.MD.PR.VT.

With a folding table.

621 —[*A work edited by Gordon.*] [Bible.] Biblia sacra cum commentariis ad sensum literae . . . Auctore R.P. Iacobo Gordono Lesmorio. Fol. 3

vols. *Lutetiae Parisiorum, sumptibus Sebastiani & Gabrielis Cramoisy*, 1632. O.C.; BRS.C⁵.CHA.D.HP.L².L⁴.LOU³.O².PA.PA³.RO².RO⁵.SOL. +

[622 *cancelled*]

Green, Thomas, *alias. See* Wakeman, T.

Green, Thomas, *O.S.B.* [*Works in which he collaborated.*] Preston, T. Appellatio [ad Paulum V], 1620. *See* no. 925.3.

—Preston, T. . . . Supplicatio [ad Gregorium XV], 1621. *See* no. 926.1.

Greenwood, Christopher. [*A disputation in which he acted as Praeses.*] Waldegrave, C. Theses ex vniuersa theologia, disputandae in Coll. Anglicano Societatis Iesu Louanii, 1620. *See* no. 1343.

623 **Griffiths, Michael,** *alias* Alford. Rosa Veralla siue de laudibus Ill. mi Principis Fabritii Card. Veralli odae tres a Martino Tondo Acad. Parth. dedicatae dum publice de philosophia disputaret in Collegio Rom. Soc. Iesu. 8°. *Romae, typis Iacobi Mascardi*, 1622. RO²(4).RO⁴.

Anon. Sommerv. (tom. 1, col. 176, correction in tom. 8, col. 1609) attributes the authorship of the poems to Griffiths on the authority of a MS note in a copy at the Jesuit Roman College.

Grinus, Thomas. *See* Green, T.

Gualpolus, Richardus. *See* Walpole, R.

H., D.R.E.O.V. *See* no. 954.

624 **Hackshott, Thomas,** *alias* Hawkshaw, *Ven.* [*Appendix.*] Relacion del martirio de Tomas Haso, inclito martir de Iesu Christo, y de Nicolas Sisburno Ingleses, y de vna muger varonil. Con otros auisos importantes, embiados por vn sacerdote del Seminario de Seuilla, testigo de vista, qne [*sic*] fue de todo. Fol. (a bifolium). [Coloph.] *Granada, en casa de Antonio Renè*, 1615. MD(V–226. n. 58). [*L.]

Thomas Hackshott (Haso) and Nicholas Tichborne (Sisburno) were both executed at Tyburn on 24 August 1601. The author of the original eye-witness account on which this printed Spanish narrative is based has not been identified.

Haddoquius, Robertus. *See* Hadock, R.

Hadock, Robert, *in religion* Robert of S. Benedict. Discours et traicté veritable du martire enduré . . . Par le Pere Iean . . . Roberts, 1611. *See* nos. 939–40.

—[*A work in which he collaborated.*] Barnes, J. Supplicatio exhibita, [1623]. *See* no. 71.

625 **Hall, Richard.** De proprictate et vestiario monachorum, aliisque ad hoc vitium extirpandum necessariis, liber vnus. 8°. *Duaci, ex officina Ioannis Bogardi*, 1585. L.O.; BRS.DAI.DE.DOU.FLO.GT.LIL².LOU³.PA.PA³. RO².RO³.TNI.

626 —De quinquepartita conscientia, I. recta, II. erronea, III. dubia, IV. opinabili, seu opiniosa, et V. scrupulosa, libri III. 4°. *Duaci, apud Ioannem Bogardum*, 1598. O.C.; AMI.C².C⁵.CHA.D.HP.KN².L².O³.O⁷.PA. PA⁴.RO²(3).VT. + +

627 —Opuscula quaedam his temporibus pernecessaria. De triɔus primariis causis tumultuum Belgicorum . . . Contra coalitionem multarum religionum . . . Libellus exhortatorius ad pacem. 8°. *Duaci, ex officina Ioannis Bogardi*, 1581. O(2).C.; AIX.BRS.C².DE.LAR.LGE.LIL³.LOU³.NCY. PA.PA³.RO⁵.WO. +

628 —Tractatus aliquot vtilissimi, pro defensione regiae et episcopalis auctoritatis, contra rebelles horum temporum. Quibus accessit Colloquium quoddam cum D. d'Incy. 8°. *Duaci, ex officina Ioannis Bogardi*, 1583. PA³.RO².

629 —[Date variant.] 1584. C.; BRS(2).DOU.DUR.GT.LGE.LOU³.MU.PA.PA³.PA⁴. RO⁶.VT.

—[*Works edited or with a dedicatory epistle by Hall.*] Fisher, J. Tractatus de orando Deum. [1576, *etc.*] *See* nos. 435–6.

—Young, J. De schismate, 1573. *See* no. 1427.

Hames, Maurus. [*A work in which he collaborated.*] [Barnes, J.]
Syllabus actorum, 1623. *See* no. 73.

630   **Hamilton, Archibald.** Caluinianae confusionis demonstratio, contra
maledicam ministrorum Scotiae responsionem. 8°. *Parisiis, apud
Nicolaum Chesneau,* 1581. DMR.DUR.E.F.KN.L¹³.LYN.NTS.O⁷.POI.RO³.
TRI.U.VI.VT. +
    Defending no. 632 against an attack by Thomas Smeton (STC
22651). Dedicated to Mary Queen of Scots. Renouard (Brumen) 262.

631   —[Imprint variant.] *Parisiis, apud Thomam Brumennium,* 1581. L.;
A(*imp.*).A².E(3).FLO.L²⁵.LOU³.MD³.MP.O².O⁴.RO.SOR.WOR.YK. +
    With Brumen's device in place of Chesneau's on the titlepage.
Forms part of a shared edition with no. 630.

632   —De confusione Caluinianae sectae apud Scotos ecclesiae nomen
ridicule vsurpantis, dialogus. 8°. *Parisiis, apud Thomam Brumenium,*
1577. L(2).O.C.; C³.E.KN.MP.NY.PA³.RO.RO².RO⁶.TRI.VAL².
    Dedicated to Mary Queen of Scots. Answered by Thomas Smeton
in STC 22651 to which Hamilton replied in no. 630. Renouard
(Brumen) 221.

633   **Hamilton, Francis.** Ad Reuerendiss: et illustriss: Principem …
Iulium, Dei gratia, Episcopum Herbipolensem, Franciae orientalis
Ducem … Oratio in solenni restitutione coenobii S. Iacobi Scotorum
Herbipoli, anno M.D.XCV. die mensis Aprilis vltimo. 4°. *Wirceburgi,
excudebat Georgius Fleischmann,* 1595. L.; E.MU.STC(*imp.*).VI.WZ.
    Hamilton was Prior of the monastery at Würzburg restored to the
Scots Benedictines by Bishop Julius in 1595. *See* Dilworth, pp.
31–2, 41–2.

634   —De sanctorum inuocatione demonstratio duplex … Ad vtramque,
pro Baccalaureatus Biblici gradu responsurus est Pater F. Franciscus
Hamiltonius Scotus … Praeside D. Petro Thyraeo. 4°. *Wirceburgi,
excudebat Georgius Fleischmann,* 1596. L.O.; AUG.DI.MU.STU.U.VI.WZ.
    A programme announcing the forthcoming defence of his thesis.

635   —Disputatio theologica de legitimo sanctorum cultu per sacras imagines
… Ad quam pro Baccalaureatu formato, in … Academia Herbi-
polensi responsurus est … Franciscus Hamiltonius Scotus. 4°. *Ex
officina typographica Georgii Fleischmanni,* 1597. L.; FU.MU.STU.U.VI.
VT.WZ.
    A programme announcing the forthcoming defence of his thesis.

636   **Harpsfield, Nicholas.** Dialogi sex contra Summi Pontificatus, monas-
ticae vitae, sanctorum, sacrarum imaginum oppugnatores, et pseudo-
martyres. Nunc primum … ab Alano Copo Anglo editi. 8°.
Antuerpiae, ex officina Christophori Plantini, 1566. L(5).O(2).C.; A.BRS.
C².CHA.D.DE(- *plate*).DUR.GTN.LOU³.MD.MTH.PA.RO⁵. + +
    Anon. With a folding plate.

637   —[Anr. issue, with a cancel title.] *Parisiis, Oliua Pet. l'Huillier,* 1566.
AMI.PA⁶.
    The sheets of no. 636 except for the title-leaf which is a cancel.
With the original colophon of Christopher Plantin at Antwerp.

638   —[Anr. ed.] 8°. *Antuerpiae, ex officina Christophori Plantini,* 1573.
L.O.C(2).; BAR².BM².BRS.C⁴.FLO.GT.HP.MD.PA.PA³.TRO.VI. +
    Anon. The text is signed: A.H.L.N.H.E.V.E.A.C. [Auctor huius
libri Nicolaus Harpesfeldus. Eum vero edidit Alanus Copus.]

639   —Historia anglicana ecclesiastica … Adiecta breui narratione de
diuortio Henrici VIII. regis … ab Edmundo Campiano. Nunc
primum in lucem producta studio & opere R.P. Richardi Gibboni.
Fol. *Duaci, sumptibus Marci Wyon,* 1622. L.C(2).; A.ANT.BRS.CHA.D.
DUR.E.GT.LOU³.MTH.PA.PA³.ST(2).USH.VT. + +
    This work includes Harpsfield's 'Historia haeresis Wicleffianae'
which was not published separately.

639.1 **Harris, Paul.**† 'Αρχτομαστιξ sive Edmundus Vrsulanus propter usurpatum judicium de tribunali dejectus. 4°. *n.p.* 1633. L.O.C.; C².C⁵.CASHEL.D.LINC.
Answers no. 861. *Pr.* [Dublin, Society of Stationers.] A&R 380, STC 12808. ERL 128.
—Illustriss. Archiepisc. & R. Episcopis per vniversam Hiberniam, [1632]. *See* no. 127.1.
Hart, John. [For editions of *Diarium Turris*]. *See* nos. 973, *etc.*
Haso, Tomas. *See* Hackshott, T.
Hawkshaw, Thomas. *See* Hackshott, T.

Hay, John.†

Original Works

640 —L'Antimoine, aux responses, que Th. de Beze faict à trente sept demandes de deux cents & six. Proposées aux ministres d'Escosse. 8°. *Tournon, par Claude Michel,* 1588. L.O.; BOR.EV.L²⁵.LOU.PA².
Beze had published anonymously at Geneva in 1586 *Response aux cinq premieres et principales demandes de F. Iean Hay (see G. Moeckli, Les livres imprimés à Genève de 1550 à 1600,* 1966, p. 115), and had evidently followed this with a supplement. The title Antimoine refers to Beze's contemptuous reference to Hay as 'Moine'.

641 —La defense des demandes proposées aux ministres de Caluin, touchant les blasphemes & mensonges, contre le libelle de Iaq. Pineton-de Chābrun. 8°. *Lyon, par Iehan Pillehotte,* 1586. BOR.LOU.LOU³.LYN. PA⁷.RO⁶.
Answering J. Pineton de Chambrun's *L'Esprit et conscience Iesuitique,* 1584, which had attacked no. 642. Hay says in his preface that he wrote the work in Latin and had it put into French by some of his students.

642 —Demandes faictes aux ministres d'Escosse: touchant la religion Chrestienne ... reueues & de l'Escossois mises en nostre langue Françoise. 16°. *Lyon, par Iean Pillehotte,* 1583. L.; AV.E.E².
A translation of A&R 389. Hay explains in a preliminary advertisement that the English original was written against the Scots Calvinists and that he has been persuaded to publish a French version for use against the Huguenots. The translator was [Michel Coyssard].

643 —[Anr. ed.] *Verdun, J. Wapius,* 1583.
Not found. Description from Sommerv. (tom. 2, col. 1599).

644 —[Anr. ed.] 16°. *Lyon, par Iean Pillehotte,* 1584. A².E².F.LOU.STA.
645 —[Anr. ed.] 12°. *Bruxelle, chez Rutger Velpius,* 1595. E.GT.LDS.
646 —[Anr. ed.] 18°. *Rouen, chez Romain de Beauuais,* 1602. TRO.
647 —[Anr. ed.] 8°. *Paris, Claude Chapelet,* 1603.
Not found. Description from Cordes catalogue, p. 97.

648 —[*German transl.*] Fragstueck des christlichen Glaubens, an die neuwe sectische Predigkandten ... Durch Sebastian Werro ... in das Teutsch gebracht. 4°. *Freyburg in Vchtlandt, bey Abraham Gemperlin,* 1585. L.O.; BNE.DI.DUS.FR.FU².KN.KN².MU(4).STG(*imp*).TB.VI.

649 —[Anr. ed.] 4°. *Freyburg in der Eydgnoschafft, bey Abraham Gemperlin,* 1586. L.; EI.FR.RG.

650 —[Date variant.] 1587. DMR.DUS.FR.KN.KN².MU.WO. [*O.]
651 —Disputationum libri duo, in quibus calumniae, et captiones ministri anonymi Nemausensis, contra Assertiones theologicas, & philosophicas in Academia Turnonia, anno M.D.LXXXII. propositas, discutiuntur. 4°. *Lugduni, apud Ioannem Pillehotte,* 1584. [Coloph.]

Excudebat Iacobus Roussin. A².AMI.AV.BOR.E.KN.MD.O¹¹.OS.PA.PA⁴.RO²
(2).TRI.VT.YK. +
> Answering an attack on the Jesuits of Tournon by the University of
> Nimes: *Academiae Nemausensis breuis et modesta responsio ad
> professorum Turnoniorum . . . assertiones,* Londini, 1584 (STC 18581).
> Hay's work was, in turn, answered by Jean de Serres in vol. 4 of
> *Anti-Iesuita,* 1586–88, and again in his *Pro vera ecclesiae catholicae
> autoritate defensio,* 1594.

Works translated or edited by Hay

652 —Carvalho, V. Iapponiensis imperii admirabilis commutatio exposita
litteris ad . . . P. Claudium Aquauiua Praepositum Generalem Soc.
Iesu, quas ex Italis Latinas fecit Io. Hayus. 8°. *Antuerpiae, sumptibus
viduae & heredum Io: Belleri,* 1604. L(2).O(2).C.; D.DI(2).GT.HEV.
MU(3).PA.RO³.SBG.TB.WO.

653 —Sisto, *da Siena.* Sixti Senensis . . . Bibliotheca sancta . . . a Ioanne
Hay . . . plurimis in locis a mendis expurgata, atque scholiis illustrata.
Fol. *Lugduni, sumptibus Sib. a Porta,* 1591. [Coloph.] *Excudebat
Stephanus Seruin,* 1591. O.; D(2).MD.PA⁴.
> Earlier editions of this work, which was first published in 1566,
> were not edited by Hay.

654 —[Anr. issue? or imprint and date variant?] *Lugduni, sumptibus Petri
Landry,* 1592. [Coloph.] *Excudebat Stephanus Seruin,* 1591. MD.STA.
TRO.

655 —[Date variant of no. 653.] *Lugduni, sumptibus Sib. a Porta,* 1593.
[Coloph.] *Excudebat Stephanus Seruin,* 1591. O.; DOL.ETON.GN.

656 —[Anr. issue? or imprint variant?] *Lugduni, sumptibus Petri Landry,*
1593. [Coloph.] *Excudebat Stephanus Seruin,* 1591. BRG.DE.GN.MD.
PA.VAL².

656.1 —[Imprint variant?] *Lugduni, apud Th. de Gabiano,* 1593.
> Not found. Reported by Sommerv. (tom. 4, col. 164).

657 —[Anr. ed.] Fol. *Parisiis, ex typographia Rolini Theodorici,* 1610. L.C.;
A.ANT³.BOR.D(2).DUR.L².L⁴.L²⁶.MD.O¹².OR.PA.PA⁴.SBG².

658 —[Anr. ed.] Vltima demum hac editione auctorum recentiorum
accessione locupletata. 4°. *Coloniae Agrippinae, ex officina Choliniana,
sumptibus Petri Cholini,* 1626. L.O.C.; A.A².CMR.DUR.FLO².L¹³.PA(3).
PLU.PR.
> Some copies have an index (sig. a–b⁴); others are without it.
> Sommerv. (tom. 4, col. 165) records what appears to be this edition
> but with date 1625; no copy with date 1625 has been found.

659 —Torres Bollo, D. de. De rebus Peruanis Rdi. P. Dieghi de Torres,
Societatis Iesu presbyteri commentarius, a Ioanne Hayo . . . ex italo
in latinum conuersus. 8°. *Antuerpiae, ex officina typographia Martini
Nutii,* 1604. L.; HEV.KN.MU(7).PA.PA⁴.PR.TRI.
> Another Latin translation of the same work, printed at Mainz in
> 1604, is not by Hay.

660 —Valignano, A. Litterae R.P. Alexandri Valignano visitatoris Societatis
Iesu in Iapponia & China, scriptae 10. Octobris 1599. ad. R.P.
Claudium Aquauiua eiusdem Societatis Praepositum Generalem: a
Ioanne Hayo . . . ex italico in latinum conuersea. 12°. *Antuerpiae, apud
Ioachim Trognaesium,* 1603. L(2).; E. HEV.O².PA.

661 —[Various authors.] De rebus Iaponicis, Indicis, et Peruanis epistolae
recentiores. A Ioanne Hayo . . . in librum vnum coaceruatae. 8°.
Antuerpiae, ex officina Martini Nutii, 1605. L(3).O.C.; ANT³.BRS.CHA.
D.DI(3).E.E².GTN.MD.MU(4).PA.RO².USH.VT. + +
> Forms vol. 2 of G. P. Maffei, *Historiarum Indicarum libri XVI,*
> Antuerpiae, 1605, but is also found separately. Hay edited the
> volume and himself translated some of the letters. Three of his

translations had already been published separately (nos. 652, 659, 660).

Hay, Romanus. [The writer of this name, sometimes taken to have been a Scotsman, who in 1639 published a reply to Caspar Schoppe's *Astrum inextinctum*, was, in fact, a German Benedictine of the Abbey of Ochsenhausen, *see* Dilworth, p. 174.]

Haydock, Robert. *See* Hadock, R.

Henfildanus, Didymus Veridicus, *pseud. See* Stapleton, T. (no. 1141).

662 **Henrietta Maria,** *Queen of England. [Appendix.]* Les royales ceremonies faites en l'edification d'vne chappelle de Capucins à Londres en Angleterre, dans le palais de la Roine; fait par son commandement & par la permission du Roy: en laquelle chappelle elle a posé la premiere pierre. 8° (in fours). *Paris, chez. Iean Brunet,* 1632. LIL. PA(2).PA⁴.

663 **Henry VIII,** *King of England.*‡ Regis Angliae Henricis huius nominis octaui Assertio septem sacramentorum aduersus Martinum Lutherum. 4°. *Lugduni, apud Guiliel. Rouillium,* 1561. O.C(2).; AV.E².F.MD.P.PA. PA³.PA⁴.POI.RO⁵.TRO.VT.

First published in 1521 (STC 13078). Does not contain Fisher's *Defensio regiae assertionis* which was added in the 1562 edition (no. 665). This edition has on its titlepage the printer's device showing an eagle mounted on a globe and column with the two entwined serpents on either side within a framework including cherubs and cornucopiae. The title is not enclosed in a border.

664 —[Anr. ed.] 4°. *Lugduni, apud Guliel. Rouillium,* 1561. L(2).; MTH.PA².
A close reprint of no. 663 from which it is distinguished by having a small piece of type-ornament in place of the device on the title-page, and the title enclosed in a woodcut border of Corinthian columns supporting a pediment.

665 —[Anr. ed., enlarged.] Assertio septem sacramentorum . . . Cui subnexa est eiusdem Regis epistola, Assertionis ipsius contra eundem defensoria. Accedit quoque R.P.D. Iohan. Roffen. Episcopi contra Lutheri Captiuitatem Babylonicam, Assertionis regiae defensio. 16°. 2 pts. *Parisiis, apud Gulielmum Desboys,* 1562. L(3: 1-pt. 2),O.; C⁵.CHA.D². DAI.DE,DUR.E.GT.HP.L².LGE³.MD.USH.VT. +
Fisher's work has its own titlepage. It was first published at Cologne in 1525. A German translation of part of it published separately in 1561 is at no. 422.

666 —[Variant imprint.] *Parisiis, apud Sebastianum Niuellium,* 1562. L(pt. 2).O.; AMI.C³.C⁵.C¹⁷.DE.HP.L¹⁵.MD.O⁴⁶.MAR.PA.STG.TB.TRO. +
With Nivelle's imprint substituted on the first of the two title-pages and his device and miprint on the second. Forms part of a shared edition with no. 665. An octavo edition with imprint *Parisiis* and date 1562, is an 18th century reprint done in Italy.

Hepburn, Bonaventure, *name in religion. See* Hepburn, J.

667 **Hepburn, James.** Lexicon S. linguae succinctum. Auctore F. Iac. Bonauentura Hepburno Scoto Minimo. 12°. *n.p.d.* [c. 1620].L(1568/ 2969).;VT(R.g.Oriente VI.1).
Hebrew and Latin. The two copies found comprise 88 numbered folios, collating: B–H¹²I⁴, i.e. lacking titlepage and preliminaries. The above title is taken from the head-title on B1ʳ. According to Roberti (vol. 2, p. 626) Hepburn, a Scottish Minim, died in 1623 while still young.

668 —Virga aurea septuaginta duobus encomiis B.V. Mariae caelata. Fol. *Philippus Thomassinus sculpsit, et excudit Romę* . . . 1616. O(Ashm. Rolls 48).

Comprising five large double folio engraved plates, unnumbered. The first plate is headed by the title as cited above, followed by a dedication to Pope Paul V signed: 'F. Iac. Bonauentura Hepburnus Scotus S.Ord. Sti Francisci de Paula'; the second bears, in its l.h. margin, the imprint and date as shown above. *Pr.* [Rome.] A facsimile of this work was published by Fernand de Mély, Paris, 1922.

669   **Hicky, Anthony.** Nitela Franciscanae religionis, et abstersio sordium quibus eam conspurcare frustra tentauit Abrahamus Bzouius. Parenti optimae Fr. Dermicius Thadaei pius filius . . . mutuam vicem reddit. 4°. *Lugduni, sumptibus Claudii Landry*, 1627. O(*imp.*).; CHAD.D.KNY(5). LYN.MTH.NP(2).NP³.PA(2).PA⁴.RO³.RO⁶.TOU.VAL².VT.

Dermicius Thadaei filius, *pseud.* Answers criticism of the Franciscans in vols. 13–18 of Bzovius's *Annales ecclesiasticae*, the sequel to Baronius published at Cologne from 1621 onwards.

—[*Works edited by him.*] Angelus, *del Paz*. Operum . . . Angeli del Pas . . . a RR.PP. Fr. Luca Wadingo & Fr. Antonio Hiquaeo . . . collectorum & reuisorum tomus secundus (-quartus), 1623–28. *See* nos. 1321–3.

—Duns Scotus, J. R.P.F. Ioannis Duns Scoti . . . Quaestiones in lib. IV Sententiarum . . . Cum commentario R.P.F. Antonii Hiquaei, 1639. *Forms vol. 8 of* no. 1326.

670   **Hill, Nicholas.** Philosophia Epicurea, Democratiana, Theophrastica, proposita simpliciter, non edocta. 8°. *Parisiis, apud Rolinum Thierry*, 1601. L.; D.PA(2).

There is a biography of Hill, a Catholic physician who retired abroad at the beginning of James I's reign, in DNB.

671   —[Anr. ed.] Accessit autem huic editioni recens Angeli Politiani πανεπιστημων. 12°. *Coloniae Allobrogum, prostant in officina Fabriana*, 1619. L(*with the words 'Coloniae Allobrogum' in the imprint blotted out in ink at an early period and the word 'Genevae' printed or stamped above them*).O.; O⁹(*as* L.).PA(2).

Hiquaeus, Antonius. *See* Hicky, A.

672   **Holdsworth, Daniel.‡** Oratio in obitum Illustrissimi D.D. Card. Sarnani tituli Sancti Petri in Monte Aureo, breuiter, & sincere eius vitam, mores, & mortem continens. Auctore R.D. Daniele Alsuorto, Anglo, Sacrae Theologiae Doct. & Illustriss. Card. Borromei familiari: ad Illustrissimum D.D. Alexandrum Perettum Card. de Montealto. 4°. *Romae, ex typographia Gulielmi Facciotti*, 1596. RO⁴.RO⁶(2).

Alsuortus [Holdsworth]. For his career, *see* Anst., vol. 1, p. 170.

673   **Holland, Henry.** Vrna aurea vel in sacrosanctam missam, maximeque in diuinam canonem . . . clara & accurata expositio. 8°. *Duaci, typis Laurentii Kellami*, 1612. AMI.AMP.DOU.KN².L⁴.MAA.PA³.PA⁶.

The privilege granting Kellam printing rights for six years is dated 15 July 1608. This supports Pits's statement (p. 808) that there was a Douai edition of 1608, but no copy has so far been found.

674   —[Anr. issue, with title:] Arca noui foederis in sacrosancto missae canone representata. *Antuerpiae, apud Petrum & Ioannem Bellerum*, 1615. C.; D.

A reissue of the sheets of no. 673 except for the titleleaf (a1) and possibly its conjugate leaf (a8).

675   **Holles, Thomas.** Oratio ad Beatissimum in Christo Patrem, ac S.D.N. Paulum V. P.M. Philippi III Hispaniarum, et Indiarum Regis Catholici nomine. Obedientiam praestante Illustrissimo . . . D. Gomesio Suarez . . . Duce Feriae . . . Habita a Thoma Holles Catalano doctore theologo, ac publico in Academia Barcinonensi professore. 4°. *Romae, apud Stephanum Paulinum*, 1607. BAR.FLO³. MD.O¹².VT(3).

Though Holles is described in the title as a Catalan, the name is English. He may have been a chaplain in the household of the Duke of Feria whose English mother, Jane Dormer, was still living.

676   **Hollings, Edmund.**‡ Poemata, religionis, virtutis, eruditionisque laude . . . F. Michaeli Hererio Ransouiensi Boio . . . et Vito Prieffero Miespachensi Boio . . . Cum V. Non. Octobris in florentissima Ingolstadiensi Academia supremam in philosophia lauream consequerentur . . . Autoribus, M. Edmundo Hollyngo Anglo [and others]. 4°. *Ingolstadii, excudebat Dauid Sartorius*, 1584. MU.

Hollings was professor of medicine at Ingolstadt. For other works by him printed at Ingolstadt which fall outside the scope of this catalogue, *see* Stalla.

677   —[*A disputation in which he acted as Praeses.*] Vietor, I. Theses, ex philosphia vniuersa, a Ioanne Vietore Monacense positae, ad publicam examen . . . Praeside Edmundo Hollyngo. 4°. *Ingolstadii, excudebat Dauid Sartorius*, 1584. DI.MU².

678   **Holywood, Christopher** (Christophorus a Sacrobosco). Defensio decreti Tridentini et sententiae Roberti Bellarmini . . . de authoritate Vulgatae editionis latinae aduersus sectarios, maxime Whitakerum . . . accessit eiusdem De inuestiganda vera ac visibili Christi ecclesia libellus. 8°. 2 pts. *Antuerpiae, apud Ioannem Keerbergium*, 1604. L.O.C.; D(3).GTN.HP.L².L²⁵.LYN.MD.MTH.O⁵.PA.TRI.VT. +

Pt. 1 is an answer mainly to Whitaker's attack on Bellarmine concerning the Vulgate (STC 25366). Pt. 2, which has its own titlepage, was possibly also issued separately in 1604 (*see* no. 679).

679   —[?Anr. issue of pt. 2] De inuestiganda vera ac visibili Christi ecclesia, libellus. *Antuerpiae, apud Ioannem Keerbergium*, 1604. O.; NI.O⁷.

The sheets of pt. 2 of no. 678 unaltered. Though copies are found separate from pt. 1 today, it is not certain that they were issued separately.

680   —[Anr. ed. of pt. 2, enlarged.] De inuestiganda vera ac visibili Christi ecclesia tractatus . . . Noua editio ab ipso auctore recognita & aucta. 8°. *Antuerpiae, apud haeredes Martini Nutii*, 1619. L.; AUG.KN.L². LIL³.TRI.

Huddleston, Richard. [Life of Richard Bristow, 1616.] *In* no. 118.

Hunt, Thomas, *alias. See* Benstead, T.

681   **Hunter, James.** Iacobi Hunteri epistolae miscellaneae. 8°. *Viennae Austriae, ex officina typographica Michaelis Rictii*, 1631. O.; EX.PA (2:-1 *imp.*).UP.VI.

Letters, some concerning religion, written to various correspondents in the course of his travels round Europe, 1620–30.

Hybernois, François. *See* Nugent, F.

I., E. Strena Catholica, 1620. *See* no. 927.1.

Ioannes, *a S. Francisco, name in religion. See* Punch, J.

Iohannes, *S. Andreae, fictitious name in religion. See* Barnes, J. (no. 70).

Ireland, *Catholic Church.* [Missals and Rituals for use in Ireland.] *See* England, Catholic Church.

682   **Irish Regular Clergy.** [*Appendix.*] Gondi, Jean François de, *Archbishop of Paris.* Censura Illustrissimi et Reuerendissimi . . . Parisiensis Archiepiscopi . . . in quasdam propositiones Hybernicas, & duos libellos Anglicanos. 8° (a quadrifolium). *Parisiis, ex officina Roberti Stephani*, 1631. PA³.PA⁴(3).RO¹⁴ (SORCE 100 ff. 131–4) [*D⁶].

Dated 30 Jan. 1631. This is a general censure of the propositions and books cited in nos. 683–5. It does not list the propositions. Reprinted with no. 1405 in 1643. An English translation [by Paul Harris] is included in A&R 224. *See Irish Theol. Quarterly*, vol. 26, 1959, pp. 110–16.

683   —Paris, *Sorbonne.* Censura propositionum ad sacram facultatem theo-

logiae Parisiensem allatarum, per D. Patricium Cahill Rectorem S. Michaelis Dublinensis, & obsignatarum ac recognitarum per ... Michaelem Cantuelem ... Iacobum Fallonum ... & Terentium Coghlanum ... quas supra dicti testati sunt passim a Regularibus in Hibernia ... publicari & praedicari. 8° (a quadrifolium). *Parisiis, ex officina typographica Natalis Charles*, 1631. C.; PA⁴(2).

> Listing eleven propositions here stated to be publicly maintained be the Regular clergy in Ireland, each followed by a censure. The censures were imposed on 7 Jan. and confirmed on 15 Jan. 1631. There is an English translation at A&R 224. Answered in no. 861.

684   —[Anr. ed., with censures against two books by English Jesuits.] Censura propositionum quarumdam, tum ex Hibernia delatarum, cum ex duobus libris Anglico sermone conscriptis in Latinum bona fide conuersis excerptarum, per sacram facultatem theologiae Parisiensis facta. 4°. *Parisiis, apud Carolum Morellum*, 1631. L.O.C.; D.D¹⁰. DUR(2).KNY.O¹².PA³(3).VT.

> The two English books censured are A&R 898 and 322; the first was censured on 5 Feb, the second on 15 Feb., 1631. The propositions objected to in the two books are the same as those listed in no. 1406 and were excerpted from an unpublished Latin translation prepared for the French bishops by a group of the English secular clergy (*see* no. 1407, and no. 685, pt. 1, p. 19). There is an English translation of the *Censura* at A&R 224. This edition of the Latin is usually found bound up with nos. 1406, 1104, 1407, all of which were also printed at Paris for C. Morel. Answered in no. 489 and parodied in no. 484. See RH, Oct. 1987, pp. 329, *et seq.*

685   —[Anr. ed., with the text re-arranged, and with further additions.] Censura propositionum quarumdam, tum ex Hibernia delatarum, cum ex duobus libris Anglico sermone conscriptis ... 12°. 2 pts. *Parisiis, apud Carolum Morellum*, 1631. DMR.

> The additions consist of texts already published separately in nos. 1407, 1406, 1104. Pt. 2 has its own titlepage with imprint: *Parisiis, iussu Cleri, excudebat Antonius Vitray.* The typography shows that Vitray, in fact, printed both parts of the book; he was evidently working for Morel whose privilege, dated 21 Feb. 1631, granting him sole publishing rights for ten years, is printed on sig. C9ᵛ of pt. 2. Reprinted in 1644.

Irland, Bonaventure. [This writer, professor of law at the University of Poitiers, was the son of a Scotsman who had settled in France. He appears to have had no links with his father's country of origin and his own publications are completely French in character. *See* P. Larousse, *Grand dictionnaire*, t. 9, p. 789.]

686   **James V,** *King of Scotland*. [*Appendix.*] Histoire, vie et mort de Iacques cinquiesme Roy d'Escosse. Ensemble l'histoire deplorable de la belle Dunglas, vray miroir de constance & chasteté. 8° (in fours). *Paris, chez Rolin Baraignes*, 1621. L.; BOR.E.PA.

> Dealing in part with the Reformation in Scotland. Internal evidence shows that this is not a translation but was written in French. An English version, made from the French, was printed in *Miscellanea antiqua*, 1710.

James, Thomas. [*A work translated by him.*] [Persons, R.] Relacion de vn sacerdote Ingles, 1592. See no. 899.

687   **Jenks, Roland.** [*Appendix.*] Histoire merueilleuse et espouuantable aduenue en Angleterre, és moys de Iuillet & Aoust derniers passez. Contenant le discours d'vne estrange maladie & mortalité aduenue en la ville & vniuersité d'Oxford, à l'instant d'vne sentence donnée contre Roland Ienkes, Catholique, & citoyen de ladicte ville: auec le nõbre des morts depuis le sixiesme Iuillet dernier, iusques au

douziesme Aoust ensuyuant. Fidelement traduict d'Anglois en François & extraict de mot à mot de l'exemplaire imprimé à Londres. 8° (a quadrifolium). *Paris, chez Iean Poupy, n.d.* [1577.] o⁹ (*cropped*). [*DMR].

> Concerning the sudden mysterious sickness and death of the judge and many other persons connected with the trial of Roland Jenks, a Catholic bookseller, at Oxford in May 1577. The text begins: 'Extraict d'vne lettre Angloise imprimée à Londres par Guillaume Bartelt, & traduicte en François . . .' No English printed version nor any MS of the text appears to be known. Collation: [a]⁴ ([a]4 blank). In the only copy found the signatures are cropped. Madan 54.

688 —[Anr. ed.] 8° (in fours). *Paris, chez Iean Poupy, n.d.* [1577]. LYN.

> Consisting of a reissue of no. 687 followed by a new quadrifolium signed b⁴. Collation: a–b⁴ (a4, b4 blank). The new quadrifolium contains an extract about similar unexplained deaths in other parts of the country, translated from Abraham Fleming's *A straunge and terrible wunder*, 1577 (STC 11050).

689 —[Anr. ed., with title:] Histoire meruelleuse aduenues [*sic*] par feu du ciel en trois villes d'Angleterre, à l'encontre de douze iuges heretiques, & de deux ministres qui voulloient persecuté [*sic*] les Catholiques. Ensemble le nom des iuges & des deux ministres à qui le Diable tordict le col dedans leur [*sic*] temples. 8° (in fours). *Paris, iouxte la copie imprimée à Rouen par Pierre Corant, n.d.* [1577]. L.O. [*DMR].

> A careless piece of work perhaps not really printed at Paris. The Rouen edition cited in the imprint has not been found. Madan 55.

690 —[Anr. ed., with title:] Histoire meruelleuse admirable aduenue en Angleterre, és moys de Iuillet & Aoust derniers passez. Contenant le discours d'vne estrange maladie & mortalité subite aduenue en la ville & vniuersité d'Oxford . . . Autres signes merueilleux & estranges aduenus en mesme moys villes & paroisses de Bongay, & Biblery, en Angleterre. Traduict sur l'exemplaire imprimé à Londres. 8° (in twos). *Paris, pour Gilles de S. Gilles, iouxte la coppie imprimée chez Iean Poupy, n.d.* [1577]. PA³(32201, pièce).

> A reprint of no. 687.

691 —[*Spanish account of some of the same incidents.*] Relacion muy verdadera de vn castigo que Dios nuestro Señor embio sobre ciertos Luteranos en la ciudad de Oxonia en el reino de Inglaterra, en este presente año de mil y quinientos y setenta y siete. Embiada de la corte de su Magestad por el Illustro Don Iuan Iofre, a esta ciudad de Valencia. 4°. *Hecha imprimir por Gabriel Ribas* [Coloph.] *En casa de Ioan Nauarro*, 1577. MD.

> This is not a translation of part of nos. 687–90 but an independent account of some of the same incidents. Though it describes the death of the judge and others at Oxford, it contains no account of the trial of Jenks. Pr. [Valencia]. Reprinted in *Relaciones de los Reinados de Carlos V & Felipe II*, 1950 (*Sociedad de Bibliófilos Españoles*, época 2, no. 25).

Joannes. *See* Ioannes.

692 **Joliffe, Henry.** Responsio venerabilium sacerdotum, Henrici Ioliffi & Roberti Ionson, sub protestatione facta, ad illos articulos Ioānis Hoperi, Episcopi Vigorniae nomen gerentis, in quibus a Catholica fide dissentiebat. 8°. *Antuerpiae, ex officina Christophori Plantini*, 1564. L.O.C.; BOR.BRS.C⁵.DMR.HP.L².L²⁶.PA.PA³.PA⁴.RO³.VT.WO. + +

> Joliffe and Jonson were canons of Worcester who refused to subscribe to Bishop Hooper's articles in 1552 under Edward VI.

—[*A work edited by Joliffe.*] Pole, R., *Cardinal*. De summo pontifice Christi in terris vicario, 1569. *See* no. 915.

693   **Jones, John,** *in religion* Leander de S. Martino.‡ Sacra ars memoriae ad
Scripturas diuinas in promptu habendas memoriterque ediscendas
accommodata . . . Annexa est Conciliatio locorum Scripturae specie
tenus pugnantium olim edita per Seraphinum Cumiranum Minori-
tam, & nunc per succinctam epitomen explicata ab eodem R.P.
Leandro de S. Martino. 8°. 2 pts. *Duaci, ex typographia Baltazaris
Belleri,* 1623. O.; AAR.AMI.ANT³. C¹⁶. CHA.DAI.DE(*imp.*).DOU.DUR.FRA.
KN(2).LOU³(pt. 2).PA.PA².PA⁴.WO. +
     Pt. 2 has its own titlepage.

—[*A work of which he was part author.*] Reyner, C. Apostolatus Benedictinorum in Anglia, 1626. *See* no. 934.

—[*Works edited by him.*] [Alliaco, P. de. Petri de Alliaco . . . opuscula
spiritualia, 1634.]
     This work, sometimes entered under Jones in library catalogues, was
not, in fact, edited by him; he merely gave the approbation for it to
be published.

694   —Arnobius. Arnobii disputationum aduersus gentes libri septem; cui
accesserunt paratitla, seu breues summulę, quibus elucidatur authoris
obscuri methodus, qua in disputando vtitur. 8°. *Duaci, ex officina
typographica Baltasaris Belleri,* 1634. L.O.C.; A.BAR².BOR.DE.DOU.DUR.
GT.PA.PA⁴.RO⁶.TOU.

695   — [Anr. issue.] *Duaci, ex officina typographica Baltasaris Belleri,* 1636.
O.; D.GT.MD.
     The sheets of no. 694 except for the first five quires, comprising the
title and preliminaries and Jones's 'Paratitla', which are reprinted.

696   —[Bible.] Biblia sacra, cum glossa ordinaria . . . nouis patrum, cum
Graecorum, tum Latinorum explicationibus locupletata . . . opera et
studio theologor. Duacensium diligentissime emendatis. Fol. 6 vols.
*Duaci, excudebat Baltazar Bellerus, suis et Ioannis Keerbergii Antuer-
piensis sumptibus,* 1617. [vols. 2–6:] *Antuerpiae, apud Ioannem Keerbergium,* 1617. L.; BOR.D.DE.LGE³.PA.RO⁸.
     The approbation names Jones as the principal editor. The titlepage
to vol. 1 is engraved.

697   —[Anr. issue.] *Antuerpiae, apud Ioannem Meursium,* 1634. AMI.ANT².
BON.BOR.BRS.D.DNPK.DUS.MTH.OR.RO⁸.VI.VT.
     Except for the titleleaves, this appears to be a reissue of the sheets
of no. 696.

—Cumiramus, S. Conciliatio omnium fere locorum totius sacrae
Scripturae, quae inter se pugnare videntur . . . Nunc nouissime per
succinctam epitomen explicata, opera & studio E. D. M. Leandri a S.
Martino, 1623. *Part 2 of* no. 693.

697.1   —Curiel, J. A. D. Ioannis Alphonsi Curielis . . . Lecturae seu quastiones
in D. Thomae Aquinatis . . . primum secundae. Fol. *Duaci, ex officina
typographica Baltazaris Belleri,* 1618. O.; D.DNPK.MD.PA.
     A note following the approbation and privilege reveals that the
Benedictine Abbot of St. Vincent's at Salamanca, who had inherited
the author's manuscripts, sent the autograph of this work to Jones in
the Low Countries with permission to see it through the press. Other
editions of this work do not bear Jones's name and may not be his.

698   —Mauburn, J. Rosetum exercitiorum spiritualium, et sacrarum medi-
tationum . . . emendatius & distinctius edidit & castigauit R.P.M.
Leander de S. Martino. Fol. *Duaci, ex typographia Baltazaris Belleri,*
1620. L.C.; AAR.AMI.BOR.BRS.CHA.DE.L²⁶.LOU³.NCY.O⁴⁹.MU.PA(2).PA³.
WO. + +
     With engraved plates.

—Sayer, G. R.P.D. Gregorii Sayri . . . opera theologica . . . hanc
editionem recensuit, & castigauit . . . D. Leander de S. Martino,
1620. *See* no. 1026.

699 —Sibylla, B. [and others]. Otium theologicum tripartitum: siue, amaenissimae disputationes . . . trium magnorum authorum. 8°. 3 pts. *Duaci, ex typographia Balthazaris Belleri,* 1621. L.C.; AMI.AUG(pt. 1). CHA.DE.DOU(2).HP.LOU³.(pt. 3).MAR.PA.VAL.X.
Pt. 1 contains Sibylla's *Speculum peregrinarum quaestionum*; pt. 2 Trithemius's *Curiositas regia. Octo quaestiones*; pt. 3 an abridgment of Tostati's *Aenigmatum sacrorum pentas.* Pts. 2, 3 have their own titlepages. Some copies have Beller's woodcut device on the general titlepage, others have a metal engraving of an arm holding up a crown, with a scroll reading 'Corona Iustitiae'.

700 —Vincent, *of Beauvais.* Vincentii . . . Speculum quadruplex, naturale, doctrinale, morale, historiale . . . opera & studio theologorum Benedictinorum Collegii Vedastini in alma Academia Duacensi. Fol. 4 vols. *Duaci, ex officina typographica Baltazaris Belleri,* 1624. L.; AMI.BOR.CHA.GT.GTN.LAR.LGE².LYN.MU.NCY.PA.PA⁴.TRO.VI. + +
Jones is not mentioned by name but, as professor of theology at the College of S. Vaast, he was one of the editors and possibly the principal. *See* Chaussy, p. 194. Vols. 2–4 have each their own title-page with title: *Bibliotheca mundi.*

—[*A work with a preface by Jones.*] Sayer, G. Clauis regia, 1619. *See* no. 1042.

Jonson, Christopher. [*A work with a dedicatory epistle by him.*] White, R. Richardi Viti . . . orationes, 1596. *See* no. 1376.1.

Jonson, Robert. Responsio venerabilium sacerdotum Henrici Ioliffi & Roberti Ionson, 1564. *See* no. 692.

701 **Kearney, Barnabas.** Barnabae Kearnaei Casselensis . . . Heliotropium, siue conciones tam de festis, quam de dominicis, quae in solari totius anni circulo occurrunt. 8°. *Lugduni, sumptibus Antonii Pillehotte,* 1622. L(*destroyed*).O.; AV.CHA.D.KN².LYN.PA.RO².RO⁴.USH.

702 —Barnabae Kearnaei Casselensis . . . Heliotropium, siue conciones de mysteriis redemptionis humanae, quae in dominica passione continentur. 8°. *Parisiis, apud Sebastianum Cramoisy,* 1633. O.; BG².CHA. D.D⁸.EX.FLO.FLO³.LX.MD(2).PA.RO².WO.

[703 *cancelled*]

Kellam, Lawrence. [Scupoli, L.] Pugna spiritualis, 1612. [With a dedicatory letter of Kellam.] *See* no. 79.1.

704 **Kellison, Matthew.**† Commentarii ac disputationes in tertiam partem Summae theologicae S. Thomae Aquinatis. Fol. 2 vols. *Duaci, ex officina Baltazaris Belleri,* 1633. O.; BRS.D.DE.MD.O¹².OR.OS.PA.PA³.RO². RO⁴.RO⁶.TNI.USH.VT.
Dedicated to Richard Smith, Bishop of Chalcedon.

705 —Examen reformationis nouae praesertim Caluinianae in quo synagoga et doctrina Caluini . . . tota fere ex suis principiis refutatur. 8°. *Duaci, typis Petri Auroii,* 1616. L.C.; AUG.BRS.DE.DOU.FLO.HP(2).L².MD.MTH. PA.RO².ST.USH(2).VT. + +
Not a translation of A&R 429–30 but a reworking of similar material.

—[*Works edited by him.*] Bristow, R. Veritates aureae, 1616. *See* no. 118.

—Douai, *English College.* Vita et martyrium D. Max-fildaei, 1616 [*etc.*]. *See* nos. 313, *etc.*

706 **Kelly, Edmund.** Conclusiones theologicae. Pro solemnitate Sancti Patritii Hyberniae Apostoli, ac tutelaris Patroni. Quaestio disputanda. Vtrum de potentia absoluta, possit vnum attributum diuinum videri, sine alio formaliter viso? Praeest R.P.M. Iacobus Pereyra Societatis Iesu, Collegii Hybernorum Vlyssiponensis Rector . . . Tuetur P. Edmundus Quelly eiusdem Societatis. Die 17. Aprilis, horis vespertinis. Fol. (a bifolium). *Vlyssipone, ex officina Antonii Aluares,* 1633. MD²(Jes. 114/95).
A programme announcing the forthcoming defence of his thesis.

707   **Knaresborough, Christopher.** Quaestio theologica. Vtrum liceat dare spiritualia pro munere ab obsequio, vel a lingua? . . . 5 Decembr. 1609. *s.sh*.fol. *n.p.d.* [1609]. DOU (Rec. A 1609/37).

       A programme announcing the forthcoming defence of his thesis at the University of Douai. For Knaresborough *see* Anst., vol. 1, p. 200. *Pr.* [Douai, widow of James Boscard.]

       Knott, Edward, *alias. See* Wilson, M.

       Kyne, Eugene. *See* Cahan, E.

       L. M.I. *See* nos. 731, 733.

708   **Laing, James.** [*Works translated by him.*] Bolsec, J. H. De vita et rebus gestis Martini Lutheri, et aliorum Speudoapostolorum [*sic*] haereseos nostri temporis &c. traductis ex sermone Gallico in Latinum. 8°. *Parisiis, apud Michalem* [sic] *de Roigny,* 1581. AV.MD.O²¹.

       A translation of Bolsec's *Histoire des vies . . . des quatre principaux heretiques de nostre temps,* 1580, which was an expanded edition of the same author's *Histoire de la vie . . . de Iean Caluin,* 1577. Dedicated to Mary Queen of Scots.

709   —[Anr. ed., with title:] De vita et moribus atque rebus gestis haereticorum nostri temporis &c. Traductis ex sermone Gallico in Latinum, quibus multa addita sunt quae in priori editione quorumdam, negligentia omissa fuere. 8°. *Parisiis, apud Michaelem de Roigny,* 1581. L(4).O.C(*imp.*); CHA.DE.E(6).E²(2).GTN.L⁸.L²⁵.MD.NCY.PA.PA³.PA⁴.RO³. Scott 119.

710   —[*German transl. made from Laing's Latin version.*] Summarische historia vnd warhafftig Geschicht von dem Leben, Lehr, Bekantnuss vnd Ableyben Martin Luthers vnd Joann Caluini . . . Erstlich auss Frantzoesischer Sprach, durch Iacobum Laingaeum Scotum . . . ins Latein gebracht . . . Mit einer . . . Vorred obgemeltes Doctoris Laingaei. 4°. *Gedruckt zu Ingolstatt in der Weissenhornischen Truckerey bey Wolffgang Eder,* 1582. AB.DI.F.KN.MU.MU².NB.NEU.PA.RG.SAL.VI. WO.

711   —Bolsec, J. H. De vita et moribus Theodori Bezae . . . et aliorum haereticorum breuis recitatio. Cui adiectus est libellus, de morte Patris Edmundi Campionis, & aliorum quorumdam Catholicorum, qui in Anglia pro fide Catholica interfecti fuerunt. 8°. *Parisii* [sic], *apud Michaelem de Roigny,* 1585. L(2).O.; A.AIX.AMS.E(2).L²⁶.LGE.³ LOU³.NI.PA.PA⁴.

       A translation of Bolsec's *Histoire de la vie . . . de Theodore de Beze,* 1582, and of the anonymous *Histoire de la mort que le R.P. Edmond Campion, et autres ont souffert en Angleterre,* 1582 (for which *see* nos. 196 *etc.*). Scott 127.

       Lanctonus, Thomas, *pseud.? See* Bourchier, T. (no. 112).

       Lascelles, Richard.‡ [*A work translated by him.*] *See* no. 1094.

       Lathom, George, *alias. See* Mainwaring, G.

       Latomus, Georgius. *See* Mainwaring, G., *alias* Lathom.

712   **Layton, Thomas,** *alias* Port. Theses ex vniuersa theologia Doctoris Angelici. Disputandae in Collegio Anglicano Soc. Iesu Louanii, 1619. Praeside P. Andrea Vito. Defendet Thomas Portus. 4°. [Coloph.] *Louanii, ex off. Bernardini Masii,* 1619.

       Not found. Description (corrected) from Sommerv. (tom. 8, col. 1092).

713   **Lea, Thomas.** [*Begin:*] Illustrissimo, ac Reuerendissimo Principi Hieronymo Vidoni S.R.E. Cardinali amplissimo. Fr. Thomas Lea S.P.S. . . . Conclusiones theologicae . . . [*End:*] Disputabuntur in Collegio S. Isidori . . . Sub tutela Reu. admodum P. Fr. Martini Angeli Valesii . . . Mense Iunii. *s.sh.*fol. *Romae, apud Ludouicum Grignanum,* 1629. RO⁸(2).

       A programme announcing the forthcoming defence of his thesis. For Lea, *see* Cleary, p. 125.

714 —[*Begin :*] Illustrissimo Domino Domino Andreae Viseo magno Angliae Priori Ordinis Melitensis, Catholicae Maiestatis Pincernae, & Consiliario Collaterali in Regno Neapolitano &c. Fr. Thomas Lea S.P.S. . . . Conclusiones theologicae . . . [*End :*] Disputabuntur in Collegio S. Isidori . . . Sub tutela Reu. admodum P. Fr. Martini Angeli Valesii . . . Mense Septembris. *s.sh.*fol. *Romae, apud Ludouicum Grignanum*, 1629. RO⁸.

A programme announcing the forthcoming defence of his thesis (postponed from June ? *See* no. 713.)

Leander, *de S. Martino, name in religion. See* Jones, J.

715 **Lee, John.** Chori in laudem Roberti Bellarmini S.R.E. Card. Ampliss. Dum philosophicas theses eidem Cardinali dicatas publice defendebat Ioannes Leus Collegii Anglicani alum. in Collegio Romano Societatis Iesu. 4° (a single quadrifolium). *Romae, apud Bartholomaeum Zannettum*, 1608. MIL².

716 **Leedes, Edward,** *alias* Courtney. In funere Elisabethae a Lotharingia Bauaria Ducis oratio Odoardi Courtnei Angli e Societate Iesu habita Leodii in templo Collegii Anglicani eiusdem Societatis. 4°. *Leodii, ex typographia Leonardi Streel*, 1635. L.O. *See* also no. 737.

717 —Thysia philosophica, siue laeta disciplinarum oblatio. Illustriss. Principi Guidoni Bentiuolio S.R.E. Card. Ampliss. Ad concentus musicos expressa, cum sub foelicissimis illius auspiciis de vniuersa philosophia disputaret in Collegio Anglicano Odoardus Courtneus eiusdem Collegii alumnus. 4°. *Romae, apud haeredem Bartholomaei Zannetii*, 1621. L.; RO².

718 **Lery, Cornelius.** Amplissimo nobilissimoque viro Domino D. Eustachio de Lys, Domino de Beauce . . . Conclusiones ex vniuersa philosophia . . . Has conclusiones . . . propugnabit Cornelius Lery Hibernus Aghideoensis. In Collegio Rhedonensi Societatis Iesu [space] die Augusti M.DC.XXXV. *s.sh.*fol. *Typis viduae Ioannis Hardy, n.d.* [1635]. C.

A programme announcing the forthcoming defence of his thesis. *Pr.* [Rennes.] Bradshaw 8658.

719 **Leslie, John,** *Bishop of Ross.*† Ad nobilitatem, populumq. Scoticum . . . Ioannis Leslaei . . . paraenesis; Scotorum historiae nuper ab eodem auctore editae, praefixa. Cui omnium regum Scotiae gencalogiae in stemmata distinctae, ac eorum . . . imagines, cum carta cosmographica accesserunt. 4°. *Romae, in aedibus Populi Romani*, 1578. C.; NH.LIL.NCY(*imp*).

With the royal arms of Scotland, incorporating the initials M.R., engraved on the titlepage. The genealogies, portraits and maps were also published as part of no. 721. Scott 101.

720 —Congratulatio Serenissimi Principi et Illustrissimo Cardinali Alberto Archiduci Austriae, etc. De fausto ac felici eius aduentu ad regimen prouinciarum Inferioris Germaniae. 8° (in fours). *Bruxellae, apud Rutgerum Velpium*, 1596. L(2).; HN.LIL.PA.PA⁴.

—De illustrium foeminarum in repub. administranda, 1580. *Part 2 of* no. 722.

721 —De origine moribus, et rebus gestis Scotorum libri decem . . . accessit noua & accurata regionum & insularum Scotiae, cum vera eiusdem tabula topographica, descriptio. 4°. *Romae, in aedibus Populi Romani*, 1578. L(2).O.C.; A.AIX(2)BAR.C².D.DUR.E(4).E².L².PA(2).RO².TRI.WO. + +

With a separate engraved map and with engravings in the text. Scott 100. Reprinted in 1675.

722 —De titulo et iure Serenissimae Principis Mariae Scotorum Reginae, quo regni Angliae successionem sibi iuste vendicat . . . Accessit ad Anglos & Scotos, vt . . . perpetua amicitia in vnum coalescant, paraenesis. 4°. 2 pts. *Rhemis, excudebat Ioannes Fognaeus*, 1580.

L(2).O.C(2).;   A(3).C²(3).D(2).DMR.DUR.E(3).E².GT.GTN.L².MD(2).PA(2). USH.WO. + +

A translation of pts. 2 and 3 of A&R 453. Pt. 2 of the Latin, entitled: *De illustrium foeminarum in repub. administranda*, which has its own titlepage, may be found separately, but the errata leaf covers both parts and shows that they were issued together. Different copies may show slight variations of setting. With a folding genealogical table. Scott 115.

723 —[Date variant; *t.p.* to pt. 1 bearing the date:] 1581. C⁹.ST.

724 —[*French transl.*] Du droict et tiltre de la Serenissime Princesse Marie Royne d'Escosse ... à la succession du Royaume d'Angleterre ... Premierement composé en Latin & Anglois, par ... Iean de Lesselie ... & nouellement mis en François par le mesme autheur. 8°. *Rouen, de l'imprimerie de George l'Oyselet, n.d.* [1587.] L(2).O.C(-*table*).; A.C³.E(2).G.LYN.M⁴.O¹¹.PA.PA⁴.SAL.

With a dedication to Henry III of France, dated from Rouen, 1587. With the same folding genealogical table. Scott 137.

725 —[*Spanish transl.*] Declaration del titulo y derecho que la Serenissima Princesa Doña Maria Reyna de Escocia, tiene a la succession del Ingalaterra ... Compuestos por ... Iohan Lesleo ... traduzido de Yngles en Latin y de Latin en Español por el mismo author. 8° (in fours). *n.p.d.* [1587.] L.; D².E.G.MD(2).PA.

With a dedication to Philip II of Spain, dated from Rouen, 4 April 1587. *Pr.* [Rouen, George l'Oyselet]. With the same folding genealogical table. Scott 138.

—Harangue funebre sur la mort de la Royne d'Escosse, [1587]. *See* no. 733.

726 —L'innocence de la tres illustre, tres-chaste, et debonnaire princesse, Madame Marie Royne d'Escosse. 8°. *n.p.*, 1572. L(4).O.; A.AIX.ANT². C³.C⁶.DMR.E(2).E².GT.LINC.M.PA(2).PA²(2).USH. +

Anon. Sometimes erroneously attributed to François de Belleforest. It includes a translation of part of Leslie's *A treatise of treasons*, 1572 (A&R 454), and also an answer to G. Buchanan's *Histoire de Marie Royne d'Escosse*, 1572 (STC 3979). A comparison of extant copies shows that a number of minor textual alterations were made in the course of printing. *See* Scott, p. 30. In some copies ll. 4–5 of the title read '... MA-/dame Marie Royne d'Escosse.' with l. 5 centred; in others '...MADAME/Marie Royne d'Escosse.' with l. 5 uncentred. Some copies have two leaves of errata at the end. Scott 85. *Pr.* [Reims, Jean Foigny].

727 —Ioannis Leslaei ... libri duo: quorum vno, piae afflicti animi consolationes, diuinaque remedia: altero, animi tranquilli munimentum & conseruatio, continentur. Ad ... Mariam Scotorum Reginam. 8°. *Parisiis, ex officina Petri l'Huillier*, 1574. L(2).O(2).; A.C⁹.DMR.E.F.L². L²⁶.O¹⁹.PA(2).RO³.TRO.VI.Y.

Scott 91.

728 —[*French transl.*] Les deuotes consolations et diuins remedes de l'esprit affligé. Liure premier. Et le Rampart et preseruatif de l'esprit tranquille. Liu. 2. 12°. *Rouen, chez Richard Petit*, 1590. E.

729 —[Anr. ed., with title:] Consolations diuines et remedes souuerains de l'esprit affligé. Liure 1. et le Rampart de l'esprit tranquille. Liu. 2. 12°. *Paris, chez Arnold Sittart*, 1593. O.; E.X.

730 —Ioannis Leslaei ... Pro libertate impetranda, oratio. Ad Serenissimam Elizabetham Angliae Reginam. 8°. *Parisiis, Oliua Pet. l'Huillier*, 1574. L.C.; C³.C⁴.E.E².E³.G.G².HN.L².MP.NY.PA.PA⁴.

This appeal, addressed to Elizabeth while Leslie wsa still a prisoner in England, was printed after his release and banishment in Jan. 1574. Scott 92.

—Libri duo, 1574. *See* no. 727.

731 —Oraison funebre sur la mort de tres-heureuse memoire, Marie Stuard, Roye [*sic*] d'Escosse, de son viuant fille, femme, & mere de roy. Auec approbation de la saincte Faculté de theologie à Paris. 8° (in fours). *n.p.*, 1587. PA(2).PA².PA³.PA⁴.
Anon. Internal evidence reveals it to be by [Leslie]. The head-title reads: 'Version Françoise d'vne oraison funebre, faicte . . . par Reuerend Pere en Dieu M.I.S.' These initials are probably a misprint for M.I.L. [M. John Leslie.]; *see* no. 733. *Tr.* [Nicolas Loiseul.] *Pr.* [Paris.] The Scots original was probably not printed.

732 —[Anr. issue?, with title:] Oraison funebre sur la mort de la Royne d'Escosse, Traduicte d'Escossois en nostre langue Françoise, par N.L.R.P. *Paris, chez Iean Charron*, 1587. PA.
Anon. N.L.R.P. [Nicolas Loiseul.] Identical with no. 731 except for the title and possibly its conjugate leaf. The title does not appear to be a cancel.

733 —[Anr. ed., with title:] Harangue funebre sur la mort de la Royne d'Escosse. Traduite d'Escossois en Françoys par N.L.R.P. 8° (in fours). *n.p.d.* [1587.] L.PA.
Anon. The head-title reads: 'Traduction Françoise d'vne harangue funebre . . . par Reuerend Pere en Dieu M.I.L.' [M. John Leslie]; cp. no. 731. *Pr.* [at Paris by the same printer as no. 732]. Scott 170.

—Pro libertate impetranda, 1574. *See* no. 730.

734 —[*A work to which he contributed.*] [Boece, H.] Scotorum historiae a prima gentis origine . . . libri XIX . . . Duo postremi huius Historiae libri nunc primum emittuntur in lucem. Accessit & huic editioni eiusdem Scotorum Historiae continuatio, per Ioannem Ferrerium Pedemontanum. Fol. *Parisiis, vaenundantur a Iacobo du Puys*, 1574. [Coloph.] *Lausannae excudebat Franciscus Le Preux . . . sumptibus Iacobi Du Puys.* L.O.C.; A.AIX.C³.C⁴.E(2).E²(2).G.M.MTH.PA.STU.WO. + +
Boece's work, originally published in [1526] (STC 3203), is here republished with a continuation by Giovanni Ferreri, a Piedmontese who had lived and worked in Scotland. In a preface addressed to James Beaton, Archbishop of Glasgow, Ferreri says that he has been helped by Leslie. *See* J. Durkan & A. Ross, *Early Scottish Libraries*, 1961, p. 96.

735 —[Date variant.] 1575. L.C.; ANT.BER.D.F.ILL.L¹³.L¹⁵.LINC.MICH.N.NY. O¹¹.PA. +

Leus, Ioannes. *See* Lee, J.

736 **Lewis, Owen,** *Bishop of Cassano.* [*Appendix.*] Fr. Ant. Gar. Epistola ad Rᵘᵐ Episcopum Cassane D. Audoenum Ludouicum Anglum. Intercepta et impressa. In qua Galliae regni praesens status et miseriae paucis et libere recensentur. Anno M.D.XCI. 8°. *n.p.d.*, [1591.] L.O.; DUR.SAL.
The author, 'Ant. Gar.'is perhaps the Antonius Guarrius,n e translator of no. 311. He dates his letter from Paris, 19 Oct. 1590. It mainly concerns French affairs but there are some references to the persecution in England. The circumstances in which it was written, intercepted and printed are obscure. Lewis was in Rome in 1590–91.

737 **Liège,** *English Jesuit College.* Serenissimo Maximiliano Boiariae vtriusque Duci, etc., has in obitu eius coniugis Elisabethae . . . laudes flebiles, lacrymas laudatrices Anglorum e Societate Iesu Leodiense Collegium, humillimis obsequiis offert D.C.Q. 4°. *n.p.d.* [1635.]
Not found. Description from Sommerv. (tom. 4, col. 1812). Theux (col. 120) cites a copy at LGE² but this is now missing. Elizabeth of Lorraine, first wife of Maximilian I of Bavaria, and a patroness of the College, died on 4 Jan. 1635. D.C.Q. who presented the address on behalf of the College has not been identified. *Pr.* [Liège].

—[*Appendix.*] Leedes, E. In funere Elisabethae a Lotharingia Bauariae Ducis oratio . . . habita Leodii in templo Collegi Anglicani, 1635. *See* no. 716.

—[*Theses defended at the College.*] *See* nos. 1024, 1248, 1259.

738   **Liège,** *English Jesuit Novitiate.* [*Appendix.*] Ernestus, *Archbishop of Cologne and Bishop of Liège.* [*Begin :*] Ernestus Dei & Apostolicae Sedis gratia Archiepiscopus Colonien: . . . Cum ad conseruandam & augendam hisce praesertim locis ac temporibus religionem orthodoxam . . . *s.sh.broadside* fol. *Leodii, typis Christiani Ouwerx, n.d.* [*n.a.* 1612.] RO⁹. (Fondo Jesuitico, 446², f. 606).

     Addressed to the parish priests of his diocese of Liège and appealing for alms to help establish the English Jesuit novitiate. Ernestus died in 1612. The novitiate was not established until 1614.

739   **Lily, George.** Chronicon siue breuis enumeratio regum et principum, in quos uariante fortuna, Britanniae Imperium diuersis temporibus translatum est. 4°. *Francoforti,* 1565. [Coloph.] *Apud Iohannem Vuolffium.* L.C(2).; C⁴.C¹⁶.C¹⁹.DMR.HAN.O¹⁰.O¹².O¹⁷.O²⁷.P.PA.PA⁴.UP.VI.

     Mainly secular but containing some church history. Versions of this work also appeared in editions of Paulus Jovius: *Descriptio Britanniae,* and Polydore Vergil: *Anglicae historiae libri viginti sex.*

740   **Lindsay,** *Sir* **Walter.** Relacion del estado del reyno de Escocia, en lo tocante a nuestra religion catolica. Este año . . . de mil y quinientos y nouenta y quatro. Fol. (a quadrifolium). *n.p.d.* [1594.] L.; E.MD.MD². (2: Jes. 102/9; 117/51).

     Anon. *Pr.* in [Spain] where the author took refuge for a time on his conversion to Catholicism. A summary in English, misdated 1586, is preserved in MS (BL. Cotton MSS. Caligula C.IX, 477): it is headed 'The content of the Discourse made by Mr Walter Lindsay of Balgays'. There is a modern English translation of the complete text in Forbes-Leith (2), pp. 351–60. Scott 185.

741   **Lisbon,** *English Bridgettine Convent.* Relacion que embiaron las religiosas del monesterio de Sion de Inglaterra, q̃ estauan en Roan de Francia, al Padre Roberto Personio . . . de su salido de aquella ciudad, y llegada a Lisboa de Portugal. Traduzida de Ingles en Castellano, por Carlos Dractan, sacerdote Ingles del Colegio de Valladolid. 8°. *Madrid, por la biuda de P. Madrigal,* 1594. L.O.; DMR.HD.MD.VT.

     Carlos Dractan [Charles Tancred or Tankard]. The *Relacion* is preceded by a 'Preambulo' on the history of the English Bridgettine foundation, written in Spanish by Robert Persons from material supplied by the nuns' chaplain, Seth Foster. The 'Preambulo' is reprinted in no. 284.

742   **Lisbon,** *English College.* Constitutiones et regulae Collegii Anglorum Vlyssiponensis. Tituli sanctorum apostolorum Petri et Pauli. Fundati a perillustri D.D. Petro Coutinio . . . Sub protectione Ill. mi ac R. mi D. Francisci a Castro episcopi, & Inquisitoris Generalis . . . Sub regimine Rmi. D. Richardi Episcopi Chalcedonensis, & saecularis in Anglia cleri presbyterorum. Fol. *Vlyssipone, apud Laurentium Craesbeeck regium typographum, n.d.* [1635.] USH.VT.[O has a fragment of the preliminaries. Douce frag. d. 13 (11).]

     These constitutions and rules, of which USH also has the original MS, were drawn up some years after the College began to admit students in 1628. The latest approbation is dated 27 March 1635.

—[*Theses defended at the College.*] *See* nos. 37, 834.

Lisbon, *Irish College.* [*Theses defended at the College.*] *See* no. 706.

Lobb, Emmanuel. Rappresentatione tragica del Zenone, 1634. *See* no. 947.

Loemelius, Hermannus, *pseud. See* Floyd, J. (nos. 485–6, 488–91.)

743   **Lombard, Peter,** *Archbishop of Armagh.* De regno Hiberniae, sanc-

torum insula, commentarius, Authore . . . Petro Lombardo Hiberno. 4°. *Louanii, apud viduam Stephani Martini*, 1632. L(3).O(2).C.; ANT². D²(*imp.*).D¹⁰.E.GTN.HA.L².L²⁶.MTH.PA.PA².ST. +

A posthumous work, written in 1600 and not previously published. An edition based on the MS in the Barberini archives was published by P. F. Moran in 1868.

744 —[Anr. issue, with cancel title:] De regno Hiberniae sanctorum insula commentarius, in quo, praeter eiusdem insulae situm, nominis originem, &c. pii conatus & res a principe O Neillo ad fidem Catholicam propagandam foeliciter gestae continentur. Authore . . . Petro Lombardo Hiberno. *Louanii, apud viduam Stephani Martini*, 1632. O(*imp.*).C.; A.ANT.D(2).F.N.NY.

Except for the titleleaf this is a reissue of the sheets of no. 743.

Louvain, English Jesuit College. [*Theses defended at the College.*] *See* nos. 523, 712, 760, 910, 1343, 1345, 1391.

Louvain, Irish Franciscan College of St Anthony of Padua. [*Theses defended at the College.*] *See* nos. 81, 82, 253, 752.

Luchranus, Patritius. *See* O'Loughran, P.

Ludovicus, Audoenus. *See* Lewis, O.

M., F.F. *See* no. 862.

M., P.M.P.Q. *See* no. 810.

MacCaghwell, Hugh† (Hugo Cavellus), *Archbishop of Armagh.* [Apologia apologiae pro Ioanne Duns Scoto, 1623.]

For this defence of MacCaghwell's *Apologia* (no. 745), published by his student, Hugh Magennis, *see* no. 756.

745 —Apologia pro Scoto Doctore Subtili contra Abrahamum Bzouium per R.P. Hugonem Cauellum. 8° (in fours). *Parisiis, ex typographia Ludouici Seuestre*, 1634. PA.

Previously published in 1620 as part of no. 749.

746 —Responsio ad quoddam scriptum anonimum, seu potius libellum famosum editum in fauorem patrum conuentualium ordinis Minorum contra Obseruantes eiusdem ordinis, & peculiariter contra magnum conuentum Parisiensem dictae obseruantiae, cui titulus est. Factum pour les Peres Cordeliers conuentuels, sine nomine Authoris, loci, vel typographi . . . Per Hugonem Cauellum. 8°. *Parisiis*, 1622. KNY.PA. STR.

The anonymous attack on the Franciscan Observants to which this is a reply has not been identified.

747 —Tractatuli duo quorum vnus vsum statutorum quae Iulii 2. dicuntur, illicitum esse ostendit fratribus minoribus, regulam S. Francisci absolute, & sine limitationibus quibus vtuntur Conuentuales, professis. Alter, communium argumentorum, quibus plurimi vtriusq; sexus, specie cuiusdam piae compassionis, erga fratres, reformari nolentes, contra reformationem vtuntur, solidas & dilucidas solutiones continet . . . Per Fratrem Hugonem Cauellum. 8°. *Parisiis*, 1622. BRU.KNY.

See Sbaralea, tom. 1, p. 53, no. 276: 'Anonymus Gallus . . . magni conventus Parisiensis alumnus scripsit publicavitque *Tractatum pro Statutis Julii II favore Franciscanorum conventualium* editus, seu pro Chordigeris Conventualibus in Gallia ea Statuta Observantibus . . . cui autori respondit Hugo Cavellus Observ. an. 1622'. The *Tractatus* has not so far been identified.

748 —[*Works edited by him.*] Duns, Ioannes, *Scotus.* Doctoris Subtilis Io. Duns. Scoti quaestiones super libris Aristotelis De anima . . . Per R.P.F. Hugonem Cauellum. 4°. *Lugduni, sumptibus Claudii Landry*, 1625. CML.KNY.USH.

Republished at Venice in 1641.

749 —Duns, Ioannes, *Scotus.* F. Ioannis Duns Scoti . . . in primum et

secundum (in tertium et quartum) Sententiarum quaestiones subtilissimae. Nunc nouiter recognitae . . . Per P.F. Hugonem Cauellum . . . Accesserunt per eundem vita Scoti, Apologia pro ipso contra P. Abrahamum Bzouium [etc.]. Fol. 2 vols, each in 2 pts. *Antwerpiae, apud Ioannem Keerbergium,* 1620. L.C(vol. 1); AUG.BRU(vol. 2).D⁶.KNY. L¹³.LOU(vol. 2).LOU³(vol. 2).MTH.OR(vol. 2).MD(vol. 2).PA(2).

Vol. 1 deals with the first and second of the Sentences, vol. 2 with the third and fourth. The 'Apologia' for Duns Scotus against the Dominican, Abraham Bzovius, the continuator of Baronius's *Annales ecclesiasticae,* was later published separately (no. 745). For a defence of the 'Apologia' against attacks on it by the Dominicans of Antwerp, by Hugh Magennis, *see* nos. 756, 750.

750 —Duns, Ioannes, *Scotus.* F. Ioannis Duns Scoti . . . Quaestiones reportatae seu repetitae in quatuor libros Sententiarum Petri Lombardi. Quaestiones item quodlibetales . . . Nunc nouiter recognitae . . . Per R.P.F. Hugonem Cauellum . . . Accessit Apologia, qua vita, et doctrina eiusdem Doctoris Subtilis . . . defenditur per R.P.F. Hugonem Magnesium. Fol. 2 pts. *Coloniae Agrippinae, sumptibus Bernardi Gualtheri & viduae Conradi Butgenii,* 1635. C.; AUG.D.D². LOU.

The 'Apologia . . . Per R.P.F. Hugonem Magnesium' is the work by Hugh Magennis first published in 1623 under the title *Apologia apologiae pro Ioanne Duns Scoto* (no. 756).

751 —Duns, Ioannes, *Scotus.* Io. Duns Scoti . . . quaestiones subtilissimae, & expositio in Metaphysicam Arist. ac conclusiones ex ipsa collectae . . . Cum annotationibus R.P.F. Mauritii de Portu Hyberni . . . nouiter recognita . . . per R.P.F. Hugonem Cauellum. Fol. *Venetiis,* 1625. *Ex officina Marci Ginammi.* KNY.STL.

—Duns, Ioannes, *Scotus.* R.P.F. Ioannis Duns Scoti opera omnia, 1639. *See* no. 1326.

752 —[*A disputation in which he acted as Praeses at St Anthony's College, Louvain.*] Barnewell, J. Vniuersa theologia iuxta mentem Doctoris Subtilis. 4°. *Louanii es typographia Bernardini Masii,* 1620.

Not found. Description from Reusens (tom. 5, p. 426) who saw a copy in the old library of Louvain University destroyed in 1914. With a dedication in Latin hexameters to Jacques Boonen, Bishop of Ghent.

—[*Appendix.*] [For a speech on the occasion of his nomination as Archbishop] *see* no. 226.

753 **Madrid,** *English College.* La fiesta que su Alteza de la Serenissima Señora Infanta Maria de Austria mandó hazer el dia de Nuestra Señora de Agosto desde año de 1623. En el seminario de Ingleses desta villa de Madrid. Fol(a bifolium). *n.p.d.* [1623]. MD.MD² Jes. 32/10).

The ceremonies were held by the English College on the feast of the Assumption, 15 Aug. 1623, in thanksgiving for the Anglo–Spanish marriage treaty which, it was thought, was about to be concluded. The account was probably written by the superior of the College, Francis Forcer. His name is here misspelt 'Forcex'. *Pr.* [Madrid.]

754 —[Anr. ed., with title:] Fiesta eclesiastica que en el Seminario Ingles de Madrid, mādó hazer . . . su Alteza de la Serenissima Infanta Maria de Austria. Dase cuenta de la nueua congregaciō de Ingleses Catolicos que en Madrid hizo el Padre Forcex. Fol(a bifolium). [Coloph.] *Seuilla, por Francisco de Lyra,* 1623. MD² (Jes. 117/82).SEV.

In spite of the changes in the title this is a reprint of no. 753.

755 —[*Appendix.*] Los motiuos que ay para fauorecer los seminarios de Ingleses, en comun, y en particular el de Madrid: en cuya fundacion ha sucedido dichosamente el patronazgo de los excelentissimos señores Condes Duques de San-Lucar, y la forma que se puede tener en su

aumento. 4° (a quire of eight). *Por Iuan de Zerain executor de la fundacion del Seminario de Madrid, en gracia de la santa Mission Anglicana*, 1632. MD² (9–3496/3).
A brief account of the foundation and history of the College, followed by an appeal for alms.

756 **Magennis, Hugh** (Hugo Magnesius), *Bishop of Down and Connor.* Apologia apologiae pro Ioanne Duns Scoto . . . in qua iacta in eum, eiusque vindicem conuitia repelluntur: eius vita, mors & doctrina, ab iniuriis, & calumniis vendicantur . . . Per F. Hugonem Magnesium. 8°. *Parisiis, apud Michaelem Sonnium*, 1623. L.O.; KNY.MD.STR.
Defending the 'Apologia' of Hugh MacCaghwell, published in 1620 as part of no. 749, against attacks on it by the Dominicans of Antwerp.

—[Anr. ed.] 1635. *Part of no. 750.*
Magnesius, Hugo. *See* Magennis, H.
Mahew, Odoardus. *See* Maihew, E.

757 **Maihew, Edward.**† Congregationis Anglicanae ordinis Sanctissimi Patriarchae Benedicti. Trophoea. Tribus tabulis breuiter comprehensa. Quarum prima, continet chronicon originis, progressus . . . eiusdē Cong. Secunda, exhibet natales sanctorum, qui in eadem pietate fuerunt celeberrimi. Tertia, recenset catalogum scriptorum. 4°. 2 vols. *Remis, ex officina Nicolai Constant*, 1619,20. O.; RO⁸.(vol. 1).
Vol. 1 comprises tabula 1; vol. 2 part of tabula 2. The rest of the work was not printed in this edition. Vol. 2 bears the date 1620 in the imprint. Attacked by John Barnes in nos. 64, 70. For the background *see* DR, 1932, pp. 108–25, 490–7; and Chaussy, pp. 103 *et seq.*

[758 *cancelled*]
759 —[An edition of the whole work, with title:] Congregationis Anglicanae ordinis Sanctissimi Patriarchae Benedicti. Trophoea. Tribus tabulis comprehensa. In quibus plurima, non tantum quae ad res Angliae, sed etiam quae ad historias Germaniae, Hyberniae, Scotiae, & Belgii spectant . . . discutiuntur. 4°. 4 vols. *Remis, apud Nicolaum Constant*, 1625. L(vols. 1, 4).O(vol. 4).; D(vols. 1, 4).D²(vols. 1–4).PA(vol. 1).RMS (vols. 1–4).
Vol. 1 comprises tabula 1; vols. 2–3, tabula 2; vol. 4, tabula 3. The titlepage to vol. 4 reads: 'Tabula tertia. Scriptorum, et aliorum eruditione praestantium virorum . . . & illustrium personarum, quae Ordinis Benedictini in Anglia fuerunt'.

—[*A work edited by him*]. *See* nos. 336.3, 336.4.

760 **Mainwaring, George,** *alias* Lathom. Theses ex vniuersa theologia Doctoris Angelici. Proposita in Collegio Anglicano Societatis Iesu Louanii, anno Domini CIƆ.IƆ.C.XIIX. Praeside Rdo P. Andrea Vito . . . Defendet P. Georgius Latomus Die 13. Iunii. 4°. *n.p.d.* [1618.]
Not found. Description from Sommerv. (tom. 8, col. 1092).

[**Malone, Daniel.**] There was no Irish writer of the name at this period. The Daniel Mallonius (Malonius) who edited Paleotti's *Historia admiranda*, [1607], (*see* no. 590) and also published a work on the second book of the *Sententiae* of Peter Lombard was not an Irishman, as is sometimes supposed, but an Italian Hieronymite.

Manrique, Pedro, *pseud. See* Creswell, J. (nos. 272–3.)

761 **Mary,** *of Guise, Queen Regent of Scotland.* [*Appendix.*] [Espence, C.d'.] Oraison funebre es obseques de tres Haute . . . Marie . . . Royne douairiere d'Escoce. Prononcée à Nostre Dame de Paris, le douzieme d'Aoust, mil cinq cens soixante. 8°. *Paris, de l'imprimerie de M. de Vascosan*, 1561. L.O.; PA.PA²(2).PA⁶.
Mary was Queen Regent from 1554 until her death in 1560. The oration draws attention to her efforts to defend Catholicism in

Scotland against the attacks of the Reformers. Dedicated by the author to Mary's daughter, Mary Queen of Scots. Scott 30.

762   **Mary,** *Stuart, Queen of Scots.* Le testament et derniers propos de la Royne d'Escosse. 8°. *Paris, pour Pierre Marin,* 1589. E.F.PA.

——[*A supposititious work.*] [Copie d'vne lettre de la Royne d'Escosse escripte de sa prison de Cheifeild touchant ses aduersitez, & le banissement de ses fidelz seruiteurs. *A Paris chez Robert Coulombel, Rue S. Jacques, a l'enseigne d'Alde,* 1572.]

Known only from a 19th century Milan 'reprint' (of which there are copies at L. and PA.). Both the letter itself and the 1572 Paris imprint are fictitious. Scott 86.

Appendix

I. *Works of declared authorship or of which the author has been identified.*

763   ——Beaulne, R. de, *Archbishop of Bourges.* Oraison funebre, de la tres-chrestienne, tres-illustre, tres-constante, Marie Royne d'Escosse, morte pour la Foy, le 18. Feburier, 1587. par la cruauté des Anglois . . . Sur le subiect & discours de celle mesme qui fut faicte en Mars, à Nostre Dame de Paris, au iour de ses obseques & seruice, & lors prononcée par R.P. Messire Renauld de Beaulne, Archeuesque de Bourges. 8°. *Paris, chez Guillaume Bichon,* 1588. AIX.E.PA(3).PA².PA⁴.

The 'Oraison' is followed by poems on Mary, some in Latin, some in French. Collation: A–I⁴. Scott 169. Renouard III, 497.

——[Anr. issue.] 1588. *Forms part 2 of no.* 809.

764   ——[Anr. ed.] 8°. *n.p.,* 1588. L.; Y.

Collation: A–F⁴.

765   ——[Anr. ed.] 8°. *Lyon, par Benoist Rigaud,* 1588.

Not seen. Description from Baudrier (tom. 3, p. 410) who cites a copy at AIX.

——[Belle-Forest, F. de.] L'innocence de la tres illustre . . . Marie Royne d'Escosse, 1572. For this anonymous work, sometimes erroneously attributed to [F. de Belle-Forest] but in fact by [J. Leslie, Bishop of Ross], *see* no. 726.

766   ——Bellièvre, P. de. La harangue faicte à la Royne d'Angleterre pour la desmouuoir de n'entreprendre aucune iurisdiction sur la Royne d'Escosse. 4°. *n.p.,* 1588. L.; PA(Bliss 146).

Anon. Bellièvre was the ambassador sent by Henri III of France to mediate with Queen Elizabeth in favour of Mary. Scott 167.

767   ——[Anr. ed., with title:] Harangue faicte à la Royne d'Angleterre par Monsieur de Bellieure. 4°. *n.p.,* 1588. CAL.

See Scott 167.

——Blackwood, A. Histoire et martyre de la Royne d'Escosse, 1589. *See* no. 100.

——Blackwood, A. Martyre de la Royne d'Escosse, 1588. *See* no. 99.

——Conn, G. Vita Mariae Stuartae, 1624 [*etc.*]. *See* nos. 264–6.

——Curle, H. Serenissimae Augustissimaeque Mariae Stuartae, Reginae Scotiae . . . 1618. *See* no. 325.

768   ——Dini, F. Vera, e compita relazione del succeso della morte della christianissima Regina di Scotia, con la dichiarazione del esequie fatte in Parigi dal christianissimo Re suo cognato e nome de'personaggi interuenutiui. 4°. *Ad instanzia di Francesco Dini da Colle, n.d.* [1587.] L.; E.FLO. [*O.]

Dini was the publisher and perhaps also the compiler. *Pr.* [Florence.] Scott 147.

[769 *cancelled*]

770 —[Anr. ed.] 4°. *In Genoua con licenza de' Superiori, n.d.* [1587.] o.; RO².
771 —[Anr. ed.] 4°. *Stampata in Genoua, e ristampata in Vico, n.d.* [1587.] PA(Bliss 282).
Scott 148.
772 —[Anr. ed.] 4°. *Milano, per Giacomo Picaglia,* 1587. E.
Scott 149.
773 —[Anr. ed., with title:] Vera relatione del sucesso della Sereniss. Regina di Scotia, condonnata a morte dalla Regina d'Inghilterra sua sorella. 8° (a quadrifolium). *In Milano et ristampata in Cremona appresso Christofero Draconi,* 1587. L.
Scott 150.
—Douai, *Scots College.* Serenissimae Augustissimaeque Mariae Stuartae, Reginae Scotiae . . ., 1618. *See* no. 325.
774 —Gatti, B. Maria Regina di Scotia poema heroico del P. Prior Bassiano Gatti monacho di S. Girolamo alla Santita di N.S. Vrbano VIII. 4°. *Bologna, per Nicolo Tebaldini,* 1633. L(2).O.; C².DMR.E.E².F.FS.ILL.O⁶. PA(*imp.*).RO².TEX.VT.Y.
The titlepage, which is engraved, shows a representation of Mary's execution surmounted by the arms of Pope Urban VIII. In some copies the imprint and date at the foot of the titlepage have been cut away. Scott 228.
775 —Herrera y Tordesillas, A. de. Historia de lo sucedido en Escocia, e Inglaterra, en quarenta y quatro años que biuio Maria Estuarda, Reyna de Escocia. 8°. *Madrid, en casa de Pedro Madrigal,* 1589. *Vēdese en casa de Iuā de Mōtoya, librero.* L.; AIX.C².E.F.HD.LGO.LINC. MD.PA.TDO.
Scott 181.
776 —[Anr. ed.] 8°. *Lisboa, por Manuel de Lyra,* 1590. L(2).O.; CHI.COI.DMR. HAN.HSA.L²⁵.LIS.LIS².MD.N.PA.
Scott 182.
777 —Julius III, *Pope.* Bulle de reconciliation pour ceux de la nouuelle religion, qui se viendront rendre à l'obeissance de nostre mere saincte Eglise. Donnée par les anciens papes de Rome, depuis Iules 3. iusques à Sixte 5. à present regnant. Presentée à la Royne d'Angleterre. 8° (in fours). *Paris, pour Michel Buffet,* 1587. PA³.(37235/10).
A French translation of the Bull *Illius qui misericors* III, promulgated 28 April 1550 (Cherubini, vol. 1, p. 696, no. 6.). The words 'Presentée a la Royne d'Angleterre' on the titlepage are an addition by the anonymous French editor. Following the text of the Bull are ten lines of French verse reproaching Elizabeth for the execution of Mary Queen of Scots. With a woodcut portrait of Mary.
—L., M.I. Harangue funebre sur la mort de la Royne d'Escosse, [1587]. [By J. Leslie.] *See* no. 733.
778 —La Guesle, J. de. Remonstrance faite à la Royne d'Angleterre, pour la Royne d'Escosse. 4°. *n.p.d.* [1587.] HA.LIL.PA.
A plea to Queen Elizabeth to spare Mary's life. Signed: Iacques de la Guesle Procureur general du Roy. Not included in the Paris 1611 edition of *Les remonstrances.*
779 —[L'Aubespine, Claude de, *Baron de Châteauneuf.*] Discours de la mort de treshaute & tres ilustre princesse Madame Marie Stouard, Royne d'Escosse. Faict le vingt troisiesme iour de Feurier 1587. 8°. *n.p.d.* [1587.] E.HN.PA(Bliss 520).
Collation: A⁴. Anon. Line 1 of text on sig. A1ʳ ends: '-troizies-' and the last line of the same page ends: 'qui fut'. Text ends on A4ᵛ (p. 8). Châteauneuf was French Ambassador in London and this is the first printed account of the execution. Scott 160.
780 —[Anr. state, with the line in the title reading 'Faict le vingt troisiesme

iour de Feurier 1587' corrected to read: 'Faict le dixhuictiesme iour de Feurier 1587'.] L.; HN (*with misprint 'tres-hute' in l. 1 of title*). MP (*? this ed.*).PA(Nm 142A).WO.

The corrected date is repeated in the title of all subsequent editions. Scott 160.

781 —[Anr. ed.] 8°. *n.p.d.* [1587.] E³.(103.d.24.)

Anon. Collation: A⁴. Line 1 of the text on sig. A1ʳ ends: '-troisiesme', and the last line of the same page ends: 'qui fut'. Text ends on A4ᵛ (p. 8). In this and subsequent editions the word 'illustre' in l. 2 of the title is spelt with double 'l'.

782 —[Anr. ed.] 8°. *n.p.d.* [1587?] PA(Nm 142).

Anon. Collation: A⁴. Line 1 of text on sig. A1ʳ ends: '-troizies-', and the last line of the same page ends: 'auec luy'. Text ends on A4ᵛ (p. 8).

783 —[Anr. ed.] 8°. *n.p.d.* [1587?] DMR.

Anon. Collation: A⁴. Line 1 of text, which in this edition begins on A2ʳ, ends: '-troiziesme', and the last line of the same page ends: 'accompa-/gné'. Text ends on A4ʳ; A4ᵛ is blank.

784 —[Anr. ed.] 8° (a quadrifolium). *n.p.*, 1587. SBG(R100 674/21).

Anon. In this edition the collation and line endings are as shown under no. 783, but the type is of a different setting and the date 1587 is printed at the foot of the titlepage.

785 —[Anr. ed., with title:] Discours de l'execution de mort. Faicte par la Royne d'Angleterre, sur la personne de tres-haute & tres-illustre Princesse Madame Marie Stouard, Royne d'Escosse . . . Ensemble les derniers propos tenuz par ladicte Dame. 8°. *Paris, par Iehan Poiteuin*, 1587. PA(Nm 141).

Anon. Collation: A⁴.

786 —[*Italian adaptation.*] Vera relatione della morte della Sereniss. Regina di Scotia nel lisola de Inghilterra. 4° (a quadrifolium). *Stampata in Perugia . . . e ristampata in Viterbo*, 1587. RO⁶(missing 1980).VT (Capponi V 364/4).

Anon. Based partly on the work by [L'Aubespine]. The Perugia edition cited in the imprint has not been found.

787 —[*Spanish transl.*] Discurso sobre la muerte de la muy alta y muy illustre Princesa Madama Maria Stouard, Reyna de Escocia. sacado ₫ copia imbiada ₫ Barcelona. 4°. *Mallorca, en casa de Gabriel Guasp*, 1587. MD². [*L].

The Barcelona edition cited in the title has not been found.

—Leslie, J., *Bishop of Ross*. De titulo et iure . . . Mariae Scotorum Reginae, 1580 [*etc.*]. *See* nos. 722–5.

——Harangue funebre sur la mort de la Royne, d'Escosse, [1587]. *See* no. 733.

——L'innocence de la tres illustre . . . Marie Royne d'Escosse, 1572. *See* no. 726.

——Oraison funebre sur la mort de . . . Marie Stuard, Roye [*sic*] d'Escosse, 1587. *See* nos. 731–3.

—[Loscho, S. Lettera di Sartorio Loscho su la morte della Reina di Scotia. Al molto illustre Signor Conte Marc'Antonio Martinengo. *Bergamo, per Comino Ventura*, 1587.]

Not found and of doubtful authenticity. Known only from a 'reprint' made at Milan c. 1860. Copy of the 'reprint' at O. Scott 146.

[788 *cancelled*]

——[Montchrestien, A. de. Escossoise, ou le desastre Tragedie par Ant. de Montchrestien Sieur de Vasteuille. *Rouen*, 1603.] Although the English government exerted diplomatic pressure on the French authorities to ban performances of this play, the author was a French Protestant and the work does not fall within the terms of this catalogue.

789 —Regnault, G. Marie Stuard Reyne d'Escosse. Tragedie. 4°. *Paris, chez Toussainct Quinet*, 1639. E.PA(3).
With an additional titlepage, engraved, depicting Mary's execution. Scott 233.

790 —[Anr. ed.] 12°. *Paris, chez Toussainct Quinet*, 1639. ANT².E.E².LGE.
With an additional titlepage, engraved, depicting Mary's execution.

791 —Roulers, A. de. Adriani Roulerii Insulani Stuarta tragoedia. Siue caedes Mariae Serenissimae Scot. Reginae in Angl. perpetrata, exhibita ludis remigialibus a iuuentute Gymnasii Marcianensis. 4°. *Duaci, ex officina typographica viduae Boscardi*, 1593. DOU.PA².WO.
A reprint edited by R. Woerner was published in *Lateinischer Litteraturdenkmaler des XV. vnd XVI. Jahrhunderts*, no. 17, Berlin, 1906.

792 —Ruggeri, C. La Reina di Scotia tragedia di Carlo Ruggeri. All'Illustriss. & Reuerendiss. Card. Spinelli. 8°. *Napoli, per Constantino Vitale*, 1604. E.E³.FLO.LYN.VT.
—S., M.I. Oraison funebre sur la mort de . . . Marie Stuard, 1587. [By J. Leslie.] *See* no. 731.
—Scotus, R., *pseud.* Summarium rationum, quibus Cancellarius Angliae et Prolocutor Puckeringius . . . persuaserunt occidendam esse . . . Mariam Stuartam, 1588 [*etc.*]. *See* nos. 1056–60.
—Turner, R. Maria Stuarta, Regina Scotiae . . . innocens a caede Darleana, 1588 [*etc.*]. *See* nos. 1271–4.

793 —Valle, F. della. La Reina di Scotia tragedia di Federigo della Valle al Sommo Pontifice, et Sig. nostro Vrbano VIII. 4°. *Milano, per gli heredi di Melchior Malatesta*, 1628. L.; DMR.E³.VT(2).
In verse. A modern edition, by Benedetto Croce, was published at Bologna in 1930. Scott 222.

794 —Vega Carpio, L. F. de. Corona tragica. Vida y muerte de la Serenissima Reyna de Escocia Maria Estuarda. A nuestro SSmo. Padre Vrbano VIII. 4°. *Madrid, por la viuda de Luis Sanchez*, 1627. *Acosta de Alonso Perez mercader de libros.* L(2).O.; A.AIX.AUG.BO.E.F.HD.HSA.LC.LYN.MD.PA(2).PEN. +
A poem, based on the life of Mary by George Conn (nos. 264–5). With a portrait. Scott 219.
—Verstegan, R. [A portrait of Mary Queen of Scots, with Latin verses]. *See* no. 1305.1.

II. *Anonymous works of which the author has not been identified.*

Compassionevole et Memorabil Caso della Morte

795 —Il compassioneuole et memorabil caso, della morte della Regina di Scotia moglie di Francesco II. Re di Francia. 4°. *Vicenza, appresso Agostino dalla Noce*, 1587. L.O. [*DMR].
Translated from a French original? Dated at the end: 'Di Parigi il di 14 di Marzo'. Scott 152.

796 —[Anr. ed.] 4°. *Parma, appresso Filandro Calestani*, 1587. L.
Dated at the end as in no. 795, but with the year 1587 added. Scott 151.

797 —[Anr. ed., with title:] Memorabil caso della morte della Sereniss. Regina di Scotia, che fu moglie del Re Francesco II. di Francia. Condannata a morte dalla Regina d'Inghilterra. 8° (a quadrifolium). *In Parma, con licenza de' Superiori, & Rist apata [sic] in Ferrara per Vittorio Baldini*, 1587. E.

De Jezabelis Anglae Parricidio . . . Poemata

798 —De Iezabelis Anglae parricidio varii generis poemata Latina et Gallica. 4°. *n.p.d.* [1587.] L.; WO. [*DMR].

Collation: A–B⁴. Unpaginated. These poems were reprinted in no. 99. The second poem in the collection is the same as that at no. 800 and is here headed: 'Aliud eiusdem argumenti, auctum & ememdatum post primam editionem'. Scott 153.

799   —[Anr. ed., enlarged.] De Iezabelis Anglae parricido [*sic*] varii generis poemata Latina et Gallica. 4°. *n.p.d.* [1587.] c².PA(Res. Yc. 858).PA⁴. Collation: A–B⁴ ²A–I⁸K²(K2 blank).

De Jezabelis Anglicae Parricidiis . . . Carmen

800   —De Iezabelis Anglicae parricidiis ad pios Mariae Scoticae Reginae manes. Carmen. *s.sh.* 4°. PA(Yc 2700).
The only known copy consists of a single leaf, unpaged and unsigned, which may be incomplete. The poem was reprinted in nos. 798–9.

Discours de la Mort

—*See* nos. 779–85.

Discours de l'Execution de Mort

—*See* no. 785.

Execution. Oder Todt Marien Stuart

—*See* Mariae Stuartae . . . Supplicium et Mors.

Gruendliche und eigentlich . . . Beschreibung

—*See* Mariae Stuartae . . . Supplicium et Mors.

Harangue faicte à la Royne d'Angleterre

—*See* nos. 766–7.

Kurtzer Ausszug . . . eines Landverreters Stucks

—*See* no. 814.

Kurtzer unnd Gründtlicher Bericht

801   —Kurtzer vnnd gründtlicher bericht, wie die Edel vnnd from Koenigin auss Schotlandt, Fraw Maria Stuarda . . . den 18. Februarii, anno 87. in Engellandt gericht worden, vnd was sie fuer ein Gottseliges end genommen. 4° (a single quadrifolium). *Gedruckt zu Muenchen, bey Adam Berg,* 1587. L.O.; c².E.
Scott 158.

802   —[*Flemish version.*] Waerachtich verhael, hoe ende in wat manieren de Coninginne van Schotlandt haer heeft ghewillichlijck begeuen ter doot, achtervolghende de sententie byde Coninghinne van Engelant ende haren Raet, den 16. Februarii 1587. gegeuen steruende int Catholicq Roomsche ghelooue. 4° (a single quadrifolium). *Gheprint Thantwerpen by Mattheus de Rische,* 1587. L.; BRS.
Scott 136.

Mariae Stuartae . . . Supplicium et Mors

803   —Mariae Stuartae Scotorum Reginae . . . Supplicium & mors pro fide Catholica constantissima. In Anglia vernacula lingua primum conscripta: ideoque multis aspersa ex hostiũ eius Reginae sententia, quae nec ipsa vnquam confessa est, nec hactenus debite probata sunt. Nunc in gratiam Catholicorum fideliter, nullis plane omissis translata & edita: vt sanctissimae Principis martyrii feruor, animiuqe inuicta

constantia, ipsorum aduersariorum testimonio comprobata, toti mundo elucescat. Additis succinctis quibusdam animaduersionibus & notis: breuiq. totius Reginae eiusdem vitae chronologia, ex optimis quibusque auctoribus collecta. 8°. *Coloniae, apud Godefridum Kempensem*, 1587. L(2).O.; BON.BRN.C.DMR.E.E².KN.MP.PA(2).TRI.WO.YK.

'Supplicium & Mors' is a translation into Latin of an unidentified hostile English account of Mary's trial and execution, together with a Catholic commentary on it. The original English account, which does not appear to have been published, is described in the drop-head title to the commentary (B3ʳ) as 'scriptum datum Londini 27 Martii 1587'. Translation and commentary are followed by Latin poems in Mary's honour and a 'Breuis chronologia' of her life. The translation and commentary were reprinted, with additional comments, in pt. 2 of nos. 1056–60. Scott 159.

804 —[*Flemish transl.*] Warachtige beschrijuinghe vant leuen ende glorioos martirie der . . . Princerssen Maria Stuart . . . Beschreuen door Jan Bernaerts Jansz . . . Met noch een corte refutatie der lasteringhen daer hare Maiesteyt van hare vyanden mede beschuldicht wort. 8°. *Tantwerpen, by de Weduwe van Gulliaem van Parijs, n.d.* [1589.] BRS. [*L.]

The order of contents is changed: the first item is a translation of the 'Brevis chronologia' of no. 803; this is followed by a translation of the hostile account and the Catholic commentary on it, and this in turn by a translation of the poems. Jan Bernaerts Jansz. refers in a foreword to 'een seker Latijns Boeccke' from which he made the translation. This foreword is dated from Mechelen 1 January 1589. The approbation was given at Antwerp on 12 March 1588.

—[*German versions of the hostile account.*] Two German versions, *Execution. Oder Todt Marien Stuart*, Koenigsperg, 1587 (Scott 187), reprinted Magdeburg 1588 (Scott 162) and *Gruendliche vnd eigentlich warhaffte Beschreibung*, Coellen, 1587, fall outside the scope of this catalogue, as they comprise only the hostile account unaccompanied by the Catholic commentary and additions.

Marie der Koenigin . . . eigentliche Bildtnuss

805 —Marie der Koenigin auss Schotlandt eigentliche Bildtnuss. Auch, wie vnd vmb was Vrsachen, dieselbig auss ihrem Koenigreich, in Engellandt kommen, vnd alda enthaupt ist worden. *Brs.fol. n.p.d.* [1587?] L.

The German text is followed by eight lines of Latin verse. The only copy known has, bound with it, a crudely coloured engraved portrait of Mary. This engraving is a poor copy, in reverse, of that described at no. 1305.1, omitting much of the detail but preserving a few of the lines of Latin verse here enclosed in an oval frame surrounding the portrait. The engraving is signed at the foot: "PM Ian. Bussem': exc." Johann Bussemacher was a Cologne printer and publisher active between 1580 and 1613. Scott 154.

Memorabil Caso della Morte

—*See* no. 797.

Mort de la Royne d'Escosse

806 —La mort de la Royne d'Escosse, Douairiere de France. Où est contenu le vray discours de la procedure des Angloys à l'execution d'icelle, la constante & royalle resolutiō de sa Maiesté defunte: ses verteueux deportements & derniers propos, les funerailles & enterremēt. 8°. *n.p.*, 1588. L.; E.E³.LINC.

Collation: a⁶b–k⁸. The lower-case signatures perhaps indicate that this edition was intended to accompany an edition of Blackwood's *Martyre* (*see* no. 100). Scott 173?

807 —[Anr. ed.] 12°. *n.p.*, 1588. A.E(*imp.*).PA².(H10922, *bound after no. 100*). VT.
Collation: A–G¹². Scott 172. *Pr.* [Paris G. Bickon?].

808 —[Anr. ed.] 16°. *n.p.*, 1589. O.; PA²(H10923). *Both these copies have the whole of pt. 1 of no. 100, except its titlepage and preliminaries (a⁴), inserted in or after the first gathering (πA⁴).*
Collation: πA⁴A–O⁸ (O7, 8 blank). Identical with pt. 2 of no. 100. Scott 179. *Pr.* [Paris G. Bickon?].

Ode sur la Mort de . . . Marie Royne d'Escosse

809 —Ode sur la mort de la tres-chrestienne tres-illustre tres-constante, Marie Royne d'Escosse, morte pour la Foy, le 18. Feburier, 1587. par la cruauté des Anglois . . . Auec l'oraison funebre prononcée en Mars à nostre Dame de Paris, au iour de ses obseques & seruice. 8°. 2 pts. *Paris, chez Guillaume Bichon*, 1588. E.E³.PA(*2 ; 1 has pt. 1 only, the other, Bliss 539, is complete*).PA⁴.(pt. 1).PML.
Collation: pt. 1, A–B⁴. pt. 2, A–I⁴. Pt. 1 consists of two odes in French; pt. 2 is another issue of no. 763. Scott 168. Renouard III. 510 (describing pt. 1 only).

P.M.P.Q.M. Advorte Hospes quod nunquam accedit hoc

810 —[*Begin :*] P.M.P.Q.M. Aduorte hospes quod nunquam accedit hoc, heus? Maria Stuarta impiatorum violentia oppressa qoiesco [*sic*] . . . 4°. *n.p.d.* [1587.] L.
An address in prose beginning as quoted above, followed by two poems, one in Latin headed 'Ad Mariam Stuartam Scotorum Reginam' and beginning 'Gentibus Arctois quae praefers lumina Princeps . . .', the other in French headed 'Sur le tombeau de Marie Stuart Royne d'Escosse . . . Elegie. En laquelle entre-parlents le passant, et la muse'. Collation: A⁴. Without pagination. P.M.P.Q.M., who has not been identified, was one of those who wrote in no. 798. Scott 161.

Proditionis ab aliquot Scotiae Perduellibus . . . Narratio

811 —Proditionis ab aliquot Scotiae perduellibus aduersus Serenissimam suam Reginam non ita pridem perpetratae breuis & simplex narratio ex amplissimi cuiusdam viri literis fideliter descripta. 8°. *Louanii, apud Rutgerum Velpiū*, 1566. L.; GT.
An account sympathetic to Mary of events leading to the murder of Rizzio. Scott 40.

812 —Anr. ed.] 4°. *n.p.*, 1566. L.O.; VT(Ferraioli IV 8890/10, -tp.). [*DMR].
Pr. [Dillingen, Sebald Mayer.] This edition contains some minor textual changes. Scott 41.

813 —[Variant, with colophon:] *Dilingae, excudebat Sebaldus Mayer*, 1566. E.(Ry. III. e.6).
—[Anr. ed.] 1573. *Part of* no. 1455.

814 —[*German transl.*] Kurtzer Ausszug vnd schlechte erzelung eines Landuerreters stucks, wider die Kuenigin in Schottland, von etlichen abfaelligen, mainaydigen, vnnd auffruerischen beschehen, vermerckt auss eines hochansehenlichen Herzens Schreiben, trewlich verteutscht. 4°. *n.p.*, 1566. L.; E. Scott 44.

Supplicium et Mors

—*See* nos. 803–4.

Vera, e compita Relazione del Successo della Morte

—*See* nos. 768–73.

Vera Relatione della Morte

—*See* no. 786.

Vera Relatione del Sucesso

—*See* no. 773.

Waerachtich Verhael

—*See* no. 802.

815   **Mary**, *Tudor, Queen of England.* [*Appendix.*] Guidi, A., *Bishop of Trau.*
Antonii Guidi oratio in funere Mariae Britanniae Reginae ad cardinales regumque & rerumpublicarum legatos. Romae habita VIII Id.
Martii M.D.LIX. 4°. *Romae, ex officina Saluiana, n.d.* [1559]. L(2).O.;
N.PA.
—[Repudio della Reina Maria d'Inghilterra, 1558.] In spite of the title,
this translation from the French, printed at Bologna in 1558, concerns Anne of Cleves and not Queen Mary, and so has no place in this
catalogue.

816   **Mason, Richard,** *in religion* Angelus a S. Francisco.†† Quaestionum
theologicarum resolutio pariter, ac collatio cum sententiis S. Augustini. 4°. *Duaci, apud Martinum Bogard*[*um*], 1637.
Not found. Description from Wadding (p. 19).

817   —Sacrarum priuilegiorum quorundam Seraphico P. S. Francisco, in
gratiam obseruantium regulam . . . a Deo O.M. indultorum, in quo
eorum veritas elucidatur . . . per F. Angelum de S. Francisco Anglum.
8° (in fours). *Duaci, typis viduae Martini Bogardi,* 1636. C.; D².DOU.
LIL.PA.PA⁴.PA⁵.RO⁸.STR.SWAF.VT(2).

Mathews, Francis, *pseud. See* O'Mahony, F. (no. 862).

Maurus, *Anglus. See* Taylor, W.

Maurus, *de S. Croix, name in religion. See* Hames, M.

Maxfield, Thomas, *Bl.* [*Appendix.*] Vita et martyrium D. Maxfildaei,
1616. *See* no. 313.

Mayhew, Edward. *See* Maihew, E.

Mayne, John, *in religion* Silvanus Mayne. [*A work edited by him.*]
Ogilvy, J., *Saint.* Relatio incercerationis . . . P. Ioannis Ogilbei, 1615
[*etc.*] *See* nos. 848–56.

Mayne, Silvanus, *name in religion. See* Mayne, J.

818   **Mead, Gerard** (Gerald). De mysterio Sanctissimae Trinitatis. Q.
theologica. Vtrum Deus sit trinus et vnus? . . . pro priore ad baccalaureatum . . . die 18. iunii 1618. *s.sh.fol. Duaci, typis Petri Telu,* 1618.
BRU²(EA 25/23).
A programme announcing a thesis to be defended at the University
of Douai. Not seen. Description from Labarre (vol. 2, p. 165) who
saw the copy cited above. A 'Geraldus Medus, S. Theol. Doctor'
figures in the list of alumni of the Irish College, Douai, in 1622,
published in no. 324.

Medus, Gerardus (Geraldus). *See* Mead, G.

Mellaghlin, Charles. Conclusiones theologicae, 1640. *See* no. 255.

Mervinea, Ioannes de, *pseud. See* Roberts, J.

819   **Messingham, Thomas.** Florilegium insulae sanctorum seu vitae et
acta sanctorum Hiberniae. Quibus accesserunt non vulgaria monu-
menta Hoc est Sancti Patricii Purgatorium, S. Malachiae prophetia de
summis pontificibus, aliaque nonnulla. Fol. *Parisiis, ex officina*

Sebastiani Cramoisy, 1624. L(3).O(3).C(3); CHA.D.D².DE.DUR.GTN.KNY.
MTH.PA.PA⁴.RO¹¹.USH.WO. + +

Includes David Rothe's *Tractatulus . . . de nominibus Hiberniae.*
With three engravings in the text sgd by the author. This issue is
dedicated to Baltazar and Remundus Lescalopier. In some copies
sigs. Ll3, Ll4 are cancels. For the lives of SS. Patrick, Bridget and
Columbanus transl. from this work *see* A&R 420.

820 —[Anr. issue.] *Parisiis, ex officina Sebastiani Cramoisy*, 1624. O.; ANG.
The sheets of no. 819, including the titleleaf, but with the bifolium
forming the inner sheet of the first quire, which contained the
dedication to B. and R. Lescalopier, replaced by a new bifolium
containing a dedication to J. F. de Gondi, Archbishop of Paris.

821 —Officia SS. Patricii, Columbae, Brigidae, et aliorum quorundam
Hiberniae sanctorum. Ex veteris membranis & manuscriptis breuiariis
desumpta. Atque ad normam officii Romani repurgata. 16°. *Parisiis,
ex typographia Hieronymi Blageart*, 1620. L(*imp.*).

822 **Miles, James.**‡ Breuis catechismus pro hereticis Anglicis, Scotis, &
aliis ad fidem captolicam [*sic*], & Apostolicam reductis. Ex Romano
catechismo Latino in Anglicum reductis. 8°. *Neapoli, apud Octauium
Beltranum*, 1635. L(*imp.*).
Text in Latin and English. ERL 153 (3). STC 17920.5.

823 —Corona ouero sacro settenario della Bma: Vergine Maria dalla stessa
Vergine riuelato. 8°. *Napoli, appresso Ottauio Beltrano*, 1631. RO⁸.
The titlepage is engraved. With woodcut illustrations.

Molanus, Ioannes. *See* Mullan, J.

More, Henry.† [*A work translated by him.*] Floyd, J. Deus et Rex, 1619.
See no. 487.

More, Thomas, *Saint.*††

Collections

824 —Thomae Mori . . . Lucubrationes, ab innumeris mendis repurgatae.
Vtopiae libri II. Progymnasmata. Epigrammata. Ex Luciano conuersa
quaedam. Declamatio Lucianicae respondens. Epistolae. Quibus
additae sunt duae aliorum epistolae, de uita, moribus & morte Mori.
8°. *Basil., apud Episcopium F[ilium]*, 1563. L(2).O.C(2); A.AMS.C².C³.
D.DMR.E.E².L²⁶.LGE³.OS.PA.VI.WO. +

825 —Thomae Mori . . . Omnia, quae hucusque ad manus nostras peruene-
runt, Latina opera: quorum aliqua nunc primum in lucem prodeunt,
reliqua vero multo quam antea castigatiora. Fol. *Louanii, apud
Ioannem Bogardum*, 1565. L.; ANT².BRN.BRS.C¹⁵.C¹⁹.CHICH.D¹⁰.HA.KN.
LIL.N.VT.Y.
The copyright was held jointly by Jean Bogard and Pierre Zangre
(*See* no. 826). The original date of copyright, 14 Oct. 1565, is
printed on the verso of the titleleaf; in some copies a printed slip
bearing a new data of copyright, 9 Feb. 1566, is pasted onto the
same page.

826 —[Imprint variant.] *Louanii, apud Petrum Zangrium Tiletanum*, 1565.
L.; BRS.D.EX.HAN.N.PA.PA⁴.
With Zangre's device and imprint substituted for Bogard's on the
titlepage. Forms part of a shared edition with no. 825.

827 —[Date variant of no. 825.] 1566. L.O(2).C.; BRU.C².C⁷.C¹⁶.D.E.E².HA.
HP(2).L⁴.L¹⁵.O¹¹.PA⁴.VI.YK. +

828 —[Date variant of no. 826.] 1566. L(2).O.; BRS.BRU.C⁴.C⁵.C⁹.D².DE.GT.
L¹⁵.LAR.MTH.PA.PA⁴. +

Single Works

829 —Doctissima D. Thomae Mori . . . Epistola, in qua non minus facete
quam pie, respondet literis Ioannis Pomerani . . . Opusculum . . . ex

Authoris quidem autographo emendato, dum viueret, exemplari desumptum, nunq. vero antehac in lucem editum. 8°. *Louanii, ex officina Ioannis Fouleri*, 1568. L.C.; AMS.G.GT(3).OS.PA(S).PA³.RO.VI.WO. —Imploratio divini auxilii. *See* nos. 426, 427.

830   —Thomae Mori V.C. Dissertatio epistolica, de aliquot sui temporis theologastrorum ineptiis; deque correctione translationis vulgatae N. Testamenti: ad Martinum Dorpium theologum Louaniensem. 12°. *Lugduni Batauorum, ex officina Elzeuiriana*, 1625. C.; GT.HAN. HN.L⁸.O².O¹¹.O³¹.PA.VT.WO.

Appendix

831   —Herrera, F. de. Tomas Moro de Fernando de Herrera. Al illustrissimo Señor Don Rodrigo de Castro Cardenal i Arcobispo de Seuilla. 12°. *Seuilla, por Alonso de la Barrera*, 1592. *Venden se en casa de Iacomo Lopez.* ESC.HSA.SEV².
       Not seen. Description from Gibson (100) and Simon Diaz (vol. xi, no. 4243) where the above copies are cited. Based in part on Stapleton's life of More (in nos. 1159–60).

832   ——[Anr. ed.] Tomas Moro de Fernando de Herrera. A Don Pedro Fernandez de Castro Conde de Lemos, de Andrade i Villalva, Marques de Sarria. 8°. *Madrid, por Luis Sãchez*, 1617. L.; HSA.Y. (*Gibson cites copies at MD and the Gleeson Library at San Francisco University; Simon Diaz cites copies of this or no. 833 at MD and the Seminario de S. Carlos at Zaragoza.*)
       Gibson 102. Simon Diaz (vol. xi, no. 4244) does not distinguish between this and no. 833. In this edition there is no portrait. The pages are numbered 1–79. Modern edition in *Archivo hispalense*, vol. 12, 1950.

833   ——[Anr. ed.] *Madrid, por Luis Sanchez*, 1617, MD.
       Not seen. Gibson (no. 101) cites a copy at L but this is an error. The MD copy is cited in Smith's *Updating* of Gibson. According to Gibson this is a pirated edition w.th a false imprint but contemporary with no. 832. It has a portrait of More by Anton Wiericx. The pages are numbered 1–75. A reprint, without the portrait but with the same imprint and date, was published at [Madrid in 1747]. The 18th century reprint (copies at C.; MD.Y) can be distinguished by the misprint 'Pernandez' for 'Fernandez' on the titlepage.
—Stapleton, T. Tres Thomae, 1588 [*etc.*]. Including the life of Thomas More. *See* nos. 1159–60.
—[For an account of More's martyrdom] *see* nos. 235–6, 1455.

More, Thomas, *S.J.* [*A work translated by him.*] Warford, W. Breuis ac methodica institutio continens praecipua Christianae fidei mysteria, 1617. *See* no. 1358.
834   **Morgan, Anthony.** Deo Optimo Maximo. Sanctissimae virgini Matri, sanctoque Thomae Aquinati ... Sacrae conclusiones theologicae. De natura & origine peccati ... Praeerit R.P. Thomas Blacklous Praeses ... Defendet Antonius Morganus Anglus in Collegio Anglorum Vlyssiponensi. Fol. (a bifolium). *Vlyssipone, ex officina Petri Craesbeeck*, 1631. O.
       A programme announcing the forthcoming defence of his thesis. Anthony Morgan may be an alias of Anthony Sanders who arrived at Lisbon from Douai in 1628 (DD.3, p. 418). He should be distinguished from Antonius Sanderus, Canon of Ypres, the author of *Bibliotheca scriptorum varia*, published at Douai in 1637. Blacklous, Thomas [T. White].
Morisanus, Bernardus. *See* Morison, B.

835   **Morison, Bernard.** Bernardi Morisani Derensis, Iberni . . . in Aris-
totelis logicam, physicam, ethicam apotelesma. 4°. *Francofurti, typis
Iohan. Weisii, impensis Petri Mareschalli,* 1625. L.O.; C³.D.O⁵.O⁷.O⁸.O¹⁸.
O¹⁹.PA.

836   —Bernardi Morisani . . . in spheram Ioannis de S. Bosco commentarius.
8°. *Francofurti, impensis Petri Mareschalli,* 1625. O.; PA.
A philosophical commentary on the astronomical theory of Joannes
de Sacrobosco. *Pr.* [J. F. Weiss].

Morley, George. [*Disputations in which he acted as Praeses.*] Theses ex
vniuersa theologia disputandae, 1622–23. *See* nos. 523, 910, 1391.

837   **Morley, Henry,** *alias* Lawrence Rigby. Triumphus religionis, virtutumque ancillantium . . . Card. Millino dicatus a Laurentio Rigbeo,
theses philosophicas in Collegio Anglicano, sustinente. 4°. *Romae, ex
typographia Alexandri Zannetti,* 1624. L.; RO².(3).
Consisting of three poems preceded by a dedication in prose.

838   **Mullan, John.** Idea togatae constantiae siue Francisci Tailleri Dubliniensis praetoris in persecutione congressus, & religionis Catholicae
defensione interitus. 12°. *Parisiis, apud viduam Petri Cheualier,* 1629.
L.; D.D⁶.DUR.F.PA.PA².(2).
Francis Taylor, the subject of this work, died in prison in Dublin in
1609. With an additional titlepage, engraved, which adds the words:
'cui adiungitur tripartita martyrum Britannicarum insularum
epitome'. The 'Epitome tripartita', which has its own titlepage,
begins on sig. P4.

838.1 **Mush, John.†** Declaratio motuum ac turbulationum quae ex con-
trouersiis inter Iesuitas iisq; in omnibus fauentem D. Georg. Black-
wellum Archipresbyterum, & sacerdotes seminariorum in Anglia. 4°.
Rhotomagi, apud Iacobum Molaeum, 1601. L.O.C.; C³.DMR.DUR.F.L².
L³⁰.O³.O⁴.P.PA.USH.W.YK. + +
Anon. Imprint false; *pr.* [London?] Law 2. Lib. 1947, p. 180.
A&R 552. STC 3102. ERL 39. Mil. vol. I, pp. 116, *etc.*

N., N. Carta, escrita a vno de los colegiales ingleses que residen en
Madrid. *See* no. 1247.

N., N., *R.P., Anglus, Oxoniensis, Societatis Iesu.* Clauis homerica. *See*
no. 938.

N., T. *See* nos. 950–2.

Neville, Thomas, *alias. See* Appleton, T.

Nixon, Iacobus de, *Hybernus & advocatus Leodiensis.* [*A work edited
by him.*] Wright, T. Quatuor colloquia, 1614. *See* no. 1426.

Northumberland, Anne, *Countess of. See* Percy, A.

Northumberland, John, *Duke of. See* Dudley, J.

839   **Nugent, Francis.** Copie d'vn tres-fameux miracle arriué en la cité de
Palerme l'an 1607. D'vn enfant mis en pieces par sa propre mere, &
remis en vie par le Seraphique Pere S. François. Enuoyée de Milan par
le R.P. François Hybernois, predicateur Capucin . . . au R.P. Gardien
des Capucins d'Arras. 8° (in fours). *Arras, par Guillaume de la
Riuiere,* 1608. AR.
François Hybernois [F. Nugent]. Consisting of a prefatory letter by
[Nugent] followed by an account of the miracle headed 'Discours
du miracle' and concluding 'Imprimé à Milan en l'Imprimerie
Archiepiscopale l'an 1607'. The Milan edition of the account, of
which this appears to be [Nugent's] translation, has not been found.

840   —[Anr. ed.] 8°. *Douay, de l'imprimerie de Laurent Kellam,* 1608. MTH.
The title is the same as in no. 839 except that the date 1605 has
been substituted for 1607 in the third line.

841   —[Anr. ed.] 8° (in fours). *Douay, de l'imprimerie de Charles Boscard,*
1608. LIL.
The date in the third line of the title is 1605.

842 —[Anr. ed., with title beginning:] Miracle tres-fameux n'agueres arriué en la cité de Palerme, d'vn enfant mis en pieces par sa propre mere . . . 8° (in fours). *Paris, iouxte la copie imprimée à Douay par Charles Boscard*, 1608. D⁶.PA(Rés. K.12 72).
There is no date in the third line of the title.

842.1 —[Anr. ed.] 8° (in fours). *Iouxte l'exemplaire imprimé, A Rouen, chez Iaques Hubault*, 1608. L.
The title is the same as in no. 842.

Oconchovair, Patricius. *See* O'Connor, P.

843 **O'Connor, Patrick.**‡ Quodlibetica decisio monastici cuiusdam casus, vbi ostenditur qualis timoris inductio, approbatae religionis professionem inualidet . . . Authore F. Patricio Oconchouair. 8°. *Parisiis, apud Ludouicum Seuestre*, 1635. D.PA.
O'Connor, an Irish Franciscan, also published at Paris in 1637 a work in praise of Louis XIII entitled *Sidus Borbonicum* which falls outside the scope of this catalogue.

O'Devany, Cornelius, Bishop of Down and Connor. [*Appendix.*] Martyrium Rmi. D. F. Cornelii Douenii, 1614. *See* no. 413.

844 **O'Donnell, Mary Stuart.** [*Appendix.*] Enriquez, A. Resolucion varonil. O viage que hiço Doña Maria Estuarda condesa de Tirconel en trage de varon . . . Dedicada a . . . Isabel Clara Eugenia Infanta de España. 8°. *Brussellas, en casa de Gouaert Schoeuaerts*, 1627. L(2).; PA³. (34400).
Describing the flight of the daughter of Rory O'Donnell, Earl of Tyrconnell, to escape persecution by the English government. She arrived in the Spanish Netherlands in 1626 to rejoin her brother, Hugh, who was in the service of the Archduchess Isabella. The family title had been forfeited on her father's attainder in 1607. (*See Complete Peerage*, vol. 12, pt. 2, pp. 111–14.)

845 —[Imprint variant.] *Brussellas, en casa de Francisco Viuieno*, 1627. MD. PA.PA³.(32094).

846 —[*French transl.*] Resolution courageuse et louable, de la Comtesse de Tirconel, Irlandoise. Ses adventures, & ses voyages en habit de caualier, estant persecutée pour la religion Catholique, en Angleterre . . . Traduicte d'Espagnol en François, par Pierre de Cadenet, Sieur de Brieulle. 12°. *Paris, chez la vefue M. Guillemot . . . et Matthieu Guillemot*, 1628. L(2).O.; PA².PA³.

847 **O'Fahy, John** [*Begin:*] Eminentissimo, ac Reuerendissimo Principi F. Felici Centino S.R.E. Cardinali amplissimo. D. Ioannes O Fahy Hibernus Seminarii Ludouisiani alumnus. S.P.F. Conclusiones theologicae . . . [*End:*] Disputabuntur publice in Collegio S. Isidori . . . Praesidente Reu. Fr. Ioanne a S. Francisco [J. Punch] . . . 1634. Mense Ianuarii. *s.sh.fol. Romae, ex typographia Ludouici Grignani*, 1634. RO⁸.
A programme announcing the forthcoming defence of his thesis.

O'Farrell. *See* Ferrall.

O'Ferrall. *See* Ferrall.

848 **Ogilvy, John,** *Saint.* Relatio incarcerationis et martyrii P. Ioannis Ogilbei natione Scoti, e Societate Iesu presbyteri. Ex autographo ipsius martyris, in carcere exarato Glasguae in Scotia octiduo ante mortem: continuata vero deinceps per eiusdem concaptiuos. qui eius martyrio interfuerunt. 8° (in fours). *Duaci, typis viduae Laurentii Kellami*, 1615. L.; A².AMI.
Put together and edited by [J. Mayne]. *See* Dilworth, pp. 56–9.

849 —[Anr. ed.] 8°. *Constantiae, ex typographaeo Leonhardi Straub*, 1616. DOE.HEI.L²⁶.SBG².

850 —[Anr. ed.] 12°. *Moguntiae, typis Ioannis Albini*, 1616. L.; BUTE.FU².MD.

851 —[Anr. ed.] 12°. *Wirceburgi, typis Conradi Schwindtlauff*, 1616. STU.

852 —[Anr. ed.] Nunc denuo recusa, & minoris congregationis Academicae

Beatiss. Virginis Annunciatae sodalibus ab illustri ... Carolo Emanuele Madrutio, eiusdem congregationis Praefecto, strenae loco oblata. 18°. *Ingolstadii, typis Ederianis apud Elisabetham Angermariam viduam*, 1616. L.; E³.PA.

853 —[*Flemish transl.*] Verhael van de geuanckenisse ende martelie van P. Ioannes Ogilbaeus. *Antwerp, Fickaert*, 1615.
Not found. Description from Sommerv. (tom. 7, col. 1311).

854 —[Anr. ed.?] Verhael, van die gheuanckenisse ende het martijrie van P. Iohannes Ogilbeus ... Ghetrouwelick ouergheset in nederduyts wt het Latijns exemplaer, ghedruckt te Doway, by de weduwe van Laurentius Kellam, anno 1615. 8°. *n.p.d.* [1615 or later.] MAA. [*L.]
Pr. [Antwerp, Frans Fickaert?]

855 —[Anr. ed.] *Antwerp, Fickaert*, 1623.
Not found. Description from Sommerv. (tom. 7, col. 1311).

856 —[*German transl.*] Relation vnd Beschreibung der Gefangcknuss vnnd Marter P. Ioannis Ogilbei ... Ersltich in Lateinischer Sprach zu Duai in Flandern aussgangen, jetzt aber ... in das Teutsch versetzt. 8°. *Constantz am Bodensee, bey Leonhart Straub*, 1616. DIL. [*O.]

856.1 —[*Spanish transl.*] Relacion de la prision y martirio del Padre Iuan Ogilveo Escoces, que la escrivio de su mano en el carcel ... de Glasconia ocho dias antes que muriese, y la continuaron los presos sus compañeros. 8°. [*n.p.d.*].
Not found. Recorded by N. Antonio, *Bibliotheca Hispana Nova* (Madrid, 1788) 2, p. 85 but without an imprint. The translator from the Latin was Marcus Lopez, who died in 1653.

857 **Oliver, John.** Praecationes de humani generis lapsu, de benedicta, & sancta Trinitate, pro sanctae Ecclesiae statu, de Spiritu sancto. De precipuis festis Saluatoris per annum ex veteris & noui Testamenti sententiis collectae. 12°. *Antuerpiae, apud Henricum Loeum*, 1571. L.
Dedicated by the author (who describes himself as 'Presbiter Anglus') to Cardinal Morone, Protector of England.

858 —Precationes horariae ex sacris literis et sanctorum Patrum sententiis collectae, De sacrosancta Trinitate. Orationes de Spiritu S. cum precibus horariis. 12°. *Louanii*, 1568. LGE².

859 —Preces horariae ex sacris literis et SS. Patrum sententiis collectae. De sacrosancta Trinitate. De dulcissimo nomine Iesu. De mysterio sacrosanctae Eucharistiae. Pro statu Ecclesiae Christianae. 12°. *Antuerpiae, apud Ioannem Bellerum*, 1567. O.; A.PA.RO³.U.
The author is described on the titlepage as 'Ioannes Oliuerus Vuigorniensis Anglus'.

860 —Preces horariae ex sacris literis & sanctorum Patrum sententiis collectae. De sacrosancta Trinitate. De Iesu Saluatore nostro. De mysterio sacrosanctae Eucharistiae. De Spiritu sancto orationes & horariae preces. 12°. *Antuerp., typ. Ae. D.*, 1568. LGE².
Pr. [Aegidius Diest.]

O'Loughran, Patrick. Martyrium ... R.D. Patriti: Luchrani, 1614.
See no. 413.

861 **O'Mahony, Francis.** Examen iuridicum censurae facultatis theologicae Parisiensis; et eiusdem ciuitatis archiepiscopi latae quasdam propositiones Regularibus regni Hiberniae falso impositas ... Auctore Edmundo Vrsulano Hiberno. 8°. *Francofurti, sumptibus generosi viri Ioannis de Witte*, 1631. L.C.; KNY.PA.PA⁴(2).STI.
Edmundus Ursulanus, *pseud.* Answering accusations against the Irish Regular Clergy in nos. 682–5. Imprint false; *pr.* [Louvain?] Answered by Paul Harris in no. 639.1. *See Coll. Hib.*, nos. 6 & 7, 1963–64, pp. 46–7; *Wadding Papers*, pp. 609, 620, 627.

862 —Exemptio fratrum et conuentuum ordinis Minor. Regularis Obseruantiae et aliorum ordinum mendicantium regni Hiberniae ... asserta ex

vetustis iudiciis, & sententiis . . . nunc recens collectis, opera F.F.M.
4°. *Louanii, typis Coenestenii,* 1632. L.
F.F.M. [Francis Mathews, *pseud.* of F. O'Mahony.]

863 **O'Sullivan Beare, Philip.** D. Philippi O Sulleuani Bearri Iberni
patritiana decas, siue libri decem, quibus de diui Patritii vita . . . de
religionis Ibernicae casibus . . . de Anglorum lubrica fide . . . de
Anglohaereticae Ecclesiae sectis . . . accurate agitur. Archicornigero-
mastix, siue Vsheri Haeresiarchae confutatio, descriptioque accessit.
4°. *Matriti, ex officina Francisci Martinez,* 1629. L(2).O(2).; D(*imp.*).
D².D⁶.L².MD(2).MTH.PA².

In part a reply to *A discourse of the religion anciently professed by the
Irish and British,* by James Ussher, later Archbishop of Armagh, of
which the first edition (now apparently no lnoger extant) was
printed at Dublin in 1623 (*see* Mil., vol. 2, p. 219).

864 —Historiae Catholicae Iberniae compendium. Domino Philippo
Austriaco IIII . . . dicatum. 4° (in eights). *Vlyssipone, excusum a
Petro Crasbeeckio,* 1621. L(3).O(2).C.; D.D⁶(3).D¹⁰.DMR.GTN.KNY.L².L²⁵.
MTH.PA.PA⁴.USH.VAL²(2). +

Including the text of the two catalogues of Irish saints and heroes
compiled respectively by Richard Conway and Henry FitzSimon.
(*See* nos. 268, 480.)

Pacenius, Bartholus, *pseud. See* Abercromby, R.

Paris, *Arras College (house of writers of the English Secular Clergy).*
[*Works subsidised by the College.*] Anderton, J., *of Lostock.* Apologia
Protestantum pro Romana ecclesia, 1615 [*etc.*] *See* nos. 27–9.

—Stapleton, T. [*Collected Works.*] Thomae Stapletoni . . . opera quae
extant omnia, 1620. *See* no. 1129.

——Propugnaculum fidei, 1619. *See* no. 1155.

Paris, *Irish College.* [*A discourse delivered at the College.*] Rothe, D.
Brigida thaumaturga, 1620. *See* no. 953.

Parsons, Robert. *See* Persons, R.

Passenius, Bartholus, *pseud. See* Abercromby, R.

Patricius, *ab Angelis, name in religion. See* Comerford, P.

864.1 **Pendryck, William,** *in religion* Eliseus of St Michael.† Meditationes
ac soliloquia in septem petitiones orationis Dominicae. Authore R.P.
F. Elisaeo a S. Michaele Carmelita Discalceato. 16°. *Antuerpiae, apud
Petrum & Ioannē Belleros,* 1624. O.C.; PA.
Dedicated to Anthony Roper of Eltham.

865 **Percy, Anne,** *Countess of Northumberland.* Discours des troubles
nouuellement aduenuz au royaume d'Angleterre, au moys d'octobre
1569. Auec vne declaration, faicte par le Comte de Nortumberland &
autres grans seigneurs d'Angleterre. 8° (in fours). *Paris, chez Nicolas
Chesneau,* 1570. L(2).; C²⁰.(*imp.*).CARP.LYN.PA(2:- Nc 154A; Bliss 122).
PA³.

Anon. For the authorship *see* Nicholas Sander's account of Thomas
Percy, Earl of Northumberland, in nos. 972–84.

866 —[Anr. ed.] 8° (in fours). *Lyon, par Michel Ioue,* 1570. L.; DI°.F.ILL.
PA(2:- Nc 154; Bliss 123).
Anon. Scott 67.

867 —[Anr. ed.] 8° (in fours). *Paris, iouxte la copie imprimée chez Nicolas
Chesneau,* 1587. PA(Nc 154B).
Anon.

868 —[Anr. ed.] 8° (in fours). *Paris, pour Iaques Blochet, iouxte la copie
impirmée* [sic] *chez Nicolas Chesneau,* 1587. PA(Nc 154C).PA³.
Anon.

869 —[Anr. ed.] 8° (in fours). *Paris, pour Laurent du Coudret, iouxte la copie
de Iacques Blochet, n.d.* [1587?]. E.PA(2:- Nc 154D; Bliss 121).PA³.
Anon. Scott 47.

870   —[Anr. ed.] 8°. *Rouen, pour Pierre l'Aignel, iouxte la forme & exemplaire imprimé à Paris*, 1587. L.
    Anon.

Pernius, Joannes, *pseud. See* Creswell, J. (no. 275).

Persons, Robert.†

ORIGINAL WORKS

Acta in Comitiis

871   —Acta in comitiis parlamentaribus Londini die X. Aprilis huius anni praesentis 1593. tam contra Catholicos quam Puritanos seu Caluinistas rigidos . . . Collecta & in sermonem latinum traducta per Ioannem Dodritium Londini commorantem. 8°. *n.p.*, 1593. O.; MD².(9–3583/6). VAL.
    Ioannes Dodritius, *pseud.* A collection of extracts from documents on the persecution of Catholics in England, put together and translated into Latin by [Persons]. *Pr.* [Antwerp, Jan van Keerberghen], and seen through the press by [Richard Verstegan]. *See* RH, Oct. 1985, pp. 341–7. STC 6989/9492.

Apologia pro Hierarchia Ecclesiastica

872   —Apologia pro hierarchia ecclesiastica a S.D.N. Clemente PP.VIII. his annis apud Anglos instituta. 8°. *n.p.d.* [1601]. L.; PA⁴(2).RO⁵.USH. VAL².VT.W.
    Anon. Translated and in part abridged [by Richard Walpole?] from A&R 613. For *Appendix ad Apologiam* [by R. Walpole?] *see* no. 1347.

Carta de un Sacerdote escrita en Londres

873   —Carta de vn sacerdote escrita en Londres. 4°. *n.p.*, 1588 [1589?]. Not found. Description from Uriarte 302. This letter, translated by Persons into Spanish from an unidentified English original dated 22 Dec. 1588, was reprinted in nos. 894, 284. *Pr.* [Spain].

De Persecutione Anglicana

874   —De persecutione Anglicana, epistola. Qua explicantur afflictiones, aerumna, & calamitates grauissimae, cruciatus etiam & tormenta, & acerbissimá martyria, quae Catholici nunc Angli, ob fidem patiuntur. 8°. *Bononiae, apud Io. Baptistam Algazarium*, 1581. L.; OS.PA.ROU.UP.
    Anon. Imprint fictitious; *pr.* [Rouen, by George Flinton, at Fr. Persons's press.] Collation: [A]²B–G⁸H⁶.

875   —[Anr. issue.] *Parisiis, apud Thomam Brumennium*, 1582. L.; AIX(2: 1 *imp.*).DIJ.DMR.L²⁶.PA⁴,TRO.WO.
    A reissue of sig. B–G⁸H⁶ of no. 874, with a reprinted sig. [A]² and the addition at the end of another quire, I⁴, containing new text, [A]² and I⁴ being printed by Brumen at Paris. Renouard (Brumen) 273.

876   —[Anr. ed., with title:] De persecutione Anglicana libellus. Quo explicantur afflictiones, calamitates, cruciatus, & acerbissima martyria, quae Angli Catholici nūc ob fidē patiuntur. Quae omnia in hac postrema editione aeneis typis ad viuum expressa sunt. 8°. *Romae, ex typographia Georgii Ferrarii, sumptibus Bartholomaei Grassi, & Caesaris Ferrarii socriorū*, 1582. [Coloph.] *Apud Vincentium Accoltum.* L(3).O.;   AIX.C².D².DE(2:-1*imp.*).DMR.E.HP.L²⁵.MD.OS.PA⁶.RO.RO³.VAL. VT. +
    Anon. Published by the English College at Rome. The final leaf

with the title 'Praesentis ecclesiae anglicanae typus' introduces six
plates with engravings representing the sufferings of the English
Catholics, copied from woodcuts in a broadsheet by Richard
Verstegan (no. 1293). The same plates are used in nos. 8, 11.

877 —[Anr. ed.] De persecutione Anglicana libellus. 12°. *Romae, apud
Franciscum Zanettum*, 1582. O.; AIX.CLIF.DE.HP.PA.PR.RO³.VT.YK.
Anon. Without plates.

878 —[Anr. ed., with title:] De persecutione Anglicana commentariolus, a
Collegio Anglicano Romano, hoc anno Domini CIƆ IƆ XXCII in
Vrbe editus, & iam denuo Ingolstadii excusus: additis literis S.D.N.
D. Gregorii Papae XIII. hortatoriis ad subueniendum Anglis, &c.
12°. *Ingolstadii, ex officina Weissenhorniana apud Wolffgangum
Ederum, anno eodem* [1582]. L(2).C.; AB.AMP.DE.DI.KN².MR.MU².OS.PA.
TB.VI.W.WO. +
Anon. Without plates. Often found bound with *Historia passionis
nouorum in Germaniae Inferioris prouincia constantissimorum
martyrum ordinis Sancti Francisci* of Florentinus Leydanus. The
letter of Pope Gregory XIII is a reprint of no. 321.

—[Anr. ed.] 1583. *In* no. 524.

—[Anr. ed.] 1588. *In* no. 525.

—[*English transl.*] See A&R 629, made from no. 879.

879 —[*French transl.*] Epistre de la persecution meue en Angleterre contre
l'Eglise chrestienne Catholique & apostolique, & fideles mēbres
d'icelle. Ou sont declarez les tres grandes afflictions, miseres &
calamitez, les tourmens tres cruelz & martyres admirables, que les
fideles chrestiens Anglois y souffrent pour leur foy & religion. 8°.
Paris, chez Thomas Brumen, 1582. L(2:-1*imp.*).O.; AIX.PA(Rothschild).
STG.WO.
Anon. *Tr.* Matthieu de Launoy. Without plates. Renouard
(Brumen) 274.

880 —[Date variant.] 1583. LAR.

881 —[Anr. ed.] 8°. *Paris, chez Thomas Brumen*, 1586. DUR.PA.WO.
Anon. Renouard (Brumen) 310.

882 —[*German transl.* of this work and of Campion's *Rationes decem.*]
Bericht von der grausamen, tyrannischen Vervolgung der Caluinisten,
wider die frommen catholischen Christen in Engellandt . . ., An jetzo
aber sampt angehenckten zehen Gründen, warumb sich P. Edmundus
Campianus mit den Caluinisten zudisputiern angebotten, trewlich ins
Teutsch gebracht durch Johann Christoff Hueber. 8°. *Ingolstadt,
getruckt durch Dauid Sartorium*, 1583. L.O.; DI.GTN(*imp.*).MU.OS.
STG.VI.
Anon (for Persons). Without plates.

883 —[*Italian transl.* of Persons's work alone.] Della persecutione de
Catolici nel regno d'Inghilterra. Per ordine di Monsig. Illustriss.
Card. Paleotti, Vescouo di Bologna. 12°. *Bologna, appresso Alessandro
Benacci*, 1582. L.; D⁶.DMR.
Anon. Without plates but with three woodcuts.

884 —[Anr. ed.?, with title:] Raccolta d'alcuni auisi della dura persecutione
d'Inghilterra contra Catholici. Nuouamente tradotti dalla lingua
Latina nella nostra Italiana. 12°. *Brescia, appresso Vincenzo Sabbio*,
1582. MIL².
Anon. Without plates or woodcuts.

*Elizabethae Angliae Reginae . . . in Catholicos
sui Regni Edictum*

885 —Elizabethae Angliae Reginae haeresim Caluinianam propugnantis,
saeuissimum in Catholicos sui regni edictum . . . Cum responsione ad

singula capita . . . Per D. Andream Philopatrum. 8°. *Augustae*, 1592.
[Coloph.] *Augustae, apud Ioannem Fabrum.* L(2).O.C.; AMI.DE.DUR.E.
E².GT.L²⁵.MD.OS(2).PA.PA².USH.VAL(2).WO. +
Andreas Philopatrus, *pseud.* The proclamation here translated and
answered is STC 8208. Imprint fictitious; *pr.* [Antwerp.] This is the
edition seen through the press by [Richard Verstegan]. *See Library*,
June 1969, pp. 143–5. An English summary is at A&R 264 (incor-
rectly entered under J. Creswell).

886   —[Anr. ed.] 8°. *Lugduni, apud Ioannem Didier*, 1592. L(2).O.C.; AIX.C².
CARP.CHA.DE.F.HP.LC.LYN.PA.PA⁴.TOU.
Andreas Philopatrus, *pseud. Pr.* [Pierre Roussin.]

887   —[Date variant.] 1593. O.; D.DI.DUR.GTN.L⁴.L²⁶.LAR.LINC.LYN.MD.MU.
PA.TOU.U. +

888   —[Anr. ed.] 4°. *Romae, ex typographia Aloysii Zannetti*, 1593. L.O.C.;
C⁹.CHA.D.DE.DUR.GTM.L²⁶.MD.PA.PA⁴(2).RO(3).RO³.ST.USH.W. + +
Andreas Philopatrus, *pseud.*

889   —[Anr. ed., with title:] Elizabethae Reginae Angliae edictum promul-
gatum Londini 29. Nouemb. Anni M.D.XCI. Andreae Philopatri ad
idem edictum responsio. 8°. *n.p.*, 1593. L.; DMR.HP.USH.VI.VI². *This or
no. 890 :* KN(3).LINC.MU.P.PR.STG.TB.U.WOR.
Andreas Philopatrus, *pseud. Pr.* [in Germany?] Collation: A–Y⁸.
This edition has on the titlepage a woodcut, roughly triangular in
shape, with arabesques and a small cherub's head and wings.

890   —[Anr. ed., with title as in no. 889.] 8°. *n.p.*, 1593. L.O.C.; AIX.ANT.C³.
CHA.D.D².DE.DMR.DUR(2).E.GT.HP(2).KNY.L⁹.PA(2).PA⁶(2).ST.VI.WO(2) +
+. *See also no. 889.*
Andreas Philopatrus, *pseud. Pr.* [in Germany?] Collation: A–Z⁸
Aa²(Aa1 errata, Aa2 blank). This edition has on the titlepage a
woodcut of a vase of flowers with, above, the sun shining and clouds
casting down a shower, the whole flanked by the legend: 'Melior
post funera vita'. Scott 184.

891   —[*French transl..*] Responce à l'iniuste et sanguinaire edict d'Elizabeth
Royne d'Angleterre. Contre les Catholiques de son royaume. Publié à
Londres le 29. Nouembre 1591 . . . Traduicte du Latin d'André
Philopatre. 8°. *Lyon, par Iean Pilehotte*, 1593. L.; AIX.CARP.F.LYN.
PA.U.
André Philopatre, *pseud.*

892   —[*German transl.*] Elisabethen der Koenigin inn Engellandt, vnd
Irrlandt, &c. Edict, den neun vnd zweyntzigrsten [*sic*] Nouembris
dess fünfftzehenhundert ein vnd neuntzigsten Jars zu Londra
öffentlich publiciert. Mit einer Erleutterung Andreae Philopatri. 4°.
1593. [Coloph.] *Ingolstatt, durch Dauid Sartorium.* L.O.; DOE.FR.GTN.
MU.PA.PR³.TB.U.ULM.VI.VI².WO.
Andreas Philopatrus, *pseud.*

Preambulo [on the History of the English Bridgettines]

—*In* no. 741.

Quaestiones Duae

893   —Quaestiones duae de sacris alienis non adeundis, ad vsum praximq;
Angliae breuiter explicatae. 12°. *n.p.*, 1607. L.O.; A.DE(*imp.*).ELY.HP.
L²⁶.OS.ST.USH.VAL.YK.
Anon. *Pr.* [S. Omer, François Bellet.]

Relacion de algunos Martyrios

894   —Relacion de algunos martyrios, que de nueuo han hecho los hereges en
Inglaterra, y de otras cosas tocantes a nuestra santa y Catolica religion.

Traduzida de Ingles en Castellano, por el padre Roberto Personio. 8°. *Madrid, por Pedro Madrigal*, 1590. L.; BAR².MD.MIL².OS.RO⁹(Hist. S.J. 72/4).SAL.

A collection of narratives on the sufferings of English Catholics, edited by Persons. Some are translated by him from English originals, others are written by him in Spanish. Includes the text of no. 965 and of the *Relacion de quatro martyrios* (below).

Relacion de Quatro Martyrios . . . de Oxonia

—Relacion de quatro martyrios . . . hechos en la villa & vniuersidad de Oxonio, 1590. *In* nos. 894, 284. No separate edition, in Spanish, has been found.

The martyrdoms occurred in July 1589. This account was either written by Persons in Spanish or translated by him from an English original now lost.

895 —*[French transl.]* Discours veritable du martyre de deux prebstres & deux laycz, aduenu l'an mil cinq cens quatre vingts neuf, à Oxfort vniuersité d'Angleterre . . . Traduict d'Italien en François, selon l'exemplaire imprimé à Romme 1590. chez Paul Diani. 8° (in fours). *Paris, chez Guillaume Chaudiere*, 1590. O.; F.PA.RO².

For the Italian version mentioned in the title *see* no. 897.

896 —*[A different French transl.]* Sommaire discours du notable martyre de deux venerables prestres & deux hommes lais, aduenu en l'vniuersité d'Oxonio en Angleterre, pour avoir purement & librement enseigné & côfessé la foy & religion chrestienne, Catholique, apostolique & Romaine. Souz la tyrannie & cruauté de la seconde Iesabel à present regnant en Angleterre. 8° (in fours). *Lyon, par Iean Patrasson*, 1590. LYN.PA.

897 —*[Italian transl.]* Breue relatione del martirio di doi reuerendi sacerdoti et doi laici, seguito l'anno M.D.LXXXIX. in Oxonio, città di studio in Inghilterra. 4°. *Roma, appresso Paolo Diani*, 1590. O.; FLO.PA³.RO⁹. (Anglia 30 II no. 575).VT(2).

898 —*[Anr. ed.]* 8° (in fours). *Brescia, stampata in Roma, et ristampata in Bressa* [sic], *appresso Vincenzo Sabbio*, 1590. DE.

Relacion de un Sacerdote Ingles
escrita a Flandes

899 —Relacion de vn sacerdote Ingles, escrita a Flandes, a vn cauallero de su tierra, desterrado por ser Catolico: en el qual le da cuenta de la venida de su Magestad a Valladolid, y al Colegio de los Ingleses, y lo que allì se hizo en su recebimiento. Traduzida de Ingles en Castellano, por Tomas Eclesal cauallero Ingles. 8°. *Madrid, por Pedro Madrigal*, 1592. L.; F.HSA.MD.PA.PR.SAL.

Anon. A translation, with additions, of A&R 636. The translator's real name was [Thomas James]. *See* RH Jan. 1972, pp. 165–78. Reprinted in no. 284.

WORKS WITH CONTRIBUTIONS BY PERSONS

—Sander, N. Nicolai Sanderi de origine ac progressu schismatis Anglicani, 1586 [*etc.*] *See* nos. 973, *etc.*, 1004, *etc.*

SUPPOSITITIOUS WORKS

—Discours de la vie abominable, 1585. For this French translation of 'Leicester's Commonwealth', *see* no. 31.1.

Philopatrus, Andreas, *pseud. See* Persons, R. (nos. 885–92).

900 **Piers, James.** Ad maiorem Dei gloriam, beataeq; virginis Mariae.

Breuis, atque dilucida in logicam introductio, quam vulgo summulas appellant. Authore D. Iacobo Piers Hiberno doctore theologo, & regio philosophiae in Collegio Aquitanico professore. 8°. 2 pts. *Burdigalae, apud Petrum de la Court*, 1635. D.

Pt. 2 comprises the author's 'Disputationes in vniuersam Aristotelis Stagiritae Logicam'.

[901 *cancelled*]

902   **Pits, Arthur.** In quatuor Iesu Christi Euangelia, et Acta Apostolorum commentarius. 4°. 4 pts. *Duaci, typis Laurentii Kellami*, 1636. O.; C^2.LOU^3.MNS.MTH.O^{12}.OS.PA^3.WOR.

903   —[Anr. issue, with title:] Obseruationes Catholicae in quatuor Euangelia, et Acta Apostolorum, contra haereses huius temporis. *Antuerpiae, apud Petrum Bellerum*, 1637. D.VT.WO.

The titleleaf is a cancel.

Pits, John. De illustrium Angliae scriptoribus. *See* no. 907, *etc.*

904   —De legibus assertiones ex theologia depromptae, quas eruditus liberalium artium Magister, & SS. Theologiae Baccalaureus formatus Ioannes Pitz Anglus secunda, tertia, & quarta responsione causa Licentię defendet in celebri Academia Treuirensi. 4°. *Augustae Treuirorum, ex officina typographica Henrici Bock*, 1592. VI.

Listing 137 theses to be defended on natural law, positive divine law and human law.

905   —Disputatio theologica de beatitudine, quam pro consequendis theologici doctoratus insignibus defendet . . . Ioannes Pittus Anglus . . . in inclita & Catholica Academia Ingolstadiensi die 13. Iunii. 4°. *Ingolstadii, ex officina typographica Wolfgangi Ederi*, 1595. O.; DMR.MU.

A programme announcing the forthcoming defence of his thesis.

906   —Ioannis Pitsii Angli . . . de peregrinatione libri septem. Iam primum in lucem editi. 12°. *Dusseldorpii, apud Bernardum Busium*, 1604. L (*imp.*).O.C.; DE.L^{25}.LGE^3.PA.SBG.TOU.WO.

907   —Ioannis Pitsei . . . Relationum historicarum de rebus Anglicis tomus primus. 4°. *Parisiis, apud Rolinum Thierry, & Sebastianum Cramoisy*, 1619. L(3: *1 with later facs. t.p.*).O(5).C.; AMP.DE.E.E^2.GTN.KNY.L^2. LOU.MD.PA.USH.WO. + +

At the end is a note by the author saying that he finished the work in September 1613. Only vol. 1 was published; it was edited and seen through the press by William Bishop who signs the dedicatory epistle. The work is generally known by the running title: 'De illustribus Angliae Scriptoribus'.

[908 *cancelled*]

909   —[Anr. issue.] *Parisiis, apud Rolinum Thierry, & Sebastianum Cramoisy*, 1623. AMP.(missing 1985).ANT^2.O^5(missing 1985).PA^2.W.

Pittus, Ioannes. *See* Pits, J.

Plantin, Francis, *alias. See* Platt, F.

Platt, Francis, *alias* Francis Plantin. [*A disputation in which he acted as Praeses.*] Savage, F. Conclusiones logicae, 1624. *See* no. 1025.

910   **Plowden, Thomas,** *alias* Edmund Salisbury. Theses ex vniuersa theologia disputandae. In Coll. Anglicano Societatis Iesu, Louanii, Anno Domini CIↃ IↃC XXII. Praeside Rdo Patre Georgio Morleo Soc. Iesu . . . Defendet P. Edmundus Salisburius eiusdem Societatis. Die 12 Iulii. 4°. [Coloph.] *Louanii, ex officina Bernardini Masii*, 1622.

Not found. Description based on Sommerv. (tom. 5, cols. 1326–7).

Pole, Reginald, *Cardinal.*†‡ Ad Henricum Octauum Britanniae Regem, pro ecclesiasticae vnitatis defensione. *See* no. 920.

911   —De concilio liber. 4°. *Romae, apud Paulum Manutium Aldi F.*, 1562. L(2).O(2); BAR^2.D^{10}.DUR(2).GTN.L^2.L^{26}.LOU^3.M.MD.N.OS.PA^3.PA^4.RO^{11}.USH (2) + +. *This or no. 912* :DE.MU.RO^5.TB.

With the author's 'De baptismo Constantini Magni Imperatoris', the two works forming a single bibliographical entity. Neither had been published previously. Pole wrote *De concilio* c. 1542–45 just before the opening session of the Council of Trent. Most copies are bound with a third work by Pole, *Reformatio Angliae*, which is bibliographically independent and is entered separately below (no. 918). In this edition of *De concilio* there are ten lines of errata after the word 'Finis' on sig. S4^r. *See* PBSA 1952, pp. 209–14; *Studies in Bibliography*, 1973, pp. 232–4. This, the original edition, consisted of 1,700 copies printed by Manutius, a personal friend of the late author; of these, 220 were despatched for sale to the Fathers at the Council of Trent.

912 —[Anr. ed.] 4°. *Romae, apud Paulum Manutium Aldi F.*, 1562. O.;D.M. PML. *See also* no. 911.
A reprint of no. 911 with the errors corrected. There is no errata list on sig. S4^r.

913 —[Anr. ed., with *Reformatio Angliae*.] Reginaldi Poli … Liber, de concilio Eiusdem De baptismo Constantini … Reformatio Angliae. 8°. *Venetiis, ex officina Iordani Zileti*, 1562. L(2).O.C(3).; BM².C².D(2). E.HP.L¹³.LOU.M.MU.PA.PA².UT.YK. +
Reformatio Angliae is here bibliographically inseparable from the rest of the book which is a reprint of the Rome edition. Cardinal Morone, on behalf of the publisher, attempted through the Apostolic Nuncio at Venice to have this edition suppressed, but evidently without success.

914 —[Anr. ed., with *Reformatio Angliae*.] Libri duo D. Reginaldi Poli … quos … ante hac in Germania nunquam excusos moriens reliquit. Primus liber de concilio agit: alter, de reformatione Angliae, sancta & huic aetati ualde commoda decreta describit. Interseritur luculenta disputatio de baptismo Constantini magni imperatoris. 8°. 1562. [Coloph.] *Dilingae, excudebat Sebaldus Mayer.* L(2).O(2).C.; AUG.BRU. C³.D.DI.FU².GT.GTN.HP.L².MU.YK. + +
The text of both works was later incorporated in the anonymous collection entitled *Concilium Tridentinum*, first published at Louvain in 1567 and many times reprinted.

915 —De summo pontifice Christi in terris vicario, eiusque officio & potestate … In modum dialogi cōscriptus olim, nunq. vero antehac editus. 8°. *Louanii, apud Iuannem Foulerum Anglum*, 1569. L(2).O(2). C(3).; AMS.BRU.C².D.DMR.GTN.L².L²⁶.LOU³.MU.O⁶.PA.RO³.USH.VI + +
Edited posthumously by Henry Joliffe.

—Epistola de sacramento Eucharistiae. *See* no. 921.

916 —Oratione del Cardinal Polo in materia di pace. A Carlo Quinto Imperatore, 1558. Forms pt. 2 of: Girardi, A. Discorso intorno alle cose della guerra, con vna oratione della pace. 4°. 2 pts. *Nell'Academia Venetiana*, 1558. L.O.C.; C².C²².M.MU.O¹¹.O³⁰.PR.VI.WO.Y.
Pole wrote his work in 1554 in an attempt to secure peace between the Emperor and the King of France. The Latin original was published at Rome in 1555. This Italian translation is reprinted from an edition published at Rome [c. 1555].

917 —[Anr. ed. of Pole's work alone.] 8°. *Milano, appresso a Giouann' Antonio de gli Antonii*, 1560. [Coloph.] *Imprimeuano i fratelli da Meda.* L.; F.MIL³.RO⁶.VT.
The text was later incorporated in the collection edited by Francesco Sansovino: *Diuerse orationi volgarmente scritti*, first published at Venice in 1561 and many times reprinted.

918 —Reformatio Angliae ex decretis Reginaldi Poli Cardinalis, Sedis Apostolicae Legati, anno M.D. LVI. 4°. *Romae, apud Paulum Manutium Aldi F.*, 1562. L(2).O(3).C(2).; DUR(3).HN.L²⁶.MD.PA.Y. *This or no. 919:* C².OS.PA(3 others).RO¹¹.TB.VI.

Containing the reforming decrees of the National Synod of the English Church which Pole, as Papal Legate, summoned and presided over, 1555–56. Not previously published. In this edition there is no comma after the word 'Angliae' in the title and there is a line of errata at the end of the text on sig. G3ᵛ. See the references cited under no. 911. Most copies are found bound with no. 911 from which, however, it is bibliographically separate.

919   —[Anr. ed.] 4°. *Romae, apud Paulum Manutium Aldi F.*, 1562. C(2).; DE.E.PML. *See also no. 918.*

A reprint of no. 918 with the errors corrected. There is a comma after the word 'Angliae' in the title and there is no line of errata on sig. G3ᵛ. Later editions form part of nos. 913–14.

920   —Reginaldi Poli Cardinalis Britanni, ad Henricum Octauum Britanniae regem, pro ecclesiasticae vnitatis defensione, libri quatuor. Nunc primum in Catholica Germaniae Academia typis excusi. 8°. *Ingolstadii, ex typographia Dauidis Sartorii*, 1587. L.O.C.; AUG.C³.CHA.D.FU².GTN. L².MTH.MU(2).O⁷.PA.VI. + +

Written in 1536 and first published [c. 1538–9] at Rome. An English translation by F. Withers of part of the work was published at London in [1560]. (STC 20087).

921   —Reginaldi Poli . . . Epistola de sacramento Eucharistiae. 8°. *Cremonae, apud Christophorum Draconium*, 1584. C.; L⁴.RO⁶.VT.

Not previously published. Edited by Deodatus Quistrus of Cremona from a MS formerly in the possession of Philomenus Patruus.

922   —Testamentum vere christianum, pium ac prudentissimum, Reuerendissimi et illustriss. . . . Reginaldi . . . Cardinalis, Archiepiscopi Cantuariensis, totius Angliae Primatis, et Apostolicae Sedis Legati. 4°. *n.p.*, 1559. L.; BUTE.C³.PA.PR.Y.

The will is dated from Lambeth, 4 October 1558, six weeks before Pole's death. *Pr.* [Dillingen, Sebald Mayer].

923   —[Anr. ed.] 4°. *Ripae*, 1562. O.; MD.NP.OS.RO³.RO⁶.VT. [*DMR].

Pr. [Jacob Marcaria].

924   —[*Appendix.*] Beccadelli, L. Vita Reginaldi Poli, Britanni, S.R.E. Cardinalis, et Cantuariensis Archiepiscopi. 4°. *Venetiis, ex officina Dominici Guerrei, & Ioan. Baptistae fratrum*, 1563. L.O(3).C.; AIX. C².C¹⁹.DE.E.L².M.O².O⁵.OS.PA².WO. +

A Latin translation of an unpublished Italian life by Beccadelli who had been Pole's secretary. The translator, who signs the dedicatory epistle, was Andreas Duditius, who had been Pole's secretary while he was Legate in England.

Ponce, John. *See* Punch, J.

Port, Thomas, *alias. See* Layton, T.

925   **Poyntz, John,** *alias* John Campion. Francisco Card. Barberino Lyricum carmen in philosophicis disputationibus Ioañis Campiani Coll. Angl. Conv. emodulatum Latina Pallas D.D. 4°. *n.p.d.* [1624.] MIL²(-tp.). RO²(2).VT(-tp.). Private owner. [*DMR.]

Ostensibly a single quire, A¹⁰, signed [A1]-A5, but the engraved title (signed with the initials of the engraver, 'G.M.') is on a separate leaf with vertical chain lines and there was never any leaf A10. At least one copy omits the words 'Coll. Angl. Conv.' from the engraved title. Poyntz left the English College, Rome, where his disputations had been held, on 17 September 1624; for his career *see* Foley, vol. 7, p. 628. The present title is recorded by Sommerv. (tom. 3, col. 131) under the name of the Jesuit professor at Rome, Alexander Donatus, who perhaps actually wrote the Latin verses for this occasion. *Pr.* [Rome, Alexander Zannettus.]

925.1   **Preston, Thomas,**† *alias* Roger Widdrington. Apologia Cardinalis Bellarmini pro iure principum. Aduersus ipsius rationes pro auctoritate papali principes seculares in ordine ad bonum spirituale deponendi. 8°. *Cosmopoli, apud Theophilum Pratum*, 1611. L.O.C(2).; A².D.DE.E.E².F(2).HP.PA⁶.ST.U.W.YK +

Answers Bellarmine's *Tractatus de potestate Summi Pontificis* (no. 1505). Rogerus Widdringtonus, *pseud.* Imprint false; *pr.* [London, Richard, Field.] Collation: ¶⁸A⁴B–Z⁸2A⁴. A&R 661. STC 25596. ERL 309. Mil. vol. 2, p. 103. This and no. 925.6 were placed on the Roman Index, 16 March 1614. *See* no. 928. Answered in no. 1540.

925.2 —[Anr. ed.] 8°. *Cosmopoli, apud Theophilum Pratum*, 1611. O.C.; CARP. DAI.DE.DUR(2).PA(2).USH.W.WO.

Rogerus Widdringtonus, *pseud.* Imprint false; *pr.* [Paris, Denis Binet?] Collation: a⁸*⁴B–Z⁸2A⁴. The errata of the English edition have been corrected. A&R 662. STC 25596.5

925.3 —Appellatio qua reuerendi patres, Thomas Prestonus, & Thomas Greenaeus Angli Benedictini, ac sacrae theologiae professores, ab ill. mis dominis cardinalibus ad Indicem deputatis ad Romanum, Summumq; Pontificem immediate prouocarunt. 4°. *Augustae, apud Baptistam Fabrum*, 1620. L.O(2).; C³.D.HP.L².L²⁶.N.Naworth Castle. OS.YK.

An appeal to the Pope by Preston and his fellow-Benedictine Thomas Green against the condemnation of Preston's books by the Sacred Congregation of the Index. Imprint false; entered in the Stationers' Register on 14 December 1620 to Edward Griffin; *pr.* [London, Edward Griffin.] A&R 677. STC 20286.3. Mil. vol. 2, pp. 107–8. ERL 354.

925.4 —Appendix ad disputationem theologicam de iuramento fidelitatis. In quo omnia argumenta, quae a Francisco Suarez . . . pro potestate papali principes deponendi, & contra recens fidelitatis iuramentū allata sunt, dilucide examinantur. 8°. *Albionopoli, apud Ruardum Phigrum*, 1616. L.O.C.; C³.D.DE.DUR.E.HP.L².L¹³.MTH.PA.W(2).YK. +

An appendix to no. 925.6 below. Rogerus Widdringtonus, *pseud.* Imprint false; *pr.* [London, Edward Griffin.] A&R 663. STC 25604. ERL 51.

925.5 —Discussio discussionis decreti magni concilii Lateranensis, aduersus Leonardum Lessium . . . nomine Guilhelmi Singletoni personatum. In qua omnia argumenta, quae idemmet Lessius pro papali potestate principes deponendi adducit . . . examinantur, & refutantur: et quaedam egregia Illustrissimi Cardinalis Peronii artificia perspicue deteguntur & refelluntur. 8°. *Augustae, apud Ioan. Libium*, 1618. L.O.C.; A²(2).D.DE.E.E².L⁹.P².PA.PA⁶.PLU.TEX.W.WO.YK. +

Answers no. 1086 erroneously attributed by Preston to Lessius, and also Du Perron's *Oration* of 1616 (English translation at A&R 287). Rogerus Widdringtonus, *pseud.* Imprint false; *pr.* [London, John Bill.] A&R 666. STC 25601. ERL 292. Mil. vol. 2, pp. 105, 129.

925.6 —Disputatio theologica de iuramento fidelitatis sanctissimo patri Paolo Papae quinto dedicata. In qua potissima omnia argumenta . . . contra recens fidelitatis iuramentum . . . examinantur. 8°. 2 pts. *Albionopoli, ex officina Theophii Fabri*, 1613. L.O.C.; D.DUR.E²(2).F.HN.L².O².PA. TEX.USH.W.YK. +

This and no. 925.1 were placed on the Roman Index, 16 March 1614. *See* no. 928. Rogerus Widdringtonus, *pseud.* Imprint false; *pr.* [London, Edward Allde.] The second part, *Rogeri Widdringtoni . . . Apologeticae responsionis . . . praefatio*, has no separate titlepage. It was originally intended for inclusion in no. 926.3. A shorter errata on A8 of pt. 1 is generally found cancelled by the longer one on A7. O. has both. A&R 667. STC 25602. ERL 359. Mil. vol. 2, p. 104.

925.7 —[Anr. ed.] 8°. *Albionopoli, ex officina Theophili Fabri*, 1614. L.; Burgensteinfast, Gymn. Arnoldinum. PA.W.

Rogerus Widdringtonus, *pseud.* Imprint false; *pr.* [Frankfurt.]
A&R 668.

—Exemplar decreti, 1614. *See* no. 928.1.

926   —Lettera di Tomaso Prestono Monaco Cassinese alla Santita di nostro
Signore Papa Gregorio XV. da Londra a 14 di giuglio 1621. *s.sh.*fol.
n.p.d. [1621.] VT²(Nunz. Fran. 416, f. 79). [*PA¹⁰].

Making submission to the Pope and promising not to write or speak
further in favour of the oath of allegiance. Probably printed in
[France] whence it was sent to Rome by the Paris Nuncio.

—Responsio apologetica, 1612. *See* no. 926.3.

926.1 —Reuerendorum patrum D. Thomae Prestoni ... & Fr. Thomae
Greenaei ... ad sanctissimum ac beatissimum patrem Gregorium
decimum quintum, Pontificem Maximum, Sanctamq; Sedem
Apostolicam, humillima supplicatio. 4°. *Augustae, apud Baptistam
Fabrum,* 1621. O.; C².HP.L².N.O³.YK.

This 'Supplicatio' addressed to Pope Gregory XV renews the
appeal previously made to his predecessor, Paul V, in no. 925.3.
Imprint false; *pr.* [London, Edward Griffin.] A&R 678. STC 20286.7.
ERL 354. Mil. vol. 2, p. 107.

926.2 —Rogeri Widdringtoni, Catholici Angli ad Sanctissimum Dominum
Paulum Quintum, Pontificem Max. humillima supplicatio. Cui
adiungitur Appendix, in quo plurimae calumniae ... deteguntur. 8°.
2 pts. *Albionopoli, apud Rufum Lipsium,* 1616. L.O.C.; C³.D.DE.E.DUR.
HP(2).L².L¹³.PA(2).ST.TRO.W.YK. +

Rogerus Widdringtonus, *pseud.* Imprint false; *pr.* [London,
Edward Griffin.] Pt. 2 has titlepage reading *Appendix ad Supplica-
tionem praecedentem.* Both parts comprise appeals to the Pope
against accusations against him made in nos. 1504 and 1540. A&R
673. STC 25605. ERL 65. Mil. vol. 2, p. 107.

926.3 —Rogeri Widdringtoni Catholici Angli Responsio apologetica ad
libellum cuiusdam doctoris theologi, qui eius pro iure principum
Apologiam tanquam fidei Catholicae aperte repugnantem ...
criminatur. 8°. *Cosmopoli apud Pratum,* 1612. L.O.C.; ANT³.C².D.DE.E.
E².HP.L².O³.OS.W.YK. +

Rogerus Widdringtonus, *pseud.* Imprint false; *pr.* [London,
Richard Field.] The author against whom Preston is replying has
not been identified. A&R 674. STC 25597. ERL 161. Mil. vol. 2, p. 104.

927   —[Anr. ed.] 8°. *Parisiis, iuxta exemplar Cosmopoli editum,* 1613. L.; TRO.
VT.WO.

A reprint of no. 926.3.

927.1 —Strena Catholica, seu explicatio breuis, & dilucida noui fidelitatis
iuramenti. Ab E.I. sacrae theologiae studioso composita. 8°. *Augustae,
apud Baptistam Fabrum,* 1620. L.O.; D.DNPK.E.L².O¹⁹.O²⁷.PA.USH.VT.

Anon. A translation, with additions, of the author's *A new-yeares
gift* (A&R 670) which is a reply to I.E. [Matthew Kellison] *The right
and iurisdiction of the prelate and the prince* (A&R 427). Imprint false;
pr. [London, John Bill.] A&R 675. STC 14050.5. Mil. vol. 2, pp. 105–6.

—Supplicatio (ad Paulum quintum), 1616. *See* no. 926.2.—(ad Gregorium decimum quintum) 1621. *See* no. 926.1.

928   —[*Appendix.*] Rome, *Sacred Congregation of the Index.* [*Begin:*]
Decretum sacrae congregationis ... Cardinalium ... ad Indicem
Librorum ... specialiter deputatorum ... *s.sh.*fol. *Romae, ex typo-
graphia Reu. Camerae Apostolicae,* 1614. BRS⁴(Arch. Jes. Prov. Gallo-
Belg. College de Saint Omer. Carton 32. Unnumbered). [*L].

Condemning Preston's *Apologia Cardinalis Bellarmini* (no. 925.1)
and *Disputatio theologica* (no. 925.6). The decree is dated 16 March
1614. Mil. vol. 2, p. 107.

928.1 —[Anr. ed., together with Preston's defence of himself.] Exemplar decreti: in quo duo libri Rogeri Widdringtoni . . . condemnantur, & authori vt se purget praeceptum imponitur atq; epistolae. quam idem Ro. Widdringtonus, ad . . . Paulum Quintum Pōtificem Max. pro se purgando transmisit. 8°. *Albionopoli, apud Theophilum Fabrum*, 1614. o(*imp.*); c⁵.

> Rogerus Widdringtonus, *pseud*. Imprint false; entered in the Stationers' Register on 1 August 1614 to William and Thomas Harper; *pr.* [London, John Beale for William and Thomas Harper.] An English translation by the author himself is at A&R 665. A&R 669. STC 25605.5.

Price, John.† [*A disputation in which he acted as Praeses.*] Wallis, F. Theses ex vniuersa theologia Doctoris Angelici, [1619]. *See* no. 1345. For Price, *see* Foley, vol. 7, p. 632.

Priceus, Gulielmus, *pseud. See* Smith, R., *Bishop of Chalcedon* (no. 1095).

Punch, John, *in religion* Ioannes a S. Francisco.‡ [Commentaries on Duns Scotus], 1639. *In* no. 1326.

—[*Disputations in which he acted as Praeses.*] Baron, B. . . . Conclusiones theologicae, 1635. *See* no. 83.

—Bray, E. . . . Conclusiones theologicae, 1634. *See* no. 114.

—Ford, E. . . . Conclusiones ex vniuersa philoosphia, 1630. *See* no. 506.

—O'Fahy, J. . . . Conclusiones theologicae, 1634. *See* no. 847.

Q., D.C. *See* no. 737.

Quelly, Edmundus. *See* Kelly, E.

Quemerford, Patrick. *See* Comerford, P.

R., A. *See* no. 17.

R., C. *See* nos. 1093, 1097.

929   **Rainolds, William**† (Gulielmus Raynoldus/Reginaldus). Caluino-Turcismus id est, Caluinisticae perfidiae, cum Mahumetana collatio, et dilucida vtriusque sectae confutatio: quatuor libris explicata . . . Authore Gulielmo Reginaldo Anglo. 8°. *Antuerpiae, in aedibus Petri Belleri*, 1597. L.O.C(2).; ANT².BRS.C².C⁵.DE.FLO.FU.GTN.HP.L².MU.OS.PA. WO. + +

> This work, left unfinished by Rainolds at his death in 1594, was completed and edited by William Gifford.

930   —[Anr. ed.] 8°. *Coloniae Agrippinae, apud Antonium Hierat*, 1603. L.O.; AMS.C².DE.F.HER.HP.KN KN².L⁹.LAR.LIL.LYN.MU.PA. +

931   —De iusta reipub. Christianae in rrges [*sic*] impios et haereticos authoritate: iustissimaque Catholicorum ad Henricum Nauarraeum & quemcunque haereticum a regno Galliae repellendum confoederatione. 8°. *Parisiis, apud Guilielmum Bichonium*, 1590. L(2).O.C.; L².L⁴. LIL.LINC.PA(3).VI.

> Anon. A defence of the League directed mainly against Henry of Navarre. The authority for Rainolds is Pits (p. 791). *Ded*. sgd.: G.G.R.A. Peregrin. Roman, initials which probably stand for Gabriel Gulielmus Rossaeus Author (*see* no. 932). 'Rossaeus' was probably a pseudonym of William (in religion, Gabriel) Gifford who edited and was perhaps part-author of the work (*see* Pits, p. 810). Renouard III.555.

932   —(Anr. ed.] G. Guilelmo Rossaeo Authore. 8°. *Antuerpiae, apud Ioannem Keerbergium*, 1592. L(2).O.C(2).; A.AMS.BRS.C².C³.DE.E².GTN. HA.L².LGE³.LOU³.MD.WO. + +

933   [*Begin:*] Reuerendissimo in Christo Patri ac Domino, D. Ioanni Baptistae Episcopo Ariminensi, et apud suam M. Christianissimam Nuntio Apostolico . . . Gulielmus Raynoldus Collegii Anglorum Rhemensis alumnus, felicitatem . . . Theses de Ecclesia eiusque monarchia et hierarchia. *s.sh.*fol. *n.p.d.* [1583.] L(Lansdowne MSS, 96, no. 55.). [*L.*DMR.]

A programme announcing the forthcoming defence of his thesis. Rainolds was then a student at the English College at Rheims. Giambattista Castelli, Bishop of Rimini, was Papal Nuncio at Paris, 1582–83. *Pr.* [Rheims, Jean Foigny.]

—[*A work translated by him.*] Allen, W. Ad persecutores Anglos, [1584]. *See* no. 18.

Rayner, William. [*Works edited or translated by him.*] Anderton, J. Apologia Protestantum, 1615 [*etc.*]. *See* nos. 27–9.

—Stapleton, T. . . . Opera quae extant omnia, 1620. *See* no. 1129.

—Propugnaculum fidei, 1619. *See* no. 1155.

Raynoldus, Gulielmus. *See* Rainolds, W.

Reginaldus, *Cardinalis. See* Pole, R. (nos. 922–3).

Reginaldus, Gulielmus. *See* Rainolds, W.

934   **Reyner, Christopher,** *in religion* Clement Reyner. Apostolatus Benedictinorum in Anglia, siue disceptatio historica, de antiquitate ordinis congregationisque monachorum nigrorum Sancti Benedicti in regno Angliae. Fol. 3 pts. *Duaci, ex officina Laurentii Kellami,* 1626. L(3).O.C(2).; AMP.AUG.BM².CHA.D(3).DAI(4).DE(2).DMR.E².HP.L².MU.PA. ST.USH. + +

Reyner edited this work on instructions from the general chapter of the English Benedictine Congregation, 1625. It answers the *Examen Trophaeorum* of John Barnes (no. 70). Its principal authors were [David Baker and John Jones].

935   **Reyner, Clement,** *in religion* Lawrence Reyner.† Tractatus de indulgentiis. 8°. *Duaci, typis Laurentii Kellami,* 1636. O.; AMP.PA.PA³.PA⁴.

An enlarged translation of A&R 711.

Reyner, Clement, *name in religion. See* Reyner, Christopher.

Reyner, Lawrence, *name in religion. See* Reyner, Clement.

Reynolds, William. *See* Rainolds, W.

Rheims, *English College.* For the English College established at Douai in 1568 which was removed temporarily to Rheims from 1578 to 1593: *See* Douai, *English College.*

Richard, *of S. Victor, name in religion. See* Wadding, R.

[936 *cancelled*]

Rigby, Lawrence, *alias. See* Morley, H.

937   **Rishton, Edward.** Synopsis rerum ecclesiasticarum. *s.sh.*fol. *Duaci, Ioannes Bogardus,* 1595.

Not found. Description from Duthilloeul 108. Written, and perhaps originally published, as early as 1577 (*see* DD 1, p. 304).

—[*A work enlarged and edited by him.*] Sander, N. Doctissimi viri Nicolai Sanderi, de origine ac progressu schismatis Anglicani, 1585 [*etc.*] *See* nos. 972, *etc.*

—[*A supposititious work.*] [For editions of *Diarium Turris* frequently attributed to Rishton]. *See* nos. 973, *etc.*

Robert, *of St Benedict, name in religion. See* Hadock, R.

938   **Roberti, Antonius,** *Anglus, pseud.?* Clauis homerica. Reserans significationes, etymologias, deriuationes, compositiones . . . quae in viginti quatuor libris Iliadis Homeri continentur . . . In gratiam studiosae iuuentutis Societatis Iesu. Huic adjicitur breuis Appendix de dialectis. Authore R.P.N.N. Anglo, Oxoniensi, Societatis Iesu. 8°. *Duaci, apud viduam Martini Bogardi,* 1636. L.O.; DOU.

A text-book for use in Jesuit colleges. With an additional titlepage, engraved, reading: 'Clauis homerica. In gratiam iuuentutis literarum graecarum studiosae, Soc. Iesu. Auctore R.P. Ant° Roberti Anglo'. Dedicated to François de la Croix, S.J., Provincial of the Gallo-Belgic Province. A second edition, with the Catholic particulars omitted, was published at London in 1638 (STC 21072a), and was thereafter frequently reprinted.

939 **Roberts, John,** *Saint.* Discours et traicté veritable du martire enduré à Londres en Angleterre. Par le R. pere Iean de Meruinia, autrement dit Roberts, religieux tres-renommé de l'ordre S. Benoist de la congregation d'Espaigne executé le 20 de decembre l'an 1610. 8° (in fours). *Douay, de l'imprimerie de Laurent Kellam,* 1611. L.C.; L²⁶.PA. [*DE.]

The first part of this work, describing Roberts's trial, was written by Roberts himself in prison while awaiting execution. The account of the execution is by Robert of St. Benedict [Robert Hadock]. The approbation states that the French is a translation of a Latin version made from the original English.

940 —[*German transl.*] Warhaffter Bericht welcher gestalt der ehrwuerdige Herr Johann von Meruinia . . . zu Londern in Engelland, wegen des Catholischen Glaubens gemartert worden . . . Auss dem zu Douay in Niderland getruckten Frantzoesischen Exemplar summarischer Weiss in das Teutsch gebracht . . . Durch Abraham Schaedlin, Catholischen teutschen Schulmaister in Augspurg. 4°. *Augspurg, bey Christoff Mang,* 1611. L.; AB.

Roche, J. *See* 396.1.

941 **Roche, Patrick.** [*Begin:*] Illmo. ac Reuermo. D.D. Marco Aurelio Maraldi Sedis Apostolicae Datario dignissimo dedicat hoc panegyricum Patricius Rocheus . . . Hibernus Capsaliensis. 4°. *Romae, ex typographia Iacobi Mascardi,* 1616. RO⁸.(2).

942 —[*Begin:*] Sanctiss. D.N. Gregorio XV. hoc poema de laetitia orbis, in foelicissimam, et optatissimam Suae Sanctitatis creationem. Dedicat vestrae Sanctitati humillimus cliens, Rochus, nobilis Hibernus, Sacrae Theologiae Doctor. 4° (a single quadrifolium). *Romae, ex typographia Guglielmi Facciotti,* 1621. MIL².RO⁸.

Gregory XV was elected 9 February 1621.

Roffensis, Joannes. *See* Fisher, John, *Saint, Bishop of Rochester.*

Roirk, Donatus, *pseud. See* Rothe, D. (nos. 955–6).

Rome, *English College.* De persecutione Anglicana libellus, 1582. Published by the English College. *See* no. 876.

943 —[*Appendix.*] Argomento d'Albano tragedia Latina che si recita nel Collegio Inglese. Con vn breue racconto atto per atto, scena per scena, di quanto in essa si tratta. 4° (a single quadrifolium). *n.p.,* 1619, VT(2).

Pr. [Rome.]

944 —Ecclesiae Anglicanae Trophaea siue sanctor. martyrum, qui pro Christo Catholicaeq. fidei veritate asserenda antiquo recentioriq. persecutionum tempore, mortem in Anglia subierunt, passiones Romae in Collegio Anglico per Nicolaum Circinianum depictae; nuper autem per Io. Bap. de Caualleriis aeneis typis repraesentate. Cum priuilegio Gregorii XIII P.M. Fol. *Romae, ex officina Bartholomaei Grassi, n.d.* [1584.] L.O.; DE.DMR.E.F.HD.HN.LN.PA.PA².RO².RO⁵. RO⁶.VT(4). *This or no. 945 :* MD.TRO.W.

Consisting of an engraved title followed by 35 etched plates numbered 2–36. Southwell (p. 314) attributes the book to William Good S.J. who probably advised on the subjects for the frescoes at the English College. In this issue the imprint is lettered in capitals.

—[Anr. issue.] 1584. *Part of* no. 1284.

945 —[Anr. issue.] *Romae, ex officina Bartholomaei Grassi, n.d.* [c. 1585–90.] L.; HP(*imp., with only 8 plates*).

The imprint has been re-lettered, this time in lower case italic. This issue is evidently later than that published in 1584 as part of no. 1284 in which the imprint of no. 944 was erased.

946 —[Anr. issue.] *Romae, Ioannes Antonius de paulis formis,* 1608. L.; DE (*imp.*).

The above imprint and date are lettered on the titlepage in place of Grassi's imprint.

947 —Rappresentatione tragica del Zenone Imperatore da farsi nel Collegio Inglese di Roma, nelle correnti vacanze del carneuale. Dedicata all'Eminentiss. et Reuerendiss. Sig. il Signor Cardinal Francesco Barberino . . . Protettore d'Inghilterra. 4° (a quire of eight). *Roma, per Francesco Corbelletti,* 1634. O.; RO².VT(2).

Not a text of the tragedy but a list of the cast and a synopsis of the action. *Ded.* to Cardinal Barberini sgd.: 'Dal Collegio Inglese di Roma li 15 di Febraro 1634 . . . Gl'Alunni del Collegio Inglese'. With the Cardinal's arms engraved on the titlepage. The play itself, here anonymous, was in fact written in Latin by the English Jesuit Emmanuel Lobb. The whole text was later published, under his alias of Joseph Simeon, in an edition printed at Rome in 1648. It is there stated to have been often performed, to great applause, in Rome, Naples, Seville, St. Omer, and elsewhere.

—Regiis Angliae diuis dithyrambus, 1627. *See* no. 1342.3.

—Thysia philosophica, siue laeta disciplinarum oblatio, 1621. *See* no. 717.

—Triumphus religionis, virtutumque ancillantium, 1624. *See* no. 837.

948 **Rome,** *Irish College.* Coronatae virtuti reuerendiss. D. Patritii Quemerfordi . . . Episcopi Waterfordiensis, & Lismorensis, inaugurati plausus Seminarii Hibernorum de Vrbe. 8°. *Romae, tipis Lud. Grignani,* 1629. O.; D⁶.KNY,RO⁸.

Published by the Irish College in honour of Patrick Comerford (Quemerford) appointed Bishop of Waterford in February 1629. In addition to an account of the struggle of the Church in Ireland it includes poems and epigrams by members of the College. The titlepage is engraved.

949 —Illustriss. Principi Ludouico S.R.E. Cardinali Ludouisio Vicecancellario, et Hiberniae Protectori. Fundatam a se Hibernicae iuuentutis domum visitanti. Gratiarum actio dicta, & dicata. 4°. [Coloph.] *Romae, apud Ludouicum Grignanum,* 1628. RO².RO³.(2).

Prose and verse in honour of Cardinal Ludovisi, the founder of the College, on the occasion of his visit. With the Cardinal's arms, and those of Ireland, engraved on the titlepage.

Rome, *Irish Franciscan College of St Isidore.* Annales Minorum, in quibus res omnes trium Ordinum a S. Francisco institutorum . . . asseruntur, 1625, [*etc.*] *See* nos. 1306–9.

—R.P.F. Ioannis Duns Scoti . . . opera omnia, 1639. *See* no. 1326.

—[*Appendix. Theses defended at the College.*] *See* nos. 83, 84, 87, 114, 128, 271, 285, 414, 506, 713, 714, 847.

Romoaldus, *Scotus. See* Scotus, Romoaldus, *pseud.?*

Rossaeus, Gulielmus, *pseud.* For this pseudonym of William Gifford, *see* nos. 931–2.

950 **Rothe, David,** *Bishop of Ossory.* Analecta sacra, noua, et mira. De rebus Catholicorum in Hibernia pro fide, et religione gestis. Diuisa in tres partes, quarum prima, quae nunc datur, continet semestrem grauaminum relationem. Secunda, Paraenesin ad martyres designatos. Tertia, Processum martyrialem quorundam fidei pugilum. Relatore & collectore T.N. 8°. *n.p.,* 1616. L.O.C.; D(2).D⁶.D⁷.D¹⁰.L².PA(2).

T.N. [David Rothe.] For Rothe's authorship of the *Analecta* and of the other works ascribed to him in this catalogue, *see* Lynch, J. *De praesulibus Hiberniae,* 1672, ed. Irish MSS Commission, 1944, vol. 1, p. 383. This edition contains pt. 1 only of the three mentioned on the titlepage. *Pr.* [Paris?] The *Analecta* was answered by Sir T. Ryves in STC 21479.

951 —[Anr. ed. of pt. 1, together with pt. 2.] 8°. *Coloniae, apud Stephanum*

Rolinum, 1617. L.O(2).C.; ANT.C².D(5).D⁶.DE.DMR.E.KNY(3).L².L²⁶.OS. PA.PA⁴.RO.ST. +

> T.N. [David Rothe.] Containing pts. 1, 2 only of the three mentioned on the titlepage. Pt. 2 begins on sig. Gg2ʳ. Imprint false; *pr.* [Paris?].

952 —[*Analecta sacra,* pt. 3, with title:] De processu martyriali quorundam fidei pugilum in Hibernia, pro complemento sacrorum analectorum. Collectore & relatore T.N. Philadelpho. 8°. *Coloniae, apud Stephanum Rolinum,* 1619. L.O.C.; D(3).D⁶.D⁸.(2).D¹⁰.DE.KNY.L¹³.L²⁶.MTH.PA(3). PA⁶.ST.TRO. +

> T.N. [David Rothe.] Imprint false; *pr.* [Paris?].

953 —Brigida thaumaturga, siue dissertatio . . . in laudem ipsius Sanctae . . . habita in Collegio Hibernorum Parisiensi Kalendis februarii die festo eiusdem Sanctae. 8°. *Parisiis, apud Sebastianum Cramoisy,* 1620. A².D.D⁶. *This or no. 954:* TRO.

> *Ded.* to Gerald FitzGerald, Earl of Kildare, sgd.: D.G. [David Rothe.] This work was attacked by Thomas Dempster in no. 296 to which Rothe replied in no. 955.

954 —[Anr. issue.] *Parisiis, apud Sebastianum Cramoisy,* 1620. L.C(2).; DI.PA.PA².PA³.PA⁴. *See also no. 953.*

> In place of the dedicatory epistle of no. 953 there is here substituted one to Jean Lescalopier, sgd.: D.R.E.O.V.H. [David Rothe Episcopus Ossoriensis Viceprimas Hiberniae.]

—De processu martyriali. *See no. 952.*

—Hiberniae siue antiquioris Scotiae vindiciae, 1621. For this work, published under the initials F.G. and sometimes attributed to Rothe, *see* no. 396.1.

955 —Hibernia resurgens. Siue refrigerium antidotale. Aduersus morsum serpentis antiqui. In quo modeste discutitur, immodesta Parecbasis Thomae Dempsteri . . . Et Hiberniae sancti sui vindicantur; ac bona fide asseruntur. Auctore Donato Roirk Hiberno. 8°. *Rothomagi, apud Nicolaum le Brun,* 1621. L(2).O.C(2).; D.D⁶.D⁷.F.MTH.N.PA.ST.

> Donatus Roirk, *pseud.* Answering no. 296. Imprint false; *pr.* [Paris, Jérome Blageart.] This issue contains preliminary verses and a dedicatory epistle to Balthasar and Raymond Lescalopier.

956 —[Anr. issue.] *Coloniae Agrippinae, sumptibus Conradi Burgeni* [*sic*], 1621. D.KNY.

> Donatus Roirk, *pseud.* Imprint false; *pr.* [Paris, Jérome Blageart.] A reissue of the sheets of no. 955 but with the preliminary verses and dedication omitted and replaced by a new bifolium of which the first leaf contains the reprinted title, *pr.* [Paris, J. Blageart] and the second is blank.

—Tractatulus . . . de nominibus Hiberniae, 1624. *In no. 819.*

Rudesindus, F., *name in religion. See* Barlow, W.

Ⓐ **S., H.** *See no.* 1061.

(S.,I. **S., M.I.** *See no.* 731. .

I.) **Sacrobosco, Christophorus a.** *See* Holywood, C.

957 **Saint Malo,** *English Benedictine Priory.* [*Appendix.*] Coppie des lettres patentes du Roy, pour l'establissement des Benedictins Anglois en la ville de S. Malo, au mois de Iuillet, l'an 1626. Fol. (a bifolium), *n.p.d.* [1626.] DE(Tracts 208, no. 3).

> The royal letters patent are followed by 'Coppie de l'Arrest de verification des lettres patentes du Roy au Parlement de Rennes, le 15 Septembre, l'an 1626.' *Pr.* [Rennes?]

Saint Omer, *English Jesuit College.* Epistola Reuerendi P.N. Generalis . . . ad patres et fratres Societatis Iesu, [1639 or 1640]. *See no.* 394.

—Exercitia spiritualia B.P. Ignatii Loyolae, 1610 [etc.]. *See nos.* 392–3.

958 —[*Plays performed by students at the College.*] Aloysius sieu saeculi fuga

dramate scenico in Collegio Anglic. Societatis Iesu Audomaropol. adumbranda. M.DC.XL. Aprilis die ... 4°. ff. 2. *n.p.d.* [1640.]
Not found. Description from Sommerv. (tom. 7, col. 434).

959   —Fratrum discordia felix siue Stanislaus fuga victor. Drama exhibendum in Collegio Anglorum Societatis Iesu Audomaropoli, inter ludos saeculares eiusdem Societatis, ab infima classe Grammatices, anno M.DC.XL. Maii die ... Habetur scena Viennae Austriae. 4°. ff. 2. *n.p.d.* [1640.]
Not found. Description from Sommerv. (tom. 7, col. 434.)

960   —Haeresis triumphata siue S. Ignatius Soc. Iesu fundator a iuuentute Anglicana in scenam productus, Audomaropoli inter ludos saeculares eiusdem Societatis. Anno a partu Virginis M.DC.XL. Habetur scena Romae. 4°. ff. 4. *n.p.d.* [1640.]
Not found. Description from Sommerv. (tom. 7, col. 434.)

961   —Sanguis sanguinem tragoedia. [*End:*] Dabitur a Poetis anno a confirmata Societate Iesu centesimo, a partu Virginis M.DC.XL. in Seminario Anglicano Audomaropoli. Mense Aprilis, die XIII. Fol. ff. 2. *n.p.d.* [1640.]
Not found. Description from Sommerv. (tom. 7, col. 434.) Sommerv. notes that the subject is taken from the history of England.

Salamanca, *Irish College.* Ianua linguarum, 1611. *See* no. 88.

962   —Vn razonamiento hecho al Reyno y Cortes de España, en Madrid, por does alūnos colegiales del Seminario Irlādes de Salamāca, año del Señor de 1610. 4°. (a single quadrifolium). *n.p.d.* [1610.] MD².(2: Jes. 9–3498/2; 9–3556bis/7).
An appeal for alms. The two students who presented the appeal on behalf of the College are not named. *Pr.* [Salamanca].

963   —Razonamiento que vn colegial del Colegio de los Irlandeses de Salamanca hizo a la Congregacion de las sanctas Iglesias destos Reynos. En Madrid, año de 1608. Traduzido de Latin en lingua Castellana. 4° (a single quadrifolium). [Coloph.] *Salamanca, en casa de Artus Taberniel,* 1608. MD (MSS 18420, n. 48).
An appeal for alms. The name of the collegian who presented it on behalf of the College is not disclosed. The Latin original has not been found.

964   —Regiorum arcanorum intimum administrum Christiane perfectum, & suis vndequaque numeris absolutissimum, ex morum disciplina, & vitae integerrimis actionibus, magni Gasparis de Guzman Comitis de Oliuares, Ducis de San Lucar, &c. quasi ex prima & cōsummatissima Idea delineatum, & transcriptum eidē patrono suo beneficentissimo, & domino aeternum colendissimo, Seminarium Ibernorum Salmanticense panegyricis concelebrabat vocibus. 4°. [Coloph.] *Madriti, ex facultate Superiorum, apud Franciscum Martinez typographum,* 1634.
HSA.
Collation: A–C⁴ (C4 blank?).

Salisbury, Edmund, *alias. See* Plowden, T.
Salisbury, John, *alias. See* Digby, J.
Sanchaeus, Gulielmus. *See* Sankey, W.

965   **Sander, Elizabeth.** Traslado de vna carta de cierta monia inglesa, llamada Isabel Sandera escrita en Ruan ciudad de Francia a Francisco Englefild cauallero ingles residente en Madrid. 4°. *Seuilla, Clemente Hidalgo, n.d.* [c. 1590.]
Not found. Described in Salvá catalogue (1872), no. 3255, and also in catalogue 79 (1897), no. 1140, of the London bookseller J. Pearson. Palau no. 257270 cites the Selvá catalogue entry but gives the title as *Relacion de vna carta ...,* which is repeated by Agulló, no. 306. The original letter, in English, was written by Elizabeth

Sander soon after she escaped from England in 1587 to rejoin the English Bridgettine community which had settled temporarily at Rouen and moved to Lisbon in 1594. This Spanish translation was also printed at Madrid in 1590 as part of Robert Persons's *Relacion de algunos martyrios* (no. 894).

Sander, Nicholas.†

DE CLAVE DAVID

966 —De claue Dauid seu regno Christi libri sex contra calumnias Acleri pro visibili ecclesiae monarchia. 4°. *Romae, in aedibus populi Romani, apud Georgium Ferrarium*, 1588. L.C.; C³.C⁹.CHA.DE.DI.FLO.L².LOU³.MU.O⁵.PS.PA⁴.RO³.YK. + +
Edited posthumously by Cardinal Filippo Sega, formerly Papal Nuncio at Madrid, with whom Sander had left the MS on his departure from Spain for Ireland in 1579. The 'Aclerus' of the title designates collectively the Protestant writers who had attacked no. 1013. *See* Mil., vol. 1, pp. 14–15.
—[Anr. ed.] 1592. *In* no. 1016.

DE JUSTIFICATIONE

967 —De iustificatione contra Colloquium Altenburgense libri sex ... Scripti ante aliquot annos a ... D. Nicolao Sandero. 8°. *Augustae Treuirorum, excudebat Emondus Hatotus*, 1585. D.L¹³.PA⁶.(–†8). *This or no. 968 or 969:* AMI.BOR.FU.FU².MU.O⁵.PR.RO⁵.TB.TRI(2).TRO.
On the Protestant discussions held at Altenburg, 1568–69. The preface, by Sander, is addressed to the English colleges at Rome and Douai, and is dated 9 September 1578. Collation: †⁸A–Vu⁸(:)⁴ (final leaf blank.) †⁸ʳ⁻ᵛ contains the beginning of 'De vita et scriptis Nicolai Sanderi' The rest of the 'De vita' is omitted from this issue. With Hatot's device and motto 'Aperto pectore et sapiente conatu' above the imprint on the titlepage.

968 —[Anr. issue.] *Augustae Treuirorum, excudebat Emondus Hatotus*, 1585. L.C.; AV.LOU³.PA.PLU.W.YK. *See also* no. 967.
The sheets of no. 967 but with an additional quire, ††⁶, containing the rest of 'De vita et scriptis Nicolai Sanderi' inserted after †8.

969 —[Anr. issue.] *Augustae Treuirorum, excudebat Emondus Hatotus*, 1585. O.; C⁵.CHA.DE.HP.RO⁶.W.
The first two quires, containing the title, preface and 'De vita et scriptis ...' are reset. The collation is now †⁸(:)⁴A–Vu⁸(:)⁴ (final leaf blank). This issue has a triangular fleuron in place of Hatot's device on the titlepage.

970 —[Anr. issue, with title and imprint:] De Lutheranorum dissidiis, circa iustificationem, libri sex ... Scripti ante annos aliquot a ... D. Nicolao Sandero ... & nunc primum post mortem eius in lucem emissi. *Coloniae Agrippinae, apud Henricum Falckenburg*, 1593. BM². PR².
A reissue of the same sheets except for the first two quires which are again reset. Collation as in no. 969.

971 —[Date variant.] 1594. BER.DI.L².LOU³.LYN.MU.PA⁴.PR².RO⁶.TB.WO.

DE LUTHERANORUM DISSIDIIS

—*See* no. 970.

DE ORIGINE AC PROGRESSU SCHISMATIS ANGLICANI

972 —Doctissimi viri Nicolai Sanderi, de origine ac progressu schismatis Anglicani, liber ... Editus & auctus per Edouardum Rishtonum. 8°.

Coloniae Agrippinae, 1585. L(3: 1 *imp*.).O(2).C.; AMP.C^4.DE(2).DUR.
HP(2).L^2.L^{26}.OS.PA.PA^2.USH.W. + +
Edited posthumously by Rishton, with additions concerning events since Sander's death in 1581. *See* Mil., vol. 1, pp. 70–2. Imprint false; *pr.* [Rheims, Jean Foigny].

973 —[Anr. ed., enlarged.] Nicolai Sanderi de origine ac progressu schismatis Anglicani libri tres . . . Aucti per Edouardum Rishtonum . . . nunc iterum locupletius & castigatius editi. 8°. *Romae, typis Bartholomaei Bonfadini*, 1586. L.O(2).; AMS.DE.DI.HP.KNY.L^{15}.L^{26}.MD.MU.OS (2).PA.PA^6.RO^2.RO^3. +
This edition contains substantial additions by Robert Persons who saw it through the press. It includes John Hart's anonymous account of his imprisonment in the Tower of London, 1580–85 (*Diarium Turris*), which is often erroneously attributed to Edward Rishton.

974 —[Anr ed.] . . . libri tres . . . Nunc vero in Germania iterum locupletius & castigatius editi. 8°. *Ingolstadii, ex officina typographica Wolfgangi Ederi*, 1586. O.; A.AUG.EI.GT.GTN(2).MD.MU.NEU.PA^4.STG.TB.

975 —[Date variant.] 1587. C.; AUG.C^2.CHA.D^6.DE.DI.E.FU.GT.L^4.L^9.LOU^3.LYN. MU.STG.TRI. +

976 —[Anr. ed.] 8°. *Ingolstadii, ex officina typographica Wolfgangi Ederi*, 1588. L.O.C.; AMP.C^4.DE.DUR.KNY.L^2.L^{26}.MD.MU(2).O^5.OS.SBG.TB. +
A close reprint of no. 974 with some errata corrected and the original errata list at the end removed.

977 —[Anr. ed., with Ribadeneira's *Appendix*.] Nunc vero addita Appendice R.P. Petri Ribadeneirae. 8°. 2 pts. *Coloniae Agrippinae, sumptibus Petri Henningi*, 1610. L(4).O.; AMS.ANT.AUG.C^5.CHA.D^8(2).DE.HP(2).MU. OS.PA.SBG.USH.VI. + +
Pt. 2 comprises the *Appendix* (sive liber quartus) which is a Latin translation of nos. 993, *etc.* It has its own titlepage.

978 —[Anr. ed., with Ribadeneira's *Appendix*, and with title:] Vera et sincera historia schismatis Anglicani . . . Nunc postremum Appendice ex R.P. Petri Ribadeneirae libris, aucta & castigatius edita. 8°. *Coloniae Agrippinae, apud Petrum Henningium*, 1628. L(4).O(2).C.; ANT^2.C^2.D. DE.DMR.DUR(2).GTN.HP(3).LOU^3.MU.OS.PA.RO^5.ST. + +
Scott 225.

979 —[Date variant.] 1629. FR.

French Translations

980 —Les trois liures de Nicolas Sander, touchant l'origine et progres du schisme d'Angleterre . . . Traduits en François, selon la copie Latine de Rome, par I.T.A.C. Et maintenant imprimé par le commandement de Monseigneur Illust. & Reuerend. Cardinal de Vaudemont, à la requeste de certains gentilzhommes Anglois refugiez pour la foy Catholique. 8°. *n.p.*, 1587. L.O.; AIX.ANT.D^6.DMR.F.FLO.L^2.L^{26}(2).NCY. NTS.PA.PA^5.PA^7.
With a prefatory note by the translator, signed I.T.A.C. and dated 9 July 1587, and with four sonnets by him on the Reformation in England. The initials have not been identified. Charles de Lorraine, Cardinal de Vaudémont, was Bishop of Toul and of Verdun. *Pr.* [Pont-à-Mousson?]

981 —[Anr. issue, with imprint:] *Ausbourg, par Hans Mark*, 1587. ou 88 [*sic*]. C(*imp*.).CHA.E.GT.L^{26}.PA(*imp*.).
The sheets of no. 980 except for the title and conjugate leaf (sig. a1. 8) which are reset. The title now ends at the initials I.T.A.C., the reference to the Cardinal de Vaudémont (who died 29 November 1587) being omitted. The Augsburg imprint is fictitious.

982   —[Anr. issue, with imprint and date:] *Ausbourg, par Hans Mark*, 1607,
      ou 1608 [*sic*]. LN.PA⁵.
      The title and conjugate leaf have again been reset.

983   —[*A different French translation.*] Les trois liures du docteur Nicolas
      Sanders, contenants l'origine & progrez du scisme d'Angleterre. 8°.
      n.p., 1587. L.O.; BRS.C².CHA.DE.GTN.HP.L².LYN.PA(2).PA²(2).PA⁴.TRO.
      VER. +
      Without initials either on the titlepage or elsewhere.

German Translation

984   —Warhaffte Engellaendische Histori, in wellicher was sich, besonder in
      Religionssachen, von LX. Jahren . . . verloffen, gründlich beschriben
      durch Edouardum Risthonum, auss denen von . . . Nicolao Sanderi
      hinderlassnen vnuerfertigten Schrifften . . . ins Teutsche vertiert
      durch . . . Johann Heuer. 4°. *Saltzburg, durch Conradum Kurner*, 1594.
      L.O.; BA.BER.DE.F.STG.VI.WO.

Appendix. [*Derivative Works.*]

985   —Davanzati, B. Scisma d'Inghilterra sino alla morte della Reina Maria;
      ristretto in lingua propria Fiorentina da Bernardo Dauanzati. 8°.
      *Roma, ad instanza di Gio. Angelo Ruffinelli, appresso Guglielmo
      Facciotto*, 1602. L.O.; C⁵(*imp.*).DMR.FLO(3).M.NM.NP³.PA.PA³.RO².RO³.
      RO⁵.VT(2). +
      Abridged and adapted from Sander's work. It goes only as far as
      the death of Queen Mary Tudor in 1558.

986   —[Anr. ed.] 8°. *Milano, per l'herede del q. Pacifico Pontio, & Gio.
      Battista Piccaglia stampatori archiepiscopali*, 1602. L.; CHI.MU.PA³.
      PEN³.VI.VT.YK.
      A reprint of no. 985 but with a different dedicatory epistle.

987   —[Anr. ed., with other works by Davanzati.] Scisma d'Inghilterra del
      Sig. Bernardo Dauanzati con altre sue operette non piu stampate. 4°.
      Fiorenza, nella nuoua stamperia del Massi, e Landi, 1637. PA.
      Containing five additional works by the author. Licensed for print-
      ing in July 1636. There are no preliminaries, and it is doubtful
      whether the book was ever intended to be issued in this state. *See*
      no. 988. Collation: A–Aa⁴Bb⁶.

988   —[Anr. issue of no. 987.] Scisma d'Inghilterra con altre operette del
      Sig. Bernardo Dauanzati al Serenissimo Ferdinando Secondo Gran
      Duca di Toscana. *Fiorenza, nella nuoua stamperia del Massi, e Landi*,
      1638. L(2).O.; AIX.BRS².DMR.FLO(2).L².L²⁶.O².PA.PA².PA³.RO².RO⁵.VT(3).
      WO. + +
      The sheets of no. 987 including the titleleaf (A1), preceded by an
      additional quire (†⁶) comprising the new titleleaf followed by pre-
      liminaries which include a dedicatory epistle to the Grand Duke, a
      biographical sketch of Davenzati, and Davanzati's original dedica-
      tory epistle from no. 985. The 1637 titleleaf, though wanting in
      most copies, was evidently not intended to be cancelled, as the
      catchword on †6ᵛ leads to it.

989   —Mayr, J. Kurtzer bericht aller gedenckwuerdigen sachen, so sich in
      Engelland in den nechsten hundert Jaren verlauffen, auss D. Niclass
      Sandero, Eduardo Risthono, vnd andern mehr Engellaendischen
      Historicis zusamen gezogen. Durch Johann Mayr. 4°. *Muenchen,
      durch Nicolaum Henricum*, 1600. L.O.; DI(2).DMR.IND.MU.PA.
      Scott 188.

990   —Pollini, G. Historia ecclesiastica della riuoluzione d'Inghilterra.
      Diuisa in cinque libri. Ne'quali si tratta di quello che è occorso in

quell'Isola, da chè Arrigo Ottauo cominciò à pensare di ripudiare Caterina sua legittima moglie, enfin'a quest'vltimi anni di Lisabetta, vltima figliuola d'Arrigo. 4°. *Fiorenza, per Filippo Giunti*, 1591. PA.PA².

Based largely on Sander's work. Dedicated by Pollini to Cardinal Allen. On 6/16 April 1592 Queen Elizabeth wrote to the Grand Duke of Tuscany asking him to suppress the work. *See* Meyer, pp. 367–8. With a colophon giving the same printer's name and address as the titlepage imprint.

991 —[Anr. issue with cancel title and final leaf.] *Bologna, ad instanza de'Giunti di Fiorenza*, 1591 [?1592]. L(formerly E³).; FLO.GTN.RO³.RO⁵. VAL².

The colophon on the cancel final leaf reproduces the changed imprint of the cancel titleleaf. Apart from the two cancel leaves the book is a reissue of the origianl sheets printed by Filippo Giunti at Florence. If the imprint was changed in consequence of Elizabeth's letter of 6/16 April 1592 (*see* note to no. 990 above), the date of this issue is [1592].

992 —[Anr. ed.] 4°. *Roma, presso Guglielmo Facciotti, ad istanza di Gio. Angelo Ruffinelli*, 1594. L(2).O.C(2).; A.C².DE(2).E.FLO.L²⁶.MD(2).MTH. OS.PA.PA³.RO².USH.WO. + +

993 —Ribadeneira, P. de. Historia ecclesiastica del scisma del reyno de Inglaterra; en la qual se tratan las cosas mas notables q̃ han sucedido en aquel reyno, tocantes à nuestra santa religion, desde que començo hasta la muerte de la Reyna de Escocia. Recogida de diuersos y graues autores. 8°. *Madrid, en casa de Pedro Madrigal*, 1588. [*t.p.* verso:] *Vendese en casa de Francisco Lopez.* L(imp.).C.; E.L⁹(coloph. covered over).MD.

Based mainly on Sander's work and partly translated from it. In this edition the Tassa on sig. †2ʳ is dated 20 June 1588 and the errata list on sig. Bbb6ʳ 17 June 1588. The colophon (on sig. Bbb6ᵛ) is dated simply 1588.

994 —[Anr. ed.] 8°. *Madrid, en casa de Pedro Madrigal*, 1588. EV.FLO².HP (imp.).MD².PA.PA².

A reprint of no. 993 with the misprints corrected. On *t.p.* verso there is a woodcut of the arms of Spain and no mention of the bookseller Francisco Lopez. The Tassa on sig. †2ʳ is dated 16 September 1588; a new errata list on sig. Bbb6ʳ is dated 15 September 1588; the colophon is dated 16 September 1588.

995 —[Anr. ed.] 8°. *Lisboa, impressa . . . en casa de Antonio Aluarez*, 1588. L.; COI.DMR.E.E³.HEI.LIS. *This or no.* 996: EV.PR(imp.).

Scott 165.

996 —[Imprint variant.] Following the imprint and date are the words: *A costa de Domingos Martinez Mercad. de lib.* MD.VV.

KING MANUEL no. 161.

997 —[Anr. ed.] 8°. *Barcelona, a costa de Hieronymo Genoues, y de Iayme Cendrad*, 1588. [Coloph.] *Impresso en Barcelona en casa de Iayme Cendrat.* BAR.BAR².BO.MD.MST.O⁷.PA².

998 —[Anr. ed.] 8°. *Çaragoça, en casa de Pedro Puig, y de la viuda de Ioan Escarrilla*, 1588. L.; MD.

999 —[Anr. ed.] 8°. *Valencia, en casa de Pedro Patricio Mey*, 1588. *Vendense en casa de Gabriel Ribas, y Martin de Esparca.* MD(imp.).RO⁸.VI(imp.).

1000 —[Anr. ed.] 8°. *Emberes, en casa de Christoual Plantino*, 1588. O.; ANT. BM².BRS.LGE³.MU.PA.ROU.U.VI.

1001 —[Anr. ed.] 8°. *Madrid, en casa de la biuda de Alonso Gomez*, 1589. MD. MD³.

1002 —[Anr. ed.] 8°. *Por Manuel de Lyra*, 1589. EV.F.LIS.MD.O¹².VV.

Pr. [Lisbon.] KING MANUEL no. 209.

1003　—[Anr. ed.] 12°. *Emberes, en casa de Martin Nucio*, 1594. L.O.; AMS.BAR. BRS.C⁷.E.FU.GT.HP.MD.MU(2).OS.USH.WO. +
　　　　Issued, and usually bound, with no. 1008 though they are bibliographically independent of each other.

1004　—Ribadeneira, P. de. Segunda parte de la historia del scisma de Inglaterra. 8°. *Alcala, en casa de Iuan Iniguez de Lequeirica*, 1593. L.; VI(-*t.p.*).
　　　　A continuation of Sander's work, describing Catholic affairs in England from 1587 to 1593. Written by Ribadeneira from material supplied by Robert Persons. Includes Barret's martyr catalogue (cp. no. 312) continued to 1593.

1005　—[Anr. ed.] 4°. *Madrid*, 1594.
　　　　Not found. Cited by Sommerv. (tom. 6, col. 1731).

1006　—[Anr. ed.] 8°. *Lisboa. Impressa en casa de Antonio Aluarez*, 1594. *A costa de Pedro de Flores, y Antonio Aluarez*. L.; COI.OP.
　　　　Collation: ✠⁸A–X⁸.

1007　—[Anr. ed.? or anr. issue?] 8°. *Lisboa, en casa de Manoel de Lyra*, 1594. CLIF.LIS.MD.
　　　　This appears to be either a reprint of no. 1006 or another issue of the sheets of the text with reprinted preliminaries. Collation: ¶⁸A–X⁸.

1008　—[Anr. ed.] 12°. *Anueres, en casa de Martin Nutio*, 1594. L.O.; BO.BRS.E. FU.GT.HP.OS.PR.USH.VI.
　　　　Issued, and usually bound, with no. 1003, though they are bibliographically independent of each other. Anr. ed. of both parts of the *Scisma* was published in pt. 2 of Ribadeneira's works printed at Madrid in 1604.

1009　—[Anr. ed.] *Madrid, la viuda de P.M.*, 1595.
　　　　P.M. [Pedro Madrigal.]
　　　　Not seen. *Catalogo colectivo* (siglo XVI, Q–R, no. 813) records a copy at Lerida B.P.

1010　—Sciacca, A. da. Relatione dello scisma anglicano, e del glorioso martirio del B.P.F. Giouanni Foresta Francescano Osseruante: e di altri santi martiri d'Inghilterra nella persecutione d'Enrico Ottauo. Breuemente raccolta dal R.P.F. Angelo da Sciacca del medesimo ordine. 4°. *Palermo, per Gio. Antonio de Franceschi*, 1597. AIX.RO³.RO⁵.
　　　　Based mainly on Sander's work.

1011　—Vernulaeus, N. Nicolai Vernulaei Henricus Octauus seu schisma Anglicanum tragoedia, exhibita ludis encenialibus, Louanii in Collegio Porcensi. 8°. *Louanii, typis Philippi Dormalii*, 1624. L.O.; BRS.F.GT.PA.
　　　　A play in Latin verse performed at Porc College, Louvain. Based in part on Sander's *De origine ac progressu schismatis Anglicani*.

DE TYPICA ET HONORARIA SACRARUM IMAGINUM ADORATIONE

1012　—De typica et honoraria sacrarum imaginum adoratione libri duo, quorum prior in adorandis sanctorum imaginibus nullum esse idolatriae periculum: posterior docet, figuralem quandam adorationem illis deberi, & naturali, & gentium, & diuino, & ecclesiastico iure. 8°. *Louanii, apud Ioannem Foulerum*, 1569. L.O.C.; AMS.BRS.C³.CHA.D. DMR.DUR.L².MD.MU.PA.O⁵.OS.RO.YK. + +

DE VISIBILI MONARCHIA ECCLESIAE

1013　—De visibili monarchia Ecclesiae, libri octo. Fol. *Louanii, Ioannis Fouleri cura & impensa, excudebat Reynerus Velpius*, 1571. L.O.C(2).; BRS.C².DE.GTN.L²⁶.LGE³.LOU³.MD.O⁵.PA.PA³.SBG. + +

For the controversy to which this work gave rise *see* Mil., vol. 1, pp. 13–15. Sander defended the work in no. 966.

1014 —[Anr. ed.] Fol. *Antuerpiae, apud Ioannem Foulerum,* 1578. O.; AMS.ANT².BRN.C⁹.CHA.DI.F.LN.MAR.MU.STG.TRI.VI.YK. + Collation: †⁶A–Z⁶a–z⁶Aa–Vu⁶Xx⁸Yy⁶.

1015 —[Anr. ed.] Fol. *Antuerpiae, et venundantur Parisiis, apud Michaelem Sonnium,* 1580. AV.CHA.GER.LYN.MD(2).PA.PA³.PA⁵.VAL.
Perhaps in part a reissue of the sheets of no. 1014 with which it shares an identical collation, but the title is not a cancel.

1016 —[Anr. ed., with *De Clave David.*] De visibili monarchia Ecclesiae . . . Accesserunt eiusdem auctoris De claue Dauid . . . libri sex. Fol. 2 pts. *Wirceburgi, apud viduam Henrici Aquensis,* 1592. L.O.C(2).; AUG.C³.CHA.D.E².FLO.FU.L².MD.PA.PA⁴.USH.W. + +
For the original edition of *De clave David, see* no. 966.

—[*Extracts.*] *In* De iustitia Britannica, 1584. *See* no. 12.

FACULA SACERDOTUM

—*See* no. 1020.

QUOD DOMINUS . . . DE SACRAMENTO EUCHARISTIAE PROPRIE SIT LOCUTUS

1017 —Quod Dominus in sexto capite Ioannis de sacarmento [*sic*] Eucharistiae proprie sit locutus, tractatus vtilis. 8°. *Antuerpiae, apud viduam & haeredes Ioannis Steelsii,* 1570. O.; AV.BM².C³.D.DI.FLO³.FR.MU(3).PR²(2).RO³.ST.STG.U.VT.

SACRIFICII MISSAE . . . EXPLICATIO

1018 —Sacrificii Missae, ac eius partium explicatio, secundum rerum ipsarum veram originem & historiam . . . Adiunctae sunt precationes dicendae dum Missa celebratur, atque aliae quaedam piis omnibus magno vsui future, collectae ex variis probatisque Catholicis authoribus. 12°. *Louanii, apud Ioannem Foulerum,* 1569. D.MU.PA.USH.

1019 —[Anr. ed.] 12°. *Antuerpiae, apud Ioannem Foulerum,* 1573. D.MU.PA.
A reprint of no. 1018.

1020 —[Anr. ed.] 1607. *Forms pt. 2 of a collection by various authors:* Facula sacerdotum. 12°. 2 pts. *Duaci, ex typographia Baltazaris Belleri,* 1607. C.; AMI.CHA.KN.NEU.OS.PA¹¹.PR³(*imp.*).VI.VT.
Pt. 2, which is a reprint of no. 1018, has its own titlepage with imprint: *Duaci, sumptibus Baltazaris Belleri,* and a colophon at the end of the text reading: *Louanii, Reynero Velpio impressore.*

SEDES APOSTOLICA

1021 —Sedes apostolica seu de militantis ecclesiae Romanae potestate, summorumq; Pontificum Romanorum primatu, atq; in omnes gentes auctoritate. 4°. *Romae, apud Paulum Parisium,* 1603. C.; EX.FR.L².L¹³.PA.PA⁴.RG.

TRES ORATIONES

1022 —Nicolai Sanderi . . . tres orationes in scholis publicis Louanii habitae, 14. Cal. Ianuarii . . . 1565. 1. De transubstantiatione. 2. De linguis officiorum ecclesiasticorum. 3. De pluribus missis in eodem templo celebrādis. 8°. *Antuerpiae, excudebat Ioannes Latius,* 1566. L.O.C.; ANT².BM².BRS.C⁹.DI.GT.L².LOU³.O⁵.PA.PA⁴.RO⁵.VT.W. +

Sanders, Anthony. *See* no. 834.

1023 **Sanderson, John.** Institutionum dialecticarum libri quatuor. 8°.
Antuerpiae, ex officina Christophori Plantini, 1589. L.O(2).C(2).; F(2).
RO³.SAL.VI.VT.
Dedicated to Cardinal Allen. Reprinted in England: STC 21698–
21700.
1023.1 —Schema catechisticum, sive doctrinae Christianae summa. [1590.]
Not found. Entered in the Plantin Catalogue (MS. M321, fol. 20ʳ)
under date 1590. *Pr.* [Antwerp, Plantin.] Pits (p. 800) attributes to
him 'Tabulae vel schema catechisticum de tota theologia morali'
which may be the same work.
1024 **Sankey, William.** Conclusiones theologicae de Incarnatione . . .
Praeside R. Patre Thoma Neuello . . . Defendet Guilelmus Sanchaeus
. . . in Collegio Anglicano Societatis Iesu Leodii, anno Domini 1637.
*s.sh.*fol. *Leodii, typis Leonardi Streel*, 1637. O(*with date 4 Aug. inserted
in MS*).
A programme announcing the forthcoming defence of his thesis.
1025 **Savage, Francis.** Conclusiones logicae . . . Praeside R.D. Francisco
Plantino . . . Defendet in Collegio Anglorum Duacensi Franciscus
Sauage Anglus. *s.sh.*fol. *Duaci, typis viduae Petri Telu*, 1624. O(*MS. e.
Museo 153*).
A programme announcing the forthcoming defence of his thesis.
The name Francis Savage does not occur in Anst., nor in DD 3, nor
in Bellenger, but two MS lecture notebooks, specially bound with
his name on the cover, are preserved at O.; one of these, which also
has the name of Francis Plantin [alias of Francis Platt] on the cover,
has this printed programme inserted in it.

Sayer, Gregory, *name in religion. See* Sayer, R.

Sayer, Robert, *in religion* Gregory Sayer.

COLLECTED WORKS

1026 —R.P.D. Gregorii Sayri . . . opera theologica. Moralis doctrinae quae ad
conscientiae directionem et solamen pertinet. Thesaurus plenissimus
quatuor tomis distinctus . . . Nouissimam hanc editionem recensuit,
& castigauit . . . D. Leander de S. Martino. Fol. 3 tom. *Duaci, ex
officina typographica Baltazaris Belleri*, 1620. L.C.; BRS.C⁰.DE.GTN.HP.
L².L²⁶.LOU³.MU(*tom. 1, 2*).O¹⁴.PA.PA³.STG.WO. +
Although much of Sayer's work had already appeared in print
separately, this was the first collected edition. Tom. 1 comprises *De
sacramentis in communi* (*see* no. 1048); tom. 2, *De censuris ecclesiasticis* (*see* nos. 1028, *etc.*); tom. 3, *Flores decisionum* (*see* nos. 1049, *etc.*)
The fourth tome, called for in the title and described in the table of
contents as 'prius separatim impressus' was the edition of *Clavis
regia* printed at Douai in 1618–19 (*see* no. 1042). Each tome has its
own titlepage, naming the contents. The general title to the whole
collection, as given above, occurs only on the half-title to tom. 1;
the imprint and date given above are taken from the full titlepage to
tom. 1. Leander de S. Martino [John Jones.].
1027 —[Date variant.] The date in the imprint to tom. 1 is 1621. C.; ANG.AUG.
BOR.HP.L².LEM.LOU³.MD⁴(*tom. 1, 2*).O².O¹³.OR.PA.TI.TNI.

SINGLE WORKS

Casuum Conscientiae . . . Thesaurus

1028 —Casuum conscientiae siue theologiae moralis thesauri . . . tomus
primus. De censuris ecclesiasticis, aliisque poenis, & canonicis
impedimentis, in septem libros distributus. Fol. *Venetiis, apud
Baretium Baretium, & socios*, 1601. O.; FB.FRA.MIL².PA.PR.SBG.SPS.TB.

The publishers appear to have originally intended to issue the work in two volumes, the first comprising *De censuris ecclesiasticis*, and the second *Flores decisionum*, but afterwards to have changed their minds and issued the latter separately under its own title (*see* nos. 1049, *etc.*). In all editions of *Casuum conscientiae . . . thesaurus* subsequent to the first, the words 'tomus primus' are omitted from the title.

1029 —[Anr. ed.] Fol. *Venetiis, apud Ioannem Baptistam Colosinum*, 1606. O.; BG.C².FLO³.HEI.MIL.PA⁵.VAL.

The title is the same as in no. 1028 except that the words 'tomus primus' are omitted.

1030 —[Anr. ed.] In hac vero tertia editione adeo mendis, & erroribus expurgatus. Fol. *Venetiis, apud Sessas*, 1609. L.; AUG.BAR².BEU.BG².D². DE.DI.GEI.LYN.PA⁵.VER.WASH.

1031 —[Anr. ed.] Hac quarta editione . . . expurgatus. Fol. *Venetiis, apud Sessas*, 1614. AB.MD.O⁸.PA⁴.RO⁵.SCG.SOL.WASH².

1032 —[Anr. ed., with title:] Thesaurus casuum conscientiae continens praxim exactissimam de censuris ecclesiasticis, aliisque poenis, & canonicis impedimentis, in septem libros distributus . . . Accesserunt in hac editione additiones . . . Francisci Baretii. Fol. *Venetiis, apud Baretium Baretium*, 1618. BG.BG².BRI.CHA.MAR.MD(2).MST.PA.STI.TUR.

1033 —[Anr. ed.] Thesaurus casuum conscientiae . . . Fol. *Venetiis, apud Baretium Baretium*, 1627. AV.BG.LOU.LOU³.PBN.RG.

1034 —[*Abridged and adapted version.*] De ecclesiasticis censuris, et aliis in . . . D. Gregorii Sayri Thesauro contentis, vna cum regulis, pro cuiuscunque Bullae in Coena Domini facili explicatione, ex eodem desumptis. Formale compendium. Per R.P.F. Antonium Ninum. 8°. *Venetiis, apud Petrum Mariam Bertanum*, 1624. C.; EI.

Clavis Regia Sacerdotum

1035 —Clauis regia sacerdotum, casuum conscientiae siue theologiae moralis thesauri locos omnes aperiens, in quibus pręcipuę canonistarum et summistarum difficultates ad communem praxim pertinentes . . . explicantur. Fol. *Venetiis, apud Baretium Baretium*, 1605. O.; A.BG². CHA.D².(-*t.p.*).FLO³.HEI.MAR.MU.PR.VI.

1036 —[Anr. ed.] In hac secunda editione a multis . . . mendis expurgatum. Fol. *Venetiis, apud Baretium Baretium*, 1607. C².CU.D.L².LOU³.MST. MU.PA.SBG².VCE.WASH.

1037 —[Anr. ed.] In hac tertia editione a multis . . . mendis expurgatum. Fol. *Venetiis, apud Baretium Baretium*, 1610. BG.BG².HER.PA⁵.VAL.WB.

1038 —[Anr. ed.] In hac quarta editione a multis . . . mendis expurgatum. Fol. *Mediolani, apud Ioan. Baptistam Bidellium*, 1615. STI.WN.

1039 —[Imprint variant?] *Mediolani, apud haer. Pacifici Pontii, & Ioan. Baptistam Piccaleum*, 1615.

Probably forming part of a shared edition with no. 1038. A copy was seen by the editors but its present whereabouts are unknown.

1040 —[Anr. ed., enlarged.] In hac quarta, & postrema editione accesserunt vtilia additamenta, nec non Catenula aurea de comparatione peccatorum . . . Paulini Berti . . . Insuper summa sacramenti poenitentiae eiusdem Sayri. Fol. 3 pts. *Venetiis, apud Baretium Baretium*, 1615. C.; BEU.BG².BRU.FLO³.FRA.GNA.MU.PA.RO⁵.SOL.

Pt. 1 comprises Sayer's *Clavis regia*; pt. 2, Sayer's *Summa sacramenti poenitentiae*; pt. 3, Berti's *Catenula aurea*. For separate editions of *Summa sacramenti poenitentiae, see* nos. 1054, *etc.* Probably the ed. from which nos. 1038–9 were reprinted.

1041 —[Anr. ed.] In hac quinta, & postrema editione aucta fuit nouis vtilibusq. additionibus R.D. Francisci Baretii Veneti. Fol. 2 pts. *Venetiis, apud Baretium Baretium*, 1618. AMS.GEI.MD.TUR.WO.

Pt. 2 comprises Sayer's *Summa sacramenti poenitentiae*. This edition omits Berti's *Catenula aurea.*

1042 —[Anr. ed. of *Clavis regia* alone.] In hac nouissima editione a multis . . . mendis expurgatum, & ad primam eiusdem Auctoris exemplaris integritatem, veramque lectionem, restitutum. Fol. *Duaci, ex officina Marci Wyon*, 1619. [Coloph.] *Duaci, typis Marci Wyon*, 1618. MNS. MOU.PA.TRO.UT.
Omitting the additions of nos. 1040–1. With a dedicatory epistle by the printer and a preface by Leander of St Martin [John Jones].

1043 —[Anr. issue of no. 1042, with a different titlepage and preliminaries.] *Antuerpiae, apud Ioannem Keerbergium*, 1619. C.; ANG.CMR.DE.HER. LYN.MD.MNS.PA.SCG.VAL.WOR.
The sheets of no. 1042 except for the title and preliinaries (*6) which are reprinted, the former dedicatory epistle and preface being replaced by a dedicatory epistle signed: 'Maurus Anglus . . . Monachus Casinas.' [William, *in religion*, Maurus Taylor].

1044 —[Anr. ed., enlarged.] Hac vero sexta, & nouissima editione aucta fuit . . . Georgii Polacchi . . . appendicibus nunquam alias impressis, praeter nouas additiones R.D. Francisci Baretii . . . Accessit insuper Summa sacramenti poenitentiae eiusdem Sayri necnon Catenula aurea de comparatione peccatorum. Fol. 2 pts. *Venetiis, apud Baretium Baretium*, 1625. CHA.ETON.FLO³.HP.L⁴.RO⁸.

1045 —[Anr. ed. of *Clavis Regia* alone.] In hac nouissima editione a multis . . . mendis expurgatum, & ad primam eiusdem Auctoris exemplaris integritatem, veramque lectionem, restitutum. Fol. *Monasterii Westfaliae, sumptibus Michaelis Dalii, & Bernardi Raesfelt*, 1628. L.C.; AV.C⁵.DI.E².FR.HAN.HP.MU(2).O¹².OR.PA¹⁰.STG.UT². +

Compendium Clavis Regiae
(A summary by Constantine of Nola of Sayer's *Clavis regia*)

1046 —Compendii Clauis regię, pars prima (pars secunda). R.P.D. Gregorio Sayro Anglo Congregationis Cassinensis Authore, et P.D. Constantino de Notariis, Nolano . . . Compilatore. 4°. 2 vols. *Venetiis, apud Bernardum Iuntam, Io. Baptistam Ciottum, & socios*, 1613. BG².STI.VI.

1047 —[Anr. ed.] Hac postrema editione . . . expurgata. 4°. 2 pts. *Venetiis, apud Io: Baptistam Ciottum, & socios*, 1621. L(2, 1 has pt. 1 only) BG².L².LYN.MIL.

De Censuris Ecclesiasticis
—*See nos.* 1028, *etc.*

De Sacramentis in Communi

1048 —De sacramentis in communi, opus theologicum, tripartitum, ac plane aureum. In quo ea omnia, quae vel ad difficillimas quasque quaestiones theologicas definiendas; vel ad casus omnes conscientiae dissoluendos; vel ad singulos haereticorum errores refellendos attinent . . . accurate explicantur. 4°. *Venetiis, ex officina Damiani Zenari*, 1599. O.; AV.BG².C⁵.DMR.FLO³.LOU³(2).MAR.MD.MU.PA.RO⁵.SOL.VI.

Decisiones Casuum Conscientiae
—*See nos.* 1052–3.

Flores Decisionum sive Casuum Conscientiae
(Sometimes called *Epitome Consiliorum Navarri*)

1049 —Flores decisionum siue casuum conscientiae, ex doctrina Consiliorum Martini ab Azpilcueta Doctoris Nauari collecti, & iuxta librorum

Iuris Canonici dispositionem in suos titulos distributi. 4°. *Venetiis, 1601.* O.C.; MD.MU.PA⁴.
Pr. [Giovanni Battista Ciotti, whose device is printed on the title-page.]

1050 —[Anr. ed.] 4°. *Venetiis, apud Baretium Baretium, & socios, 1601.* AV.FLO³.FR.RO⁵.SPS.VI.

1051 —[Anr. ed.] 4°. *Venetiis, apud Baretium Baretium, 1611.* MAR.PA.

1052 —[Anr. ed., with title:] Decisiones casuum conscientiae ex doctrina Consiliorum Martini ab Azpilcueta Doctoris Nauarri collectae. Fol. *Venetiis, apud Baretium Baretium, 1619.* [Coloph.] *Venetiis, ex typographia Baretii Baretii, 1618.* BRI.MAR.MD(S).MST.PA.STI.TUR.
Usually found bound after no. 1032 with which it was probably issued.

1053 —[Anr. ed., with title as in no. 1052.] Fol. *Venetiis, apud Baretium Baretium, 1627.* AV.LOU.LOU³.RG.VI².
There is no colophon. Probably issued with no. 1033.

Sacramenti Poenitentiae Summa

1054 —Sacramenti. poenitentiae summa, ex commentariis Doctoris Nauarri in septem distinctiones de poenitentia, colecta. 8°. *Venetiis, 1601.* D.
Pr. [Giovanni Battista Ciotti, whose device is printed on the titlepage].

1055 —[Anr. issue? with fresh preliminaries and with title beginning:] Summa sacramenti poenitentiae, ex eruditissimis commentariis Doctoris Nauarri... *Venetiis, apud Baretium Baretium, & socios, 1601.* C.; MD.MU.RO⁵.VI.
—[Anr. ed.] 1615. *Part of no.* 1040.
—[Anr. ed.] 1618. *Part of no.* 1041.

Summa Sacramenti Poenitentiae
—*See no.* 1055.

Thesaurus Casuum Conscientiae
—*See nos.* 1032–3.

Sayrus, Gregorius. *See* Sayer, R.
Scepreus, Gulielmus. *See* Shepreve, W.
Scotland, *Catholic Church.* [Missals and Rituals for use in Scotland.] *See* England, *Catholic Church.*
—[*Appendix.*] Litaniae et preces recitandae pro fide Catholica Romana in regnis Angliae, & Scotiae, 1603. *See no.* 336.10.
—[An account by Sir Walter Lindsay of the state of Catholicism in Scotland in 1594.] *See no.* 740.
—[A report by Patrick Anderson on the state of Catholicism in Scotland in 1612.] *See no.* 26.
Scottish Catholics. [*Appendix.*] [A petition by Hugh Semple to the King of Spain on behalf of Scottish Catholics, 1623.] *See nos.* 354–7.

1056 **Scotus, Romoaldus,** *pseud.?* Summarium rationum, quibus Cancellarius Angliae et Prolocutor Puckeringius Elizabethae Angliae Reginae persuaserunt occidendam esse Serenissimam Principem Mariam Stuartam ... vna cum responsionibus Reginae Angliae et sententia mortis: quae omnia Anglice primum edita sunt, et Londini a typographo regio impressa ... His additum est Supplicium et mors Reginae Scotiae, vna cum succinctis quibusdam animaduersionibus, & confutationibus eorum, quae ei obiecta sunt. Opera Romoaldi Scoti. 8°. *Ingolstadii, ex officina Wolffgangi Ederi, 1588.* L(4).O.C.; BM².DE.DI.DMR.E(2:1 *imp.*).E².E⁴(*misdated 1587 in catalogue*).GTN.MU(6).PA.PA⁴.STG.TB.VI. + +

The first part (*Summarium rationum*) is a translation into Latin, with a Catholic commentary, of the English government's account of Mary's condemnation and execution which forms part of STC 6052; the second (*Supplicium et mors*) is an enlarged edition of the first two items in no. 803 of this catalogue. Romoaldus Scotus has not been identified. Scott 171.

[1057 *cancelled*]

1058   —[Anr. ed.] 4°. *n.p.*, 1588. L(*imp.*).; C²(*imp.*).DMR(*imp.*).GTN.MU.PA.PA⁴. WO(2).
         Pr. [Trier, Heirs of Emond Hatot].

1059   —[Abr. ed.] 8°. *Coloniae, sumptibus Petri Henningii*, 1627. L(2).O(2).C(2).; AMI.ANT².C²(2).DE.DMR.E².GT.GTN.HP.MU(2).PA.PA².VAL.WO. +
         Usually found bound with nos. 978, 1272. Scott 221.

1060   —[Imprint variant.] *Bambergae, apud Augustinum Crinesium. Sumptibus Petri Henningii*, 1627. BA.DMR.NEU.
         Forms part of a shared edition with no. 1059.

Semple, Hugh‡ [A petition to the King of Spain in favour of Scottish Catholics, 1623.] *See* nos. 354–7.

1061   —Motiuos para fauorecer la religion Catolica en la nacion Escocesa. Escritos por H. S. Fol. (a bifolium). *n.p.d.* [1635]. E.MD²(2: Jes. 113/48; 130/12(*imp.*).)
         [H. S. Hugh Semple.] The conjectured date of publication [1635] is based on internal evidence. Scott 230. This is a different work from the petition which forms part of nos. 354–7. *Pr.* [Spain]

Seville, *English College.*

APPEALS BY THE COLLEGE FOR ALMS

1062   —Algunos motiuos y razones que ay, para fauorecer los seminarios Ingleses. 4° (a single quadrifolium). *n.p.d.* [*n.b.* 1599, *n.a.* 1612.] MD²(9–3496/2).
         An appeal for alms. *Pr.* [Spain]. Although the title says 'los seminarios Ingleses', this is, in reality, a plea for special help for the College at Seville. The limiting dates are fixed by a reference in the text to no. 284, printed in 1599, and by the omission of any reference to the English College at Madrid, founded in 1612.
         —Creswell, J. Informacion a la ciudad de Seuilla, por parte del Colegio Ingles de la misma ciudad, 1604. *See* no. 279.

DOCUMENTS ISSUING FROM THE COLLEGE
Documents of 1599

1063   —Nueuos auisos de Inglaterra, de diez y seys del mes de Enero, de este año de mil, y quientos y nouenta y nueue, en los quales se da quēta de muchas particularidades de cosas de guerra, y de sucessos, y persecuciones de los Catholicos. Fol. (a bifolium). *Seuilla, en la imprenta de Rodrigo de Cabrera*, este año de nouenta y nueue [1599]. MD²(Jes. 102/3). [*L.].
         The first part of this newsletter deals with secular events; the second, headed 'Auisos de algunos Catholicos q̄ estan reclusos en los carceles de Londres, y de otros que se han librado' is based on reports sent from England to the English College at Seville.

Documents of 1600

—Relacion del martirio de los dos sacerdotes, el padre Tomas Benested, que fue del Colegio Ingles de Seuilla; y de N. Sprat . . ., 1600. *See* no. 91.

Documents of 1603

1064 —La declaracion que hizo el Conseio de Estado de la Reyna Isabela de Inglaterra difunta. En fauor de Iacobo quinto [*sic*] Rey de Escocia, por heredero y sucessor de aquella corona. A tres dias de Abril de 1603. Fol. (a bifolium). *Seuilla, en casa de Iuan de Leon*, 1603. SEV(63.9.82/25). [*L.]

A translation into Spanish of the Proclamation issued by the English Privy Council on the day of the Queen's death, 24 March/3 April, 1603 (STC 8297–8300). Preceding the text are comments that reflect reports from England recently received at the English

Ⓐ 1064.1 College. *See* RH, May 1981, pp. 316–18.

Documents of 1614

1065 —Peralta, Francisco de. Copia de vna carta, que el padre Francisco Peralta . . . Rector del Collegio de los Ingleses de Seuilla. Escriuio al padre Rodrigo de Cabredo Prouincial de Nueua España. En que se da quenta, de la dichosa muerte que tuuo en Londres la sañcta señora doña Luysa de Carauajal . . . Y de las honras, que se la hizieron, en la yglesia de San Gregorio Magno, apostol de Inglaterra: en el Collegio Ingles de Seuilla, en 11. de mayo de 1614. 4°. 2 pts. *n.p.d.* [1614.] BO.HSA.MD(2: 1 -*t.p.*).

Pr. [Seville.] Pt. 2 comprises a funeral sermon in honour of Luisa de Carvajal preached in the College chapel by Iuan de Pineda, poems in her praise, and documents (translated into Spanish) sent to the College from England and Flanders. Included among the documents is the text of no. 1. For Luisa de Carvajal who devoted her life and fortune to the cause of the English Catholics and died in England in 1614, *see* C. A. Abad, *Una misionera española en la Inglaterra del siglo XVII*, Comillas, 1966. *See* also this catalogue, nos. 1618–19.

1066 ——[*An extract from the same letter.*] Admirable y breue relacion, sacada sumariaments de algunas clausulas de vna carta, que escriuio el padre Rector de los Ingleses de Seuilla, a el padre Prouincial de la Compañia de Iesus de Mexico: en que se trata quien fue doña Luysa de Caruajal, su grande y rara santidad, el motiuo que tuuo para yr a Inglaterra, y el estado de aquel reyno. Fol. (a bifolium). [Coloph.] *Sacada por su original impressa en Seuilla, y en los Reyes con licencia por Francisco del Canto*, 1615. PA(Rés. 01.285/30).

1066.1 —[Anr. ed. of no. 1066.] Fol. (a bifolium.) *Sevilla, Diego Perez*, 1618. Not seen. Probably a reprint of the earlier Seville ed. from which no. 1066 was reprinted. Diego Gomez Flores, catalogue 54 (*Barcelona* 1987) no. 74.

Documents of 1615

1067 —Algunos auisos de Inglaterra de la persecucion grande que aora de nueuo ay en aquel reyno contra los Catolicos. Fol. (a bifolium). *Seuilla, por Alonso Rodriguez Gamarra*, 1615. L[11](SP. 14/80, f. 93). MD[2](4: Jes. 145/48 +*3 others*).SEV[2]. [*L.]

Extracts from three letters, two from England and one from Brussels, sent to the English College, Seville. The first letter from England is by an unnamed English priest, formerly a student of the College.

—Relacion del Martirio de Tomas Haso . . . Con otros auisos importantes, embiados por vn sacerdote del Seminario de Seuilla, 1615. *See* no. 624.

1068 —Luna, Martin de. Relacion verdadera, embiada al Seminario de Seuilla, por vn padre de la Compañia de Iesus q̃ esta preso en Inga- laterra, entre otros muchos sacerdotes: dase cuenta de la prision de diez y seis mil Christianos, y de los crueles martyrios que algunos han padecido por nuestra santa Fe Catolica . . . Compuesta por el Padre Martin de Luna, de la Casa Professa de Toledo, que aora vino de Ingalaterra. 4°. (a single quadrifolium). *Impresso en Cuenca, en casa de Saluador Viader, 1615.* MD. [*L.]

> A poem based on the documents printed in no. 1067 but treating the subject with much poetic licence. Martin de Luna may perhaps be a pseudonym.

1069 Ⓐ —[Anr. ed.?] Fol. 2 leaves. *Granada, Bartolomé de Lorençana, 1615.*

> Not found. Description from Uriarte 2891. The title is the same as in no. 1068 except that the words 'Compuesta por el Padre Martin de Luna . . .' [etc.] are omitted and the following are substituted: 'Vista y examinada por el Padre Geronimo de Tamayo de la Compania de Iesus'.

Documents of 1616

1070 —Peralta, F. de. Relacion que el P. Francisco de Peralta . . . Rector del Colegio de San Gregorio, de los Ingleses de Seuilla, escriuio a don Antonio Vigil de Quiñones y Pimentel, Conde de Luna y Mayorga. En que se da quenta del estado que oy tienen las cosas de la religion Catolica de Inglaterra, y la persecucion que padecen los catolicos. Y del martirio, que el mes de Março passado padecieron dos sacerdotes, y vn lego. 4°? *Seuilla, por Alonso Rodriguez Gamarra, 1616.* MD (varios 58–98). [*L.]

> The only copy known, which is in a very decayed state, consists of ff. [2] 1–14. The three martyrs referred to in the title were Thomas Atkinson, John Thules and Roger Wrenno.

Documents of 1623

1071 —Relacion de la venida en secreto y por la posta desde Londres a Madrid, del Principe don Carlos de Inglaterra . . . Embiada de Madrid al P. Rector del Colegio de Ingleses de Seuilla. Fol. (a bi- folium). *Lo imprimió en Seuilla Iuan Serrano de Vargas y Vreña, 1623.* SEV(63–7–14, no. 16). [*L.]

> For accounts of Prince Charles's journey to Madrid in 1623 appended to the proposed articles of marriage between Charles and the Infanta, *see* nos. 1562, *etc.* Other accounts, where there is no explicit reference to Catholics in England or to their institutions abroad, fall outside the scope of this catalogue.

Documents of 1626

—Noticias de Inglaterra y sobre el estado de los Catolicos, 1626. *See no.* 387.

Ⓐ —Verissima relacion en que se da quenta en el estado en que estan los 1071.1 Catolicos de Inglaterra, 1626. *See no.* 386.

APPENDIX

1072 —Copia de vna relacion hecha en el cabildo de la ciudad de Seuilla, que mãdo imprimir el Assistente della Don Bernardino Gonçales Del- gadillo de Avellaneda, sobre vn caso, si la ciudad tratando de su desempeño, y aviendo quitado para el mismo fin otras mercedes y limosnas podia continuar la que hazia al Seminario de los Ingleses. Con pareceres de theologos sobre el mismo caso. Fol. [Coloph.]

Sevilla, por Clemente Hidalgo, 1604. MD². (Jes. 14/7, no. 23, imp.). VT². (Arm. I, t. 15, ff. 1–14).

The question for the theologians was whether the 600 ducats which the city gave yearly to the College ought not rather to be used for the redemption of captives taken by the Moors. The balance of opinion was in favour of the College. For a plea by Joseph Creswell that the allowance to the College should continue, *see* no. 279.

1073 —Luque Fajardo, Francisco de. [Editor.] Relacion de la fiesta que se hizo en Seuilla a la beatificacion del glorioso S. Ignacio fundador de la Compañia de Iesus. 4°. *Seuilla, por Luis Estupiñan*, 1610. MD(2).SEV².

On 14 Jan. 1610 students of Jesuit universities in Spain took part in a verse competition, held at Seville, in honour of the beatification of Ignatius of Loyola. This volume, published to celebrate the occasion, includes a section (ff. 27ᵛ–48ʳ) giving the Latin prize poems submitted by ten students (named) of the English College at Seville. Gallardo 2854 prints the names of all the contestants.

1074 **Seville,** *Irish College*. Breue relacion de la presente persecucion de Irlanda. Contiene vna carta embiada de Irlanda por vna persona graue: y otra d'el Rey de Inglaterra, con dos editos de su Virrey contra los Catholicos. Dedicada a don Feliz de Guzman arcediano, y canonigo de la S. Iglesia de Seuilla . . . Por el Colegio de la Immaculada Concepcion de la Virgen Madre de Dios de Seuilla. 4°. *Seuilla, por Gabriel Ramos Vejarano*, 1619 DE.KNY(*archives*).MD².(9–3556, bis/6).RO⁹(Anglia 41, ff. 120–45).

A collection put together by priests of the Irish College, Seville. With the arms of Felix de Guzman printed on the titlepage. The KNY copy bears a contemporary MS note ascribing the authorship of the 'Carta embiada de Irlanda' to 'Fra Patricius ab Angelis [Patrick Comerford].' The 'Carta' is dated 31 Oct. 1618.

1075 —[*Latin version.*] Persecutio Hiberniae, [1619].

Not found. O'Reilly cites a copy at RO⁸ but it does not now appear to be there.

Shelley, *Sir* Richard. [*A work translated by him.*] Dudley, J., *Duke of Northumberland*. Ioannis Dudlaei . . . ad populum Londinensem concio, 1570. *See* no. 331.

1076 **Shepreve, William.** Conexio literalis Psalmorum, in officio B. Mariae Virg. et corroboratio ex variis linguis . . . vna cum mysticis sensibus elaborata per Gulielmum Scepreum. 4°. *Romae, apud Aloysium Zannettum*, 1596. O.; BG.BG².C³.D.FLO.MD.NP.PA.PA⁴.RO⁶.TOU.VT.

1077 **Sherlock, Paul.**‡ Anteloquia in Salomonis canticorum canticum, ethica pariter, & historica. Opus, in quo memoranda plurima de vtroque, sacro, & profano, Sponso . . . integro subiiciuntur examini. Fol. *Lugduni, sumptibus Iacobi Cardon*, 1633. C.; D⁶.FLO³.L⁴.LYN.PA.PA⁴. SCG.VT.WO.

This is vol. 1 of a work in three volumes; for vol. 2, *see* nos. 1081, *etc.*; for vol. 3, *see* no. 1085. The title is printed within an elaborate engraved frame.

1078 —[Anr. ed. of vol. 1.] Fol. *Venetiis, ex typographia Ducali Pinelliano*, 1639. L.; LOU³.VI.

1079 —[Imprint variant.] *Venetiis, apud Franciscum Babam*, 1639. BG.

Forming part of a shared edition with no. 1078.

1080 —[Anr. ed. of vol. 1, with title:] Anteloquia cogitationum in Salomonis canticorum canticum, historica simul & concionatoria. Volumen primum . . . Hac secunda editione insigni auctuario nobilitata. Fol. *Lugduni, sumpt. Iacobi & Petr. Prost*, 1640. BOR.D.F.GTN.MD.MIL². MTH.OR.PA.RO⁵.STI.UT.

The second Lyon edition. The title is printed within an elaborate engraved frame.

1081 —[Vol. 2, with title:] Cogitationes in Salomonis canticorum canticum, ex triplici vestigatione: humana, sacra, didactica. Volumen secundum. Fol. *Lugduni, sumptib. Iacobi Prost*, 1637. O.; BOR.C⁵.D(2).D⁶.F.FLO.LC. LOU³.MD.VT.WO.
The titlepage is engraved.

1082 —[Anr. ed. of vol. 2.] Fol. *Venetiis, ex typographia Ducali Pinelliana*, 1639. L.; LOU³.

1083 —[Imprint variant.] *Venetiis, apud Franciscum Babam*, 1639. BG.VI².
Forming part of a shared edition with no. 1082.

1084 —[Anr. ed. of vol. 2.] Fol. *Lugduni, sumpt. Iacobi & Petr. Prost*, 1640. BOR.F.FLO.RO⁵.

1085 —[Vol. 3.] Cogitationes in Salomonis canticorum canticum . . . Volumen tertium. Fol. *Lugduni, sumpt. Iacobi & Petri Prost*, 1640. O(2).; D.D⁶. F.FLO.LOU³.MD.MTH.OR.RO⁵.STI.
The title is printed within an elaborate engraved frame.

Simeon, Joseph, *alias. See* no. 947.

1086 **Singleton, William.** Discussio decreti magni Concilii Lateranensis, et quarundam rationum annexarum, de potestate Ecclesiae in temporalibus; & incommoda diuersae sententiae, Authore Guilhelmo Singletono. 8°. *Moguntiae, ex officina Ioannis Albini*, 1613. L.O(3).; D.D².L⁴.L¹³.LOU³.LYN.PA⁴.PR.ST.TRO.WO(2).YK.VT.
Sometimes erroneously attributed to Leonardus Lessius. For the background, and Singleton's own statement that he was the author, *see* RH, Oct. 1979, pp. 114–15. Answered by no. 925.5.

Sion Convent. *See* Lisbon, *English Bridgettine Convent.*

Sirenus, Thomas. Theses ex vniuersa theologia, 1639. *See* no. 254.

Sisburno, Nicolas. *See* Tichborne, N.

Smith, Nicholas, *pseud. See* Wilson, M. (nos. 1400–04.)

Smith, Ralph, *alias. See* Babthorpe, R.

Smith, Richard,†‡ *Bishop of Chalcedon.*

Single Works

1087 —Apologia Iesuitarum Anglorum pro Rmo Episcopo Chalcedonensi, ejusque authoritate episcopali super Catholicos laicos in Anglia tempore persecutionis. 8° (in fours). *n.p.*, 1631. L(2: 1 -t.p.).O.; F.O¹⁰. PA.PA³(2).USH(3).W.
Anon. For [Smith's] authorship *see* RH, Oct. 1982, p. 145. A MS note by M. A. Tierney in one USH copy refers to a contemporary MS of an English translation of this work corrected and interlined in Smith's own hand. *Pr.* [Paris, at the press of Jérome Blageart.]

1088 —Breuis et necessaria declaratio juris episcopalis, quod R. mus Episcopus Chalcedonensis habet super Catholicos in Anglia. 8° (in fours). *Coloniae*, 1631. L(2).O.C.; PA.PA³.USH.
Anon. For [Smith's] authorship *see* RH, Oct. 1982, p. 144. Imprint false; *pr.* [Paris, at the press of Jérome Blageart.] An English version, apparently not now extant, was printed at Douai in 1631. Answered in no. 490. For declarations by groups of English Catholics concerning Smith's authority, *see* nos. 358–62.

1089 —Collatio doctrinae Catholicorum ac Protestantium cum expressis S. Scripturae verbis. 4°. *Parisiis, ex typographia Ioannis Laquehay*, 1621. L.C.; AMP.DUR.HP.L⁹.P.USH.WOR.
An English translation was published at Douai in 1631 (A&R 774).

1090 —[Date variant.] 1622. O.; AUG.BOR.C².D².DAI.DE.E.FU².HP.KNY.L⁴.L²⁵.PA⁶. (*imp.*).ST.TRO. +

1091   —[Anr. issue, with a cancel titleleaf.] 4°. *Parisiis, apud Melchiorem Mondiere*, 1624. O.C.

1092   —De auctore et essentia Protestanticae ecclesiae et religionis. 8°. *Parisiis, apud Mathurinum Mauperlier*, 1619. L.O.C.; AMP.AUG.C².CHA. DE.HP.KNY.L².OS.PA.PA⁶.ST.USH. + +
       An English translation was published in 1621 (A&R 776).

1093   —Duplicatio aduersus nuperrimam replicam T. Mortoni, pro defensione suae pseudo-catholicae Apologiae. Auctore C.R. Theologo. 8°. *Coloniae*, 1638. O.; BOR.C².CSL.DUR.PA.PA⁶(4).ST(2).USH.
       C.R. Theologus [R. Smith]. Answers Thomas Morton's *Replica*, 1638 (STC 18193) which was itself an answer to no. 1097. Imprint false; *pr.* [Paris, at the press of Jérome Blageart.]

1094   —Epistola historica de mutuis officiis inter Sedem Apostolicam & Magnae Britanniae reges Christianos, Anglice olim scripta, ad Seren. M. Britanniae Regem Iacobum. Per Richardum Smitheum, nunc Episcopum Chalcedonensem. Latine versa per Richardum Lascelles. 12°. *Coloniae*, 1637. DUR.O¹⁸.PA.PA³.RO⁶.VT.
       A translation of an address written by Smith in English and presented by him to James I at the beginning of his reign. The English original would appear to have been printed c. 1603–4, but no copy has been found. For the background *see* Chaney, pp. 29–31. Imprint false; *pr.* [Paris, at the press of Jérome Blageart.] The Latin was reprinted in Smith's *Florum historiae ecclesiasticae gentis Anglorum libri septem*, 1654. An English version, calling itself the third edition, was printed in 1652 (Clancy 911, copies at D. & PA.).

1095   —Manifestatio circa Declarationem Iesuitarum Anglorum, falso editam sub nomine laicorum Catholicorum Angliae aduersus authoritatem, quam Rmus D. Episcopus Chalcedonensis in eosdem vendicat. Authore Gulielmo Priceo. 8° (in fours). *Coloniae*, 1631. O.; PA.PA³(2). USH.W.
       Gulielmus Priceus, *pseud.* For [Smith's] authorship, *see* RH, Oct. 1982, p. 145. Answering no. 358. Imprint false; *pr.* [Paris, at the press of Jérome Blageart].

1096   —Monita quaedam vtilia pro sacerdotibus, seminaristis praesertim, quando primum veniunt in Angliam. 12°. *Duaci, typis Baltazaris Belleri*, 1630. USH.
       A spiritual guide for priests coming on the English mission. New editions were published in 1647, 1695, 1741.

1097   —Refutatio Apologiae pseudocatholicae Thomae Mortoni. Pars prima, in qua refutantur quadraginta nouem priora capita suae Apologiae ... Auctore ... C.R. Theologo. 8°. *Coloniae*, 1638. O.C.; C².CARL.HP. O².PA.USH.
       C.R. Theologus [R. Smith]. Morton's *Apologia* to which this is a reply was originally printed in 1605 (STC 18173.5). It is possible that Smith was provoked into answering it so long after its first appearance by a more recent edition which has not survived. Imprint false; *pr.* [Paris, at the press of Jérome Blageart.] Answered by Morton in his *Replica*, 1638 (STC 18193) to which Smith, in turn, replied in no. 1093.

1098   —Vita illustrissimae, ac piissimae dominae Magdalenae Montis-acuti in Anglia vicecomitissae: scripta per Richardum Smitheum ... qui illi erat a sacris confessionibus. 8°. *Romae, apud Iacobum Mascardum*, 1609. L(2).; C⁵.CHA.DE.FLO³,MU(2).OS.PA.PA³.RO²(2).RO⁵.STG.W.
       Smith had been chaplain to Lady Montague (d. 1608) at Battle Abbey. Dedicated to Odoardo Farnese, Cardinal Protector of England, whose arms are printed on the titlepage. An English translation was published in 1627 (A&R 775).

1099   —[*German transl..*] Frawenzimmer Spiegel, das ist: das Leben der Hoch vnnd Wolgebornen, auch Gottsfoerchtigen Frawen, Frawen

Magdalena, Marggraefin zu Scharpffenberg in Engellandt ... in Lateinischer Sprach beschriben, vnd jetzo ... auff vnser Teutsche Sprach vbersetzt. 8°. *Augspurg, bey Chrysostomo Dabertzhofer, n.d.* [1611.] L.; FR.MU.PR³.VI. [*O.]

The dedication is dated from Augsburg, 'Am Tag Maria Geburt' 1611, and signed: Chrysostomus Dabertzhofer. Scharpffenberg is a rendering of the Latin Mons acutus.

1100 —[*A different German transl.*] Gottseligs Leben, der Hochwolgebornen Frawen, Frawen Magdalena, Graefin zu Scharpfenberg, in Engelland ... Auss dem Lateinischen Exemplar, so zu Rom gedruckt worden, in die Teutsche Sprach gebracht. 8°. *Augspurg, bey Sara Maengin wittib.* 1619. MU(2). [*O.]

The dedication is dated 4 Oct. 1619 and signed: C.H.C.B.V.A.P.

Appendix

1101 —Bref narré de ce qui s'est passé ensuite du different meu entre l'Euesque de Chalcedoine, delegué du Pape aux Royaumes d'Angleterre & d'Escosse, & les Iesuites Anglois. 8° (in fours). *n.p.d.* [1633.] L.O.; PA(3).PA³(2).PA⁴.USH.

The author has not been identified but would seem from the text to have been a foreigner. The last date mentioned in the text is 1633. *Pr.* [Paris.]

1102 —Disquisitio decreti Sacrae Congregationis ... Cardinalium ... ad Indicem Librorum ... specialiter deputatorum, d. XIX Martii M.DCXXXIII. Ad Eminentissimos et Reuerendiss. Cardinales ipsi Sacrae Congregationi praefectos ac deputatos. 8°. *n.p.*, 1633. PA. PA³(2).

A protest on behalf of the Bishop of Chalcedon against the decree of the Index of 19 March 1633 forbidding the publication by either side of any further works in his controversy with the Jesuits (*see* no. 1103). Reprinting the text of the decree. *Pr.* [Paris.] Answered by [John Floyd] in nos. 485–6. No. 486 reprints the text of the *Disquisitio.*

—Rationes reditae, pro impressione librorum in causa sacerdotum Anglorum, [1631]. Upholding the right of the seculars to defend the Bishop of Chalcedon against the Jesuits. *See* no. 396.

1103 —Rome, *Congregation of the Index.* Decretum Sac. Congregationis ... Cardinalium ... ad Indicem Librorum ... specialiter deputatorum ... [*Text begins:*] Cum inter Chalcedonensem Episcopum, & Regulares Anglię postremis hisce annis nonnullae controuersiae ortae sint ... *s.sh.*fol. *Romae, ex typographia Reu. Camerae Apostolicae,* 1633. BRS⁴(Arch. Jes. Prov. Gallo-Belg. Coll. de S. Omer, Carton 31, unnumbered.) [*L.]

The decree is dated, Rome, 19 March 1633. It refers back to the Brief *Britannia* of Urban VIII, dated 9 May 1631, and reaffirms the Pope's prohibition against publishing any further works in the controversy. For a protest against the decree, *see* no. 1102; for a defence of it, *see* nos. 485–6; both the protest and the defence reprint the text. The text was again reprinted in 1642 (copies at L.; DAI—Weldon IV, p. 201).

—Urban VIII, *Pope.* [For the Brief *Britannia* of 9 May 1631 in which the Pope sought to end the controversy over Smith's authority.] *See* no. 41.

1104 —Urban VIII, *Pope.* Exemplar Breuis Sanctiss. D. N. Vrbani PP. VIII. Per quod episcopalis authoritas Chalcedonensi Episcopo demandatur. 4° (a single quadrifolium). *n.p.d.* [1631.] L(2).O.C.; D(2). DUR(2).L²⁷ᴬ(A17 no. 18).PA³.PA⁴.PA⁸.YK.

The Brief *Ecclesia Romana sollicita* of 4 Feb. 1625 granting faculties to Smith on his appointment as bishop for England in succession to William Bishop. Published by Smith after his withdrawal to Paris in 1631. *Pr.* [Paris, for Charles Morel.] Usually found bound after no. 684 which was printed for Morel at Paris in 1631.

1105 **Smith, Richard,** *Dean of St Peter's, Douai.* Confutatio eorum quae Philippus Melancthon obijcit contra Missae sacrificium propitiatorium. Cui accessit & repulsio calumniarum Ioannis Caluini, & Musculi, contra Missam, & Purgatorium. 8°. *Louanii, apud Ioannem Bogardum,* 1562. [Coloph.] *Typis Stephani Valerii.* O.; AUG.BRU.F.GT.LGE³.PA⁶.
Mainly an answer to Melanchthon's *Iudicium . . . de controuersia Coenae Domini,* 1560. Collation: A–D⁸.

1106 —[Anr. ed.] 16°. *Parisiis, apud Michaelem Iulianum, n.d.* [1562.] L.; PA.R.
Collation: A–E⁸F².

[1107] —[Anr. ed., enlarged.] Confutatio eorum quae Philippus Melanchthon obiicit contra Missae sacrificium propitiatorium . . . Cui accessit & repulsio calumniarum Ioannis Caluini, & Musculi, & Ioannis Iuelli, contra Missam, eius canonem, & Purgatorium, denuo excusa. 8°. *Louanii, apud Ioannem Bogardum,* 1562. [Coloph.] *Typis Stephani Valerii.*
This is part 2 of no. 1114 but may also have been issued separately. Collation: a–h⁸.

1108 —Defensio compendiaria, et orthodoxa, sacri, externi et visibilis Iesu Christi sacerdotii. Cui addita est sacratorum Catholicae Ecclesiae altariũ propugnatio, ac Caluinianae communionis succincta refutatio. 8°. *Louanii, apud Ioannem Bogardum,* 1562. L.O(2).C(2).; AUG(3).BRS.CHA.D(2).E.E².GT.KN².L².LOU³(2).PA⁴.PA⁶(2).RO⁵. +

1109 —De infantium baptismo, contra Ioannem Caluinum, ac de operibus supererogationis, & merito mortis Christi, aduersus eundem Caluinum, & eius discipulos. 8°. *Louanii, apud Ioannem Bogardum,* 1562. L(2).O(2).C(2).; AUG(2).BRS.CHA.D(2).E.E².GT.L²(2).LOU³(2).MU.PA.PA⁶.WO. + +

1110 —[Anr. ed.] 8°. *Coloniae, excudebat Godefridus Ceruicornus, & Theodorus Baum,* 1563. L.; FLO³.HA.MU.STU.X.

1111 —De libero hominis arbitrio aduersus Ioannem Caluinum, & quotquot impie illud auferunt, Lutherum imitati. 8°. *Louanii, ex officina Ioannis Bogardi,* 1563. L.O.; AMI.AUG(2).D.DI.E².GT.HA.KN.L².L⁴.MU.PA.TRI.U.

1112 —De Missae sacrificio, succincta quaedam enarratio. 8°. *Louanii, apud Ioannem Bogardum,* 1562. AUG.BRU.D.DMR.GT.LGE³.PA⁶.
Collation: A–D⁸E². In this edition the title ends at the word 'enarratio'.

1113 —[Anr. ed.] 16°. *Parisiis, apud Michaelem Iulianum,* 1562. L.; PA.
Collation: A–H⁸I⁴. Title as in no. 1112.

1114 —[Anr. ed., revised, with anr. ed. of no. 1105.] De Missae sacrificio, succincta quaedam enarratio, ac breuis repulsio praecipuorum argumentorum, quae Philippus Melanchthon, Ioannes Caluinus, & alii sectarii obiecerunt aduersus illud, & Purgatoriũ. 8°. 2 pts. *Louanii, apud Ioannem Bogardum,* 1562. [Coloph.] *Typis Stephani Valerii.* L.O.C.; AUG(2).C⁴.D.E.EI.L².L⁴.L³⁵.LIL³.LOU³.PA.PA⁶.RO⁵.YK. *Pt. 2 only:* O(1 copy); C(1 copy); D(1 copy).DE.LOU³(1 copy).
Collation: (pt. 1) A–G⁸ (G7, 8 blank). (pt. 2) a–h⁸. Pt. 2, which has its own titlepage, may also have been issued separately. *See* no. [1107].

1115 —Refutatio locorum communium theologicorum, Philippi Melanchthonis, Germani, M. Lutheri discipuli primarii, dedicata principum illustrissimo, ac catholicissimo Philippo, Regi Hispaniarum, &c. 8°. *Duaci, typis Iacobi Boscardi*, 1563. [Coloph.] *Duaci, typis Iacobi Boschaert*. L.C.; ANT².BOR.C¹⁸.D.DI.DMR.DOU.FU.L⁴.LEM.PA.⁷WO. *This or no. 1116, 1117, 1118* : GTN.TB.

1116 —[Anr. state.] A printed slip of one line, bearing the words: *Prostant apud Nicolaum Lapidanum* has been pasted over the line reading *Typis Iacobi Boscardi, Typographi iurati* of the original imprint. O.C.; AUG.CHI.GT.IO.MU.PR.U.

1117 —[Anr. state.] The pasteover slip of no. 1116 has been replaced by one reading: *Prostant apud Iacobum Doff.* ABV.D.PA.

1118 —[Anr. state.] A printed slip of three lines, bearing the words: *Prostant apud Nicolaum Lapidanum/Typis Iacobi Boscardi. Cum Gra. & Pri. R.M./Duaci*, has been pasted over the whole of the original imprint. A copy of this was seen by the editors but its location is not now known.

—[*A work doubtfully attributed to Smith.*] Religionis et regis aduersus exitiosas Caluini, Bezae & Ottomani coniuratorum factiones defensio prima, 1562 [*etc.*] This anonymous tract, of which editions appeared at Paris and Cologne in 1562 and at Venice in 1563, is sometimes found entered under Smith in library catalogues. There appears to be no sound evidence to support the attribution.

Smith, Rodolphus, *alias. See* Babthorpe, R.

Smythaeus, Richardus. *See* Smith, R.

1119 **Southwell, Henry.** I diuini sepolcri e pie lagrime idilii di Henrico Southuel canonico di S. Marco all'illustrissima & eccell. Signora Elisabetta Dudley Southuel Contessa di Waruick & Leicester dedicati. 12°. *Venetia, appresso Antonio Pinelli, n.d.* [1620]. DMR(-*tp*.).VCE².

Poems, mainly religious. *Ded.* dated from Venice, 19 Nov. 1620. For Elizabeth Southwell and her relationship with Sir Robert Dudley, styled Earl of Warwick (1574–1649), *see* his entry in DNB. and *Complete Peerage*, vol. 9, pp. 726–7.

1120 **Southwell, Robert,** *Saint.*† Corten reghel van een goedt leuen. Door P. Robertus Southwellus, verduytsch door P. Iacobus de Villegas, beyde priesters der Societeyt Iesu. 12°. *t'Antwerpen, by Jan Cnobbaert, by het Professenhuys der Societeyt Iesu, in S. Peeter*, 1625. LW. [*L.]

A translation into Flemish of *A Short Rule of Good Life* (A&R 787–91). With a foreword to the reader, signed by the translator, Jacobus de Villegas, and dated from Antwerp, 3 March 1625. Villegas belonged to the Flandro-Belgic Province S.J.; Sommer-vogel's reference (tom. 7, col. 410) to a Spanish translation by a Jesuit of this name appears to be a false inference.

1121 —[Anr. ed.] 12°. *t'Antwerpen, by Jan Cnobbaert, by het Professen-huys de Societeyt Iesu, in S. Peter*, 1626. LW. [*L.]

A reprint of no. 1120.

Southwell, Thomas, *alias. See* Bacon, T.

Sprat, N. *See* Sprott, Thomas.

Sprott, *alias* Sprat, Thomas. *Bl.* Relacion de martirio . . . de N. Sprat [i.e. T. Sprott], 1600. *See* no. 91.

Stafford, Ignatius, *alias. See* Badduley, R.

Stanihurst, Richard. Breuis praemunitio pro futura concertatione cum Iacobo Vsserio. *See* no. 1126.

—De rebus in Hibernia gestis. *See* no. 1127.

1122 —De vita S. Patricii, Hiberniae apostoli, libri II. Nunc primum in lucem editi. 8°. *Antuerpiae, ex officina Christophori Plantini*, 1587. L(2).C(2: 1 *imp.*).; ANT².C⁵.C¹⁷.D⁶.D⁷.D¹⁰.DUR.F.MD.PA.RO⁵.SAL.VI.

1123 —Hebdomada eucharistica ex sacris litteris atque orthodoxis Catholicae Romanae Ecclesiae patribus collecta. 12°. *Duaci, ex officina Baltazaris Belleri*, 1614. L.O.; AAR.D.GN.RO⁶.

1124   —Hebdomada Mariana, ex orthodoxis Catholicę Romanę Ecclesiae patribus collecta: in memoriam septem festorum Beatissimae Virginis Mariae, per singulos dies hebdomadae distributa. 12°. (in eights). *Antuerpiae, ex officina Plantiniana, apud Ioannem Moretum*, 1609. L.O.C.; AMI.ANT².ANT³.BRS².D.D¹⁰.L⁴.L²⁶.MD.NP.RO⁶.TNI.UT².

     Some copies (e.g. L.BRS².RO⁶.) have a metal engraving on the title-page and seven full-page engravings in the text; in some (e.g. NP.) these engravings are replaced by woodcuts; in some others (e.g. O.) the titlepage illustration is a woodcut but the seven illustrations in the text are engraved. Fine paper copies have the engravings in metal, the others have woodcuts.

1125   —Psalmi, litaniae, et orationes, quae coram Augustissima Eucharistia perapposite recitari possunt. Tertia editio, castigatior & auctior. 32°. *Antuerpiae, apud Ioannem Moretum*, 1598. DAI(*imp.*).

     Imprimatur dated from Antwerp, 'Nonis Septembr. 1597'. The first and second editions have not been found.

1126   —Richardi Stanihursti ... Breuis praemunitio pro futura concertatione cum Iacobo Vsserio ... qui in sua historica explicatione conatur probare, Pontificem Romanum ... verum & germanum esse Antichristum. 8°. *Duaci, ex typographia Baltazaris Belleri*, 1615. L.O(2). C.; BRS².D.D¹⁰.L².L¹³.O¹⁸.PA⁴.

     Answers STC 24551. See Mil., vol. 2, pp. 175–6.

1127   —Richardi Stanihursti ... De rebus in Hibernia gestis, libri quattuor ... Accessit ... Appendix, ex Siluestro Giraldo Cambrensi ... collecta; cum eiusdem Stanihursti adnotationibus. 4°. *Antuerpiae, apud Christophorum Plantinum*, 1584. L(3).O(3).C(3).; A.ANT².BRS.C². D(4).DAI.E(2).GT.L².LOU³.PA.PA⁴.ST(2).USH.WO. + +

     This work was criticised by Stephen White S.J. in an unpublished MS entitled: *Apologia pro innocentibus Ibernis olim temere traductis per Ricardum Stanihurstum* (Poitiers MS 260).

1128   —[Imprint variant.] *Lugduni Batauorum, ex officina Christophori Plantini* 1584. O.C.; BOU.C².DE.DUR.F.MD.SAL.VI.

1128.1 **Stapleton, Theobald.** Catechismus, seu doctrina Christiana, Latino-Hibernica, per modum dialogi, inter magistrum et discipulum ... apposita est methodus facilis legendi linguam Hibernicam, cum charactere Romano. Catechismus. Adhon, an Teagasc Criostuí ... Agus deis an chlair modh vras leighte na teangan Ghaoilaige à leitreacha Romhanacha. 4°. *Bruxellis, typis Huberti Anthonii Velpii*, 1639. L(2).O(2).; D.D⁸.DE.KNY.N.O¹⁷.TALL.

     The text has Latin and Irish in parallel columns. A&R 795. STC 23230.5. ERL 387.

Stapleton, Thomas.†

COLLECTED WORKS

1129   —Thomae Stapletoni ... opera quae extant omnia ... in quatuor tomos distributa ... Tomus primus (- quartus). Fol. 4 tom. *Lutetiae Parisiorum*, 1620. [Coloph.] *Sumptibus Roberti Fouet, Nicolai Buon, Sebastiani Cramoisy*. L.O.C(2).; A.C².D.DUR.E.E².GTN.HA.HP.L².LOU³.MD. MU.PA.RO¹⁰.ST.USH. + +

     Edited by [William Rayner] and other English priests at Arras College, Paris, which subsidised the publication. See RH, May 1982, p. 41, n. 81.

SINGLE WORKS

(Except *Promptuarium Catholicum*
and *Promptuarium Morale*
for which *see* nos. 1167–1209, 1210–43)

An Politici horum temporum in numero
Christianorum sint habendi

1130 —An politici horum temporum in numero Christianorum sint habendi. Oratio academica. 12°. *n.p.*, 1602. ANT².ANT³.C².DI.DOE.GTN.HP.PA. PEN.PR².SBG.STG.VI.WO.
Pr. [in Germany.]

1131 —[Anr. ed.] 12°. *n.p.*, 1606. PR².
Pr. [in Germany.]

1132 —[Anr. ed., with title:] Oratio academica. An politici horum temporum in numero Christianorum sint habendi. 4°. *Impressum Monachii*, 1607. DUR.MU(5).TB.

1133 —[Anr. ed.] 4°. *Primo impressa Monachii*, 1608. L.O.; DUR.F.HD.HEI. MU(3).OR.P.PR².STG.ULM.VI.WO(4).
A reprint of no. 1132 but from a different press. The typography suggests that it may have been printed considerably later than 1608.

Antidota Apostolica

1134 —[Tom. 1.] Antidota apostolica contra nostri temporis haereses . . . In Acta Apostolorum: to. primus. 8°. *Antuerpiae, apud Ioannem Keerbergium*, 1595. L(-*port*).C.; AMS.AUG(2).BM².C⁹.D.DE.DMR.L¹³.LOU³(2). MU.OS.PA.ST.USH. + +
Titlepage engraved. With an engraved portrait of Pope Clement VIII.

1135 —[Tom. 2.] Antidota apostolica contra nostri temporis haereses . . . In Epistolam B. Pauli ad Romanos: tomus II. 8°. *Antuerpiae, apud Ioannem Keerbergium*, 1595. C.; AMS.BM².C⁹.D.FU².L².LOU³(2).MU.OS. PA.PA⁴.ST.STG.W. +

1136 —[Tom. 1 & 2.] Antidota apostolica contra nostri temporis haereses . . . In Acta Apostolorum, inque Epistolam Diui Pauli ad Romanos. 8°. *Lugduni, sumptibus Ioannis Baptistae Buysson*, 1596. L.O.; BAR³.BOR. C¹².CHA.DE.DI.HP.L⁹.LYN.MTH.OS.PA.RO¹⁰.TRO. + +

1137 —[Anr. ed. of no. 1136.] 8°. *Lugduni, sumptibus Ioannis Baptistae Buysson*, 1599.
Not found. Description from Baudrier, vol. 5, p. 134.

1138 —[Tom. 3.] Antidota apostolica contra nostri temporis haereses. In duas B. Pauli Epistolas ad Corinth. Tomus III. 8°. 2 pts. *Antuerpiae, apud Ioannem Keerbergium*, 1598. C.; AMS.ANT²(pt. 2).D(2).L².MU.PA. PA⁴.PR.SOL.ST.STG.VAL².VI.VT. +
Pt. 2 has its own titlepage reading *Antidota apostolica . . . tomi tertii pars altera.*

Antidota Evangelica

1139 —Antidota euangelica contra horum temporum haereses. In quibus quatuor Euangeliorum, quibus vel haeretici hodie (maxime Caluinus & Beza) ad sua dogmata propugnanda vti solent, vel ad haereticorum dogmata impugnanda Catholici vti possunt. 8°. 2 vols. *Antuerpiae, Ioannem Keerbergium*, 1595. L(vol. 2); AMP.AUG(2).BRN.DMR.FLO³.FR. FU(2).GT.HP.L¹³.LOU³.MU.OS.SAL.SOL.W. +
Titlepage engraved.

1140 —[Anr. ed.] 8°. 2 vols. *Lugduni, sumptibus Claudii Chapellet bibliopolae Parisiensis*, 1595. [Coloph.] *Ex typographia haeredum Petri Roussin*. A.AV.BOR.C¹².CHA.DE.HP.KYN.LYN.MD.MTH.OS.PA.PA⁴.TB.USH. +

Apologia pro Rege Catholico

1141 —Apologia pro Rege Catholico Philippo II. Hispaniae, & caet. Rege. Contra varias & falsas accusationes Elisabethae Angliae Reginae. Per edictum suum 18. Octobris Richemondiae datum, & 20. Nouembris Londini proclamatum, publicatas & excusas ... Authore Didymo Veridico Henfildano. 8°. *Constantiae, apud Theodorum Samium, n.d.* [1592.] L.O.C.; AB.AIX.D.DE.DUR(2).F.GT(3).HA.L²⁵.L²⁶.LIL.PA.PA²(2). + Didymus Veridicus Henfildanus, *pseud.* Imprint false; *pr.* [Antwerp?] Answering Elizabeth's proclamation *A declaration of the great troubles* of 18 Oct. 1591 (STC 8207). Dated at the end: March 1592. Some copies have an inserted bifolium in quire F, containing the text of a letter to Elizabeth from the Sultan of Turkey. For the controversy of which this work forms part, *see* Mil. vol. 1, pp. 113–14.

> *Authoritatis Ecclesiasticae circa*
> *S. Scripturarum Approbationem*
> *... Defensio*

1142   —Authoritatis ecclesiasticae circa S. Scripturarum approbationem, adeoque in vniuersum, luculenta & accurata defensio libris III. digesta. Contra disputationem de Scriptura Sacra Guilielmi Whitakeri. 8°. *Antuerpiae, apud Ioannem Keerbergium,* 1592. L.; AMP.AMS.AUG.C⁹.DE. DI.LOU³(2).MD.MU.OS.PA.PA⁴.RO.USH. + +
Answers STC 25366. Whitaker replied in STC 25363 to which Stapleton replied in pt. 2 of no. 1154. *See* Mil., vol. 1, pp. 149–50.

> *Laudatio in Funere Francisci Richardot*

1143   —Laudatio in funere Francisci Richardot. 8°. *Atrebati,* 1598.
Not found. Cited by Le Long (*Bibl. historique,* 1719, no. 3342) who also cites the reprint in the 1620 *Opera omnia* of Stapleton (no. 1129). It was also reprinted in vol. 2 of *Orationes academicae,* 1600 (no. 1147), and in the 1608 Douai edition of Richardot's *Orationes.*

> *Manuale Peccatorum*

1144   —Manuale peccatorum, siue de septem capitalibus peccatis orationes catecheticae duodecim. 8°. *Antuerpiae, apud Ioannem Keerbergium,* 1598. L.; AMS.ANT.D.DI.FU².GT.HP.L².L¹³.MD.OS.PA.ST.TRI. + +
1145   —[Anr. ed.] 8°. *Lugduni, apud Horatium Cardon,* 1599. [Coloph.] *Ex typographia Iacobi Roussin.* CHA.HP.MD.O⁷.OS.PA.PA⁴.RO.SBG.ST.TDO.ZA.
1146   —[*An extract.*] Oratio catechetica praeclarissima de luxuriae fuga, & remediis contra eam. 4°. *Napoli, per Gio Giacomo Carlino, e Constantino Vitale,* 1608. RO².
This is Oratio catechetica 9 in the *Manuale peccatorum.*

> *Oratio academica. An politici*
> *horum temporum ...*

—*See* no. 1132.

> *Oratio Catechetica ... de*
> *Luxuriae Fuga*

—*See* no. 1146.

> *Orationes Academicae*

1147   —Orationes academicae, miscellaneae triginta quatuor. 8°. 2 vols. *Antuerpiae, apud Ioannem Keerbergium,* 1600. BM².BOR.BRU.CHA.D.DE. DI.GTN.HP(*imp.*).L².LOU³(2).MU.P(vol. 1).PA⁴.USH.W. + +
Edited by Thomas Worthington.

Orationes Sex

1148 —Orationes sex, tres funebres, dogmaticae tres: his temporibus apprime vtiles, et necessariae. 8°. *Antuerpiae, apud Iohannem Foulerum Anglum*, 1576. [Coloph.] *Excudebat vidua Ludouici de Winde, cura & impensa Iohan. Fouleri.* O.C.; AMS.ANT².C¹⁰.DE.DI.E.HP.LGE³.MU.PA⁴(2). PBN.STG.VI. +
Pr. [Douai.]

Orationes Theologicae

1149 —Orationes theologicae celebriores, in funere diuersorum praesulum, et aliae miscellaneae. 8°. *Duaci, ex officina typographica Balthazaris Belleri*, 1603. BOR.DOU.HEI.LGE³.MU.PA.TB.VI.

Principiorum Fidei Doctrinalium Demonstratio

1150 —Principiorum fidei doctrinalium demonstratio methodica per controuersias septem in libris duodecim tradita. Fol. *Parisiis, apud Michaelem Sonnium*, 1578. BM².C².C⁹.DI.FLO³.L²⁶.LEM.MU.O⁵.OR.P. PR.VI.
In Bk. 4, ch. 10, 11 of this work Stapleton answers W. Fulke's *Two treatises*, 1577 (STC 11458). Fulke published a *Responsio* in 1579 (STC 11418) to which Stapleton replied in no. 1157, the text of which also formed Bk. 13 of the present work added in the 1581 edition (no. 1152). *See* Mil., vol. 1, pp. 148–9.

1151 —[Date variant.] 1579. O.; AV.BER.C⁵.DAI.FR.HP.KN².MD.MU(2).N.PA⁵.RO¹¹. ST.STG. +

1152 —[Anr. ed., with additions.] Editio altera ab Authore recognita ... cui etiam accesserunt, Successionis Ecclesiasticae defensio accuratior ... Contra Gulielmi Fulconis Angli inanes cauillationes aduersus huius operis lib. 4 capita 10. & 11. editas. Liber decimus tertius & Speculum prauitatis haereticae per orationes decem ad oculos demonstratae: item aliae orationes tres funebres. Fol. *Parisiis, apud Michaelem Sonnium*, 1581. ANG.C³.C¹⁹.CMR.LEM.MD³.MST.MU.NA.PR.
See note to no. 1150. *Speculum prauitatis* had appeared separately in 1580 (no. 1156).

1153 —[Date variant.] 1582. L.; BOR.BRG.C¹⁵.CHA.CMR.D.LYN.MTH.MU.NCY. PA⁴.RO.TRO.WOR. +

Principiorum Fidei Doctrinalium Relectio

1154 —Principiorum fidei doctrinalium relectio scholastica & compendiaria. Per controuersias, quaestiones et articulos tradita. Accessit per modum Appendicis Triplicatio inchoata aduersus Gulielmum Whitakerum Anglocaluinistam pro authoritate Ecclesiae. 4°. 2 pts. *Antuerpiae, apud Ioannem Keerbergium*, 1596. L.O.C.; ANT².BRS.D.DE.GTN.HP.L².LOU³(2). MD.MU.OS.PA.RO⁵.W. + +
. The general titlepage is engraved; pt. 2, the 'Triplicatio' has its own, printed titlepage. Pt. 2 answers STC 25363 which was itself a reply to no. 1142. Pt. 2 is sometimes found on its own and may have been issued thus.

Propugnaculum Fidei

1155 —Propugnaculum fidei primitiuae Anglorum, quo fides illa, quae Anglis, ante mille annos per S. Augustinum tradita fuit, & quae tunc temporis ac deinceps per vniuersam Christi Ecclesiam semper viguit, quam nunc Protestantes Papisticam vocant, orthodoxam esse, vereq;

Christianam, asseritur & probatur ... Nunc primum Latine editum interprete Guilielmo Rainerio. Fol. *Lutetiae Parisiorum, apud Robertum Fouet Nicolaum Buon Sebastianum Cramoisy,* 1619. ANG.LOU. A translation into Latin of A&R 797. The publication was subsidised by Arras College, Paris, of which the translator, William Rayner, was a member. *See* note to no. 1129.

Speculum Pravitatis Haereticae

1156   —Speculum prauitatis haereticae per orationes quodlibeticas sex ad oculum demonstratae. 8°. *Duaci, ex officina Ioannis Bogardi,* 1580. C.; BM².DE.DI.DOU.FR.FU².MOU.MTH.MU.OS.PA.
Reprinted in nos. 1152–3.

Successionis Ecclesiasticae
Defensio

1157   —Successionis ecclesiasticae defensio amplior ... *Duaci,* 1580.
Not found. Description from Duthilleul, 1530. A reply to STC 11418. Reprinted in nos. 1152–3. *See* note to no. 1150.

[A Table of the Sects.]

1158   —[A table listing the various Protestant sects and briefly describing them.] Fol. *Louanii, apud eundem Io. Foulerum,* 1565. L(Lansdowne MSS, 96, nos. 52, 51 – *in that order*). [*DMR.]
The only known copy lacks the leaf containing the title and the first part of the text. Of the two surviving leaves, the first begins: 'Descriptio sectarum qui supra in ramis sunt collocatae ...', and the second concludes: 'Autore Frederico Staphylo ... ex cuius Apologia in hanc formam redacta est haec Tabula, primum quidem Anglice, opera Thomae Stapletoni, nunc vero Latine edita opera Ioannis Fouleri' and the imprint and date as shown above. Stapleton's English translation of the *Apologia* of F. Staphylus, on which this Table is based, was published in the same year, 1565 (A&R 794). No English version of the Table itself has so far been found.

Tres Thomae

1159   —Tres Thomae. Seu De S. Thomae Apostoli rebus gestis. De S. Thoma Archiepiscopo Cantuariensi & martyre. D. Thomae Mori Angliae quondam Cancellarii vita. His adiecta est oratio funebris in laudem R.P. Arnoldi de Ganthois Abbatis Marchennensis. 8°. *Duaci, ex officina Ioannis Bogardi,* 1588. L(2).O(2).C(2).; AMS.ANT.C⁹.DE.DI.DUR. GTN.HP.L².L²⁶.MU(3).RO⁵.ST. + +
With an engraved portrait of Thomas More.

1160   —[Anr. ed., with title:] Tres Thomae seu res gestae S. Thomae Apostoli. S. Thomae Archiepiscopi Cantuariensis & martyris. Thomae Mori Angliae quondam Cancellarii ... Additis duobus indicibus. 8°. *Coloniae Agrippinae, sumptibus Bernardi Gualteri,* 1612. [Coloph.] *Excudebat Stephanus Hemmerden.* L(2).O.C.; C²(2).D².DAI.DE.DI.FU.HA. HP(2).L⁴.LOU³.MU(3).OS.PA.USH. + +
This edition omits the 'Oratio funebris' of no. 1159.

—[*A work partly based on Stapleton's life of More.*] Herrera, F. de. Tomas Moro, 1592 [*etc.*] *See* nos. 831–3.

Triplicatio

—Triplicatio inchoata aduersus Gulielmi Whitakeri ... Duplicationem, 1596.
Part 2 of no. 1154.

Universa Justificationis Doctrina
hodie controversa

1161 —Vniuersa iustificationis doctrina hodie controuersa. Libris duodecim tradita. Fol. *Parisiis, apud Michaelem Sonnium*, 1581. ANG.FR.MU(2). NA.PR.RO⁶.TNI(*imp.*).VI.

1162 —[Date variant.] 1582. AMS.BM².BOR.C⁹.C¹⁵.CHA.D(2).DI.GTN.MD.MU(2). O¹¹.PA⁴.PA⁶.TRO.VAL. +

Vere Admiranda

1163 —Vere admiranda, seu, De magnitudine Romanae Ecclesiae libri duo. 4°. *Antuerpiae, ex officina Plantiniana, apud Ioannem Moretum*, 1599. L.O.C.; ANT².BRS.C⁵.CHA.D.DE.DI.DUR.HA.L²⁶.LOU³.MD.MU(4).PA.RO⁶.USH. WO. + +

1164 —[Anr. ed.] Editio secunda correctior. 8°. *Romae, ex bibliotheca Bartholomaei Grassi, apud Nicolaum Mutium*, 1600. L.O.; MU.

1165 —[Anr. issue, with the *Admiranda* of J. Lipsius.] Admiranda et Vere admiranda, siue de magnitudine et vrbis et ecclesiae Romanae. Auctoribus Iusto Lipsio . . . Belga, & Thoma Stapletono Anglo . . . Coniunctim nunc primum editi. Curante Gasp. Schoppio Franco. 8°. 2 pts. *Romae, ex bibliotheca Bartholomaei Grassi, apud Nicolaum Mutium*, 1600. O.; D.ETON.FLO³.HA.MST.MU.NB.PA.RO².VI.

Pt. 1 contains the work of Lipsius; pt. 2 that of Stapleton.

[1166 *cancelled.*]

PROMPTUARIUM CATHOLICUM

Parts 1 & 2
Sundays and Feastdays

1167 —Promptuarium Catholicum ad instructionem concionatorum contra haereticos nostri temporis, super omnia Euangelia totius anni, tam Dominicalia, quam de Festis. 8°. *Parisiis, apud Michaelem Sonnium*, 1589. HD.HP.LYN.P.PA.

1168 —[Anr. ed.] 8°. *Lugduni, in officina Iuntarum*, 1591. C⁹.CHA.CMR.DI.MD³. MU.O⁷.PA⁵.PA⁶.RO⁵.3AL.VAL.

1169 —[Anr. ed.] 8°. 2 vols. *Antuerpiae, in aedibus Petri Belleri*, 1592. FR. KDN.KNY(vol. 1).SOL.

1170 —[Anr. ed.] 8°. *Coloniae, apud Godefridum Kempensem*, 1592. [Coloph.] *Typis Godefridi Kempensis.* O.C.; ANT³.BER.CMR.D⁸.EX.FU.FU².MD.MTH. PR.TB.WB.X.YK. +

1171 —[Anr. ed.] 8°. *Coloniae Agrippinae, in officina Birckmannica, sumptibus Arnoldi Mylii*, 1592. BRN.FU².

1172 —[Anr. ed.] Hac quinta editione . . . locupletatum. 8°. *Coloniae Agrippinae, in officina Birckmannica, sumptibus Arnoldi Mylii*, 1594. L.O.; AMS.BER.CHA.CMR.DE.E⁴.KN².MU(2).OS.PA¹⁰.STG.TB.VI. + +

1173 —[Anr. ed.] 8°. *Venetiis, apud Minimam Societatem*, 1594. BAR².HP.MD. MD⁴.NA.NI.SBG.SCG.W.

1174 —[Anr. ed.] Hac sexta editione . . . locupletatum. 8°. *Antuerpiae, in aedibus Petri Belleri*, 1595. L.O.; AMP.ANT².C³.D.LIL³.NI.OS.PR².ST.USH.

1175 —[Anr. ed.] 8°. *Venetiis, apud Petrum Dusinellum*, 1596. IND.MD.

1176 —[Anr. ed.] Hac sexta editione . . . locupletatum. 8°. *Venetiis, apud haeredes Melchioris Sessae*, 1598. BRN.CHI.DMR.L⁹.MD⁴.PA¹⁰.

In some copies the titlepage of the second 'part' (sig. Aa1ʳ) has the imprint: *Venetiis, apud Minimam Societatem.*

1177 —[Imprint variant.] *Venetiis, apud Minimam Societatem*, 1598. MD⁴.

Both titlepages have this imprint.

1178   —[Anr. ed.] 8°. *Lugduni, apud Horatium Cardon*, 1601. [Coloph.] *Ex typographia Claudii Morillon*. L.; AV.KNY.MD.

1179   —[Anr. ed.] 8°. *Coloniae Agrippinae, in officina Birckmannica, sumptibus Arnoldi Mylii*, 1602. ANT.EI.FR.FRA.KDN.MAA.MR.MU².OS.PA⁶.RG².SOU. VI.X.

1180   —[Anr. ed.] 8°. *Parisiis* [a shared ed. with variant imprints], 1606. With imprint: *Apud Adrianum Beys*. HP.; *Apud Ioannem de Heuqueuille*. AV.; *Apud. viduam Dominicum Salis*. HA.STL².; With imprint and date: *Apud Petrum Bertault*, M.C.VI [*sic*].LOU³.; *Apud Abraham Saugrain*, M.C.VI [*sic*].BRS².; With imprint *Abraham Saugrain* and date corrected to 1606 (in Arabic numerals).O¹¹.

1181   —[Anr. ed.] 8°. *Coloniae Agrippinae, in officina Birckmannica, sumptibus Hermanni Mylii*, 1608. DE.HD.KN².LOU³.MR.NI.RG².STG.TB.TI.UT².VI. W.X.

1182   —[Anr. ed.] Hac sexta editione . . . locupletatum. 4° (in eights). 2 vols. *Venetiis, apud Petrum Ricciardum*, 1608. FLO³.RO.STI.VT.

1183   —[Anr. ed.] Hac sexta editione . . . locupletatum. 4° (in eights). 2 vols. *Brixiae* [a shared ed. with variant imprints], 1608. With imprint: *Apud Franciscum Tebaldinum*. MIL².; *Apud Io. Baptistam, & Antonium Bozzolas*. RO⁶.; *Apud Cominum Praesenium*.LOU³.

1184   [Anr. ed.] 8°. *Coloniae Agrippinae, in officina Birckmannica, sumptibus Hermanni Mylii*, 1613. L.; A.CHA.DE.FOR.FU².MU.PA.TB.TIL.WI.X.

1185   —[Date variant.] 1614. FR.TB.

1186   —[Anr. ed.] 8°. *Parisiis* [a shared ed. with variant imprints], 1617. With imprint: *Ex typographia Ioan Libert*. L.; *Apud Martinum Durandum*. LYN.; *Apud Hieronymum Drouart*.NM².UT².; *Apud Petrum de Forge*. AUG.PA⁶.; *Apud Franciscum Iacquin*.O.; MSM.; *Apud Laurentium Sonnium*.L.USH.; *Apud N. de la Fosse*.CHA.TRO. All copies seen have a titlepage to the second 'part' (sig. S6ʳ) bearing the imprint: *Apud Franciscum Iacquin*.

1187   —[Anr. ed.] 8°. *Aschaffenburgi, sumptibus Hermanni Mylii Birckmanni* [at Cologne], *excudebat Balthazar Lippius*, 1622. CHA.DE.HA.MFL.MR. MU.OS.PR².SBG².TB.TIL.UT².W.X. +

1188   —[Anr. ed.] 8°. *Coloniae Agrippinae, in officina Birckmannica, sumptibus Hermanni Mylii*, 1624. ERL.GSN.MR.OS(*imp*.).ROT².SPS.TB.X.

1189   —[Anr. ed.] 8°. *Moguntiae, sumptibus Hermanni Mylii Birckmanni* [at Cologne], *excudebat Hermannus Meresius*, 1631. O.; BM².(*imp*.).DE.ERL. HA.LOU.LW.NI.NT.PR.PR².TNI.USH.VI³.X.

German Translation

1190   —Kirchen- vnd Hausspostill, oder Catholisches Zeughauss. Das ist, Feste, wolgegruendte Eroerterung vnd Ausslegung der fuernembsten Stellen aller Euangelien, so an Son- vnd Festtaegen, durch das gantze Jar, der Christlichen Gemeyn pflegen fuergelesen zuwerden . . . inn Hochteutsch gebracht, durch F. Aegidium Sturzium. 4°. 2 vols. *Ingolstatt, durch Wolffgang Eder*, 1595, 96. EI.LIL³.(vol. 1).MU.PR². (vol. 1).SBG.(vol. 2).STU.ULM(vol. 2).VI.(vol. 2).

     Vol. 1, dated 1595, comprises the texts for Sundays, vol. 2, dated 1596, those for Feast Days.

1191   —[Anr. ed.] 4°. 2 vols. *Ingolstadt, in der Ederischen Truckerey, durch Andream Angermayer*, 1602. MU.TB.WO.

Part 3.
Weekdays in Lent

1192   —Thomae Stapletoni . . . Promptuarium Catholicum, ad instructionem concionatorum contra nostri temporis haereses, super Euangelia ferialia per totam Quadragesimam. 8°. *Coloniae Agrippinae, in* officina *Birckmannica, sumptibus Arnoldi Mylii,* 1594. [Coloph.] *Typis Godefridi Kempensis.* L.; BRN.DE.DUR.MU.OS.PR³.SAL.TRI.VI.W.

1193 —[Anr. ed.] 8°. *Lugduni, sumptibus Petri Landri,* 1594. [Coloph.] *Typis Ioannis Tholosan.* GER.MD.NA.RO.SAL.VAL².

1194 —[Date variant.] 1595. L.; AV.COR.LYN.MD.MTH.PA⁵.STI.

1195 —[Anr. ed.] 8°. *Antuerpiae, in aedibus Petri Belleri,* 1595. L.O.; ANT³.C³. L².NI.OS.PR².ST.

1196 —[Anr. ed.] 8°. *Parisiis* [a shared ed. with variant imprints], 1595. With imprint: *Apud Laurentium Sonnium.* L.ILL.O⁷.P.; *Apud Michaelem Sonnium.* DE.HP.

1197 —[Anr. ed.] 8°. *Venetiis, apud Petrum Dusinellum,* 1596. O.; FBH.MD. MIL².RO².VIL.VT.

1198 —[Anr. ed.] 8°. *Venetiis* [a shared ed. with variant imprints], 1598. With imprint: *Apud haeredes Melchioris Sessae.* DMR.; *Apud Minimam Societatem.* BRN.CHI.MD⁴.

1199 —[Anr. ed.] 8°. *Coloniae Agrippinae, in officina Birckmannica, sumptibus Arnoldi Mylii,* 1602. [Coloph.] *Typis viduae Godefredi Kempensis.* MAA.OS.SOU.VI.

1200 —[Anr. ed.] 8°. *Lugduni, sumptibus Petri Landry,* 1602. [Coloph.] *Ex typographia Claudii Morillon.* LYN.MD.RO⁵.TB.VES.WASH².

1201 —[Anr. ed.] 8°. *Parisiis* [a shared ed. with variant imprints], 1606. With imprint: *Apud Adrianum Beys.* BRU.HP.; *Apud Ioannem de Heuqueuille.* AV.; *Apud viduam Dominicum Salis.* HA.STL².; with imprint and date: *Apud Petrum Bertault,* M.C.VI. [*sic*].HA.LOU³.; with imprint: *Apud Abraham Saugrain,* and date 1606 in Arabic (*see* no. 1180). BRS².DE.

1202 —[Anr. ed.] 8°. *Coloniae Agrippinae, in officina Birckmannica, sumptibus Hermanni Mylii,* 1608. [Coloph.] *Typis Stephani Hemmerden.* CHA.DE. ERL.HD.LOU³.U.

1203 —[Anr. ed.] 4° (in eights). *Venetiis, apud Petrum Ricciardum,* 1608. RO.

1204 —[Anr. ed.] 4° (in eights). *Brixiae* [a shared ed. with variant imprints], 1608. With imprint: *Apud Franciscum Tebaldinum.* MIL².; *Apud Cominum Praesenium.* LOU³.

1205 —[Anr. ed.] 8°. *Coloniae Agrippinae, in officina Birckmannica, sumptibus Hermanni Mylii,* 1614. [Coloph.] *Typis Stephani Hemmerden.* L.; FR. PA.TB.TI.UT².WASH³.WI.X.

1206 —[Anr. ed.] 8°. *Parisiis* [a shared ed. with variant imprints], 1617. With imprint: *Ex typographia Ioan. Libert.* O.; *Apud Martinum Durandum.* LYN. *Apud Hieronymum Drouart.*NM².UT².; *Apud Petrum de Forge.* AUG.PA⁶.; *Apud Franciscum Iacquin.* L.AV.; *Apud Laurentium Sonnium.* L.

1207 —[Anr. ed.] 8°. *Aschaffenburgi, sumptibus Hermanni Mylii Birckmanni* [at Cologne], *excudebat Balthazar Lippius,* 1622. DE.

1208 —[Anr. ed.] 8°. *Coloniae Agrippinae, in officina Birckmannica, sumptibus Hermanni Mylii,* 1624. O.; ANT³.BM².DE.HA.KDN.LOU.MU.OS.PR.USH. VI³.W.X.

1209 —[Anr. ed.] 8°. *Moguntiae, sumptibus Hermanni Mylii Birckmanni* [at Cologne], *excudebat Hermannus Meresius,* 1631. DE.FU².NI.

PROMPTUARIUM MORALE

Sundays. Pars Hiemalis.–Pars Aestivalis.

1210 —Promptuarium morale super Euangelia dominicalia totius anni ... Pars hyemalis (Pars aestiualis). 8°. 2 vols. *Antuerpiae, ex officina Plantiniana, apud viduam, & Ioannem Moretum,* 1591. AMS.ANT(*p.h.*). ANT²(*p.a.*).C⁹.FU²(*p.h.*).KN².L².LOU(*p.a.*).MR.MU.O⁷.TB(*p.h.*).VI.W(*p.a.*). X (*p.h.*).

1211 —[Anr. ed.] Editio altera. 8°. 2 vols. *Antuerpiae, ex officina Plantiniana, apud viduam, & Ioannem Moretum,* 1592. FU²(*p.h.*).MU(*p.h.*).PA.RO³.TB. TRI.

1212 —[Anr. ed.] 8°. 2 vols. *Lugduni, apud Ioannem Baptistam Buysson,* 1592. [Coloph.] *Excudebat Petrus Roussin.* O.; BRN(*p.a.*).FR.GER(*p.a.*).HP (*p.h.*).MD.PAL.SAL.STI.UEB.

1213 —[Anr. ed. of p.h.] 8°. *Antuerpiae, in officina Plantiniana, apud viduam, & Ioannem Moretum,* 1593. AUG.SBG.USH.
     Collation: ✱–✱✱⁸✱✱✱⁴A–Bbb⁸Ccc⁴. pp. 750. Sig. ✱✱✱3ᵛ contains the last 16 lines of the Proemium, sig. ✱✱✱4 is blank. Titlepage has (l. 10) … *Authoribus* …, and imprint: ANTVERPIÆ,/IN OFFICINA …

1214 —[Anr. ed. of p.a.] 8°. *Antuerpiae, in officina Plantiniana, apud viduam, & Ioannem Moretum,* 1593. AUG.NI.USH.
     Collation: †⁸A–Ss⁸. pp. 640. Titlepage has (l. 10) … *Authoribus* …, and imprint: ANTVERPIÆ,/IN OFFICINA … Sig. A1ʳ (p. 1) has (ll. 2–3): … SVPER EVAN-/GELIA DOMINICALIA.

1215 —[Anr. ed. of p.h.] 8°. *Antuerpiae, in officina Plantiniana, apud viduam, & Ioannem Moretum,* 1593. ANT².HP.WO.
     Collation as in no. 1213. Sig. ✱✱✱4ʳ contains the last 13 lines of the Proemium followed by an ornamental tailpiece showing a head surrounded by arabesques. Titlepage has (l. 10) … *authoribus* …, and imprint: ANTVERPIAE,/IN OFFICINA …

1216 —[Anr. ed. of p.a.] 8°. *Antuerpiae, in officina Plantiniana, apud viduam, & Ioannem Moretum,* 1593. DAI.DMR.HP.O⁵.
     Collation as in no. 1214. Titlepage has (l. 10) … *authoribus* …, and imprint: ANTVERPIAE,/IN OFFICINA … Sig. A1ʳ (p. 1) has (ll. 2–3): … SVPER EVAN-/GELIA DOMICALIA [*sic*].

1217 —[Anr. ed. of p.h.] 8°. *Antuerpiae, in officina Plantiniana, apud viduam, & Ioannem Moretum,* 1593. L.; KNY.
     Collation as in no. 1213. Sig. ✱✱✱4ʳ contains the last 13 lines of the Proemium followed by printer's type-ornament in the form of a rough cross. Titlepage has (l. 10): … *authoribus* …, and imprint: … ANTVERPIAE,/IN OFFICINA …

1218 —[Anr. ed. of p.a.] 8°. *Antuerpiae, in officina Plantiniana, apud viduam, & Ioannem Moretum,* 1593. ST.
     Collation as in no. 1214. Titlepage has (l. 10): … *authoribus* …, and imprint: ANTVERPIAE,/IN OFFICINA … Sig. A1ʳ (p. 1) has (ll. 2–3) … SVPER/EVANGELIA DOMINICALIA.

1219 —[Anr. ed. of p.h.] 8°. *Antuerpiae, in officina Plantiniana, apud viduam, & Ioannem Moretum,* 1593. DAI.
     Collation as in no. 1213. Sig. ✱✱✱3ᵛ contains the last 29 lines of the Proemium, sig. ✱✱✱4 is a blank. Titlepage has (l. 10): … *authoribus* …, and imprint: ANTVERPIÆ,/IN OFFICINA …

1220 —[Anr. ed. of p.h.] 8°. *Antuerpiae, ex officina Plantiniana, apud viduam, & Ioannem Moretum,* 1593. DE.USH(*Lisbon Collection*).
     Collation: ✱–✱✱⁸A–Z⁸a–y⁸. pp. 694. The Proemium ends on sig. A1ᵛ (p. 2) and is followed by a tailpiece made up of ornamental scrolls. Titlepage has (l. 10): … *authoribus* …, and imprint: ANTVERPIÆ,/EX OFFICINA … In spite of the imprint and Plantin's compasses device on the titlepage, this edition is clearly from a different press from that of nos. 1213–19.

1221 —[Anr. ed. of p.a.] 8°. *Antuerpiae, ex officina Plantiniana, apud viduam, & Ioannem Moretum,* 1593. ANT³.USH(*Lisbon Collection*).
     Collation: †⁸A–Z⁸a–p⁸. pp. 592. Titlepage has (l. 10): … *authoribus* …, and imprint: ANTVERPIÆ,/EX OFFICINA … Sig. A1ʳ (p. 1) has (ll. 2–3): … SVPER/EVANGELIA DOMINICALIA. This edition is from the same press as no. 1220.

—[The following libraries have copies of one or both parts bearing the same imprint and date as nos. 1213–21: BRN.C³.C¹³.CHA.FR.FU.FU².GT. MNS.MR.MTH.MU.TDO.UT.W.WB. + + The editions to which these copies belong have not been determined.]

1222 —[Anr. ed. of both parts.] 8°. 2 vols. *Lugduni, apud Ioannem Baptistam Buysson*, 1593. BRN(*p.a.*).D(*p.h.*).D²(*p.h.*).MD⁴(*p.h.*).VES.

1223 —[Anr. ed.] 8°. 2 vols. *Lugduni, sumptibus Ioannis Baptistae Buysson*, 1594. BRN.CHA.LOU(*p.a.*).MD.RO².SAL.STG.

1224 —[Anr. ed.] 8°. 2 vols. *Venetiis, apud Minimam Societatem*, 1594. D(*p.a.*).FLO³.LOU²(*p.a.*).MD.NA.OS(*p.h.*).RO⁸.VAL(*p.h.*).

1225 —[Anr. ed.] 8°. 2 vols. *Lugduni, sumptibus Ioannis Baptistae Buysson*, 1595. EX(*p.a.*).MD.PAL.SAL.SCG.TAR.TDO.

1226 —[Date variant.] 1596. AMP(*p.a.*).DAI(*p.h.*).DMR(*p.a.*).DUR²(*p.h.*).LYN (*p.a.*).PA(*p.a.*).PAL(*p.a.*).SAL(*p.h.*).STI.

1227 —[Anr. ed.] 8°. 2 vols. *Venetiis* [a shared ed. with variant imprints], 1596. With imprint: *Apud Petrum Dusinellum*. GER(*p.h.*).MD³.SCG.VAL.; *Apud Florauantem Pratum*. L.; BAR(*p.a.*).BAR².PAL.VT(*p.a.*).

1227.1 —[Date variant of no. 1227.] 1597. With imprint: *Apud Florauantem Pratum*, USH.

1228 —[Anr. ed.] 8°. 2 vols. *Venetiis* [a shared ed. with variant imprints], 1597. With imprint: *Apud Societatem Minimam*. TAL(*p.a.*).; *Apud haeredes Melchioris Sessae*. REG.RO⁶(*p.a.*).

1229 —[Date variant of no. 1228.] 1598. With imprint: *Apud Societatem Minimam*. MD(*p.h.*).TAL(*p.h.*); *Apud haeredes Melchioris Sessae*. FLO³. HP(*p.h.*).MSM(*p.h.*).

1230 —[Anr. ed.] 8°. 2 vols. *Parisiis* [a shared ed. with variant imprints], 1598. [Coloph.] *Excudebat Leodegarius Delas*. With imprint: *Apud Dominicum Salis*. O(*p.h.*).PA(*p.h.*).PA⁵(*p.h.*).PAL(*p.h.*).; *Apud Franciscum Gueffier*. LYN.PA(*p.a.*).R(*p.a.*).

1231 —[Anr. ed.] 8°. 2 vols. *Lugduni* [a shared ed. with variant imprints], 1602. With imprint: *Sumptibus Horatii Cardon*. BAR(*p.h.*).MIL².O¹¹. PA⁶(*p.h.*).; *Apud Ioannem Pillehotte*. DMR(*p.h.*).

1232 —[Anr. ed.] 8°. 2 vols. *Parisiis* [a shared ed. with variant imprints], 1602. [Coloph.] *Excudebat Franciscus Iacquin*. With imprint: *Apud Franciscum Iaquin*. BRS².X(*p.h.*).; *Apud Sebastianum Niuellium*. DE(*p.h.*).WB.; *Apud Carolum Chastellain*. PA⁶(*p.a.*).

[1233 *cancelled*.]

1234 —[Anr. ed.] 8°. 2 vols. *Parisiis* [a shared ed. with variant imprints], 1606. [Coloph.] *Lutetiae, excudebat Franciscus Iacquin*. With imprint: *Apud Franciscum Iaquin*. ANT³.NTS.; *Apud viduam Petri Bertault*. DE (*p.h.*).FRA(*p.a.*).; *Apud Robertum Fouët*. HER(*p.a.*).

1235 —[Anr. ed.] 8°. 2 vols. *Venetiis, apud Petrum Ricciardum*, 1608. MD.

1236 —[Anr. ed.] 8°. 2 vols. *Moguntiae, apud Balthasarum Lippium, sumptibus Ioannis Moreti* [at Antwerp], & *Hermanni Mylii* [at Cologne], 1610. L(*p.a.*).; BEU.COR.DMR(*p.a.*).LW.O².O³(*p.h.*).PA.TB.

1237 —[Anr. ed.] 8°. 2 vols. *Antuerpiae, ex officina Plantiniana, apud viduam & filios Io. Moreti*, 1613. L.; AMP(*p.h.*).ANT(*p.h.*).CHA(*p.a.*).D²(*p.a.*). FU(*p.h.*).HP(*p.h.*).LOU³.LW.MD(*p.h.*).NM².OS(*p.a.*).STU.UT.X. + +

1238 —[Anr. ed.] 8°. 2 vols. *Coloniae Agrippinae, ex officina Birckmannica, sumptibus Hermanni Mysii*, 1615. CHA(*p.h.*).DE(*p.a.*).PA⁶(*p.a.*).PN.PR². UEB.

1239 —[Anr. ed.] 8°. 2 vols. *Parisiis* [a shared ed. with variant imprints], 1617. With imprint: *Apud Franciscum Iacquin*. O(*p.h.*).; KNY(*p.a.*).; *Apud Laurentium Sonnium*. PA(*p.a.*).; *Apud Sebastianum Chappelet*. NBTS(*p.h.*).

1240 —[Anr. ed.] 8°. 2 vols. *Coloniae Agrippinae, in officina Birckmannica, sumptibus Hermanni Mylii*, 1620. A.AMP(*p.h.*).D(*p.h.*).DAI(*p.h.*).DE.FU². HP.KN².KNY(*p.h.*).NT(*p.a.*).O⁵(*p.a.*).PLU.RO².SBG.TB.TI. + +

1241   —[Anr. ed.] 8°. 2 vols. *Parisiis* [a shared ed. with variant imprints],
       1627. With imprint: *Apud Franciscum Iacquin.* AMP(*p.a.*).E(*p.a.*).HP
       (*p.h.*).PA(*p.h.*).PA¹⁰(*p.h.*).; *Apud Nicolaum du Fossé et Petrum Hury.*
       O(*p.a.*).

German Translation

1242   —Promptuarium morale das ist, sittliche Speisskämer darinnen heyl-
       same Lehren, Gottselig, Christlich, Catholische Vnderweysungen,
       von loeblichen Sitten vnd Tugenden, wider allerley Suend vnd Laster,
       vber die Sontaeglichen Euangelien dess gantzen Jars, begriffen vnd
       verwahret ... in die gemeyne Teutsche Sprach transferiert vnd
       vbersetzt: Wintertheyl (Sommertheyl). Fol. 2 vols. *Ingolstatt, durch
       Wolffgang Eder,* 1596, 97. BON.MU(2).WO.
       The titlepage of vol. 1 (Wintertheyl) bears the date 1596, that of
       vol. 2 (Sommertheyl) 1597.
1243   —[Date variant.] Both vols dated 1597. BEU.BRN.CMR.FR.MU.NI.PBN.PR².
       VI.Y.

PROMPTUARIUM MORALE

Feast Days

*This part of the 'Promptuarium' was written by Lawrence Beyerlinck,
Canon of Antwerp, and falls outside the scope of the present catalogue.*

1244   **Stephens, Thomas.** Discurso sobre a vinda de Jesu Christo nosso
       Saluador ao Mundo. *Impresso em Rachol com liçenca da Santa Inqui-
       sição, e Ordinario no Collegio de todos os Santos da Companhia de Jesus,*
       1616.
       Not found. For the description and history of this work, *see* C. R.
       Boxer, 'A Tentative Check-list of Indo-Portuguese Imprints,
       1556–1674' (*Boletim do Instituto Vasco da Gama,* 1956), no. 17.
1245   —Doutrina Christam em lingoa Bramana Canarim. Ordenada amaneira
       de dialogo, pera ensinar os mininos. Cōposta pollo padre Thomas
       Esteuâo da Companhia de Iesus. natural de Lōdres. 8°. *Empressa no
       Collegio de Rachol da Cōpanhia de Iesus,* 1622. LIS.VT.
       See Boxer, *op. cit.* (no. 1244), no. 18. Facsimile reprint ed. M.
       Saldanha, 1945.
1246   —Iesus Maria Arte da lingoa Canarim composta pelo padre Thomaz
       esteuâo da Companhia de Iesus & acrecentada pello padre Diogo
       Ribeiro da mesma Cōpanhia E nouemente reuista, & emendada por
       outros quatro padres da mesma Companhia. 4°. *Com licença de S.
       Inquisicam & Ordinario em Rachol no Collegio de S. Ignacio da
       Companhia de Iesus,* 1640. EV. L⁵¹.LIS.
       See Boxer, *op. cit.* (no. 1244), no. 22.
1247   **Stile, Lewis.** Carta, escrita a vno de los colegiales ingleses que residen
       en Madrid, por su padre, para apartarle de su resolucion de ser
       sacerdote: traduzida en nuestra lengua. [With, sig. ¶4ʳ: 'La respuesta
       del hijo a su padre'.] 4° by imposition, 12° by folding. *n.p.d.* [1611.]
       L.; MD. [*O.]
       Anon. The father's letter is dated 1 June 1611 and is signed
       'Vuestra Padre N.N.'; the son's reply is dated 4 September 1611
       and is signed: 'Su obediente y amado hijo A.A.' Internal evidence
       reveals that the son is [Lewis Stile] who arrived at the English
       College, Madrid in 1611, after two years at S. Omer; he died at
       Valladolid in 1615. *See* CRS 29, pp. 85–6, 146; CRS 30, p. 118. *Pr*
       [Madrid.]

1248 **Stillington, William.** Theses ex theologia Sancti Thomae. Propositae in Collegio Anglicano Societatis Iesu Leodii. Anno Domini CIƆ IƆC XXVII. Praeside Rdo Patre Andrea Vito . . . Defendet P. Gulielmus Stillingtonus . . . Mense Augusto. 4°. *Leodii, typis Leonardi Streel, n.d.* [1627.]
Not found, Description from Sommerv. (tom. 8, col. 1092).

Stouard, Maria. *See* Mary, *Queen of Scots.*

Stuard, Marie. *See* Mary, *Queen of Scots.*

Stuart, Mary. *See* (1) Mary, *Queen of Scots;* (2) O'Donnell, Mary Stuart.

T., G. [A newsletter from London, dated 30 July 1585.] *See* no. 1457.

T., G. In sacrae scholae calumniatorem & calumniae duplicatorem sententia iuris, 1632. *See* no. 1257.

Taillerus, Franciscus. *See* Taylor, F.

Talbot, Adrian, *alias. See* Fortescue, A.

Tancred (Tankard), Charles. [*A work translated by him.*] Relacion que embiaron las religiosas del monesterio de Sion de Inglaterra, 1594. *See* no. 741.

Taylor, Francis. [*Appendix.*] Mullan, J. Idea togatae constantiae [on F. Taylor], 1629. *See* no. 838.

Taylor, Maurus, *name in religion. See* Taylor, W.

Taylor, William, *in religion* Maurus Taylor. [*A work with a dedicatory epistle by him*] Sayer, R. Clauis regia, 1619. *See* no. 1043.

1249 **Thirry, William.** De prouida status electione oratio theologica. In qua . . . quid cuique tam ad statum vitae eligendum, quam ad electum in salutis consecutionem dirigendum, expediat, liquido demonstratur . . . Habita in Collegio Ibernorum Duaci in festo S. Patricii die 17 Martii, anno 1623. 4°. *Antuerpiae, apud Petrum & Ioannem Belleros,* 1624. LYN.

1250 —Discursus panegyrici de nominibus, tribulationibus, et miraculis S. Patricii Ibernorum Apostoli, cum exhortatione ad persecutiones pro fide patienter ferendas, & Apostrophe ad Iberniam, qui . . . habiti sunt in Collegio Ibernorum Duaci, anno 1616. 8°. *Duaci, ex officina Balta-zaris Belleri,* 1617. L(3).O.; D.D⁶.DOU.KNY.MTH.O³.OS.PA³.ST.
Editor's *ded.* sgd.: F. Patricius Donouanus.

1251 **Thomson, George,** *pseud.?* De antiquitate Christianae religionis apud Scotos. Authore Georgio Thomsono, Scoto. 4°. *Romae, ex typographia Bartholomaei Bonfadini,* 1594. L.; E.NP.PA.RO⁶.RO⁹(Anglia 42, ff. 87–92). VT(2).
An appeal for support of the Scots College, recently moved from Pont-à-Mousson to Douai. Sometimes attributed to [James Tyrie S.J.] On the authorship *see* T. G. Law in *Publications of the Edinburgh Bibliographical Society,* vol. 3, 1899, pp. 137–40.

1252 —[Anr. ed.] 12°. *Duaci, typis Balthasaris Belleri,* An. XCIIII [1594]. E.E³.PA.
A reprint of no. 1251. Reprinted by Antonio Possevino in *Bibliotheca selecta,* Cologne, 1607, vol. 2.

Throckmorton, Thomas. [*A Work translated by him.*] Discours de la vie abominable, ruses, trahisons . . . desquelles a vsé . . . my Lorde de Lecestre, 1585. *See* no. 31.1.

[1253 *cancelled*]
Thunder, Henry. [Locupletatio animae, 1634.]
Southwell's reference, p. 332, describes a work in English which will be listed in our vol. 2.

Thyraeus, Gulielmus. *See* Thirry, W.

Tichbourne, Nicolas, *Ven.* [*Appendix.*] Relacion del martirio de . . . Nicolas Sisburno [Tichborne], 1615. *See* no. 624.

Tirconel. *See* Tyrconnell.

1254   **Tully, Francis,** *in religion* Franciscus de S. Maria. Illustrissimo
       Principi Andreae Peretto S.R.E. Cardinali Amplissimo. F. Franciscus
       de S. Maria . . . perpetuam felicitatem exoptans theolog. haec
       theoremata D.C. . . . Praecipuae controuersiae theologicae ex libris
       Sententiarum Scoti Doctoris Subtilis, & partibus D. Tho. Doct.
       Angel. depromptae. *s.sh.fol. Romae, typis Iacobi Mascardi,* 1625. RO².
       Announcing the theses he would defend at a public academic con-
       test at Rome at which he had been selected to represent his Province.
       See Cleary, pp. 81–2.
       —[*Disputations in which he acted as Praeses.*] Baron, B. . . . Conclusiones
       theologicae, 1634. *See* no. 84.
       —Cahan, E. . . . Conclusiones theologicae, 1634. *See* no. 128.
       —Cornin, J. . . . Conclusiones theologicae, 1634. *See* no. 271.
       —Curcy, J. . . . Conclusiones theologicae, 1633. *See* no. 285.
       —Ferrall, J. . . . Conclusiones theologicae, 1634. *See* no. 414.

1255   **Turnbull, George.** Imaginarii circuli quadratura Catholica, de formali
       obiecto, & regula fidei. Aduersus calumniosam disputationem
       Roberti Baronis. 8°. *Remis, excudebat Simon Fognaeus,* 1628. E.
       The first issue. Collation: †⁸A–K⁸L⁴ (L4 blank). Answers STC 1494.
       Baron replied in STC 1493 which Turnbull answered in no. 1257.

1256   —[Anr. issue, enlarged.] *Remis, excudebat Simon Fognaeus,* 1628. C.;
       A².C⁵.HP.MTH.ST.VAL².
       Collation: †⁸A–R⁸ (R8 blank except for the printer's device). A re-
       issue of the sheets of no. 1255 as far as sig. K8. The first three
       leaves of sheet L are reset and the rest is new. The additions consist
       of six new chapters and an epilogue.

1257   —In sacrae scholae calumniatorem & calumniae duplicatorem sententia
       iuris. Pro Tetragonismo Georgii Turnebulli . . . De obiecto, & regula
       fidei. 8°. *Remis, excudebat Simon de Foigny,* 1632. L.; A²(3).GT.
       Sgd.: G.T. [George Turnbull]. Answers STC 1493. *See* notes to
       no. 1255.

1258   **Turner, Bartholomew.** Assertiones, ex vniuersa philosophia naturali
       depromptae et ad publicam disputationem in . . . Ingolstadiensi
       Academia die [space] Iunii proposiṭẹ: a Bartolomaeo Turnero
       Salisburgensi, philosophiae studioso. 4°. *Ingolstadii, ex officina typo-
       graphica Ederiana,* 1598. MU.
       Not seen. Description from Stalla (1243) who cites the MU copy.
       In spite of the author's English name, the epithet of origin may
       signify Salzburg rather than Salisbury.

1259   **Turner, Bernard.** Templum honoris Bauarici nominis aeternitati
       sacrum et accinentibus Musis in Collegio Anglicano Societatis Iesu
       Maximiliano Serenissimo Bauariae Duci dedicatum, cum eiusdem
       auspiciis philosophicas conclusiones publice defenderet Bernardus
       Turnerus ex nobilium Anglorum conuictu. 12°. *Leodii, excudebat
       Leonardus Streel,* 1629. ANT²(*imp., lacking first and last leaf*).
       In verse. Description from Sommerv. (tom. 4, col. 1820–1) as the
       only copy found lacks the title.

       Turner, Robert.

                         Collections
               In chronological order of publication

       —Roberti Turneri Panegyrici sermones duo, 1583. *Part 2 of* no. 1260.
1260   —Roberti Turneri . . . Orationes XIV . . . Commentationes in loca
       Scripturae, expressa ad imitationem antiquorum Ecclesiae doctorum.
       Panegyrici duo, de duobus triumphis post natos homines clarissimis,
       illo Romae in translatione Gregorii Nazianzeni, hoc Leodii in
       inauguratione Ernesti Ducis Bauariae & Electoris iam Coloniensis.

8°. 2 pts. *Ingolstadii, ex officina typographica Dauidis Sartorii*, 1584. L.O.; AB.BRN.CMR.DE.DI.EI.L⁹.MU(3).PR.RG.SBG.STG.TB.VI. + +

Pt. 2, comprising *Panegyrici sermones duo*, has its own titlepage. This part bears the date 1583 in the colophon and (in some copies) the imprint. It includes Turner's Latin translation of no. 196. *Orationes XIV* was also printed in the 1584 Ingolstadt edition of M. A. Muretus, *Epistolarum . . . liber*.

1261 —Roberti Turneri . . . Orationes XIV. Accessit oratio funebris in exequiis Illustriss. Princ. Eystensis, & epistola ad Alanum Cardinalem. 8°. *Antuerpiae, apud Gummarum Sulsenium*, 1597. ANT.ANT².C¹⁵.E. FLO.L².O⁵.VAL.VER.

For a separate edition of the funeral oration and the letter to Cardinal Allen, see no. 1275.

—Roberti Turneri . . . Orationes XVI, 1599. Part 2 of no. 1262.

1262 —Roberti Turneri . . . Panegyrici duo, de duobus triumphis clarissimis, illo Romae in translatione Gregorii Nazianzeni; hoc Leodii in inauguratione Ernesti Ducis Bauariae . . . Eiusdem Orationes XVI et tres commentationes in loca Scripturae . . . Additae sunt eiusdem epistolae. Editio secunda. 8°. 2 pts. *Ingolstadii, ex typographia Adami Sartorii*, 1599. L.; CMR.E².EI.MU(2).PA.SBG.

This is the second edition, enlarged, of no. 1260. Pt. 2, comprising *Orationes XVI*, *Commentationes*, and *Epistolae*, has its own titlepage. Including Turner's Latin translation of no. 196.

1263 —Roberti Turneri . . . Posthuma. Orationes septemdecim, tractatus septem, epistolarum centuriae duae . . . Accesserunt Edmundi Campiani . . . orationes, epistolae, tractatus de imitatione rhetorica. a Roberto Turnero Campiani discipulo collecta, omnia nunc primum e m.s. edita. 8°. 2 pts. *Ingolstadii, typis Ederianis, apud Andream Angermarium*, 1602. L(2: 1 *imp.*).O.C.; C⁵.CMR.DE.DI.GTN.HP.MU.O⁵.OS. PA.PA³.PR.SBG.YK.X.

Campion's *Opuscula* occupy pt. 2 which has its own titlepage with imprint: *Ingolstadii, ex officina typographica Ederiana, apud Andream Angermarium*.

1264 —Roberti Turneri . . . Panegyrici duo, de duobus triumphis clarissimis, illo Romae in translatione Gregorii Nazianzeni; hoc Leodii in inauguratione Ernesti Ducis Bauariae . . . Eiusdem orationes XVI. et tres commentationes in loca Scripturae . . . Additae sunt eiusdem epistolae. 8°. 2 pts. *Ingolstadii, ex typographeo Adami Sartorii*, 1609. L.C.; AB.C².DMR.F.PBN.PR.STG.VI².WO.

Another edition of no. 1262, including Turner's Latin translation of no. 196. Pt. 2, comprising the *Orationes*, the *Commentationes* and the *Epistolae*, has its own titlepage.

1265 —Roberti Turneri . . . Orationum volumen primum . . . Seorsim editae sunt orationes et tractatus posthumi; nec non epistolae, quotquot reperiri potuere? [*sic*] Accesserunt P. Edm. Campiani orationes, epistolae, & tract. De imitatione rhetorica. Nusquam antehac coniunctim edita. 8°. *Coloniae Agrippinae, sumptibus Ioannis Kinckhes*, 1615. C.; A.ANT.D.DAI.DUR.F.L⁴.L⁹.L¹⁵.STG.VAL².VI.

This volume comprises sixteen *Orationes*, three *Commentationes*, two *Panegyrici*. For the *Orationes et tractatus posthumi* and Campion's *Opuscula* see nos. 1266–7. For the *Epistolae* see no. 1268.

1266 —[vol. 2.] Roberti Turneri . . . Posthuma. Orationes XVII. Tractatus VII. Nusquam vnquam ante hac edita. Accesserunt Edmundi Campiani . . . Orationes, Epistolae, Tractatus de imitatione rhetoric. a Roberto Turnero . . . collecta. 4°. *Coloniae Agrippinae, apud Ioannem Kinckhes*, 1615. A.C⁵.D.DAI.FR.HP.L⁹.MU.PA.PA⁴.STG.VAL².VI².

1267 —[Anr. issue of vol. 2, with a cancel title:] Roberti Turneri . . . Orationum volumen secundum. Recens in lucem editum. Accesserunt

Edmundi Campiani . . . Orationes, Epistolae Tractatus de imitatione rhetorica a Roberto Turnero . . . collecta. *Coloniae Agrippinae, apud Ioannem Kinckhes*, 1615. ANT.L⁴.

1268   —[vol. 3.] Roberti Turneri . . . Epistolae, quae reperiri potuere, additis centuriis duabus posthumis, antehac nusquam coniunctim editae. 8°. *Coloniae Agrippinae, apud Ioannem Kinckhes*, 1615. L(2).C(2).; ANT.C².
D.DMR.E.L⁹.LN.MFL.MU.PA(*imp*.).PA⁴.R.VI.

An earlier collection of Turner's letters was published in the 1584 Ingolstadt edition of M. A. Muretus, *Epistolarum . . . liber*.

1269   —[Anr. ed. of vol. 2, enlarged.] Roberti Turneri . . . Orationum, volumen secundum, recens in lucem editum. Accesserunt Edmundi Campiani . . . Orationes, Epistolae, Tractatus de imitatione rhetorica a Roberto Turnero . . . collecta. 8°. *Coloniae Agrippinae, apud Ioannem Kinckium*, 1625. L.; D⁸.E.L.¹⁵PBN.WZ. [*O.]

To this edition have been added Campion's *Rationes decem* and Turner's Latin translation of no. 196.

1270   —Roberti Turneri . . . Orationum volumina duo. Accesserunt R.P. Edm. Campiani Soc. Iesu Orationes, Epistolae, & Tract. de imitatione rhetorica. 8°. *Coloniae Agrippinae, apud Ioannem Kinckium*, 1629. E.PR.WZ.

Only the first volume, which is a reprint of no. 1265, has been found in this edition. The collective title suggests that the publisher may have issued the volume with surplus stock of nos. 1267–9 instead of reprinting the whole. Campion's *Opuscula* mentioned in the title do not form part of this first volume.

Single Works

1271   —Maria Stuarta, Regina Scotiae, Dotaria Franciae, Haeres Angliae et Hyberniae, martyr Ecclesiȩ, innocens a caede Darleana: vindice Oberto Barnestapolio. 8°. *Ingolstadii, ex officina Wolfgangi Ederi*, 1588 L(5).O.C.; AC².DE(2).DI.E.E².L².MD.MU(6).OS.PA(2).STG. + +

Obertus Barnestapolius, *pseud*. Written for Germany, to combat the writings of George Buchanan against Mary, twice published there. Dedicated to Cardinal Allen. Scott 164.

1272   —[Anr. ed.] 8°. *Coloniae, sumptibus Petri Henningii*, 1627. L(2).O.C(2).; AMI.D.DE.DUR.E².FR.HP(2).L².MU(2).PA².U.YK. + +

Obertus Barnestapolius, *pseud*. Usually found bound with no. 1059. *Pr*. [Bamberg, Augustin Crinesius]. Scott 220.

1273   —[Imprint variant.] *Bambergae, apud Augustinum Crinesium, sumptibus Petri Henningii Bibliopolae Coloniensis*, 1627. L.; BA.DMR.E².

1274   —[*French transl*.] L'histoire et vie de Marie Stuart, Royne d'Escosse, d'Oiriere de France, heritiere d'Angleterre & d'Ibernye, en laquelle elle est clairement iustifiée de la mort du Prince d'Arlay son mary. Composée en Latin par Obert Barnestapolius, & faicte Françoise, par Gabriel de Guttery Clunisois. 12°. *Paris, chez Guillaume Iulien*, 1589. L.O.; PA.PA².

Obert Barnestapolius, *pseud*. Scott 178.

1275   —Roberti Turneri . . . Oratio & epistola de vita & morte . . . Martini a Schaumberg, Principis & Episcopi Eystadiani: illa in funere 3. Non. Iul. An. 1590. Eystadii habita: haec scripta Romam ad . . . Gulielmum Alanum S.R.E. Cardinalem. 8°. *Ingolstadii, typis Wolfgangi Ederi*, 1580 [*sic* for 1590]. L.; AB.BUTE.ERL.FR.GTN.HAN.MR.MU.PA.PAS.VI.WO.

The date 1580 in the imprint is a misprint for 1590, the year in which the Bishop died. Reprinted in 1597 as part of no. 1261.

Tyrconnell, Mary Stuart, sometimes styled *Countess of Tyrconnell*. *See* O'Donnell, Mary Stuart.

Tyrie, James. *See* Thomson, George, *pseud.?*

Ursulanus, Edmundus, *pseud. See* O'Mahony, F. (no. 861).
V., R. *See* nos. 1288–92; 1295–1305.
Valesius, Martinus Angelus. *See* Walsh, M.
Valgravius, Franciscus. *See* Walgrave, F.
Valisius, Franciscus. *See* Wallis, F.

1276   **Valladolid,** *English College.* [*Appendix.*] Razonamiento a la Serenissima Reyna Doña Margarita nuestra Señora . . . Hecho a 26. de Março, de 1603. 4° (a bifolium, the second leaf blank). *n.p.d.* [1603.] MD(V–996, n. 28.).

An address to the Queen of Spain by a group of unnamed English priests about to set out from their seminary [Valladolid] for the English mission. It begins: 'Todos estos sacerdotes que V.M. vee (Serenissima Reyna) salimos de nuestra Patria en n̄ra tierna edad, huyendo de la persecuciō . . .' *Pr.* [Spain]

1277   —Ortiz, A. Relacion de la venida de los Reyes Catolicos, al Colegio Ingles de Valladolid, en el mes de Agosto Año de. 1600. Dirigida a la Serenissima Señora Infanta de España Doña Isabel Clara Eugenia; por Don Antonio Ortiz. 4°. 2 pts. *Madrid, por Andres Sanchez,* 1600. L.O(pt. 1).C.; BAR².EV.HSA(pt. 2).MD.MD²(pt. 2. 9–3556 bis 5).PA(pt. 2. 01.410).RO³.RO⁶.

Pt. 2, which recounts the reception by the College of the statue of the Blessed Virgin mutilated by the English soldiery at the sack of Cadiz in 1596, has its own titlepage reading 'Recebimiento que se hizo en Valladolid a vna imagen de Nuestra Señora . . . Por D. Antonio Ortiz' and the imprint: *Madrid, imp. de la Tina,* 1600. Antonio Ortiz has not been identified. For an English translation of part of the work, *see* A&R 584.

—Ortiz, A. Recebimiento que se hizo en Valladolid a vna imagen de Nuestra Señora, 1600. *Part 2 of no.* 1277.

[1278 *cancelled*]

Verementanus, Fidelis Annosus, *pseud. See* Floyd, J. (nos. 492–4.)
Veridicus, Didymus Henfildanus, *pseud. See* Stapleton, T. (no. 1141).

1279   **Verstegan, Richard.**†‡ Anatomie van Caluiniste calumnien. ghetoont in eenen Dialogus oft t'samensspreecken, tusschen eenen Brabander en eenen Hollander. Aengaende een placcaet, onlancks in Hollandt gepubliceert door eenighe die hun seluen naem toe eyghenen van Hooghe ende Moghende Heeren Staeten. 8°. *n.p.,* 1622. AM3. [*L.]

Signed at the end: 'Wt Ceulen den 8. Aprilis 1622. V.L. seer dienstwillighen D.N. For [Verstegan's] authorship, *see* RH, Oct. 1986, pp. 128–42. *Pr.* [Antwerp?] An English translation was printed at [S. Omer, Eng. Coll. press] in the same year (A&R 566). The Placcaet referred to in the title was printed at the Hague in 1622 (Knuttel 3349).

1280   —Brief et veritable discours, de la mort d'aucuns vaillants et glorieux martyrs, lesquelz on a faict mourir en Angleterre, pour la foy & religion Catholique, l'an passé de 1600. Et semblablement aussi en ceste presente année de M.D.CI. 8°. *Anuers, chez Hyerosme Verdussen,* 1601. L.; BRS.W.

Anon. Petti 9a. For a full description and analysis of this work, *see* RH, April 1959, pp. 82–5.

—Briefue description des diuerses cruautez. *See* no. 1285.

1281   —[*Flemish transl.* of no. 1280.] Cort ende waerachtich Verhael van het lijden van sommighe vrome ende glorieuse martelaers, die om de H. Catholijcke religie in Enghelandt ghedoodt zijn int voorleden Iaer van gratien, 1600. Ende desghelijcx oock in desenteghenwoordighen Iare 1601. 8°. *t'Hantwerpen, by Hieronymus Verdussen,* 1601. DE.GT.

Anon. Petti 9b.

1282 —Een cluchtich verhael, van eenen gepredestineerden cappuyn. Midts-
ghaeders eenighe vonnissen in dicht die daer ouer zijn ghegheuen. 4°.
T'Hantwerpen, by Abraham Verhoeuen, 1619. ANT.LN.
Anon. Petti 18. Rombauts, pp. 198–9, 302–10.
—Cort ende waerachtich Verhael. *See* no. 1281.

1283 —Descriptiones quaedam illius inhumanae et multiplicis persecutionis,
quam in Anglia propter fidem sustinent Catholicè Christiani. Fol.
n.p.d. [1583–84.] W.
Anon. Consisting of six leaves, the first containing prose text, the
remainder (which are engraved) illustrations with comments and
verses. The plates are [Verstegan's] own work. *Pr.* [secretly at
Paris, under Verstegan's direction]. Petti 2 (replacing 2a, *see* RH,
April 1966, pp. 290–1). For a full description and an account of the
printing of this work, *see* RH, April 1959, pp. 70, *et seq.*

1284 —[Anr. ed.] Fol. *Romae, apud Franciscum Zannettum*, 1584. L(*leaf 1
only*); DE.DMR.F.L³⁰(*leaf 1 only*).RO¹⁰.ST.W.
Anon. In this edition the engraved plates are by G. B. Cavalieri.
Petti 2b. Issued with a set of the plates of no. 944 in which the
imprint of Bartolomeo Grassi on the engraved title has been erased.

1285 —[*French version.*] Briefue description des diuerses cruautez que les
Catholiques endurent en Angleterre pour la foy. Fol. *n.p.d.* [1583–84.]
PA(Coll. L'Etoile). [*DMR.]
Anon. One leaf of French text and five numbered plates with
French explanatory text and the same Latin verses as 1284. *Pr.*
[secretly at Paris under Verstegan's supervision, by the printer of
no. 1283]. Petti 2c (revised no., *see* RH, April 1966, p. 291).

1286 —De droeuige traenen, van eene Hollandt-sche Bibelsuster. Waer by
gheuoeght is de lamentatie van noch meer andre van de Reformatie.
4°. *T'Hantwerpen, by Abraham Verhoeuen, n.d.* [1626.] ANT².
Anon. Petti 24. Rombauts pp. 198, 307, 309.

1287 —Ian Iosepsens droom, gheschreuen door ziinen goeden vrient aen
den welcken hy t'selue verhaelt heeft. 4°. *t'Hantwerpen, op. de
Lombaerde Veste inde gulde sonne*, 1619. ANT.
Ⓐ Anon. *Pr.* [Abraham Verhoeven.] Petti 19. Rombauts, pp. 198–9,
1287.1 305–7.
—Miroir des chrestiens abusés. *See* no. 1294.

1288 —Oorloge gheuochten met die wapenen van die waerheydt, en van die
reden, in twee bataillien. Teghen tvve valsche pretentien vande
rebellighe Hollanders. 8°. *T'Hantwerpen, by Ian Knobbaert*, 1628.
BRS.
Ded. sgd.: R.V. Petti 25. Rombauts, pp. 191, 284.
—Orspronck ende teghenwoordighen staet van de Calvinische secte.
See no. 1292.

1289 —L'origine et present estat de la secte Caluinienne, comme elle est
maintenant deuisée en quatre principales parties. *s.sh.*fol. *Anuers,
chez Robert Bruneau*, 1611. PA.
Ded. sgd.: R.V. Petti 13a.

1290 —[Anr. ed.] *s.sh.*fol. *Iouxte la coppie imprimée en Anuers par Robert
Bruneau, n.p.d.* [1611] PA(Dupuy 844 f. 327 bis).

1291 —[Anr. ed.] *s.sh.*fol. *Paris, chez Iacques Honervogt . . . iouxte la coppie
imprimée à Lyon et premierement à Anuers*, 1611. PA(D 2204 bis).
Petti 13b. The Lyon edition cited in the imprint has not been
found.

1292 —[*Flemish transl.*] Oorspronck ende teghenwoordighen staet van de
Caluinische secte, alsoo die nu versheyden is in vier principale deelen.
*s.sh.*fol. *Nae de copye ghedruct t'Antwerpen, by Robert Bruneau*, 1611.
n.p.d. [1611?] HA(2).LN.
Ded. sgd.: R.V. Petti 13c. *Pr.* [Spanish Netherlands]

1293 —Praesentis Ecclesiae Anglicanae typus. *s.sh.*fol. *n.p.*, 1582. w.
Anon. Comprising six woodcuts with accompanying Latin poems, followed by further poems. *Pr.* [Rheims, Jean Foigny.] Petti 1a (revised no., *see* RH, April 1966, pp. 288–91). For a set of plates derived from this work, *see* no. 876.

1294 —Speculum pro Christianis seductis . . . Ista tabula, collecta opera & industria D. Richardi Verstegani. *s.sh.*fol. *Antuerpiae, ex officina Plantiniana*, 1590. ANT².OS(*lower half only*). [*DMR(OS).]
Includes four engravings by Verstegan himself. Petti 5. A version in French, *Miroir des Chrestiens abusés*, was printed but no copy has been found (Petti B1).

1295 —De spiegel der Nederlandsche elenden. Getoont door een lief-lebber der waerheyt ende der Nederlanden weluaert. 8°. *Tot Mechelen, by Hendrick Iaye*, 1621. L.; AMS.ANT.BRS(7).GT(2).LN.NI.
Ded. sgd.: R.V. Petti 21a. An English translation was printed at [S. Omer, Eng. Coll. press] in the same year (A&R 579). *See* RH, Oct. 1986, pp. 128–42.

1296 —[Anr. issue.] *Tot Mechelen, by Hendrick Iaye*, 1621. L(*imp.*).
In this issue the titlepage bears Jaye's woodcut device of a tower on an island surrounded by the legend: 'Turris fortitudinis nomen Domini'. Petti 21b.

1297 —Theatrum crudelitatum haereticorum nostri temporis. 4°. *Antuerpiae, apud Adrianum Huberti*, 1587. L.; ANT³.BRS.D⁶.DMR(2).E.HAN.LAR.LIL². NCY.NI.NM.POI.UP.VI. +
Preliminary address sgd.: R.V. The titlepage is engraved and there are 29 other engravings, all by [Verstegan] himself. Petti 4a. For a full description and analysis of this work, *see* RH, April 1959, pp. 78, *et seq.* Scott 155.

1298 —[Anr. ed.] 4°. *Antuerpiae, apud Adrianum Huberti*, 1588. L.; MU.PA(2). w.
Petti 4b.

1299 —[Anr. ed.] 4°. *Antuerpiae, apud Adrianum Huberti*, 1592. L(2).O.; AMP. ANT².C².D⁸.DE.HA.KN².LIL.MTH.MU.PA(Bliss 729).STG.VI. +
Petti 4c.

1300 —[Anr. ed.] Editio altera emendatior. 4°. *Antuerpiae, apud Hadrianum Huberti*, 1604. L.O.C.; ANT.ANT².C².DE.E.HA.KN².MFL.MU.OS.RO⁷.ST. VI. +
Petti 4d.

1301 —[*French transl.*] Theatre des cruautez des hereticques de nostre temps par M. Richard Versteganus. 4°. *Anuers, chez Adrien Hubert*, 1587. AMS.
A piracy. For genuine editions published by Hubert at Antwerp in 1588 and 1607, *see* nos. 1302–3. The titlepage of the piracy is not engraved and the plates are poor copies of the originals in no. 1297. Petti 4e.

1302 —[Anr. ed.] 4°. *Anuers, chez Adrien Hubert*, 1588. L.O.; ANT.BRS.E.F.GT. O⁶.PA.
Genuine edition by Hubert. With the original engravings as in no. 1297. Petti 4f.

1303 —[Anr. ed.] La seconde edition, augmentée & plus correcte. 4°. *Anuers, chez Adrien Hubert*, 1607. L(2).; AIX.ANT².BRS.CH.DMR.E².F.HAN(-*t.p.*)). L³⁸.LYN.N.VI.
Genuine edition by Hubert. Petti 4g.

1304 —[*A different French transl.*] Theatre des cruautez des hereticques de nostre temps. 4°. *Anuers, chez Adrien Hubert*, 1588. AMS.BRS.BRS².F. GT.HN.LIL(*imp.*).
With an added prologue and a fuller commentary. With the original engravings as in no. 1297. Petti 4h.

1305 —Typus Ecclesiae Catholicae. et signa quibus ea cognoscitur. Typus
      haereticae synagogae et eiusdem proprietates. *s.sh.*fol. *n.p.d.*(?) [1585.]
      PA.(Coll. L'Etoile). [*DMR.]
      Ded. dated from Paris, 3 Jan. 1585 and sgd.: Richardus Verste-
      ganus Anglus. Includes two engravings sgd.: R.V. and dated 1585.
      In the only known copy any imprint there may have been has been
      cut off. Petti 3.

1305.1 —[A portrait of Mary Queen of Scots, including vignettes of her
      execution and twenty lines of Latin verse signed: 'G.Cr. Scotus'. The
      whole engraved anonymously by Richard Verstegan at Antwerp in
      1587?] *Brs.* fol. Copies in the following print-rooms, museums and
      other collections: L.; BRS.; Brunswick, Herzog Anton Ulrich;
      Coburg; DMR.; Dresden; PA.; Rotterdam, Boymans; Vienna,
      Albertina.
      This is the well-known 'Antwerp' engraved portrait of Mary
      usually attributed to Wiericx but which has close affinities with the
      engravings in Verstegan's *Theatrum crudelitatum* (nos. 1297, *et seq.*)
      which first appeared in the same year. The likeness of the Queen in
      this engraving is taken from the portrait by Thomas de Leeu. The
      verses have been attributed to William Crichton the Jesuit but are
      more probably by George Crichton (1555–1611) who was a noted
      writer of Latin verse. Not in Petti. *See* also no. 805.

Viseus, Andreas. *See* Wise, A.
Vitus. *See* White.
Voton, Piquerin. *See* Wotton, Pickering.
W., G., *Evulgator. See* nos. 481–3.
W., T. *See* no. 1417.

Wadding, Luke.††

Original Works

1306 —Annales Minorum, in quibus res omnes trium ordinum a S. Francisco
      institutorum ex fide ponderosius asseruntur, calumniae refelluntur,
      praeclara quaeque monumenta ab obliuione vendicantur. Authore
      R.P.F. Luca Waddingo Hiberno. [Tom. 1.] Fol. *Lugduni, sumptibus
      Claudii Landry,* 1625. O.C.; ANT.AV.AV.CMR.D.GEI.HA.LOU³.MD.MU.NI.
      PEN.RO³.STR.TB. +

1307 —Tomus secundus. Fol. *Lugduni, sumptibus Claudii Landry,* 1628.
      O.C.; ANT.AV.D.DUS.FLO³.HA.MD.NI.PA.PEN.RO³.STR.TOU. +

1308 —Tomus tertius. Fol. *Lugduni, sumptibus Claudii Du-Four,* 1635. O.C.;
      ANT.AV.D.D².FLO³.STR.TOU(*with date 1636*).UT².

1309 —Tomus quartus. Fol. *Lugduni, sumptibus Claudii Du-Four,* 1637. O.C.;
      ANT.AV.D.D².FLO³.L⁴.MD.NI.PA.PEN.RO³.STR.TOU.
      A further four volumes of the work were published between 1642
      and 1657.

1310 —Apologeticus de praetenso monachatu Augustiniano Sancti Francisci,
      in quo deteguntur, & refelluntur varii errores ex vna controuersia
      exorti. 4°. *Matriti, apud D. Theresiam Iuntam,* 1625. C.; D.PA.PA¹¹.RO⁸.
      A second edition, printed before 1641, has not been found. A third
      edition, enlarged with an answer to Thomas de Herrera (who had
      published a reply to the *Apologeticus* at Bologna, c. 1635) was
      printed at Lyon in 1641 (copies at AV.LYN.RO⁸).

1311 —[*Spanish transl.*] Respuesta apologetica contra los que pretenden auer
      sido N.P.S. Francisco frayle de los Ermitaños de S. Agustin, antes que
      fundasse su religion: en que se descubren, y refutan varios errores de
      historia, ocasionados desta controuersia . . . Traducida en Castellano
      por el Padre Fray Pedro Nauarro . . . Difinidor de la Prouincia de

Castilla. 4°. *Madrid, en la Imprenta Real*, 1625. [Coloph.] *Madrid, por Teresa Iunti, impressora del Rey N. Señor.* BAR.MD.VI.

—De Hebraicae linguae origine, praestantia, & ad sacrarum literarum studiosos interpretes, opusculum, 1621. *See* no. 1325.

1312 —Illustre martyrium quatuordecim Fratrum Minorum regularis obseruantiae, ab haereticis Pragae Bohemiae pro fide Catholica occisorum. Authore Fre Hieronymo Strasser eiusdem instituti theologo et per Superiorem Germaniā Generali Commissario. 4°. *Viennae Austriae, excudebat Matthaeus Formica*, 1624. PR(Tres. Rd. 24).
Wadding, in his entry under Strasser in *Scriptores Ordinis Minorum*, 1650 (1906 ed., p. 119), says that he himself wrote this work and sent the MS to Strasser in Germany, adding: 'Correxit ille, expoliuit, emisit'. There is no mention in the published volume of Wadding's authorship. With an engraved plate representing the martyrdoms, and with the arms of the Emperor Ferdinand engraved on the titlepage.

1313 —Πρεσβεια siue legatio Philippi III et IV regum Hispaniarum ad ... Paulum PP.V et Gregorium XV. De definienda controuersia immaculatae conceptionis B. Virginis Mariae, per Antonium a Trejo ... Descripta ac concinnata per ... Lucam Waddingum. Fol. *Louanii, ex officina Henrici Hastenii*, 1624. L.O(2).C(2: 1 imp.).; AMI.ANT².C⁵.D².DI. GT.GTN.HP.L².LOU³(imp.).MU(3).PA(2).RO².VT(2).WO. + +
With an additional titlepage, engraved. Reprinted at Antwerp in 1641.

1314 —[*An extract from no. 1313.*] *In* Pineda, Juan de. Oratio panegyrica de immaculata conceptione B. Mariae Virginis ... Nunc primum Latine edita, vna cum monitione, de occasione & fructu, huius aliarumque orationum, ex R.P. Fr Luca Waddingo Minorita. 12°. *Coloniae, apud Petrum a Brachel*, 1626. PR.
Pineda's *Oratio* to which the extract from Wadding is here attached is a Latin translation of a sermon originally given in Spanish at Seville in 1615 (Palau 226373–5).

1315 —Vita et res gestae. B. Petri Thomae Aquitani. Ex ordine B. Mariae Virginis a Monte Carmelo Patriarchae Constantinopolitani et Sedis Apostolicae legati. 8°. *Lugduni, sumptibus Laurentii Durand* (1637). C.; AV.BAR².BAR³.C².FLO³.KNY(2).LYN(2).LYN².MD.PA.RO²(2).RO³.RO⁵.RO⁸(2). +
With an additional titlepage, engraved. The date 1637 occurs in the imprint on the engraved titlepage only.

1316 —Le vray S. reliquaire de l'esprit seraphique du B.P.S. François sous la lettre de ses propres oraisons, cantiques, epistres, admonitions, conferences, & de tout le reste de sa doctrine; partie en Latin-François, ou Italien-François, mot à mot, pour conseruer l'esprit de l'Autheur; partie abbregée en seul François, & rangée en ordre des vertus. Le tout hors des vieux originels ... recueillis par le R.P. Lucas Wadingus. 8°. *Liege, de l'imprimerie des heritiers Sauueur*, 1632. UT².
Collation: π²A–Cc⁸.

1317 —[Anr. issue? or titlepage variant? With title beginning:] L'esprit seraphique du tres-heureux pere S. François sous la lettre de ses propres oraisons, cantiques, epistres [etc., as in no. 1316] ... *Liege, de l'imprimerie des heritiers Sauueur*, 1632. AIX.LGE.LGE².STR.
Collation as in no. 1316.

1318 —[Anr. ed.? or anr. issue? With title as in no. 1316.] 8°. *Liege, chez Iean van Milst*, 1637. LOU³.NM².
Collation as in nos. 1316–17. This is either a page for page reprint or a reissue of the original sheets except for the first gathering (π²).

1319 —[Latin verses and epigrams.] *In* Francisco, de Sosa. Tratados. 4°. *Salamanca, por Antonio Vazquez*, 1623. MD.

The verses and epigrams are contained in Tratado 9, entitled: *Sanctorale seraphicum . . . Sancti Francisci, & eorum qui ex tribus eius Ordinibus relati sunt inter sanctos; cum elogiis, versibus & deprecationibus, pro seraphici instituti deuotis.* Palau 319803.

1320 —[*Flemish transl.,* enlarged, of *Sanctorale seraphicum.*] Seraphische historie van het leuen der heijligen des oordens S. Francisci van Assysien ende van syn eerste ghesellen . . . ghestelt door . . . Cornelius Thielmannus. Fol. *Louen, Cornelius Coenesteyn,* 1630. SHT².

Works edited by Wadding

1321 —Angelus, *del Paz.* Operum . . . Angeli del Pas . . . a RR.PP. Fr. Luca Wadingo & Fr. Antonio Hiquaeo . . . collectorum & reuisorum tomus secundus. Complectens commentaria in Marci Euangelium. Fol. *Romae, typis & sumptibus Ildefonsi Ciacconi,* 1623. C.
     Titlepage partly engraved. An edition in five volumes of the works of Angelus del Paz was planned but only vols. 2, 3, 4, edited by Wadding and Hicky, were published.

1322 —Tomus tertius. Complectens primam partem comentariorum in Lucae Euangelium. Fol. *Romae, typis et sumptibus Ildefonsi Ciacconi,* 1628.PA.RO⁷.RO⁸.RO¹⁰.
     Titlepage partly engraved.

1323 —Tomus quartus. Complectens secundam partem commentariorum in Lucae Euangelium. Fol. *Romae, typis et sumptibus Ildefonsi Ciacconi,* 1625. RO⁷.RO⁸.RO¹⁰.
     Titlepage partly engraved.

1324 —Anthony, *of Padua, Saint.* S. Antonii de Padua concordantiae morales sacrorum Bibliorum . . . Quibus accessit egregium Promptuarium S. Scripturae, Anonymi cuiusdam Franciscani Hyberni . . . Nunc primum extracta ex m.ss. . . . industria R.P.F. Luca Waddingi Hyberni. 4°. 2 pts. *Romae, apud Alphonsum Ciacconum,* 1624. O.C.; D.FU.KN.KN².KNY.PA.RO².RO⁷.RO⁸.RO¹⁰.STR.
     Pt. 2, comprising the *Promptuarium,* has its own titlepage.

1325 —Calasius, M. Concordantiae Sacrorum Bibliorum Hebraicorum. Fol. 4 vols. *Romae, apud Stephanum Paulinum,* 1621(–22). L.O.; CHI.D.PA. PH.RO⁸(*missing 1976*).Y.
     Wadding edited the work after Calasius's death, appending to it his own *De Hebraicae linguae origine, praestantia, & ad sacrarum literarum studiosos interpretes, opusculum.*

1326 —Duns, Joannes, *Scotus.* R.P.F. Ioannis Duns Scoti . . . opera omnia, quae hucusque reperiri potuerunt. Collecta, recognita, notis, scholiis, & commentariis illustrata, a PP. Hibernis, Collegii Romani S. Isidori professoribus. Fol. 12 vols. *Lugduni, sumptibus Laurentii Durand,* 1639. L.O.C.; ANG.HEI.L⁴.LIL.LYN.MD.MU(2).PA.PA⁴.SBG.SOL.VI.UT. +
     Edited under the direction of Wadding who signs the Epistle to the Reader. His principal assistant was Hugh MacCaghwell. Vol. 8 comprises *Quaestiones in lib. IV Sententiarum . . . Cum commentario R.P.F. Antonii Hiquaei.* The commentaries in vol. 7, pt. 2 are by John Punch.

1327 —Francis, *of Assisi, Saint.* B.P. Francisci Assisiatis opuscula . . . Nunc primum collecta . . . Notis et commentariis asceticis illustrata, per Fr. Lucam Waddingum. 4°. *Antuerpiae, ex officina Plantiniana, apud Balthasarem Moretum, et viduam Ioannis Moreti, et Io. Meursium,* 1623. L.O.C.; AMI.ANT.ANT³.BRS(2).CHA.D⁶.HA.KNY.LOU³.MD.MU.PA(2). RO².+ +
     The titlepage is engraved.

1328 —[*Anr. ed., abridged.*] Opuscula B.P. Francisci Assisiatis: iampridem ab adm. R.P. Fr. Luca Waddingo . . . collecta, distincta, notis, & commentariis asceticis illustrata. Nunc tandem, ad commodiorem vsum, instante Fr. Io. Baptista a Frescarolio eiusdem Ord. hoc contractiori volumine excussa, & euulgata. 32°. *Alexandriae, ex officina Ioannis Soti*, 1629. RO².

1329 —[Anr. ed. of no. 1328.] 16°. *Neapoli, apud Lazarum Scorigium*, 1635. C.; AMS.BO.NP².RO².SBG.SCG.USH.UT².

1330 —[*A different abridgment.*] Sancti Francisci Assisiatis . . . opuscula. Olim a R.P.F. Luca Waddingo . . . collecta, digesta, & commentariis illustrata, nunc vero . . . in Enchiridion redacta. 32°. *Lugduni, - sumptibus Laurentii Durand*, 1637. BO.KNY.PA(2).

> Edited by Ludovicus Cavalli, O.F.M., who dedicates it to the General of the Order, Baptista a Campanea, who had ordered the redaction to be made.

1331 —Luis, *da Cruz.* R.P. Fr. Ludouici a Cruce . . . Disputationes morales in tres bullas apostolicas, Cruciatae, Defunctorum et Compositionis. 4°. *Lugduni, apud Iacobum Prost*, 1634. PA.

> Edited by [Wadding]. Wadding himself says that he edited it in his entry under Luis da Cruz in *Scriptores Ordinis Minorum*, 1650 (1906 ed., p. 163).

1332 —[Variant imprint.] *Lugduni, sumptibus Nemesii Trichet*, 1634. HNC.

> Forms part of a shared edition with no. 1331.

1333 —Rodrigues, Manoel. Summa casuum conscientiae, omnium quae hucusque in lucem exiere copiosissima, confessariis et animarum curam gerentibus ad quascunque materiarum moralium resolutiones vtilissima . . . Translata nunc primum in Latinum . . . opera Baltazaris de Canizal. 4°. *Duaci, ex typographia Baltazaris Belleri*, 1614. L.; AAR.AMI.CHA.LYN.MU.PA.VES.

> Canizal's Latin translation abridged and edited by [Wadding?]. In his entry under Rodrigues in *Scriptores ordinis minorum*, 1650 (1906 ed., p. 73), Wadding says that his superiors asked him to edit the Latin translation, and that he compressed the two volumes of the original into one which was published at Zaragoza in 1616. As no 1616 edition, published anywhere, has been found, there may possibly be some confusion as to place and date. The 1614 Douai edition appears to correspond in every other respect to Wadding's own description. One of the two approbations is by Henry Mailer, Professor of Theology at the English College, Douai.

1334 **Wadding, Peter.**‡ Breuis refutatio calumniarum quas Collegio Societatis Iesu Pragensi. impegit scriptor famosi libelli cui titulus Flagellum Iesuitarum. 4°. *Nissae, impressit Ioannes Schubarth*, anno XXXIIII [misprint for XXXVIII, i.e. 1638]. L.; HD.PR.PR².RO. RO²(2).

> Defending Jesuit control of the University of Prague against [Caspar Schoppe's] *Flagellum Iesuitarum, dass ist, Iesuiter Geissel*, 1632. A prefatory note by the printer says that Wadding's MS, written in 1632 and sent from Prague into Germany to be printed, remained unprinted for six years because 'iniquitas temporis negavit opportunitatem Latini typi'. The date of printing, therefore, is 1638.

1335 —De natura, propietatibus et notis verae Christi Ecclesiae: disputatio theologica ex Catechesi Heidelbergensi . . . Quam publice proponit, & . . . tuebitur Fredericus Adolphus Reuter . . . Assistente Reu. P. Petro Wadingo Societ. Iesu, S. Theologiae Professore, Antuerpiae in Collegio Societatis Iesu 3. Februarii & sequentibus, CIɔ.IɔC.XXI. hora locoq. solitis. 4°. *n.p.d.* [1621]. O.

> *Pr.* [Antwerp?]

1336 —Disceptatio placida super famosa quaestione. An hoc tempore legitimae sint causae, vt quaedam monasteria alterius instituti monachis, vel militaribus institutis dentur? 4°. *n.p.*, 1631.

Anon. Not found. Description from Sommerv. (tom. 8, col. 929) correcting an earlier erroneous attribution (in tom. 4, col. 1592) to the German Jesuit, P. Layman.

1337 —Ferdinando III Austriaco. Per Romani Imperii fasces abauos atauos, numerare solito . . . ex totius Pragensis Vniuersitatis voto vitam felicitatemq; exoptat. Humillimus cliens. Petrus Wadingus. In eadem Academia Sac. Theologiae. Professor. 4°. *n.p.d.* [1637.] PA (Rés. m. Yc. 936/18).

A panegyric on behalf of the University of Prague for the Emperor, Ferdinand III, elected 22 Dec. 1636. *Pr.* [at Prague?]

1338 —Laudatio funebris dicta . . . in metropolitana ecclesia Pragensi cum clerus et proceres regni exequias celebrarent . . . Ferdinandi Secundi. 4°. *Viennae, typis Matthaei Formicae*, 1638.

Not found. Description from Sommerv. (tom. 8, col. 930).

1339 —R.P. Petri Wadingi . . . Tractatus de Incarnatione. Ad Sereniss. Ferdinandum III Bohemiae & Vngariae Regem. 4°. *Antuerpiae, apud Martinum Nutium*, 1636. L.O.; ANT³.BAR³.D(3).D².E²(*imp.*).HP.LYN.MD. MTH.PA.RO.RO².UO.X. +

Walsh (no. 628) cites an edition with this imprint dated 1634 at MTH, but this appears to be an error.

1340 —[*Disputations in which he acted as Praeses.*] Bauters, B. Disputatio theologica de praedestinatione et gratia . . . Eam proponit Praeside R.P. Petro Wadingo Soc. Iesu . . . Balthasar Bauters, eiusdem Societatis, Antuerpiae in Collegio Societ. Iesu. 8. Iunii, hora [space] meridiem. 4°. *Antuerpiae, typis Martini Nutii*, [1621?]. HP.

In the only copy found the date has been cut away. Sommerv. (tom. 8, col. 928) gives the date as 1521, clearly a misprint for 1621. The thesis discusses opinions expressed at the Synod of Dort in 1618–19.

1341 —[Anr. issue? or anr. ed.? of the same programme, with a different Respondent.] . . . Eam proponit Praeside R.P. Petro Wadingo Soc. Iesu . . . Petrus Darcaeus Hibernus. 4°. *Antuerpiae, typis Martini Nutii*, 1521 [misprint for 1621].

Not found. Description from Sommerv. (tom. 8, col. 928–9) who gives the date as : M.D.XXI.

1342 —Cruyce, I. B. van den. D.O.M. [Disputatio] theologica. Praeside R. Patre Petro Wadingo . . . Defendet P. Ioannes Baptista van den Cruyce Societatis Iesu. Die [space] hora 9 et 3 post meridiem. 4°. *Louanii, typis Henrici Hastenii*, 1622.

Not found. Description from Sommerv. (tom. 8, col. 929).

1342.1 **Wadding, Richard,** *in religion* Richard of S. Victor. [*Begin :*] Illustrissimo Principi, ac reuerendissimo Domino Ludouico Ludouisio S.R.E. Card. . . . Hiberniae Protectori. Doctor Frater Richardus de S. Victore Hibernus Augustinensis D.V.C. . . . Theoremata selectiora ex vniuersa theologiae summa pro comitiis generalibus Ord. Eremit. M.P. Augustini Romae celebrandis deprompta. [*End :*] Tuebitur P. F. Richardus de S. Victore . . . in celebri Conimbricensium Academia Doctor Theologus, & Prouinciae Portugalliae in praedictis comitiis generalibus discretus: in Conuentu M.P. Augustini Romano. Maii die 26. Anno Domini M.DC.XXV. 4°. *Romae, apud haeredem Bartholomaei Zannetti*, 1625. RO⁸.

For the Irish Augustinian, Richard Wadding, *see Archivum Hibernicum*, xix, (1956) 61–134, pp. 127, 129.

1342.2 **Wadsworth, James,** *the Elder.*† Las leyes nueuamente hechas en el Parlamẽto de Inglaterra este año de M.DC.VI. contra los Catolicos Ingleses, que llaman Recusantes, traduzidas de su original impresso en Ingles. Fol. (a single quadrifolium). *n.p.d.* [1606.] MD²(2: Jes. 94/16; 112/37). SIM(E 2512/129). [*L.]

Anon. A summary in Spanish of the anti-Catholic legislation of 1606 following the Gunpowder Plot, and of various letters by English Catholics describing the persecution. The evidence for [Wadsworth], correcting an attribution to [Andrew Wise and Joseph Creswell] advanced by A. J. Loomie in *Guy Fawkes in Spain*, p. 51, and *Spain and the Jacobean Catholics*, vol. 1, p. 174, is to be published in his forthcoming edition of the English original of no. 274. *Pr.* [Madrid?]

1342.3 **Wakeman, Thomas,** *alias* Green. Regiis Angliae diuis dithyrambus Praeside Octauio Card. Bandino in disput. Thomae Grini Coll. Angl. alum. emodulatus. Fol. *Romae, apud Franciscum Corbellettum,* 1627. L(2).; MIL²(3).RO²(5).

Complimentary verses addressed to Cardinal Bandini on the occasion of his presiding over a thesis defended at the English College. For Wakeman, *see* Foley, vol. 7, p. 801. The titlepage is engraved. Some words of the title are printed in reverse.

1343 **Waldegrave, Charles,** *alias* Flower. Theses ex vniuersa theologia, disputandae in Coll. Anglicano Societatis Iesu Louanii anno Domini CIƆ IƆC XX. Praeside R. Rdo Patre Christophoro Greenwood, Soc. Iesu . . . Defendet Carolus Florus, eiusdem Societatis. 4°. *Louanii, ex officina Bernardini Masii,* 1620.

Not found. Description from Sommerv. (tom. 3, col. 1729).

1344 **Walgrave, Francis.** [*A work edited by him.*] Ioannis Gersen Abbatis Vercellensis Italo-Benedictini De imitatione Christi libri quatuor A nonnullis olim Ioanni Gerson, ab aliis nuper Thomae a Kempis falso tributi . . . Cum animaduersionibus apologeticis F Francisci Valgrauii A.B. ad titulum & textum. 12°. *Parisiis, apud Sebastianum Huré,* 1638. O.; CARP.O³.PA².TRO.

A French version of the text with Walgrave's annotations was published in 1643, and another edition of the Latin c. 1650. *See* Chaussy, p. 151. For the authorship controversy *see* P. L. Puyol, *L'auteur du 'De Imitatione Christi'*, 2 vols., Paris, 1899–1900.

—[*A work written at his instigation.*] Barnes, J. Examen Trophaeorum Congregationis praetensae Anglicanae Ordinis S. Benedicti, 1622. *See* no. 70.

1345 **Wallis, Francis.** Theses ex vniuersa theologia Doctoris Angelici. Disputandae in Coll. Anglicano Societatis Iesu Louanii, Anno Domini CIƆ IƆC XIX. Praeside P. Ioanne Pricio Soc. Iesu . . . Defendet P. Franciscus Valisius eiusdem Societatis. Die [space] Iulii. 4°. *n.p.d.* [1619.]

A programme announcing the forthcoming defence of his thesis. Not found. Description from Sommerv. (tom. 6, col. 1225). For Wallis *see* Foley, vol. 7, p. 805. *Pr.* [Louvain].

Walpole, Henry, *Saint.* [*Appendix.*] Creswell, J. Historia de la vida y martyrio que padecio . . . el P. Henrique Valpolo, 1596. *See* nos. 276–7.

——Histoire de la vie . . . du pere Henry Valpole, 1597. *See* no. 278.

Walpole, Michael.† [*A work based partly on MS material left by him.*] Muñoz, L. Vida y virtudes de la venerable virgen doña Luisa de Caruaial, 1632. *See* no. 1619.

[1346 *cancelled*]

1347 **Walpole, Richard.**† Appendix ad Apologiam pro hierarchia ecclesiastica . . . Qua Latinus eiusdem Apologiae interpres R.G. iudicium suum, censuramque fert de octo libellis famosis sub inquietorum presbyterorum nomine recens in lucem editis. 8°. *n.p.,* 1602. L.O.; D.O⁴.RO.YK.

R.G. [Richard Gualpolus? i.e. R. Walpole?] *See* RH, April 1962, p. 223. This is a sequel to Robert Persons's *A Briefe Apologie*

(A&R 613) by the English Jesuit who translated that work into Latin in 1601 (no. 872). It is a different work from the English *An Appendix to the Apologie* (A&R 612).

—[*A work translated by him?*] Persons, R. Apologia pro hierarchia ecclesiastica, [1601]. *See* no. 872.

Walsh, Angelus, *name in religion. See* Walsh, M.

1348 **Walsh, Martin,** *in religion* Angelus Walsh.‡ Incomparabili vitae, mortis, ac miraculorum excellentia gloriosissimo Seraphicę Religionis syderi . . . Iacobo a Marchia . . . primos musaei flores consecrat . . . Frater Angelus a Neapoli . . . Conclusiones philosophicae . . . [*End:*] [Disputabun]tur publice in Neapolitano Montis Caluariae Seminario . . . Respondebit . . . Angelus a Neapoli . . . Assistet . . . Martinus Angelus Valesius ab Hibernia. *s.sh.fol. Neapoli, ex typographia Domin*[*ic*]*i Maccarani,* 1625. RO⁸(*mutil.*)

A programme announcing the forthcoming defence of a thesis.

1349 —Paraenesis poetica in aduentu Caroli Walliae Principis . . . *Matriti, in typographia regia,* 1624.

A poem on Prince Charles's visit to Madrid to woo the Infanta in 1623. Not found. *See* Wadding, p. 169. A copy noted by T. Wall (IER, 5th ser. vol. 69, p. 720) at D¹⁰ in 1947 cannot now be found.

1350 —Seraphicae religionis obsfrantissimae [*sic*] . . . inuictae Cantabriae Prouinciae, Fr. Martinus Angelus Valesius obsequentissimus eius filius . . . Corollaria philosophica ex principiis deducta theosophicis de augustissimo Sacramento. Controuersia principalis, Vtrum conuersio sit ratio formalis qua corpus Christi constituitur praesens in Eucharistia? . . . Fretus praesidio . . . P. Fr. Thomae de Guessalla enitetur horum reddere rationē Fr. Martinus Angelus Valesius Manapiensis in comitiis prouincialibus Victoriae celebrandis anno 1619. *s.sh.fol. n.p.d.* [1619.] RO⁸. *Pr.* [Spain?]

—[*Disputations in which he acted as Praeses.*] Lea, T. . . . Conclusiones theologicae, 1629. *See* nos. 713–14.

Ward, Francis. Conclusiones theologicae, 1639. *See* no. 253.

1351 **Ward, Mary.** [*Appendix.*] Urban VIII, *Pope.* S.D.N.D. Vrbani Diuina Prouidentia Papae VIII. Suppressio praetensae Congregationis Iesuitissarum. Fol. (a quadrifolium). *Romae, ex typographia Reu. Cam. Apost.,* 1631. L²⁷ᴬ(16/1 n. 7).MD²(Jes. 118/108).RO⁶.RO⁹ (Anglia 35 I no. 1).

The Brief *Pastoralis Romani Pontificis* suppressing Mary Ward's first Institute. Though the Brief itself bears the date 13 Jan. 1630 it was not registered in the Secretariate of Briefs until 21 May 1631 (*see* sig. A4ᵛ). With a woodcut of the arms of Urban VIII on the titlepage. Collation: A⁴.

1352 —[Anr. ed.] 4°. *Romae, MDCXXI* [*sic*]. *Ex typographia Reu. Cam. Apost. Et Venetiis, apud Andream Babam, n.d.* [1631]. LINC.WO(3).

A reprint of no. 1351. Collation: A⁴.

1353 —[Anr. ed.] 4°. *Bruxellae, typis Ioannis Mommartii,* 1631. ANT².ANT³ BRS².GT.LOU.SBG.

A reprint of no. 1351. Collation: A⁴B² (B2 blank).

1354 —[Anr. ed.] 4°. *Romae, deinde Cracouiae, in officina Andreae Petricouii,* 1631. KR.KR².VI.WR².

A reprint of no. 1351. Collation: A⁴.

1355 —[Anr. ed., with other documents.] 4°. *Iuxta exemplar Bruxellae impressum. Typis Ioannis Mommartii,* 1631. [1643 *or later*]. MU. [*O.]

A reprint of no. 1353 followed by other documents, all of them hostile to Mary Ward. Internal evidence shows that this edition cannot have been printed before 1643. Collation: A–G⁴ (G4 blank?).

1356 —[Anr. ed. of the Brief alone.] S.D.N. Dn. Vrbani diuina Prouidentia Papae VIII. Suppressio praetensae Congregationis Iesuitissarum.

Romae ex typographia Reu. Camerae Apostolicae. M.DC.XXXII. 4°. *n.p.*, 1636. L.O.; C².CHA.D.D².FU.GT.L².L⁴.NP.SBG.STG.TB.WO(3). + Though copies of this edition may be found on their own, it is, in fact, the final part of a collection published in 1636 by [Caspar Schoppe] under the pseudonym Alphonsus de Vargas, entitled: *Relatio ad reges et principes Christianos*. Collation (of this section): ¶⁴. (pp. 1–8). It is a reprint of no. 1351, some copies of which may have borne the date 1632.

1357 —[*Flemish transl.*] Onser alderheyligsten Vaders ende Heeren Urbani by den ghedooghe Godts des VIII. Paus, suppressie van de vermeynde Vergaderinghe der Jesuiterssen. 4°. *Brussel, by Jan. Mommart*, 1631. ANT².BRS.GT.

1358 **Warford, William.**† Breuis ac methodica institutio continens praecipua Christianae fidei mysteria: e Sacra Scriptura, SS. Patribus & Conciliis collecta. Addita est compendiaria methodus conscientiam ad confessionem generalem discutiendi ... Latine nunc primum edita mandante Reuerendissimo Domino Iacobo Blasaeo Audomarensi Episcopo. 8°. *Antuerpiae, apud haeredes Martini Nutii*, 1617. VT (Stamp. Barb. V. XIV. 101).

Anon. An enlarged translation [by Thomas More S.J.] of A&R 877 and 880. The printer's foreword says of the English original: 'Datum est praelo in Hispania, a Georgio Doulaeo anno Domini 1603'. The authorities for [Warford] and [More] are the 1632 Catalogue and Alegambe (pp. 171, 434). The English originals may have been the result of collaboration between [Warford] and [William Bathe] for Alegambe has entries for them under both these authors (pp. 171, 169). *Pr.* [S. Omer, Charles Boscard]. This appears to have been a shared edition: Alegambe gives the imprint as 'Audomari', though no copy with that imprint is now known. The translation is sometimes erroneously ascribed to Bishop Blaise who commissioned it.

1359 **Weston, Edward.**† De triplici hominis officio, ex notione ipsius naturali, morali, ac theologica; institutiones orthodoxae, contra atheos, politicos, sectarios. 4°. 3 pts. *Antuerpiae, apud Ioannem Keerbergium*, 1602. L.O.C.; C².D.D².DI.FU.GTN.HP.L².LYN.MU(2).O⁵.PA. PA⁶,WO. + + The titlepage is engraved.

1360 —[Anr. issue, with title:] Antiatheus, antipoliticus, & antisectarius. Tribus institutionum libris, triplex hominis officium, naturaliter, moraliter, ac theologice complectens. *Duaci, apud Baltasarem Bellerum*, 1609. C.; BOR.LYN.PA⁵.SOI. The sheets of no. 1359 except for the first quire (a⁴) which is reset.

1361 —[Anr. issue, with title:] De vere Christiani hominis officiis libri tres. *Antuerpiae, apud Ioannem Keerbergium*, 1609. O.; ANT.MST. With the first quire (a⁴) again reset.

1362 —Iesu Christi Domini Nostri Coruscationum, simulque earum vi dictorum, factorumque quarumdam personarum, eodem Christo praesente, in euangelica historia recensitorum enarrationes sacrae, philosophice, theologice, et historice tractatae. Fol. *Antuerpiae, ex officina Hieronymi Verdussii*, 1631. AV.MD.MU.WO. [*O.] The text concludes: 'Finis partis prioris'. No subsequent part has been found.

1363 —Iuris pontificii sanctuarium. Defensum ac propugnatum contra Rogeri Widdringtoni in Apologia & Responso apologetico impietatem. 8°. *n.p.*, 1613. L.O.C.; D.D².DE.DUR(2).HP.L².L¹³.L²⁶.MTH.O⁴.PA⁴.PA⁶. RO¹¹.USH. Answers no. 925.1 and no. 926.3. Answered by no. 925.6. *See* Mil., vol. 2, pp. 103–4, and RH, Oct. 1979, pp. 111–14.

—Probatio seu examen veritatis Christianae, 1614.
Cited by Duthilleul (no. 1594) and Labarre (vol. 2, no 621) but probably an error for the English work at A&R 885.

1364 —Theatrum vitae ciuilis ac sacrae; siue de moribus reipub. Christianae commentaria. Fol. *Brugis Flandrorum, ex officina Guilielmi de Neue*, 1626. L.O.; AMI.ANT(2).BRS.E².GTN.HA.MD.MU.OR.RO⁵.USH.VAL.VT(2). WO. +

1365 —[Anr. issue, with imprint;] *Antuerpiae, prostant apud Gulielmum a Tongris*, 1626. C.; GTN.ULM.
The sheets of no. 1364 except for the first quire (✠⁴) which is reset and signed: *⁴. The date in the imprint is misprinted: M.CD.XXVI.

White, Andrew.‡ [*Disputations in which he acted as Praeses.*] Layton, T. Theses es vniuersa theologia Doctoris Angelici. Disputandae in Collegio Anglicano Soc. Iesu Louanii, 1619. *See* no. 712.

—Mainwaring, G. Theses ex vniuersa theologia Doctoris Angelici. Proposita in Collegio Anglicano Societatis Iesu Louanii, [1618]. *See* no. 760.

—Stillington, W. Theses ex theologia Sancti Thomae. Propositae in Collegio Anglicano Societatis Iesu Leodii, [1627]. *See* no. 1248.

White, Edward, *alias. See* Gifford.

White, John James, *Abbot of Ratisbon. See* Whyte, J. J.

1366 **White, Richard.**‡ Breuis explicatio martyrii sanctae Vrsulae et vndecim millium virginum Britannarum, per R.V.B. 8°. *Duaci, ex typographia Petri Auroii*, 1610. L(2).C.; BRS².
R.V.B. [Richard White (Vitus) of Basingstoke.] This is an extract from Book 6 of the author's *Historiae* (no. 1370).

1367 —Breuis explicatio priuilegiorum iuris, et consuetudinis, circa venerabile sacramentum Eucharistiae. Per R.V.B. 8°. *Duaci, apud Carolum Boscardum*, 1609. L.
R.V.B. [Richard White (Vitus) of Basingstoke.]

1368 —De reliquiis et veneratione sanctorum. *Duaci*, 1609.
Not found. Description from Labarre 404, citing BCNI 5552, following Foppens 1073. Its existence is confirmed by Pits, p. 807.

1369 —Ricardi Viti . . . Historiarum libri, 1. Ab origine ad Brotum. 2. Ab illo ad Malmutium. 3. Ab hoc ad Helium. 4. Ab isto ad Lucium. 5. Ab eo ad Constantium. Cum notis antiquitatum Britannicarum. 8°. *Atrebati, ex officina Gulielmi Riuierii*, 1597. L(2).O(2).C(2).; A.AIX. C².C⁸.D(2: 1 *imp.*).DE(2).DUR.GT.L².L¹³.LOU³.VI. + +

1370 —Historiarum Britanniae liber sextus. Quo vis armorum in campis, & authoritas litterarum in scholis, atque religio Christiana in orbe terrarum publicata, demōstratur. 8°. *Duaci, apud Carolum Boscardum*, 1598. [Coloph.] *Atrebati, ex typogr. Gulielmi Riuerii.* L(2).O.; A.AMI. C².C³.C¹⁰.C¹⁷.D.D².DE.F.GT.LOU³.M.RNN.VNS.

1371 ——Liber septimus. Quo verus ad eam insulam Saxonum ingressus, & permansio declaratur. 8°. *Duaci, apud Carolum Boscardum*, 1600. L.O.; A.C².C³.C¹⁰.C¹⁷.D.D².DE(*imp.*).L¹³.LIL.LOU³.M.RNN.

1372 ——Liber octauus. Quo vera causa excidii, regni Brtionum [*sic*] in insula, demonstratur. 8°. *Duaci, apud Carolum Boscardum*, 1600. L.O.; A.C².C³.C¹⁰.C¹⁷.D.D².DE.F.L¹³.LOU³.M.RNN.
Some copies have the titlepage misprint corrected (e.g. O.)

1373 ——Liber nonus, quo fundamenta regni, & ecclesiae Anglorum in insula exponuntur. 8°. *Duaci, apud Carolum Boscardum*, 1602. L.O.; A.C².C³.CARP.D.D².DE.GTN.L¹³.LOU³.O³.PA.RNN. +

1374 ——Liber decimus, quo monarchiae Anglorum constitutio, variis Dacorum irruptionibus perturbata, demonstratur. 8°. *Duaci, apud Carolum Boscardum*, 1606. L.; E.LOU³.RNN.

1375 ——Liber vndecimus. In quo totius exercitus Angloru̅, Dacorumque conflictatione, per annos multos ... peruenitur. 8°. *Duaci, apud Carolum Boscardum*, 1607. L.; E.LOU³.RNN.

1376 —[Anr. issue of bks. 1–9.] Ricardi Viti ... *Historiarum Britanniae insulae, ab origine mundi, ad annum Christi octingentesimum, libri nouem priores. Apud Carolum Boscardum*, 1602. L(2).O(-*t.p.*).C.; C²⁰. D.E.F.L².L⁴.U.
The sheets of nos. 1369–73 reissued with an additional quire (signed: *a*⁸) at the beginning, comprising the general titlepage and preliminaries. *Pr.* [Douai.]

1376.1 —*Richardi Viti ... orationes*: 1. De circulo artium & philosophiae. 2. De eloquentia & Cicerone. 3. Pro diuitiis regum. 4. Pro doctoratu. 5. De studiorum finibus. Cum notis rerum variarum & antiquitatis. 8°. *Atrebati, ex officina Gulielmi Riuerii*, 1596. L(2).O.; GN.GT.PA.
The first and second of these *Orationes* had been published in London in 1565–66 with a dedicatory epistle by Christopher Jonson of Winchester College (STC 25403). The present edition reprints Jonson's epistle.

1376.2 —[Anr. ed., enlarged with two additional *Orationes*.] 8°. *Duaci, typis Caroli. Boscardi*, 1604. DOU('*Oratio septima*' only).O('*Oratio septima*' only).RMS.
'Oratio septima' has its own titlepage with imprint and date: *Duaci, ex typographia Caroli Boscardi*, 1604, but the pagination and signatures continue those of no.s 1–6.

1377 **White, Stephen.** [*Disputations in which he acted as Praeses.*] Christelius, N. Disputatio theologica. De actibus humanis in Catholica et celebri Academia Dilingana publice proposita anno Salutis M.DC.XII die [space] Iunii, Praeside P. Stephano Vito. *Dilingae, apud Ioannem Mayer, n.d.* [1612.]
Not seen. Sommerv. (tom. 8, col. 1093–5) records a copy of this and nos. 1378–88 at the Cistercian Abbey of Stams in the Tyrol, but not traced there in 1985.

1378 —Fischer, I. G. Disputatio theologica. De poenitentia quam in inclita, orthodoxa Vniuersitate Dilingana III Nonas Decembres praeside ac promotore Staphano Vito ... publice defendet ... Ioannes Georgius Fischer ... anno Christiano M.DC.XIII. 4°. *Dilingae, apud Ioannem*
(A) *Mayer, n.d.* [1613.]
1378.1 Not seen. See note to no. 1377.

1379 —Kempf, Ioannes. Disputatio theologica de iure, iustitia, et aliquot eiusdem actibus, quam in alma et Catholica Vniuersitate Dilingana, anno Christi M.DC.XXI. Mense [space] die [space] Praeside Stephano Vito, Societatis Iesu ... Publice proposuit R.D. Ioannes Kempf ... candidatus pro prima & secunda theologiae laurea. 4°. *Dilingae, apud Vdalricum Rem, n.d.* [1621]. LOU³.
See also note to no. 1377,

1380 —Keyslin, A., & Vogt, A. Disputatio theologica, de augustissimo Eucharistiae sacramento, quam in inclita, orthodoxa Vniuersitate Dilingana anno salutis M.DC.XV. die [space] Septembris praeside ac promotore Stephano Vito ... proponent ... Albertus Keyslin, et Andreas Vogt. 4°. *Dilingae, apud viduam Ioannis Mayer, n.d.* [1615.]
Not seen. See note to no. 1377.

1381 —Kranzegger, I. L. Disputatio theologica, de sacramento Baptismi, et Confirmationis. Quam in ... [Catholica Academia] Dilingana, anno M.DC.XIV. die XXIII Septembr. praeside Stephano Vito ... publice proponet Ioannes Ludouicus Kranzegger. 4°. *Dilingae, apud Ioannem Mayer, n.d.* [1614].
Not seen. See note to no. 1377.

1382 —Lintz, W. Disputatio theologica, de humanis actionibus bonis et malis vniuersim. Quam D.O.M.A. in Catholica celebri Vniuersitate

Dilingana anno M.DC.XIX die [space] Martii praeside Stephano Vito ... publice propugnabit R.F. Wolfgangus Lintz. 4°. *Dilingae, apud viduam Ioannis Mayer, n.d.* [1619.]
Not seen. *See* note to no. 1377.

1383   —Mindler, J. Positiones theologicae de Deo Vno et Trino, quas mense Martio die [space] in inclita, orthodoxa Vniuersitate Dilingana, praeside ac promotore Stephano Vito ... proposuit Ioannes Mindlerus. 4°. *Dilingae, typis academicis, apud Vdalricum Rem,* 1620.
Not seen. *See* note to no. 1377.

1384   —Peischel, G. De sanctissimae Trinitatis mysterio disputatio. Quam ... in Catholica ... [Vniuersitate Dilingana] II Iunii publice proponet ... Georgius Peischelius ... Praeside et promotore Stephano Vito. 4°. *Dilingae, typis academcis, apud Melchiorem Algeyer,* 1620.
Not seen. *See* note to no. 1377.

1385   —Scheilz, G. Theses theologicae ex omnibus D. Thomae partibus in Catholica Vniuersitate Dilingana, ad publicam disputationem propositae. Praeside P. Stephano Vito ... Ad diem XIV. Iunii. Anno M.DC.XXII. 4°. *Dilingae, apud Vdalricum Rem, n.d.* [1622.]
Not seen. *See* note to no. 1377.

1386   —Schmid, V. Disputatio theologica de Incarnatione Filii Dei, quam in Catholica et celebri Academia Dilingana anno 1614. die 1 Iulii, praeside Stephano Vito ... publice proponet Valentinus Schmid. 4°. *Dilingae, apud Ioannem Mayer, n.d.* [1614.]
Not seen. *See* note to no. 1377.

1387   —Stöcklin, A. Disputatio theologica, de religiosorum Ecclesiae Christianae ordinum status natura, dignitate, obligationibus, effectis ... Quam D.O.M.A in Catholica, celebri Vniuersitate Dilingana, anno Christi M.DC.XIX. die 1 Iulii praeside Stephano Vito ... publice ... propugnabit R.P. August. Stöcklin. 4°. *Dilingae, apud viduam Ioannis Mayer, n.d.* [1619.]
Not seen. *See* note to no. 1377.

1388   —Weiss, M. Disputatio theologica, de sacramento matrimonii. Quam in alma et Catholica Academia Dilingana, die [space] Ianuarii, praeside Stephano Vito ... proponet ... Matthaeus Weiss ... Anno Salutis M.DC.XVI. 4°. *Dilingae, apud viduam Ioannis Mayer, n.d.* [1616].
Not seen. *See* note to no. 1377.

—[For an unpublished MS by White entitled: *Apologia pro innocentibus Ibernis olim temere traductis per Richardum Stanihurstum :*] *See* note to no. 1127.

White, Thomas.†‡ [*A disputation in which he acted as Praeses.*] Morgan, A. ... Conclusiones theologicae, 1631. *See* no. 834.

White, William, *in religion* Claudius de S. Benedicto. Constitutiones missionis Benedictinorum, 1633. *See* no. 338.

1389   **Whyte, John James,** *Abbot of Ratisbon.* Theses theologicae: de syncera ac solida verbi Dei, in religionis potissimum controuersiis dirimendis, interpretatione, ad publicam disputationem propositae: quas ... R.P.F. Ioannes Iacobus Albus, Ordinis D. Benedicti, Monasterii S. Iacobi Scotorum Prior, Calend. Febr. & sequentibus diebus tuebitur: in Aula Episcopali Ratisponensi. 4°. *Ingolstadii, ex officina typographica Wolfgangi Ederi,* 1588. AB.MU.RG.
Announcing the theses to be defended in a public disputation with the Protestants. For Whyte's career, *see* Dilworth, pp. 28–56.

1390   —Theses theologicae, oder Fuerhalt einer geistlichen theologischen Disputation: von der reinen, vnuerfaelschten, bestaendigen, vnfehlbaren Ausslegung dess Worts Gottes, nach welcher, fuernaemblich die, in Religionssachen eingefallene Strittigkeiten entscheyden vnd eroertert werden sollen vnd muessen: zu Regenspurg in Bischofflichen Hoff den 30. Januarii vnd 1 Februarii gehalten. 4°. *Ingolstat,*

durch Wolffgang Eder, 1588. AB.DIL.EI.ERL.MU.RG.VI.
A summary in German of his defence of the theses announced in no. 1389. The author's preface to the reader sgd.: Frater Iohan. Iacobus Albus.

Widdrington, Roger, *alias. See* Preston, T.

1391 **Wigmore, Richard,** *alias* Campion. Theses ex vniuersa theologia disputandae. In Coll. Anglicano Societatis Iesu, Louanii, Anno Domini CIↃ IↃC XXII. Praeside Rdo Patre Georgio Morleo Soc. Iesu ... Defendet P. Richardus Campianus eiusdem Societatis. Die [space] Iunii. 4°. [Coloph.] *Louanii, ex officina Bernardi Masii,* 1622. Not found. Description from Sommerv. (tom. 5, col. 1326–7).

1392 **Williams, Lewis.** Q. theologica. Vtrum vita alia sit actiua, alia contemplatiua? &, an haec in sola consistat Dei contemplatione? ... Ludouicus Williams Anglus, in schola theol. hora consueta. 19 Februarii. 1611. *s.sh.*fol. *Duaci, typis viduae I. Boscardi, n.d.* [1611]. DOU(A 1611/1).
A programme announcing theses to be defended at the University of Douai. For Williams, *see* Anst., vol. 2, p. 357.

1393 **Williamson, Edward.** Quaestio theologica. Vtrum omne periurium sit peccatum mortale? ... Eoduardus [*sic*] Williamsonus Anglus, in schola theol. hora consueta. 7 Nouembris. 1609. *s.sh.*fol. *Duaci, typ. viduae Iac. Boscardi, n.d.* [1609.] DOU(A 1609/33).
A programme announcing theses to be defended at the University of Douai. For Williamson, *see* Anst., vol. 2, p. 357.

1394 **Wilson, John.**† Exercitium hebdomadarium, collectore Ioanne Wilsono sacerdote Anglo, in gratiam piorum Catholicorum. 12°. *Antuerpiae, ex officina Plantiniana apud Balthasarem Moretum, & viduam Ioannis Moreti, & Io. Meursium,* 1621. L.; RO⁵.
A collection of prayers and offices. The printer's mark on the title-page is engraved. There are eight other engravings.

1395 —[Anr. ed.] 12°. *Antuerpiae, ex officina Plantiniana Balthasaris Moreti,* 1630. L.C.; ANT²(2).BM².BRS.DE.RO⁵.USH.
With the same engravings as no. 1394.

1396 [*Extracts.*] Exercitia quotidiana cum suis sacris litaniis aliisq; piis precibus ex Ioanne Wilsono et aliis probatis auctoribus collecta. In gratiam Catholicorum. 32°. *Antuerpiae, apud Ioan. Cnobbarum,* 1630. O.; DAI.
The titlepage is engraved and there are numerous small engravings in the text.

1397 —[Anr. ed., enlarged, of no. 1396.] Exercitia quotidiana pia et Mariana cum sacris litaniis aliisq; piis precibus ex Joanne Wilsono et aliis probatis auctoribus collecta. In gratiam Catholicorum. 32°. 2 pts. *Antuerpiae, apud Ioan. Cnobbarum,* 1633. VT(Chigi VII.103).
The titlepage is engraved and the text contains many of the engravings from no. 1396. Pt. 2 has its own titlepage reading: *Exercitia Mariana seu officium purissimae & immaculatae conceptionis cum litaniis, hymnis, aliisque precibus ad Dei-param Virginem Mariam.* The imprint on the titlepage to pt. 2 is: *Antuerpiae, apud Ioan. Cnobbaert.*

1398 —[*A doubtful attribution.*] Officium Passionis Iesu Christi, ex oraculis prophetarum desumptum. 12°. *Antuerpiae, ex officina Plantiniana,* 1621. L.
Anon. The only copy found is bound at the end of no. 1394 but the approbation given by the Bishop of Antwerp says that the work was sent to the printer from Rome, which makes it doubtful whether Wilson had any connection with it.

1399 —[Anr. ed.] 12°. *Antuerpiae, ex officina Plantiniana Balthasaris Moreti,* 1630. C.

Anon. The titlepage is engraved.

—[*A Spanish translation of a work put into English by him.*] Vando y leyes del Rey Iacobo de Inglaterra contra la fé catolica. Con su respuesta. [1611]. *See* no. 280.1.

1400 **Wilson, Matthew,**†‡ *alias* Edward Knott. Modesta ac breuis discussio aliquarum assertionum D. Doctoris Kellisoni quas in suo de ecclesiastica hierarchia tractatu probare conatur: auctore Nicolao Smitheo. 12°. *Antuerpiae, ex officina Plantiniana Balthasaris Moreti*, 1631.

Nicolaus Smitheus, *pseud.* A translation of A&R 898 in which the author had answered A&R 431. Alegambe (p. 99) attributes the translation to George Wright, but this is incorrect. Wright says, in the Appendix added to nos. 1402–4, that he merely commissioned the translation. With numerous approbations from universities in Flanders and Germany, the earliest dated 7 July 1630 and the latest 28 October 1630. For Wright's identity and the background to this publication, *see* RH, Oct. 1987, pp. 329, *etc.* (esp. pp. 379–82). This is the first issue; no separate copy has been found but its composition is revealed by certain copies of the reissue at no. 1402. Collation: A–K¹² (K11, 12 blank).

1401 —[Anr. issue.] *Antuerpiae, ex officina Plantiniana Balthasaris Moreti*, 1631. L(*in original vellum as issued.*)

The sheets of no. 1400 unaltered except for the final quire, K¹², which is partly reset. The approbations now end on sig. K11ʳ (p. 237), K11ᵛ (unpaged) bears a Summa Privilegii (absent in no. 1400) dated 6 Feb. 1631, K12ʳ (unpaged) has Moretus's compasses device, K12ᵛ is blank.

1402 —[Anr. issue, with an Appendix.] *Antuerpiae, ex officina Plantiniana Balthasaris Moreti*, 1631. *With K¹² as in no. 1400:* DIJ.HP. *With K¹² as in no. 1401 :* O.C(2).; ANT²(2).D².DE.L².L⁹.MU(2).PA.PA⁶.U.USH.

The sheets of either no. 1400 or no. 1401 unaltered, but with the addition at the end of a new quire, L¹², containing an Appendix signed: Georgius Wrightus Sacerdos saecularis. Sigs. L1ʳ–L11ᵛ are paginated 241–62. L12 is blank except for a colophon on the recto: *Antuerpiae, ex officina Balthasaris Moreti* M.DC.XXXI. Some copies (e.g. HP) have an inserted leaf, unsigned and unpaged, before the Appendix, containing errata to the work itself and a note to the reader explaining that the Appendix which follows is intended as a preface to the whole work and would have been printed at the beginning if it had not come too late to the printer. Some copies (e.g. USH) have at the end of the Appendix a quadrifolium, unsigned and unpaged, of which the recto of the first leaf bears the printer's device and the remaining leaves are blank.

1403 —[Anr. issue.] *Antuerpiae, ex officina Plantiniana Balthasaris Moreti*, 1631. PA⁴(*with K¹² as in no. 1401*).

The sheets in one or other of the states described under no. 1402, but with the addition, before the Appendix, of an unsigned bifolium, paginated 237–40, containing further approbations, the latest being dated 16 March 1631.

1404 —[Anr. ed.] Vna cum Appendice R. Domini Georgii Wright. Qua libri argumentum & eiusdem Latine edendi occasio explicatur. Quae nunc ad modum praefationis praefigitur. Editio altera. 8°. *Leodii, typis Leonardi Streel*, 1631. O².HAN. [*L.]

Appendix

—[Bacon, T.] Vindiciae pro Nicolao Smitheo, contra censuram nomine Facultatis Parisiensis editam, 1631. *See* nos. 34–34.1.

1405 —France, *Bishops*. Epistola Archiepiscoporum et Episcoporum Parisiis nunc agentium, ad Archiepiscopos & Episcopos Regni Galliae super animaduersione duorum libellorum quorum tituli sunt: prioris quidem,. Modesta & breuis discussio ... Posterioris vero, Apologia pro modo procedendi Sanctae Sedis Apostolicae. 4°. *Parisiis, iussu Cleri, excudebat Antonius Vitray*, 1631. L.O.; DUR(2).TOU.YK. *This or no. 1406 :* D.O³.POI.

The two books referred to are [Wilson's] *A modest briefe discussion* (A&R 898, of which no. 1400 above is a translation) and [John Floyd's] *An apologie* (A&R 322). The letter bears 34 signatures and is dated from Paris, 10 Feb. 1631. Collation: A⁴. This edition does not contain the text of the propositions objected to; it can be identified by the absence of a catchword at the foot of sig. A4ᵛ. The *Epistola* is answered in no. 488. Reprinted with no. 682 in 1643.

1406 —[Anr. ed., with the text of the propositions.] Epistola Archiepiscoporum et Episcoporum Parisiis nunc agentium ... 4°. *Parisiis, iussu Cleri, excudebat Antonius Vitray*, 1631. HP(BX 2008. var. 2.).PA.PA³(6). Collation: A–D⁴E². The first quire (A⁴) is a resetting of no. 1405 from which it can be distinguished by the catchword 'PROPO-' at the foot of A4ᵛ leading to *head-title* 'Propositiones collectae ...' on B1ʳ. The propositions, which occupy B–D⁴E², are the same (and in the same Latin translation) as those condemned by the Sorbonne (*see* no. 684) but are here printed without the Sorbonne's censures. This edition was probably set up in type between 5 and 15 Feb. 1631, for in the HP copy the censures of the Sorbonne on Wilson's work (5 Feb.) but not those on Floyd's (15 Feb.) have been added in contemporary MS. *Pr.* by Vitray [for Charles Morel].

—[Anr. ed., with the text of the propositions together with the censures of them by the Sorbonne.] Epistola Archiepiscoporum et Episcoporum Parisiis nunc agentium ... 12°. *Parisiis, iussu Cleri, excudebat Antonius Vitray*, 1631.

This edition forms pt. 2 of no. 685.

1407 —France, *Bishops.* [*Begin :*] Monseigneur, on a publié depuis quelques mois deux liures Anglois, contenants plusieurs chefs preiudiciables à l'Eglise ... *s.sh.*fol. (folded). *n.p.d.* [1631.] L.O.; DUR(*imp.*).L²⁷ᴬ.PA.PA³.

A covering letter, signed 'Les Agens Generaux du Clergé de France' and dated from Paris, 20 Feb. 1631, printed to accompany copies of nos. 684, 1405, 1406, being sent on behalf of the Bishops resident in Paris to the rest of the Bishops of France. *Pr.* [Paris, for Charles Morel.] Reprinted with a Latin translation in no. 685.

1408 —France, *Jesuits.* Declaration et desadueu des Peres Iesuites. 4° (a bifolium). *n.p.d.* [1633.] CARP.L²⁷ᴬ(A. 16.1/9).PA.

A disavowal by the French Jesuits of the positions maintained by [Wilson and Floyd]. Dated from Paris, 23 March 1633 and signed by Louis de la Salle and others. *Pr.* [Paris]

—Paris, *Sorbonne.* Censura propositionum quarumdam, cum ex Hibernia delatarum, tum ex duobus libris Anglico sermone conscriptis in Latinum bona fide conuersis excerptarum, 1631. *See* nos. 684–5.

1409 —Spain, *Inquisition.* Auto que proueyò el Consejo de su Magestad de la santa General Inquisicion de España, sobre el libro de Nicolas Smitheo. *s.sh.*fol. *n.p.d.* [1637.] BRS⁴(Arch. Jes. Prov. Gallo-Belg. Coll. S. Omer. Carton 32. Unnumbered.) [*L.]

Pr. [Madrid?] The decree, dated from Madrid, 8 Oct. 1637, is signed by the six members of the Council, including the secretary, Sebastian de Huerta. It declares that the work entitled 'Modesta, ac breuis discussio ... Auctore Nicolao Smitheo' contains sound Catholic doctrine and may be permitted to circulate without restriction in the King of Spain's dominions.

1410   —[Author unknown.] Deprauationes deprehensae in Latina versione duorum librorum qui nuper a S. Facultate Parisiensi damnati sunt, facta a Jesuitis Anglis ex Anglico idiomate, nimirum libri Nicolai Smithaei, cui titulus est Modesta & breuis discussio, &c & libri Danielis a Iesu qui inscribitur Apologia pro processione Sanctae Sedis Apostolicae, &c. 4°. *n.p.*, 1631. DUR.L²⁷ᴬ(Cath. Tracts vol. 5, no. 2).PA(D10760).PAᴬ(MSS. Fr. 15734, ff. 294, *et seq.*).PA³(2).
    Claiming that the Jesuits altered the sense of certain passages when translating them from English into Latin. The author cites passages in the original English (from A&R 898 and 322) and compares them with the Latin versions in this catalogue nos. 1400 and 481. *Pr.* [Paris, at the press of Jérome Blageart.] *See* RH, Oct. 1987, pp. 382–4.

1411   **Winzet, John.** In canonicam D. Iacobi epistolam breuis commentarius, sub assertionum fere forma, ad publicam disputationem in Catholica Ingolstadiensi Academia propositus: praeside Petro Steuartio. 4°. *Ingolstadii, excudebat Dauid Sartorius*, 1591. L.; MU.

1412   —Oratio de purificatione B. et intemeratae Deiparae Virginis Mariae, Reuerendissimo . . . Nythardo, Ecclesiae Bambergensis Episcopo, et Herbipolis praeposito . . . dicata a Ioanne Winzeto . . . in Collegio ibidem Eloquentiae Professore. 4°. *Bambergae, excudebat Antonius Horitz, n.d.* [c. 1595.] BA.STG. [*O.*DMR.]
    An address delivered on the feast of the Purification (2 February); the year is not indicated.

1413   —Oratio de sacerdotis dignitate, in honorem Reuerendi . . . Ioannis Kuna Scheslitzensis, Reuerendissimi . . . Nythardi Ecclesiae Bambergensis Episcopi, et Herbipolensis praepositi &c. alumni, quando die 10. mensis Augusti . . . anno M.D.XCV. in Collegio eiusdem . . . Principis, primum ad tremenda iila mysteria . . . accessit, conscripta a Ioanne Winzeto . . . in Collegio ibidem Eloquentiae Professore. 4°. *Bambergae, excudebat Antonius Horitz, n.d.* [1595.] BA.FR. [*O.*DMR.]

1414   **Winzet, Ninian.**† Flagellum sectariorum, qui religionis praetextu seditiones iam in Caesarem, aut in alios orthodoxos principes excitare student . . . Accessit velitatio in Georgium Buchananum circa Dialogum, quem scripsit de iure regni apud Scotos. 4°. *Ingolstadii, ex officina typographica Dauidis Sartorii*, 1582. L(2: 1 *consisting of the Velitatio only*); AB.AUG.DI.DMR.DUR.E.EI.HAN.MU(5, +3 *of the Velitatio only*).NEU.PA⁶.TB.VI.WO. +
    The *Velitatio* answers STC 3973. Collation: a⁴A–Z⁴a–o⁴. In some copies, two additional quires, *⁶ containing an index to the *Flagellum*, and **⁴ containing a titlepage and dedicatory epistle to the *Velitatio*, are inserted as an afterthought between the end of the first work (sig. T4) and the beginning of the second (sig. V1).
    —Velitatio in Georgium Buchananum, 1582. *See* no. 1414.

1415   **Wise, Andrew.** Fratris Andreae VVise Hyberni Prioris Angliae Ode Dicolos Tetrastrophos. 4° (a single quadrifolium). *Neapoli, apud Ioannem Iacobum Carlinum*, 1616. RO⁸.
    A hymn of 23 strophes headed 'Ad Diuum Benedictum'.
    —[*Works translated by him.*] Allen, W. Copia d'vna lettera scritta all'illustrissimo Cardinal d'Inghilterra . . . con la risposta, 1588. *See* no. 16.
    —[For *Las leyes nueuamente hechas*, 1606, formerly thought to have been translated by him:] *see* no. 1342.2.
    —[*A thesis defended under his patronage.*] Lea, T. . . . Conclusiones theologicae, 1629. *See* no. 714.

1416   **Worthington, Thomas.**† Catalogus martyrum pro religione Catolica in Anglia occisorum, ab anno Domini 1570. regni Elizabethae duodecimo, ad annum 1610. qui est Regis Iacobi octauus. De aliis vero martyribus sub Henrico octauo summatim scripsit insignis doctor Nicolaus Sanderus lib. 7. de visibili Monarchia Ecclesiae. 8°. *n.p.*, 1610. VT(Barb. H. I. 213 bis, int. 2).

Anon. A collection of narratives put together and edited by [Worthington]. The authority for Worthington's editorship is Pits, p. 808. A printed note, signed A.B., on the verso of the titlepage says that the work is to be printed but not yet published. In the only copy found the following emendations have been made by pen in an early hand: the dates 1610 in the title and imprint have been altered to 1612, the word 'octauus' on the titlepage changed to 'decimus', and the initials A.B. in the note on the verso of the title-page altered to T.W. For martyr relations published by Worthington in English *see* A&R 916–17.

1417 —[Anr. ed., enlarged.] Catalogus martyrum pro religione Catholica in Anglia occisorum. Ab anno Domini 1570. regni Elizabethae duodecimo, ad annum 1612. qui est Regis Iacobi decimus. Cui praemittitur Narratio de origine seminariorum Anglorum, & de missione sacerdotum, etiam variorum ordinum, in Angliam. 8°. *n.p.*, 1614. O.; EH.OS.

Anon. With the same printed note on the verso of the titlepage as in no. 1416 but signed T.W.

1418 —Ratio et modus constituendi sodalitatem sacerdotum Anglorum, qui seinuicem in spiritualibus & temporalibus adiuuabunt. 8°. (a quadrifolium). *n.p.d.* [1616.] L²⁷ᴬ(16/1 n. 1).

Anon. The only copy found bears a contemporary MS note by an unnamed secular priest, reading: 'this is Dr. Worthington's design, but disliked by my Ld of Chalcedon, and the cheefe of the clergye and so I neuer stirred in it'. For Worthington's attempts to form a sodality for English secular priests and laymen, see the contemporary account by John Bennet printed in HMC, 5th rep., vol. 1, p. 185, and Worthington's own MS. account written in 1624, in AAW B. 26. The rules of the proposed sodality printed here are dated 1616.

1419 —Rosarium siue psalterium beatae Virginis Mariae. Cum aliis piis exercitiis ... a T.W.A. editum. 12°. *Antuerpiae, apud Ioannem Keerbergium,* anno M.VIᶜ [1600]. L.; BRS.DE.MU³.O⁵.W(*imp.*).

T.W.A. [T. Worthington.] Preface sgd.: T.W.B. [T. Worthington.] and dated 24 June 1599. The approbation is dated 25 January 1599 [o.s.] This appears to be the work attributed to Worthington by Pits (p. 808) under the title 'De mysteriis rosarii'. Collation: ✱¹²A–F.¹² The titlepage is engraved and there are engravings in the text. An English version is at A&R 918.

1420 —[Anr. ed., enlarged.] Rosarium siue psalterium beatae Virginis Mariae a T.W.A. editum. Cui accessere litaniae plurimae, & pia exercitia varia. 12°. *Antuerpiae, apud Ioannem Keerbergium,* anno M.D.C. [1600.] ANT³.E.L²⁵(*imp.*).O⁴.RO⁵.

The preface is signed and dated as in no. 1419. With an approbation bearing the date 6 July 1600. Collation: ✱¹²A–K¹²L². The titlepage is engraved and there are engravings in the text.

1421 —[Anr. ed.] 12°. *Antuerpiae, apud Ioannem Keerbergium,* 1602. AB.DMR. NI.WO. [✱O.]

A reprint of no. 1420 reproducing the preface and approbation signed and dated as in that edition. The titlepage is engraved and there are engravings in the text.

1422 —[Anr. ed.] 12°. *Ingolstadii, ex officina Ederiana, apud Andream Angermarium,* 1603. AB.EI.O⁴.

A reprint of no. 1420 reproducing the preface (but not the approbation) signed and dated as in that edition. The titlepage is not engraved but printed. This edition has woodcut copies of the original engravings.

1423 —[Anr. ed.] 12°. *Antuerpiae, apud Ioannem Keerbergium*, 1604. HP.MU. O⁴.OLD.OA⁴.RO⁵.RO⁶.W.

A reissue of no. 1421, with engraved titlepage and engravings in the text.

1424 —[Anr. ed.] 12°. *Antuerpiae, apud Ioannem Keerbergium*, 1613. BM². DMR.L²⁵(*imp*.).

The titlepage is engraved and there are engravings in the text.

—[*Works edited by Worthington.*] Bristow, R. Richardi Bristoi ... motiua, 1608. *See* no. 117.

—Stapleton, T. Orationes academicae, 1600. *See* no. 1147.

1425 **Wotton, Pickering.** Bekehrung, Herrn Piquerin Votons ... von der Ketzerey der Protestanten, zu dem rechten, waren, alten, Catholischen ... Glauben. 4°. *Ingolstatt, in der Ederischen Truckerey, durch Andream Angermeyr*, 1606. L.; DUS.MU(3).VI.WO.

An account, by Wotton himself, of his conversion to Catholicism which took place at Valladolid on 17 Oct. 1605, followed by several other accounts of notable conversions, all of them foreign. Pickering Wotton was son and heir of the English diplomat, Edward, Baron Wotton of Marly. No English original of his work is known; for a Spanish version, in MS, *see* ARSI Anglia 30, pt. 2, no. 597 (APSI film 15), and Julian Paz, *Catálogo de documentos españoles existentes en el archivo del Ministerio de negocios extranjeros de Paris*, 1932, nos. 903–4.

Wright, George. [*Works translated or with contributions by him.*] Floyd, J. Apologia Sanctae Sedis Apostolicae, 1631. *See* nos. 481–3.

—Wilson, M. Modesta ac breuis discussio, 1631. *See* nos. 1400–4.

1426 **Wright, Thomas.**† Quatuor colloquia inter Rdum dominum Thomam Wrightum Anglum ... & illustrem dominum Thomam Roe equitem auratum Anglum ad aquas Spadanas habita ... 1613. Opera Iacobi de Nixon Hyberni & aduocati Leodiensis collecta, & typis mandata. 8°. *Mechliniae, apud Henricum Ieay*, 1614. L.

The four colloquies, which took place at Spa in July 1613, dealt with the following subjects: the uncertainty of the remission of sins, the Calvinistic communion service, transubstantiation and the real presence of Christ in the Eucharist, the infallibility of the Pope. Sir Thomas Roe's brother, William, answered this account in 1615 (STC 21152).

1427 **Young, John.** De schismate, siue de ecclesiasticae vnitatis diuisione liber vnus: in duodecim capita eleganti methodo sectus, in quibus multa nostris his temporibus accommodata continentur. Authore Iohan. Giouano. 8°. *Louanii, apud Iohannem Foulerum, Anglum*, 1573. L.O.C.; AUG.BRS.C⁵.C⁹.E.L¹³.MD.O⁷.OS.PA.TRI.VI.VT.WO. +

Iohannes Giovanus [J. Young.]. Edited by Richard Hall who signs the dedicatory epistle.

1428 —[Anr. issue, with title:] Pacis ecclesiasticae perturbator, siue de schismate tractatus historicus, in quo multa nostris temporibus accommodata continentur. Autore Ioanne Giouano ... Opera & studio Richardi Halli. *Duaci, ex officina typographica Baltazaris Belleri*, 1603. PA⁶.WO.

Notwithstanding the lapse of thirty years, this is a reissue of the sheets of no. 1427 except for the first quire (*⁸) which has been reprinted.

Catalogue Part II (Subject Section)

Headings in this section are arranged chronologically; the following is an alphabetical list of subject-headings used:

Appeal to Pope Sixtus V to support an invasion of England (1588).
Campaign against the Catholics in Ireland (1595–1599).
Catholic propaganda. A spurious letter (1626).
Catholic propaganda in favour of the Emperor Ferdinand's claim to the kingdom of Bohemia (1619).
Constable of Castile and Catholicism in England (1604).
Elizabethan Religious Settlement (1562, etc.).
Excommunication of Elizabeth (1570, etc.).
French Marriage (1625, etc.).
German attack on Protestant persecution of Catholics in England (1588).
Luisa de Carvajal (1632, etc.).
Oath of Allegiance and loyalty of English Catholics (1606, etc.).
Persecution of Catholics. The Act against Jesuits and Seminary Priests (1585).
Queen Henrietta Maria's chaplains (1626).
Recantation of M. A. de Dominis (1622).
Reformation in Scotland (1581).
Report about an anti-Catholic play on the London stage (1586).
Satire on the English Protestant clergy (1588).
Spanish Marriage negotiations (1623).
Sufferings of English and Scottish Catholics (1573).

1562 [etc.]
The Elizabethan Religious Settlement
(*Mil., vol. 1, pp. 18–19;
Sou., pp. 119–20*)

1429   **Dalmada, E.,** *Bishop of Angra.* Epistola . . . aduersus Epistolam Gualteri Haddoni . . . contra . . . Hieronymi Osorii Lusitani, Episcopi Syluensis, Epistolam, nuper aeditam. 4°. *Antuerpiae, ex officina Gulielmi Silvii,* 1566. L.O.C(2).; BRS.C².C⁵.C¹⁹.D².L².L²⁵.MD(2).PLU.O⁵. R.RO⁵.
A reply to Haddon's *Pro Reformatione Anglicana epistola,* 1563, which was itself a reply to no. 1430.

1430   **Osorio da Fonseca, J.** *Bishop of Sylva.* [*Epistola ad Elizabetham.*] Epistola Hieronymi Osorii ad Serenissimam Elisabetam Angliae Reginam. 8°. [Coloph.] *Olysippone, apud Ioannem Blauium Typographum Regium excusum,* 1562. COI.EV.HD.
An English translation by Richard Shacklock is at A&R 585–6. Answered by ·Walter Haddon in *Pro Reformatione Anglicana epistola apologetica,* printed at Paris in 1563, to which Osorio replied in no. 1442. For another reply to Haddon *see* no. 1429. For editions of Osorio's letter to Elizabeth published together with his reply to Haddon, *see* nos. 1443–51. Osorio's *Opera omnia* were published at Rome in 1592.

1431   —[Anr. ed.] 4°. *Louanii, ex officina Ioannis Bogardi,* 1563. L.; AB.BRU.C¹¹.
1432   —[Anr. ed.] 4°. *Venetiis, ex officina Iordani Zileti,* 1563. L.O.; C⁴.C⁷.DI.F. MU(3).PA.PR.VI.VT.WO.
1433   —[Anr. ed., preceded by letters of the Emperor Ferdinand I, and with title:] Exemplar literarum Ferdinandi Romanorum Imperatoris, ad

Pium iiii. Pontificem Maximum . . . Epistola etiam, cuiusdam docti hominis, natione Lusitani, ad Elizabetam Reginam Angliae. 8°. (in fours). *Parisiis, apud Nicolaum Chesneau,* 1563. L.O.; PA.PA⁴.

Osorius's letter occupies ff. 8–40. His name is revealed in the privilege and also in the text.

1434   —[Anr. ed., without the letters of Ferdinand.] Epistola Reuerendissimi D. Hieronymi Osorii Episcopi Syluensis, ad Serenissimam Elisabetam Angliae Reginam. 4°. *Olysippone, excudebat Antonius Riberius, expensis Ioannis Hispani,* 1575. L.; C⁸.F.ILL.LIS.

This edition forms pt. 2 of *D. Hieronymi Osorii . . . De regis institutione & disciplina, lib. 8 . . . Quibus accessit eiusdem Authoris Epistola ad Elizabetham Angliae Reginam,* of which pt. 1 had been published in 1572 (copies of pt. 1 at C⁸.LIS.P.).

1435   —[*French transl. of no. 1433.*] Les graues et sainctes remonstrances de l'Empereur Ferdinãd, à nostre sainct pere le Pape . . . Plus, vne bien longue & docte epistre, escrite par certain personnage Portugallois . . . à Ma-Dame Elizabeth, Royne d'Angleterre. 8°. *Paris, chez Nicolas Chesneau,* 1563. L.; HA.NY.PA.

1436   —[Anr. ed., without the letters of the Emperor, and with title:] Remonstrance chrestienne en forme d'epistre, contenant vn beau et docte discours touchant les affairs du monde . . . Traduict du Latin de Hierosme Osorius, Portugallois. 8°. *Paris, chez Nicolas Chesneau,* 1565. AV.VT.WO.

1437   —[Anr. ed. of no. 1436, with title:] Remonstrance à Madame Elizabeth Royne d'Angleterre, et d'Irlande: touchant les affaires du monde, gouernement politique des royaumes, republiques, & empires: & restablissement de l'ancienne Catholique religion . . . Faicte Françoise du Latin de Hierosme Osorius Portugallois. 8°. (in fours). *Paris, chez Iean Poupy,* 1575. PA².PA⁴.

Collation: A–O⁴(O4 blank).

1438   —[Anr. ed.? or anr. issue?] 8° (in fours). *Paris, chez Nicolas Chesneau & Iean Poupy,* 1577. CARP.PA.PA².

Collation as in no. 1437.

1439   —[Anr. ed.] 8° (in fours). *Paris, pour Michel Roigny,* 1587. PA.PA³.

1440   —[Anr. ed.] 8° (in fours). *Lyon, prins dur la coppie imprimée à Paris,* 1587. O.; DMR.PA.SBG.

Without name of printer or publisher, but probably for [Jean Pillehotte].

1441   —[Anr. ed.] 8°. *Lyon, L. Tantillon,* 1587.

Not found. Description from Baudrier, vol. 2, p. 406.

1442   **Osorio da Fonseca, J.** *Bishop of Sylva.* [*In Gualterum Haddonum.*] Amplissimi atque doctissimi viri D. Hieronymi Osorii, Episcopi Syluensis, in Gualterum Haddonum Magistrum Libellorum Supplicum apud . . . Helisabetham Angliae, Franciae, & Hiberniae Reginam, libri tres. 4° (in eights). *Olissipone, excudebat Franciscus Correa Regius Typographus,* 1567. L.O.C.; BRU.C⁵.C¹⁷.D.DUR.F.HSA.L²⁶. LIS.MD.MTH.VI. +

See note to no. 1430. This edition is without the letter to Elizabeth.

1443   —[Anr. ed., with *Epistola ad Elizabetham.*] Domini Hieronymi Osorii . . . in Gualterum Haddonum . . . de religione libri tres. Praefixa est eiusdem . . . viri Epistola, ad eandem Principem . . . quam idem Haddonus . . . oppugnandam suscepit. Opus eruditissimum & nunc primum in Germania editum. 8°. *Dilingae, ex officina Sebaldi Mayer,* 1569. L(2).O(2).C(2).; C².C⁴.DI.FU².GTN.HP.L²⁶.MU(3).PA.ST.USH.VI. + +

1444   —[Anr. ed. of both works.] 8°. *Dilingae, ex officina Sebaldi Mayer,* 1574. C.;A².AMP.C¹⁵.L².L²⁵.

1445   —[Anr. ed. of both works.] Editio tertia, prioribus emendatior. Accessit recens Christophori Longolii . . . non dissimilis argumenti oratio.

16°. *Dilingae, excudebat Sebaldus Mayer*, 1576. L.O.; C².C⁵.DI.DMR. E(*imp.*).FR.FU².GSN.HAN.KN².L²⁶.MU.STG.TB. +

1446 —[Anr. ed. of both works.] Editio quinta. Accessit Christophori Longolii ... oratio. 12°. *Coloniae, apud Gosuinum Cholinum*, 1585. L.; CMR.FR.FU.FU².HAN.L².L¹³.L¹⁵.L²⁶.MU.SBG.TB.USH.WO. +

1447 —[Imprint variant.] *Treueris, apud Emundum Hattot*, 1585. BRU.CHA. FU².PA.PR³.ROT.STG.USH.VI.
Forms part of a shared edition with no. 1446.

1448 —[Anr. ed. of both works.] Editio sexta. 12°. *Coloniae, apud Gosuinum Cholinum*, 1588. FU.PA.PBN.PR. *This or no. 1449 :* SPS.TB.

1449 —[Imprint variant.] *Coloniae, apud Petrum Horst*, 1588. FU².
Forms part of a shared edition with no. 1448.

1450 —[Date variant of no. 1448.] 1589. BOR.CHA.P.
1451 —[Date variant of no. 1449.] 1589. DMR.F.FU².MFL.X.

1570 [*etc.*]
Excommunication of Elizabeth
The Bull Regnans in Excelsis
(*Pollen, pp. 142–59*)

1452 **Pius V**, *Saint, Pope.* S.D.N. Pii Papae V. Sentententia declaratoria contra Elisabeth praetensam Angliae Reginam, & ei adhaerentes hereticos. Qua etiam declarantur absoluti omnes subditi a iuramento fidelitatis & quocunque alio debito et deinceps obedientes anathemate illaqueantur. *s.sh.fol. n.p.d.* [1570.] L.; HD.VT²(Misc. Arm. IV, t. 31, f. 49).[*DMR.]
The text is dated from Rome 24 Feb. 1569 [i.e. 1570 *n.s.*]. This, the original Roman edition, has the arms of Pius V, flanked by medallions representing SS. Peter and Paul, printed at the head of the text. *Pr.* [Rome, heirs of Antonio Blado.]

1453 —[Anr. ed.] S.D.N.D. Pii. Papae V. sententia declaratoria contra Elisabeth praetensam Angliae Reginam, & ei adhaerentes haereticos ... *s.sh.fol.* [1570 or later.] L¹¹(SP 12/49, n. 53.)[*L.]
This edition has no papal arms or other insignia, and no medallions of SS. Peter and Paul, at the head of the text. The date and place of printing have not been established. It is not from the press of the heirs of Antonio Blado at Rome.

1454 —[Anr. ed., with title beginning as in no. 1453.] *s.sh.fol. n.p.d.* [1579–80?] RO²(68.13.E.1/98).LF.VT².
Pr. [Rome, heirs of A. Blado.] This may be the reprint known to have been made at Rome in preparation for the invasion of Ireland in 1580 (*see* CRS, vol. 53, pp. 232–3). It has the medallions of SS. Peter and Paul at the head of the text, but between them, in place of the papal arms, are printed the insignia (cross-keys and umbrella) used Sede vacante. This may have been done to spare embarrassment to Gregory XIII who was reigning at the time.

1573
Sufferings of English and Scottish
Catholics. Dulken's 'Trophoea'.

1455 **Dulken, V. a.** Illustria Ecclesiae Catholicae trophoea, ex recentibus Anglicorum martyrum, Scoticae proditionis, Gallicorumq. furorum rebus gestis grauiss. virorum fide notatis. Charae posteritati ... erecta. 8°. [Coloph.] *Monachii, excudebat Adamus Berg*, 1573. L(2).O.; AMS.CMR.D.DE.F.L²⁶.N.O⁶.OS.U.USH.VI.W(2).
A collection which includes reprints of the 1550 edition of Maurice Chauncy, *Historia aliquot nostri saeculi martyrum* (including the

first part on More and Fisher as well as the second on the Carthusians), and of the anonymous defence of Mary Queen of Scots, *Proditionis ab aliquot Scotiae perduellibus . . . narratio*, 1566 (nos. 811–14).

1581
The Reformation in Scotland

1456   **Benoist, R.,** *Bishop of Troyes.*†‡ Ad pios et Catholicos Scotos, impiae Geneuensis factionis ministrorum truculenta atque sathanica barbarie et ferocitate diuexatos & oppressos: pro fide & religionis antiquae . . . professione atque persuasione, firmissimae semper retinenda, simplex & catholica cohortatio. 8°. *Parisiis, apud Nicolaum Chesneau*, 1581. L.; MU.O⁷.PA.PA³.
Benoist had formerly been confessor to Mary Queen of Scots. His other polemical writings fall outside the scope of this catalogue, except for a Scottish translation of another work by him (not in A&R, but ERL 393; STC 1884.5) which will be described in our volume 2.

1585
Persecution of Catholics. The Act against Jesuits and Seminary Priests (27 Eliz. c. 2)

1457   [Author unknown.] Crudelitatis Caluinianae exempla duo recentissima ex Anglia. Quorum primum, continet barbarum ac saeuum Caluinianorum edictum recenter editum contra Catholicos: alterum vero, exhibet indignissimam mortem illustrissimi viri comitis Northumbriae in castro Londinensi occisi mense Iulio huius anni. 1585. Praemissa est praefatio ad principes populosque Catholicos de cladibus quas haeresis infert Rebuspub. . . . adiectum est in fine exemplar quarundam literarum ex Anglia. 8°. *n.p.*, 1585. L(2).O.; BRS².C².KN.L².L⁴.L²⁶.PA².PA⁴(3).ST.STA. *This or no. 1458 :* D⁸.LINC.MD. MU(4).UT.VT.
The text of the Act is printed here with an extensive commentary. The Catholic newsletter from England, added at the end of the book, is dated from London, 30 July 1585 and signed: G.T. Collation: A–D⁸ (D7, 8 blank). *Pr.* [Cologne, Godefridus Kempensis.]

1458   —[Anr. ed.] 8°. *n.p.*, 1585. D.DE.LX.PA.PA³.USH.W. *See also note to no. 1457. Pr.* [Rheims, Jean Foigny.] Collation: A–C⁸D⁴.

1459   —[*German transl.*] Der Caluinisten Grausambkeit. In zweyen Exempeln, so in Engellandt newlich fuergelauffen, beschrieben vnnd begriffen . . . Zu Endt ist Copia der Koenigin Schreibens, an ettliche Reichs-Fuersten, neben noch mehr andern Brieffen auss Engellandt geschrieben, hinzugesetzt. 4°. *n.p.*, 1586. L.; FU.FU².MU(6).SBG.TB.UT. WO.
Pr. [Ingolstadt, David Sartorius?] Gillow's assertion (vol. 5, p. 260) that the work was also published in French, Italian and Spanish appears to be an error.

[1460 *cancelled.*]

1586
Report about an anti-Catholic play on the London stage

1461   Copia de vna lettera venuta nouamente dalla fortezza di Cales nella magn. città di Venezia nella quale si legge il grande & spauentoso succeso auuenuto ne Lōdra, città principale d'Ingh. alli 24 d'Apr. 1586. Oue s'intēde, che in essa città si recitaua vna comedia in dis-

pregio della S. Fede iui spauenteuolmente apparsero molti diauoli dell-inferno & via se ne riportorno i recitanti, con la morte de'molti & altre cose notabili, & marauigliose da sapere. 4°. *Milano, appresso Gio. Battista Colonio,* 1586. MIL[3].
Not seen. Description from G. Bologna, *Le Cinquecentine della Biblioteca Trivulziana* (1965), no. 263.

1588
*Appeal to Pope Sixtus V to support
an invasion of England*

1462 **Piccha, G.** Gregorii Picchae V.I.D. Oratio ad Sixtum V. Pont. Max. aliosq. Christianos principes, et respubl. Pro Britannico bello indicendo. 4°. *Romae, ex typographia Vincentii Accolti,* 1588. L(2).O.C.; NY.PA.RO[2].RO[4].RO[6].STAN.VI.

1588
*German attack on Protestant persecution
of Catholics in England*

1463 **Hanson, P.** Warnung an alle getrewe, Gottsfoerchtige, ehr vnd fridliebende Teutschen, vor der Caluinisten gefaehrlichen Practicken vnd toedtlichem Gifft. 4°. *Ingolstadt, durch Dauid Sartorium,* 1588. O.; DI. DOE.FR.FU.STG.UEB.ULM.VI.
Including material on the persecution of Catholics in England under Henry VIII and Elizabeth, based mainly on the works of Nicolas Sander and on [Robert Persons's] *De persecutione Anglicana* (nos. 874, *etc.*). The letter transl. as no. 1464 occupies pp. 76–9.

1464 —*[French transl.* of part of no. 1463.] Coppie de la requeste presentée au Turc par l'Agent de la Royne d'Angleterre, le 9. de Nouembre 1587. Traduicte sur la coppie imprimée en Allemand en la ville d'Ingolstad, chez Dauid Sartorius 1588. & inserée dedans le liure de Pierre Hanson de Saxe, portant ce tiltre, Admonition ou aduertissement aux fideles Germains, pour se garder des Caluinistes. 8° (in fours). *Verdun, pour Iacques Eldreton,* 1589. O.; E.HAN.PA(2).PA[3].PA[12]. [*DMR.]
Prefaced to Elizabeth's letter to the Sultan is an address by the French editor drawing attention to the apparent readiness of the English government to ally itself with infidels. *See* Strype, *Annals,* IV, pp. 213–24. Following the letter are verses, some in Latin and some in French, attacking Elizabeth.

1465 —[Anr. ed., enlarged.] Copie de la requeste presentée au Turc ... Ensemble la copie de certaines lettres du Sultan à la Royne d'Angleterre. 8° (in fours). *n.p.,* 1589. L(2).; BRS.LIL.PA.
This edition omits the verses of no. 1464 but adds the text in Latin and French of a letter from the Sultan to Elizabeth dated 9 Aug. 1588.

1588
*Satire on the English
Protestant Clergy*

1466 Discours plaisant et recreatif de la vie, & faitz des ministres d'Angleterre, qui en ces années dernieres ont annoncé la loy de Luther, au Royaume d'Angleterre. Traduict d'Anglois, en François. 8° (a quadrifolium). *Paris, chez la vefue de François Plumion,* 1588. L(C.37.a.55.).
A collection of scandalous stories. Perhaps based on material supplied by English Catholic exiles. No English original has been found. The writer of the epistle 'au Lecteur' calls himself a French-

man recently in England. In this edition English place-names are frequently mis-spelt.

1467   —[Anr. ed.] 8° (in fours). *n.p.*, 1588. L (1192.e.42); PA.
In this edition English place-names are correctly spelt.

[1468 *cancelled*]

1595–1599
*The Campaign against the Catholics
in Ireland*

1469   Auuiso della rotta, che ha data il Signor d'Odonnel all'essercito dell'-asserta Reina d'Inghilterra condotto da Giouan Noris in Hibernia Sul principio del mese di Nouembre M.D.XCVI. Publicato da Bernardino Beccari da Sacile alla Minerua. 8° (a quadrifolium). *Roma, per Nicolò Mutii,* 1596. RO⁴.(Gall.14.A25/121).VT(CapponiV.681/102.)
In this and the following newsletters published by Beccari the Irish resistance is represented as a crusade for the Catholic religion.

1470   —[Anr. ed.] 8° (a quadrifolium). *In Roma, & ristampato in Bologna, per Gio : Battista Bellagamba,* 1596. RO³ (Misc. Ant. XIV.b.32.26.)

1471   Ragguaglio de i successi dell'Isola d'Hibernia à fauor de'Cattolici. Dal mese di Settembre del 1598. fino al mese di Luglio 1599. Doue s'intendono particolarmenre [*sic*] due rotte date da i detti Cattolici à gli Inglesi. Publicato per Bernardino Beccari alla Minerua. 8° (a quadrifolium). *Roma, appresso Nicolò Mutii,* 1599. L.; D⁶.

1472   Relatione della guerra d'Hibernia, tra la Lega de'Catholici di quel regno, & l'asserta Reina d'Inghilterra. Doue s'intende i progressi marauigliosi fatti da essa Lega contro gli Heretici, dal principio dell'anno presente 1595 . . . Publicata per Bernardino Beccari alla Minerua. 8° (a quadrifolium). *Roma, per Domenico Gigliotto,* 1596. D¹⁰.RO⁴.VT.

1473   —[*French transl.*] Briefue relation de la guerre d'Irlande, entre ceulx de la Ligue de cestuy royaume, et Isabelle Royne d'Angleterre . . . Le tout prins hors d'vne copie nagueres mis en Italien, par Bernardino Beccari alla Minerua, present ausdictes seruices, imprimée à Milan par Francisco Paganelli. 8° (a quardifolium). *Bruxelles, par Rutger Velpius,* 1596. C.
The Milan edition of the Italian, referred to in the title, has not been found.

1474   —[Anr. ed.] 8° (a quadrifolium). *Lille, chez Guillaume Stroo-bant,* 1596. *Ioxte* [sic] *la copie imprimé* [sic] *à Bruxelles.* LIL.NY.PA.

1604
*The Constable of Castile and
Catholicism in England
(CRS vol. 64, pp. 26–44)*

1475   **Fernandez de Velasco y Tobar, Juan de,** *Constable of Castile.* Relacion de la iornada del Excmo. Condestable de Castilla, a las pazes entre Hespaña y Inglaterra, que se concluyeron y iuraron en Londres, por el mes de Agosto, año M.DC.IIII. 4°. *Anueres, en la emprenta Plantiniana por Iuan Moreto,* 1604. L.O.; CARP.F.MD.PA.PR³.VI.
The Constable's report to Philip III on the state of Catholicism in England. It should not be confused with the accounts of the events and ceremonial of his visit to England which also appeared in print but which fall outside the scope of this catalogue. Following the report are Latin verses by scholars of the English Jesuit College of S. Omer presented to the Constable when he passed through the town on his return from England to Spain.

1476   —[Anr. ed.] Fol. *Valladolid, por los herederos de Iuan Yniguez,* 1604.
L.; BAR.MD.MD²(Jes.102/33).NY.
    A reprint of no. 1475.

1477   —[Anr. ed.] 4°. *Valēcia, jūto al Molino de Rouella,* 1604. *Vendense en
casa de Francisco Miguel, y en casa Alexãndre Martinez, libreros.* HD.

1478   —[Anr. ed.] 4°. *Milan, por Pandolfo, y Marco Tulio Malatesti,* 1605.
L(2).

1479   —[*Latin transl., with additions.*] Legatio illa celeberrima, summae
grauitatis, & prudentiae plena, qua ... Ioannes Fernandus Velascus.
Comes-stabilis Castellae ... Philippi III. nomine, cum Sereniss.
Iacobo Britanniae Rege pacem conciliauit ... Hispano sermone
descripta, & in Latinum conuersa. 4°. *Mediolani, apud haer. Pacifici
Pontii, & Io. Baptistam Piccaleum,* 1606. L(*slightly imp.*).
    Following the Latin verses by the scholars of S. Omer is added a
Latin translation from the Spanish of an account of the events and
ceremonies of the Constable's visit to England.

1606 [*etc.*]
*The Oath of Allegiance and the
Loyalty of English Catholics
(See Mil. vol. 2, pp. 89, et seq.)*

1480   **Becanus, M.** Controuersia Anglicana. De potestate regis et pontificis,
contra Lancellottum Andream, Sacellanum Regis Angliae, qui se
Episcopum Eliensem vocat, pro defensione Illustrissimi Cardinalis
Bellarmini. 8°. *Moguntiae, ex officina Ioannis Albini,* 1612. O(2).; BRS.
C⁵.DUR.E.L⁴.MU.NCY.O³.O⁵.O⁷.PA.PR.STG.VT.WO.
    A fuller study than that contained in no. 1486. Mainly answering
STC 626. Propositions from this book were condemned by the Sor-
bonne, 1 Feb. 1613. Answered in STC 1703(which prints in pt. 2 the
text of the Sorbonne's condemnation) and in STC 4116.

1481   —[Anr. ed.] Controuersia Anglicana de potestate pontificis et regis;
recognita et aucta ... Vbi etiam defenditur Illustrissimus Cardinalis
Bellarminus. 8°. *Moguntiae, apud Ioannem Albinum,* 1613. L.C.;
BRS².DI(2).DUS.ERL.L².L⁴.MU(2).O³.OS.PA.PA⁴.USH.VT.WO. +
    Sommerv. (tom. 1, col. 1102) lists a Paris edition of 1613 but this
would seem to be an error; he also lists a Mainz edition of 1618
where the date is probably a misprint for 1613.

1482   —Dissidium Anglicanum de primatu regis, cum breui praefatione ad
Catholicos in Anglia degentes. 8°. *Moguntiae, ex officina typographica
Ioannis Albini,* 1612. L.O.; D(3).DUR.FU.FU².GT.GTN.L².L²⁶.MD.MU(2).
PA.SBG.STG. + +
    Answers mainly STC 24119, 24032, 4118, all of which had attacked
no. 1486. An English translation was printed at the English College
press, S. Omer, in 1612 (A&R 80). The *Dissidium* was answered in
STC 12814 to which Becanus replied in no. 1484.

1483   —Duellum Martini Becani ... cum Guilielmo Tooker, Anglicanae
theologiae professore, & decano Ecclesiae Lichefeldensis. De primatu
Regis Angliae. 8°. *Moguntiae, ex officina typographica Ioannis Albini,*
1612. L.O.; CARP.D(2).DI.FU.GT.L².MU(2).O².PA.ST.STG.VI.VT.WO. + +
    Answers STC 24119 which was itself an answer to no. 1488. This is
a fuller answer to STC 24119 than that in no. 1482.

1484   —Examen Concordiae Anglicanae. De primatu Ecclesiae regio. 8°.
Moguntiae, apud Ioannem Albinum, 1612. UP.
    Answers STC 12814 which was itself an answer to no. 1482. Answered
in STC 12815.

1485   —[Date variant.] 1613. C.; CARP.D.GT.HP.L⁴.L¹³.PA³.PA⁴.SBG.ST.STG.TRO.
USH.WO.YK. +

Sommerv. also records an 'Editio secunda' printed at Mainz in 1613 but this probably refers only to this date variant.

1486 —Refutatio Torturae Torti seu contra sacellannm [*sic*] Regis Angliae, quod causam sui Regis negligenter egerit. 8°. *Moguntiae, typis Ioannis Albini*, 1610. L.O.C.; BRS.C⁹.CHA.DMR.DUR.FU.GTN.L⁴.L²⁶.O⁷.PA(2).PA³. SBG.ST.VT.WO. + +

An answer to STC 626 which was itself an answer to Bellarmine's *Responsio* (no. 1502). An English translation of the *Refutatio* was published at the English College press, S. Omer, in 1610 (A&R 77). Answered by STC 4118 and 24032. Collation of this edition: A–D⁸E⁴.

1487 —[Anr. ed.] 12°. *Moguntiae, typis Ioannis Albini*, 1610. BRS(2).D² (*date altered by stamping to 1611*).GT.HP(*date altered by stamping to 1612*). LOU³.MD.PA.

Collation of this edition: A–C¹² (C11, 12 blank). The word 'Sacellanum' in the title is correctly printed.

1488 —Serenissimi Iacobi Angliae Regis Apologiae, & monitoriae Praefationis ad Imperatorem, Reges & Principes, refutatio. 8°. *Moguntiae, typis Iohannis Albini*, 1609. L.; FU.FU².HEI.MU.PR.SBG².SPS.STG.WN.WO.

Answers STC 14401. Answered by STC 24119 to which Becanus replied in no. 1483. Collation of this edition: A–L⁸ (L8 blank).

1489 —[Date variant.] 1610. L.O.C.; ANT².CARP.DI(4).DMR.E.FU².HA.L⁴.LOU.O³. PA.ST.VT.WO. + +

1490 —[Anr. ed.] 12°. *Moguntiae, typis Ioannis Albini*, 1610. BRS(2).D²(*date altered by stamping to 1611*).HP(*date altered by stamping to 1612*).LOU³. MD.

Collation of this edition: a⁶A–F¹²G⁶ (G6 blank).

1491 **Bellarmine, Robert,** *Saint, Cardinal.* Apologia Roberti S.R.E. Cardinalis Bellarmini, pro Responsione sua ad librum Iacobi Magnae Britanniae Regis, cuius titulus est, Triplici nodo triplex cuneus; in qua refellitur Praefatio monitoria Regis eiusdem. Accessit eadem ipsa Responsio iterum recusa, quae sub nomine Matthaei Torti anno superiore prodierat. 4°. *Romae, apud Bartholomaeum Zannettum*, 1609. O.; D.DMR.E.FLO.GT.LOU³.MD.MD⁴.MP.MST.RO⁵.SBG.USH.VT. + +

The *Apologia* answers STC 626 and James I's 'Praefatio monitoria' published in STC 14405. It is followed by the reprinted text of the *Responsio* (*see* nos. 1502–3), here called 'Editio tertia' of which Bellarmine now acknowledges himself the author. The *Apologia* was answered by STC 604.

1492 —[Anr. ed. of both works.] Editio altera. 4°. *Romae, apud Bartholomaeum Zannettum*, 1610. L(2).C(3).; A.C³.C⁵(2).LINC.LOU.O⁵.PA.PA⁴. VAL. Imprint false; *pr.* [S. Omer, Eng. Coll. press.]

1493 —[Anr. ed. of both works.] 8°. *Ad exemplar Rom. editum, n.p.*, 1610. L.; BRS².HA.L²⁵.LIL.LOU.PA.PA⁶.TRO.VER.YK. *Pr.* [Paris.]

1494 —[Anr. ed. of both works.] 8°. 2 pts. *Coloniae Agrippinae, apud Ioannem Kinckes*, 1610. AUG.DAI(*imp.*).LAR.MAR(pt. 1).MTH.VI(pt. 1).WO(pt.1). *This or no.* 1495 : BRS².FRA.LOU.PR.SBG².WOR.

Collation: (pt. 1) (*)⁶A–T⁸. (pt. 2): A–L⁸. Colophon to pt. 1 (T8ʳ): *Coloniae Agrippinae, apud Ioannem Kinckes.* Imprint to pt. 2 (A1ʳ): *Coloniae Agrippinae, apud Ioannem Kinckes.* Colophon to pt. 2 (L8ʳ): *Coloniae Agrippinae, excudebat Stephanus Hemmerden, sumptibus Ioannis Kinckii.*

1494.1 —[Anr. issue of both parts of no. 1494, with a cancel title to pt. 1 bearing the imprint:] *Coloniae Agrippinae, excudebat Stephanus Hemmerden, sumptibus Ioannis Kinckii*, 1610. L(860.f.15.)

1495 —[Anr. ed. of no. 1494, pt. 1, with a reissue of pt. 2.] 8°. 2 pts. *Coloniae, apud Ioannem Kinckes*, 1610. O.C.; C³.D².DMR.L¹³.L²⁶.LGE³.LOU³.OS.PA. *See also note to no. 1494.*

Collation of pt. 1: A–T⁸V⁴. Colophon to pt. 1 is the same as in pt. 2 of no. 1494. Pt. 2 is a reissue of the sheets of pt. 2 of no. 1494.

1496 —[Anr. issue of no. 1495, pt. 1, with anr. ed. of pt. 2] 8°. 2 pts. *Coloniae, apud Ioannem Kinckes,* 1610. ANT².FRA(*with 2 copies of pt. 2, one in the new ed., the other in the original.*)
Pt. 1 is a reissue of the sheets of no. 1495. Collation of pt. 2: A⁶ B–K⁸L⁴. Pt. 2 has imprint (A1ʳ): *Coloniae Agrippinae,* 1610.

1497 —[Anr. ed. of both works.] 8°. *Coloniae, apud Georgium Gartnerum,* 1610. D.DIJ.GER.PA.PA³.PA⁴.TAL.WO.

1498 —[Anr. ed. of both works.] 4° (in eights). *Cremonae, apud Mar. Antonium Belpierum,* 1610. BG.MD.VT(3).

1499 —[Anr. ed. of both works.] 4° *Vilnae, apud Ioannem Karcanum,* 1610. KR.UP(2).WR².

1500 —[*French transl.* of both works.] Apologie de l'Illustrissime Robert Bellarmin . . . pour la response dudit sieur, au liure du Serenissime Roy de la Grand Bretaigne . . . Auec la Responce cy-deuant publiée, sous le nom de Matthieu Torty. 8°. *n.p.,* 1610. L³⁰ᴬ.MP.PA.PA².

1501 —[*Anr. French transl.* of both works.] Responce du Cardinal Bellarmin. A la preface, & à l'Apologie du Roy de la Grand' Bretaigne. Auec la refutation des principales heresies de ce temps . . . Traduit du Latin, par François de Rosset, & dedié, à Monseigneur le Cardinal Duperron. 8°. *n.p.,* 1611. CARP.NI².

1502 —Responsio Matthaei Torti presbyteri, et theologi Papiensis, ad librum inscriptum, Triplici nodo triplex cuneus. 8°. *Coloniae Agrippinae, sumptibus Bernardi Gualtheri,* 1608. L.C.; ANT.CARP.FLO.HP.RO⁶.USH.VI.
Answers STC 14403. Matthaeus Tortus, *pseud.* Answered in STC 626 and defended by Bellarmine in his *Apologia* (*see* nos. 1491, *etc.*).

1503 —[Anr. ed.] Editio altera. 4°. *n.p.,* 1608. O.C.; A.C²(2).C³(2).HP.L².L⁴. LINC.OS.P.PLU.
Pr. [S. Omer, Eng. Coll. press.] Later editions, whether in Latin or in translation, were published together with the *Apologia* (*see* nos. 1491, *etc.*).

1504 —Roberti S.R.E. Card, Bellarmini Examen ad librum falso inscriptum Apologia Card. Bellarmini pro iure principum, &c. auctore Rogero Widdrinctono Catholico Anglo. 8°. *Romae, ex typographia Bartholomaei Zannetti,* 1612. RO³.VAL.VT.
Answers no. 925.1. The reason for its rarity is that it was never put into general circulation. The text was incorporated, in 1613, in a larger answer to no 925.1 by Adolf Schulcken (no. 1540). *See* Sommerv., tom. 1, col. 1225, and Mil., vol. 2, p. 103.

1505 —Tractatus de potestate Summi Pontificis in rebus temporalibus. Aduersus Gulielmum Barclaium. 8°. *Romae, ex typographia Bartholomaei Zannetti,* 1610. AIX.AV.BAR³ BRS.C²(2).FLO.FRA.GTN.MD.MU.PA POI.RO.RO.STI.WO. + +
Answers William Barclay's *De potestate Papae,* 1609 (no. 53.1). Answered by John Barclay in his *Pietas,* 1612 (no. 52), by Thomas Preston in his *Apologia,* 1611 (no. 925.1) and by [N. Le Jay] in *Le Tocsin,* 1610 (English translation STC 1845). Condemned by the Paris Parlement. 26 Nov. 1610. The work by Anthony Hoskins, *A briefe and cleare declaration,* 1611 (A&R 405) is not, as sometimes stated, an abstract of this work but of that by L. Lessius on the same subject (no. 1534).

1506 —[Anr. ed.] Recens ad exemplar Romanum impressus. 8°. *Coloniae Agrippinae, sumptibus Bernardi Gualtheri,* 1610. O.; AMS.CARP.CHA. DE(-*t.p.*).L².L³.LYN.NI.RO⁶.UT².WO.

1507 —[Date variant.] 1611. L.O.; D(2).E.GT.L⁴.ST.TNI. *This or no. 1508:* C². ERL.FU².HA.LAR.LOU.MD.MU.PA³.PR(2).SBG.STG.TB.VAL.VI. +
May be distinguished from no. 1508 by the signature positions, e.g.:

B [in Italic] 2 here occurs beneath the words *dominio, veliudicio*;
*V*2 beneath the words *quis verò*.

1508 —[Anr. ed.] Recens ad exemplar Romanum impressus. 8°. *Coloniae
Agrippinae, sumptibus Bernardi Gualtheri*, 1611. SOL.USH. *See also
no. 1507.*
A close reprint of no. 1507 from which it may be distinguished by
the signature positions, e.g.: B [in Roman] 2 here occurs beneath the
words *verum illos*; *V*2 beneath the words *verò Regum*.

1509 **Capelli, M. A.** F.M. Antonii Capelli . . . aduersus praetensum prima-
tum ecclesiasticum Regis Angliae Liber in quo Iacobi Regis, & eius
Eleemosynarii confutantur scripta. 4°. *Bononiae, ex typographia Bar-
tholomaei Cocchii*, 1610. L.O.C(2).; AB.BOR.CARP.DMR.L^{13}.O^2.O^9.O^{12}.PA^4.
RG.VT(2).
Answers STC 14405 and 626.

1510 —[Anr. ed.] Nunc primum in Germania editus. 8°. *Coloniae, apud
Seruatium Erffens*, 1611. L.O.; ANT^3.AV.D.D^2.ERL.FR.FU^2.HAN.HP.MD.
MNS.O^7.TRO(*misdated 1640 in printed catalogue*).WO.YK.

1511 **Coeffeteau, N.,** *Bishop of Marseille.* Apologie pour la response à
l'aduertissement du Serenissime Roy de la Grande Bretagne. Contre
les accusations de Pierre du Moulin. 8°. *Paris, en la boutique de
Niuelle, chez Sebastien Cramoisy*, 1614. L.; AV.IO.L^2.VT.
Answers the Huguenot, Pierre du Moulin's *Defense de la foy
Catholique contenue au liure de Iacques* I, 1610 (2nd ed. 1612), which
had attacked no. 1511.1.

1511.1 —Responce à l'aduertissement, adressé par le Serenissime Roy de la
Grande Bretagne, Iacques I. à tous les princes & potentats de la
Chrestienté. 8°. *Paris, par François Huby*, 1609. AMI.E.LYN.
Answers STC 14408. Answered by STC 5474 and by P. du Moulin in
Defense de la foy Catholique, 1610, to which Coeffeteau replied in
no. 1511.

1512 —[Date variant.] 1610. L.O.C.; C^2.JH.L^{25}.O.PA.SAI.

1513 —[Anr. ed.] 12°. *Rouen, chez Iean Osmont*, 1610. MD.PA.

1514 —[Anr. ed.] 12°. *Lyon, par Claude Morillon*, 1610. L.; PA.

1515 —[Anr. ed.] Derniere edition, reueue, augmentée de beaucoup, & corrigée par l'Autheur. 8°. *Paris, en la boutique de Niuelle, chez Sebastien
Cramoisy*, 1615. LOU.PA^7.VT.

1515.1 —[German transl.] Refutatio Apologiae. Das ist Gründtliche Wider-
legung vnd Gegenantwort auff die Ermahnung, so Iacobus dises
Nammens der erst König in Engellandt . . . hat lassen aussgehen . . .
Von Ioanne Meisero . . . in die gemeine Teutsche Sprach gebracht.
8°. *Getruckt in Freyburg im Breyssgaw, bey Martin Böckler*, 1614. WO.

1516 **Coqueau, L.** Examen praefationis monitoriae, Iacobi I. Magnae Britanniae et Hiberniae Regis, praemissae Apologiae suae pro iuramento
fidelitatis. Fol. *Friburgi Brisgoiae, apud Ioannem Strasserum*, 1610.
L.C.; BRS.D.DI.FLO.L^{25}.LYN.MD.MU.O^2.PA.PA^4.RO^5.VT.WO. + +
Answers STC 14401.

1517 —[Date variant.] 1611. MU.U.

1518 —[Anr. ed.] Fol. *Mediolani, sumptibus haeredum Pacifici Ponti et Ioannis
Baptistae Piccalei, impressorum Archiepiscopalium*, 1616. TRO.

1519 **Dassier, I.** Discours sur la response du Sr Casaubon, au nom du Roy
d'Angleterre, à l'epistre de Monseigneur le Cardinal du Perron.
Par I. Dassier M. 8° (in fours). *Paris, par Fleury Bourriquant*, 1614. PA.
Answering STC 4740 which was itself an answer to no. 1521.

1520 —[Anr. ed.] 8° (in fours). *Lyon, par Iean Poyet, iouxte la coppie imprimée
à Paris*, 1614. LYN(imp.).VER.

1521 **Du Perron, J. D.,** *Cardinal.* Lettre de Monseigneur le Reuerend Cardinal du Perron. Enuoyée à Monsieur Casaubon estant de present en
Angleterre. 8° (in fours). *n.p.*, 1612. PA(D33199).

Appealing to Casaubon to persuade King James to lead his subjects back to the true faith. The letter is dated 30 Aug. 1611. This is the first edition, published without the author's knowledge. There is no preface. *Pr.* [Paris.] Casaubon's reply is at STC 4740.

1522   —[Anr. ed.] Lettre de Monseigneur l'Illustriss. Card. du Perron. Enuoyée à Monsieur Casaubon estant en Angleterre. 8° (in fours). *Rouen, iouxte la coppie imprimée à Paris*, 1612. DMR.LC.LIL.LOU.N. PA(D22050/5).RMS.WO.
A reprint of no. 1521.

1523   —[Anr. ed., corrected by the Author.] Lettre de Monseigneur le Cardinal du Perron. Enuoyée au Sieur Casaubon en Angleterre. 8° (in fours). *Paris, de l'imprimerie de Iean Laquehay . . . et Iean Bouillette*, 1612. O.; CARP.F.HA.LINC.PA(D33198).VI.WO.
With a preface by Du Perron saying that this edition supersedes the unrevised and corrupt text of nos. 1521, 1522 which were published without his knowledge. The letter here bears the date 15 July 1611. The corrected text is reprinted in the preliminaries to no. 1525. An English translation of it is at A&R 286.

1524   —[Anr. ed. of the corrected text.] 4°. *Paris, chez Pierre Durand*, 1612. L.; BRS.PA(D10732).PA⁴.VI.WO.
A reprint of no. 1523.

1525   —Replique à la Response du Serenissime Roy de la Grand Bretagne. Fol. *Paris, par Antoine Estiene*, 1620. O.C.; AUG.D².DIJ.HP.KN.L².L²⁵. LAR.LOU.O³(2).PA.PA⁴.SBG.VT. + +
Answering STC 4740 in which Casaubon had replied to Du Perron's *Lettre* (nos. 1521, etc.). The preliminaries contain the text of the *Lettre* in its corrected form. The *Replique* was published posthumously. There is a full-page portrait of Du Perron on the verso of the titleleaf. For an English translation of part of this work see A&R 288.

1526   —[Anr. ed.] Seconde edition, enrichie de tables. Fol. *Paris, par Antoine Estiene*, 1622. C.; ANG.CHA.FLO.HAN.L².LOU.MD.MNS.MRB.O⁶.PA.RO³. TOU.VT. +

1527   —[Anr. ed.] Troisiesme edition, enrichie de tables. Fol. *Paris, chez Pierre Chaudiere*, 1633. AMI.ANT.C².C⁵.CHA.DMR.GTN(3).LYN.O².O¹⁸. POI.TRO.WO.

1528   **Eudaemon Ioannes, A**. Parallelus Torti ac Tortoris eius Cicestrensis : siue responsio ad Torturam Torti pro Illustrmo. Card. Bellarmino. 8°. *Coloniae Agrippinae, apud Ioannem Kinckium*, 1611. L.C.; C².D.DUR(2). HP.L²⁶.LOU³.MD.O⁷.O⁸.OS.PA(2).PA³.RO³.VT. + +
Answers STC 626. Answered by STC 4117 and 5563.

—R.P. Andreae Eudaemon-Ioannis . . . Epistola monitoria, 1613. *See* no. 53.

1529   [**Gretser, J**.] Antitortorbellarminianus Ioannes Gordonius Scotus pseudodecanus et capellanus Caluinisticus, nuper in Germaniam hirsuto et hispido capillo delatus, nunc sine pectine quidem, sed tamen satis eleganter tonsus ac pexus, & iucundi spectaculi ergo ad Serenissimum Magnae Britanniae Regem Iacobum remissus. 4°. *Ingolstadii, ex typographeo Adami Sartorii*, 1611. O.; CHICH².DIJ.HA. LGE³.
Answers John Gordon, Dean of Salisbury's *Antitortobellarminus*, 1610 (STC 12054).

1530   —Βασιλικον Δωρον siue Commentarius exegeticus in Serenissimi Magnae Britanniae Regis Iacobi Praefationem monitoriam; et in Apologiam pro iuramento fidelitatis. 4°. *Ingolstadii, ex typographeio Adami Sartorii*, 1610. L.O.; D.DUR.E.FU.GTN.HA.HD.HP.L².LGE³.MD(2). O².PA.RO⁵. + +
Answers STC 14405. Scott 204.

1531   **Harlay de Champvallon, F.**, *Archbishop of Rouen*, Francisci Archiepiscopi Rothomagensis . . . Apologia Euangelii, pro Catholicis, ad Iacobum, maioris Britanniae Regem. Fol. *Lutetiae Parisiorum, apud Antonium Stephanum,* 1625. o^{12}.PA(2).PA^3(2).PA^4.PLU.RO^5.
Disputing James's claim that the Anglican Church is truly Catholic.

1532   —[*French transl.* of the Preface only.] Preface de l'apologie de l'Euangile, pour tous les Catholiques: adressée au Serenissime Roy de la Grand'Bretaigne . . . Traduitte du Latin en François, par Monsieur le Marquis de Breual, son frere. Fol. *Paris, par Antoine Estiene,* 1625. PA.PA^3.

1533   **Kermadec, François de.** Relation veritable enuoyée au Serenissime Roy de la Grand'Bretagne, de plusieurs diuers iugemens faits en France. Sur le sujet de la Declaration de S.M. pour le droit des Rois & l'independance de leurs couronnes. 4°. *Caen, sur la coppie imprimée à Nantes,* 1615. L(3).O.; AIX.FLO^3.L^2.MIN.NTS.PA.PA^4(2).PA^7.TOU.VT.Y.
The 'Declaration' referred to in the title is STC 14367. *See* RH Oct. 1979, pp. 92–4. The Nantes edition of the *Relation* has not been found.

1534   **Lessius, L.** Defensio potestatis Summi Pontificis, aduersus librum Regis Magnae Britanniae, Guilielmi Barclaii Scoti, & M. Georgii Blacuelii. 4°. *Caesaraugustae, apud Christophorum Iouium,* 1611. L^2 (*imp.*).NP.VT.
Answers STC 14405, 1408 (= no. 53.1 in this catalogue) and part of 3103. Imprint false; *pr.* [S. Omer, Eng. Coll. press]. This book was suppressed by Rome and never generally distributed. For the background, *see* K. van Sull, *Léonard Lessius de la Compagnie de Jésus,* Louvain, 1930, pp. 219–32. A 17th century MS of the work is in the Bibliothèque Royale, Brussels, MS no. 1754. A&R 405 is an English abstract of the work. Answered in STC 25602 (no. 925.6 in this catalogue). Another work by Lessius, in answer to part of STC 14405, *De Antichristo,* 1611, falls outside the scope of this catalogue as it is not directly concerned with the allegiance of English Catholics.
  —Discussio decreti magni Concilii Lateranensis, 1613. *See* no. 1086.

1535   **Pelletier, T.** La religion catholique soustenue en tous les poincts de sa doctrine. Contre le liure adressé aux rois, potentats & republiques de la chrestienté par . . . Iacques I. Roy d'Angleterre. 8°. *Paris, par Iean Iannon,* 1610. L.O.; C^2.L^2.PA.PA^2.TRO. *This or no. 1536 :* BOR.L^{25}.
Purporting to answer the 'Praefatio monitoria' in STC 14405 but, in fact, containing little reference to James's work.

1536   —[Imprint variant.] *Paris, chez Iean Gesselin,* 1610. PA.
Forming part of a shared edition with no. 1535.

1537   **Schoppe, C.** Gasp. Scioppii Collyrium regium Serenissimo D. Jacobo Magnae Britanniae Regi . . . Vna cum Syntagmate de cultu et honore iam tertium edito. 8°. *Apud Holofernem Kriegsederum,* 1611. L.O(2). c(2).; C^2.D.GT.GTN.L^2.L^6.L^{25}.MD.PA.TRO.VI.WO. +
The *Collyrium,* here published for the first time, answers James I's 'Praefatio monitoria' in STC 14405; the *Syntagma* is a new edition of another work by Schoppe which has no special reference to England. Imprint fictitious; *pr.* [Ingolstadt, Andreas Angermayer?].

1537.1   —[Anr. ed. of both works, with title:] Gasp. Scioppii Syntagma de cultu adorationis et honore. Editio quarta. Cui praemissum est eiusdem Collyrium regium. 8°. *n.p.* 1616. L.; CHI.D.PA.

1538   —Gasp. Scioppii Ecclesiasticus Auctoritati Serenissimi D. Iacobi Magnae Britanniae Regis oppositus. 4°. *Hartbergae,* 1611. L.O.C(2).; AMP.ANT.C^2.D.E^2.FLO^3.GTN.L^2.L^6.MD.PA.VI(2).WO. +
A further answer to STC 14405. Imprint fictitious; *pr.* [Ingolstadt, Andreas Angermayer?]

1539 —Gasp. Scioppii Scorpiacum Hoc est: nouum ac praesens aduersus Protestantium haereses remedium . . . quo aduersus Serenissimum D. Iacobum Magnae Britanniae Regem recitatis Magdeburgensium centuriatorum testimoniis luculentissime demonstratur: Ecclesiae Romanae fidem omnibus saeculis inde ab Apostolorum aetate in vniuerso mundo annunciatum fuisse. 4°. *Moguntiae, ex officina typographica Ioannis Albini*, 1612. L.O.C.; ANT.D.E.FLO³.GTN.L².L⁶.MD.PA. PA⁴.VI.WO. +

A further answer to STC 14405. Another work by Schoppe, *Alexipharmacum regium*, published at the same press in 1612, though dedicated to King James, does not concern itself with the question of Catholic allegiance.

1540 **Schulcken, A.** Apologia Adolphi Schulckenii . . . pro Illustrissimo Domino D. Roberto Bellarmino . . . De potestate Romani Pont. temporali. Aduersus librum falso inscriptum, Apologia Card. Bellarmini pro iure principum, &c. Auctore Rogero Widdringtono Catholico Anglo. 8°. *Coloniae Agrippinae, sumptibus Bernardi Gualtheri*, 1613. [Coloph.] *Typis Stephani Hemmerden.* O(2).C.; ANT².AUG.D.DMR.L². L¹³.L²⁶.LGE³.LOU³.P.PA.PA⁴.TRO.USH. +

An answer to no. 925.1. Sommerv. (tom. 1, col. 1225) rejects Thomas Preston's attribution (in A&R 664) of this work to Bellarmine himself and considers it a genuine work by Schulcken. It incorporates the text of Bellarmine's *Examen* (no. 1504).

1541 **Suarez, F.** Defensio fidei Catholicae, et apostolicae Aduersus Anglicanae sectae errores, cum responsione ad Apologiam pro iuramento fidelitatis, & Praefationem monitoriam Serenissimi Iacobi Angliae Regis. Fol. *Conimbricae, apud Didacum Gomez de Loureyro Academiae typographum*, 1613. L.O.C.; CHA.E.E².GT.HP.LYN.OS.

Answers STC 14405. Answered in no. 925.4 and in STC 6994 and 47.

1542 —[Anr. ed.] Fol. *Coloniae Agrippinae, in officina Birckmannica, sumptibus Hermanni Mylii*, 1614. C.; C².DI.EX.FRA.FU.LOU³.LYN.MU.PA.PA⁴.PA⁸. TB.VI.YK. +

1543 —[Anr. ed.] Fol. *Moguntiae, sumptibus Hermanni Mylii Birckmanni* [at Cologne]. *Excudebat Balthasar Lippius*, 1619. C.; A.C⁵.CHA.D².E.FLO³. GTN.HA.HER.HP(2).LGE³.MU(2).TB.WOR. +

1544 —[Extracts.] Excerpta ex libro cui titulus est R.P. Francisci Suarez . . . Defensio fidei Catholicae & Apostolicae aduersus Anglicanae sectae errores . . . Coloniae Agrippinae, in officina Birckmannica, sumptibus Hermanni Mylii . . . Anno CIƆ.IƆ.C.XIV. 4°. *n.p.d.* [1614]. PA(D10068).PA⁴.

Comprising passages from Bk. 3, chapters 23 and 29, and Bk. 6, chapters 4, 6 and 8, which were singled out and condemned by the Parlement of Paris (26 June 1614) as prejudicial to the sovereign rights of kings. Probably intended to be issued as a supplement to editions of the Parlement's decree printed in the same year. Collation: A⁴B² (A3 blank). *Pr.* [Paris?]

1545 —[Anr. ed.] 4°. *n.p.d.* [1614.] PA(D10069).
Collation: A–C². *Pr.* [Paris?]

1546 **Varin de Perrières, P.** Epistre à tres-haut . . . Prince, Iacques . . . Roy de la Grande Bretagne. Sur son Apologie pour le serment de fidelité qu'il requiert de tous ses sujets. 8°. *Rouen, chez Iean Petit*, 1610. PA(Nc 226/2).

Answers STC 14405.

1547 [Author unknown.] Le Roy et la foy d'Angleterre combatus. 8°. *A Couloigne, n.d.* [1609.] L.O(2).; AIX.PA.VER.

Answers STC 14405. Imprint false; *pr.* [France.]

1619

*Catholic propaganda in favour of the Emperor Ferdinand
II's claim to the Kingdom of Bohemia against James I's
son-in-law, Frederick Elector Palatine.
For Catholic pamphlets in English on this controversy, see
A&R 303 (and another translation of the same not in A&R, to
be described in our volume 2) and 260.*

1548 **[Schmid von Schmiedebach, Augustin.]**‡ Informatio fundamentalis
super discursu quodam circa modernum Bohemiae statum facto. Cui
adiectus est tenor bullae aureae Caroli quarti. 4°. *n.p.* 1619 [o.s. =
1620] O.; OS.[*DMR.].

> The original text was drawn up by [von Schmiedebach] for presen-
> tation to the King of Denmark and to the princes of the 'sächssischer
> Kreis' by the imperial delegation which set out from Vienna at the
> beginning of January 1620. Editions of the Latin (entitled *Infor-
> matio fundamentalis super hodierno Bohemiae statu*) and of a transla-
> tion into German were printed at Frankfurt and elsewhere in
> Germany in 1620 and 1621. The present Latin edition was printed
> [secretly in England, at the 'Birchley Hall' press in Lancashire]. On
> 22 July 1620 Archbishop Abbot informed William Trumbull, King
> James's Agent at Brussels, that it was 'Padre Maestro' (Assistant
> to Gondomar, the Spanish Ambassador in London) who was
> responsible for having it printed in England. The copy sent by
> Abbot to Trumbull is now at O. The 'Discursus' opposing the
> Emperor's claim referred to in the title of the present edition has
> not been identified. STC 3207.5. Answered in STC 3205, 3206. *See*
> Gebauer, J., *Die Publicistik über den böhmischen Aufstand von 1618*,
> 1892, pp. 41–2; Hurter, F. E. von, *Geschichte Kaiser Ferdinands II
> und seiner Eltern*, 1850–62, vol. 8, pp. 213–14; Downshire MSS
> (Berkshire County Record Office, Reading), vol. 1, no. 42.

[1549 *cancelled*]

1622

*Recantation of M. A. de Dominis.
It strengthened the morale of English Catholics shaken by
his earlier apostasy and his acceptance of office in the
Anglican church. See Mil., vol. 2, pp. 187–93. English
translations were published at S. Omer and 'Liège' in 1623.
(A&R 272–3).*

1550 **Dominis, M. A. de,** *Archbishop of Spalatro.* Marcus Antonius de
Dominis . . . sui reditus ex Anglia consilium exponit. 4°. *Romae, ex
typographia Reu. Camerae Apostolicae,* 1623. CHA.GER.GT.L².MD.PA.
PA².PA³.RO².RO³.RO⁴.RO⁵.RO⁶.RO⁸.VT(2).

> Dated from Rome, 24 November 1622. This, the original Roman
> edition, may be recognised by the large ornament above the imprint,
> showing a crowned eagle in an elaborate cartouche. Answered in
> STC 7006; 5975; 18039; 18421.

1551 —[Anr. ed.] 4°. *Romae, ex typographia Reu. Camerae Apostolicae,* 1623.
O.

> A reprint [done in Germany?] of no. 1550, repeating the original
> Roman imprint. The ornament above the imprint is much smaller
> than in no. 1550 and shows a mask surrounded by scrolls; it
> resembles that on the titlepage of no. 1576.

1552 —[Anr. ed.] 4°. *Romae, ex typographia Reu. Camerae Apostolicae,* 1623.
[Coloph.] *Louanii, typis Henrici Hastenii,* 1623. L.; BRS².HA.LOU³.YK.

A Louvain reprint repeating the original Roman imprint on the titlepage.

1553   —[Anr. ed.] 4°. *Romae, ex typographia Reu. Camerae Apostolicae*, 1623. *Et Mediolani, apud impressores Archiepiscopales.* LIL³.MIL².

1554   —[Anr. ed.] 4°. *E. Romano exemplari . . . edito . . . Dilingae, apud Vdalricum Rem*, 1623. L.O.; DUR(2).DI(5).FR.MU.O⁸.TB.ULM.UP.

1555   —[Anr. ed.] 8°. *Coloniae Agrippinae, sumptibus Bernardi Gualtheri*, 1623. LINC.

1556   —[Anr. ed.] 4°. *Moguntiae, ex typographia Antonii Stroheckeri*, 1623. E². MRB.SBG.TB.VI.WO.

1557   —[Anr. ed.] 8°. *Parisiis, apud Sebastianum Cramoisy*, 1623. CARP.CHA. L².O⁵.O⁶.O¹⁷.PA.U.

1558   —[Anr. ed.] 8° (in fours). *Iuxta exemplar Romae, Parisiis, apud Ioannes le Begue*, 1623. BOR.DE.PA.PA⁴.

1558.1 —[Anr. ed.] 8°. *Tornaci, apud Reginaldum Laurentium (ex officina Adriani Quinqué)*, 1623. TNI².
        Not seen. Description from Desmazières no. 77.

1559   —[*Flemish transl.*] Redenen van Marcus Antonius de Dominis . . . ghegheuen ouer zijn wedercompste wt Enghelandt . . . Ouerghezedt wt het Lattijn in onser Nederlandsche tale. 4°. *t'Hantwerpen, by Abraham Verhoeuen, naar de coppije van Romae, ex typographia Reu. Camerae Apostolicae*, 1623. L.; HA.

1560   —[*French transl.*] La declaration de Marc-Antoine de Dominis . . . sur son retour d'Angleterre . . . traduit de Latin en François sur l'exemplaire romain, par C.M.S. 8° (in fours). *Iouxte la coppie imprimée à Rome. Paris, chez Iean le Begue*, 1623. D².LEM.PA(2).PA³.
        The translator, C.M.S., has not been identified.

1561   —[*German transl.*] Marcus Antonius de Dominis . . . zeigt an vñ erklaeret seine bewegliche vrsachen, warumb er auss Engelland von der falschen, widerumb zu der wahren vnd allein seligmachenden Catholischen Roemischen Kirchen getretten sey . . . in die Teutsche Sprach versetzt, durch Thomam Vitum Fuerstlichen Augspurgischen Registratorem zu Dillingen. 4°. *Dilingen, in der Academischen Truckerey, bey Vlrich Rem*, 1623. DI.ERL.MU.TB.ULM.WO.

1562   —[*Polish transl.*] Marcus Antonius de Dominis . . . swego zwrocenia sie z Angliey, rade przekłada . . . z Láćinskiego ná Polski iezyk, przetłumáczona, y w druk podána. 4°. *w Wilnie w drukárni akademiey Societatis Iesu, n.d.* [1623]. KR.

1623

The Spanish Marriage Negotiations

I.

Nine articles signed by King James I and Prince Charles in January 1623, These included a promise to allow limited toleration to Catholics in England. They proved unacceptable to the Pope and to Philip IV and were replaced in July 1623 by a revised set of articles which also came to nothing. (Gardiner, vol. 2, pp. 283, et seq.). An edition of the earlier articles, printed at Antwerp, probably in English and Spanish, and which has not so far been found, appears to have been the original of the following translations.

562.1 [*French.*] Articles du mariage entre le Prince de Gales, et l'Infante d'Espagne. En faueur de la Religion Catholique Apostolique & Romaine. Auec quelques nouuelles de son voyage & de son sejour en la cour du Roy d'Espagne. Suiuant la coppie imprimée Anuers.

Et traduitte en François. 8° (in fours). *Paris, de l'imprimerie de Iean Laguehay*, 1623. L.O.; NCY.PA(2).PA³.ROU.

Following the articles is a brief account of the journey of Charles and Buckingham to Madrid, their arrival there on 7/17 March 1623 and their reception at the Spanish court.

1563   —[Anr. ed.] 12° (a quadrifolium). *Grenoble, de l'imprimerie de P. Marniolles*, 1623. CARP.

The title follows that of no. 1562.1 as far as the words 'En faueur de la religion Catholique Apostolique & Romaine' after which it terminates. The text is a reprint of no. 1562.1.

1564   —[Anr. ed.] 8° (in fours), *Lyon, par Claude Armand, dit Alphonse*, 1623. LYN.

The title follows that of no. 1563.

1565   [*Italian.*] Copia de capitoli fatti per il matrimonio del Serenissimo Prencipe Carlo de Valles Infante d'Inghilterra, et la Serenissima Infante di Spagna dona Maria d'Austria. Tradotta dalla lingua Inglese nell'Italiana. 4° (a single quadrifolium). *Milano, per Gio Battista Malatesta, n.d.* [1623.]. L.; F(*wants frontisp.*).RO³.TUR.

The account of the journey of Charles and Buckingham here stops short at their arrival at Paris on 18/28 February. With an engraved frontispiece copied from the titlepage of *Rosa Hispani Anglica* (STC 7376), a collection of complimentary pieces on the Spanish marriage published in England under the name of Michael Duval. *Rosa Hispani Anglica* does not include the articles of marriage.

1566   —[Anr. ed.] 8° (a quadrifolium). *In Milano, & in Piacenza, per Giacomo Ardizzone*, 1623. NCY.

1567   —[Anr. ed.] 8° (a quadrifolium). *In Milano, & in Bologna, per gli heredi del Cochi*, 1623. BG(Av Tab. I NIII vol. 264/50).

1568   —[Anr. ed.] 4° (a bifolium). *Napoli, per Secondino RAsagliolo*, 1623. *Si vendono da Gio. Orlandi*. RO³(Misc. Ant. XIV. d. 27/6).

2.

Spanish theological opinions submitted to Philip IV concerning the proposed marriage.

1569   **Araujo, F. de.** Parecer del M. fray Francisco de Araujo, de la orden de Santo Domingo, sobre el matrimonio de la Infanta doña Maria con el Principe de Gales. Madrid. 29 de abril 1623. 4°. *n.p.d.* [1623.] MD² (Jes. 86/21. *Missing 1977*).

Not seen. Description from MS catalogue of the Jesuit collection at MD². *Pr.* [Madrid?]

1570   **Carrillo, Martin,** *Bishop of Osma.* Parecer afirmatiuo de casamiento de la Serenissima Infanta doña Maria de Austria, con el Principe de Gales don Carlos. Y se responde a los exemplares, que por la parte negatiua se han propuesto. Fol. (a quadrifolium). *n.p.d.* [1623.] L(Egerton MSS, 339, ff. 201–4).

An opinion in favour of the marriage. There are five approbations, all from Zaragoza, the last dated 1 Aug. 1623. *Pr.* [Zaragoza?]

1571   **Francisco** [Jodar], *de Jesus.* Los papeles que por mandado del Rey nuestro Señor ha hecho Fray Francisco de Iesus su Predicador. Sobre el tratado del matrimonio, que el Principe de Gales pretende con la Serenissima señora Infante Maria. Segun los diferentes estados que ha ido teniendo esta materia. 4°. *En la Imprenta Real, n.d.* [1623.] O.; PA.STU.

Comprising four papers by Francisco, dated between 21 April and 1 Aug. 1623, dealing with various aspects of the proposed marriage. At the end of the last paper he refers to the conflicting opinions of the theological junta set up by the King to examine the question. *Pr.* [Madrid.] An edition was published in 1869 by S. R. Gardiner (Camden Soc. vol. 101) from B.L. Add. MS. 14043.

1572 **Gonzalez de Mendoza, P.** Copia del parecer del Padre Gonzalez de Mendoça de la Compañia de Iesus, cerca del casamiento entre la Señora Infanta de España Doña Maria, y el Señor Principe de VVales. Fol. *n.p.d.* [1623.] HSA.MD²(Jes. 126/52).

Comprising two pareceres of Gonzalez de Mendoza under the date 1 July 1623. These are followed by a postscript saying that, in spite of the unfavourable opinion of Gonzalez and some others, the majority of the theological junta resolved on 14 July that consent should be given to the marriage provided that the Pope's conditions for granting his dispensation were guaranteed by the King of Spain. *Pr.* [Madrid?]

1573 **Montemayor, J. de.** Parecer que dio en el Iunta el padre Iuan de Montemayor de la Compañia de Iesus, acerca del casamiento de sus Altezas. 4°. *n.p.d.* [1623.] O.

Insisting that guarantees be obtained from the King of England that the conditions imposed by the Pope, and particularly those concerning toleration for English Catholics, will be met. Collation: A–D⁴. *Pr.* [Salamanca?]

1574 —[Anr. ed.] 4°. *n.p.d.* [1623.] MD(MSS 2354, ff. 227, *et seq.*). Collation: A–E⁴F².

3.

Letter of Pope Gregory XV to Prince Charles, urging him to lead England back to the Faith, 10/20 April 1623. An English translation, printed in London, is at STC 13257.

1575 [*Latin.*] Breue S.D.N. Papae Gregorii XV. Ad Carolum nobilissimum VValliae Principem Iacobi Magnae Britanniae filium. 4°. *Antuerpiae, apud Abrahamum Verhouium,* 1623. BRS(VB 10102).

1576 —[Anr. ed., with the Latin text of Charles's reply of 18/28 June 1623.] Epistola Gregorii XV. Pontif. Max. Ad Serenissimum Principem, Carolum, Jacobi Britanniarum Regis filium, Principem Walliae. Ad exemplum Parisiense recusa. Cui recens accedit Serenissimi Principis ad eam Responsio. 4°. *n.p.,* 1623[?]. GTN.HAN.HEI.MU.PR.PR³.WO. [*O.]

The typography suggests that it was printed later than the date shown on the titlepage which is the date of the original edition. *Pr.* [in Germany?] The ornament on the titlepage resembles that on the titlepage of no. 1551. For a 1623 Paris edition of the Latin text of the Pope's letter, together with a French translation, *see* no. 1583.

1577 [*Latin and Spanish.*] Breue S.D.N. Papae Gregorii XV. nobilissimo Walliae Principi Magnae Britanniae Regis filio. (Breue de la Santidad de Gregorio Papa XV. traduzido de Latin en Castellano. Al nobilissimo Principe de Gales, hijo del Rey de la Gran Britania.) Fol. (a bifolium). [Coloph.] *Madrid, por Luis Sanchez, n.d.* [1623.] HSA.MD² (Salazar A1). RO³.SCG.

The Latin text occupies the recto and verso of one leaf, the Spanish the recto and verso of the other. In some copies the sheet is folded in reverse, so that the Spanish comes first and the Latin second. Following the Spanish text is the statement: 'Traduzido en Madrid por el Doctor don Mateo Renzi, Capellan de su Magestad, a 28 dias de Mayo de 1623 años' and the colophon.

1578 [*Spanish only.*] IHS Breue de la Santidad de Gregorio Papa XV. traduzido de Latin en Castellano. Al nobilissimo Principe de Gales, hijo del Rey de la Gran Britania. Fol. (a bifolium). [Coloph.] *Madrid*, 1623. L(T.90*/27).; HD.HSA.MD²(Jes. 132/33).

The translation is that of Mateo Renzi (*see* no. 1577). Collation: A². In this edition the last line on sig. A1ʳ begins: 'Real Anglicana . . .' and sig. A2ᵛ is blank.

1579 —[Anr. ed.] Fol. (a bifolium). [Coloph.] *Madrid*, 1623. HD.HSA.MD² (Jes. 201/8).

Collation: A². In this edition the last line on sig. A1ʳ begins: 'esso que . . .', and sig. A2ᵛ is blank.

1580 —[Anr. ed.] Fol. (a bifolium). *n.p.d.* [1623.] L(Add. MSS. 28453, f. 108.) Without signatures. In this edition the last line on the recto of the first leaf begins: 'y amparo . . .' and the verso of the second leaf contains 'Recibimiento que se le hizo al Principe de Gales en Inglaterra' recording the Prince's departure from Madrid and his arrival in London [on 5 Oct. 1623].

1581 —[Anr. ed.] Fol. (a bifolium). [Coloph.] *Seuilla . . . por Gabriel Ramos Jejarano*, 1623. L(593.h.17/1).; HSA.MD²(Jes. 93/32).

1582 —[Anr. ed., with additions.] Breue de la Santidad de Gregorio Papa XV. traduzido de Latin en Castellano. Al nobilissimo Principe de Gales, hijo del Rey de la Gran Britania. Contiene la respuesta que dio de palabra al Nuncio, quando le visito de parte de su Santidad. Gregorio Papa XV. Fol. (a bifolium). *Valladolid*, 1623.

Not found. Description from Vindel 319.

1583 [*French and Latin.*] Bref de nostre S. Pere le Pape Gregoire V [*sic*]. Au tres-noble Prince de Galles, fils du Roy de la grande Bretagne. 8° (in fours'. *Paris, chez Denys Langlois*, 1623. PA(Nc 263). Huth Sale, pt. 5, June 1912, lot 1500 (*present whereabouts not known*).

The text is here given first in French and then in the Latin of which the French is a translation. An abbreviated version of the French is printed in *Le Mercure François*, tom. 9, pp. 510–14.

1584 —[Titlepage variant.] Lettre de nostre S. Pere le Pape Gregoire V [*sic*] . . . *Paris, chez Denys Langlois*, 1623. PA(Nc 3452).PA⁴.ROU.

Apart from the substitution of the word 'Lettre' for 'Bref' in the title the setting is the same as in no. 1583.

1585 —[Anr. ed.] Lettre de nostre S. Pere le Pape Gregoire XV. Au tres noble Prince Charles de Galles, fils vnique du Roy de la grande Bretagne. 8° (a quadrifolium). *Iouxte la copie imprimée à Madril. Chez Denis Langlois, au mõt sainct Hilaire au Pelican*, 1623. LIL.

Imprint false; *pr.* [Lille, Christoffe Beys.]

1586 —[Anr. ed., with the name of Pope Urban VIII substituted for that of Gregory XV in the title.] 4°. *Iouxte la copie imprimée à Madril, chez Dominico de Gabianis*, 1623. F(DA 396A3/C3 Cage).

Gregory XV died 8 July 1623, Urban VIII was elected 6 Aug. 1623. The text of the letter is unchanged. *Pr.* [Lille, Christoffe Beys.]

1587 [*French and German.*] Lettre de nostre S. Pere le Pape Gregoire XV. Au tres-noble Prince de Valles, fils du Roy de la Grande Bretagne. Schreiben Bapst. Gregorii dess Fuenffzehenden an den Printzen von Wallis . . . Auss obgesetztem Frantzoesischen, zu Paris bey Deonysio L'Anglois . . . getrucktem Exemplar verteutscht. 4°. *Strassburg, bey Johann Andrea*, 1623. PA(Nc 264, *missing* 1977.).STG.ULM.WIE.

1588 [*Flemish.*] Vertaelden brief, gheschreuen door Paus Gregorius den XV. Aen d'Hooghgeuooren Prince van Walles, soon van den Hooghmachtigen Koningh van groot Brittange. 4°. *n.p.d.* [1623.] GT.HA.

The letter is here misdated 20 May (for 20 April) 1623. *Pr.* [Antwerp?] The translation is not the same as that found in the Dutch Protestant publication, *Copye van twee Brieven*, Amsterdam, 1642.

1589   [*Italian.*] Breue della Santita di Gregorio Papa XV. Tradotto dal Castigliano in Italiano. Al nobilissimo Principe di Gales figliuolo del Rè della gran Bretagna. Fol. (a bifolium). [Coloph.] *In Milano, nella R.D. Corte, per Gio. Battista Malatesta*, 1623. WO(316.5.Th./14).

1590   —[Anr. ed.] Lettera in forma di breue della Santita di N.S. Gregorio Papa XV. Tradotta dal Castigliano in Italiano. Al nobilissimo Principe di Gales figliuolo del Rè della gran Bretagna. 4° (a bifolium). [Coloph.] *Stampata in Milano, nella R.D.C. per Gio. Battista Malatesta.* 1623. *Et in Napoli, per Secondino Roncagliolo.* HP(BX.124.Pam./1).RO³.

4.

Letter of Pope Gregory XV to Enrique Pimentel, Bishop of Cuenca and Inquisitor General of Spain, urging him to use his influence with the King of Spain to persuade Prince Charles to become a Catholic. 9/19 April 1623.

1591   [*Latin and Spanish.*] Gregorius PP. XV. Venerabili fratri Episcopo Concheñ. in Hispaniarum Regnis Inquisitori generali. (Gregorio Papa decimoquinto. Al Venerable hermano Obispo de Cuenca, Inquisidor general de las Españas.) Fol. (a bifolium). *n.p.d.* [1623.] L(593.h.22. *wanting the leaf containing the Latin*).O.; MD²(2: Jes. 117/72; Jes. 31/38, imp.).ND.

    Without signatures. The Latin text occupies the recto and verso of one leaf, the Spanish the recto and verso of the other, and in some copies the sheet is folded in reverse so that the Spanish comes first and the Latin second. In some copies (e.g. O) the verso of the leaf containing the Latin has only thirteen lines and there is an omission in the text; in others (e.g. ND.MD²(Jes. 31/38)) have the correct text in a new setting of sixteen lines.

1592   —[Anr. ed., with the Spanish preceding the Latin.] Fol. (a bifolium). [Coloph.] *Con licencia del Señor Licenciado Veas Velon, Oydor de Audiencia de la Ciudad de Seuilla, por Gabriel Ramos Vejarano,* 1623. MD²(Jes. 145/52).

    Collation: A². The Spanish occupies A1ʳ⁻ᵛ, the Latin A2ʳ⁻ᵛ.

1593   —[Anr. ed., with the Spanish preceding the Latin.] Fol. (a bifolium). *n.p.d.* [1623.] MD²(Jes. 93/30).

    Collation: A². Pr. [Seville, Gabriel Ramos Vejarano.] There is no colophon; types and ornaments are the same as in no. 1592 but the type has been reset.

5.

Prince Charles's reply to the Pope's letter, no. 3 above. 18/28 June 1623. Contemporary English versions are preserved in MS at L¹¹ (SP14/147, no. 10).

1594   [*Spanish and Latin.*] Copia de la respuesta del Serenissimo Principe de Gales a la carta de su Santidad. Fol. (a bifolium). *n.p.d.* [1623.] MD² (Jes. 93/29).

    The text is here given first in Spanish and then in the Latin of which the Spanish is a translation. Pr. [Spain]

1595   —[Anr. ed.] Fol. (a bifolium). [Coloph.] *Sevilla, por Gabriel Ramos Vejarano,* 1623. HSA(*wanting the first leaf containing the Spanish text*). MD²(2: Jes. 93/31; Jes. 31/37 & 41).

1596   [*Spanish only.* With anr. ed. of no. 1604.] Respuesta del Principe de Inglaterra a la carta de su Santidad . . . y a dos de su Magestad. Fol. (a bifolium). *n.p.d.* [1623.] HD.HSA.MD(*V–1016,18*).

    For the letter from Prince Charles to Philip IV, *see* §6 below. *Pr.* [Spain]

1597   —[Anr. ed. of no. 1596.] Fol. (a bifolium). [Coloph.] *Lima, por Geronymo de Contreras*, 1624. PA(Rés. 01.785/27).

1598   [*French*. The letter to the Pope only.] Lettre du Serenissime Prince de Galles. Enyoyée au Pape. 8°. *Iouxte la coppie imprimée en Espagne, 1623.* HN(*formerly Huth 1501*).
      Without the original Latin. Pr. [France?]

1599   —[Anr. ed. of no. 1598, with the name of Pope Urban VIII substituted for that of Gregory XV in the title.] Responce de Charles Prince de Galles fils vnique du Roy de la Grande Bretagne. A la lettre de nostre sainct Pere le Pape Vrbain VIII. 4°. *Iouxte la copie imprimée à Madril, chez Dominico de Gabianis,* 1623. F.
      See no. 1586. The text is unchanged. Pr. [Lille, Christoffe Beys.]

1600   [*Italian*. The letter to the Pope only.] Resposta del Principe d'Inghilterra. Alla lettera della Santita di N.S. Papa Gregorio XV ... Tradotta dal Castigliano in Italiano per Giouanne Orlandi. 4° (a bifolium). [Coloph.] *Stampata in Milano, nella R.D.C. per Gio. Battista Malatesta.* 1623. *Et in Napoli, per Secondino Roncagliolo.* HP(BX.124.Pam./2).
      The Milan edition from which this Naples reprint was made has not been found.

6.

Letter from Prince Charles to Philip IV answering letters from Philip himself and from Count Olivares. [June 1623.] In his letter Charles renews an earlier promise of limited toleration for Catholics in England.

1601   [*Spanish*.] Copia de vn papel que el Smo. Principe de Gales embiò, en respuesta de otro de S.M. Catolica del Rey nuestro Señor. Fol. (a bifolium). *n.p.d.* [1623.] MD²(Jes. 75/102).
      This Spanish version may be distinguished from that at no. 1604 by the opening words of the text which here begins: 'Señor. Auiendo visto y considerado el Serenissimo Principe de Gales el papel que la Iunta de teologos presento ...'

1602   —[Anr. ed., with title:] Copia de vn papel que el Smo. Principe de Gales embiò, en respuesta de su Magestad Catolica del Rey nuestro Señor. Fol. (a bifolium). *n.p.d.* [1623]. HSA.

1603   —[Anr. ed., with title:] Memorial que el Serenissimo Principe de Gales dio, en razon de que se concluya el casamiento con la Señora Infanta. Refierense las condiciones deste casamiento, y iuramento que haze de cumplirlas el Principe de Inglaterra. Fol. (a bifolium). [Coloph.] *Impresso en Madrid y por su original en Seuilla ... por Francisco de Lyra, n.d.* [1623.] MD²(Jes. 117/81).SEV².

1604   [*A different Spanish version of the same letter.*] Respuesta que el Principe de Gales embiò a su Magestad Filipo 4 nuestro Señor, sobre la junta que uvo, en que la Infanta no saliesse de España, dentro de el tiempo propuesto. Fol. (a bifolium). *Sevilla, por Gabriel Ramos,* 1623. MD² (Jes. 93/22, *formerly 93/24*).
      In this version the text begins: 'En dos de Iunio de 1623 presento su Magestad al Principe de Gales vn papel de la iunta de los teologos ...' For editions of this version published together with a letter from Charles to the Pope, *see* nos. 1596–7.

1605   [*French*.] La responce du Prince de Galles aux dernieres propositions du Roy d'Espagne, sur le faict de son mariage, auec l'establissement de la liberté de conscience en Angleterre. Traduict de l'Espagnol en François par le Sieur Demalespert. 8°. *Paris, par Guillaume Citerne,* 1623. PA(Nc 262).

7.

A collection of French translations of documents of 1622–1623 concerning the relaxation of the penal laws against Catholics in England, in anticipation of the Spanish marriage.

1606 Lettres des heureuses alliances faictes entre Charles Prince de Galles fils du Roy d'Angleterre, & de la Serenissime Infante doña Maria, soeur de Philippe quatriesme Roy des Espaignes . . . Auec la lettre du Grand Chancelier adressée aux iuges du Royaume d'Angleterre par le commandement du Roy pour le faict des Catholiques d'Angleterre. 8°. *Amiens, chez Iacques Hubaut,* 1623. PA³(33578).

Comprising translations of two letters that passed between Madrid and London in January 1623 on the proposed Anglo-Spanish marriage, followed by other material, including the complete text of *Recit veritable* . . . and *Lettre de l'Euesque de Lincolne* . . . which had been issued together as an independent publication in 1622 (*see* nos. 370–2).

1607 —[Anr. ed., with title beginning:] Les heureuses alliances faictes entre Charles Prince de Galles filz du Roy d'Angleterre . . . 4°. *Amiens, chez Iacques Hubaut,* 1623. LIL.

The type is partly reset.

1625 [etc.]
The French Marriage

1.

The marriage treaty, signed 10/20 November 1624, contained a number of 'articles généraux' guaranteeing the rights of Henrietta Maria and her household to the free exercise of their religion, and three 'articles particuliers' granting limited toleration to Catholics in England. The full text of all the articles was printed in Le Mercure françois, tom. 10, Paris 1625, pp. 480–7. The following publications contain only the 'articles généraux'.

1608 [*French.*] Articles accordez entre les commissaires du Serenissime Roy de la Grande Bretagne d'vne part: et ceux du Roy tres-Chrestien de France & de Nauarre d'autre. Pour le mariage, entre le Serenissime Prince de Galles . . . & Madame Henriette Marie. 8° (in fours). *A Paris,* 1625. O.; CARP(M739).PA³(37233/17).VT²(Nunz. Fran. 416. f. 395).

Collation: A–B⁴. pp. [1–2] 3–15 [16].

1609 —[Anr. ed. ? or anr. issue ?, with title:] Les articles du mariage. Entre le Roy de la Grande Bretagne & Madame Soeur du Roy. 8° (in fours). *A Paris,* 1625. CARP(M208/28).

Collation as in no. 1608. Charles succeeded to the throne 27 March 1625.

1610 [*Italian.*] Capitoli del matrimonio tra il Rey della Gran Bertagna, & Madama Henrietta Maria sorella del Christianissimo Re di Francia. Con il trionfo, ordine, e ceremonie in esso osseruate. Tradotti dal Francese in Italiano. 4°. *Parigi, MDCXXV. E di nuouo in Torino, per li Caualleris,* [1625]. L.

In spite of the statement in the title, there is no description of the ceremony.

1611 [*A different Italian version.*] Capitoli accordati sopra il matrimonio fra'il Serenissimo Prencipe di Galles figlio del Sereniss. Rè d'Inghilterra, et Madama sorella del Christianissimo Rè di Francia. Dedicati all'Illustrissimo, & Eccellentissimo Sig. & Padron colendissimo. Il

Sig. Thomaso Dempster Barone di Muresk. 16°. *Bologna, per gl'heredi del Moscatelli*, 1625. BG(AV Tab. IN. III. vol. 264/14).

2.

Renewed persecution of Catholics in England in spite of the provision of the treaty.

1612 **Urban VIII**, *Pope.* Copia de vna carta de nuestro muy S. Padre Vrbano VIII. Para el Christianissimo Rey de Francia, en que le pide, haga que el Rey de Inglaterra cumpla las condiciones con que se hicieron las capitulaciones de la Christianissima Reyna de Inglaterra su hermana. Traduzida de Latin en Romance. Fol. (a bifolium). *n.p.d.* [1626.] MD²(Jes. 76/82).

　　The letter, dated from Rome 30 May 1626, complains that the conditions in the articles of marriage, which included toleration for Catholics in England, are not being honoured. It is printed in Spanish and in the Latin of which the Spanish is a translation. *Pr.* [Madrid?].

1613 —[Anr. ed.] Fol. (a bifolium). [Coloph.] *Seuilla, por Pedro Gomez de Pastrana*, 1626. L.; MD²(Jes. 87/31).

1614 [Author unidentified.] [Le fidele François au Roy d'Angleterre touchant l'iniustice de ces armes contre la France.] 8° (in fours). [*Paris, pour Jacques Brisson?* 1626?] WO(511.1.Hist./16. *Wants t.p.*).

　　Complaining about English support for the Huguenots of La Rochelle and the renewed persecution of Catholics in England in spite of the terms of the marriage treaty. Collation: A–B⁴. pp. [1–2] 3-[16]. p. 16 is misprinted: 12. The only copy found wants the titleleaf. *See* the imprint of no. 1615.

1615 —[Anr. ed.] Le fidelle François, au Roy d'Angleterre. Touchant l'iniustice de ses armes contre la France. 8° (in fours). *Paris, chez Pierre Ramier, iouxte la coppie imprimée pour Iacques Brisson*, 1627. CARP.

　　Collation and pagination as in no. 1614, but the misprinted numeration of p. 16 is corrected.

[For a newsletter about the renewed persecution of Catholics in England in 1626:] *See* nos. 384–7.

1626
*Catholic propaganda. A spurious letter purporting to
be written by the Lord Chancellor, John Williams,
Bishop of Lincoln, to the Chancellor of France*

1616 Punition de Dieu arriuée à Londres en Angleterre. Du grand nombre des morts en 24. heures, & marquez d'vne main sur le corps, qui remplit de craincte & tremblement les royaumes d'Escosse & d'Angleterre. 8° (in fours). *S. Omer, imprimé sur les lettres d'Angleterre ce present mois*, 1626. L.

　　This letter, purporting to be by Williams, speaks of 200,000 people having died in London on one day, and cites the disaster as an instance of God's judgment against heretics. The writer concludes by expressing repentance for his own evil life. *Pr.* [Charles Boscard?] STC 25730 (rejected).

1626
Queen Henrietta Maria's Chaplains

1617 Ce qui s'est passé en l'assemblée tenue de nuict, en Angleterre, entre les ecclesiastiques de la Reyne d'Angleterre, et les ministres Puritains

de la ville de l'Ondres [*sic*] en Angleterre. 8°. *Imprimée sur les copies d'Angleterre*, 1626.
Pr. [Lille, Charles Beys.] Not found. Description from Houdoy, no. 72. No English original has been traced.

1632 [*etc.*]
Luisa de Carvajal. Documentation concerning her life and sanctity.
For earlier accounts of her, see nos. 1065–6.

1618 **Doyega de Mendieta, Juan de.** Interrogatorio de preguntas, para la informacion, que por autoridad ordinaria se pretende hazer, de la vida, virtudes, santidad, y milagros de la sierua de Dios, y venerable señora D. Luisa de Carbaial y Mendoça, nacida en la villa de Iaraizejo en Estremadura, obispado de Plasencia. Fol. *n.p.d.* [*before* 1640.] MD²(Jes. 118/11).
An inquiry ordered by the Bishop of Plasencia into Luisa's reputation for sanctity, as a preliminary stage in a process of beatification. Signed by the ecclesiastical officer conducting it, Juan de Doyega de Mendieta. Among the miracles attributed to Luisa's intervention are several attested by members of the English College at Valladolid. *Pr.* [Salamanca?]

1619 **Muñoz, Luis.** Vida y virtudes de la venerable virgen doña Luisa de Caruaial y Mendoça. Su jornada a Inglaterra, y sucessos en aquel Reyno. Van al fin algunas poesias espirituales suyas . . . Por el licenciado Luis Muñoz. 4° (in eights). *Madrid, en la Imprenta Real*, 1632. L(2).O.C.; BAR².DMR.ESC.F.GTN.HSA.MD(2).MD².NY.OS.PA.
Muñoz says in his dedicatory epistle that the work is based partly on some of Luisa's own writings which have been entrusted to him and partly on unpublished material left by her English confessor, Michael Walpole, S.J. With two engraved portraits. A French translation was published in 1647.

Index of Titles

NOTE: This index embraces the titles of all the works described in Volume I, together with such other contemporary publications as are named in the annotations by their *titles*, as distinct from those quoted only by abbreviated bibliographical references (e.g. STC, A&R numbers). Other works are either identified when quoted or, if cited in a shortened form, will be found in the list of SHORT REFERENCES (pp. xxii–xxvii) together with the abbreviations used for them.

The letters i/j and u/v have in this index always been conformed to modern usage to simplify alphabetisation, which is strictly by the actual spelling found in the opening words, other than the definite article. But when the first words of the titlepage or heading comprise either:

an author's name in the genitive case

a phrase addressed to, or describing, a patron or dedicatee

a motto or ejaculation

such words are disregarded and the true title is taken from subsequent wording.

Index of Printers and Publishers

NOTE: As far as possible this index is set out under the present-day English names of countries, listed alphabetically, so as to establish the part played by each country in the production of the books described in the Catalogue. Within each country, places are arranged alphabetically (also under their modern English forms) and the names of printers, generally in their vernacular form, are in alphabetical order under each place, with their output under dates followed by the relevant *catalogue* numbers. More than one printer sharing the same Christian names and surnames are distinguished by (I), (II) etc.

Dates inside square brackets are not stated in the books themselves but are supplied by the editors; similarly, where the catalogue numbers are inside *square* brackets the place/printer is not stated in the book but has been supplied. A catalogue number inside a *round* bracket indicates a printer or place named as the original source of a reprinted edition.

Some false imprints are placed under their alleged place of printing; these are distinguished by having an asterisk prefixed to each entry. Other alleged places of printing are obviously meant to appear merely imaginary; these are grouped after the Country headings in a single alphabetical sequence under the heading MISCELLANEOUS FICTITIOUS IMPRINTS.

Many entries in the catalogue in fact carry no imprint at all; only when it has not been possible to suggest any attribution have such entries been grouped under the heading UNATTRIBUTED and listed year by year. This chronological arrangement has also been used (under the abbreviation 'n.p.n.', standing for 'no printer named') when the place of origin is known but the actual printer has not been identified, e.g. 'Madrid, n.p.n.'

To make it easier to find any particular press, a single ALPHABETICAL LIST OF PLACES AND PRINTERS is appended to this Index, giving references back to the Index itself. This final list also includes cross-references from unfamiliar Latin or vernacular place-names and from alternative forms of the family names of printers.

AUSTRIA

GRAZ
Widmanstetter, Georg
  1588—146
SALZBURG
Kürner, Konrad
  1594—984
VIENNA
Formica, Margaretha, Widow of
Leonhard
  1607—191
Formica, Matthäus
  1624—1312
  1638—1338
Jesuit College
  1572—613

Kolb, Franz
  1594—149
  1599—187
Rickhes, Michael
  1631—681
Stainhofer, Kaspar
  1572—612, [613?]
Vienna, n.p.n.
  1640—469

BELGIUM

ANTWERP
Bax, Andreas
  1581—22
  1611—540, 541
  1616—542

France, DOUAI, —cont.
Bogard, Martin
 1630—323
Bogard, Widow of Martin
 1636—817, 938
 1637—816
Bogard, Pierre
 1628—330
Borremans, Pierre
 1605—473
 1611—541
Boscard, Charles
 1598—1370
 1600—1371, 1372
 1602—1373, 1376
 1604—1376.2
 1606—1374
 1607—1375
 1608—841, (842)
 1609—1367
Boscard, Jacques
 1563—1115, 1116, 1117, 1118
Boscard, Widow of Jacques
 1593—791
 1605—473
 [1609]—80, [707], 1393
 [1611]—1392
Doff, Jacobus
 1563—1117
Fampoux, Jean de
 1632—171
Kellam, Lawrence (I)
 1604—336.3, 336.4
 1608—673 note, 840
 1610—336.5
 1611—939
 1612—79.1, 673
Kellam, Widow of Lawrence (I)
 1615—79, 848
 1616—313, 531, 532, (533)
 1619—74, 75, 76, 77, 78
Kellam, Lawrence (II)
 1626—934
 1633—338, 339
 1636—902, 935
Lapidanus, Nicolaus
 1563—1116, 1118
Patté, Gérard
 1633—569
Pinchon, Gérard
 1628—323.1
 1630—457
 1631—533
 1632—451
Télu, Pierre
 1618—818
Télu, Widow of Pierre
 1622—225, 327

1623—223
1624—1025
Winde, Loys van de
 1576—6
Winde, Widow of Loys van de
 1576—1148
Wyon, Marc
 1619—1042
 1620—544
 1622—639
Douai, n.p.n.
 1580—1157
 1609—1368
FLÈCHE, LA
Hébert, Louis
 1620—168
GRENOBLE
Marniolles, Pierre
 1623—1563
LILLE
Beys, Christophe
 1623—[1585], [1586], [1599]
 1626—[1617]
Stroobant, Guillaume
 1596—1474
LYONS
Armand, Claude
 1623—1564
 1625—348
Beraud, Symphorien
 1585—24
Berlerius, Antonius
 1627—69
Buysson, Jean-Baptiste
 1592—1212
 1593—1222
 1594—1223
 1595—1225
 1596—1136, 1226
 1599—1137
Cardon, Horace
 1599—1145
 1601—1178
 1602—1231
Cardon, Jacques
 1630—565.1 [See Addenda]
 1633—1077
Chard, Antoine
 1628—572
 1634—287, 288
 1635—289
 1638—577
Charlot, Jean Pierre
 1619—132
Didier, Jean
 1592—886
 1593—887
Du-Four, Claude

GERMANY

ASCHAFFENBURG

Lipp, Balthasar
1622—1187, 1207

AUGSBURG

Dabertzhofer, Chrysostomus
[1611]—1099
*Faber, Baptista
1620—72, 925.3, 927.1
1621—926.1
*Faber, Joannes
1592—885
*Libius, Joannes
1618—925.5
Mang, Christoph
1611—940
Mang, Sara, Widow of Christoph
1619—1100
*Mark, Hans
'1587, ou 88'—981
'1607, ou 1608'—982

BAMBERG

Crinesius, Augustin
1627—1060, [1272], 1273
Horitz, Anton
1595—1413

COLOGNE

Baum, Dietrich
1563—1110
Birckmann, Heirs of Arnold
1558—417
1559—419
1561—423
1564—421
1568—424
1569—245
1570—246
1581—248
Birckmannica, Officina
(continued by)
Mylius, Arnold
Mylius, Hermann
Brachel, Peter von
1626—1314
*Brunus, Bernardus
1640—286
*Bütgen, Konrad
1621—956
Bütgen, Widow of Konrad
1635—750
Bussemacher, Johann
[1587?]—805
Calenius, Gerwin
1561—422
Cervicornus, Gottfried (I)
1563—1110
Cholinus, Goswin
1585—1446

1588—1448
1589—1450
Cholinus, Maternus
1558—416
1559—418
1564—420
1585—[115, 116]
Cholinus, Peter
1626—658
Christoffel, Johann
1620—502
Crith, Johann
1610—455
1614—616
Egmondt, Cornelius von
1626—120
Erffens, Servas
1611—1510
*Fabritius, Simon
1631—481
Falckenburg, Heinrich
1593—970
1594—971
Gartner, Georg
1610—1497
Gymnich, Johann (IV)
1600—188
1629—565
Hemmerden, Stephan
1608—1202
1609—517
1610—1494, 1494.1
1612—1160
1613—1540
1614—1205
Henning, Peter
1610—977
1612—25
1627—1059, 1060, 1272, 1273
1628—978
1629—979
Hierat, Anton (I)
1603—930
Horst, Peter
156[-]—425
1588—1449
1589—1451
Kempen, Arnold von
1614—413
Kempen, Gottfried von
1585—[1457]
1587—803
1592—1170
1594—1192
Kempen, widow of Gottfried von
1602—1199
Kinckius, Johann
1610—1521, 1494, 1494.1, 1495,

Bellagamba, Giov. Battista
  1596—1470
Benacci, Alessandro
  1579—308
  1582—883
Bonardo, Fausto
  [1598?]—310
Bonardo, Pellegrino
  '1581' [1582]—201
Bonomi, Sebastiano
  1620—297
Cochi, Bartolomeo
  1607—111
  1610—1509
Cochi, Heirs of
  1623—1567
Golsarino, Pellegrino
  1623—299
Moscatelli, Heirs of
  1625—1611
Tebaldini, Nicolò
  1621—263, 292
  1622—291, 295, 298, 380
  1623—293, 299
  1627—294
  1633—774
Bologna, n.p.n.
  1591 [1592?]—991
BRESCIA
Bozzola, Antonio
  1608—1183
Bozzola, Gio. Battista (II)
  1608—1183
Presegni, Comino
  1608—1183, 1204
Sabbio, Vincenzo di
  1582—363.1, 884
  1590—898
Tebaldini, Francesco
  1608—1183, 1204
CREMONA
Belpiero, Marc Antonio
  1610—1498
Draconi, Cristofero
  1584—921
  1587—773
FERRARA
Baldini, Vittorio
  1587—797
  1590—309.1
FLORENCE
Dini da Colle, Francesco
  [1587]—768
Giunta, Filippo (II)
  1591—990, 991
Landi
  1637—987
  1638—988

Marescotti, Giorgio
  1588—17
Massa, Amatore
  1637—987
  1632—988
Pignoni, Zenobio
  1623—300
GENOA
Pavoni, Giuseppe
  1630—266
Genoa, n.p.n.
  [1587]—770, (771)
MACERATA
Martellini, Sebastiano
  1583—8
  1585—11
MANTUA
Osanna, Aloisio
  1620—195
Osanna, Ludovico
  1620—195
Mantua, n.p.n.
  [1622]—379, (380)
MESSINA
Brea, Pietro
  1629—86
MILAN
Antonii, Giov. Antonio degli
  1560—917
Bidelli, Giovanni Battista
  1615—1038
  1625—134
Colonio, Giovanni Battista
  1586—1461
Impressores Archiepiscopales
  see Ponte, Heirs of Pacifico
  Piccaglia, Gio. Battista
Locarno, Pietro Martire
  1606—237
Malatesta, Giov. Battista
  1623—3, 357, 1589, (1590),
    (1600)
  [1623]—1565, (1566)
Malatesta, Marco Tullio
  1605—1478
  1614—272
Malatesta, Heirs of Melchior
  1628—793
Malatesta, Pandolfo
  1605—1478
  1623—381
Meda, Fratelli da
  1560—917
Paganello, Francesco
  1596—(1473)
Piccaglia, Giacomo
  1582—200
  1587—772

Italy, MILAN—*cont.*
Piccaglia, Giov. Battista
1602—986
1606—1479
1615—1039
1616—1518
1623—1553
Ponte, Pacifico da
1582—137
Ponte, Heirs of Pacifico da
1602—986
1606—1479
1615—1039
1616—1518
1623—155
Ponte, Paolo Gotardo da
1584—9
Tini, Pietro
1584—9
Milan, n.p.n.
[1590?]—309.1
MODENA
Cassiani, Giuliano
1634—504
NAPLES
Beltrano, Ottavio
1631—823
1635—822
Carlino, Giovanni Giacomo
1592—439
1608—1146
1616—1415
Cesare, Cesare
1584—10
Maccani, Dominico
1625—1348
Orlandi, Gio.
1623—1568
Pace, Antonio
1592—439
Roncaglio, Secondino
1623—1568, 1590, 1600
Salviani, Horatio
1584—10
1592—439
Scorigio, Lazaro
1635—1329
Vitale, Costantino
1604—792
1608—1146
*Zangarus, Joannes Baptista
1585—115, 116
Naples, n.p.n.
1627—195 *note*
ORVIETO
Colaldi, Antonio
1588—[309?]

PALERMO
Franceschi, Gio. Antonio dei
1597—1010
PARMA
Calestani, Filandro
1587—796, (797)
PERUGIA
n.p.n.
1587—(786)
PIACENZA
Ardizzone, Giacomo
1623—1566
Bazzachi, Giovanni
1593—437
PISA
n.p.n.
1618—131
REGGIO, nell'Emilia, and RIVA
See Addenda
ROME
Accolti, Vincenzo
1582—876
1588—1462
1592—[275]
Blado, Heirs of Antonio
[1570]—[1452]
[1570?]—[332?]
1575—363
[1579-80]—[1454]
1582—321
1586—322
Blado, Paolo, 'impressores
camerales'
[1593]—[326]
Bonfadino, Bartholomeo
1584—143
1586—973
1594—1251
Beccari, Bernardino
1596—1469, (1470), 1472
1599—1471
Camera Apostolica
1603—336.10
1614—928
1623—1550, *1551, (1552),
(1553), (1554), (1558),
(1559), (1560)
1626—226
1631—1351, (1352)
1633—1103
Ciacconus, Alphonsus
1623—1321
1624—1324
1625—1323
1628—1322
Corbelletti, Francesco
1626—301
1627—1342.3

1583—412
1584—403, 407
[1586]—401
1586—402
1590—408, [410?], 411
VILNA
Jesuit College press
1623—1562
Karcan, Jan
1610—1499
Radziwill, Mikola Kristof
1584—192
[1584-85]—[193]
1585—144
Poland, n.p.n.
1587—[404?]
1592—[405?]

PORTUGAL
COIMBRA
Gomes de Loureyro, Diogo
1613—1541
LISBON
Alvarez, Antonio
1588—995, 996
1594—1006
1633—706
1639—35
Blavio, João
1562—1430
Correa, Francisco
1567—1442
Craesbeeck, Lourenzo
[1635]—742
Craesbeeck, Pedro
1621—864
1631—834
Espanha, João de
1575—1434
Flores, Pedro de
1594—1006
Lyra, Manuel de
1589—1002
1590—776
1594—1007
Martinez, Domingos
1588—996
Ribeiro, António
1575—1434
[1579?]—[471]
Rodrigues, Matías
1632—37
Viña, Geraldo de la
1626—385
Lisbon, n.p.n.
[1597?]—[470?]

SPAIN
ALCALA
Iñiguez de Lequerica, Juan
1593—1004
BARCELONA
Cendrat, Jaime
1588—997
Cormellas, Sebastian de
1612—282
Genovés, Jeronimo
1588—997
Liberós, Estevan
1622—376
[1622]—375
Barcelona, n.p.n.
1587—(787)
1613—[273.1]
BURGOS
Junta, Philippo de
1583—235, 236
CADIZ
Gracián, Manoel
1622—374
Rey, Fernando
1616—505
CUENCA
Viader, Salvador
1615—1068
GRANADA
Diaz de Montoya, Fernando
[1603]—1064.1
Lorençana, Bartolomé de
1615—1069
Renè de Lazcano, Antonio
1615—624
MADRID
Abarca de Angulo, Francisco
1621—307
Español, Diego
1622—373, (374)
Flamenco, Diego
1623—1, (2)
*Gabianis, Dominico de
1623—(1586), (1599)
Gómez, Widow of Alonso
1589—1001
Guzmán, Bernardino de
1626—384
Imprenta Real
[1623]—1571
1624—1349
1625—1311
1632—1619
Junti, Teresa
1625—1310, 1311
Lopez, Francisco (II)
1588—993
Madrigal, Pedro

Morillo, Gerónimo
[1623]—354, 382
Valladolid, n.p.n.
1623—1582
ZARAGOZA
Escarilla, Widow of Juan
1588—998
*Jovius, Christophorus
1611—1534
Lanaja y Quartaret, Juan
1629—466
Puig, Pedro
1588—998
Robles, Lorenço de
1596—277
Tavano, Angelo
1596—277
Zaragoza, n.p.n.
[1623]—[1570?]
Spain, n.p.n.
1583—[364?]
1588—[873]
[1594]—[740]
[1599-1612]—[1062]
[1603]—[1276]
[1612]—[26?]
[1619]—[1350]
[before 1621]—[268?]
[1623]—[356?], [383?], [1574?],
  [1594?], [1596?]
[1635]—[1061]

SWITZERLAND

BASEL
Episcopius, Nicolaus (II)
1563—824
Henricpetri, Sebastian
1611—249
CONSTANCE
*Samius, Theodorus
[1592]—1141
Straub, Leonhard (II)
1616—849, 856
FRIBOURG
Gemperlin, Abraham
1585—648
1586—649
1587—650
GENEVA
Fabri, François
1619—671
La Rovière, Pierre de
1612—251
LAUSANNE
Le Preux, François

1574—734
1575—735
RORSCHACH
Crasebomius
1608—162
Schnell, Bartholomäus
1606—160
1608—162

MISCELLANEOUS FICTITIOUS IMPRINTS
*Brixiae Catacorum, ex officina
  Caroli Pensae. 1638—215
*Cosmopoli, apud Theophilum
  Pratum. 1611—925.1, 925.2
    1612—926.3
    1613—(927)
*Fastemburgi, apud Petrum
  Baretium, a Ioh. Astemium.
  1634—213
*Francopoli, ex officina Matriniana.
  [1606-16]—45
*Hartbergae. 1611—1538
*Intercatiae Orniacorum, apud
  Ioannem Simonis. 1610—306
*Lutetiae Britannorum, apud Isaac
  Iacobi. 1609—304-05
*[no place] Apud Holofernem
  Kriegsederum. 1611—1537

UNATTRIBUTED
1566—814
[1570 or later]—1453
1587—784, 983
[1587]—778, 779, 780, 781, 782, 783,
  798, 799, 810
1588—99, 764, 766, 767, 806, 1467
[1588]—15
1589—1465
[1591]—736
1610—1416, 1500
1611—1501
[1611]—1290
1614—1417
1616—1537.1
[1616]—1418
1619—1075
[c. 1620]—667
[1623]—1580, 1601, 1602
1628—389
1631—1336, 1355
[1631]—484, 484.1
1636—1356
n.d.—800, 856.1

ALPHABETICAL LIST OF NAMES OF PRINTERS AND PLACES

Abarco de Angulo, Fran. *Madrid*
Academia Venetiana *Venice*
Accolti, Vincenzo *Rome*
Aedes Populi Romani *see* Popolo Romano, casa del
Albin, Johann *Mainz*
Albionopoli *see* London
ALCALA *Spain*
ALESSANDRIA *Italy*
*Algazarius, Io. Bapt. *Bologna*
Algeyer, Melchior *Dilligen*
Allde, Edward *London*
Alphonse *see* Armand
Alvarez, Antonio *Lisbon*
Amberes *see* Antwerp
AMIENS *France*
AMSTERDAM *Netherlands*
Andreae, Balthasar *Danzig*
Andreae, Johann *Strassburg*
Angelieri, Giorgio *Venice*
Angermaier, Andreas *Ingolstadt*
Angermaier, Elizabeth *Ingolstadt*
Antonii, Giov. Antonio degli *Milan*
Antonius, Widow of Hubertus (I) *Brussels*
Antonius, Hubertus (II) *Brussels*
Antonius, Peter *Hanau*
ANTWERP *Belgium*
Aquensis, Henricus *see* Heinrich von Aachen
Ardizzone, Giacomo *Piacenza*
Armand, Claude *Lyons*
ARRAS *France*
ASCHAFFENBURG *Germany*
*Astemius, Joh. *Misc. Fict.*
Atrebati *see* Arras
Audomaropoli *see* Saint-Omer
AUGSBURG *Germany*
Augspurg *see* Augsburg
Augustae *see* Augsburg
Augustae Pictonum *see* Poitiers
Augustae Trevirorum *see* Trier
Augustoriti Pictonum *see* Poitiers
Avenione *see* Avignon
AVIGNON *France*

Baba, Andrea *Venice*
Baba, Francesco *Venice*
Bacx *see* Bax
Baillet, Pierre *Paris*
Baldini, Vittorio *Ferrara*
BAMBERG *Germany*
Baragne, Rollin *Paris*
BARCELONA *Spain*

*Baretius, Petrus *Misc. Fict.*
Barezzi, Barezzo *Venice*
Barrera, Alonso de la *Seville*
Barrois, Jacques *Paris*
'Bartelt', Guillaume *London*
Bartoli, Flaminio *Reggio*
BASEL *Switzerland*
Baum, Dietrich *Cologne*
Bax, Andreas *Antwerp*
Bazzachi, Giovanni *Piacenza*
Beauvais, Romain de *Rouen*
Beccari, Bernardino *Rome*
Behem, Kaspar *Mainz*
Behourt, Jean-Baptiste *Rouen*
Bellère, Balthazar *Douai*
Bellère, Widow of Balthazar *Douai*
Bellère, Widow and Heirs of Jean (I) *Antwerp*
Bellère, Jean (II) *Antwerp*
Bellère, Peter (I) *Antwerp*
Bellère, Widow and Heirs of Peter (I) *Antwerp*
Bellère, Peter (II) *Antwerp*
Bellet, François *Saint-Omer*
Bellet, Jean *Ypres*
Belpiero, Marc Antonio *Cremona*
Beltrano, Ottavio *Naples*
Benacci, Alessandro *Bologna*
Beraud, Symphorien *Lyons*
Berg, Adam *Munich*
BERGAMO *Italy*
Bergomi *see* Bergamo
Berlerius, Antonius *Lyons*
Bernard, François *Reims*
Bernard, Melchior *Pont-à-Mousson*
Bertault, Widow of Pierre *Paris*
Berthelin, Jean *Rouen*
Besogne, Jacques (I) *Rouen*
Bessin, Jehan *Paris*
Bevilacqua, Heirs of Nicolò *Turin*
Beys, Adrien *Paris*
Beys, Christophe *Lille*
Bichon, Guillaume *Paris*
Bidelli, Giov. Battista *Milan*
Bill, John *London*
Bindoni, Francesco *Venice*
Bindoni, Gasparo (I) & fratelli *Venice*
Binet, Denis *Paris*
'Birchley Hall' press *Great Britain*
Biturigibus *see* Bourges
Bivas, Antonio *Seville*
Blado, Heirs of Antonio *Rome*
Blado, Paolo *Rome*
Blageart, Jérosme *Paris*
Blageart, Françoise, Widow of Jérosme *Paris*
Blanchet, Jean *Poitiers*
Blavio, João *Lisbon*

Blocher, Jacques *Paris*
Bock, Heinrich *Trier*
Böckler, Martin *Freiburg im Breisgau*
Bogard, Jan *Louvain*; *Douai*
Bogard, Martin *Douai*
Bogard, Widow of Martin *Douai*
Bogard, Pierre *Douai*
BOLOGNA *Italy*
Bonardo, Fausto *Bologna*
Bonardo, Pellegrino *Bologna*
Bonfadino, Barthol. *Rome*
Bonomi, Sebastiano *Bologna*
Bononiae *see* Bologna
BORDEAUX *France*
Borremans, Pierre *Douai*
Boscard, Charles *Douai*; *Saint-Omer*
Boscard, Jeanne, Widow of Charles
    Saint-Omer
Boscard, Jacques *Douai*
Boscard, Widow of Jacques *Douai*
Boschaert *see* Boscard
Bosck, Henry *Brussels*
Bouillette, Jean *Paris*
Boulenger, Louis *Paris*
BOURGES *France*
Bourriquant, Fleury *Paris*
Bozzola, Antonio *Brescia*
Bozzola, Giov. Batt. (II) *Brescia*
Brachel, Peter von *Cologne*
Bramereau, Jacques *Avignon*
Branchu, Jean *Paris*
Brandt, Marten Jansz *Amsterdam*
Brea, Pietro *Messina*
BRESCIA *Italy*
Brisson, Jacques *Paris*
Britannus, Ricardus *see* Floyd
Brixiae *see* Brescia
*Brixiae Catacorum *Misc. Fict.*
BRNO *Czechoslovakia*
Bruenn *see* Brno
BRUGES *Belgium*
Brumen, Thomas *Paris*
Bruneau, Robert *Antwerp*
Brunel, Jean *Paris*
*Brunus, Bernardus *Cologne*
Bruslé, Nicolas *Paris*
BRUSSELS *Belgium*
Bruxellae *see* Brussels
*Bütgen, Konrad *Cologne*
Bütgen, Katharina, Widow of
    Konrad *Cologne*
Buffet, Michel *Paris*
Buon, Nicolas *Paris*
Burdigalae *see* Bordeaux
Burey, Pierre *Paris*
Burgen, Conrad *see* Bütgen
BURGOS *Spain*
Busius *see* Buyss

Bussemacher, Johann *Cologne*
Buyss, Bernhard *Düsseldorf*
Buysson, Jean-Baptiste *Lyons*

Cabrera, Juan de *Seville*
Cabrera, Rodrigo *Seville*
CADIZ *Spain*
Cadomi *see* Caen
CAEN *France*
Caesaraugustae *see* Zaragoza
Calenius, Gerwin *Cologne*
Calestani, Filandro *Parma*
Camera Apostolica *Rome*
Canto, Francisco del *Lima*
Çaragoça *see* Zaragoza
Carampello, Bartolomeo *Venice*
Cardon, Horace *Lyons*
Cardon, Jacques *Lyons*
Cassiani, Giuliano *Modena*
Catalauni *see* Châlons-sur-Marne
Cavalleris, li *Turin*
Cavelier, Adam *Caen*
Cavellat, Denyse, Widow of
    Guillaume *Paris*
Cea Tesa, Francisco de *Salamanca*
Cendrat, Jaime *Barcelona*
Cervicornus, Gottfried (I) *Cologne*
Cesare, Cesare *Naples*
Cezary, Franciszek *Cracow*
CHÂLONS-SUR-MARNE *France*
Chappelet, Claude *Paris*
Chappelet, Sébastien *Paris*
Chappellain, Charles *Paris*
Chard, Antoine *Lyons*
Charles, Noël *Paris*
Charlot, Jean Pierre *Lyons*
Charron, Jean (II) *Paris*
Chastellain, Charles (I) *Paris*
Chastellain, Charles (II) *Paris*
Chastellain, Marie, Widow of
    Charles (I) *Paris*
Chaudière, Guillaume (I) *Paris*
Chaudière, Pierre *Paris*
Chaudière, Regnault (II) *Paris*
Chesneau, Nicolas *Paris*
Chevalier, Clement *see* Knight
Chevalier, Elizabeth, Widow of
    Pierre (II) *Paris*
Chevillot, Pierre *Troyes*
Cholinus, Goswin *Cologne*
Cholinus, Maternus *Cologne*
Cholinus, Peter *Cologne*
Christoffel, Johann *Cologne*
Ciacconus, Alphonsus *Rome*
Ciotti, Giov. Battista *Venice*
Citerne, Guillaume *Paris*
Clavijo, Matías *Seville*
Cnobbaert, Jan *Antwerp*

265

Cochi, Bartolomeo *Bologna*
Cochi, Heirs of Bartol. *Bologna*
Coellen *see* Cologne
COIMBRA *Portugal*
Colaldi, Antoinio *Naples*
Colin, Étienne *Paris*
COLOGNE *Germany*
Coloniae Agrippinae *see* Cologne
Coloniae Allobrogum *see* Geneva
Colonio, Giov. Battista *Milan*
Colosini, Giov. Battista *Venice*
Commelinus, Janus *Heidelberg*
Company of Stationers *see* Societas
   Bibliopolarum Londinensium
Conimbricae *see* Coimbra
Conincx, Arnold *Antwerp*
CONSTANCE *Switzerland*
Constant, Nicolas *Reims*
Contreras, Jerónimo de *Lima*
Coppens, Gilles *Antwerp*
Corbelletti, Francesco *Rome*
*Cordatus, Eubulus *Reims*
Cormellas, Sebast. de *Barcelona*
Correa, Francisco *Lisbon*
Corswaremia, Arnoldus a *Liège*
*Cosmopoli *Misc. Fict.*
Coulombel, Robert *Paris*
Courant, Nicolas *Rouen*
Courant, Pierre *Rouen*
COURTRAI *Belgium*
Cousturier *see* Le Cousturier
Crabbe, Antoine *Saint-Omer*
CRACOW *Poland*
Craesbeeck, Lourenzo *Lisbon*
Craesbeeck, Pedro *Lisbon*
Cramoisy, Gabriel *Paris*
Cramoisy, Sébast. *Paris*;
   Pont-à-Mousson
Crasebomius *Rorschach*
Creede, Thomas *London*
CREMONA *Italy*
Crinesius, Augustin *Bamberg*
Crith, Johann *Cologne*
CUENCA *Spain*

D., Ae. *see* Coppens, Gilles
Dabertzhofer, Chrysostom.
   Augsburg
Dale, Michael von *Münster*
DANZIG *Poland*
David, Mathieu *Paris*
Dehors, Fiacre *Paris*
Delas, Léger *Paris*
DENDERMONDE *Belgium*
Desboys, Guillaume *Paris*
Diani, Paolo *Rome*
Diani, Tito *Rome*
Diaz de Montoya, Fern. *Granada*

Didier, Jean *Lyons*
Diesthemius, Aegidius *see* Coppens,
   Gilles
DILLINGEN *Germany*
Dini da Colle, Francesco *Florence*
Doff, Jacobus *Douai*
Dormael, Philip van *Louvain*
DOUAI *France*
Draconi, Cristofero *Cremona*
Drouart, Jérome *Paris*
Duaci *see* Douai
DUBLIN *Great Britain*
*Du Bois, François *Pont-à-Mousson*
Du Carroy, Jean *Paris*
Du Coudret, Laurent *Paris*
DÜSSELDORF *Germany*
Du Fossé, Nicolas *Paris*
Du Four, Claude *Lyons*
Dumesnil, Louis (I) *Rouen*
Du Petit Val, David *Rouen*
Du Puys, Jacques (I) *Paris*
Durand, Laurent *Lyons*
Durand, Martin *Paris*
Durand, Pierre *Paris*
Dusinelli, Pietro *Venice*

Eder, Elizabeth *Ingolstadt*
Eder, Wilhelm *Ingolstadt*
Eder, Wolfgang *Ingolstadt*
EDINBURGH *Great Britain*
*Eldreton, Jacques *Verdun*
Eliot's Court press *London*
Elzeviriana, Officina *Leyden*
Emberes *see* Antwerp
England *see* Great Britain
English College press *Saint-Omer*
Episcopius, Nicolaus (II) *Basel*
Erffens, Servas *Cologne*
Escarilla, Widow of Juan *Zaragoza*
Espanha, João de *Lisbon*
Español, Diego *Madrid*
Esparza, Martin de *Valencia*
Estienne, Antoine *Paris*
Estienne, Robert (III) *Paris*
Estupiñán, Luis *Seville*
*Euridicus, Uplaus *Lyons*

F., Barthol. Albertus *see* Forman
F.[ilius], Episcopius *see* Episcopius,
   Nicolaus (II)
*Faber, Baptista *Augsburg*
*Faber, Joannes *Augsburg*
*Faber, Theophilus *London*
Fabri, François *Geneva*
*Fabritius, Simon *Cologne*
Faciotto, Guglielmo *Rome*
Falckenberg, Heinrich *Cologne*
Fampoux, Jean de *Douai*

*Fastemburgi *Misc. Fict.*
Feburier, Jean *Paris*
Feburier, Pierre-Louis *Paris*
FERRARA *Italy*
Ferrari, Caesar *Rome*
Ferrari, Giorgio *Rome*
Fevrier *see* Feburier
Fickaert, Frans *Antwerp*
Field, Richard *London*
Fiorenza *see* Florence
Firenze *see* Florence
Flamenco, Diego *Madrid*
FLÈCHE, LA *France*
Fleischmann, Georg *Würzburg*
Fleishmann, Stephan *Würzburg*
Flexiae *see* La Flèche
*Fleysben, Gaspar *Antwerp*
Flinton, George *Rouen*
FLORENCE *Italy*
Flores, Pedro de *Lisbon*
Floyd, Richard *Saint-Omer*
Fognaeus *see* Foigny
Foigny, Jean (I) de *Reims*
Foigny, Simon de *Reims*
Forge, Pierre de *Paris*
Forman, Bartol. Albrecht *Brno*
Formica, Margaretha *Vienna*
Formica, Matthäus *Vienna*
Fouet, Robert *Paris*
Foulerus *see* Fowler
Fowler, Alice, Widow of John
    Louvain
Fowler, John *Antwerp*; *Louvain*
Franceschi, Gio. Antonio dei
    Palermo
Francese, Hercole *see* François
*Francois, Hercule *London*
*Francopoli *Misc. Fict.*
FRANKFURT AM MAIN *Germany*
FREIBURG IM BREISGAU *Germany*
Fremy, Claude *Paris*
Freyburg in der Eydgnoschafft *see*
    Fribourg
Freyburg in Uchtland *see* Fribourg
FRIBOURG *Switzerland*

*Gabianis, Dominico de *Madrid*
Gabiano, 'Th.' [*sic*] de *Lyons*
Gadoulleau, Michel *Paris*
Galignani, Heirs of Simon *Venice*
*Gallus, Adamus *Mons*
Ganaraeus, Ludovicus *Lyons*
Gandavi *see* Ghent
*Garnich, Jacques *Pont-à-Mousson*
Garriz, Juan Crisóstomo *Valencia*
Gartner, Georg *Cologne*
Gelli, Giovanni Paolo *Rome*
Gemperlin, Abraham *Fribourg*

GENEVA *Switzerland*
GENOA *Italy*
Genovés, Jeronimo *Barcelona*
Gesselin, Jean *Paris*
GHENT *Belgium*
Gigliotto, Domenico *Rome*
Ginammi, Marco *Venice*
Giunta, Filippo (II) *Florence*
Giunta *see also* Junta
GÖRLITZ *Germany*
Golsarino, Pellegrino *Bologna*
Gómez, Widow of Alonso *Madrid*
Gómez de Pastrano, Pedro *Seville*
Gracian, Manoel *Cadiz*
Graecii *see* Graz
GRANADA *Spain*
Grassi, Bartólomeo *Rome*
GRAZ *Austria*
'Greenstreet House' press *Stonor
    Park*
Grégoire, Jacques *Paris*
GRENOBLE *France*
Griffio, Alessandro *Venice*
Grignano, Ludovico *Rome*
Grosius, Henning *Leipzig*
*Gryphius, Sebastianus *Lyons*
Gryphius *see also* Griffio
Gualtherus *see* Wolter
Guarisco, Marco *Venice*
Guasp, Gabriel *Palma*
Gueffier, François (I) *Paris*
Guerra, Domenico *Venice*
Guerra, Giov. Battista *Venice*
Guillemot, Marie, Widow of
    Mathieu (I) *Paris*
Guillemot, Mathicu (II) *Paris*
Guzmán, Bernardino de *Madrid*
Gymnich, Johann *Cologne*

Haenlin, Georg *Ingolstadt*
HANAU *Germany*
Handle, Jiří *Olomouc*
Hanoviae *see* Hanau
Hardy, Jaquine, Widow of Jean
    Rennes
*Hartbergae *Misc. Fict.*
Hastens, Hendrik van *Louvain*
Hastens, Widow of Hendrik van
    Louvain
Hatot, Emund *Trier*
Hatot, Heirs of Emund *Trier*
Hébert, Louis *La Flèche*
Hécart, Nicolas *Reims*
HEIDELBERG *Germany*
Heil, Nikolaus *Mainz*
Heinrich, Nikolaus *Munich*
Heinrich von Aachen *Würzburg*
Heinrich von Aachen, Ursula,

Widow of *Würzburg*
Hemmerden, Stephan *Cologne*
Henault, Mathurin *Paris*
Henning, Peter *Cologne*
Henricpetri, Sebastian *Basel*
Henricus, Nicolaus *see* Heinrich
Herbipoli *see* Würzburg
Heuqueville, Jean (II) de *Paris*
Heyll *see* Heil
Hidalgo, Clemente *Seville*
Hierat, Anton (I) *Cologne*
Hispanus, Joannes *see* Espanha, João
Holomúcy *see* Olomouc
Honervogt, Jacques *Paris*
Horitz, Anton *Bamberg*
Horst, Peter *Cologne*
Houssaye, Denis *Paris*
Hubault, Jacques *Amiens*; *Rouen*
Huberti, Adriaen *Antwerp*
Huby, François (I) *Paris*
Huby, François (II) *Paris*
*Huldric, Helie *Pont-à-Mousson*
Huré, Sébastien (I) *Paris*
Hury, Pierre (I) *Paris*
Hury, Pierre (II) *Paris*

Ieay, Henricus *see* Jaye
Imprenta Real *Madrid*
Impressores Camerales *Rome*
INGOLSTADT *Germany*
Iñiguez de Lequerica, Juan *Alcala*
Iñiguez de Lequerica, Heirs of Juan *Valladolid*
*Intercatiae Orniacorum *Misc. Fict.*
Iovius *see* Jovius
Ipris *see* Ypres
Iunta *see* Junta
Iunti *see* Junti

*Jacobi, Isaac *Misc. Fict.*
Jacquin, François *Paris*
Jannon, Jean *Paris*
Jaye, Henry *Mechlin*
Jesuit College *Prague*
Jesuit College *Rachol*
Jesuit College *Saint-Omer*
Jesuit College *Vienna*
Jesuit College *Vilna*
Jove, Michel *Lyons*
*Jovius, Christophorus *Zaragoza*
Julien, Guillaume *Paris*
Julien, Michel *Paris*
Junta, Philippo da *Burgos*
Juntarum, Officina *Lyons*
Junti, Teresa *Madrid*

Karcan, Jan *Vilna*
KASSEL *Germany*

Keerberghen, Jan van *Antwerp*
Kellam, Lawrence (I) *Douai*
Kellam, Widow of Lawrence (I) *Douai*
Kellam, Lawrence (II) *Douai*
Kempen, Arnold von *Cologne*
Kempen, Gottfried von *Cologne*
Kempen, Widow of Gottfried von *Cologne*
Kinckius, Johann *Cologne*
Knight, Clement *London*
Knobbaert *see* Cnobbaert
Kolb, Franz *Vienna*
Kortrijk *see* Courtrai
Krakow *see* Cracow
*Kriegsederus, Holofernes *Misc. Fict.*
Kürner, Konrad *Salzburg*
Kuntzen, Joh. Balthasar *Mainz*

La Coste, Jean de *Paris*
La Coste, Nicolas de *Paris*
La Court, Pierre de *Bordeaux*
Laet, Jan *Antwerp*
La Flèche *see* Flèche, La
La Fosse, Nicolas de *see* Du Fossé
*La Fosse, Pierre de *Paris*
Laignel, Pierre *Rouen*
Lallemant, Richard (II) *Rouen*
Lanaja y Quartaret, Juan *Zaragoza*
Landi *Florence*
Landry, Claude *Lyons*
Landry, Pierre *Lyons*
Langenhove, Joos van *Dendermonde*
Langlois, Denis *Paris*
La Noüe, Marie, Widow of Guillaume *Paris*
Lantzenberger, Michael *Leipzig*
Lapidanus, Nicolaus *Douai*
La Porte, Sibille de *Lyons*
Laquehay, Jean *Paris*
La Rivière *see* Rivery
La Rochelle *see* Rochelle
La Rovière, Pierre de *Geneva*
Laurent, Regnault *Tournai*
LAUSANNE *Switzerland*
Lazari, in Officina *see* Łazarz
Łazarz [Andrysowic] *Cracow*
Le Begue, Jean *Paris*
Le Blanc, Mathieu *Paris*
*Le Brun, Nicolas *Rouen*
Le Cousturier, Jean *Rouen*
LEIPZIG *Germany*
Leodii *see* Liège
León, Juan de *Seville*
Le Preux, François *Lausanne*
Le Roy, Théophile *La Rochelle*
*Le Sage, Pierre *London*

Lesteens, Guilliam *Antwerp*
LEYDEN *Netherlands*
L'Huillier, Pierre *Paris*
Liberós, Estavan *Barcelona*
Libert, Jean *Paris*
*Libius, Joannes *Augsburg*
LICH *Germany*
LIÈGE *Belgium*
LILLE *France*
LIMA *Peru*
Lipp, Balthasar *Aschaffenburg*;
    Mainz
Lipsiae *see* Leipzig
*Lipsius, Rufus *London*
LISBON *Portugal*
Locarno, Pietro Martire *Milan*
Loe, Hendrick van der *Antwerp*
LONDON *Great Britain*
Lopez, Francisco *Madrid*
Lopez, Jacomo *Seville*
Lorençana, Bartolomé de *Granada*
LOUVAIN *Belgium*
Loven *see* Louvain
L'Oyselet, Georges *Rouen*
Lugduni *see* Lyons
Lugduni Batavorum *see* Leyden
*Lutetiae Britannorum *Misc. Fict.*
Lutetiae Parisiorum *see* Paris
LYONS *France*
Lyra, Francisco de *Seville*
Lyra, Manuel de *Lisbon*

M., Widow of P. *see* Madrigal
Maccarani, Dominico *Naples*
MACERATA *Italy*
MADRID *Spain*
Madrigal, Pedro *Madrid*
Madrigal, Widow of Pedro *Madrid*
Maes, Bernardinus *Louvain*
Maes, Jan (I) *Louvain*
Maes, Jan (II) *Louvain*
MAINZ *Germany*
Malatesta, Giov. Bapt. *Milan*
Malatesta, Marco Tullio *Milan*
Malatesta, Heirs of Melchior *Milan*
Malatesta, Pandolfo *Milan*
Malines *see* Mechlin
Mallasis, Étienne *Rouen*
Mallorca *see* Palma
Manilius, Gualterus *Ghent*
MANTUA *Italy*
Manuzio, Paolo *Rome*
Marcaria, Jacob *Riva*
Marcigay, Pierre *Saint-Malo*
Mareschall, Peter *Frankfurt am
    Main* .
Marescotti, Giorgio *Florence*
Marin, Pierre *Paris*

*Mark, Hans *Augsburg*
Marnef, Jérome de *Paris*
Marniolles, Pierre *Grenoble*
Marsilius, Alexander *Lyons*
Martellini, Sebastiano *Macerata*
Martinez, Alexandre *Valencia*
Martinez, Domingos *Lisbon*
Martinez, Francisco *Madrid*
Martinus, Widow of Stephanus
    Louvain
Mascardi, Giacomo *Rome*
Massa, Amatore *Florence*
*Matriniana, Officina *Misc. Fict.*
Matriti *see* Madrid
Mauperlier, Mathurin *Paris*
Mayer, Barbara, Widow of Johann
    Dillingen
Mayer, Johann *Dillingen*
Mayer, Sebald *Dillingen*
Meaux, Abraham de *Paris*
Mechelen *see* Mechlin
MECHLIN *Belgium*
Meda, Fratelli da *Milan*
Mediolani *see* Milano
Mercator, Martinus *Pont-à-Mousson*
Meres, Hermann *Mainz*
Mesnier, Antoine *Poitiers*
Messanae *see* Messina
MESSINA *Italy*
Mettayer, Pierre *Paris*
Meursius, Jan *Antwerp*
Mey, Pedro Patricio *Valencia*
Michael *see* Michel
Michel, Claude *Tournon*
Michel, Étienne *Lyons*
Miguel, Francisco *Valencia*
MILAN *Italy*
Millanges, Jacques *Bordeaux*
Millanges, Simon de *Bordeaux*
Millot, Didier *Paris*
Minima Societas *Venice*
MODENA *Italy*
Modona *see* Modena
*Molaeus, Jacobus *Rouen*
'Molina de Rovella' *see* Garriz, Juan
    Crisóstomo
Mommaert, Jan (I) *Brussels*
Monachii *see* Munich
Monasterii Westfaliae *see* Münster
Mondière, Melchior *Paris*
Mongiroud, Claude *Bordeaux*
MONS *Belgium*
Montibus *see* Mons
Montluel *see* Vimiaci
Montoya, Juan de *Madrid*
Moreau, Denis *Paris*
Moreau, Sylvestre *Paris*
Morel, Charles *Paris*

Morel, Fédéric (II) *Paris*
Moretus, Balthasar *Antwerp*
Moretus, Jan (I) *Antwerp*
Moretus, Martina, Widow of Jan (I)
  Antwerp
Morillo, Gerónimo *Valladolid*
Morillon, Claude *Lyons*
Moscatelli, Heirs of *Bologna*
Mourentorf *see* Moretus
Muenchen *see* Munich
MÜNSTER *Germany*
Muguet, Louis *Lyons*
MUNICH *Germany*
Mussiponti *see* Pont-à-Mousson
Mutii, Nicolò *Rome*
Mylius, Arnold *Cologne*
Mylius, Hermann *Cologne*

*Nafield, Jean *Edinburgh*
NANTES *France*
NAPLES *Italy*
Navarro, Juan *Valencia*
Neapoli *see* Naples
NEISSE *Germany*
Neve, Gulielmus de *Bruges*
Neyss *see* Neisse
Nissae *see* Neisse
Nivelle, Sébastien *Paris*
Nutius *see* Nuyts
Nuyts, Martin (II) *Antwerp*
Nygrin, Giří *Prague*

Oliverius, Joannes *Louvain*
OLOMOUC *Czechoslovakia*
Olysippone *see* Lisbon
Orlandi, Gio. *Naples*
ORVIETO *Italy*
Osanna, Aurelio *Mantua*
Osanna, Ludovico *Mantua*
Osmont, Charles *Rouen*
Osmont, Jean (I) *Rouen*
Ouwerx, Christian *Liège*
Ouwerx, Jan *Liège*
Ouyn, Adrien *Rouen*

Pace, Antonio *Naples*
Pagaeus, Franciscus *Poitiers*
Paganello, Francesco *Milan*
PALMA *Spain*
PALERMO *Italy*
Paolino, Stefano *Rome*
Parijs, Widow of Willem van
  Antwerp
PARIS *France*
Parisius, Paulus *Rome*
PARMA *Italy*
Patrasson, Jean *Lyons*
Patté, Gérard *Douai*

Paulinus *see* Paolino
Paulis formis, Joannes Antonius de
  Rome
Pavoni, Giuseppi *Genoa*
Pelé, Guillaume *Paris*
*Pensa, Carolus *Misc. Fict.*
Percheron, Claude *Paris*
Pérez, Alonso *Madrid*
Pérez, Diego *Seville*
Persons, Robert *Rouen*
Peterle, Michael *Prague*
Petit, Jean (III) *Rouen*
Petit, Richard *Rouen*
Petricovius *see* Piotrkowczyk
Phaeus, Andreas *see* Fei
*Phigrus, Ruardus *London*
PIACENZA *Italy*
Piccaglia, Giacomo *Milan*
Piccaglia, Giov. Batt. *Milan*
Piccaria *see* Piccaglia
Pictavis *see* Poitiers
Pignoni, Zenobio *Florence*
Pillehotte, Antoine *Lyons*
Pillehotte, Jean *Lyons*
Pinchon, Gérard *Douai*
Pinelli, Antonio *Venice*
Piotrkowczyk, Andrzej (I) *Cracow*
Piotrkowczyk, Andrzej (II) *Cracow*
PISA *Italy*
Placentiae *see* Piacenza
Plantin, Christophe *Antwerp*;
  Leyden
Plantin, Jeanne, Widow of
  Christophe *Antwerp*
Plantiniana, Officina *Antwerp*
Plumion, Widow of François *Paris*
POITIERS *France*
PONT-À-MOUSSON *France*
Ponte, Pacifico da *Milan*
Ponte, Heirs of Pacifico da *Milan*
Ponte, Paolo Gotardo da *Milan*
Popolo Romano, Casa del *Rome*
Porta. Sib. a *see* La Porte
Posnaniae *see* Poznań
Poupy, Jean *Paris*
Poyet, Jean *Lyons*
POZNAŃ *Poland*
Praesenius *see* Presegni
PRAGUE *Czechoslovakia*
Prati, Fioravanti *Florence*
*Pratus, Theophilus *Misc. Fict.*
Presegni, Comino *Brescia*
Prevosteau, Étienne *Paris*
Prost, Jacques *Lyons*
Prost, Pierre *Lyons*
Puig, Pedro *Zaragoza*

Quentel, Arnold *Cologne*

Quentel, Heirs of Johann *Cologne*
Quinet, Toussaint *Paris*
Quinqué, Adrien *Tournai*

RACHOL *India*
Rode, Gilles van den *Antwerp*
Radziwiłł, Mikoła Kristof *Vilna*
Raesfeldt, Bernhard *Münster*
Raesfeldt, Lambert *Münster*
Rambau, Hans *Görlitz*
Ramier, Pierre (II) *Paris*
Ramos Vejarano, Gabriel *Seville*
REGGIO nell' Emilia *Italy*
Regii *see* Reggio
Regius, Theophilus *see* Le Roy
REIMS *France*
Reinheckel, Andreas *Neisse*
Rem, Ulrich *Dillingen*
Remis *see* Reims
Renè de Lazcano, Antonio *Granada*
RENNES *France*
Reyes, Los *see* Lima
Rezé, Jacques *Paris*
Rhemis *see* Reims
Rhode, Jakob(1) *Danzig*
Ribas, Gabriel *Valencia*
Ribeiro, Antonio *Lisbon*
Ricciardus, Petrus *Venice*
Richard, Thomas *Paris*
Rickhes, Michael *Vienna*
Rictius *see* Rickhes
Rigaud, Benoît *Lyons*
Rigaud, Simon *Lyons*
Ripae *see* Riva
Rische, Matheas de *Antwerp*
RIVA *Italy*
Rivery, Guillaume *Arras*
Rivierius *see* Rivery
Robles, Lorenço de *Zaragoza*
ROCHELLE, LA *France*
Rodrigues, Matías *Lisbon*
Rodriguez Gamarra, Alonso *Seville*
Roigny, Michel de *Paris*
*Rolinus, Stephanus *Cologne*
ROME *Italy*
Roncagliolo, Secondino *Naples*
Ronsier, Pierre *Lyons*
RORSCHACH *Switzerland*
Rothomagi *see* Rouen
ROUEN *France*
Rouillard, Charles *Paris*
Rouillé, Guillaume *Lyons*
Roulliard *see* Rouillard
Roussin, Jacques *Lyons*
Roussin, Pierre *Lyons*
Roussin, Heirs of Pierre *Lyons*
Ruffinelli, Giacomo *Rome*
Ruffinelli, Giov. Angelo *Rome*

Rupellae *see* La Rochelle

Sabbio, Vincenzo di *Brescia*
Saint Gilles, Gilles de *Paris*
SAINT-MALO *France*
SAINT-OMER *France*
SALAMANCA *Spain*
Salis, Dominique *Paris*
Salis, Jacqueline, Widow of
  Dominique *Paris*
Salmanticae *see* Salamanca
Salvio, Horatio *Naples*; *Rome*
SALZBURG *Austria*
*Samius, Theodorus *Constance*
Sánchez, Andreas *Madrid*
Sánchez, Luis *Madrid*
Sánchez, Widow of Luis *Madrid*
Sartorius, Adam *Ingolstadt*
Sartorius, David *Ingolstadt*
Sassenus, Servatius *Louvain*
Saugrain, Abraham *Paris*
Saugrain, Espérance, Widow of
  Abraham *Paris*
Sauveur, Heirs of François *Liège*
Schnell, Bartholomäus *Rorschach*
Schoevaerts, Govaert *Brussels*
Schubart, Johann *Neisse*
Schwindtlauff, Konrad *Würzburg*
Scorigio, Lazaro *Naples*
Serrano de Vargas y Vreña, Juan
  Seville
Servain, Étienne *Lyons*
Sessa, Melchiorre *Venice*
Seutin, Georges *Saint-Omer*
Sevestre, Louis (II) *Paris*
SEVILLE *Spain*
Silvius, Guillaume *Antwerp*
*Simonis, Joannes *Misc. Fict.*
Sittart, Arnold *Paris*
Smits, Geeraerd *Antwerp*
Snell *see* Schnell
Societas Bibliopolarum
  Londinensium *Frankfurt am
  Main*
Soly, Michel *Paris*
Sonnius, Laurent *Paris*
Sonnius, Michel (I) *Paris*
Sonnius, Michel (II) *Paris*
Sotus, Joannes *Alessandria*
Stainhofer, Kaspar *Vienna*
Steels, Aegidius *Antwerp*
Steels, Widow and Heirs of Joannes
  Antwerp
Stephanus *see* Estienne
Stonor Park *Great Britain*
STRASSBURG *Germany*
Strasser, Johann *Freiburg im
  Breisgau*

Straub, Leonhard (II) *Constance*
Streel, Leonaerdt *Liège*
Stroobant, Guillaume *Lille*
Sulsenius, Gummarus *Antwerp*
Symonet, Jean *Vimiaci*

Taberniel, Artus *Salamanca*
Tantillon, Louis *Lyons*
Taupinart, Adrien *Paris*
Tavano, Angelo *Zaragoza*
Tebaldini, Francesco *Brescia*
Tebaldini, Nicolò *Bologna*
Télu, Pierre *Douai*
Télu, Widow of Pierre *Douai*
Thévenyn, Jacques *Châlons-sur-Marne*
Thiboust, Samuel *Paris*
Thierry, Rolin *Paris*
Tholosan, Jean *Lyons*
Thomassinus, Philippus *Rome*
Thoreau, Julien *Poitiers*
Tina, Imprenta de la *Madrid*
Tinghi, Philipe *Lyons*
Tini, Pietro *Milan*
Tongris, Guilielmus a *Antwerp*
Torino *see* Turin
Tornaci *see* Tournai
TOURNAI *Belgium*
TOURNON *France*
Treveris *see* Trier
Trichet, Nemesius *Lyons*
TRIER *Germany*
Trognesius, Joachim *Antwerp*
TROYES *France*
TURIN *Italy*
Typographia Regia *see* Imprenta Real

Ulyssipone *see* Lisbon
Unckel, Hans Karl *Frankfurt am Main*

VALENCIA *Spain*
VALLADOLID *Spain*
Van Milst, Jan *Liège*
Vascosan, Michel de *Paris*
Vaticana, Typographia Apostolica *Rome*
Vazquez, Antonio *Salamanca*
Velpius, Reyner (II) *Louvain*
Velpius, Rutger (I) *Louvain*
Velpius, Rutger (II) *Brussels*
Velpius *see also* Antonius, Hub.
VENICE *Italy*

Ventura, Comino *Bergamo*
VERDUN *France*
Verdussen, Guilliam *Antwerp*
Verdussen, Hieronimus *Antwerp*
Vereul, Étienne *Rouen*
Verhoeven, Abraham *Antwerp*
Verstegan, Richard *Antwerp*; *Paris*
VICENZA *Italy*
VICO DI SORRENTO *Italy*
VIENNA *Austria*
Villery, Jacques *Paris*
Villiers, Thomas de *Hanau*
VILNA *Poland*
VIMIACI *France*
Viña, Geraldo de la *Lisbon*
Vitale, Costantino *Naples*
VITERBO *Italy*
Vitré (Vitray) Antoine *Paris*
Vivien, François *Brussels*
Voegelin, Ernst *Leipzig*

Wapy, Jean *Verdun*
Weiss, Johann Friedrich *Frankfurt am Main*
Willerianis, Typis *see* Villiers
Wilnie *see* Vilna
Wilno *see* Vilna
Winde, Loys van de *Douai*
Winde, Widow of Loys van de *Douai*
Wirceburgi *see* Würzburg
Witte, Everard de *Louvain*
*Wolfangho, Hercules *London*
Wolrab, Jan (I) *Poznań*
Wolter, Bernhard *Cologne*
Wolter, Heirs of Bernhard *Cologne*
WÜRZBURG *Germany*
Wyon, Marc *Douai*

Yniguez *see* Iñiguez
YPRES *Belgium*
Yvrard, François *Lyons*

Zanetti, Alessandro *Rome*
Zanetti, Aloyse *Rome*
Zanetti, Bartholomeo *Rome*
Zanetti, Heirs of Barthol. *Rome*
Zanetti, Francesco *Rome*
*Zangarus, Joannes Baptista *Naples*
Zangrius, Peter *Louvain*
ZARAGOZA *Spain*
Zarain, Juan de *Madrid*
Zenaro, Damiano *Venice*

Chronological Index

NOTE: References are to the catalogue entries under each year from 1558–1640.

Square brackets enclose entries where a date is wanting (or misprinted) in the original and has therefore been supplied by the editors.

General Index of Proper Names

(Numbers refer to catalogue entries)

NOTE: This index does not include names which are found as main headings in Part I, the Personal section of the catalogue (nos. 1–1428), unless a subsidiary mention is made of them elsewhere (such as that of Thomas Dempster in no. 380) which is not already covered by a cross reference under their main heading. But all the authors, etc. who, because they were either not English or not Catholic, therefore could not figure as headings in Part I, are indexed here. In addition, this index includes all persons and places mentioned, throughout both Parts of the catalogue, in titles or in our annotations, with the exception of:
  names of countries (e.g. Spain, Scotland, England)
  — of religious bodies (e.g. Catholics, Lutherans)
  — of religious Orders (e.g. Benedictines, Franciscans, Jesuits)
  — of places and persons found in imprints; these are listed separately in the INDEX OF PRINTERS (pp. 241–272)
  — of secondary sources and modern authorities; those most often quoted are listed under SHORT REFERENCES (pp. xxii–xxvii)

Abbot, George *abp. of Canterbury* 1548
Accolti, Benedetto *Cardinal* 300
Aelred *Saint, O. Cist. Abbot of Rielvaulx* 531–33
Agent (L') de la Royne d'Angleterre *see* Harborne, William
Agen(t)s (Les) Généraux du Clergé de France 1407
Ailly, Pierre d' *Cardinal, after* 693
Albano (a tragedy) 943
Albert *Archduke, Governor of the Netherlands* 225, 324, 720
Alfield, Thomas *Bl.* 196
Alfredus (a play) 329
Allen, William *Cardinal* 1023, 1261, 1271–74, 1275
Alliaco, Petrus de *see* Ailly, Pierre d'
Almada, Emmanuel de *see* Dalmada, E.
Aloysius (a play) 958
Alpharabius *see* Muhammad Ibn Muhammad, al Farabi
Altenburg 967–71
Aluredus (a play) 329
Amadeus *Saint, bp. of Lausanne* 534–36
Amurath III *Sultan of Turkey* 1141, 1464–65

Anchin *O.S.B. Abbey of Saint Sauveur, Douai* 544
Andrews, Lancelot *bp. of Ely* (Tortor Cicestrensis *pseud.*) 1480–81, 1486–87, 1509–10
Androzzi, Fulvio *S.J.* 537
Angelus *a Neapoli, O.F.M.* 1348
Angelus *del Paz, O.F.M.* 1321
Angra *Portuguese see* 1429
Annat, François *S.J.* (Eugenius Philadelphus Romanus *pseud.*) 213
Anselm *Saint, abp. of Canterbury* 219–20, 517.1, 517.2
Antony *of Padua, Saint, O.F.M.* 1324
Antwerp 139, 536, 804, 1120–21, 1398
— Dominicans 749, 756
— Jesuit College 1335, 1340–41
Aquaviva, Claudio *S.J., General of the Jesuits* 26, 478–79, 652, 660
Aquinas *see* Thomas *Aquinas, Saint*
Aquitanicum, Collegium *see* Bordeaux, Collège de Guienne
Araujo, Francisco de *O.P.* 1569
Argensola, Bartolome Leonardo 466
Aristotle 42.1, 42.2, 241.1, 241.2, 748, 751, 835
Armenta, Juan de *S.J.* 505

277

Addenda and Corrigenda

NEW ENTRIES

119.1 **Brown, John.** In Benedictiones XII. Patriarcharum commentaria et quaest. analyticae . . . Authore R.P.F. Ioanne Bruno Scoto Ordinis Minimorum. 8°. *Venetiis, apud Ioan. Baptistam Collosinum*, 1604. L.O.; PA.
   For the author, *see Innes Review* II (1951), pp. 77–81.

Brunus, Ioannes, *Scotus. See* Brown, J. (above).

565.1 **Gibbons, Richard.** [Anr. ed. of no. 565.] 8°. *Lugduni, sumptibus Iacobi Cardon*, 1630. DNPK.

S., I.I. *See* no. 1287.1 (below).

1064.1 **Seville.** [Anr. ed. of no. 1064] *Granada, Fernando Diaz de Montoya,* [1603]. GRAN.

1069 **Seville.** [Revised entry.] Relacion verdadera embiada al Seminario de Seuilla por vn padre de la Compania de Iesus . . . Fol. 2 leaves. *Granada, Bartolome de Lorencana,* 1615. GRAN.
   Not another edition of the poem at no. 1068 but a work in prose on which that poem was probably based. Like no. 1068 it draws on documents printed in no. 1067.

1071.1 **Seville.** [*Documents of c. 1630.*] Breue proposicion de algunos de los motiuos que ay para fauorecer los seminarios ingleses y en particular este de San Gregorio de Seuilla. 4°? *n.p.d.* [c. 1630.] GRAN.
   An appeal for alms. It mentions that the number of students is now down to twelve. *Pr.* [Seville.]

1287.1 **Verstegan, Richard.** [Anr. ed. of no. 1287.] 8°. *Gheprent te druckendorp, door t'bestier, van sweeten inct, en vvit pampier.* anno 1619. L.
   [By R. Verstegan.] Sgd. at the end: I.I.S. *Pr.* [in the Spanish Netherlands.] This edition not in Petti.

1378.1 **White, Stephen.** [*Disputations.*] Hvober, G. Disputatio theologica, de Deo vno et trino. Quam in catholica et celebri [Universitate Dilingana] Anno M.DC.XVI die vii Octobris. Praeside Stephano [Vito] publice proponet Georgius Hvober. 4°. *Dilingae, apud Viduam Ioannis Mayer,* [1616].
   Not seen. *See* note to no. 1377.

ADDITIONAL LIBRARY SYMBOLS

BRN² Brno, Cathedral Library; GRAN Granada, Biblioteca Universitaria; SBR Saint-Brieuc, Bibliotheque Municipale.

FURTHER COPIES

2 – SEV²	542 – DMR	1093 – DNPK
4 – BRS	574 – DNPK	1097 – DNPK
15 – [*DMR]	599 – SBR	1344 – DNPK
103 – POI	740 – [*O*DMR]	1488 – DNPK
127 – DMR	790 – PA(Bliss 611)	1502 – DNPK
155 – O²	947 – [*DMR]	1572 – SEV²
159 – O²O³	977 – PA(Bliss 619)	1578 *or* 1579 – SEV
190 – BRN²	1004 – PA(Bliss 619)	1592 – SEV
276 – GRAN	1062 – GRAN	1594 – SEV
386 – SEV²	1064 – SEV²	1596 – SEV
395 – [*DMR]	1065 – SEV²	1603?– SEV
435 – [*DMR]	1074 – GRAN	1604 – SEV²

ADDENDA TO INDEX OF PRINTERS (p. 258)

REGGIO, nell'Emilia
  Bartoli, Flaminio
    1621 – 259
    1628 – 260

RIVA
  Marcaria, Jacob
    1562 – [923]

CORRIGENDA

Page				
	viii	line 10	*read*	borderline
	38	no. 252.1	*read*	Gregorium XIV
	57	no. 379	*read*	[Mantua]
	92	no. 670	*read*	Democritiana
	112	nos. 807 808	*read*	[Paris, G. Bichon?]
	222	Title Index	*add*	Disputatio theologica, de Deo uno et trino 1378.1 (*Addenda*).
	223		*read*	Disquisitio
	223		*read*	Divini (I)
	223		*read*	(*last entry under D*) krotka . . . Gaspra
	225		*read*	(*3rd entry under F*) fatto
	226		*read*	Historia admiranda . . . sacrae
	227		*read*	In librum duodecim
	229		*read*	Liberté (La)
	229		*read*	Meditationes ac Soliloquia . . . 864.1.
	230		*read*	Missale parvum . . . itinerantibus
	230		*read*	Narratio eorum . . . Ignatii
	230		*read*	Opera omnia [Osorio da Fonseca]
	232		*read*	Paraenesis . . . napominania . . . nowowiernych
	232		*read*	Philosophia . . . Democritiana
	238		*read*	Traitté singulier, pour l'esclarcissement
	260	Printer Index	*add*	(*under* Venice, Colosini) 1604 – 119.1
	262		*read*	(*under* Seville, n.p.n.) [c.1630] – 1071.1 (*Addenda*)
	266		*read*	(*under* Colaldi) Antonio *Orvieto*
	274	Chronological Index	*read*	(*under* 1604, *for* 119.5) 119.1.
	275		*read*	(*under* 1630, *for* [1071.5]) [1071.1]
	279	General Index	*read*	Cauchon de Maupas du Tour
	280		*read*	(*for* Cuminanus) Cumiramus
	287		*add*	(*after* S., C.M.) S., I.I. (*Addenda* no. 1287.1.)